THE WORLD

OF NABOKOV'S

STORIES

LITERARY

MODERNISM

SERIES

· · · · · · · · · · · · ·

Thomas F. Staley, Editor

The World of Nabokov's Stories

Maxim D. Shrayer

. . . .

UNIVERSITY OF TEXAS PRESS, AUSTIN

Copyright © 1999 by the University of Texas Press
All rights reserved
Printed in the United States of America
First paperback printing, 2000
Requests for permission to reproduce material from this work
should be sent to Permissions, University of Texas Press, Box 7819,
Austin, TX 78713-7819.
♾ The paper used in this publication meets the minimum require-
ments of American National Standard for Information Sciences—
Permanence of Paper for Printed Library Materials,
ANSI Z39.48-1984.

Library of Congress Cataloging-in-Publication Data
Shrayer, Maxim, 1967–
The world of Nabokov's stories / Maxim D. Shrayer.
    p.   cm. — (Literary modernism series)
Includes bibliographical references and index.
Romanized record.
ISBN 0-292-77733-7 (alk. cl.)
ISBN 0-292-77756-6 pbk.
1. Nabokov, Vladimir Vladimirovich, 1899–1977—Criticism and in-
terpretation.   I. Title.   II. Series.
PG3476.N3Z864   1999   813'.54—dc21   98-5898

FOR EMILIA

AND

DAVID SHRAYER

Его (поэта) поэзия, как и письма, черновики, как и воспоминания друзей — говорят нам о его внутреннем мире; мы забываем, что она может быть порывом в другой, потусторонний, сияющий, бессмертный мир.
—Владимир Вейдле, „Умирание искусства"

His (the poet's) poetry, as well as his letters, his drafts, as well as the memoirs of his friends, tell us about his inner world; we forget that his poetry might be a flight into a different, radiant, deathless other world.—Vladimir Veidle, *The Dying of Art* (1937)

. . . .

Total grandeur of a total edifice,
Chosen by an inquisitor of structures
For himself. He stops upon this threshold,
As if the design of all his words takes form
And frame from thinking and is realized.
—Wallace Stevens, "To an Old Philosopher in Rome" (1952)

. . . .

... напротив, это была самая дюжинная комнатка, с красным полом, с ромашками, намалёванными на белых стенах, и небольшим зеркалом, наполовину полным ромашкового настоя, — но из окошка было ясно видно озеро с облаком и башней, в неподвижном и совершенном сочетании счастья.
—Владимир Набоков, „Облако, озеро, башня"

On the contrary, it was a most ordinary room, with a red floor, daisies daubed on the white walls, and a small mirror half filled with the yellow infusion of the reflected flowers—but from the window one could clearly see the lake with its cloud and its castle, in a motionless and perfect correlation of happiness.
—Vladimir Nabokov, "Cloud, Castle, Lake" (1937)

Contents

. . . .

Illustrations

· ·

Acknowledgments

. . . .

The research for this book began in the spring of 1991 in Vladimir E. Alexandrov's seminar on Nabokov at Yale. Professor Alexandrov introduced me to Nabokov studies and encouraged me at all stages of this project. Robert L. Jackson's seminars on Dostoevskii, Chekhov, Tolstoi and Turgenev are partly responsible for shaping my perspectives on authorship, textuality, and reading.

I would like to thank my teachers, both undergraduate and graduate, for contributing to my training: Albert Cook and Victor Terras at Brown; Janet Walker, Stephen Walker, Catharine R. Stimpson, Uri Eisenzweig, and Serge Sobolevich at Rutgers–New Brunswick; Vladimir E. Alexandrov, Victor Erlich, Harvey Goldblatt, and Robert L. Jackson at Yale.

This book would never have been completed without the expert help of the following dedicated librarians and archivists: Stephen Crook and Edward Kasinec, both of the New York Public Library; Fredrick W. Bauman Jr. and Mary Wolfskill, both of the Library of Congress; Vincent Giroud of Beinecke Rare Book and Manuscript Library (Yale University); Richard D. Davies of the Leeds Russian Archive, Brotherton Library (University of Leeds, England); Milena Klímová, Jiří Vácek, and Helena Musátová, all of the Slavonic Library (Prague, The Czech Republic).

My research was partly funded by two short-term grants from the Kennan Institute for Advanced Russian Studies (1993, 1996) and a research expense grant from Boston College (1996). The financial support of these institutions is gratefully acknowledged.

I am grateful to Dmitri Nabokov (Montreux) for granting me access to Vladimir Nabokov's unpublished materials at the Library of Congress and the New York Public Library. I would also like to express my gratitude to the late Militsa E. Greene (Edinburgh) and to Richard D. Davies (Leeds) for allowing me to work with the unpublished papers of Ivan and Vera Bunin at the Leeds Russian Archive. Ivan Bunin's unpublished letters to Andrei Sedykh and Roman Gul', as well as Nabokov's book inscription, are quoted and reproduced with the kind permission of Vincent Giroud (Beinecke Rare Books and Manuscript Library, Yale University). I also thank Ellendea Proffer for permission to reproduce photographs of Vladimir Nabokov. I am deeply grateful to the late Nina Berberova, who responded to my queries about Nabokov and Bunin and whose enthusiastic voice on the telephone line was another justification for continuing my work.

Throughout this project, I depended upon the advice, assistance, and friendship of colleagues, whose contribution I acknowledge with much appreciation: Richard D. Davies, D. Barton Johnson, Laurence Mintz, M. J. Connolly, Lawrence G. Jones, Cynthia Simmons, and Margaret Thomas. I would like to thank my editors at the University of Texas Press, Jim Burr and Kathy Lewis, and Stephen Vedder of Boston College's Audiovisual Services for his help with photographs.

Although one always thanks one's parents, my grateful words of admiration for Emilia and David Shrayer have a special meaning in the case of this book. It is to my parents, who—as Jewish Refuseniks—paid a dear price for emigration from the former Soviet Union, that I owe the privilege of being able to write freely about Vladimir Nabokov.

Parts of this study, modified for publication, have appeared elsewhere:

"'Cloud, Castle, Lake' and the Problem of Entering the Otherworld in Nabokov's Short Fiction." *Nabokov Studies* 1 (1994): 131–53.

"Ivan Bunin i Vladimir Nabokov: poètika sopernichestva" (Ivan Bunin and Vladimir Nabokov: The Poetics of Rivalry). In *I. A. Bunin i russkaia literatura XX veka* (Ivan Bunin and Twentieth-Century Russian Literature), 41–65. Moscow: Nasledie, 1996.

"Pilgrimage, Memory and Death in Vladimir Nabokov's Short Story 'The Aurelian.'" *The Slavic and East European Journal* 40:4 (Winter 1996): 700–725.

"Mapping Narrative Space in Vladimir Nabokov's Short Fiction." *The Slavonic and East European Review* 75:4 (October 1997): 624–641.

"Decoding Nabokov's 'The Return of Chorb.'" *Russian Language Journal* 51:168–170 (1997): 177–202.

Note on Transliteration, Dates, and References

. . . .

Unless otherwise specified, a parenthetical date in the text refers to the first publication of a literary work; in some cases the date of completion is also provided if it differs significantly from the date of publication. For information on the history of the creation and publication of Nabokov's short stories, see the Appendix. Parenthetical dates for critical studies always refer to the date of publication.

Since pre-1918 Russian publications, most pre–World War II Russian émigré publications, and all of Nabokov's and Bunin's Russian manuscripts utilized the so-called old Russian orthography (*staryi stil'*), certain changes had to be made in quotations. I have altered the originals in those instances where case endings or prefixes differ from modern Russian spelling rules (e.g. "mërtv*ogo*" instead of "mërtv*ago*"; "Russk*ie* zapiski" instead of "Russk*iia* zapiski"; "*ras*skazyval" instead of "*raz*skazyval"). In cases where the text (published or unpublished) contained a trivial misprint or misspelling, I have corrected it silently. I have, however, marked with "[*sic*]" those instances where an authorial misspelling seems meaningful or intentional.

A slightly simplified Library of Congress system for transliterating the Russian alphabet is used throughout. The only exceptions are Nabokov's own transliterations of Russian names in his works ("Vasiliy" vs. "Vasilii").

Unless otherwise indicated, all citations from the English text of the Bible are from *The Revised English Bible* (Oxford/Cambridge); from the

Russian text of the Bible from *Bibliia* (Izdanie Moskovskoi Patriarkhii, 1992).

Where sources of translations from the Russian are not included, the translations are mine. My translations do not aspire to capture the originals' artistry, but rather attempt to be literal insofar as that is possible.

List of Abbreviations

· ·

The following abbreviations for books only are used throughout this study in the main text, Notes, and Appendix. For detailed information about Nabokov's short stories, see the Appendix. For information on Nabokov's periodical publications cited in this study, see Works Cited.

Books by Nabokov

Ada	*Ada or Ardor: A Family Chronicle.* New York: Vintage Books, 1990.
BS	*Bend Sinister.* New York: Vintage Books, 1990.
CE	*Conclusive Evidence: A Memoir.* New York: Harper and Brothers, 1951.
DS	*Details of a Sunset and Other Stories.* Tr. Dmitri Nabokov in collaboration with the author. New York: McGraw-Hill Book Company, 1976.
Gift	*The Gift.* Tr. Michael Scammel in collaboration with the author. New York: Vintage Books, 1989.
Glory	*Glory.* Tr. Dmitri Nabokov in collaboration with the author. New York: Vintage Books, 1991.
Gogol	*Nikolai Gogol.* New York: New Directions, 1961.
GP	*Gornii put'.* Berlin: Grani, 1923.
Grozd'	*Grozd'.* Berlin: Gamaiun, 1923.
Kniga	*Rasskazy. Priglashenie na kazn'. Èsse, interv'iu, retsenzii.* Ed. A. A. Dolinin and R. D. Timenchik. Moscow: Kniga, 1989.

Krug	*Krug*. Ed. N. I. Tolstaia. Leningrad: Khudozhestvennaia literatura, 1990.
L	*The Annotated Lolita*. Ed. Alfred Appel Jr. New York: Vintage Books, 1991.
LATH	*Look at the Harlequins!* New York: Vintage Books, 1990.
LL	*Lectures on Literature*. Ed. Fredson Bowers. New York: Harcourt Brace Jovanovich/Bruccoli Clark, 1980.
LRL	*Lectures on Russian Literature*. Ed. Fredson Bowers. New York: Harcourt Brace Jovanovich/Bruccoli Clark, 1981.
Mary	*Mary*. Tr. Michael Glenny in collaboration with the author. New York: Vintage Books, 1989.
ND	*Nabokov's Dozen*. Garden City, NY: Doubleday, 1958.
NQ	*Nabokov's Quartet*. New York: Phaedra Publishers, 1966.
NS	*Nine Stories*. Norfolk, Conn.: New Directions, 1947 (*Direction*, no. 2).
P'esy	*P'esy*. Ed. Iv. Tolstoi. Moscow: Iskusstvo, 1990.
Pnin	*Pnin*. New York: Vintage Books, 1989.
PP	*Poems and Problems*. New York: McGraw-Hill Book Company, 1970.
PSS	*Perepiska s sestroi*. Ann Arbor: Ardis, 1985.
RB	*A Russian Beauty and Other Stories*. Tr. Dmitri Nabokov in collaboration with the author. New York: McGraw Hill, 1973.
RLSK	*The Real Life of Sebastian Knight*. New York: Vintage Books, 1992.
S	*Sogliadatai*. Paris: Russkie zapiski, 1938.
SL	*Selected Letters, 1940–1977*. Ed. Dmitri Nabokov and Matthew J. Bruccoli. San Diego: Harcourt Brace Jovanovich, 1989.
SM	*Speak, Memory: An Autobiography Revisited*. New York: Vintage Books, 1989.
SO	*Strong Opinions*. New York: Vintage Books, 1990.
SSoch	*Sobranie sochinenii v chetyrëkh tomakh*. Moscow: Pravda, 1990.
Stikhi 1916	*Stikhi*. [St. Petersburg]: n.p., 1916.
Stikhi	*Stikhi*. Ann Arbor: Ardis, 1979.
Stikhotvoreniia	*Stikhotvoreniia, 1929–1951*. Paris: Rifma, 1952.
Stories	*The Stories of Vladimir Nabokov*. New York: Vintage Books, 1997.

TD	*Tyrants Destroyed and Other Stories.* Tr. Dmitri Nabokov in collaboration with the author. New York: McGraw-Hill, 1975.
VCh	*Vozvrashchenie Chorba: rasskazy i stikhi.* Berlin: Slovo, 1930.
Vén	*La Vénitienne et autres nouvelles.* Ed. Gilles Barbedette. Paris: Gallimard, 1990.
VF	*Vesna v Fial'te.* New York: Izdatel'stvo imeni Chekhova, 1956.
Wilson Letters	*The Nabokov-Wilson Letters: Correspondence between Vladimir Nabokov and Edmund Wilson, 1940–1971.* Ed. and intro. Simon Karlinsky. New York: Harper Colophon, 1980.

Works by Bunin and Chekhov

Bunin	*Sobranie sochinenii v deviati tomakh.* Moscow: Khudozhestvennaiia literatura, 1965–1967.
Chekhov	*Polnoe sobranie sochinenii i pisem v tridtsati tomakh.* Moscow: Nauka, 1974–1985.

Archival Materials

Bunin Leeds	The Papers of Ivan Bunin and Vera Muromtseva-Bunina at the Leeds Russian Archive, Brotherton Library, University of Leeds.
VN Berg	Vladimir Nabokov's Papers at the Berg Collection of American Literature, New York Public Library.
VN LC	Vladimir Nabokov Collection at the Division of Manuscripts and Archives, Library of Congress.
ZSh LC	Zinaida Shakhovskaia (Shakhovskoy) Collection at the Division of Manuscripts and Archives, Library of Congress.

Other Works

Boyd, *RY*	Brian Boyd. *Vladimir Nabokov: The Russian Years.* Princeton: Princeton University Press, 1990.
Boyd, *AY*	Brian Boyd. *Vladimir Nabokov: The American Years.* Princeton: Princeton University Press, 1991.

Introduction

· ·

Vladimir Nabokov (1899–1977) left a corpus of some seventy short stories, written between 1921 and 1951 and revised thereafter. The vast majority of the stories were created during his Russian period—in the 1920s and 1930s in Germany, Czechoslovakia, and France—and appeared first in the leading émigré periodicals (*Rul'*, *Sovremennye zapiski*, *Poslednie novosti*, etc.); many were later collected in the three volumes *Vozvrashchenie Chorba* (The Return of Chorb, 1930), *Sogliadatai* (The Eye, 1938), and *Vesna v Fial'te* (Spring in Fialta, 1956). Beginning with 1943, Nabokov wrote short stories in English while also "Englishing" the Russian stories.[1] (He composed his last Russian story in 1939.) A sampling of English and Russian short stories was published as an English-language collection, *Nine Stories* (1947), and later expanded into *Nabokov's Dozen* (1958). In the early seventies, when he was already in Switzerland, Nabokov revisited his Russian stories: two-thirds of them were translated into English by the author's son, Dmitri Nabokov, in collaboration with the author. Four other original collections of short stories appeared in English: *Nabokov's Quartet* (1966), *A Russian Beauty and Other Stories* (1973), *Tyrants Destroyed and Other Stories* (1975), and *Details of a Sunset and Other Stories* (1976). The appearance of *The Stories of Vladimir Nabokov*, a volume of sixty-five short fictions edited by Dmitri Nabokov, in 1995 gave readers an opportunity to put in perspective Nabokov's contribution to the genre: it is an impressive and truly bilingual body of short stories by one of the major literary figures in the twentieth century. Nabokov's stories frequently appear in anthologies of short fiction and are widely taught in universities.[2]

The study of Nabokov's short stories is no longer the virgin territory that it was in the 1960s when Slavicists and Americanists were beginning to rediscover Nabokov's pre–World War II gems. Scholars began to turn their attention to his short stories in the 1960s for several reasons, including the 1956 publication of the collection *Spring in Fialta*, one of the best collections of Russian stories ever to appear; the gradual translation of the Russian stories into English and their publication in leading periodicals (*The Atlantic Monthly, The New Yorker*, etc.) and in separate American and British editions; and the success of *Lolita* (1955) and the subsequent heightened interest in anything by Nabokov. Few among the early workers in the field of Nabokov's short stories had been aware of the vast pre–World War II literature about him, dispersed throughout numerous Russian émigré publications. The rich materials included reviews of Nabokov's individual stories or entire collections (the third collection was announced as forthcoming in 1939 but was published only in 1956).[3] Seminal articles by the leading Russian émigré critics and writers of the time, including Georgii Adamovich, Iulii Aikhenval'd, Al'fred Bem, Pëtr Bitsilli, Zinaida Gippius, Vladislav Khodasevich, Pëtr Pil'skii, Gleb Struve, Vladimir Veidle, some full of praise, others bilious and skeptical, were preparing "native grounds" for a unified scholarly inquiry into the poetics of Nabokov's short stories. Had it not been for the peripeties of World War II and the disintegration of Russia Abroad, as well as Nabokov's "disappearance" from Europe and his subsequent place as a recluse in post–World War II Russian émigré culture, a study of his stories might have been born directly out of the rich émigré context of the 1920s–1930s.[4] History made other arrangements.

With a few exceptions, Nabokovians of the 1960s–1970s had to start essentially from scratch. The vast émigré culture—both the substratum and the milieu for Nabokov's Russian stories—had been buried in the collective graves of libraries and archives, all but forgotten.[5] The very sense of the literary and cultural contexts for Nabokov's achievement in his Russian short stories was difficult to restore. The undertakings of Nabokovians in working the post–World War II field of the short stories were a heroic effort and deserve both admiration and gratitude. A monograph, several doctoral dissertations, and sections of books and some fifty articles analyze Nabokov's short stories.[6] Notable attention has been given to narrative structure. A case in point is Pekka Tammi's monumental *Problems of Nabokov's Poetics* (1985). Tammi's study provides an exhaustive narratological analysis of Nabokov's entire corpus of texts, considering novels, memoirs, plays, and many Russian and all English short stories as compendia of narrative devices. Tammi's examination of the short stories is limited to a number of literary devices (types of narrator, framing, irony, etc.) also to be found, albeit in a different proportion, in other literary texts, both Russian and non-Russian. Such a narrative approach to Nabokov's works is therefore device-specific, not Nabokov-specific. It seeks neither to make value judgments about his contribution to the genre of the short story nor to link the structure of his stories with their implied philosophical outlook or cultural contexts. It might help one see how Nabokov is like other writers, but not how he is unlike them.

In addition to studying narrative poetics, critics in the West have produced exemplary thematic readings of Nabokov's short stories, focusing largely on such topics as memory and exile, love and adultery, madness, self versus other, and the artist in the modern world. Although these themes enjoy a prominent status in Nabokov's oeuvre, they by no means distinguish him from his great Russian coevals, such as Isaak Babel' and Andrei Platonov, to name but two, or his stories from his novels. Overall, while post–World War II studies have introduced a significant frame of structural and cultural references, they have not answered the two questions—separate albeit interconnected—which the Russian émigré critics had begun to tackle in the 1930s when they hailed Nabokov as the new star of Russian prose: What makes Nabokov's short stories unique as compared to the other short stories of the great Russian tradition, from Aleksandr Pushkin to Lev Tolstoi and from Anton Chekhov to Ivan Bunin? and What places Nabokov the writer of short stories in a peerless position on the map of Russian modernism? These questions still remain largely unanswered.

The year 1993 was marked by the appearance of *A Small Alpine Form,* the first collection of scholarly articles devoted entirely to Nabokov's short fiction, both Russian and English. The biggest achievement of the collection lies in its insistence on recognizing Nabokov's "smaller butterflies" not merely as footnotes to his novels but as deserving a place among the world's finest short stories.[7] The recent surge of interest among both scholars and readers signals a need for an approach to the short stories based on searching for poetic paradigms that are solely Nabokovian.[8]

The World of Nabokov's Stories is the first examination of Nabokov's entire Russian career as a major writer of short stories. My goal is to highlight Nabokov's original contribution to the Russian tradition, to the genre of short story, and to modernism. My main concern is to map out the dynamics of the interaction between his growing mastery of the short story and his worldview, also in the process of development. To accomplish my task, I will trace Nabokov's ripening literary practices from the apprentice stories of the early 1920s to the masterpieces of the 1930s. The reader will note my insistence on using the term "originality" when speaking of his threefold contribution. Nabokov's short stories belong, as do such celebrated works as Gustave Flaubert's *Three Stories* (1877) and James Joyce's *Dubliners* (1914), to the main line of a major writer's developing career. The Russian stories are indispensable for understanding Nabokov's entire life in letters, including the Russian and English novels, especially given his literary bilingualism and his experience as an exile in Europe in the 1920s–1930s. My particular interest in these stories also stems from a belief that the short story as genre is the ultimate test of a writer's perfection. A superb writer of short stories is likely to become a great novelist (as did Lev Tolstoi or F. Scott Fitzgerald), while a fine novelist is not necessarily equipped to write short stories (Ivan Goncharov or Samuel Beckett). To quote one of this century's foremost writers of short stories, Nabokov's contemporary and fellow-exile Isaac Bashevis Singer (1904–1991), "[the short story] constitutes the utmost challenge to the creative writer. Unlike the novel, which can absorb and even forgive lengthy digressions, flashbacks, and loose construction, the short story must aim directly at its climax."[9]

Three principal contexts have facilitated my understanding of Nabokov's short stories: the world of Russian exiles between the two world wars; the history of modernism in Russia; and the history of the short story as genre.

The events depicted in Nabokov's stories resulted from historical and sociopolitical cataclysms during the first half of the twentieth century, chiefly the pre-1917 turmoil in Russian society, the October 1917 Revolution and the Civil War of 1918–1922, the influx of Russian exiles into Europe, Asia, and the Americas, the emergence of Weimar Democracy, and the rise of Nazism in Germany and Stalinism in the Soviet Union. Additionally, any discussion of Nabokov's stories would be unthinkable without reference to the history and culture of the Russian diaspora in the 1920s and 1930s.[10] This also entails outlining his contacts with other Russian émigré authors and his reception by Russian émigré critics. Having left Russia in 1919 as a young man, Nabokov emerged as a writer in exile, and for nearly twenty years he supported himself as a contributor to émigré publications. A society within society, for nearly twenty years Russia Abroad provided outlets for publishing his short stories (and honoraria, however meager), a demanding reading audience, and, last but not least, the raw existential material that informed his fictions. The majority of

Nabokov's Russian stories feature Russian émigré protagonists, are set in interwar Europe, and address issues of the exiles' spiritual and physical survival.

Nabokov occupies a problematic position in the realism-modernism line of development in the history of Russian and European letters during the first third of the twentieth century. In the 1980s–1990s large-scale interpretations of his career have negotiated his unique status as a Russian writer. In particular, Vladimir E. Alexandrov has argued in *Nabokov's Otherworld* (1991) that the otherworld—both a sui generis core of metaphysical beliefs and a structural and thematic foundation—underlies Nabokov's writings and makes them so distinct from much else in twentieth-century Russian letters.[11] In *Nabokov's Art of Memory and European Modernism* (1993), John Burt Foster Jr. has demonstrated that Nabokov was truly at home in European literatures. His polylingual and polycultural works point to European modernism, notably such great masters as James Joyce (1882–1941) and Marcel Proust (1871–1922).

While Nabokov's masters of the novel might have lain outside the Russian literary tradition, his short stories were forged in the course of a dialogue with his predecessors in *russkii rasskaz* (the Russian short story). Based in part on archival materials, my study makes a case for understanding Nabokov's career as a triangular dialogic relationship with his Russian masters, Chekhov and Bunin. Both Anton Chekhov (1860–1904) and Ivan Bunin (1870–1953) are recognized as supreme masters of the Russian short story. More than once, Nabokov recorded his great admiration for Chekhov's art of short story writing.[12] Even more than such Western masters as Rudyard Kipling, Guy de Maupassant, or Edgar Allan Poe, Chekhov truly defined the modern short story as a major, self-sufficient generic form. He brought representational short fiction to a point of stylistic perfection and precision that signals a covert modernist war against narrative conventions, an offensive against linear time and traditional structure of closure. The short stories of Bunin, Nabokov's senior contemporary, an émigré, and the first Russian writer to win the Nobel Prize (1933), embody a modernist obsession with poetic absolute language that focuses on the linguistic material itself. At the same time, Bunin's stories employ traditional love triangles as their structural foundation and probe the artistic limits of depicting desire. A growing tension between the language, communicating its own preoccupation with verbal artistry, and the narrative structure, revealing—like a palimpsest—layers and layers of narrative topoi, lies at the core of Bunin's short fiction. The unprecedented harmony of Nabokov's stories—language, narrative, and world vision—

was his answer to the great masters. His stories obtain much of this harmony from their metaphysical dimension, which warrants their artistic longevity and popularity with both Russian and non-Russian readers.

This book also continues the work of dismantling a popular critical myth about Nabokov's *nerusskost'* (non-Russianness). Rather than regard Nabokov, as have notable critics, both émigré and Western, as a Russian literary anomaly—a foreign genius somehow accidentally working in the Russian language, I will treat his career in short fiction as being at once an exile's gradual farewell and a unending tribute to his Russian masters. I will place the Russian short story tradition, especially Chekhov and Bunin, at the root of Nabokov's art. Only in perspective, by reading along and against the grain of the Russian tradition, can one see his artistic innovations clearly.

Nabokov certainly had in mind exemplary Russian short story subtexts, such as Chekhov's "Gusev" (1890), "Ionych" (1898), and "Dama s sobachkoi" (Lady with a Lap Dog, 1899) or Bunin's "Lëgkoe dykhanie" (Light Breathing, 1916), "Petlistye ushi" (Loopy Ears, 1916), and "Gospodin iz San Franstisko" (Gentleman from San Francisco, 1915).[13] An anxiety of influence gave Nabokov impetus to eclipse the finest achievements of Russian realism and modernism by leaning upon his native tradition and refashioning it from without, from the vantage point of being a Russian exile in Europe and America.[14]

Several generic and methodological aspects of my approach need to be explained. In this study I will adhere to a rather traditional and transparent definition of the short story as literary form and genre. By "short story" I will mean here a relatively short work of fiction that centers on a limited number of protagonists (often on one protagonist), focuses on a singular concurrence of events which is localized both temporally and spatially, and creates, develops, and undoes an intrigue much less diversified than that of a novel.[15] To quote Isaac Bashevis Singer once again, "[The short story] must possess uninterrupted tension and suspense. Also, brevity is its very essence. The short story must have a definite plan; it cannot be what in literary jargon is called 'a slice of life.' The masters of the short story, Chekhov, Maupassant, as well as the sublime scribe of the Joseph story in the Book of Genesis, knew exactly where they were going. One can read them over and over again and never get bored."[16]

Additionally, as an astute connoisseur, prolific author of short stories, and Nabokov's editor at *The New Yorker*, William Maxwell, pointed out, "stories read better one at a time. They need air around them. And they need thinking about, since they tend to have both an explicit and an un-spelled-out meaning."[17]

In an 1971 interview with Stephen Jan Parker, Nabokov said: "In rela-tion to the typical novel the short story represents a small Alpine, or Polar, form. It looks different, but is conspecific with the novel and is linked to it by intermediate clines."[18] Critics have inquired into the mean-ing of Nabokov's statement and the light it sheds upon the study of his short stories.[19] By "conspecificity," I believe, Nabokov meant most of all that his "short stories are *produced* in exactly the same way as [his] novels and informed by their [a]uthor and his subtexts [italics added]."[20] Na-bokov's working and somewhat tentative definition, based primarily on the criterion of textual length, lacks a second criterion related to the struc-ture of composition. When working on his "small Alpine forms," I expe-rienced a need to draw a line between the short stories and the transitional or hybrid forms. The latter include two short novels, *Sogliadatai* (The Eye, 1930) and *Volshebnik* (The Enchanter, 1939, published 1986) and two chap-ters of an abandoned novel ("Solus Rex," 1940, and "Ultima Thule," 1942) which appeared in periodicals and collections in the guise of separate short fictions.[21] I have decided to exclude them from my analysis. At the same time, I could not leave several of the early plotless fictions out of my study. Virtually eventless, "Groza" (The Thunderstorm, 1924) satisfies the criterion of length, but not of structure, as I have conceived of it in this study. A few, like the very early "Nezhit'" (The Woodsprite, 1921) or "Slovo" (The Word, 1923), correspond to the genre of creative nonfiction. Finally, there is also the exhilarating case of "A Guide to Berlin," which is not a short story but a sequence of five vignettes of the type that Ernest Hemingway inserted between his short stories in the collection *In Our Time* (1925).

The second methodological issue concerns the shape of narrative clo-sure. Ever since Aristotle's *Poetics,* to quote the narratologist Gerald Prince, critics have "pointed out that the end occupies a determinative position because of the light it sheds (or might shed) on the meaning of the events leading up to it. The end functions as the (partial) condition, the magne-tizing force, the organizing principle of narrative: reading (processing) a narrative is, among other things, waiting for the end, and the nature of the waiting is related to the nature of the narrative."[22] My interest in the com-position of the ending in Nabokov's short stories stems from two factors. First, as I hope to demonstrate, Nabokov deemed crucial the structure of the ending in a literary text: much of his dialogue with his Russian mas-ters, Chekhov and Bunin, focused on the relationship between the raw material of fiction and the way a story comes to a closure. Second, in current literary studies the notion of an open/closed ending, while commonly used, remains loosely defined. To quote a recent overview of Nabokov's short stories, "Most of the short stories . . . are open-ended, expansive rather than circuitous."[23] My survey shows a nearly 40 percent / 60 percent breakdown between the "open endings" and "closed endings" in his Russian stories. Clearly, the authors of the overview and I operate with different formal criteria of what constitutes an "open ending" and what qualifies as a "closed ending."

Hereafter I will employ open ending and closed ending as narratological concepts that describe how a short story comes to an end, resolves its plot, and completes its action. An open ending allows the reader to project narrative action in several directions, thereby creating a sense of indeterminacy since the reader is likely to speculate about "what is going to happen?" A good example of an open-ended short story is Chekhov's "Lady with a Lap Dog." Chekhov's reader is left speculating—beyond the physical ending of the story—whether or not Anna and Gurov will get married, break up, or continue their adulterous relationship. A letter to Chekhov from his admirer S. S. Remizova in October 1903 illustrates a typical reader's response to an open-ended short story: "You have abandoned your readers, so to speak, in the most critical time of their lives, when a decision should be made, but what kind? There is a difficult question. You will probably choose not to write a continuation of this story, so will you be so kind as to drop a few lines about what you would do in Gurov's place . . . how you would resolve this complicated situation . . ." (Chekhov 10:426).

Conversely, upon finishing a closed-ended story, the reader is unlikely to speculate about what happens beyond the closure. A closed ending offers a resolution of the actions in the story. The shapes of resolutions may vary and include solving a mystery (Honoré de Balzac's "Sarrasine"), finding the saint (O. Henry's "The Last Leaf"), locating the missing object (Poe's "The Purloined Letter"), killing off the protagonist (J. D. Salinger's "A Perfect Day for Bananafish"), and so forth. A closed ending makes the outcome of the story's action determinate for the reader. In some cases, as in Bunin's "Loopy Ears," it may be said about a closed-ended story that its narrative potential has been exhausted and the action calls for a resolution. In other cases, however, the narrative conflict may be shown to be unresolvable. For instance, many stories dealing with a murderer's confession during a trial possess such closed endings. In Bunin's "Delo korneta Elagina" (The Affair of Cornet Elagin, 1925), the narrative pieces together all the evidence—the prosecutor's remarks, witnesses' testimony, and the protagonist's confession of murder—thereby captivating the reader. Once Elagin has finished his confession, and all his motives have been disclosed, the story is over, leaving no potential for the reader's quest beyond its ending.[24]

The third and final issue centers on the model of the act of reading that I will advocate in this study. This issue entails three separate albeit interconnected problems: Nabokov's own view of reading, the distinction I will make between "textual memory" and "reader's memory," and, finally, the notion of the "ideal reader," also stemming from Nabokov's discursive writings. In his provocative lecture "Good Readers and Good Writers," Nabokov stated that, "curiously enough, one cannot *read* a book: one can only reread it. A good reader, a major reader, an active and creative reader is a rereader" (*LL*, 3). Such a singular understanding of the act of reading as a series of continuous rereadings/recollections relates to the distinctive role memory plays in the functioning of Nabokov's texts. Research over the past decade has broadened our understanding of his art of memory from the domain of the novels and memoirs to that of the short stories, both Russian and English. In addition to Nabokov's discursive statements in *Speak, Memory* (1966) and elsewhere, his short stories themselves signal his self-awareness as an artist of memory.[25] Several of his Russian stories, especially "Govoriat po-russki" (Russian Spoken Here, 1923), "Rozhdestvo" (Christmas, 1924), "Pis'mo v Rossiiu" (A Letter That Never Reached Russia, 1925), "Britva" (Razor, 1926), "Pamiati L. I. Shigaeva" (In Memory of L. I. Shigaev, 1934), and "Sovershenstvo" (Perfection, 1932), foreground a distinction between two kinds of memory operating in the process of reading. A need for such a distinction is manifest in a seminal passage from the story "Putevoditel' po Berlinu" (A Guide to Berlin, 1925): "I think that here lies the sense of literary creation: to portray ordinary objects as they will be reflected in the kindly mirrors of future times; to find in the objects around us the fragrant tenderness that only posterity will discern and appreciate in the far-off times when every trifle of our plain everyday life will become exquisite and festive in its own right: the times when a man who might put on the most ordinary jacket of today will be dressed up for an elegant masquerade" (*Stories*, 157). Speaking about the "fragrant tenderness" which "our successors" ("nashi potomki"; *VCh*, 97) would sense in the ordinary objects of the past recorded by the text, Nabokov thereby suggests a distinction between the text of a given short story as produced by its creator and the text of the same story as perceived by its future readers, removed from the moment of creation by the passage of time. Such a distinction between the author's text and the reader's text is familiar in modern critical theory. For instance, Wolfgang Iser writes that "the literary work has two poles, which we might call the artistic pole and the aesthetic: the artistic pole is the author's text, and the aesthetic is the realization accomplished by the reader."[26] However, Nabokov's concern was not so much in defining the boundaries of text per se, but rather in exploring the nature of textual memory. Nabokov links his experience as a writer concerned with immortalizing memory via language to that of a reader to whom the recorded memory of his story is ultimately addressed.

By the "textual memory" of a short story I mean the totality of information that its text encodes. In several respects, my notion of textual memory is kindred to Wolfgang Iser's useful notion of textual "repertoire" as it appears in *The Act of Reading* (1978): "The repertoire consists of all the familiar territory within the text. This may be in the form of references to earlier works, or to social and historical norms, or to the whole culture from which the text emerged—in brief, to what the Prague structuralists have called the 'extratextual reality.'"[27] The information stored in textual memory includes facts of a plot, as they inevitably refer to specific (if fictionalized) events, as well as the structure of a given narrative. As opposed to the self-reflecting textual memory, an all-absorbing, spongelike depository of the text's various contexts, the reader's memory of the text is selective. By the "reader's memory" of the text I mean the selections from the textual memory which have been recorded in the reader's individual memory and become part of it. During the initial act of reading, the reader becomes privy to textual memory. What will be selected and etched in the reader's memory is dependent upon many factors, pertaining both to the individual qualities of the reader and to her or his time and milieu. While the textual memory is, in a manner of speaking, unalterable so long as the text remains intact, the reader's memory is mobile and undergoes alterations. Rereading/revisiting the text constitutes one of the sources of alteration of the reader's memory.[28] The reader's memory could also be altered due to changes in the contexts of the reader's time or in the reader's awareness of these contexts. Also, the mere duration of the reader's life can be the main reason behind an alteration of the reader's text: coming of age often compels the reader to reevaluate the earlier perception of a given work. The reader's memory not only records portions of the textual memory and shapes them according to historical and personal time, but also reflects the reader's responses to the text as accumulated over the duration of the acts of rereading. While the textual memory is the text's memory of itself, the reader's memory is the reader's memory of the act of reading. Finally, one might posit a hypothetical situation where the textual memory nears the reader's memory. This situation, in some respects ideal for a reception of the text, may take place when the author serves as the reader of her or his own text.

I realize that both the notion of a semiotic totality stored in the textual memory and my tendency to approach the reader's memory of the text as a determinate entity may elicit criticism. However, I am not the first and most certainly not the last student of literature to risk opening a theoretical can of worms. In fact, several scholars, including Wolfgang Iser, E. D. Hirsch Jr., and Umberto Eco, have raised similar problems of interpretation and introduced similar distinctions as essential to our understanding of the poetics of a literary text. For instance, in *Validity in Interpretation* (1967), Hirsch sets up a decisive opposition between "meaning" (as the author's view/intention) and "significance" (as the reader's construction).[29] No matter how one reads a given text, it is bound to contain both determinacies and indeterminacies. Given that all perceptions are mediated, I do not see a way around this hermeneutic problem. How can a critic ascertain some distinction between the text as such and the textual imprint it leaves on the perceiver (in my terms, between "the textual memory" and "the reader's memory") without being accused of having a deterministic view of reading? As I hope to demonstrate in this study, the notions of the textual memory and the reader's memory are not merely a part of some theoretical agenda of mine but rather stem from Nabokov's aesthetic practices. One hopes that a critic may share her or his subject's dose of determinism.

Nabokov's understanding of the role the reader plays during the act of reading was indeed deterministic, as becomes apparent from his unpublished notes, entitled "Lectures on Style and Short Stories." Presumably, he prepared these notes for a course on creative writing, a version of which he taught at Stanford University in the summer of 1941.[30] The lectures are handwritten and in places employ a telegraphic style and abbreviations. They must have been planned for a course that would combine intense reading and discussion of selected short texts with the students' own creative work. The short fictions covered in the course included Wilkie Collins's "[The Traveler's Story of] a Terribly Strange Bed" (1852), Henry James's "The Special Type" (1890), Thomas Hardy's "The Melancholy Hussar of the German Legion" (1890), R. L. Stevenson's "The Sire de Malétroit's Door" (1878), Joseph Conrad's "The Inn of the Two Witches" (1913), Saki's "The Reticence of Lady Anne" (1910), and Anton Chekhov's

"Lady with a Lap Dog" (1901). The last lecture of the course, entitled "Great Overture. The Philosophy of Fiction," contains Nabokov's version of reader-response criticism. His statement articulates—in more precise and plain terms than elsewhere in his discursive writings—the problem of the text's bearing on the model of its own reading:

> The material of fiction necessarily includes the mind of the reader. Of the human relationships with which a work of fiction may deal, that of the reader is the most important and the controlling relationship. . . . Any attempt to construe material apart from the reader, as if fiction were produced in a vacuum and uttered in a void, must result in failure. . . . A writer has an idea of a reader, and in this respect the idea of a reader may be said to be one of the characters of the book. But this ideal reader is really the author's double—and has nothing to do with any of the readers an author can imagine in terms of definity [sic] presumably, time, race, local interests, etc. In other words the reader an authentic writer imagines is himself or a man like himself that is with the same capacity of receiving impressions as he has.[31]

This passage was written soon after Nabokov's arrival in the United States and sums up his formal quest in almost sixty Russian short stories and eleven novels. Rendered in a newly adopted language and addressed to future American fiction writers, his remarks attribute great significance to the author's virtual presence during the act of reading. For Nabokov, the author constructs the text with a reader in mind by encoding in the text a set of reader-response expectations. These expectations take the form of various "signs and symbols"—to adapt the title of the 1948 story—and manifest themselves to the reader during the act of rereading. When Nabokov speaks of an ideal reader who is like his own double against the text of a given short story, he wishes for a reader who would succumb to the text and allow it to perform in its full capacity.

I have divided Nabokov's stories into four periods, the Early period (1921–1929), the Middle period (1930–1935), the High period (1936–1939), and the American period (1940–1951). The criteria employed in devising this system of periodization are not merely chronological, historical, or philological. It is certainly true that each of the three Russian periods centers on the stories included in Nabokov's three Russian collections of short stories, *The Return of Chorb* (1930), *The Eye* (1938), and *Spring in Fialta* (1956; it would have come out in 1939 had it not been for the outbreak of

World War II). In addition, the temporal boundaries between the Early and Middle and the Middle and High periods correspond to natural intervals in Nabokov's creative work. Prior to writing "Pil'gram" (The Aurelian, 1930), he had not produced a single short story for over a year, in contrast to the steady yearly output of the 1920s. Such a hiatus marked a transition to a decidedly new understanding of the structure of the short story in "The Aurelian" and the subsequent works of the 1930s. "Mademoiselle O" celebrates the beginning of Nabokov's High period for two reasons: it was written in French and already bespeaks his shifting linguistic orientation (eventually resulting in his permanent switch from Russian to English), but also his forthcoming move to France, preempting a second emigration. My periodization takes into account the maturation of Nabokov's poetics. The stories of the Early period exemplify his artistic laboratory. During the Middle period, he developed an innovative poetics while also perfecting his skills as a professional belletrist. The High period, the briefest of all, produced a series of absolute masterpieces that receive the highest score in Nabokov's dialogic competition with Chekhov and Bunin. This period yielded his best stories, wherein the writer's philosophical outlook dovetails with his craft in the most harmonious fashion.

A division into three periods also corresponds organically to the distribution of Nabokov's novels over the Russian years. The Early period produced *Mary* (1926), *King, Queen, Knave* (1928), *The Defense* (1929), and *The Eye* (1930); the Middle, *Glory* (1931), *Kamera obskura* (1932–1933), *Despair* (1934), and *Invitation to a Beheading* (1935–1936); the High, *The Gift* (1937–1938), *The Real Life of Sebastian Knight* (1939; 1941), and *The Enchanter* (1939; 1986). For the American period, the language of the stories was an obvious criterion. Although in the course of this study I will make occasional references to several of the ten American stories, I have chosen not to engage in a full-length discussion of their poetics. The main reason behind this decision is that all ten stories of the American period have elicited much more attention than their Russian counterparts.[32]

While working with Nabokov's short stories, I faced a need to examine not only the texts included in his collections, but also the original publications in the Russian émigré periodicals. When the latter were unavailable—as in the case of "Paskhal'nyi dozhd'" (Easter Rain), until recently believed to have been lost, or in the case of the Russian stories still unpublished in the original—I went back to the surviving original manuscripts and corrected typescripts.[33] While it would be impossible to account for every single variant in the known versions of each short story, I have tried to incorporate a series of observations dealing with Nabokov's methods of reworking his short stories, from drafts to final versions, as well as the textual discrepancies between the different published versions. In several cases, especially that of "The Aurelian," I will provide a detailed account of the significant changes from first draft to fair copy to the journal version to the collected text. Since many of the Russian stories exist as a nearly bilingual body of works, I was compelled to examine and compare all the parallel Russian and English versions.[34] In many cases, I have consulted the manuscripts of Nabokov's translations in order to understand the kind of linguistic and stylistic choices the writer opted for after his second glance at his Russian works.

Finally, brief comments on the structure of this book are in order. Chapter 1 examines in chronological fashion the parallel evolution of Nabokov's sui generis metaphysical outlook and the poetics of his short stories. The chapter traces the evolution of a number of devices paradigmatic of Nabokov's stories, including his use of various forms of markedness (prosodic, iconic, etc.) to signal to the reader that she or he has approached a privileged textual passage. Viewing Nabokov's entire oeuvre as a single aesthetic and philosophical continuum, I will also demonstrate that he frequently used his expertise in versification to introduce devices of poetry into prose.

Interlude considers the techniques Nabokov devised and employed in order to depict the space where the events of his short stories occur.

Chapter 2 includes four case studies of exemplary short stories from the Early, Middle, and High periods of Nabokov's career. Each section anatomizes a short story in light of paradigms outlined in Chapter 1 against the backdrop of the entire corpus of his short fiction. The first section negotiates the status of the author in the text of a remarkable early short story, "The Return of Chorb." The second focuses on the way Nabokov's view of fate and death structures the narrative closure of a fine butterfly story, "The Aurelian." The third section considers "Cloud, Castle, Lake," one of the best achievements of the Russian short story, as a culmination of Nabokov's pre–World War II metaphysical quest. Finally, the fourth section analyzes his last Russian short story as a metaliterary testament regarding its author's place in Russian poetry, as well as his pronouncement on the future of Russian culture in exile.

Chapter 3 discusses Nabokov's apprenticeship to Chekhov. The second half focuses on Nabokov's multilevel dialogue with "Lady with a Lap Dog" (1899), an emblem of Chekhov's poetics. The case of Ivan Bunin, Nabokov's fellow-exile, gave me an opportunity to elaborate the notion of the poetics of rivalry. Chapter 4 thus explores the impact of the writers' personal and literary relationship on the dynamics of their poetics and shows that the two masters, the older Bunin and the younger Nabokov, challenged each other to a fierce competition in the genre of the short story.

Coda inquires into the generic mutability of Nabokov's short stories and explores the relationship between his short stories and his epistolary and autobiographical heritage. The short stories, perhaps more than the novels, elucidate the equation between Nabokov's life and his art. The applicability of Poststructuralist theory to his writings is questioned.

My chief theoretical interest in this book is to arrive at a theory of reading Nabokov's short fiction that bridges his life and his art by negotiating between biography and poetics. Several overarching themes or theoretical leitmotifs recur throughout this study. Each section not only offers another perspective on the short stories, but also reconsiders the conclusions of the earlier sections in a different hermeneutic tonality. If the following pages have captured some of the poetic melodies and prosaic harmonies of Nabokov's short stories, my efforts have not been in vain.

1 Writing and Reading the Otherworld

. . . .

We should always remember that the work of art is invariably the creation of a new world, so that the first thing we should do is to study that new world as closely as possible, approaching it as something brand new, having no obvious connection with the worlds we already know.[1]—Vladimir Nabokov, "Good Readers and Good Writers"

Véra Nabokov was the first to point to the centrality of *potustoronnost'* (otherworldliness) for Nabokov's life and art. In her foreword to the 1979 posthumous collection of her late husband's verses, Nabokov's wife wrote:

> Теперь, посылая этот сборник в печать, хочу обратить внимание читателя на главную тему Набокова. Она, кажется, не была никем отмечена, а между тем ею пропитано всё, что он писал; она, как некий водяной знак, символизирует всё его творчество. Я говорю о „потусторонности", как он сам её назвал в своём последнем стихотворении „Влюблённость".
> (*Stikhi*, 3)

> (I would like to call the reader to a key undercurrent in Nabokov's work, which permeates all that he has written and characterizes it like a kind of watermark. I am speaking of a strange otherworldliness, the "hereafter" (*potustoronnost'*), as he himself called it in his last poem, "Being in Love" [translation deviates somewhat from the original]).[2]

Covert claims regarding the fundamentally metaphysical nature of Nabokov's art had been made by the émigré critics in the 1930s and carried over into the 1950s. Vladimir Varshavskii came closest among Russian émigré critics to the "metaphysical view" of Nabokov. Varshavskii's book *Nezamechennoe pokolenie* (The Generation Unnoticed 1956) summed up his observations about Nabokov's art: "at times . . . one even regrets that Nabokov is engaged in belles-lettres rather than metaphysics."[3] Western students of Nabokov did not turn their attention to his metaphysics until the late 1970s, and it was not until the 1990s that their voices became audible in the chorus. In a pioneering dissertation, "Cosmic Synchronization and Other Worlds in the Work of Vladimir Nabokov" (1979), Jonathan Borden Sisson argued that through his fiction and poetry Nabokov shared with the reader his transrational awareness of the existence of other worlds outside mundane reality. Sisson was particularly illuminating in his exploration of Nabokov's artistic means of evoking "aesthetic bliss"—the total effect the writer's works have upon the reader. Sisson also explored the seminal notion of "cosmic synchronization," Nabokov's prerequisite of artistic creation defined in his autobiography, *Speak, Memory,* as "the capacity of thinking several things at a time" (*SM,* 218). Cosmic synchronization enables Nabokov and his readers to "perceive—or to seem to perceive—all things in space and all moments in time simultaneously," which also underwrites the existence in Nabokov's works of "simultaneous but mutually exclusive fictional worlds presented in ambiguous contraposition in order that the reader's habits of perception are violated, thus liberating the reader's mind and stimulating it to a greater capacity of consciousness."[4]

In an influential study, *Worlds in Regression* (1985), D. Barton Johnson established that a self-reproducing "two-world" model operates in Nabokov's novels and "describes their underlying cosmology": "the fictional world inside that of the author-persona who in turn aspires to that of his author (the real one from our point of view) who stands in the same relationship to his author *ad infinitum:* worlds in infinite regression." Johnson claimed that the relationship between Nabokov's metaphysics and the formal aspects of his art was a reciprocal one: while the inferable cosmology of Nabokov's works may be a "projection of a personal cosmology," the "aesthetic cosmology may provide a personal cosmology."[5] In 1989 Ellen Pifer expanded our understanding as she splendidly placed Nabokov's transcendent notion of love at the heart of "Nabokov's universe": "love is quite literally the power that exposes human beings to 'alien worlds'; love opens them to the world of other people and to the even stranger realm of 'the beyond. . . .'"[6] Finally, in 1991 Vladimir E. Alexandrov demonstrated in *Nabokov's Otherworld* that Nabokov's novelistic and discursive works are underlain and triggered by the writer's "sui generis faith in a transcendent realm."[7] Arguing against the conventional view of Nabokov as primarily a metaliterary writer, Alexandrov proposed that the metaliterary serves as a model for his metaphysical beliefs. Alexandrov also introduced the seminal notion of Nabokov's metaphysics, ethics, and aesthetics as "names for a single continuum of beliefs, not for separate categories of Nabokov's interests."[8]

Brian Boyd's acclaimed two-volume biography (1990, 1991) emphasized the centrality of a metaphysical quest in Nabokov's career while reexposing the great Russian-American writer to a wide readership.[9] Paradoxically, even most educated readers still perceive Nabokov as a brilliant yet soulless conjurer, a literary gamesman if not an aestheticizing pornographer. It should come as no surprise that the post–World War II American writers who have most explicitly claimed Nabokov as their predecessor are the so-called postmodernists: Donald Barthelme, Robert Coover, Stanley Elkin, John Hawkes, and others.[10] The lasting and one-sided view of Nabokov as a metaliterary writer continues to be buttressed by critics who are reluctant to recognize the intimate connections between Nabokov's art and his sui generis metaphysics. Such formulations as Richard Rorty's remark that "for [Nabokov] the distinctions among art, religion, and metaphysics—like the distinction between inventing and intuiting—just don't matter" provide an additional compelling motivation for the present discussion, especially since little has been written about the metaphysics of Nabokov's short stories.[11]

While our current ideas about Nabokov's metaphysics have been elaborated and tested largely on the material of the novels, it was in the short stories that he progressively embraced his sui generis cosmology. In fact, not until *Zashchita Luzhina* (The Defense, 1929), Nabokov's third Russian novel, did the otherworld emerge as the central thematic and structural cluster in his fictions. *The Defense* was preceded not only by two Russian novels rather free of metaphysics—*Mashen'ka* (Mary, 1926) and *Korol', dama, valet* (King, Queen, Knave, 1928)—but also by thirty-three short stories where one observes on an atomistic level the gradual and parallel changes in Nabokov's poetics and world vision. Surely this is good reason to launch a full-scale exploration of the otherworld in the stories.

Of Nabokov's own statements about the metaphysics of his art, "Being in Love," the poem referred to in his wife's preface, seems indispensable to the analysis of the short stories. It was written by the protagonist of his last finished novel, *Look at the Harlequins!* (1974), Vadim Vadimych (cf. Nabokov's first name and patronymic, Vladimir Vladimirovich). A Russian émigré writer like his author, Vadim Vadimych composes "on the night of . . . a more oblique, more metaphysical little poem" which he recites— first in Russian—to a young English woman named Iris:

Влюблённость

Мы забываем что влюблённость
Не просто поворот лица
А под купавами бездонность,
Ночная паника пловца.

Покуда снится, снись, влюблённость
Но пробуждением не мучь,
И лучше недоговорённость
Чем эта щель и этот луч.

Напоминаю что влюблённость
Не явь, что метины не те,
Что может быть потусторонность
Приотворилась в темноте.
(*LATH*, 25; cf. *Stikhi*, 317–318)

In the text of the novel, the poem appears in Nabokov's English transliteration, followed by Vadim Vadimych's prose translation, which is also furnished with occasional remarks:

> I have it here on the back. It goes like this. We forget—or rather tend to forget—that being in love (*vlyublyonnost'*) does not depend on the facial angle of the loved one, but is a bottomless spot under the nenuphars, *a swimmer's panic in the night* (here the iambic tetrameter happens to be rendered—last line of the first stanza, *nochnáya pánika plovtsá*). Next stanza: While the dreaming is good—in the sense of "while the going is good"—do keep appearing to us in our dreams *vlyublyonnost'*, but do not torment us by waking us up or telling too much: reticence is better than that chink and that moonbeam. Now comes the last stanza of this philosophical love poem.... *Napomináyu*, I remind you, that *vlyublyonnost'* is not wide-awake reality, that the markings are not the same (a moon-striped ceiling, *polosatyy ot luny potolok*, is, for instance, not the same kind of reality as a ceiling by day), and that, maybe, the hereafter stands slightly ajar in the dark. (*LATH*, 25–26)[12]

In Vadim Vadimych's recital of "Being in Love" lies a quintessential situation wherein a Nabokovian literary persona formulates and delivers a semitransparent key to Nabokov's own poetics. The poem establishes links between the verbal limitations of writing about love and love's metaphysical nature. Being in love offers the *innamorati* glimpses of a different reality ("vliublënnnost' ne iav'") with distinctive manifestations of time and space ("metiny ne te"). A person in love becomes privy to a different world which reveals itself clandestinely to this person ("potustoronnost' / priotvorilas' v temnote"). In his English translation and commentary, Vadim Vadimych refers to the reciprocal reality of being in love as "the hereafter." This choice of an English equivalent for *potustoronnost'* does not seem ideal, for it suggests a temporal diachrony between this reality (*iav'*) and the one which follows it, the hereafter. In the Russian poem, nothing of the kind is suggested. *Potustoronnost'* (literally, the-other-sided-ness, from *po tu storonu*, on that side, as opposed to *po siu storonu*, on this side) is a domain that exists synchronically with and influences the reality of the mundane world (which Nabokov terms "wide-awake reality"), and being in love allows the chosen person to partake of this other, idealized reality during her or his lifetime.[13] *Potustoronnost'*, which Alexandrov aptly translates as the "otherworld," reveals itself to the chosen subjects (in the poem, to those in love) through glimpses or intimations ("priotvorilas'": stands slightly ajar).[14] The first and second stanzas also suggest the otherworld as the source, locus, and ultimate object of love. In the first stanza, "Bezdonnost' pod kupavami" is not merely a "bottomless spot" under "water-lilies" that astonishes a night swimmer, but also a fathomless otherworld that opens itself ("priotvorilas' v temnote"; from the Russian *otvorit'sia*, to have opened oneself) to a person chosen to be in love. The second stanza also paints being in love as an otherworldly dream ("snis', vliublënnost'"); communicating the meaning of the dream would amount to awakening the person and interrupting the dream. Such an awakening from the perfect dream is likened to the painful effect of sunlight presumably falling through a chink in the blinds. Ultimately, the poem speaks of language (and literary language as its special variety) as incommensurate with the transcendent experience of love.

In this chapter, I will show that the otherworld distinguishes Nabokov's short stories from those of his predecessors and contemporaries in Russian literature. I will regard the otherworld as a privileged space in the textual memory that positions the reader vis-à-vis the text of a Nabokov short story so as to ensure both a deeply personal reception and a firm place in the reader's memory. Nabokov's otherworld is not a domain where the souls of the deceased dwell in traditional metaphysical systems. It is a sui generis dimension which exists simultaneously with the author's mundane reality and which is both a source and an addressee of artistic creation. Ontologically, Nabokov's otherworld is akin to the domain beyond the looking glass where Lewis Carroll's Alice discovers that all the mundane laws of existence have been overturned.[15] Aesthetically, it is a realm where "false commonsense"—the enemy of literary imagination—"must be shot dead," "right then, just before it blurts out the word *s, e, double-l*" (*LL,* 380). Emotionally, this otherworld is a domain of idealized timeless love, impossible in the mundane world and yet aspired to by a gamut of characters from Nikitin in the early story "The Seaport" (1924) to Vasen'ka (Victor) in the late "Spring in Fialta" (1936). Overall, Nabokov's otherworld is an antiworld with respect to the reality of this world, and not much more can be said about it in terms other than Nabokov's own. Even Nabokov hesitates to speak in conventional terms about his "main secret":

> Эта тайна, та-та, та-та-та-та, та-та,
> а точнее сказать я не вправе.

> That main secret, tra-tá-ta, tra-tá-ta tra-tá
> —and I must not be overexplicit.

> (*PP,* 110–111)

As early as the mid-1920s, Nabokov's short stories begin to exhibit elements of a metaphysical exploration. In several stories of the Early period, glimpses of a timeless idealized realm show through openings, "chinks" in the quotidian world. Encounters with the otherworld privilege certain of Nabokov's characters, not infrequently the estranged protagonist of a given story, over individuals who surround them. In the short stories, Nabokov creates a unique type of a protagonist, the author's representative (*predstavitel'*). Ellen Pifer poignantly called Nabokov's otherworld "solicitous": he endows his privileged characters with the gift of being able to see otherworldly beatitude and love despite the *poshlost'* (untranslatable Russian term for a combination of vapidness, vulgarity, and philistinism) of quotidian existence.[16]

Memory plays a crucial role when the otherworld manifests itself to the chosen characters. The otherworld in the short stories serves as a depository of idealized memories of things unattainable or lost—often but not always a beloved woman, a deceased person, or a distant homeland. Nabokov's privileged characters communicate with their idealized and exalted memories during moments when the door to the otherworld "stands slightly ajar." In accordance with the Nabokovian model of reading which I will pursue in this study, when the ideal reader identifies with an experience of a privileged character, her or his consciousness grows to join with that of the character. Since Nabokov shares with some of his protagonists his experience of the otherworld, the reader too becomes privy to such experiences, thereby entering the cycle which D. Barton Johnson has termed "worlds in infinite regression."[17]

In depicting manifestations of the otherworld as perceived by his characters, with an intensely sensual apprehension of reality in its variegated particulars, Nabokov faces a paradoxical need to employ precise and controlled linguistic and narrative means to record inexplicable and often evanescent experiences. When he records otherworldly experiences in textual memory, he writes the otherworld. A reader partaking of the character's otherworldly experience reads the otherworld and copies it into the reader's memory. While revisiting a particular glimpse of the otherworld now etched in the reader's memory, one rereads Nabokov's otherworld and even rewrites it to a certain degree.

Given Nabokov's steady output of short stories, averaging 3.5 per year throughout the Early period, 3.2 throughout the Middle period, and 1.8 throughout the High period, the stories reflect the smallest changes that his metaphysics underwent throughout the 1920s–1930s. One can trace the sources of his remarkable achievements of the 1930s, such as "Spring in Fialta" or "Cloud, Castle, Lake," back to the early 1920s. In several stories of the Early period, Nabokov explores the fusion of traditional Judeo-Christian metaphysics with elements of the fantastical and/or supernatural. Later he would repudiate such experimentation with angels and paradises for the sake of a transcendent realm sustained by no religious or mythological references but by language, memory, and imagination alone.

Such pieces as the plotless and impressionistic "Slovo" (The Word, 1923) and "Groza" (The Thunderstorm, 1924) abound in elements of biblical mythopoetics and imagery. Stylistically, they are also reminiscent of symbolist works (especially of Fëdor Sologub's short fictions) and the ornamentalism and folklorism of Aleksei Remizov. Remizov's ornamental style, the narrative technique of *skaz,* and pagan mythopoetics are most manifest in Nabokov's embryonic story "Nezhit'" (The Woodsprite, 1921), where a wood goblin finds himself exiled from his native Russia. In "The Word," published in a Christmas issue of the Berlin newspaper *Rul'* (The Rudder) in 1923, an angel visits the nostalgic narrator to grant him hope and consolation.[18] The angel utters only one word ("molvil edinstvennoe slovo") that throws the narrator into rapturous tears. The reader never finds out what the angel actually said. In "The Thunderstorm," the narrator witnesses another apparition, this time by Elijah the Prophet, the mighty figure from the Old Testament (1 Kings, 2 Kings) also omnipresent in Russian folklore as *Il'ia-prorok.* Elijah addresses the narrator as Elisha (Elisei)—the peasant who in biblical mythopoetics witnesses Elijah's chariot of fire while plowing a field. "Udar kryla" (Wingstroke, 1924), Nabokov's fourth short fiction, culminates in a long sequence with angels taking part. The sentence follows a conversation between the psychologically tormented suicidal protagonist, an Englishman named Kern, and a homosexual philosopher of death and dying, an Italian by the name of Monfiori. The conversation is set in an Alpine lodge in Switzerland, and the story seems to have been informed by Nabokov's vacation in the Swiss Alps in the company of a Cambridge classmate, the half-Italian Bobby de Calry.[19] Prior to his encounter with the angel, Kern rejects the biblical God by calling him "gazoobraznoe pozvonochnoe" (gaseous vertebrate), following Monfiori's suggestion that "there is God, after all" ("A Bog vsë taki est'"; Stories, 36).[20] After his conversation with Monfiori (in whom he confides his decision to die), Kern returns to his room. He is disturbed by barking which emanates from behind the wall. In the room next door lives Isabel, a stunning young Englishwoman and an object of Kern's desire (her image anticipates that of Iris in Look at the Harlequins!). When Kern storms into Isabel's room, he discovers a furry doglike angel who has apparently been making love to her. Kern struggles with the angelic beast and violently overpowers him. Thus, as early as 1923 Nabokov combined traditional religious imagery with psychological aberrations. He would soon find this path to be fruitless. Toward the end of the story, Isabel, a fine athlete—whom Kern characterizes as "letuchaia" (literally, airy with all the subtleties of this word's connotations)—jumps in a skiing competition only to die in midflight. The angel's revenge "crucifie[s Isabel] in midair" ("raspiataia v vozdukhe" in the Russian; Stories, 42). Features of a sui generis otherworld gradually oust traditional Judeo-Christian attributes. At this point one finds hints of the otherworldly, such as a reference to "rainbow-colored gods" ("raduzhnye bogi"; Stories, 50) in "Bogi" (Gods, late 1923).[21] Structured as a confession to the narrator's beloved and containing autobiographical references, "Gods" anticipates several of Nabokov's addresses to an idealized otherworldly beloved in the stories of the High period or in The Gift. There is also the story "Zvuki" (Sounds, late 1923) in which the village schoolmaster Pal Palych splits into two halves; one, his otherworldly double, glitters as a reflection on the surface of water: "a second Pal Palych quivered in the black ripples" (cf. the Russian: "drugoi Pal Palych drozhal na ziabi vody"; Stories, 24). In 1937, in the masterful story "Cloud, Castle, Lake," a shimmering reflection on the surface of a lake signifies the boundary between this world and the otherworld.

The year 1924 yielded the highest (fourteen) annual number of stories in Nabokov's entire career (see Appendix). "Katastrofa" (Details of a Sunset, literally, The Catastrophe, 1924), Nabokov's thirteenth story to date, presents us with the most explicit otherworldly motif to appear thus far.[22] A triangular intrigue sets the plot into motion. Mark, a German salesclerk, a philistine described bathetically as a "demigod," does not suspect the return of his fiancée's former love, "the handsome ruined foreigner who last year rented a room from her mother" (*Stories, 79*). Mark spends his days in a state of bliss. He holds his fiancée, Klara, in an idealized realm while refusing to take heed of his mother's warnings that Klara is not to be trusted. Mark perceives the world around him as colored by his beloved's presence:

> He glanced at his watch and decided to go straight to his fiancée's without stopping at his mother's. His happiness and the limpidity of the evening air made his head spin a little. An arrow of bright copper struck the lacquered shoe of a fop jumping out of a car. The puddles, which still had not dried, surrounded by the bruise of dark damp (the live eyes of the asphalt), reflected the soft incandescence of the evening. The houses were as gray as ever; yet the roofs, the moldings above the upper floors, the gilt-edged lightning rods, the stone cupolas, the colonnettes—which nobody notices during the day, for day-people seldom look up—were now bathed in rich ochre, the sunset's airy warmth, and thus they seemed unexpected and magical, those upper protrusions, balconies, cornices, pillars, contrasting sharply, because of their tawny brilliance, with the drab façades beneath.
>
> "Oh, how happy I am," Mark kept musing, "how everything around celebrates my happiness." (*Stories, 82*)

One detects a note of light irony in the omniscient narrator's voice. This, however, does not diminish the importance of the motif of transcendent designs shimmering behind the façades of the mundane world as perceived by those in love (i.e., the motif of Vadim Vadimych's poem in *Look at the Harlequins!*). Heady with anticipation, Mark rides a streetcar to Klara's house at sunset. The otherworldly motifs are about to culminate. As Mark jumps to the ground, he undergoes an experience that the narrator presents through Mark's own eyes. The reader is never quite certain exactly what happened. Apparently, Mark was run down by a bus: "He felt as if a thick thunderbolt had gone through him from head to toe, and then nothing" (*Stories, 83*). In a near-death vision, "he saw, at a distance, his own figure, the slender back of Mark Standfuss, who was walking . . . as if nothing had happened. Marveling, he caught up with himself in one easy sweep, and . . . his entire frame filled with a gradually diminishing vibration" (*Stories*, 83). The world which Mark has now entered continues to be painted in otherworldly colors:

> The street was wide and gay. The colors of the sunset had invaded half of the sky. Upper stories and roofs were bathed in glorious light. Up there, Mark could discern translucent porticoes, friezes and frescoes, trellises covered with orange roses, winged statues that lifted skyward golden, unbearably blazing lyres. In bright undulations, ethereally, festively, these architectonic enchantments were receding into the heavenly distance, and Mark could not understand how he had never noticed before those galleries, those temples suspended on high.
> (*Stories*, 83)

Nabokov's narrator speaks of the fact that Mark is looking at the familiar architectural ensembles of his home city and seeing it anew, in an otherworldly "glorious" light. The perception of the otherworld is beholder-specific, and the otherworld itself is synchronic with the mundane world.

In his near-death vision, Mark proceeds to Klara's house to find her in the company of several strangers. All he is able to utter as an explanation is a cryptic phrase, "The foreigner is offering the aforementioned prayers on the river . . ." (*Stories*, 84). A foreigner's offering prayers on the river also recalls—*mutatis mutandis*—Christ's preaching by the river Jordan. This is one of the last instances of Nabokov's use of biblical mythopoetics in the short stories. Soon thereafter, the otherworld would carry traces of nothing but "those temples suspended on high" ("ètikh khramov, povisshikh v vyshine"; *VCh*, 154). For a short while, Mark regains consciousness in a hospital ward, "lying supine, mutilated and bandaged." His last thought is about his beloved Klara. Then, as the narrator concludes his story, "Mark no longer breathed, Mark had departed—whither, into what other dreams, none can tell" (*Stories*, 85). Ending with Mark's death in a hospital bed, the story suggests that dying is not to be equated with entering the space of the otherworld, much as glimpses of the otherworld itself are not to be equated with vestiges of the hereafter as the domain of the dead.

During the exceptionally prolific year 1924, Nabokov, like an alchemist, mixed elements of Judeo-Christian mythopoetics with the supernatural, pagan, or fairy-tale elements. In "Drakon" (The Dragon) he parodied the medieval topos of dragon-slaying in the setting of a modern industrial society. In this modern fairy-tale a dragon wakes up hungry in his cave and comes to a big city where two major tobacco companies are at war. One of them uses the dragon to advertise its cigarettes. The other tobacco company literalizes the dragon-slaying metaphor by building a giant knight whose armor is pasted over with ads for its products. Terrified, the poor dragon flees to die in his cave. The story was never published in Nabokov's lifetime.[23] One may speculate that he found it artistically schematic and therefore unsatisfactory. Toward the end of 1924, his search for unparalleled themes and plots began to lead him away from traditional religious and mythological topoi.

It would be wrong to infer that Nabokov's sole concern during the Early period was to find artistic expression for his increasingly unorthodox metaphysical vision. A number of stories from the period—for the most part originally published in Berlin's *The Rudder* and the Riga newspaper *Segodnia* (Today)—testify to Nabokov's growth as a professional belletrist. One should always keep in mind that throughout the 1920s and 1930s honoraria for Nabokov's short stories constituted a significant part of his income. Two-thirds of his Russian stories came out first in newspapers. Writing short fiction that had to appeal to both a newspaper editorial staff and a newspaper audience imposed definite limitations on length, subject, narrative structure, and philosophical outlook. The quality of the leading Russian émigré newspapers such as *Rul'* (The Rudder), *Poslednie novosti* (The Latest News), and *Segodnia* (Today) tended to be remarkably high. In fact, the Russian émigré press presents students of culture in exile with an unprecedented concentration of superb littérateurs contributing to daily newspapers. (Nabokov's co-contributors in Berlin, Paris, Prague, Riga, Sofia, Warsaw, Belgrade, and Shanghai included Georgii Adamovich, Konstantin Bal'mont, Ivan Bunin, Evgenii Chirikov, Zinaida Gippius, Aleksandr Kuprin, Dmitrii Merezhkovskii, Irina Odoevtseva, Aleksei Remizov, Ivan Shmelëv, Nadezhda Tèffi, Marina Tsvetaeva, Vladimir Veidle, Boris Zaitsev, and many others.) Still, at times the very urge to dash off a story must have outweighed Nabokov's experiments with writing the otherworld. Nonetheless, his later achievements, such as the stories "Spring in Fialta" or "The Aurelian," where narrative perfection runs apace with a focus on otherworldly beatitude, would have been unthinkable without both his belletristic apprenticeship and metaphysical quest in the 1920s.

Stories of the 1920s introduce motifs, devices, and tropes that Nabokov would later utilize and perfect in either the short stories or novels. The protagonist of "Port" (The Seaport, 1924), the émigré Nikitin, comes to Marseilles looking for work and his Russian beloved.[24] When he mistakes a French prostitute for a distant beloved, his state of disarray is described as follows: "V pamiati u nego proneslos' chto-to, kak sorvavshaiasia zve-zda . . ." (Something akin to a falling star hurtled through his memory; *VCh*, 25/*Stories*, 65). Nikitin experiences a spell of happiness as he "recog-nizes" the woman: "Bozhe moi, kak khorosho . . ." (God, this is wonder-ful . . .; *VCh*, 25; *Stories*, 65). Later, when Nikitin has realized the misap-prehension, his loneliness and longing are encoded in the description of the night: "Prokatilas' paduchaia zvezda s neozhidannost'iu serdechnogo pereboia" (A falling star shot by with the suddenness of a missed heart-beat; *VCh*, 26/*Stories*, 66). What was earlier a metaphor of a powerful recollection ("falling star") has now been transferred to a depiction of a physical heartache. Links between an aching heart and an otherworldly experience recur in several short stories, including "Lik," "Perfection," and "Cloud, Castle, Lake," and novels *Priglashenie na kazn'* (Invitation to a Beheading, 1938) and *Pnin* (1957). In addition, both Nikitin of "The Sea-port" and Luzhin, the protagonist of "Sluchainost'" (A Matter of Chance, 1924), inform the character of Galatov in *Mary*. All three identify their beloved women with an idyllic otherworldly Russia of their past. All three find it impossible to face anything short of a perfect recollection. As well as being independent works of art, the early short stories frequently served as test-sites for future explosions of style and theme.

To return to Nabokov's experiments with writing the otherworld, "Ve-netsianka" (La Veneziana, 1924) deserves special attention because it em-ploys elements of the fantastical in order to explore the connections between desire, painting, and the otherworld as sources of artistic inspira-tion and expression. The longest among the early stories and only recently published in the original, "La Veneziana," like "Kartofel'nyi Èl'f" (The Potato Elf, 1924) and "Mest'" (Revenge, 1924), is set in England.[25] Nabo-kov's experience as a student in Cambridge must have fed into two of the story's characters, college roommates presumably at Oxford or Cam-bridge. One of them, Simpson, is spending a weekend at the castle of his roommate's father. The father, an English aristocrat referred to as the Colonel, is a prominent collector of paintings. The reader learns that the Colonel resents his son Frank, an aspiring painter, for wasting his time in-stead of making the most of his studies at the university. The main triangle of desire entails one McGore, an old art dealer and the Colonel's friend and adviser, his young wife, Maureen, and Frank. McGore and his wife are at the castle because he has located a rare canvas by a fifteenth-century Italian and sold it to the Colonel (the published Russian original renders the artist's name as "Sebastiano Luchiano," the English translation as "Se-bastiano Luciani").[26] Sebastiano Luciani, called Sebastiano del Piombo

(1485–1547), was a Renaissance painter of the Venetian School. Nabokov might have seen del Piombo's famous painting *Ritratto femminile* ("*Dorotea*") in Berlin (see Figure 1). The landscape vista in the background of del Piombo's painting—a common feature of Italian Renaissance painting—symbolizes an alluring *otherspace*, with a dissimilar set of parameters.

Maureen and Frank are in the midst of a tempestuous affair. As if the double intrigue was not convoluted already, Simpson himself feels an irresistible attraction to Maureen. After looking at the Colonel's new painting, a portrait of a woman with fruit, Simpson notices an uncanny resemblance between Maureen and the woman on the canvas. To add to Simpson's fascination, McGore shares a "secret": years of dealing with paintings have taught him that through an act of concentrated will one can enter the space of a given painting and explore it from within. Simpson is equally drawn to Maureen and the Venetian woman in the painting. At night, some otherworldly magnetism draws him to the gallery where the new canvas hangs. Literalizing McGore's supernatural metaphor, Simpson walks into the space of the portrait, where the beautiful Maureen / La Veneziana offers him a lemon. Simpson "grows" into the canvas, becomes part of its painted space. The story's fantastical spring has now almost unwound itself. In the morning McGore discovers that his wife has eloped with Frank. Naturally, this infuriates the Colonel. What maddens him even more is a discovery of "poor Simpson's portrait" painted next to the woman's face on the new acquisition. McGore spends the morning scraping Simpson's presence off the canvas and restoring its original look. After he has finished, he tosses the rags with the flakes of paint out of the window. The remains of Simpson's portrait land on the lawn. Later, the Colonel's gardener stumbles onto Simpson sleeping on the lawn. Holding a lemon in his hand, Simpson reports having had a "monstrous dream" (*Stories*, 114). McGore confesses to the Colonel that the portrait of the Venetian Woman is actually the result of a scam: intending to prove his talent as an artist to his father, Frank had talked McGore into a fraudulent scheme. Frank is the actual creator of the magnificent portrait. The Colonel's response concludes the story: "I'm proud of my son" (*Stories*, 115).

Why such a long retelling and commentary? I believe the story embodies several key elements that would become central to Nabokov's poetics. Afloat in the story's enchanting and elegant syntax, and never fully synthesized and harmonized, these elements call for scrutiny. One should pay increasing attention to Nabokov's concern with the problem of entering a space whose parameters differ from the regular space enveloping a character. In addition, he constructs this otherspace to host visually perfect

1. Sebastiano del Piombo. *Bildnis einer jungen Römerin*. Staatliche Museen zu Berlin—Preußicher Kulturbesitz. Gemäldegalerie. Photo: Jörg P. Anders. Reproduced by permission.

images. In the case of La Veneziana's portrait, the pictorial space of the canvas becomes charged with the features of the beautiful Maureen. Remarkably, both the creator of the portrait, Frank, and the explorer of its otherspace, Simpson, perceive it through a prism of eternity. For Frank, the artist and visionary, creating the portrait was not only an opportunity to settle the score with his skeptical father, to prove his own worth as an artist, but also a way of immortalizing his beloved, the stunning and sensuous Maureen, for whom he longed while away in Italy. The motif of what Nabokov later defined, in "Cloud, Castle, Lake," as longing for "that lady, another man's wife" (*Stories*, 430) is nascent in several early short stories, including "Bakhman" (Bachmann, 1924), in which the protagonist's beloved is described as having "the face of a madonna that had not quite come out" (*Stories*, 116). In "La Veneziana" the "madonna" did come out perfectly.

One is also reminded of the pictorial context of the Italian High Renaissance, and of the Venetian School in particular, often blurring the boundary between secular portrayal of feminine seductive beauty and ecclesiastic representation of an idealized Madonna. Frank charges his creation with extraordinary perfection to further his love for the original and thereby not repeat Pygmalion's tragic mistake. In contrast to Frank, his friend Simpson falls in love with an image of idealized feminine beauty, which appears to him even better than the possessor of this beauty in flesh and blood. Simpson succumbs to the magnetism of the otherworldly pictorial space, which gleams through an opening in his mundane reality. In his consciousness, the image of beauty wins over beauty itself. To put it differently, when Simpson reads the text of the otherworld within the story by gazing deeply at the portrait, he is compelled to become part of that text. During the act of reading, the reader who follows Simpson in his lunatic exploration thus experiences a textual simulacrum of the pictorial space which Simpson transgresses in the story. What we have then is a story, a verbal text, which frames another text—the pictorial text of the otherworld rendered by a linguistic medium—and thereby foregrounds a specific model of its reading.

D. Barton Johnson has drawn attention to Nabokov's remark from a 1967 interview: "I think that what I would welcome at the close of a book of mine is a sensation of its world receding in the distance and stopping somewhere there, suspended afar like a picture in a picture: *The Artist's Studio* by Van Bock" (*SO*, 72–73). Johnson saw in this formulation, based on a painting by a fictitious Flemish artist (Nabokov's mystification: cf. the invented French philosopher Delalande in *The Gift*; Van Bock is an ana-

gram of Nabokov), a model of his "aesthetic cosmology." The real pictorial subtext behind Nabokov's alleged painting is Jan Van Eyck's *Giovanni
Arnolfini and His Bride* (also known as *Wedding Portrait* [1434]; National
Gallery, London). Van Eyck's painting depicts "a young couple solemnly
exchanging marriage vows in the privacy of their bridal chamber. They
seem to be quite alone, but as we scrutinize the mirror, conspicuously
placed behind them, we discover in the reflection that two other persons
have entered the room. One of them must be the artist, since the words
above the mirror . . . tell us that . . . Jan Van Eyck was here in the year
1434." [27] On the basis of this information, Johnson concluded that "the two
paintings, . . . , one imaginary and one real, constitute a concise paradigm
of Nabokov's art: *ut pictura poesis.*" [28] The fruitful connections between
painting, writing, and reading the otherworld are all explored in "La
Veneziana." Nabokov's lifelong interest in painting might in part be explained by the parallels he saw between the acts of reading a literary text
and a pictorial text. In his Cornell lectures, Nabokov discussed this subject: "When we read a book for the first time the very process of labori-
ously moving our eyes from left to right, line after line, page after page,
this complicated physical work upon the book, the very process of learning in terms of space and time what the book is about, this stands between
us and artistic appreciation. When we look at a painting we do not have to
move our eyes in a special way even if, as in a book, the picture contains
elements of depth and development. The element of time does not really
enter in a first contact with a painting" (*LL,* 3). [29] Something very similar
to what Nabokov described in his lecture takes place during the act of
reading "La Veneziana."

Finally, the story exhibits a vanishing element of traditional religion.
A watchman referred to as a "guardian angel" (*Stories,* 109) flies by the
reader only to dissolve in the expanding textual space. Such an angelic disappearance literally signals that time-honored biblical mythopoetics give
way to Nabokov's original poetics sustained by intuitions of the beatific
and beneficent otherworld. Such an intuition would be best described in
Nabokov's fourth, underappreciated novel, *Podvig* (Glory, 1931), where the
beliefs of the protagonist's mother are characterized thus:

> She firmly believed in a certain power that bore no resemblance to
> God as the house of a man one has never seen, his belongings, his
> greenhouse and beehives, his distant voice, heard by chance in an
> open field, bear to their owner. It would have embarrassed her to call
> that power "God," just as there are Peters and Ivans who cannot

pronounce "Pete" or "Vanya" without a sensation of falsity, while there are others who, in reporting a long conversation to you, will pronounce their own names or, still worse, nicknames, with gusto twenty times or so. This power had no connection with the Church, and neither absolved nor chastised any sins. It was just that she sometimes felt ashamed in the presence of a tree, of a cloud, of a dog, or of the air itself that bore an ill word just as religiously as a kind one. And now Sofia, as she thought about her unpleasant, unloved husband and about his death, even though she repeated the words of prayers natural to her ever since childhood, actually strained her whole being so that—fortified by two or three happy memories, through the mist, through great extensions of space, through all that would always remain incomprehensible—she might give her husband a kiss on the forehead. (*Glory*, 11)

The coupling of the motifs of human love (as a source of perfect happiness) and the otherworld (as a locus of idealized dreams and memories) may be traced in several stories of the Early period, including "Pis'mo v Rossiiu" (A Letter That Never Reached Russia, 1925), "Uzhas" (Terror, 1927), and "Vozvrashchenie Chorba" (The Return of Chorb, 1925). While in "La Veneziana" and "The Return of Chorb" only glimpses of the otherworld are recorded in the text, nowhere in the Early period is the otherworldly experience more powerful than in the 1924 masterpiece "Rozhdestvo" (Christmas).[30]

Written some two years after V. D. Nabokov's murder by Russian ultra-rightists, "Christmas" reverses the situation of a son who communicates with a presence of his deceased father.[31] The story also anticipates a theme in the novel *The Gift*. Having buried his teenaged son, the protagonist, Sleptsov, finds the live memories of the boy slipping away. Only the father's fathomless sorrow remains. After sitting for an hour beside the family burial vault, Sleptsov returns to his country home feeling "as if there [i.e., beside his son's grave] he had been even further removed from his son than here, where the countless summer tracks of his rapid sandals were preserved beneath the snow" (*Stories*, 133). Sleptsov clings desperately to any signs of his late son's presence. He goes to what used to be his son's room to immerse himself in the atmosphere that had surrounded his beloved boy the summer before his death. At first, an influx of memories throws Sleptsov into a fit of weeping: "and suddenly, dropping his head onto the desk, he started to shake, passionately, noisily, pressing first his lips, then his wet cheek, to the cold, dusty wood and clutching at its far corners"

(*Stories*, 134). In his son's desk Sleptsov discovers two groups of objects: notebooks with his son's summer diary and equipment for butterfly collecting. The equipment characterizes a side of the boy's personality that is all too familiar to his father. In fact, an "English biscuit tin" contains "a large exotic cocoon" originally from India. In his deathbed delirium, the boy talked of this cocoon and regretted not having it. Sleptsov assumes, however, that "the chrysalid inside [is] probably dead" (*Stories*, 134). The text of the diary promises to offer the mourning father consolation by offering keys to the cherished if fading memories of his son. Before reading it, Sleptsov notices that a servant has "placed a . . . fir tree in a clay pot . . . and was just attaching a candle to its cruciform tip" (*Stories*, 135). Sleptsov asks for the tree to be removed: he has completely blocked out the fact that it is Christmas Eve ("sochel'nik"). Even after the servant's reminder that the following day is a holiday ("prazdnichek zavtra"; *VCh*, 72), Sleptsov still insists on taking away the fir tree. Thus, symbolically, Nabokov's text rejects the Christian holiday of the Nativity as of no use to Sleptsov's sorrow and, perhaps, its own metaphysics. Still, one must not forget that the story's title and its first appearance in the 1925 Christmas issue of *The Rudder* set a familiar pattern for the reader's expectations.

The text of the boy's diary weaves together references to butterflies and a certain girl, the object of his summertime adolescent love. The writer of the diary employs a private code to record his love. He does not refer to the girl by name: "Deliberately rode by her dacha twice, but didn't see her . . . Our eyes nearly met. My darling, my love . . ." ("Moia prelest', moia radost' . . ."; *Stories*, 135/*VCh*, 73). The screen of feminine pronouns separates Sleptsov as the reader of his son's diary from the object of his son's first love. Sleptsov is both drawn to read more of the diary ("avidly deciphering the childish handwriting") and disappointed that he would never encounter an entire facet of his son's life: "This is unthinkable . . . I'll never know" (*Stories*, 135). The reader faces a profoundly tragic predicament: a text of love (diary) serves as a living connection between the dead son and the mourning father who has outlived him.

The diary's last entry deserves a closer look:

Сегодня — первый экземпляр траурницы. Это значит — осень. Вечером шёл дождь. Она, вероятно, уехала, а я с нею так и не познакомился. Прощай, моя радость. Я ужасно тоскую... (*VCh*, 73)

(Saw a fresh specimen of the Camberwell Beauty today. That means autumn is here. Rain in the evening. She has probably left, and we

didn't even get acquainted. Farewell, my darling. I feel terribly sad. . . ;
Stories, 135)

Unlike its English equivalent, the Russian name of the butterfly, *traur-nitsa* (deriving from *traur,* mourning), points to death. The Russian name of Camberwell Beauty reflects the solemn and austere design of its coloring: the fringes of the dark-brown wings are marked by thin white lines. Death and dying are indeed in the air, the dying of the summer, the end of the eternally romantic *dachnyi sezon* (countryside vacation season), the disappearance of summer butterflies, the departure of the girl, whom Sleptsov's son never meets in person and only loves from a distance. The pure and naïve young *innamorato* writes his diary without imposing any overarching structure on his reflections. At the same time, the last entry also records how his first love—even in its dying—transforms the boy into an adult, a man. Note also that Sleptsov's son belongs to the cohort of Nabokov's characters who love unattainable women. These characters love from afar, creating exaltation as a source of the language of love directed at an ultimate female addressee. As does Sleptsov's son in "Christmas," many of Nabokov's enamored characters idealize the remote objects of their love, for one is more likely to idealize someone one does not know than someone one knows well and routinely communicates with. The English again neutralizes the diary's romantic language of love and longing by translating "Ia uzhasno toskuiu" (*VCh,* 73) as "I feel so terribly sad" (*Stories,* 135). The Russian verb *toskovat'* (to long for someone/something) undoubtedly belongs to an adult's vocabulary. The last entry—the boy's imitation of the language of adult love, intertwined as it is with reflections on the dying of the season and the "mournful" butterfly—throws his father into "yet another onrush of hideous sobs": "I-can't-bear-it-any-longer . . . I-can't-bear-it-any-longer" (*Stories,* 135).

A remarkable situation thus emerges. Sleptsov comes to feel that only via his own death will he be able to restore the disrupted link with his son. Instead of fulfilling its earlier promise to reconnect the father with his dead and unattainable son, the diary only worsens Sleptsov's pain. Butterflies, of course, signal Nabokov's authorial presence in the story—his other career was in lepidopterology. Butterfly collectors, Nabokov stressed in *Speak, Memory* and elsewhere, explore the world of nature's artistically perfect and transcendent creations. The language of the diary conflates the boy's passion for butterflies with his adolescent love. In fact, because the name of the butterfly, *traurnitsa,* is a feminine noun in Russian, this blurs the boundaries between *ona* (she) as the antecedent of *moia radost'* (my darling) and the butterfly of which the boy speaks in the preceding sentence. The reader wonders whether the boy's farewell is addressed to the butterfly (*traurnitsa*) or to the girl (*ona, radost'*). Such a conflation is hardly gratuitous, for here butterfly collecting shares something with the state of being in love.

One may recall that in his son's desk Sleptsov locates a cocoon with a chrysalid of an Indian butterfly. The cocoon's thick walls separate a life dormant inside from the dead boy's father. He believes the Oriental butterfly to be dead, like his son. And now Sleptsov himself turns toward death. Again, Christmas as a holiday of life is brought up and denied in his internal monologue: "It's Christmas tomorrow . . . and I'm going to die. Of course. It's so simple. This very night . . ." (*Stories,* 136). Sleptsov teeters on the verge of a suicide which, he supposes, would reunite him with his boy. The otherworldly transformation in the story occurs at the moment when Sleptsov experiences a moment of horror and total disillusionment with his existence apart from his son: "Sleptsov pressed his eyes shut, and had a fleeting sensation that earthly life lay before him, totally bared and comprehensible ["do kontsa obnazhena zemnaia zhizn'"]—and ghastly in its sadness, humiliatingly pointless, sterile, devoid of miracles . . ." (*Stories,* 136/*VCh,* 74). He needs a miracle to reaffirm the meaning of life. The narrative of "Christmas" needs an otherworldly transformation to make it into Nabokov's unorthodox Christmas story. The conclusion offers such a miracle: "The cocoon in the biscuit tin had burst at its tip, and a black, wrinkled creature [*smorshchennoe sushchestvo*] the size of a mouse was crawling up the wall above the table. It stopped, holding on to the surface with six black furry feet, and started palpitating strangely [*stranno trepetat'*]" (*Stories,* 136/*VCh,* 74).

The reader finds out that the creature "emerged . . . because a man overcome with grief had transferred a tin box to his warm room, and the warmth had penetrated its taut leaf-and-silk envelope" (*Stories,* 136). As if to give the reader time enough to appreciate the miracle, the texture of the language here intones a very gradual metamorphosis of death into life. First described as a mouselike creature, the butterfly "slowly and miraculously [*chudesno,* recalling the earlier "devoid of miracles"] expand[s]" (*Stories,* 136). The description of the "creature" turning into a butterfly defies Darwinian evolutionary principles—which Nabokov never found convincing—and suggests an alternative schema.[32] In this story a creature which at first resembles a mouse, a mammal occupying an evolutionary step much higher than a butterfly, metamorphoses into an evolutionarily "lower" butterfly, an insect. An alternative direction of evolution seems to be at stake here, an evolution toward what is aesthetically superior: "instead of a little lump of life, instead of a dark mouse, was a great *Attacus* moth [*nochnaia babochka*]" (*Stories*, 136). Nabokov's text also invokes the notion of the transcendent transformation of a chrysalid into a butterfly. He describes the butterfly's unfolding wings as "now . . . developed to the limit set for them by God [*polozhennogo im Bogom*]" (*Stories*, 136/*VCh*, 75). This direct linkage of an aesthetic and incommunicable experience to God is an exhilarating synthetic moment in terms of Nabokov's artistic development. The complexity of what is happening should not be overlooked. When Nabokov speaks of "it becom[ing] a winged thing" ("stalo krylatym"), this also evokes an angelic presence (cf. the angels in early stories like "The Word" and in his early Russian poetry). In addition, the gradual metamorphosis of death into otherworldly beatitude is likened to the way "a maturing face imperceptibly becomes beautiful" ("stanovitsia prekrasnym muzhaiushchee litso"; *Stories*, 136/*VCh*, 74). Like Sleptsov, the reader is bound to remember how the discourse of the dead boy's diary gradually metamorphoses into that of an adult under love's transforming radiance. Finally, to add verisimilitude to the fresh miracle, Nabokov offers very specific information about the great moth that has emerged. We learn its species (in the Englished text it is even given in Latin) and habits: "fly, birdlike [another evolutionary twist or merely an indication of the creature's size?], around lamps in the Indian dusk" (*Stories*, 136). The Russian is even more specific: "vokrug fonarei Bombeia" (literally, around streetlamps of Bombay; *VCh*, 74).

What exactly is happening in terms of the emerging poetics of the otherworld? Sleptsov seeks but does not find consolation in his son's diary that documents the dying of love. When he finds himself on the verge of committing suicide in order to join his son, he undergoes a cathartic experience: the wondrous transformation of a dead cocoon into a beautiful butterfly offers Sleptsov a cognitive metaphor of access to his son's spirit. Mundane life, "devoid of miracles," expands "miraculously" in the text of the story. However, we do not know and never will know what happens to the protagonist. The story openly ends right at the height of writing an otherworldly metamorphosis. This transformation may or may not rescue Sleptsov from the black hole of death. But it does offer the reader a glimpse into eternity, a moment of unearthly joy which is etched in the reader's memory: "And then those thick black wings, with a glazy eyespot on each and a purplish bloom dusting their hooked foretips, took a full breath under the impulse [*v poryve*] of tender, ravishing, almost human happiness" (*Stories*, 136).

The end of the story underscores that death is not a passage to the otherworld. Seeking to preserve his connections with the deceased beloved son, Sleptsov first decides to die so as to restore their severed communication. At the same time, reading his son's diary prepares him for the imminent miracle. To recall my earlier suggestion, the boy's diary conflates love (an otherworldly state in Nabokov's works) and butterfly collecting (as a markedly aestheticized passion) into a single continuum of transcendent desire. Owing to a miraculous metamorphosis, Sleptsov is able to resist the temptation of suicide, a death which would literalize (and, for that matter, sever) his desperate attempts to communicate with the dead boy. Sleptsov's catharsis, the "human happiness" that crowns the text of the story, shows that while Nabokov's otherworld may harbor an idealized presence of the deceased, it is never to be equated with a conventional afterlife in traditional religions.

Nabokov's Middle period opens with "Pil'gram" (The Aurelian, 1930), a masterpiece for all times that I will consider in detail in Chapter 2. The way in which "The Aurelian," "Perfection," and "Terra Incognita"—the best stories of the Middle period—position their readers may be likened to the effect of the modern technological concept of "virtual reality," which creates an audiovisual cyberspace simulacrum of being inside a real space, be it the space of an office, an art museum, or a tropical forest.[33] One reads such a "virtually real" story by envisioning its simulated space and interacting with it.

The stories of Nabokov's Middle period fall into two uneven groups. Only a minority of stories break new ground in terms of his individual growth and in terms of the Russian short story tradition. Something seems to be amiss in many of the stories of the Middle period. Their popular themes and unoriginal plots were not equal to their superb writing. The verbal texture of Nabokov's sentence began to reach the level of perfection that would define his signature style of the High period. At the same time, the narrative grammar of the stories seemed to have reached a temporary plateau. Many stories of the Middle period follow familiar paths in the Russian short story tradition without trying to challenge or elevate Nabokov's own earlier achievements. Why did Nabokov the writer of short stories put on hold his artistic quest for the otherworld in favor of feuilletonistic pieces for almost half a decade?

Out of the nineteen stories of the Middle period, only one had to wait twenty-five years to be published ("Usta k ustam" [Lips to Lips, written 1931; 1956]); the rest appeared in émigré periodicals in the early 1930s. Fifteen of the eighteen published stories appeared in the newspaper The Lat-

est News and one each in the review *Contemporary Annals*, the semi-tabloid magazine *Illiustrirovannaia zhizn'* (Illustrated Life), and the Riga Russian newspaper *Segodnia* (Today).³⁴ The stories in newspapers appeared on average a month after their completion. By the early 1930s, Nabokov had become a regular contributor to the leading Russian émigré newspaper abroad, the Paris daily *The Latest News* (Berlin's *The Rudder* ceased to exist in 1931). His stories were now in demand, which on the one hand stimulated the writer and kept him productive, but on the other imposed certain thematic and formal constraints upon his creative output.

A notable example of a feuilletonlike short story is "Vstrecha" (The Reunion, 1931). Borrowing from Nabokov's immediate surroundings, Russian Berlin in the late 1920s–early 1930s, it concerns a topic which was sure to find a response among the Russian émigré readers: maintaining contacts with relatives remaining in Soviet Russia. Lev, an émigré littérateur living in Berlin, receives a call from his elder brother Serafim, whom he has not seen for over ten years. While Lev emigrated after the Revolution, Serafim stayed and became a "spets," an abbreviation from *spetsialist,* a professional trained before the Revolution who was willing to serve the Bolshevik regime. Having never been very close and now grown even further apart—psychologically and ideologically—the two brothers experience much discomfort during their "reunion" of sorts.

This trivial scenario possesses two redeeming features. "The Reunion" initiates a recurrent motif that culminates in Nabokov's unfinished American story "Scenes from the Life of a Double Monster" (1950).³⁵ This motif, an antirelationship between two brothers as recalled by one from the vantage point of posterity, culminates in Lev's recollection of Serafim just before their failed reunion:

> He pictures Serafim, his meaty, sloping shoulders, his huge rubbers, the puddles in the garden in front of their *dacha,* the death of their parents, the beginning of the Revolution. . . . They had never been particularly close—even when they were at school, each had his own friends, and their teachers were different. . . . One day, while swimming in a river, Serafim had nearly drowned. . . . These were Lev's more colorful recollections of his brother, and God knows they didn't amount to much. . . . Nevertheless, Serafim was still his brother. He ate a lot. He was orderly. What else? One evening, at the tea table. . . .
> (*Stories*, 306)

It is interesting to compare this passage with Nabokov's reminiscences of his brother Sergei in *Speak, Memory:*

For various reasons I find it inordinately hard to speak about my other brother [as opposed to Nabokov's younger brother Kirill, with whom he was relatively close]. . . . Except for two or three poor little adventures I have sketched in earlier chapters, his boyhood and mine seldom mingled. He is a mere shadow in the background of my richest and most detailed recollections. I was the coddled one; he, the witness of the coddling. Born, caesareanally, ten and a half months after me, . . . , he matured earlier than I and physically looked older. We seldom played together. . . . He was quiet and listless, and spent much more time with our mentors than I. . . . We attended different schools. . . . (*SM*, 257)

At the end of the meeting, probably their last one, the two brothers in the story are nearly reunited by shared memories of their common childhood. This gives birth to the motif of reaching into the depths of one's memory, a motif connected with Nabokov's seminal notion of "cosmic synchronization." Both brothers struggle to recall the name of a dog, a black poodle who used to belong to their summer house neighbors: "Chto-to vrode Tushkana . . . Toshka . . . Tashka . . ." (It was something like Turk . . . Trick . . . No, it won't come. It's hopeless; *S*, 141/*Stories*, 311). They never figure it out together; only later, already alone, Lev experiences the liberating moment of recollection as his memory expands: "'Dai lapu, Shutik!' Shutik! Kak prosto. Shutik . . ." ("Give me your paw, Joker." Joker! How simple it was. Joker . . . ; *S*, 141/*Stories*, 311). Something very similar would be described twenty years later in Chapter 7 of *Speak, Memory*. In the chapter, also known as the English-language short story "First Love," the narrator reminisces about spending a summer in Biarritz at age ten and being in love with a French girl named Colette. After a number of painstaking attempts, the name of Colette's dog finally comes back to the narrator: "I try again to recall the name of Colette's dog—and, triumphantly, along those remote beaches, over the glossy evening sands of the past, . . . here it comes, echoing and vibrating: Floss, Floss, Floss!" (*SM*, 152/*Stories*, 610).

Another striking feature of the Middle period is that many of its stories represent beginnings of larger projects, some of which never developed beyond their early stages. Thus, for instance, "Obida" (A Bad Day, 1931) and "Lebeda" (Orache, 1932) may be viewed as fragments of a semiautobiographical Bildungsroman about a boy named Putia Shishkov. Critics have noted the obvious biographical subtext for the events narrated in "Orache": V. D. Nabokov's 1911 duel with the publisher Mikhail Suvorin. In addition, both stories about Putia Shishkov's childhood, especially "Orache," contain intertextual parallels with the childhood chapters of

Nabokov's autobiographies. "Krasavitsa" (A Russian Beauty, 1934), another story with a subtext in his personal and family past, reveals a connection to Nabokov's sister Olga, four years his junior: "Olga, of whom we are about to speak, was born in the year 1900, in a wealthy carefree family of nobles. A pale little girl in a white sailor suit [*v beloi matroske*], with a side parting in her chestnut hair and such merry eyes that everyone kissed her there, she was deemed a beauty since childhood" (*Stories*, 385). This description echoes Olga's appearance on a surviving 1918 photograph of Nabokov with his four brothers and sisters. In addition to the sailor suit, one is especially struck by the "enchanting" expression "of her closed lips."[36] Another short fiction, "Pamiati L. I. Shigaeva" (In Memory of L. I. Shigaev, 1934), belongs stylistically with several real obituaries which Nabokov published during his Russian years.[37] As for "Krug" (The Circle, 1934), in an English-language preface Nabokov referred to it as a "small satellite separated . . . from the main body of [*The Gift*]" (*Stories*, 653). Later in the same preface he also projected the shape of the reader's interaction with "The Circle": "the story will produce upon readers who are familiar with the novel a delightful effect of oblique recognition, of shifting shades enriched with new sense, owing to the world's being seen not through the eyes of Fyodor, but through those of an outsider . . ." (*Stories*, 653–654).

Several stories of the Middle period served Nabokov primarily as battlegrounds of various sorts: political, moral, literary-critical. In "Lips to Lips," he unveiled a contemporary literary scandal involving his literary nemeses, the "two Georges," critic Adamovich and poet Ivanov, and the funding of their lavishly printed Parisian periodical, *The Numbers*.[38] "Lips to Lips" struck so recognizably close to reality that the editors of *The Latest News* discerned the scandalous subtext and withdrew the story. "Korolëk" (The Leonardo, 1933) may be considered Nabokov's earliest offensive against rising Nazism in Germany and in that respect a testing ground for the later masterpiece "Cloud, Castle, Lake," which also deals with an attack by chauvinistic thugs on a conspicuous foreigner. "Khvat" (A Dashing Fellow, 1932) exposes the spiritual emptiness and corruption of a traveling Russian émigré salesman, a scoundrel and a cheat. The pathos of antivulgarian rhetoric overpowers the narrative to such an extent that Nabokov even opts for the irksome "we"-variety of discourse largely employed in feuilletons: "Our suitcase is carefully embellished with bright-colored stickers. . . . Tonight we arrive in a voluptuous little town. . . . Oh, woman, thy name is Goldie! That's how we called Mamma and, later, our wife Katya" (*Stories*, 259).

Busy as they were with fighting the battles of their time and milieu, only a few stories of the Middle period continued writing the otherworld. In "Torpid Smoke," an amorphous meditation on the rapturous mysteries of literary creation, two features point beyond their immediate milieux. The protagonist, a young émigré poet and a very distant literary cousin of Fyodor Godunov-Cherdyntsev (the main character of *The Gift*), is capable of what the Russian text labels "iasnovidenie" (literally, clairvoyance; *VF*, 76) and the English version terms "second sight" (*Stories*, 397).[39] About "Torpid Smoke" Sisson has written that "in Nabokov's experience of cosmic synchronization, the mind not only sees everything in the universe, but expands physically through all space and time. Thus, Nabokov's young poet Grisha . . . lies in a clairvoyant trance as his being expands to fill his apartment, his neighborhood, the sky."[40] By means of a special concentration of imagination, the protagonist is able to send the eye of his consciousness traveling across spaces other than his dark, quiet bedroom in a household charged with oppressive domesticity: "As he lay flat on his couch, he felt carried sideways by the flow of shadows and, simultaneously, he escorted distant foot-passengers, and visualized now the sidewalk's surface right under his eyes (with the exhaustive accuracy of a dog's sight), now the design of bare branches . . . or else the alternation of shop windows: a hairdresser's dummy . . ." (*Stories*, 397).

The protagonist also envisions his surroundings as assuming the shapes of his own body parts: "the lane on the other side of the house might be his own arm"; *Stories*, 397). Since the protagonist's consciousness forks during the moments of "second vision," the narrative seeks to find a corresponding mixed mode. Much as in the earlier "Details of a Sunset" where Mark Standfuss catches up with his own figure walking away from him, the narrator of "Torpid Smoke" "over[takes] his own self" (*Stories*, 399) as he moves around his apartment. In the finale the narrative shifts from one diegetic perspective, closest to free indirect discourse, to another, nominally first person, within a single sentence: "On his way out of the dining room he noticed his father turn his whole torso in his chair to face the wall clock as if it had said something, and then begin turning back—but there the door I was closing closed, and I did not see that bit to the end" (*Stories*, 400). The "he-I" shift of narration puts "Torpid Smoke" on one of the satellite orbits of *The Gift*, where, as Alexandrov explains it, the "widespread and, at first, bewildering alternations between Fyodor as 'he' in one sentence and 'I' in the next . . . are due to [his] speaking from the viewpoint of an author and that of a character."[41]

"Muzyka" (Music, 1932) may very well be the only short story where the word *potustoronnii* (otherworldly) is found in the text. In fact, in the surviving manuscript of the first draft the word *potustoronnii* is inserted above the line of the text as though it represents a final stage of editing.[42] In "Music," which bears the title "Ograda" (The Fence) in the manuscript, a Russian émigré encounters his ex-wife at a music recital. He divorced her upon discovering her adulterous affair; now, separated from her by the "fence" of music for which he has no appreciation, he recollects the joy and happiness of their love: "The barrier [*ograda*] of sounds remained just as high and impenetrable. The spectral hands [*potustoronnie ruki*] in their lacquered depths continued to go through the same contortions. 'We'll be happy forever'—what melody in that phrase, what shimmer!" (*Stories*, 334/*S*, 179). *Potustoronnii*, here rendered as "spectral," suggests the presence of an immaterial if haunting spirit, perhaps the phantom of the ex-couple's happiness together. The reference to the pianist's hands reflected in the grand piano's black lacquered surface is followed immediately by the leitmotif of the couple's brief happiness. Music allows the lonely protagonist to enter the idealized realm where his memories of the ex-wife now dwell. Formerly a barrier, music has turned into a salutary link only to "dissolve" at the end of the recital. As his wife makes her hasty departure, the protagonist realizes "that the music, which before had seemed a narrow dungeon where, shackled together by the resonant sounds, they had been compelled to sit face to face some twenty feet apart, had actually been incredible bliss, a magic glass dome that had embraced and imprisoned him and her, had made it possible for him to breathe the same air as she; and now everything had been broken and scattered . . ." (*Stories*, 336).

A student of Nabokov's short stories will find "Zaniatoi chelovek" (A Busy Fellow, 1931) a gratifying case study of the writer's gradual discovery of how to write the otherworld. Two major sign systems are at work in the story. The first entails references to the Gospel narratives of Christ's self-prophesied death and subsequent resurrection, as well as Apocalypse, while the second constructs a semiotic model of the otherworld that exists parallel to the mundane world and reveals itself—by way of glimpses—to the privileged protagonist. Two features bridge the two disparate metaphysical systems in the story: narrative irony and a secondary character, a certain Engel, who serves as the protagonist's guardian-angel but also as Nabokov's authorial representative (*predstavitel'*).[43] The protagonist, a small-time Russian littérateur, lives alone in Berlin, convinced that he will die at Christ's age in accordance with an adolescent dream. The double nature of authorial irony with respect to Graf It's idiosyncrasy manifests itself early on:

An ever-increasing insistence. The figure 33—the theme of that dream—had got entangled with his unconscious, its curved claws like those of a bat, had got caught in his soul, and there was no way to unravel that subliminal snarl [cf. the original *dushevnyi koltun*, literally, soul's plica]. According to the tradition, Jesus Christ lived to the age of thirty-three and perhaps (mused Graf, immobilized next to the cross of the casement frame), perhaps a voice in that dream had indeed said: "You'll die at Christ's age"—and had displayed, illumined upon a screen, the thorns of two tremendous threes ["'Umrësh' v vozraste Khrista', — posle chego osvetilis' na èkrane ternii dvukh ogromnykh troek"; note the modern cinematic setting of the dream and the deliberate *r*-alliterations in the Russian and *t*-alliterations in the English of the last several words]. (*Stories*, 287/*S*, 159)

The description of Graf It's dream is followed by a first glimpse of a metaphysical domain, reminiscent of the otherworldly cityscape in "Details of a Sunset": "It was lighter without than within, but streetlamps had already started to glow. Smooth clouds [recurrent markers of the otherworld in Nabokov's stories] blanketed the sky; and only westwards, between ochery housetops, an interspace was banded with tender brightness. Farther up the street a fiery-eyed automobile had stopped, its straight tangerine tusks plunged in the watery gray of the asphalt. A blond butcher [*blondin-miasnik*] stood on the threshold of his shop and contemplated the sky" (*Stories*, 287). A series of semantic shifts transforms ordinary objects into those of an otherworldly realm, in this case also colored by gentle irony (e.g., "blond butcher"). As Graf It gets closer to the fatal date of the prophecy and expects and fears to die at Christ's age, the intimations of the sui generis otherworld occur increasingly and develop parallel to features of a Christological scenario. For instance, Graf It first interprets the "strange agitation" ("strannoe volnenie") which "was spreading around in the streets" as his "heart contracted from the tenderness of early lights" as meaning "the end of the world" (*S*, 162/*Stories*, 289). Then, "suddenly with a numbing tingle [*zamiraniem*] in every part of his frame, he understood [*ponial*]" (*S*, 162–163/*Stories*, 289). A colon follows, and the reader is never told what Graf It "understood." A magnificent description evokes an atmosphere that is difficult to explain: ". . . there, there, across the deep vista between buildings, outlined softly against a clear golden background, under the lower rim of a long ashen cloud, very low, very far, and very slowly, and also ash-colored, also elongated, an airship was floating by. The exquisite, antique loveliness of its motion, mating with the intolerable beauty of the evening sky, tangerine lights, blue silhouettes of people, caused the contents of Graf's soul to brim over" (*Stories*, 289). The protagonist feels that the otherworldly airship is "a celestial token, an old-fashioned apparition [*znamenie*]" (*S*, 163/*Stories*, 289; "celestial token" was added to the Englished text). The weight of traditional associations finally compels him to conclude that the airship reminded him that he was "reaching the established limit of his life [*do predela polozhennoi emu zhizni*]" (*Stories*, 289/*S*, 163).

From this point until the culmination of the story, Graf It torments himself with thoughts about the shape of the "hereafter" ("zagrobnyi mir") to which he hopes his immortal soul will soon proceed. The narrator presents his protagonist's state as pitiful: as a modern skeptical subject, Graf It is in no way convinced either that his soul is indeed immortal or that entering the Christian hereafter is a safe enterprise. He begins a phase of what Nabokov's ironic narrator terms "transcendental cowardice," an idiosyncratic fear of anything likely to cause his death. Enter Graf It's neighbor, a Russian German by the name of Engel (which means "angel" in German), who is described as a representative of "some kind of foreign (very foreign, perhaps, Far-Eastern or Celestial) firm" (*Stories*, 292). "Far-Eastern" literally refers to the large and affluent Russian émigré communities in Kharbin and Shanghai between the two world wars while also signaling remoteness, unattainability, or exoticism. The guardian Engel envelops his neighbor with care and helps him pull through the time of anticipation until the day Graf It turns thirty-four. Again, the two sign systems in the story are conflated in Engel's character. The Celestial firm which he "represents" in the text could very well stand for the Christian paradisal hereafter, with Engel as an angelic envoy. But Engel is also an early variant of the narrator's authorial representative in the text, a figure to gain much prominence in Nabokov's short fictions of the High period but also in the novel *The Gift*.

On the day when Graf It turns thirty-four, he undergoes a profound experience in which Engel plays a notable part: "Around eight o'clock, at the very moment that Graf, after nicely laying the table [he is expecting guests], leaned out of the window, the following happened: at the corner of the street, where a small group of men had collected in front of the pub, loud angry cries rang out followed suddenly by the cracking of pistol shots. Graf had the impression that a stray bullet whistled past his face, almost smashing his glasses, and with an 'akh' of terror, he drew back" (*Stories*, 294). A messenger brings a telegram for Engel which—as Graf It later finds out—contains two Russian words: "SOGLASEN PRODLENIE (extension agreed)." Again, the source of the telegram may either be a conventional hereafter or the author who grants his character a different sort of immortality: never having to die into a fictional narrative. Graf It lives on to see an otherworldly dream: "Gradually Graf dozed off in a chair and in his dream he saw . . . Engel singing couplets in a garden of sorts and fanning his bright-yellow, curly-feathered wings" (*Stories*, 295). He wakes up when "the lovely June sun was lighting little rainbows in the landlady's liqueur glasses, and everything was somehow soft and luminous and enigmatic—as if there was something he had not understood, not thought through to the end, and now it was already too late, another life had begun . . ." (*Stories*, 295–296). Graf It's memory has been cleansed of the troubling reminiscence of an adolescent premonition. One thing is almost clear: Graf It's new life after the "death" of the "meaningless memory" ("umerlo pustiachnoe vospominanie")—ironically his textual "resurrection"—will never be the same. The "luminous and enigmatic" may refer to the otherworld that has revealed itself to Graf It, which he initially mistook for an omen of physical death.

In sum, which sign system—a traditional Christian or a sui generis otherwordly one—has more bearing on the story's meaning? This still depends upon the mode of reading, on the reader's willingness to make a leap of faith toward the inexplicable miraculous "airship" rather than read this story as a modern tragicomic or even feuilletonistic evocation of the Gospel narrative. In subsequent stories, the metaphysics are those of Nabokov, who claimed to have no interest in "organized tours through anthropomorphic paradises" (*SM*, 297) and who, in the words of his privileged narrator from "Spring in Fialta," could not "imagine any heavenly firm of brokers [cf. Celestial firm in "A Busy Man"] that might consent to arrange [for him] a meeting with [his beloved] beyond the grave" (*Stories*, 415).

Nabokov continues to investigate the relationship between the otherworld, death, and writing in "Terra Incognita," one of the most memorable short stories in the Middle period.[44] It deserves special attention because it foregrounds a model of the otherworld different from those found anywhere else in his short fiction. "Terra Incognita" poses an intriguing question: What if, instead of embodying a perfect alternative to the mundane world, the otherworld is actually a realm of horror? This horrific realm, much like the idealized otherworldly realm in Nabokov's stories, could possess a magnetism of its own, a result of an esoteric conception of space and time. The very title of the story, "Terra Incognita," suggests an unknown textual zone, a territory inviting to be explored and read.

The narrator, the naturalist Vallière, describes a tropical expedition he undertakes with two European companions, his fellow explorer Gregson and the opportunist Cook. Also present through the first part of their journey is a group of African porters. The expedition heads for a remote and unexplored region, presumably located in West Central Africa. The narrator provides only a few geographical landmarks. Zonraki, the name of the place where the African porters were "engaged," does not appear in atlases, maps, or reference guides to the African continent. The porters are referred to as "big, glossy-brown Badonians" (*Stories,* 297). Although no nation or tribe with this or any remotely close name seems to inhabit the world, there is a town called Badon in southeastern Senegal close to the Senegal-Guinea border. The "projected itinerary, across as yet unknown country," is said to lie "toward Gurano Hills" (*Stories,* 298). A thorough geographical search revealed no Gurano Hills, but it did reveal Mt. Gura, located in central Nigeria. Another reference—a local drink named "vongho"—seems to be the fruit of Nabokov's (or the hallucinating narrator's) imagination. Commentators have also referred to the fictitious names of tropical plants, "limia" and "acreana."[45] Another floral reference is to a real plant, ipecacuana (known in Russian as *rvotnyi koren'*, literally, vomiting root), a native of the South American rain forest, but not Africa.

One more element of tropical flora in the story deserves attention: a plant called *Vallieria mirifica*. This is the only plant with a full Latin taxonomic designation. Fictitious as it appears to be, the Latin name easily succumbs to decoding. *Vallieria* entails the entire name of the narrator, Vallière, while *mirifica* means "causing wonders." The connection between the narrator and the plant is not immediately apparent. The name of the narrator is used only once by his leader, Gregson, in the middle of the story. The name of the plant, however, occurs on the first page. In the Russian text the name of the plant is printed in the Latin alphabet, while the name Vallière is in Cyrillic, "Вальер," which makes the association less apparent to a Russian reader. Such a verbal gesture—encrypted and concealed in a typically Nabokovian fashion—points towards the story's narrative principle. It is my hypothesis that in "Terra Incognita" the narrator's association with making wonders (*Vallieria mirifica*) suggests not only an explorer's interest in a wondrous space, but also the narrator's special powers: the narrative wonders which he creates in the story.

What exactly are these narrative wonders? Vallière narrates the culmination of the expedition into the heart of the otherspace, a *terra incognita*. The title of the story refers not only to exploration in Africa, but also to the textual space that Vallière's narrative creates for the reader to enter and explore. Vallière's narrative commences at the point when the explorers are about to enter a territory yet untrodden by Europeans: "The sound of the waterfall grew more and more muffled . . . and we moved on through the wildwood of a *hitherto unexplored region*" (*Stories*, 297; italics added). For a short while the reader has no difficulty following the narrator across the tropical forest. Soon the reader learns that the African porters—led by Cook, who knows their dialect—have "deserted" the explorers and taken away all their equipment. This is the first crucial point in the act of reading: Vallière and Gregson must decide "whether to return to Zonraki or continue our projected itinerary, across as yet *unknown country*, toward the Gurano Hills" (*Stories*, 298; italics added). As Vallière puts it, "the unknown won out [*nevedomoe perevesilo*]. We moved on" (*Stories*, 298/*S*, 118).

It is also important to note that Vallière suffers from a severe tropical fever, and his senses are "deafened by quinine" (*Stories*, 298), which he takes in large quantities. Vallière is "tormented by strange hallucinations" (*Stories*, 298). However, what increasingly makes Vallière's narrative a reading puzzle is the way his hallucinations affect the narrative mode. At first, one ponders the nature of the hallucinations: "I gazed at the weird tree trunks, around some of which were coiled thick, flesh-colored snakes; suddenly I thought I saw, between the trunks, as though through my fingers, the mirror of a half-open wardrobe with dim reflections . . ." (*Stories*, 298). Half a page later Vallière gazes at the tropical sky and sees "whitish phantoms of plaster, stucco curlicues and rosettes, like those used to adorn European ceilings . . ." (*Stories*, 299). A page later Vallière describes how "at times Gregson and Cook seemed to grow transparent, and I thought I saw, through them, wall-paper with an endlessly repeated design of reeds," and still later, "listing among the repetitious reeds, what seemed a large armchair but was actually a strange, cumbersome grey amphibian . . ." (*Stories*, 300).

By now the reader has apprehended the code of Vallière's hallucinations: in his delirium the settings of a European room show through his tropical African surroundings. But then something else happens that is bound to confuse the reader. Vallière conflates two hitherto distinct diegetic planes: that of the tropical African reality and that of the European hallucinations: "I raised myself up from my pillow and leaned my elbow on the resilient surface of the rock . . ." (*Stories*, 300). Another confusion follows a page later: "The rock was as white and as soft as a bed. I raised myself a little, but promptly fell back on the pillow" (*Stories*, 300). What is happening here? The next "delirious vision" does not change much but only enhances the diegetic confusion: "The lines of a dim ceiling stretched and crossed in the sky. A large armchair rose, as if supported from below, out of the swamp. Glossy birds flew through the haze of the marsh and, as they settled, one turned into the wooden knob of a bedpost, another into a decanter. Gathering all my will power, I focused my gaze and drove off this dangerous trash" (*Stories*, 301–302).

Everything in Vallière's presentation—the syntax, the colloquiality, the structure of transitions—betrays an oral narrative, a story told to a listener or group of listeners. In an oral narrative act, the sudden illogical transition from the diegetic plane of Vallière's hallucination to that of his physical location within an African *terra incognita* does not have to create an obstacle for the listener. This is not, however, an oral narrative per se: Vallière's narrative somehow gets wondrously recorded, and its written textual form is made available to the reader. The reader, I maintain, questions not so much the reliability of Vallière as a narrator, but the actual way in which he records his narrative on paper. That question becomes increasingly unavoidable after Vallière declares that he is at the last stage of a mortal illness and about to die in a few minutes. This happens right after his companions, Gregson and Cook, get into a fight and kill each other. Vallière is now alone face to face with the tropical otherspace. His tone becomes lofty, suffused with the pathos of someone who has found the answer:

> But suddenly, at this last stage of my mortal illness—for I knew that in a few minutes I would die—in these final minutes everything grew completely lucid: I realized that all that was taking place around me was not the trick of an inflamed imagination, not the veil of delirium, through which unwelcome glimpses of my supposedly real existence in a distant European city (the wallpaper, the armchair, the glass of lemonade) were trying to show. I realized that the obtrusive room was fictitious, since everything beyond death is, at best, fictitious: an imitation of life hastily knocked together, the furnished rooms of nonexistence. I realized that reality was here, here beneath that wonderful, frightening tropical sky. . . ." (*Stories*, 303)

In a provocative analysis of "Terra Incognita," Sisson has shown that the narrative paradox here resembles that of a Chinese sage, Chuang Chou, who wakes from his dream wondering "whether Chuang Chou dreamed he was a butterfly, or a butterfly is dreaming that he is Chuang Chou." According to Sisson, the pleasure of reading the story, that "aesthetic bliss" which Nabokov sought to award his readers, derives from the story's "perceptual indeterminacy, which is a permanent feature of human consciousness."[46] My interests here are somewhat different from those of

Sisson. His reading of "Terra Incognita" focuses primarily on establishing a pattern of indeterminacy in its interrelation with Nabokov's overarching concerns with "alternative realities."[47] I am most intrigued by the way the narrator records his narrative and passes it on to the readers, given his indeterminately bispatial standing in the story as well as the disappearance of his notebook at the end. In this connection, and given Nabokov's view of reading a verbal text as a pictorial text (*LL*, 2), I find especially stimulating Sisson's discovery of a visual model of Vallière's place in Nabokov's narrative, Henri Rousseau's painting *Le rêve* (The Dream, 1910).[48] The painting depicts a nude woman resting on a sofa surrounded by a magical jungle. Commenting on the meaning of his painting, Rousseau remarked with the genial literality of a primitivist, "This woman sleeping on this sofa [the resting woman is actually not sleeping; at least her eyes are open] dreams that she is transported into the middle of this forest, hearing the notes of the charmer's pipe. This gives the motive for the sofa being in the picture."[49]

Because of the nature of Rousseau's pictorial text, the dose of indeterminacy which "The Dream" gives its reader/viewer does not change; the painting is frozen in time. Conversely, the dose of indeterminacy in Nabokov's "Terra Incognita" increases as the narrative unravels. In the narrative's progress toward a wondrous culmination, there comes a point when the reader can no longer tell which diegetic plane Vallière occupies. Is he recording a real tropical expedition during which he experiences mind-boggling shifts of narrative perspective (from the tropical forest to a bedroom in Europe)? Or is he indeed dying in a hospital bed in Europe and experiencing delirious visions of Africa possibly informed by his past travels? But there is more to the narrator's troubles and the reader's questions. Having pronounced his monologue, Vallière crawls over to his friend and leader, Gregson, only to find him "dead, quite dead" (*Stories*, 303). As head of the expedition, Gregson is instrumental in insisting on continuing the exploration of the *terra incognita* even when all the odds seem against it. With Gregson dead, Vallière has no one urging him to continue the exploration of an unknown territory. All alone in his own narrative, Vallière feels the current of *terra incognita*'s horrifying magnetism. His problems as narrator culminate when he tries—in his African nightmare or European hallucination?—to fix in writing the death of his fellow explorer Gregson as well as his own nearing death: "Fumbling with my enfeebled hands, I took a thick notebook out of my shirt pocket, but here I was overcome by weakness; I sat down and my head drooped. And yet I conquered this impatient fog of death and looked around. Blue air, heat, solitude . . . And how sorry I felt for Gregson, who would never return home—I even remembered his wife and the old cook, and his parrots, and many other things" (*Stories*, 303).

The mention of Europe with the recognizable realia of a Western lifestyle creates a familiar space on the fringes of the text. In contrast to the horror-charged space of *terra incognita* that occupies a major part of the text, the marginal space of the European world is filled with clichés of a mundane existence. Vallière's memories of Europe are ipso facto connected with the vaguely mapped space of his bedroom, one of the two presumed locales of narration. Such an opposition between the unpredictable African *terra incognita* and the more or less predictable European *terra cognita* reverses Nabokov's scheme of an otherworld showing through the chinks in mundane reality, as outlined in the paradigmatic poem "Being in Love" and actualized in a number of stories. This situation is in stark contrast to such a classic tale of European explorers in the tropics as Joseph Conrad's *Heart of Darkness* (1899), where the narrator, Marlow, tells his horrific story in Europe and provides closure for the plot by visiting the fiancée of Kurtz, who died in Africa.

Glimpses of a European reality obfuscate the reader's understanding of the narrator's location. These glimpses occur at the point when the reader feels quite uncertain not only about the narrator's location and state of mind, but also about the future of the narrative. For it seems that if Vallière dies there will be nobody left to finish his narrative. Vallière unequivocally states that there is no one else with him—wherever he may be—to witness what is happening: "I was alone" (*Stories*, 303). The story thus ends on a most indeterminate note: "Everything around me was fading, leaving bare the scenery of death—a few pieces of realistic furniture and four walls. My last motion was to open the book, which was damp with my sweat, for I absolutely had to make a note of something [*koe-chto zapisat' nepremenno*]; but, alas, it slipped out of my hand. I groped all along the blanket, but it was no longer there" (*Stories*, 303/*S*, 128).

We then have the notebook, a journal, which Vallière fails to write. Finding it impossible to write the otherworld in the story, he lets the notebook slip twice in the conclusion. Yet the reader has just finished reading a text entitled "Terra Incognita"—Vallière's narrative. Thus, the reader's ultimate question is likely to be: who creates the text of Vallière's narrative if he himself drops out?

The only person who might have narrated the hallucinatory expedition is Vallière himself, which could only be possible if he indeed survived the deadly disease. In this case, his narrative would be constructed as one of a surviving witness of either his own real expedition into the heart of the African tropics or his own real hallucinations on his deathbed back in Europe. In either case, Vallière would not need to be the actual scribe of his narrative (recall the oral rhetorical and structural elements in his presentation), although he might be.

It is (I agree with Sisson's conclusion) quite impossible to decipher the story's narrative mode conclusively, given that "the reader does not know whether the narrator is alive or dead."[50] Such an indeterminacy is intentional on Nabokov's part. On the one hand, in keeping with his discursive and fictional statements ("That main secret, tra-tá-ta tra-tá-ta tra-tá— / and I must not be overexplicit"; *PP*, 111), the otherworld does not facilitate its own verbal description or guarantee a transparent narrative mode. On the other hand, it may also be the case that, unlike the idealized perfect otherworld of texts like the early "Christmas," the horrific otherworld of "Terra Incognita" appears *too indeterminate* to write. This may explain the way the story comes to its closure: the narrator's incomprehensible surrendering of his responsibilities to the reader. Occupying an unparalleled position among the short stories of the transitional Middle period, "Terra Incognita" shows Nabokov experimenting with writing an alternative reality which is drastically different from the mundane reality and is not a perfect counterpart, but rather a nightmarish locus of absurdity and death. In contrast to the *terror incognitus* of this experimental story, idealized timeless love serves as the main aesthetic, ethical, and metaphysical correlative of the sui generis realms in Nabokov's subsequent short stories.

Writing about the otherworld becomes a chief artistic concern for Nabokov by the mid-1930s, not only in the genre of the short story, but also in novels, poetry, drama, and even his early attempts at memoirs ("Mademoiselle O"). While in the mid-1920s and early 1930s he "set [himself] to illustrate the principle of making a short poem contain a plot and tell a story" (*PP*, 14), by the mid-1930s he was able to build a lyrical poem lacking a deliberate narrative structure, based upon glimpses and intimations of that which is unutterable. Consider, for instance, the confessional poem "Kak ia liubliu tebia . . ." (How I Love You . . . ; 1934), which Adamovich labeled "Pasternakovian"[51]:

Какой зелёный, серый, то есть
весь заштрихованный дождём,
и липовое, столь густое,
что я перенести — уйдём.
Уйдём и этот сад оставим,

и дождь, кипящий на тропах....
(*PP*, 78/*Stikhi*, 252)

Kind of green, kind of gray, i.e.
striated all over with rain,
and the linden fragrance, so heady,
that I can hardly—Let's go!
Let's go and abandon this garden
and the rain that seethes on its paths. . . .
(*PP*, 79)

As the continuation of the poem shows, a locus of the ineffable, a chink, a hiatus, is situated between "ia perenesti" (I can hardly) and "uidëm" (let's go). Initially, the reader co-intuits this otherworldly glimpse, while the final stanza offers more palpable contours of the perfect otherworld colored by timeless love:

Как я люблю тебя. Есть в этом
вечернем воздухе порой
лазейки для души, просветы
в тончайшей ткани мировой.
(*PP*, 80/*Stikhi*, 252–253)

How I love you! In this
evening air, now and then,
the spirit finds loopholes, translucences
in the world's finest texture.
(*PP*, 81)

A short story, unlike a poem, requires a narrative capsule. In a poem like "How I love you . . ." an elliptical dash indicates an opening—a privileged textual space of silence which the lyrical voice cannot render through words and marks with a punctuation mark and a pause. Conversely, a short story depicting a comparable otherworldly experience would have to employ more deliberate narrative and linguistic means. In his short stories Nabokov not only introduced into modern Russian prose fiction the motif of entering the otherworld, but also elaborated a corresponding system of devices that signal to the reader the nearness of an otherwordly experience. The logic of his artistic discovery might be as follows: if there exists an otherworld (filled as it is with love, perfect memories, and airy hopes) which communicates with the privileged characters, then it is only to be expected that such characters would want to enter the otherworld during their lifetime.

Nabokov's concern was first and foremost an artistic one, when the main function of writing is not to reflect metaphysical ideas, however profound, but to cognize and simultaneously construct an otherworld via writing it. What happens after death is shrouded in mystery, and even within the religions with which Nabokov was most familiar (Christianity, Judaism) theologians disagree as to the shape of the afterlife and the terms of access to it. As early as the 1924 story "Christmas," the protagonist Sleptsov first considers suicide but then experiences an epiphany which rescues him and points to a way of maintaining the perfect memories of his dead son. It is necessary to keep in mind Nabokov's insistence upon the otherworld's synchronic and not diachronic relationship to the mundane world. In his short fictions, death does not offer a path into the otherworld. "None of Nabokov's other worlds," Sisson emphasized, "is the conventional 'hereafter,' about which he frequently speculates jocularly, but . . . his other worlds cannot be demonstrated empirically, and Nabokov is always obscure about the nature of the various other worlds, many of which do involve some form of survival of consciousness after death." [52]

A focus on entering the otherworld gives Nabokov's stories an enthralling thematic direction and narrative movement. The High period yields a record number of stories dealing with their characters' attempts and failures to enter a privileged otherspace. Works of a great master of the short story, they demonstrate an exceptional harmony and consistency of poetic means. As writing the otherworld reaches its highest point in Nabokov's short fiction, the stories develop an intricate system of markers of otherworldly experiences. These markers may be classified as indexical, iconic, sonic, and metrical. Metrical markers are Nabokov's signature devices. He uses them in delineating the boundaries of the otherworld. Many writers before him turned to various forms of prosodic markedness in order to emphasize the meaning of their prose, to accentuate privileged textual loci. A writer's rationale for employing prosodic structures was superbly explicated by I. A. Richards in his classic *Principles of Literary Criticism* (1924): "Meter adds to all the variously fated expectancies which make up rhythm a definite temporal pattern and its effect is not due to our perceiving a pattern in something outside us, but to our becoming patterned ourselves. With every beat of the meter a tide of anticipation in us turns and swings, setting up as it does so extraordinarily extensive sympathetic reverberations." [53]

Nabokov begins to experiment with metrical markedness during the Early period, and the results of his first experiments are visible in "Mest" (The Revenge, 1924) or "Vozvrashchenie Chorba" (The Return of Chorb,

1925). Nabokov employs syllabo-tonic meters, but also such a twentieth-century Russian accentual meter as the *dol'nik,* to enhance the semantic effect of a passage. Among the writers particularly important for Nabokov's development, Ivan Turgenev and Anton Chekhov in the nineteenth and Ivan Bunin and Andrei Belyi in the twentieth century experimented with rhythmization of their prose.[54] Belyi wrote about the use of prosodic markedness in the preface to his novel *Maski* (Masks, 1932): "My prose is not at all prose; it is a long poem written in anapests and printed as prose only for the sake of the economy of space; my verses of prose were composed during walks, in the woods, rather than while I was sitting at the desk. . . . Any passage in this prose I hear as verses."[55] Metrical markedness acquires a specialized function in Nabokov's narratives as compared to Belyi's uniformly rhythmicized prose. Nabokov designedly and discriminately uses metrical patterns to highlight passages where the protagonists undergo otherworldly experiences. Six out of seven stories in the High period employ metrical markedness to emphasize the impact of the otherworld upon a character or to delineate its boundaries.

Consider an example from "Lik" (1938). In the passage below, Nabokov's narrator discusses his protagonist's daydreams. He introduces Lik, a Russian actor in a provincial French troupe, as someone with vague intuitions which he can never develop into full-fledged otherworldly experiences:

> ...*этой* двери Александр Лик не отворил, а попал на актёрский путь, по которому шёл без увлечения, с рассеянным видом человека, ищущего каких-то путевых примет, которых нет, но которые, пожалуй, снились или, быть может, принадлежат другой, как бы не проявленной местности, где ему не бывать никогда, никогда. (*VF,* 132)

> (. . . Lik had failed to open *that* door [the one presumably opening into the otherworld], taking instead the Thespian path, which he followed without enthusiasm, with the absent manner of a man looking for signposts [note the markedly semiotic language] that do not exist but that perhaps have appeared to him in a dream, or can be distinguished in the undeveloped photograph of some other locality that he will never, never visit; *Stories,* 462–463)

In the heavily edited manuscript of the first draft, the passage also included a clause that identifies Lik's vague intuition of the existence of something beyond everyday reality. Nabokov crossed out a clause that follows the word *cheloveka* (genitive singular of "man"): "chuvstvuiushchego, chto mesto, v kotorom on okazalsia, khorosho-to khorosho, no est' za uglom luchshee" (literally, feeling that no matter how good the place where he has found himself, there is a better one around the corner).[56] Two lines below, this "place" was originally referred to as "voobrazënnoe mesto" (imagined/envisioned place/space). In both the Russian manuscript and the printed version the final clause of the passage is anapaestic: "gde emu ne byvát' nikogdá, nikogdá." The repetition of *nikogda* (never) reaffirms the final clause of the sentence as a metrical cluster, either as a long line of anapaestic tetrameter (An4) with a caesura or as two lines of anapaestic dimeter (An2). The English version, usually a reliable proof of the authorial intent, is here rendered as an iambic tetrameter (Ia4) with a feminine clausula: "that he will néver néver vísit."

The text of "Lik" also exemplifies a syncretic form of marking the otherworld: images of heart pain. Reminiscent of both Aleksandr Kuprin's fine story "Kak ia byl aktërom" (How I Worked as an Actor, 1906) and the plot of Ruggero Leoncavallo's celebrated opera *Pagliacci* (1892), "Lik" dwells on certain parallels between two sets of disparate spaces, stage vs. life, and otherworld vs. this world. Lik plays the part of a young Russian with a heroic name (Igor', after Prince Igor') in a mediocre French play entitled *L'Abîme* (The Abyss). The plot of this play—whether or not it actually existed outside Nabokov's imagination—recalls and trivializes Ivan Turgenev's *Mesiats v derevne* (A Month in the Country, 1850), a firm part of the European repertoire since the 1860s. Set on country estates, both *The Abyss* and *A Month in the Country* focus on a triangle of desire involving a mother, a daughter, and a young man both love. Before going onstage, the lonely and troubled Lik dreams of the vague possibility that his role as a passionate Russian lover might offer him an onstage place in the play's fanciful otherworld:

> For instance, Lik might hope, one vague and lovely night, in the midst of the usual performance, to tread, as it were, on a quicksandy spot; something would give, and he would sink forever in a newborn element [*ozhivaiushchei stikhii*], unlike anything known—independently developing the play's threadbare themes in ways altogether new. He would pass irrevocably into this element, marry Angélique, go riding over the crisp heather, receive all the material wealth hinted at in the play, go live in that castle, and moreover, find himself in a world of *ineffable tenderness* [*v neveroiatno nezhnom mire*]—*a bluish, delicate world where fabulous adventures of the senses occur, and unheard-of metamorphoses of the mind.* As he thought about all this, Lik imagined for some reason that when he died of heart failure—and he

would die soon—the attack would certainly come on-stage, as it had been with poor Molière, barking out his dog Latin among the doctors [a reference to Molière's legendary death while performing in his own *The Imaginary Invalid* (1673)]; but that he would not notice his death, *crossing over instead into the actual world of a chance play,* now blooming anew because of his arrival, while his smiling corpse lay on the boards, the toe of one foot protruding from beneath the folds of the lowered curtain. (*Stories,* 465/*VF,* 137; italics added)

His heart aching, Lik wonders whether death might be a bridge between the quotidian and the eternal. But more importantly, as Nabokov's character, Lik peers into art's capacity to create other worlds and thereby apprehends the metaphysical designs of his creator.

In the remaining pages of this chapter, I would like to concentrate on "Poseshchenie muzeia" (The Visit to the Museum, 1938), a story which typifies the motif and design of entering the otherworld. Exhibiting several of Nabokov's hallmark devices, his antepenultimate Russian short story has been relatively popular with the critics.[57] My brief remarks will focus almost exclusively on the significance of entering the otherworld and the role memory plays in recognizing an otherworldly space. The opening paragraph introduces a two-world system. Moreover, the paragraph adumbrates one of the story's central cognitive tasks: testing the limits of one's imagination and fantasy. The protagonist's friend, a Russian émigré like himself, asks him to visit a local museum in the fictional French town of Montisert and inquire about purchasing his grandfather's portrait, which is supposedly deposited there. At first, the protagonist does not heed his friend's semiobscure request "chiefly because [he] had always had doubts about my friend's capacity to remain *this side of fantasy*" (*Stories,* 277; italics added). In the original, the same phrase appears as "glavnoe potomu, chto vsegda somnevalsia v sposobnosti moego druga ostavat'sia po siu storonu fantazii" (*VF,* 101; italics added). *Po siu storonu fantazii* is easily recognized as the opposite of *po tu storonu fantazii* (the other side of fantasy). Beyond this side, the side of mundane reality, lies the other side, presumably the area of fantasy, into which the protagonist will be drawn by otherworldly magnetism.

To the narrator's great surprise, he does locate the portrait in the provincial French museum. This initiates a series of fantastical transformations that go so far as to bring the narrator beyond his dreams, into a realm charged with the exile's cherished and embellished memories of Russia. The novelty of "The Visit to the Museum" lies in its insistence upon the narrator's initial unwillingness to enter or even approach the otherworld.

This distinguishes him from many of Nabokov's privileged characters in the short stories who seek the otherworld as both a source of salvation and a beatific refuge. The narrator gets involved in his friend's whim. However, once he has located the old portrait, he finds himself under the spell of the museum's liminal space and wishes to investigate the matter further. As he admits, "It is fun to be present at the coming true of a dream [*pri vo-ploshchenii mechty*], even if it is not one's own" (*Stories*, 279/*VF*, 105). At this point, as the narrator proceeds to investigate the portrait, which was painted in the first decade of the twentieth century, the first signs of the otherworld manifest themselves. Nabokov employs a device of charging familiar objects with slightly surreal or absurdist characteristics, which suggests to the reader the imminence of something beyond common-sense.[58] Consider the four sentences following the comment about "the coming true of a dream": "I left the museum [he has to go to the director's house] with a brisk, resonant step, and found that the rain had stopped, blueness had spread across the sky, a woman in besplattered stockings was spinning along on a silver-shining bicycle, and only over the surrounding hills did clouds still hang. Once again, the cathedral began playing hide-and-seek with me, but I outwitted it. Barely escaping the onrushing tires of a furious red bus packed with singing youths, I crossed the garden gate of M. Godard" (*Stories*, 279–280). One senses lightness and play in the at-mosphere, and the image of a cathedral engaged in a game of hide-and-seek with the narrator supports the airy mood. However, this would not be a Nabokov story if the narrative merely followed a predictable course without a series of reversals. What started for the narrator as an explo-ration of his friend's preposterous fantasy turns out to be a visit to a terri-tory where the narrator could only dream of setting his feet.

The narrator returns to the museum in the company of the curator, Monsieur Godard. When they enter the building, the red bus is brought to the reader's attention again, now parked outside. The bus transported a group of "members of some rural athletic organization" ("molodtsy iz . . . sel'sko-sportivnoi korporatsii"; *Stories*, 281/*VF*, 108) to the museum. The youths amuse themselves by playing collective vulgar games with the ob-jects on display, trying on medieval armor, swearing, evading the old mu-seum guard. The narrator describes disapprovingly how the "swarm[ing]" group disrupts his exploration of fantasy: ". . . their motion and voices cre-ated a condition of crush and thick noise" (*Stories*, 281). The collective "noisy fun" of the youths—rendered in the Russian by the word *izdevat'sia* (literally, to mock at, to scoff at, to insult)—is juxtaposed with the narra-tor's preoccupation with the ancestral portrait. The portrait goes back to the time of the Russo-Japanese War and therefore represents a facet of the narrator's prerevolutionary Russian past, the time that Russian émigrés chose to idealize. By investigating the portrait, the narrator also explores an alluring private connection with his Russian past. The noisy youths have no sense of history and refer to the man on the portrait as "old ape" ("Kto èta staraia obez'iana?"; *Stories*, 282/*VF*, 109). It makes sense that the narrator would try to get away from the collective experiences of the members of the agricultural corporation.

As the narrator tries to escape the collective pursuers, he falls under the impact of what Liudmila Foster appropriately described as phantasmagoric narrative magnetism.[59] Exhibit halls lead to yet more rooms: "There was an exit, which I had not noticed previously, at the end of the hall and we thrust our way through it" (*Stories*, 282). Soon the narrator loses his companion, only to face the increasingly "alarm[ing]" signs and signals. The narrator proceeds through a section of Ancient Sculpture into a room with Oriental fabrics and then into rooms with paintings that bespeak their High Renaissance or Baroque origins: "the oblique sheen of large paintings, full of storm clouds, among which floated the delicate idols of religious art in blue and pink vestments" (*Stories*, 283). The change of exhibits along the narrator's way suggests a history of human civilization from antiquity to modernity; before the narrator gets lost "among models of railroad stations," the following absurdist scene catches his attention: "a crowd of gray-haired people with umbrellas examining a gigantic mock-up of the universe" (*Stories*, 283). An exhibit of locomotives follows a room "dedicated to the history of steam machines" (*Stories*, 283). The brief history of civilization covers not only the arts, but also production and industry. "Beyond the fan of wet tracks," the exhibits lose any sense of order or logic and include "numerous office cabinets and elusive, scurrying people . . . a thousand musical instruments . . . a pool with a bronze Orpheus atop a green rock" (*Stories*, 283).[60]

Critics have speculated that the narrator's visit to a provincial museum in Montisert was informed by Nabokov's visit to the local museum in Menton in the winter of 1938. During a research trip to the French Riviera in September 1994, I decided to visit Menton's Musée Municipal, which, according to travel guides, prides itself on possessing the thirty-thousand-year-old skull of "Menton Man," also known as "Grimaldi Man" (cf. the custodian's remark in the story: "'And now I call your attention to this skull!'"; *Stories*, 278). Writing to the émigré writer Mark Aldanov in February 1938, Nabokov described the museum's collection as follows: "It has everything from paintings by Ferdinand Back to a ramshackle collection of faded butterflies. And do you know what two statues stand at the entrance? Pushkin and Peter the Great . . . ."[61] Such a bizarre "mixture of France and Russia," Nabokov's biographer suggested, "lit Nabokov's fancy."[62] Instead of the statues that Nabokov described in the letter, pseudoclassical statues stand at the entrance to Menton's modern-day museum, whose façade is adorned with a semi-Latin sign, "MVSEE," and the French flag (see Figure 2); the museum is located on rue Lorédan-Larchey). The description of the building's exterior bears only a remote likeness to the description in the story: "It was a building of modest proportions, constructed of many-colored stones, with columns, a gilt inscription over the frescoes of the pediment, and a lion-legged stone bench on either side of the bronze door" (*Stories*, 278). There is, however, something in Menton's Musée Municipal that resembles the absurd atmosphere of the fictional museum in Nabokov's short story. A figure of a prehistoric man, wearing a military helmet, stands inside at the entrance to the exhibit (cf. "trying not to look at some statues at the entrance . . . , I entered the main hall"; *Stories*, 278). The materials on exhibit include local maps, minerals, and old agricultural tools (cf. "a group of porous fossils; . . . a red-and-green map of Montisert in the seventeenth century; and a trio of rusted tools . . .—a spade, a mattock and a pick" (*Stories*, 279). None of the paintings exhibited on the walls was a male portrait; none bore the signature of Leroy. The custodians knew nothing about a catalogue and, for that matter, had no idea about the museum's pre–World War II collection.

It might be too speculative to claim a direct link between the historical prototype and the fictional museum in the story. However, the visit to Menton's pre–World War II museum probably gave Nabokov the idea to use the museum as a model of history in its making. Sergej Davydov has argued that "time and space in the museum are compressed and virtually devoid of boundaries and directions; every new step reveals a new century, epoch, continent, civilization."[63] If the protagonist of Nabokov's story indeed takes an esoteric tour of history, then Davydov's suggestion might explain why in Nabokov's design the description of the narrator's passage is laden with signs of an imminent historical cataclysm:

> Now and then, on one side or the other, stone stairs, with puddles on the steps, which gave me a strange sensation of fear, would descend into misty abysses, whence issued whistles, the rattle of dishes, the clatter of typewriters [the writing of history?], the ring of hammers and many other sounds, as if, down there, were exposition halls of some kind or other, already closing or not yet completed. Then I

2. Menton, France, Musée Municipal. Photo by the author.

found myself in darkness and kept bumping into unknown furniture until I finally saw a red light and walked out onto a platform that changed under me. . . . (*Stories,* 283)

What historical catastrophe is being evoked before the eyes of the protagonist? The narrator finds himself in a "bright parlor, tastefully furnished in Empire style [*ampir*], but not a living soul, not a living soul . . ." (*Stories,* 283). He tries to retrace his steps but cannot. He is in a deserted anteroom of the collapsed Russian Empire, without a single "living soul" around him. It is perhaps the historical association with the Russian Empire that makes the narrator "indescribably terrified" (*Stories,* 283). Moreover, from the Empire-style parlor the narrator proceeds to "a greenhouse with hydrangeas and broken windowpanes" (*Stories,* 283). In the original Russian, "greenhouse" is rendered as "zimnii sad" (literally, winter garden), perhaps a subtle allusion to Zimnii Dvorets (Winter Palace), the St. Petersburg residence of the Russian tsars. The storming of the Winter Palace—according to the Soviet myth the last stronghold of the anti-Bolshevik forces in the former capital—left parts of the palace's exterior decor damaged, windows broken.[64] The narrator continues his surreal journey across Russian history only to find himself in a room "with coatracks monstrously loaded down with black coats and astrakhan hats." Apparently, an enormous gathering of people is taking place behind the door, judging by the "bursts of applause" (*Stories,* 284). Again, an encoded historical reference—perhaps to the Second Congress of Soviets convening during the storming of the Winter Palace and arrest of the Provisional Government—might be at work. Behind the door, the narrator finds no theater, but "splendidly counterfeited fog with perfectly convincing blotches of indistinct streetlights. More than convincing!" (*Stories,* 284). Now a miraculous transformation takes place, the swift unraveling of history is over, and the narrator enters a space that gives him "a joyous and unmistakable sensation of reality" that replaces "all the unreal trash" (*Stories,* 284; probably referring to historical allusions evoked during the narrator's passage).

The paradox of recognition shapes the next page of the story, as the narrator treads the "real sidewalk powdered with . . . newly fallen snow." Recognition, the culmination of the narrator's experience, occurs gradually as he finds the weather, the buildings, the pedestrians "somehow strikingly familiar" (*Stories,* 284). The narrator characterizes his passage as having "escaped" ("vyshel na voliu"; literally, came out into freedom) "from the museum's maze" (*Stories,* 284). The recognition is accompanied by heart pains, a sure marker of a privileged experience in Nabokov's artistic writing (cf. "Lik"). Earlier, as the narrator was crossing the railroad tracks, "spasms shook" his heart. Now he feels a "twinge" in his heart ("kol'nulo v serdtse") as he recognizes the buildings which he used to pass while still living in Russia. Finally, when the narrator makes out in the decrepit shop the sign ". . . inka Sapog" ("". . . oe Repair'," lacking the hard sign after the *g* which it would have had under the pre-1918 orthography—still prevalent in Russian émigré letters and used by Nabokov himself), complete recognition is punctuated by a "pounding" heart. The narrator's reaction deserves a full quotation:

> ... и я уже непоправимо знал, где нахожусь. Увы! это была не Россия моей памяти, а всамделишная, сегодняшняя, заказанная мне, безнадёжно рабская и безнадёжно родная. Полупризрак в лёгком заграничном костюме стоял на равнодушном снегу, октябрьской ночью, где-то ночью, где-то на Мойке или на Фонтанке, а может быть и на Обводном канале, — и надо было что-то делать, куда-то идти, бежать, дико оберегать свою хрупкую, свою беззаконную жизнь. О, как часто во сне мне уже приходилось испытывать нечто подобное, но теперь это была действительность, было дей-

ствительным всё, — и ещё незамёрзший канал, и рыбный садок, и особенная квадратность тёмных и жёлтых окон. (*VF*, 115)

(. . . and already knew, irrevocably, where I was. Alas, it was not the Russia I remembered, but the factual Russia of today, forbidden to me, hopelessly slavish, and hopelessly my own native land. A semiphantom in a light foreign suit, I stood on the impassive snow of an October night [another allusion to the October Revolution?], somewhere on the Moyka or the Fontanka Canal, or perhaps on the Obvodny, and I had to do something, go somewhere, run; desperately protect my fragile, illegal life. Oh, how many times in my sleep I had experienced a similar sensation! Now, though, it was reality. Everything was real—the air that seemed to mingle with scattered snowflakes, the still unfrozen canal, the floating fish house, and that peculiar squareness of the darkened and the yellow windows; *Stories,* 285)

In the narrator's revelatory monologue every single word, every punctuation mark, possesses a precise, carefully weighed function both in the story's poetics and in the larger span of Nabokov's oeuvre. The pathos of recognition collapses the previously binary opposition between the idyllic, otherworldly, familiar Russia of the narrator's reveries, dreams, and memories and the Russia under Bolshevik rule, both forbidden and alien to the émigrés. The narrator makes an express pronouncement on his status in Soviet Russia. The narrator's term "semiphantom" fulfills two complementary roles. On the one hand, it reminds the reader of the fantastical nature of what is happening to him. On the other, it connotes the official Soviet view of the Russian emigration as a conglomeration of ghosts of the tsarist past, as a community of the living dead. In 1927 Nabokov published the poem "Bilet" (The Ticket) in Berlin's *The Rudder.* It elaborates the motif of an exile's return to his homeland. An official Soviet poet, Dem'ian Bednyi, printed a satirical response in *Pravda,* a leading Soviet newspaper. Entitled "Bilet na tot svet" (Ticket to the Hereafter), Bednyi's satire proclaimed that all émigrés—including the "poor little poet Sirin—[would] die before the Soviet fist open[ed] for [them]."[65]

The leitmotif of entering Bolshevik Russia illegally runs through Nabokov's fiction from the 1920s until the 1970s and is most explicit in the novel *Glory.* The motif of traveling across the Russian border in one's dreams also surfaces in his poetry. For instance, the poem "Rasstrel" (Execution, 1927) begins with a recollection of its émigré protagonist's habitual nightmare about being executed in Russia. Waking up restores the "cover" of a safe exile ("blagopoluchno[e] izgnan'[e]"; *PP*, 46–47), which both facilitates such dreams and prevents them from being realized. In the four-part poem "K Kn. S. M. Kachurinu" (To Prince S. M. Kachurin, 1947), Nabokov replays his prominent scenario again, this time by creating a lyrical persona, an émigré who undertakes a trip to Russia under the guise of being an American minister. Incidentally, in *Speak, Memory* he admitted to "sometimes . . . fanc[ying] [him]self revisiting [his former Russian surroundings] with a false passport, under an assumed name" (*SM*, 250). The poem opens with the following stanza:

Качурин, твой совет я принял
и вот уж третий день живу
в музейной обстановке, в синей
гостиной с видом на Неву.
(*PP*, 134/*Stikhi*, 278)

Kachurin, your advice I've accepted
and here I am, living for the third day
in a museumist setup: a blue
drawing room with a view on the Neva.
(*PP*, 134–135)[66]

The reference to a "museum atmosphere" recalls the museum in the story. The poetic persona also speaks of the new denizen of Russia, the "broad-shouldered provincial and slave" (*PP*, 138–139). The "slave" ("rab") in the poem recalls the "rabskaia" (slavish) Russia in the story. Finally, in Nabokov's last published novel, *Look at the Harlequins!* (1974), the protagonist, Vadim Vadimych, also undertakes a trip to Russia in disguise. An émigré Russian poet and a former Petersburgian himself, he experiences no "thrill of recognition" when visiting his native city. Like the persona of "To Prince S. M. Kachurin," the author of the emblematic poem "Being in Love" finds nothing otherwordly during his visit to Leningrad: "it was an unfamiliar, if not utterly foreign, town, still lingering in some other era: an undefinable era, not exactly remote, but certainly preceding the invention of body deodorants" (*LATH*, 210). Thirty-five years separate "The Visit to the Museum" and *Look at the Harlequins!* Over these years, Nabokov gradually relinquished his idealistic, otherworldly perspective on Russia, a view that had informed and shaped the short stories of the Russian period. In 1938 Nabokov was still capable of regarding Russia as "hopelessly slavish, hopelessly my own native land" (*Stories*, 285). In 1947, at the end of "To Prince S. M. Kachurin," the poet is tired of visiting the barely familiar territory of his ex-homeland. His new home, America, with its "enchanting chaparral" and "texases," lures him back.

At the end of "The Visit to the Museum," the reader beholds a two-world system within a two-world model. The story starts as an exploration of the other side of fantasy ("po tu storonu fantazii") against the background of life's routine, "this side." The narrator leaves behind the mundane space of a provincial French town and enters—via the liminal labyrinth of a quaint museum—into a space which promises a meeting with his idealized Russian past. After a brief chaotic tour of history-making, the narrator finally arrives at a space that is charged with two sets of parameters. One set strikes the narrator as being completely alien to both his memories and his expectations. That is the Bolshevik Russia of the 1930s. The other is composed of the signs of the past that trigger a familiar mechanism of nostalgic recognition.

Remarkably, several details of the narrator's evening in Leningrad seem to recall at least two of Aleksandr Blok's famous poems. Blok (1880–1921), Russia's great twentieth-century poet and one of the key figures in Nabokov's Silver Age aesthetic education, created images of St. Petersburg which became part of the émigrés' standard cultural baggage. Perhaps the "eshchë nezamërzshii kanal" (still unfrozen canal) goes back to "Noch'. Ulitsa. Fonar'. Apteka" (Night. Street. Lamp. Apothecary), part 2 of Blok's 1912 cycle "Pliaski smerti" (Dances of Death), with its celebrated "ledianaia riab' kanala" (the icy shiver of the canal)? Also, Nabokov's "osobennaia kvadratnost' tëmnykh i zhëltykh okon" (peculiar squareness of the darkened and yellow windows) evokes the yellow windows and symbols of darkness in the 1903 poem "Fabrika" (The Factory): "V sosednem dome okna zholty . . . Nedvizhnyi kto-to, chërnyi kto-to . . ." (In the building next door the windows are yellow . . . Somebody immobile, somebody dark . . .). Finally, a prosodic analysis of Nabokov's Blokian passage reveals that both in the Russian and in the English (a fine test!) several marked clauses are metrical or nearly metrical. "Býlo deistvítel'nym vsë" and "kák by proséiannyi snégom" are dactylic (D3). "I eshchë nezamërzshii kanál" is perfectly anapaestic (An3), while its English version, "the stíll unfró[o]zen canál," is iambic (Ia4). "I osobennaia kvadratnost'" is near-anapaestic (An3; a missing first syllable of the third feet), "tëmnykh i zhëltykh ókon" is nearly dactylic (D3). The English version yields an entire clause that is nearly anapaestic, with an extra syllable at the end of the second foot: "that peculiar squareness of the darkened and yellow windows"; notice that "tëmnykh" is rendered as "darkened" and not merely "dark" in order to maintain a ternary beat.

The narrator himself belongs to the otherwordly (dreamy, Blokian, metrically marked) past which shows through the chinks in the Soviet present at the culmination of the story, and he is bound to be recognized and detained. The story ends right there, with a brief description of the narrator's vain attempts to conceal his identity and a summary of his "arrest," "subsequent ordeals," and return "back abroad." The narrator is Orpheus-like (at which the bronze statue in the museum may hint) only insofar as he attempts to rescue his Russian past, which is no more—just as Euridice is no longer in the world of the living. What began as an exploration of a vague connection with the Russian past—a fruit of a friend's fantasy—has now led him to space which he will soon recognize as Russia—not the idyllic Russia of his past, but the real Soviet Russia of the 1930s. What started as the whim of a friend's outlandish fantasy ends in a firm decision not to carry out "commissions entrusted one by the insanity of others" (*Stories*, 285). "The Visit to the Museum" thus occupies a conspicuous place among Nabokov's models of entering the otherworld. The "visit" may be considered successful in the sense that the protagonist does end up in an otherspace, although this space turns out to be different from the one he previously visited in his dreams.

I will argue in Chapter 3 and Chapter 4 that Nabokov's best short stories capitalize on the artistic practices of his Russian masters, Chekhov and Bunin, and eclipse their canonical achievements. As a way of summing up the results of Nabokov's metaphysical quest in the Russian short stories, I propose to examine briefly the endings of two short stories he particularly admired and was likely to consider his literary models, Chekhov's "Lady with a Lap Dog" (1899) and Bunin's "Light Breathing" (1916).[67] Both stories raise an interesting problem: how are we to account for a passage in the text that seemingly offers the reader no narrative information but that matters a great deal for the story's metaphysics?

Bunin's remarkable story centers on three interconnected episodes from the short life of its protagonist, Olia Meshcherskaia, a high-school queen in a city in southern Russia.[68] The episodes are woven together by a dispassionate narrator who combines omniscient storytelling with quoting lengthy passages from Olia's diary, which he claims to have read. In chronological order, the three episodes are Olia's seduction by her father's friend, a man much older than she; Olia's conversation with her headmistress; and Olia's murder by her lover, a Cossack officer. The reader learns that Olia is dead at the very beginning of the story: the three episodes are framed by a scene at the cemetery in which Olia's former teacher visits her grave. The end bracket of the narrative frame consists of two parts which contribute very little to the story's events. The first focuses on Olia's homeroom teacher and her visits to the cemetery. In the second part, the narrator constructs a penetrating meditation on beauty, death, and immortality. The omniscient narrator lifts information from the teacher's memory: the teacher recollects a conversation between Olia and her girlfriend overheard sometime prior to Olia's death. In the conversation, Olia relates to her girlfriend a passage from her father's "old, funny book" describing "what female beauty should be like" (Bunin 4:360). This description tops the list of female perfection with "light breathing" ("lëgkoe dykhanie"), which Olia claims to possess. Her light breathing then traverses the boundaries of the teacher's recollection to enter into the story's last sentence. The last words of the story, the end of its physical text, presumably belong to the narrator: "Now that light breathing has been dispersed again in the world, in the cloudy sky, in this cold vernal wind" (Bunin 4:360).

What is the relationship between the story's narrative and its two final paragraphs, the teacher's recollection and the narrator's closing meditation on the immortality of Olia's soul? In "Lady with a Lap Dog" Chekhov's narrator also concludes the story with a meditation: "And it seemed that just a little longer, and the solution would be found, and then a new, beautiful life would begin; and it was clear to them both that the end lay far ahead of them and that the most complicated and difficult times were only beginning" (Chekhov 10:143). Chekhov's meditation invites the reader to construct a continuation of the story, promising a "solution" to be found and increasing the narrative distance between the actual open ending of the story and the presumed closed ending of a reader's would-be continuation. As Nabokov put it in his Cornell lectures, "the story does not really end, for as long as people are alive, there is no possible and definite narrative conclusion to their troubles and dreams" (*LRL*, 263). Chekhov's exemplary short story celebrates the indeterminacy of its ending. The narrator's meditation at closure invites the reader to wonder about the future of its characters. Conversely, Bunin's closed ending reinstates death as the locus of determinacy and yet, in the closing meditation on immortality, invites the reader to a different sort of wondering.

Given Nabokov's notion that "one cannot read a book: one can only reread it" (*LL*, 3), how does the "light breathing" meditation function in the act of reading Bunin's story? While rereading the cemetery scene that frames the narrative of Olia's death, the reader faces what I will call a textual opening. Unlike the reader of Chekhov's "Lady with a Lap Dog,"

Bunin's reader does not wonder about the future of the protagonist: Olia has no future in the reader's memory. Instead, the reader joins the narrator in pondering the mystery of immortality.

A textual opening is a privileged textual zone that positions the reader in such a way as to ensure its exclusive status in the reader's memory of a given text. During the act of rereading, a textual opening reemerges and compels the reader to pause and meditate. A textual opening such as the one crowning Bunin's "Light Breathing" produces a mesmerizing effect upon the reader because it communicates a set of powerful signals. Such signals describe the most fundamental human experiences, be they love, birth, death, or the transcendent. I have named only a few not because the semantic aura of a textual opening is somehow restricted to a finite set of fundamental notions, but because I am modeling the most likely possibilities. Nabokov employs a variety of markers in constructing his textual openings and flagging their presence for the reader. They include alliteration, cadence, prosodic structures, quotes from familiar mythological and literary subtexts, as well as syncretic methods (e.g., *ut pictura poesis* in "La Veneziana"). The term "textual opening" refers not only to a privileged passage in the text but also to the reader's experience of the text, whereby the reader's consciousness expands and makes a cosmological leap. A textual opening compels the reader to synchronize all the narrative information in order to achieve a state which Nabokov himself has described as "aesthetic bliss, that is a sense of being somehow, somewhere, connected with other states of being where art (curiosity, tenderness, kindness, ecstasy) is the norm" (*L*, 314–315). Awarding the reader a foretaste of eternity, a textual opening may be likened to what Belyi—speaking of the role of symbols in communicating a religious revelation—called "okno v Vechnost'" (window onto Eternity).[69] This attribution is especially relevant given Nabokov's roots in the aesthetics and metaphysics of the Russian Silver Age.[70] Nabokov himself, wearing a transparent disguise of a forgotten émigré critic (strangely reminiscent of Adamovich), likened his works to "windows giving upon a continuous world . . . a rolling corollary, the shadow of a train of thought" (*SM*, 288).[71]

A textual opening—such as the scene describing the salutory metamorphosis at the end of "Christmas"—thus allows Nabokov to extend his sui generis vision to the reader. What I have described as a textual opening stems from his "methods of evoking an aesthetic bliss that enlarges consciousness to a point of awareness of cosmic synchronization and of 'other worlds' beyond ordinary physical laws." Nabokov, Sisson explained, "plays a shamanic role in stimulating the reader to a shared awareness of other worlds as an outgrowth of a simulated omniscience which Nabokov derives from love and which, in transcending a deterministic view of the universe, educes the acausal (hence 'aesthetic') love (hence 'bliss') necessary for an intuition of cosmic coherence."[72] A "shamanic" writer like Nabokov expects from the reader a specific spectrum of responses to his text. His notion of the ideal reader suggests that the writer encodes in the text a projected range of responses by means of language, narrative structure, complex ironies, characterization, mapping of the narrative space, etc. In keeping with Nabokov's inherently deterministic working definition, the ideal reader is an author's double—someone capable of partaking in the same experiences as the author and the author's privileged characters. Through a textual opening, the reader accesses an alternative reality (also a diegetic plane) that is fundamentally other than the mundane reality of the plot. A textual opening embodies the results of Nabokov's quest for the shape of a short story which would ensure both a highly personalized reception and an intimate relationship between the reader and the text. The discovery of a textual opening is concomitant with the shaping of Nabokov's otherworldly metaphysics, and in a number of his short stories, including several I will consider in detail in Chapters 2, 3, and 4, the protagonist's otherworldly experiences culminate in a textual opening.

Nabokov's artistic quest in the 1920s–early 1930s has been identified with both cognizing and constructing the otherworld through writing. I have traced the evolution of Nabokov's otherworldly motifs from the very early short stories such as "La Veneziana" and "Christmas" to masterpieces of the Middle and High periods, "Terra Incognita" and "The Visit to the Museum." I have proposed that Nabokov's short stories develop a major theme: entering the otherworld. In my search for paradigms that brand his short stories with a mark of peerlessness, I have paid special attention to his elaborate devices for marking a character's encounter with the otherworld, signaling to the reader that she or he has entered a privileged textual zone through a textual opening.

Through the otherworldly travails of the privileged characters, Nabokov's short stories explore the artistically fruitful fusion of love, memory, and writing, a fusion best articulated in his bilingual poem "Being in Love." The otherworld lures his characters because it radiates both love (usually romantic love but also such human passions as butterfly collecting) and perfect memories of the deceased or the unattainable, people and places alike.

Nabokov is interested in the possibility of entering the otherworld. He cognizes not via abstract reasoning but through writing various models of what the otherworld might be like. In writing the otherworld, Nabokov (re)creates a space where love and memory are in harmony, where past and future, life and death, cease to be antinomies. The experience of entering the otherworld embodies an émigré's plight. If exile does affect a writer's performance, both negatively and positively, Nabokov's otherworld seems a perfect solution for writing in exile, where the author lives his text only insofar as the text compensates for the author's irrevocable losses.

Interlude: Mapping Narrative Space in Nabokov's Stories

. . . .

A convention of literary criticism is to view a narrative as a textual entity characterized by unique figurations of two parameters, a temporal one and a spatial one. The spatial analysis of literary texts in the West received an impetus in the writings of Joseph Frank.[1] Additionally, ever since the introduction of Mikhail Bakhtin's very useful term "chronotope" to wide critical audiences, the idea of a narrative possessing two characteristics, some sort of time and some sort of space, has taken root in contemporary critical strategies.[2] This chapter inquires into the figurations of space in the texts of Nabokov's short stories.

Any narrative strives to (re)create a simulacrum of "real" space. Any narrative set on the earth and carrying at least some traits of representationality is bound to possess a three-dimensional space which corresponds to the conventionally three-dimensional space of our human existence. Writers then face a fundamental dilemma of which only some of them are fully conscious: how does one present—with maximum precision and adequacy—a full-fledged three-dimensional space via words printed on two-dimensional paper? Nabokov's oeuvre in general and his short stories in particular stand out against the background of twentieth-century Russian prose in the way they render narrative space. He describes narrative space via mapping it, by analogy with the notion of mapping the physical space of a given territory in cartography. *Mutatis mutandis,* Nabokov faces a problem vis-à-vis the space of his narrative similar to the problem of cartographers with respect to the physical space they are mapping. Because a conventional map is flat (two-dimensional) and the physical space volumetric (three-dimensional), cartographers have to employ various substitute devices to render the third dimension, including use of color and density: elevations are presented via contour lines or in shades of brown and depressions in shades of green, areas of water in shades of blue; the darker the shade, the higher/lower a given point. A rendition of a three-dimensional space on a two-dimensional plane inevitably leads to some distortion. To minimize those distortions, cartographers use maps of small formats, thereby achieving greater precision and detail. Nabokov renders the narrative space of his stories in a kindred fashion. The scientist, the entomologist-morphologist, in Nabokov most likely influenced the way Nabokov the writer describes physical space.[3] His syntactic and lexical sophistication as well as the semantic intonation, sound orchestration, and rhythm of his text correspond functionally to color, density, and other means of rendering space in cartography.

Two interconnected issues can be distinguished in a discussion of Nabokov's approach to describing narrative space. The first has to do with rendering three-dimensional space on an atomistic scale, that of a paragraph or episode in a short story. Examples of his detailed and skillfully composed maps of a frozen park, nighttime Berlin, and a Russian forest in the summer will be given below.

The second issue concerns the way an entire narrative serves as a guide to its own space; the experience of reading such a short story can be compared to that of finding one's way around a given space (a city, a region, a country) via a travel guide.

The first group of examples illustrates the diverse linguistic means through which Nabokov overcomes the flatness of narrative space and enhances the perception of its multidimensionality. The first example comes from the story "Rozhdestvo" (Christmas, 1924), a recognized early masterpiece from the collection *The Return of Chorb*. Sleptsov, the protagonist, brings a coffin with the body of his teenage son to his country estate to be buried in the family sepulcher. On the morning after his arrival, Sleptsov walks through the park, where every object triggers new memories of his dear son:

> Перед крыльцом чуть *вздувались над гладким снегом* белые *купола клумб, а дальше сиял высокий парк*, где каждый чёрный сучок окаймлён был серебром, и ёлки *поджимали* зелёные лапы под пухлым и сверкающим грузом. . . . Он заметил даже, что оснеженный *куст похож на застывший фонтан*, и что на *склоне* сугроба — пёсьи следы, шафранные пятна,

прожёгшие наст. Немного дальше *торчали* столбы мостика. (*VCh*, 68–69; italics added)

(The creamy white *mounds of what were flower beds* in summer *swelled* slightly *above the level snow* in front of the porch, and *further off loomed the radiance of the park*, where every black branchlet was rimmed with silver, and the firs seemed to *draw in* their green paws under their bright plump load. . . . He even noticed that a snow-covered *bush resembled a fountain* and that a dog had left a series of saffron marks on the *slope* of a snowdrift, which had *burned through* its crust. A little further, the supports of a foot bridge *stuck out* of the snow; *Stories*, 132; italics added)

I have italicized instances where the language communicates the three-dimensionality of the space it depicts. Nabokov opted for metaphorical constructs which emphasize a vertical movement or a downward/upward direction. His English text, frequently a fine test of the author's being fully conscious of his designs in the original, follows the Russian closely and even translates the adjective "gladkii" (smooth) as "level" as if suggesting that the surface of the snow was a kind of level above which the snow-frosted flower beds "rise" ("swell") as "domes" ("kupola") in the Russian and "mounds" in the English. When Nabokov (through the eyes of Sleptsov, who is walking the reader across the narrative space of the story) likens a snowy bush to a "petrified fountain" ("osnezhennyi kust pokhozh na zastyvshii fontan"), a similar effect of spatial three-dimensionality is achieved. A fountain is immediately associated with an upward movement, and this quality is being transferred to a bush, which, generally speaking, does not have specific spatial associations.

An analogous technique is employed in the story "Pis'mo v Rossiiu" (A Letter That Never Reached Russia, 1925). The émigré protagonist is trying to convey his relationship with the shadowy world of nighttime Berlin to a distant Russian beloved. He claims that at night "one perceives with a special intensity the immobility of objects" (*Stories*, 137). The protagonist is taking his routine walk and—to create a contrast with the quietude and immobility of his surroundings—he must stress the three-dimensionality of the objects he describes in the letter: "doma — kak tumany, na tram-vainoi ostanovke stoit stekliannyi, nalityi zhëltym svetom, stolb" (*VCh*, 44; literally, buildings are like fogs; at the tram stop there stands a glass pole filled with yellow light). The metaphoric comparison of houses and fogs achieves much the same result as the earlier likening of a bush to a fountain; in both instances a habitual spatial image (house, bush) is replaced by a new, defamiliarized one. The English does not preserve "doma — kak tumany," but it does render what follows in the Russian with precision: "A glass column, full of liquid yellow light, stands at the streetcar stop" (*Stories*, 137). Again, here a vertical stream of light falling from a streetlamp is likened to a "glass column" and presented in an estranged shape which is even more three-dimensional in the English, where the adjective "liquid" is added to "yellow light."

The next example elucidates Nabokov's brilliant and subtle rendering of a natural space, a Russian forest. "Obida" (A Bad Day, 1931) contains the following passage:

> Сначала ехали лесом. Скользящие по синеве великолепные облака только прибавляли блеска и живости летнему дню. Ежели снизу смотреть на вершины берёз, они напоминали пропитанный светом прозрачный виноград. По бокам дороги кусты дикой малины обращались к жаркому ветру бледным исподом листьев. Глубина леса была испещрена солнцем и тенью — не разберёшь, что ствол, что просвет. Там и сям райским изумрудом вдруг вспыхивал мох; почти касаясь колёс, пробегали лохматые папоротники. (*S*, 89)

> (The first part of the way went through the woods. Splendid clouds gliding across the blue only increased the glitter and vivacity of the summer day. If one looked from below at the tops of the birches, their verdure reminded one of sun-soaked translucent grapes. On both sides of the road bushes exposed the pale underside of their leaves to the hot wind. Shine and shade specked the depth of the forest: one could not separate the pattern of tree trunks from that of their interspaces. Here and there a patch of moss flashed its heavenly emerald. Floppy ferns ran past, almost brushing against the wheels; *Stories*, 269)

This narrative guide to the forest follows the brief opening of the story, from which we learn that the protagonist, a boy named Putia, is being driven to a neighbor's country estate to attend a party. Putia is at odds with the people around him (his sister, the coachman); as in the case of several other estranged characters in Nabokov's short stories (cf. Vasiliy Ivanovich in "Oblako, ozero, bashnia" [Cloud, Castle, Lake, 1937]), the landscape becomes the object of his attention. It is impossible to ascertain the exact consciousness that perceives the forest as so magnificently three-dimensional: as is frequently the case with Nabokov's privileged characters, the narrator shares his estranged vision with them.

Not every narrative depiction of a forest renders it as nearly three-dimensional as Nabokov's in "A Bad Day." When Fëdor Dostoevskii in part 3, book 8, of *The Brothers Karamazov* talks of Dmitrii Karamazov's ride through the Chermashnia forest, there is nothing in the language besides the word "les" (both forest and lumber) to suggest the three-dimensionality of the actual physical wooded space. In Nabokov's description of the forest space, the sense of three-dimensionality is enhanced in several ways. First we have a reference to the clouds, which establishes the upward vertical perspective. "Snizu" (from below) enhances this perspective of an upward glance, this time covering the tops of the birch trees. The wood is presented as having volume, filled and/or pierced with light (verdures are likened to "sun-soaked translucent grapes"; the "glubina" (depth) of the forest is "specked" by "shine and shade"). Finally, the ferns, known for their long patterned flat leaves, are set in motion ("probegali": ran past), thereby overcoming the stillness of a flat surface; the adjective "lokhmatye" (floppy) evokes—at least in the Russian—an image of long-eared hunting dogs running along with the carriage.

Several of Nabokov's short stories, including such masterpieces of the 1930s as "Pil'gram" (The Aurelian, 1930) and "Cloud, Castle, Lake," fashion themselves as travel guides to their narrative space. The protagonist of "The Aurelian" puts together a guide to the privileged space of his daily "impossible" dreams about traveling to the areas of butterfly-collecting: "Out of localities cited in entomological works he had built up a special world of his own, to which his science was *a most detailed guide-book*. In that world there were no casinos, no old churches, nothing that might attract a normal tourist. Digne in Southern France, Ragusa in Dalmatia, Sarepta on the Volga, Abisko in Lapland—these were the famous sites dear to butterfly collectors. . ." (*Stories*, 253–254; italics added).

A short piece stands out from the entire corpus of Nabokov's short fictions because of its insistence on guiding the reader through narrative space. Its project is suggested as early as the title of the story, "Putevoditel' po Berlinu" (A Guide to Berlin, 1925). Although not a short story in the strict sense, but rather a series of fragmented sketches/vignettes unified not by a plot but by an underlying theme, that of Berlin's attractions, "A Guide to Berlin" nevertheless offers many insights into the problem of describing narrative space in Nabokov's short fictions.[4]

"A Guide to Berlin" is Nabokov's travel guide to the streets of Berlin in the 1920s. Like any tourist map, it assumes that the reader (tourist) is unfamiliar with the space it describes. However, the excursions to attractions and landmarks are selected with specific criteria in mind: this guide is a

Russian exile's tour of Berlin. The immediate addressee of this guide is designated here as "priiatel'" (pal; friend). A little vignette, introducing the main text of this guidebook, shows the narrator entering a beer hall with his "friend and usual pot companion" (*Stories*, 155). They sit down, and the actual text of the tour begins thereafter. The tour-guide consists of five small chapters, each dealing with one locality: "Truby" (The Pipes), "Tramvai" (The Streetcar), "Raboty" (Work), "Èdem" (Eden), and "Pivnaia" (The Pub). Not every tourist enjoys the excursions/walks/trips recommended by a guidebook; sure enough, at the end of the story the "friend" abstains from completing the entire route of the tour which the narrator maps out for him. The last part of the tour contains information about the beer hall where the two are sitting; we learn that the friend is not happy with this peculiar tour:

> Это очень плохой путеводитель, — мрачно говорит мой постоянный собутыльник. — Кому интересно знать, как вы сели в трамвай, как поехали в берлинский Аквариум?
>
> ("That's a very poor guide," my usual pot companion says glumly. "Who cares about how you took a streetcar and went to the Berlin Aquarium?"; *VCh*, 100/*Stories*, 159)

The friend does not see the criteria the narrator used to select material for his guide. He does not bother to look at the legend to this map of Berlin's space, to figure out the hermeneutic codes that are contained in the text and that explain how to use the guide.

Two codes are employed in the mapping of Berlin in the story. One parodies a number of Dantesque motifs and a structural principle from *The Divine Comedy*. The other introduces a view of art (and, consequently, of describing narrative space) that is an alternative to Viktor Shklovskii's *ostranenie* (making strange, estrangement).

The progress of the tour of Berlin in Nabokov's story recalls that of Dante's excursion in *The Divine Comedy*. Dantesque codes are also put to use elsewhere in Nabokov's Berlin works, as in *Korol', dama, valet* (King, Queen, Knave, 1928), where Franz allegorizes his passage from a third-class to a second-class compartment as leaving Inferno, going through Purgatory, and entering Paradise.[5] Dante's guide is Virgil, a poet. The narrator of Nabokov's story who guides his friend through Berlin is also a writer, which is revealed in several statements he makes on the nature of literary creation. Might the chapters of this tour of Berlin exhibit correspondences to parts and locales in *The Divine Comedy*?

The first part of the tour centers on sewage pipes that are being laid under the ground:

Перед домом, где я живу, лежит вдоль панели *огромная чёрная труба*, и на аршине подальше — другая, а там — третья, четвёртая: *железные кишки улиц*, ещё праздные, ещё не спущенные в *земляные глубины*, под асфальт (*VCh*, 94; italics added).

(In front of the house where I live a *gigantic black pipe* lies along the outer edge of the sidewalk. A couple of feet away, in the same file, lies another, then a third and a fourth—the *street's iron entrails,* still idle, not yet lowered into the ground, deep under the asphalt; *Stories,* 155; italics added)

One notes the infernal signification of this opening passage, more explicit in the Russian, which contains such a marked expression as "zemlianye glubiny" (literally, depths of the earth but possibly connoting the setting of Inferno, the first part of Virgil's tour). Later, we also learn about boys crawling "on all fours through those round tunnels" and about an illumined streetcar reflected in its tracks like "bright-orange heat lightning"; the tunnels of the pipes are described as possessing a "tainstvennaia glubina" (literally, mysterious depth).

While in "The Pipes" the text describes boys crawling through the infernal bowels of the earth, Chapter 3, entitled "Work," contains parodic allusions to the torments to which humans are subjected in Hell: "But perhaps fairest of all are the carcasses, chrome yellow, with pink blotches, and arabesques, piled on a truck, and the man in apron and leather hood with a long neck flap who heaves each carcass onto his back and, hunched over, carries it across the sidewalk into the butcher's red shop" (*Stories,* 158). The Inferno motifs—steeped in the aesthetic contexts of Weimar Berlin at the height of German expressionist cinema (early to middle 1920s) with its mixture of horror and absurd—are here echoed in the estranged presentation of a butcher shop.[6] Subsequently, a movement toward Paradise is signaled by another parodic shift: "A young white-capped baker flashes by on his tricycle; there is something angelic about a lad dusted with flour" (*Stories,* 157).

While "A Guide to Berlin" creates no equivalent of Dante's Purgatory (perhaps to avoid obviating the author's hypertextual intent), the mock-Dantesque motifs culminate in the penultimate chapter, "Eden," which describes Berlin's parodic paradise. In fact, "Eden" is the last part of the tour, its ultimate goal. The paradise of Nabokov's tour is situated in Berlin's famous zoo. Again, he employs a strong dose of irony—even more manifest in English than in Russian—when mapping his Eden:

If churches speak to us of the Gospels, zoos remind us of the solemn, and tender, beginning of the Old Testament. The only sad part is that this artificial Eden is all behind bars, although it is also true that if there were no enclosures the very first dingo would savage me. It is Eden none the less, insofar as man is able to reproduce it, and it is with good reason that the large hotel across from the Berlin Zoo is named after that garden. (*Stories*, 158)

The parodic allusions to Dante elucidate Nabokov's criteria for selecting certain sites of his tour around Berlin. The "Eden" chapter not only epitomizes the Dantesque code, but also links it with the second code, related to Viktor Shklovskii. Critics have alluded to the connections between Shklovskii's epistolary novel *Zoo. Pis'ma ne o liubvi, ili Tret'ia Èloiza* (Zoo: Letters not about Love, or the Third Héloïse, 1923) and Nabokov's "A Guide to Berlin."[7] The site of the Berlin Zoo plays an important structural and mythopoetic role in both texts; the teeteringly Soviet Shklovskii and the émigré Nabokov both lived in Berlin in the early 1920s. Both frequented the Berlin Zoo and its beer halls, as becomes apparent from the texts. Shklovskii's *Zoo* was published in Berlin by Gelikon Publishing House and could not have passed unnoticed by Nabokov who actively wrote and reviewed for the émigré editions. It is not unlikely that "A Guide to Berlin," published on December 24, 1925, in *The Rudder*—one of the leading émigré newspapers—was his belated response to Shklovskii's stance at the end of *Zoo*, where he writes a letter to the VTsIK (All-Union Central Executive Committee) and requests permission to return to Russia, which was granted in the fall of 1923. Shklovskii's position of a returnee—however complex was his personal situation—would have been ethically unacceptable to Nabokov. Also, one could speculate that the "friend and pot companion" in his story is not an émigré proper but rather one of the Russian writers who lived in Berlin temporarily in the early 1920s (Viktor Shklovskii, Aleksei Tolstoi, Il'ia Èrenburg, et al.) and wrote about the alien world of the West.[8] In "The Pub" chapter the friend exclaims: "A boring, foreign city, and expensive to live in, too. . ." (*Stories*, 159).

However, the superficial connection between *Zoo* and "A Guide to Berlin" points to a more significant dialogic response that Nabokov offers to Shklovskii's seminal definition of art as making strange in "Iskusstvo kak priëm" (Art as Device) in 1917. Shklovskii wrote:

The goal of art is to give the feeling of a thing as seen rather than recognized; the device of art is the device of "making things strange" and the device of complicating form which increases the difficulty and length of perception, for the process of perception in art is a goal to itself and should be prolonged; art is a means of living through the making of a thing, while that which is already made does not matter in art.[9]

Shklovskii's view of literary evolution charges the artist with the function of distorting form by reacting to an earlier form. Alterity is the aim of new art. If Nabokov is indeed polemicizing with Shklovskii, the following passage addresses the same problem that Shklovskii tackles in the definition above: namely the way a writer (artist) treats the objects he or she is depicting, including the space described. In Chapter 2 of "A Guide to Berlin," as the narrator is riding a streetcar, he concludes:

I think that here lies the sense of literary creation: to portray ordinary objects as they will be reflected in the kindly mirrors of future times; to find in the objects around us the fragrant tenderness that only posterity will discern and appreciate in the far-off times when every trifle of our plain everyday life will become exquisite and festive in its own right: the times when a man who might put on the most ordinary jacket of today will be dressed up for an elegant masquerade. (*Stories,* 157)

For Shklovskii of "Art as Device," the writer's creative consciousness serves as the agent of estrangement; such a writer measures innovation against the background of the past culture. For Nabokov of "A Guide to Berlin," time rather than the artist is the chief agent of estrangement. Objects in a given space, the space of Berlin in the 1920s, become estranged due to passage of time, which adds the quality of having been made strange. From the vantage point of the 1990s, a reader/user of Nabokov's "A Guide to Berlin" is bound to feel this "difficulty" of form in the precise anatomical descriptions of a streetcar, a baker's apron, a mundane jacket—objects most familiar for their time in the 1920s, rendered by Nabokov with maximum faithfulness of detail and strange to us in the 1990s. The act of reading "A Guide to Berlin" might be likened to that of using an actual travel guide from the 1920s and trying to tour Berlin with it today. For Nabokov, the "kingly mirrors of time" are the writer's greatest help because posterity "discerns" and "appreciates" the effort the writer took to map the space of the narrative.

Nabokov's views of making strange are further explicated in the final chapter, "The Pub," where at the very end the pub's interior is presented through the eyes of a boy:

> There, under the mirror, the child still sits alone. But he is now look-ing our way. From there he can see the inside of the tavern—the green island of the billiard table, the ivory ball he is forbidden to touch, the metallic gloss of the bar, a pair of fat truckers at one table and the two of us at another. He has long since grown used to this scene and is not dismayed by its proximity. Yet there is one thing I know. Whatever happens to him in life, he will always remember the picture he saw every day of his childhood from the little room where he was fed soup. He will remember the billiard table and the coatless evening visitor who used to draw back his sharp white elbow and hit the ball with his cue, and the blue-gray cigar smoke, and the din of voices, and my empty right sleeve and scarred face, and his father be-hind the bar, filling a mug for me from the tap. (*Stories,* 158–160)

The English brings back the important notion of the "mirrors of time"—missing in the Russian—from an earlier and conceptually crucial passage in the story. Introducing this guide to the pub's interior space, the mirror hanging above the child's head (locus of human memory) antici-pates the concluding statement of "A Guide to Berlin." The pub, seen through the eyes of an observant child, is a case of Shklovskian estrange-ment where a habitual (and expected) perspective of an adult frequenter of a pub is being replaced with that of an innocent child seeing objects afresh. At the end of Nabokov's story we have its narrator, a Russian writer living in Berlin, confessing that he has just looked at the pub through the boy's eyes, that he is in fact only recording the description of the pub the way a child would see it were he indeed in the narrator's place. The narra-tor's interlocutor does not understand his interest in mapping the pub's interior: "I can't understand what you see down there." Instead of an-swering his unimaginative friend directly, the narrator addresses a brief and poignant statement to the reader, the ultimate receiver of "A Guide to Berlin": "What indeed! How can I demonstrate to him that I have glimpsed somebody's future recollection? [*budushchee vospominanie*]"; (*Stories,* 160/*VCh,* 102).[10]

Just as an old guidebook to any space, city or country, inevitably be-comes an estranged guide to the space which is no longer there in its prior shape, Nabokov's "A Guide to Berlin," a projected memoir of a present space, embodies the same intrinsic tendency of becoming a carefully mapped space for future self-estrangement. Such a project of mapping a given space with utmost attention to detail and then surrendering it to time, the master agent of estrangement, constitutes Nabokov's intriguing correlative to Shklovskii's ground-breaking theory of literary dynamics.

Any map or travel guide is designed with a traveler in mind. No map (unless it is merely a decoration) contains gratuitous details. A map always reflects both the reality of the space it encodes and an awareness of the way a traveler through such space would interact with it. A map allows one to read its real space via mapped space. The same must be true for the map of a narrative space. The only difference is that in cartography a map of a physical space employs a number of codes that are stored in the map's legend and allow one to read the map, to decode the space it renders in order to be able to travel/walk through it. Conversely, Nabokov's narrative maps do not imply the reader's a priori knowledge of the map's codes. This means, in turn, that a reader of his narrative map faces a double task: figuring out the private (often clandestine) codes employed by the author in mapping the space of a given story (or parts thereof) and reading this space with these codes in hand.

Examples of Nabokov's use of various codes in mapping the space of his short stories are legion. Several of them have been offered above: codes of three-dimensionality in "Christmas," "A Letter That Never Reached Russia," and "A Bad Day"; the parodic Dantesque code in the travel guide to Berlin's space. Another telling example of the way his short stories contain clues to how the maps of their own space might be read occurs in one of the masterpiece short stories of the 1930s, "Sovershenstvo" (Perfection, 1932).

In some ways, "Perfection" is the pinnacle of Nabokov's narrative mapping, for both the shape of the mapped space of the narrative and the codes employed here in mapping correspond to the shape and codes of the protagonist's consciousness and memory that the story foregrounds. Mapping is at the heart of the story's poetics, as alluded to in the first sentence ("here we have two lines") and overtly stated in the third paragraph. Ivanov, the protagonist, was trained in Russia as a geographer, only to be earning a meager living in Berlin as a tutor to émigré families:

> He had taken his degree in geography but his special knowledge could not be put to any use: dead riches, a highborn pauper's magnificent manor. How beautiful, for instance, are ancient charts! Viatic maps of the Romans, elongated, ornate, with snake-like marginal stripes representing canal-shaped seas; or those drawn in ancient Alexandria, with England and Ireland looking like two little sausages; or again, maps of medieval Christendom, crimson-and-grass col-

ored, with the paradisian Orient at the top and Jerusalem—the world's golden navel—in the center. (*Stories*, 338)

Unable to apply his training professionally, Ivanov makes mapping the center of his private life. Because the omniscient narrator presents the world through the eyes of his privileged protagonist, the majority of the descriptions of the space are maps compiled by Ivanov. Also, since Ivanov launches himself into daily imaginary travels across the spaces that he knows largely through his training in geography, the reader ends up following Ivanov along the maps of his travels. His consciousness in the story is constructed through spatial associations. For instance, this is how Ivanov explains the evolution of the human mind to the Russian-Jewish boy he tutors, as they walk in a Baltic forest: "'We should cherish the woods,' Ivanov said in an attempt to divert his pupil. 'It was the first habitat of man. One fine day man left the jungle of primitive intimations for the sun-lit glade of reason. Those bilberries appear to be ripe, you have my permission to taste them'" (*Stories*, 344). Several things in this passage are remarkable. First, while walking through the forest and commenting upon its space, Ivanov is compelled to present the evolution of the human mind in a twofold fashion: allegorically as a passage from the darkness of ignorance to the brightly lit glade of reason and literally as a gradual perfection of a landscape, from a tangled thick jungle to a clear forest glade. More strikingly, Ivanov makes a direct metonymic transition from a spatial image of a human mind as forest glade to the glade in the actual physical forest where he is walking with his pupil, David. Ivanov's memory possesses a phenomenal capacity to progress via spatial associations—triggered by the act of mapping itself—from the space of his present moment to any number of past spaces whose maps are stored inside his memory. For example, when Ivanov learns that he might be accompanying David to a seaside resort in Pomerania, he begins to envision a seascape in his mind and moves from there to a recollection of his last visit to the Baltic Sea in Estonia: "He had last seen the sea in 1912, eighteen years ago when he was a university student. The resort was Hungerburg in the province of Estland. Pines, sand, silvery-pale water far away—oh, how long it took one to reach it, and then how long it took it to reach up to one's knees! It would be the same Baltic Sea, but a different shore" (*Stories*, 341).

From here, in a remarkable sweep of nostalgic recollection-in-mapping, Ivanov travels via memory routes to the space where he last went swimming, this time in the Luga River, southwest of Petersburg and not far from the Nabokovs' country estate, Vyra:

However, the last time I went swimming was not at Hungerburg but in the river Luga. Muzhiks came running out of the water, frog-legged, hands crossed over their private parts: pudor agrestis. Their teeth clattered as they pulled on their shirts over their wet bodies. Nice to go bathing in the river toward evening, especially under a warm rain that makes silent circles, each spreading and encroaching upon the next, all over the water. But I like to feel underfoot the presence of the bottom. (*Stories,* 341)

Ivanov's memory might be likened to a depository of maps of various spaces, both real and fictional, both traveled through and imagined.

The reader finds out that Ivanov suffers from a heart ailment: "the blundering but dutiful beat of his long-ailing heart" (*Stories,* 336). Mapping plays a significant role in the depiction of his severe heart pains. In fact, I would suggest that the heart pains are not merely described but also mapped, rendered in spatial terms with parallel references to the physical space which surrounds Ivanov and even causes his pains. The first time he sees the Baltic Sea in the German resort in Pomerania,[11] a very complex series of spatial associations creates a map of his heart pain:

When they came down to the beach after a fifteen-minute walk, Ivanov instantly became conscious of an acute discomfort in his chest, a sudden tightness followed by a sudden void, and out on the smooth, smoke-blue sea a small boat looked black and appallingly alone. Its imprint began to appear on whatever he looked at, then dissolved in the air. . . . The way back was uphill; Ivanov's heart now drifted away, then hurried back to perform anyhow what was expected of it, only to escape again, and through all this pain and anxiety the nettles along the fences smelled of Hungerburg. (*Stories,* 342)

Again, within a single sentence, a spatial transition is made from Ivanov's being conscious of his heart pain to a seascape's map. The "appalling" loneliness of the boat parallels the loneliness of Ivanov's aching heart (David, his pupil, is unaware of his tutor's condition). The heart pain is metonymized into a boat, part of a seascape with which Ivanov's consciousness now melds. The process of "eë" (Russian feminine pronoun that refers to "lodka," boat; "eë" is rendered as "its" in the genderless English) being imprinted upon "whatever he looked at" could be seen as a twofold mapping in which the little black boat serves as a landmark. As a physical landmark, it centers the physical map of a seascape upon itself; this black boat also holds the same position as the heart on the map of

Ivanov's heart pain. Finally, another spatial transition is made, this time via memory, from the map of an aching heart to a recollected map of Hungerburg, the Estonian resort where Ivanov last saw the Baltic Sea as a university student. The map of the actual seascape first yields the map of his heart pain in Ivanov's consciousness and later connects it to a similar map of a seaside resort that rests in his memory ("the same Baltic Sea, but a different shore"; *Stories*, 344). Later Ivanov's pain, this time the result of a severe sunburn, is represented spatially as "a symmetrical archipelago of fiery pain" (*Stories*, 344), another instance of mapping.

Like Timofey Pnin from the later, eponymous novel (1957), Ivanov is capable of experiencing states of unique fusion of the past and the present through memory; these moments have been compared to what Nabokov himself termed "cosmic synchronization" (defined in *Speak, Memory* as "the capacity of thinking of several things at a time") and occur precisely during moments of severe heart pains.[12]

Two other Nabokovian protagonists, Lik and Graf It, also experience recurrent heart pains that mark intimations of the otherworld. Intense heart pains accompany the emergence of perfect visions which, as the manuscript of "Lik" informs us, "he could only dream of" ("kotorye emu tol'ko snilis'"), visions of an "endlessly-airy world" ("beskonechno-vozdushnom mire," also crossed out in the manuscript).[13] Although Lik does not belong to the group of Nabokov's privileged characters (Ivanov in "Perfection," Vasiliy Ivanovich in "Cloud, Castle, Lake," and Pnin in the eponymous novel) capable of sharing their creator's otherworldly experiences, his heart pains do prompt a connection. Just as Ivanov does, Lik both fears the sea and marvels at its expanse. Lik's heart pain colors his vision of the space (sea coast) outside his room:

> He crushed a red-bellied mosquito on the wall, then sat for a long time on the edge of the bed, afraid to lie down, afraid of palpitations. The proximity of the sea whose presence he divined beyond the lemon grove oppressed him, as if this ample, viscously glistening space, with only a membrane of moonlight stretched tight across its surface, was akin to the equally taut vessel of his drumming heart, and, like it, was agonizingly bare, with nothing to separate it from the sky. . . . (*Stories*, 466)

Like that of Ivanov—also a skinny, lonely, poor Russian émigré who sleeps naked and suffers from an ailing heart—the actor's existence is suspended in anticipation of the otherworldly abyss that the readers never see in "Lik" but encounter in "Perfection."

The highest state of "cosmic synchronization" is achieved by Ivanov when he drowns as result of a massive heart attack at the end of the story. Jokingly, David pretends he is drowning, and Ivanov dashes off into the sea to rescue him. He has not been well for a long time; his fear for David's life and the contact with cold water cause heart failure. The last paragraph of "Perfection" describes what goes on in Ivanov's consciousness after he appears to have crossed the boundary between this world and the otherworld. Its very last sentence, the single longest one in the story and one of the longest in Nabokov's oeuvre, sums up the same art of gradual associative mapping of the physical space surrounding Ivanov, the space of his heart pain, and the recollected space of his memories. Cosmic synchronization here allows a perfect superimposition of these various maps in some otherworldly order. In the final moment of absolute clarity, Ivanov's consciousness becomes a perfect map of his entire being, of all the routes he has taken, mundane and otherworldly alike. In the legend to this map, if the reader were to deduce one, death serves as the central code:

Ровный, матовый туман сразу прорвался, дивно расцвёл, грянули разнообразные звуки — шум волн, хлопанье ветра, человеческие крики — и Давид стоял по щиколотки в яркой воде, не знал, что делать, трясся от страха и не смел объяснить, что он барахтался в шутку, а поодаль люди ныряли, ощупывали до дна воду, смотрели друг на друга выпученными глазами и ныряли опять, и возвращались ни с чем, и бежал человек с краснокрестной повязкой на рукаве,..., и Балтийское море искрилось от края до края, и поперёк зелёной дороги в поредевшем лесу лежали, ещё дыша, срубленные осины, и чёрный от сажи юноша, постепенно белея, мылся под краном на кухне, и над вечным снегом Новозеландских гор порхали чёрные попугайчики, и, щурясь от солнца, рыбак важно говорил, что только на девятый день волны выдадут тело. (*S*, 223–224)

(The dull mist immediately broke, blossomed with marvelous colors, all kinds of sounds burst forth—the rote of the sea, the clapping of the wind, human cries—and there was David standing, up to his ankles in bright water, not knowing what to do, shaking with fear, not daring to explain that he had not been drowning, that he had struggled in jest—and farther out people were diving, groping through the water, then looking at each other with bulging eyes, and diving anew, and returning empty-handed, while others shouted to them from the shore, advising them to search a little to the left; and a fellow with a Red Cross armband was running along the beach, . . . , and the Baltic Sea sparkled from end to end, and, in the thinned-out forest, across a green country road, there lay, still breathing, freshly cut aspens; and a youth, smeared with soot, gradually turned white as he washed under the kitchen tap, and black parakeets flew above the eternal snows of the New Zealand mountains; and a fisherman, squinting in the sun, was solemnly predicting that not until the ninth day would the waves surrender the corpse; *Stories,* 347)

Describing the various types of space in his short stories by means of "mapping" techniques, Nabokov continues the tradition of Russian prose that attributes enormous significance to representing the space where a given narrative unwinds and where characters interact. This tradition, manifest in the works of Lev Tolstoi and Ivan Turgenev, also includes Anton Chekhov and Ivan Bunin as its two representatives crucial for Nabokov's artistic development. One could also claim that there exists a counter-tradition in Russian prose, which attributes little weight to rendering the space of its narratives. Where Fëdor Dostoevskii (with the exception of Petersburg cityscapes and house interiors) and such twentieth-century writers as Zinaida Gippius, Fëdor Sologub, and Evgenii Zamiatin—to take those whose work Nabokov knew well—verbalize their narrative space merely by alluding to it, Tolstoi, Bunin, and Nabokov render the maps of their narrative space in great detail. In Dostoevskii, the narrative space functions at best as minimalist theatrical sets, background for entangled narratives, and at worst does not function at all in the poetics of the text.[14] In Nabokov, narrative space is mapped with such heightened attention not only because it hosts his space-traveling characters, but also because space itself, and not only the human beings inhabiting it, becomes the subject of his art.

. . . .

The Creative Laboratory in "The Return of Chorb" (1925)

Nabokov wrote "Vozvrashchenie Chorba" (The Return of Chorb) in October 1925 in Berlin, having taken a break before revising his first novel, *Mary*, also written during the productive fall of 1925.[1] The hiatus resulted in his twenty-third story, his second best after "Christmas" in the Early period. The story possesses a conspicuous and memorable Russian title with a near-perfect mirror symmetry between the vowels and consonants: vowel-labiodental-liquid-vowel-sibilant: *o-v-r-a-shch* vs. sibilant-vowel-liquid-labial-vowel: *ch-o-r-b-a*. This, in addition to the intriguing aura of the word "return," made the story's title a sound candidate for the name of Nabokov's first collection (1930). Apparently, he thought a great deal of "The Return of Chorb," for he chose to have it retranslated in the 1970s; Gleb Struve's earlier apt British translation was diagnosed as "too tame in style and too inaccurate in sense to [Nabokov's] present purpose" (*Stories*, 648). Nabokov regarded the story "a good example of [his] early constructions" (*Stories*, 648). I would add that "The Return of Chorb" offers numerous keys to his changing artistic predilections during the Early period. This short text is indeed so rich in material, so dense in various literary devices in their (re)making, so abundant with references to works of art and mythological systems, and so charged with the youth and fervor of its creator that its decoding awards many pleasures.

The protagonist Chorb, a Russian émigré writer living in Germany, marries the only daughter of a certain Herr Keller, presumably a Baltic German, and his Russian wife. During their half-year honeymoon, Chorb's young wife dies by accidentally touching a "live wire of a storm-felled pole" (*Stories*, 148). After the fatal accident, the grief-stricken widower undertakes to retrace the steps of their journey across Germany, Switzerland, and France—in order to make his dead wife's fleeting image complete and therefore immortal in his memory. Chorb's last stop brings him back to the "pacific German city" (*Stories*, 147) where his wife grew up, where they were married and spent their first wedding night in a cheap, disreputable hotel. Realizing that he will not be able to endure being alone in the same room where they stayed before, Chorb hires a prostitute to keep him company. Nothing sexual ever happens between them, because Chorb seeks not sex but a likeness of his dead wife beside him in bed. In the middle of the night he scares the prostitute as he mistakes "the white specter of a woman" (*Stories*, 153) next to him for his wife. Chorb has now overcome his last temptation, and his "ordeal" (*Stories*, 153) comes to an end. Or does it? The story halts at an open ending as the door of his room opens to let the prostitute out and his in-laws in. A Gogolian silence akin to that of the end of *The Inspector-General* (1836) leaves the reader wondering what will "happen next":[2] "But in the room all was silence. It seemed incredible that inside there should be three people. Not a single sound came from there. 'They do not speak,' whispered the lackey and put his finger to his lips" (*Stories*, 154).

"The Return of Chorb" is a story about love, loss, obsession, and values that contradict philistine commonsense. It is also about the role memory plays in an attempt to communicate with the deceased. The protagonist, an exile whose very name sounds strange, snatches his wife away from the philistine world of her bourgeois parents ("bourgeois in Flaubert's sense is a state of mind, not a state of pocket"; *LRL*, 309). He is without means, an artist and a dreamer. Everything he has to offer his wife goes against her parents' world of genteel vapidness, depicted by the narrator with such unsparing verisimilitude:

> Immediately upon coming home from church she [Chorb's wife] ran up to her room to change, while downstairs the guests were gathering for supper.... Her mother ... led her closest friends, two by two, to inspect the bedroom meant for the young couple: with tender emotion, whispering under her breath, she pointed out the colossal eiderdown, the orange blossoms, the two pairs of brand-new bedroom slippers—large checkered ones, and tiny red ones with pompons— that she had aligned on the bedside rug, across which a Gothic inscription ran: "WE ARE TOGETHER UNTO THE TOMB." Pres-

ently, everybody moved toward the *hors d'oeuvres*—and Chorb and his wife, after the briefest of consultations, fled through the back door, and only the following morning, half an hour before the express train was to leave, reappeared to collect their luggage. Frau Keller had sobbed all night; her husband, who has always regarded Chorb (destitute Russian émigré and littérateur) with suspicion, now cursed his daughter's choice, the cost of the liquor. . . . And several times, after the Chorbs had gone, the old man went to look at the black hotel [where the newlyweds spent the night], and henceforward that black, purblind house became an object of disgust and attraction to him like the recollection of a crime. (*Stories*, 149–150)

In the story, the reader is offered two perspectives on Chorb, that of his wife's parents and that of the omniscient narrator. The parents, Frau and Herr Keller, perceive him as a dubious character, a dark adventurer, who is a threat to their bourgeois status quo. After Chorb's "return" to the hometown of his deceased wife, he calls on his in-laws, who happen to be out. He talks to the maid, who later describes his behavior to her employers:

. . . what struck her first was the fact that Chorb remained standing silently on the sidewalk, although she had unlocked the little gate at once. ". . . I asked him why he was alone. His eyes were blazing, their look terrified me. . . . He said softly: 'Tell them that she is ill.' I asked: 'Where are you staying?' He said: 'Same old place,' and then added: 'That does not matter. I'll call again in the morning.'" (*Stories*, 151)

After hearing the maid's account, the Kellers conclude that "the man is insane" (*Stories*, 152). The news that the Chorbs are staying again in "that vile hotel" confirms the parents' worst fears and expectations. They do not, of course, suspect that their daughter is dead, and that a night in the same hotel promises Chorb the resolution of his "agonizing and yet blissful test" ("muchitel'nyi i sladkii iskus"; *Stories*, 152/*VCh*, 12). The Kellers expect to find their daughter in the hotel with Chorb. Dramatic irony is at work in the final scene: "At this moment the sound of voices and footsteps came from the corridor [the prostitute hears this]. One could hear the voice of the lackey repeating mournfully: 'But look here, there's a lady with him.' And an irate guttural voice kept insisting: 'but I'm telling you she's my daughter'" (*Stories*, 154).

The Kellers want to rescue their daughter from the "insane" Chorb. They intrude, still thinking their daughter is alive and seeking to reestablish patriarchal order. They have no idea that a vulgar substitute, a prostitute, has taken their daughter's place. At the same time, the prostitute herself perceives Chorb's actions at first as suspicious ("This fellow likes kinky stuff" ("s fokusom" in the Russian, literally weird, crazy; *Stories*, 153/*VCh*, 14) and later, after Chorb's ordeal is over, as insane and terrifying. Both the narrator and the reader have the advantage of knowing the goal of Chorb's quest. However, neither the narrator nor the reader perceives this quest as unequivocally moral and meaningful.

Unlike the Kellers, who have built their burghers' world upon "square" commonsense—"sense made common, . . . so everything is comfortably cheapened by its touch" (*LL*, 372)—the omniscient narrator, the sober witness of Chorb's "ordeal," makes no ethical or psychological pronouncements about his protagonist. At the same time, like the dispassionate narrators of many a Chekhov story, Nabokov's narrator ends up anatomizing—with great precision and knowledge—the nuances of Chorb's character. While the narrator makes no judgments about Chorb's morality, the reader still constructs the protagonist's nature—via characterization and verbal play—as ambiguous and maniacal. Chorb's duality—seeker of the mystery of death and patron of prostitutes—is signified by several means; the most central are his polysemous name, his silence, and his numerous links with forms of blackness and darkness throughout the story.

In "The Return of Chorb," Nabokov explores the phenomenon of grief and its impact upon an artist's sensibility. Devastated by his wife's death and naturally endowed with an artistic sensibility, Chorb decides to collect every bit of the past they ever shared. He wishes to retrace every step of their honeymoon backward from the point of his wife's death to their first wedding night, when "he had kissed her once—on the hollow of the throat—that had been all in the way of love-making" (*Stories*, 150). Like a writer who scrupulously collects the missing information in order to assemble a narrative whole, Chorb somehow believes that a catalogue of restored memories will offer him a consolation, a virtual image of his deceased beloved. His tragic mistake lies in his having confused the immortality of memory and the physical irreversibility of death.

My working method in decoding "The Return of Chorb" is to treat this short story as Nabokov's creative laboratory. The short story offers many insights into his artistic pursuits in the mid-1920s, when Nabokov was actively writing short fiction and testing his poetic preferences. This was also the time when his artistic devices were being shaped under the impact of his major Russian teachers, Chekhov and Bunin.

Various signifying systems—crowding the text—generate the meaning of the story. This analysis will first consider how etymological interpretations of Chorb's name shed light on his exploit. It will inquire into Nabokov's revamping of the classical myth of Orpheus and Eurydice and then connect the culminating scene of Nabokov's short story with a scene from Bunin's earlier story. Since one of my overarching concerns in this study is to bridge poetics and biography, I will also examine how Nabokov records and settles scores with his personal past. Finally, I will point out several devices of markedness that Nabokov employs in order to signal to the reader the loci of privileged meaning.

The name of the story's protagonist, Chorb, casts a number of shadows of meaning upon the text. What kind of name is this? It is the only way Nabokov's omniscient narrator refers to the "destitute émigré and *littérateur*" ("nishchii èmigrant i literator"; *Stories*, 150/*VCh*, 9). It is clearly not a Russian name, nor is it a German or other European name. (In his English translation, Gleb Struve rendered it as Tchorb, possibly emphasizing its Germanness; Nabokov stuck to the exact transliteration of the Russian Чорб.) In fact, the reader of the Russian version is never positive whether Chorb is a last name, a first name, or some sort of a nickname or penname. Nabokov offered the English reader a clue in his remarks prefacing the translated text: "The place is a small town in Germany half a century ago. I notice that the road from Nice to Grasse where I imagined poor Mrs. Chorb walking was still unpaved and chalky with dust around 1920" (*Stories*, 648). In addition, where the Russian text has "molodye" (*VCh*, 10), here meaning "the newlyweds," the English version opts for "the Chorbs" (*Stories*, 150).

The sign "Chorb" amounts to Nabokov's authorial gesture toward decoding his story. One might recall that his fondness for literary codes had already found its way into his literary practices by 1925. He had already invented several anagrams for his own name, including an early *nom de plume*, "Cantab," under which he published poetry in *The Rudder*.[3]

The most obvious suggestion would be to explore the connections between "Chorb" and *chërt*, the Devil/Satan of the Russian popular imagination and pre-Christian and Christian mythology.[4] In fact, an alternative spelling of this word, *chort*, prevailed in the pre-1918 Russian orthography, which Nabokov the émigré followed as a matter of principle. Linda Saputelli Zimmermann has commented on the *chërt*-Chorb connection, claiming that it creates a sense of a dark mystery surrounding the protagonist's name.[5] Indeed, one finds some textual support for the protagonist's identification with dark powers. A mystique of darkness and silence surrounds Chorb in the eyes of his in-laws and the reader, although the reader knows his innermost motivations from the omniscient narrator. At several points in the text, Chorb is linked with signs of blackness and darkness, especially the word *chërnyi* (black). Although *chërnyi* and *chërt* may not be related etymologically, the former is a traditional euphemistic substitute for the latter.

In this short text, blackness figures ten times. Also, on the sonic level, the presence of the phoneme *ch* (as in "Chorb" and *chërnyi*) is supported by repetitions of *ch* in adjacent words, as in the following passage describing Chorb's ride from the train station to the hotel:

> Было около восьми **часов** вечера. За домами башня собора отчётливо **чернела** на червонной полосе зари. На площади перед вокзалом стояли гуськом всё те же дряхлые извозчики. Покрикивал тот же газетчик глухим вечерним голосом. Тот же **чёрный** пудель с равнодушными глазами поднимал тонкую лапу у рекламной тумбы прямо на красные буквы афиши: Парсифаль. (*VCh*, 8; emphasis added)

The English text cannot recreate the same color-sound correspondence, although the repetition of the sound *s* plays a similar part in the passage:

> It was around eight o'clock of the evening. Beyond the houses the cathedral tower was sharply **set** off in **black** against a golden-red stripe of sunset. In the station **square** stood in file the selfsame decrepit fiacres. The identical same **black** poodle with apathetic eyes was in the act of raising a thin hind leg near a Morris pillar, straight at the scarlet lettering of a playbill announcing *Parsifal*. (*Stories*, 149; emphasis added)

Chekhov frequently employed the chiaroscuro technique to cement a juxtaposition of two characters. A telling example may be found in the story "Vragi" (The Enemies, 1887). There black/white and light/darkness oppositions punctuate the failure of the two main characters—the physician Kirillov and the landowner Abogin—to communicate. In Nabokov's story, forms of blackness (linked with Chorb) are counterbalanced by forms of whiteness.[6] The word "belyi" (white) and its derivatives occur six times throughout the story. Symbolically, whiteness enhances the aura of innocence enveloping Chorb's wife. In the long passage describing their blissful honeymoon, Nabokov experiments with the blackness/whiteness opposition to underscore the couple's union of extremes, the "dark" stranger Chorb and his pure "white" wife:

> And just as he had tried, on the southern beach, to find again that *unique rounded black pebble with the regular little white belt,* which she had happened to show him on the eve of their last ramble, so now he did his best to look up all the roadside items that retained her exclamation marks: the special profile of a cliff, a hut roofed with a layer of silvery-gray scales, *a black fir tree and a footbridge over a white torrent. . . .* (*Stories,* 148; italics added)

Death severs the couple's union of black and white and plunges Chorb into a dark chasm of loneliness.

In addition to Chorb's links with blackness/darkness and *chërt* (Devil), his name also evokes several biblical associations. These associations surround the protagonist's name with a complex and ambiguous aura, which conflates Chorb's deeply humane if obsessive quest and his status as dark adventurer and evildoer in the eyes of his wife's parents.

In *Speak, Memory* Nabokov reminisced about his infatuation with reading the Vladimir Dal' dictionary, a combined Russian equivalent of the *Oxford English Dictionary* and *Webster's,* while studying at Cambridge.[7] His fondness for the shape and origins of words might have led him to create a name that would carry a rich spectrum of religious, cultural, and literary connotations. A Russian émigré reader without an especially acute awareness of the drastic transformations of sounds and roots in different Indo-European languages was unlikely to notice that Chorb and the English "Cherub" sound similar and share four graphemes. In Russian, of course, the Greek shape of the Hebrew root (χεϱουβ, pl. χεϱουβιμ) bears little resemblance to the protagonist's name: Чорб cf. Херувим. This is due in part to the Russian practice of adopting some foreign plurals as singulars. In sum, for an average Russian reader Чорб does not evoke Херувим (Cherub) the same way it does for an English-language reader.

What are the possible connections between Chorb's characterization and the complex ecclesiastical connotations of the sign "Cherub"?

"Cherub" points to at least two distinct biblical notions. The first (pronounced *chéruhb,* etymology uncertain) refers to an angel of a high order found in the earliest books of the Old Testament. In Genesis 3:24, we read: "When he drove [Adam] out, God settled him to the east of the garden of Eden, and he stationed the cherubim and a sword whirling and flashing to guard the way to the tree of life." The fullest description of the cherubim is found in Ezekiel 1 where the prophet creates a vision of the many-winged, many-eyed, four-faced creatures (man, lion, ox, and eagle) identified with fire, lightning, and bright sparkling: "The appearance of the creatures was as if fire from burning coals or torches were darting to and fro among them; the fire was radiant, and out of the fire came lightning" (Ezekiel 1:13). In the story Chorb's association with storm and electricity also flits by: Mrs. Chorb dies after touching a "live wire of a storm-felled pole" (*Stories,* 148) while on a walk with her husband. Finally, Ezekiel's cherubim "had rims, and the rims were covered with eyes all around" (Ezekiel 1:18). When the terrified prostitute in the story turns on the light after Chorb's inhuman scream, she sees that "Chorb was sitting among his tumbled bedclothes, his back to the wall, and through his spread fingers one eye could be seen burning with a mad flame" ("sumasshedshim bleskom gorel odin glaz"; *Stories,* 153/*VCh,* 15). One detects a strange likeness to a cherublike creature in Chorb's posture: his rimlike fingers frame an eye; his glance is fiery.

The terms *cherub* (sg.) and *cherubim* (pl.) are omnipresent in the Old Testament and the Apocrypha.[8] For Christian theologians the cherubim symbolize God's highest potencies, sovereignty, and goodness. The cherubim are identified with knowledge in contrast to the seraphs, whose distinctive feature is love.[9] In the Jewish tradition, cherubs are believed to have been created prior to the Garden of Eden and served as a model used by God in the creation of humankind. Among other things, they are instrumental in manifesting God's will to humans and bringing the soul of a sleeping man to God. Nabokov employs the austere biblical repertoire of the term in constructing the mystical and singular aura of his character.[10] Chorb seeks complete knowledge and understanding of the phenomenon of death. He also seeks absolute proximity with his dead wife, for which he needs to create her perfect *obraz,* in Russian both image and icon. Like the cherub guarding the gates of Eden, Chorb screens his dead wife's perfect image from the world: "he wished to possess his grief all by himself, without tainting it by any foreign substance and without sharing it with any other soul" (*Stories,* 148). This is why he never informs his wife's parents of her death until he has "gather[ed] all the little things they had noticed together" (*Stories,* 149).

The second set of connotations which the word "cherub" evokes has to do with specific Old Testament narratives depicting the return of the Jewish exiles from Babylonian captivity. In this respect, graphic but not sound resemblance connects Cherub (pronounced *kéruhb;* etymology other than from the Hebrew *cherubim*) with Nabokov's Chorb. In Ezra 2:59, Nehemiah 7:61, and 1 Esdra 5:36, "Cherub" ("Kerub" in some English texts of the Bible, *Kherub* in the Russian; here always capitalized) refers either to the leader of the group of Jews who returned to Israel but failed to prove their genealogy or to an unknown place in Babylon where these people came from. The latter connotations of "Cherub" have a direct significance for the image of Chorb in the story. Chorb, like the biblical Jewish exiles, is an émigré with a keen sense of uprootedness. In fact, the reader knows nothing about his background. The only detail of his past surfaces when Chorb speaks about Russian birches to his future wife: ". . . ivy never grew on birches in Russia" (*Stories*, 151). Chorb is said to be a littérateur, but we have no idea what he writes. One also notices that he is virtually silent in the text: he pronounces only a handful of phrases, while his wife's speech is rendered indirectly if at all. Such an ambiguous status of verbal communication in the story supports Chorb's marginal place as an exile.

Other characters in the story perceive Chorb as distinctly alien to their world. This is not only true for his German father-in-law, but also for his Russian mother-in-law, as well as for the prostitute and the lackey at the hotel. Chorb's only real label is that he comes from Russia. He exemplifies an exile par excellence—someone likely to be perceived as devoid of origins, much like the group of Jewish exiles returning from Cherub. Also, the very notion of return(ing)—announced in the story's title—lies at the heart of Chorb's journey, which originates and ends in the same place, his wife's hometown. Elsewhere in the Old Testament, we find information about one Chorbe (pronounced *Kórbee, Khorve* in the Russian), another exile returning from Babylon. This Chorbe (1 Esdra 5:12; also known as Zacchai in Ezra 2:9 and Nehemiah 7:14) succeeded in his journey and returned to Israel.

This detailed exploration of the possible origins of the protagonist's name is necessary to construct a model of Nabokov's creative laboratory around 1925, when his poetics were only in the process of being shaped. It is therefore essential to consider as broad a semantic field of connotations as possible that might have informed the protagonist's synthetic name. Any such possibilities or combinations might have contributed to the making of Chorb's controversial character. Most likely, Nabokov adopted Chekhov's method of utilizing and/or conflating distinct elements and motifs of religious mythopoetics, be it Christmas and paschal motifs in "On Christmas Eve" (1881), the Psalms in "Rothschild's Fiddle" (1894), or St. George the Dragonslayer in "On the Road" (1886).[11]

In sum, the associations that the name Chorb evokes fall into three main groups: *chërt* (the Russian Devil/Satan), the biblical cherubim, and

Jewish exiles in search of their identity. The semantic equation to describe the meaning of Chorb's name would then be Чорб = чёрт + херувим (Chorb = devil + cherub). In the eyes of his wife's parents, Chorb is the Devil who tempts their innocent daughter, lures her away, and brings death upon her. At the same time, in the eyes of the reader, Chorb's solemn quest has something purely angelic (or specifically cherubic), for he seeks to possess the mystery of death and soul's immortality, that is seeks knowledge of the meaning of life. Overall, for the dispassionate narrator, his character conflates angelic and satanic features. Such a conflation is also supported by another possible interpretation: Chorb as a black cherub, a fallen angel. Satan, before his fall, is believed to have been a supreme angel in the choir of cherubim. The allegorical equation which explains the origins of Chorb's name might also be Чорб = чёрный херувим (Chorb = black cherub). The association with a black cherub is supported textually by Chorb's linkage with the color black and ipso facto compels the reader to establish a symbolic connection: Chorb-black. The conflation of angelic and satanic features within his character might explain his duality and ambiguity in the story. However pure Chorb's motivations, there is still something blasphemous in his attempt to wrestle with the powers of death.

"The Return of Chorb" appears saturated with various mythopoetic associations. In addition to the biblical motifs considered above, Nabokov's short story subtextualizes several major literary works from antiquity, the Middle Ages, the Renaissance, and the twentieth century. Nabokov scholars have pointed out the parallels between "The Return of Chorb" and the classical myth of Orpheus, which finds its best-known literary manifestation in Ovid's *Metamorphoses,* Book 10.[12] In Nabokov's story, the prostitute contemplates the night streets from the window of Chorb's hotel room:

> Behind the curtain the casement was open and one could make out, in the velvety depths, a corner of the opera house, the black shoulder of a stone Orpheus outlined against the blue of the night and a row of light along the dim façade which slanted off into darkness. Down there, far away, diminutive dark silhouettes swarmed as they emerged from bright doorways onto the semi-circular layers of illumined porch steps, to which glided up cars with shimmering headlights and smooth glistening tops. (*Stories,* 153)

In the classical myth, the celebrated pre-Homeric poet Orpheus descends to Hades, to rescue his wife, Eurydice. Chorb, like Orpheus, is a writer. Like the Thracian poet, he undertakes to reunite with his wife, the nameless Euridyce of Nabokov's story. Like Eurydice, Chorb's wife dies instantaneously, the former bitten by a venomous serpent on her ankle, the latter electrocuted by a live wire. In Hades Euridyce leads a vague and shadowy existence. Orpheus finds her "limping a little / From her late wound, with the new shades of Hell."[13] Chorb's wife, in addition to being nameless, is also linked in the text with shadows, weightlessness, and transparency. At one point, she is described as "light as a dead leaf" ("lëgk[aia], kak blëklyi list"; *Stories*, 151/*VCh*, 11). It is noteworthy that the passage quoted above immediately precedes the description of Chorb's horrifying awakening with a prostitute next to him in bed. At first, the prostitute's point of view (she is looking through the window at the opera house below) constructs Chorb's room as the space of the living, while the dark streets below are the space of the dead. The text emphasizes ("down there, far away") the location of Chorb's Hades behind the statue of Orpheus. In Ovid's Hades "pale phantoms" dwell in the "vast kingdom's silences."[14] Nabokov's is a modern Hades, inhabited by "dark silhouettes" but also equipped with automobiles. Remarkably, after the Hadean perspective has been established, the prostitute switches off the light and joins Chorb, already sleeping in bed. Chorb's sleep completes his Orphean journey into the netherworld. He wakes up and confronts death eye to eye:

> Он крикнул ужасно, всем животом. Белая женская тень соскочила с постели. Когда она, вся дрожа, зажгла свет, — Чорб сидел в спутанных простынях, спиной к стене, и сквозь растопыренные пальцы сумасшедшим блеском горел один глаз. Потом он медленно открыл лицо, медленно узнал женщину. (*VCh*, 15)

> (He screamed horribly, with visceral force. The white specter of a woman sprang off the bed. When, trembling, she turned on the light, Chorb was sitting among the tumbled bedclothes, his back to the wall, and through his spread fingers one eye could be seen burning with a mad flame. Then he slowly uncovered his face, slowly recognized the girl; *Stories*, 151)

The English text here surpasses the Russian in its emphasis on Chorb's sudden awakening, which brings recognition and ends his "ordeal" (the Russian "iskus"). The noun "specter" not only evokes "shadow," but also suggests "phantom," "spirit," and "apparition." Nabokov responds to Ovid's story with bitter irony. Orpheus ruins his undertaking by turning back and glancing at his beloved Euridyce. He can never bring her back.

Chorb, this modern Orpheus of an exile, creates a mock-up model of an Orphean exploit first by hiring a prostitute to play the part of his wife, then by falling asleep and descending into a domain where he and his dead wife are together, and, finally, by waking up to discover the terrifying discrepancy between his wife's perfect image fresh in his memory and the "white specter," a blemished live replacement. Note also that the first thing the prostitute does upon hearing Chorb's scream is to turn on the light and thereby complete his return from Hades into this world. Chorb's Eurydice is "gone in a moment." Turned into a prostitute, she "[dies] for the second time."[15] While Orpheus clearly fails in his mission, his modern variant ends on a more ambiguous note which suits his character and anticipates the open-ended silence in the closing scene. The reader is left to speculate about the meaning of the narrator's remark about the end of Chorb's "ordeal." While the prostitute dresses hastily, Chorb is said to contemplate her with "a meaningless smile" ("s ravnodushnoi ulybkoi"; *Stories,* 153/*VCh,* 15). This incomprehensible smile is the last the reader knows of him.

Ivan Bunin's pre-émigré short stories were instrumental in Nabokov's development during the 1920s. Bunin's story "Petlistye ushi" (Loopy Ears, 1916)—an account of its protagonist's sadistic experiment with murdering a prostitute—offered Nabokov a point of departure for the scene where Chorb hires a prostitute to complete his obsessive experiment.[16] First published in 1917, Bunin's story was reprinted several times during his émigré period, notably in his major post-1917 collection, *Roza Ierikhona* (The Rose of Jericho, 1924), published in Berlin by Slovo, the publishing house which later put out *The Return of Chorb* (1930). Nabokov clearly knew Bunin's work very well as early as the mid-1920s. The details of their relationship will be investigated in Chapter 4; it will suffice to say for now that Nabokov owned a number of Bunin's émigré collections, several editions presented to him (or to his father) by Bunin himself. In the 1920s alone, "Loopy Ears" was reprinted in two collections, *The Rose of Jericho* and *Sny Changa* (Chang's Dreams, 1927).[17]

The goals of the two protagonists are starkly different. Bunin's maniacal protagonist plans and commits a vicious premeditated crime. Nabokov's Chorb is engaged in a humane quest, a wrestle with irreversible death. The former wants to kill a woman, while the latter attempts to resurrect one from the dead. However, both use the same method to execute their plans.

"Loopy Ears" focuses on a single evening in the life of one Adam Sokolovich, a killer with a biblical first name. Sokolovich strikes everyone by his excessive exterior resemblance to the Devil. He is described as "extremely tall, skinny, and ill-built, long-legged and with large feet, with a . . . yellowish rather sparse goatee under a distinct lower jaw; with a grim, unpleasant, and focused countenance. . . ."[18] Walking up and down the Nevskii Prospect in St. Petersburg, Sokolovich elicits the following reaction from the crowd: "Oh, again this horrible man."[19] A Pole, Sokolovich appears to his drinking companions, two Russian sailors, to be alien, incomprehensible, and terrifying, much as Chorb does to everyone in the story except his wife. Sokolovich prefers to call himself "syn chelovecheskii" (son of man) rather than "panskii syn" (son of a Polish nobleman). The sailors "[do not] know well and [cannot] comprehend either [Sokolovich's] character, or his past, or his present homeless and idle existence."[20] This makes Sokolovich an exile of sort, similar to Chorb in this respect.

After a night of drinking, Sokolovich leaves a cheap tavern to pace alone up and down the Nevskii. Eventually, he heads for the Nevskii's "red-light district" and hires a prostitute. Bunin's description of his protagonist's way toward the "dark incomprehensible Pole [*polius*]"[21] (no double-entendre in the Russian) anticipates Chorb's own walk along the "city's main avenue" to the "secret by-street where one could buy love" (*Stories*, 152). Also kindred, both in spirit and in design, are the encounters between the protagonists and the prostitutes in the two stories. While narratives that describe hiring a prostitute may share common features, the language and characterization of the encounters suggest something more than an inherited topos. In Bunin's story, "nodding her head with a fake pretense of being at ease, even with some awareness of the irresistibility of her sex . . . she suddenly stood in the path of Sokolovich, who walked in a stooped fashion. He, measuring her with one good look, called the night cabby waiting at the corner."[22] In Nabokov's text, Chorb, who is earlier portrayed as "hunching a bit," "accosted at once the first girl who hailed him. 'The night,' said Chorb, scarcely unclenching his teeth. The girl cocked her head, swung her handbag, and replied: 'Twenty-five.' He nodded" (*Stories*, 152). Both prostitutes are not devoid of attractiveness, although their clothes and their faces are "jaded." Trying to be coquettish and seductive, both try to assume an intimate tone with their clients. Walking with Chorb down the corridor to the hotel room, "the girl looked at [him] with an expression of cold playfulness" (*Stories*, 152). When Sokolovich and his prostitute are riding in a cab to some hotel in a "desolate area," the prostitute makes "another attempt at being a woman: she startled suddenly and sought to press herself to his body."[23] In fact, neither Sokolovich nor Chorb wishes to communicate with his midnight companion.

Chorb cannot wait to fall asleep and complete his project. Brooding and determined to execute his murderous plan, Sokolovich does not respond to the prostitute's seductive behavior. In both cases, the prostitutes have already been to the hotel with previous clients, and the lackeys acknowledge them with a "frown" (Bunin) and an "amiable look" (Nabokov).

Both episodes in the hotel rooms construct a hellish perspective. In "The Return of Chorb," the prostitute contemplates the shadowy night town (with references to Orpheus's descent to Hades) from the window of the room. In "Loopy Ears," "from outside the room, through black windows, deaf voices wafted, a noise of some machinery was heard, and a crimson light of a huge torch burned as in hell." Chorb's prostitute closes the curtain after getting a view of the night town. In Sokolovich's room, the lackey draws the curtain to cover the hellish scene outside. Soon thereafter, the room, "behind whose window an ominous flame burned and the secret night job made its deaf noises, was charged with mystery."[24] The mystery solves itself in the early morning, after Sokolovich has already departed, leaving the prostitute sleeping in the room. The lackey finds his room "terribly quiet, so quiet that it didn't seem there was a sleeping person in it."[25] At the end of Nabokov's story, the lackey and the prostitute "exchanged a frightened glance and bent their heads to listen. But in the room all was silence. . . . Not a single sound came from there" (*Stories*, 154). The lackey in Bunin's story discovers that "shadows wandered through the dim room, and on the bed the short legs of a lifeless woman stuck out from under the blanket. Her head was smothered by two pillows."[26]

Despite the parallels in the ways the two stories evoke hellish atmosphere right before their culminations,[27] one detects a marked difference in the authorial balance of good and evil, resulting in the disparate structures of closure in Bunin's and Nabokov's stories. Bunin's serial killer, a monster with "loopy ears," undertakes a perfectly calculated if psychopathic research. Despite his ambiguously humanistic philosophizing over cognac, Sokolovich does commit a "crime without punishment."[28] The reader is left with the impression that he will not be caught. "Loopy Ears" is paradigmatic of Bunin's stories with a closed ending. In such stories as "The Affair of Cornet Elagin" or "Syn" (The Son, 1916) no questions can be entertained following the act of reading, and the reader leaves the text with a feeling of the awful weight of having co-participated in a crime. Conversely, "The Return of Chorb" partakes in Chekhovian open-endedness, when the narrative halts at its most questionable point and launches the reader into wondering. Chorb's in-laws are prepared to see him as a criminal type, all evil and malice. The prostitute thinks he is crazy. The lackey, one of Chorb's readers within the story, makes a gesture toward decoding the story's ambiguity, its characters' silence: "Oni molchat" (They don't speak; *Stories*, 154/*VCh*, 16).

In a narratological study of Nabokov's poetics, Pekka Tammi notes the presence of "covert self-references" in "The Return of Chorb."[29] I believe that not only covert but also overt references to Nabokov's own past permeate the text. They give the story its incredible energy and coherence, as well as its focus on love, memory and remembering, and nostalgia for lost pastoral.

Nabokov's biographer Brian Boyd claims that "had he not been married, Nabokov could have written neither *Mary*, nor "The Return of Chorb": it needed the confidence of his love for Véra for him to set Lyussya Shulgin [Nabokov's first love, the Tamara of the autobiographies] behind him in *Mary*, and his dread of any harm befalling her to charge 'The Return of Chorb' with such helplessness before the losses time can bring."[30] While what we know of Nabokov's first love makes a convincing case for Boyd's first attribution, quite a different personal subtext, namely Nabokov's failed engagement to Svetlana Siewert (Zivert), helps elucidate the poetics of "The Return of Chorb."

Svetlana Siewert was a daughter of Roman Siewert, a Russian émigré living in Berlin in the 1920s.[31] Nabokov met her and her sister Tat'iana through his Cambridge roommate Mikhail Kalashnikov, the Siewerts' cousin, in June 1921.[32] Soon thereafter, the twenty-two-year-old Nabokov found himself utterly in love with the seventeen-year-old Russian beauty. Boyd, who interviewed Nabokov's former fiancée in the 1980s, wrote about album poems that Nabokov composed for his beloved "punning on her name."[33] Svetlana's name lent itself to poetic wordplay, since it was derived from the Russian word *svet* (light). The name had been mythologized in Russian Romantic poetry, beginning with V. A. Zhukovskii's famous ballad "Svetlana" (1812), which centers on the Russian folk ritual of divination. Several of Nabokov's poems from 1921 to 1922 encode references to his fiancée via forms of the word *svet*, like the following short example of his juvenilia written a month after their acquaintance:

От взгляда, лепета, улыбки
в душе глубокой иногда
свет загорается незыбкий,
восходит крупная звезда.

И жить не стыдно и не больно;
мгновенье учишься ценить,

и слова одного довольно,
чтоб всё земное объяснить.
(*Stikhi,* 52)

From a glance, a prattle, a smile
sometimes in a deep soul
an unshimmering *light* shines,
a large star ascends.

And living is not shameful or painful,
one learns to value moments,
and one word is enough,
to explain all that is earthly.
(italics added)

Consider also the 1922 poem "Znaesh' veru moiu?" (Do you know my faith?), which ends with "spasibo, chto svetish'" (thank you for shining; Krug, 77). Even as late as 1924, after the engagement had already been broken, Nabokov composed a balladlike poem, "Gadan'e" (Divination), in which the lyrical voice addresses a girl named Svetlana and follows the mode of Zhukovskii's ballad.[34]

Earlier I noted Nabokov's use of the chiaroscuro technique in order to augment the opposition between Chorb's darkness and his wife's purity and whiteness. One finds a similar opposition in the story between forms of the word *noch'* (night) and the word *svet* (light), the latter referring to Svetlana Siewert in the biographical context of the story. Forms of the word "light" occur eleven times in the Russian text of the story, which roughly corresponds to the number of times (eight) one encounters forms of the word "night." Nabokov places light at the very core of the following description of the death of Chorb's wife:

Ему сдавалось, что её смерть — редчайший, почти неслыханный случай, что ничего не может быть чище вот такой именно смерти, — от удара электрической струи, которая, перелитая в стёкла, даёт самый чистый и яркий *свет. (VCh,* 6; italics added)

(Her death appeared to him as a most rare, almost unheard-of occurrence; nothing, it seemed to him, could be purer than such a death, caused by the impact of an electric stream, the same stream which, when poured into glass receptacles, yields the purest and brightest *light; Stories,* 148; italics added)

In addition to cognates of *svet* ("svetlyi," "osveshchat'"), one finds ten references to electricity, light bulbs, wires, and lanterns in the Russian text. In the context of the passage quoted above, references to light and electricity evoke the young woman's accidental death.

Nabokov and Svetlana Siewert became engaged in June 1922, and the engagement was broken off in January 1923. Svetlana's parents were afraid to entrust their young daughter to the young émigré littérateur and demanded that Nabokov get a steady job.[35] The Siewerts, like the Kellers in the story, objected to their daughter's involvement with a "destitute émigré and *littérateur*" (*Stories,* 150). Several other parallels can be identified. The name of Chorb's mother-in-law is Varvara Klimovna, which, as Nabokov explains in his English preface, bespeaks her origins in the merchant class. The name of Svetlana Siewert's mother is Klavdiia, also a name probably marking a member of the Russian merchant class with its set of distinct customs and traditional names even as late as the 1900s.[36] Like Chorb's father-in-law, the father of Svetlana Siewert also bore a German last name.

Nabokov was devastated by the Siewerts' decision and by Svetlana's seemingly easy acquiescence.[37] Several poems of the time, especially the one entitled "Finis," served as his private diary. They present the young poet in pain of rejection, plunged into despair and heartbroken. But nothing testifies better to Nabokov's condition after the broken engagement than a letter he sent his ex-fiancée from Solliès-Pont in southern France on May 25, 1923, some five months after their parting. The letter was written from a Russian-owned farm (Domaine Grand Beaulieu) where Nabokov worked during the spring and summer of 1923, healing his wounds and writing a great deal. In the letter, he addresses his ex-fiancée as "Svet" (literally, light but actually a common vocative form of the name Svetlana, the reduced "Sveta"). The letter contributes to the understanding of Nabokov's personal drama, which had a lasting impact upon his fiction. Nabokov explains that distance has awarded him the freedom of being able to say the most affectionate things to Svetlana Siewert; as the addressee she will not be able to undo them, but will have to read them instead. He also speaks of the great difficulty of cutting off a live memory of his love. At the same time, he admits that, thanks to what happened, he has found some new words and is a better writer now. He writes about his plan to go as far as Biskra (a town in North Africa) in order to forget Svetlana. Finally, he suggests that all poetry is constructed upon the kind of tragic love that he experiences.[38]

Nabokov did not settle in North Africa. Instead, he returned to Berlin in August of 1923 to leave his grief behind, embark on a lifelong relationship with his future wife, Véra Slonim, and enter a new creative phase. A shift toward prose was underway: four stories written in the fall of 1923 and fourteen during 1924. Several of the stories from the time of Nabokov's posttraumatic creative upsurge, such as "Wingstroke," "The Seaport," "Revenge," "La Veneziana," and "Christmas," include elements of their author's biography. In "The Return of Chorb," Nabokov conflated taxing memories of his failed engagement with the blissful new impressions of a recent honeymoon journey.

In his story Nabokov offers palpable outlines of the young couple's honeymoon route. It started in the fall, when they left the quiet German city to hike through Schwarzwald, the vast forest in the south of Germany. Afterward, they spent the winter in Switzerland and then went farther south to the French Riviera, where Chorb's wife was killed "on the road from Nice to Grasse" (*Stories*, 648).

In August 1925 Nabokov took Véra to Czechoslovakia for two weeks to meet his family.[39] The honeymoon was interrupted when he went to the Baltic resort of Zoppot as escort to his student, Aleksandr Zak. On August 27 Nabokov and Sak set off to tour Schwarzwald. They visited the city of Freiburg, where Nabokov admired its famous Gothic cathedral. The atmosphere of the old German city, located on the western boundary of Schwarzwald, enters into the text of "The Return of Chorb": "In that pacific German city, where the very air seemed a little lusterless and where a transverse row of ripples had kept shading gently the reflected cathedral for well over seven centuries . . ." (*Stories*, 147). Between August 31 and September 4 (cf. the Chorbs' autumn in Schwarzwald) Nabokov and his fellow sojourner climbed Mt. Felberg and covered the long trail between St. Blasien and Wehr, ending their tour in Säckingen, near the German-Swiss border. On September 4 Nabokov took a train to Constance (Konstanz), also on the Swiss border, where he met Véra and stayed for a week in a pension. After their trip through Schwarzwald, which began in a city resembling Freiburg, Chorb and his wife "wintered" in Switzerland. "The Return of Chorb" was written in October when Nabokov's impressions of his honeymoon were fresh. The new impressions were woven together with the now-crystallized memories of Svetlana Siewert. If Nabokov, whose own pen-name, Sirin, shared with Chorb's its mythological aura, was indeed coming to terms with his failed love for Svetlana while also recording within the same text the bliss of his marriage to Véra, this might add to the previous explanations of Chorb's duality and ambiguity. The open-ended text of "The Return of Chorb" commemorates both an authorial drama in the closed-ended past and authorial victory over it in the open-ended present.

As I have proposed in Chapter 1, Nabokov employs various markers of privileged meaning in his short stories. The function of such markers is comparable to the instructions—regarding both speed and emphasis—that composers place in their notes. Nabokov's markers prompt the readers about the ways to read a given story. The ambiguity of Chorb's character finds expression through various signifying systems in the story. Nabokov utilizes the Chekhovian technique of loading the text with overriding fixations upon a single object or interplay between two objects or attributes. In his classic study of Chekhov's stylistics, Pëtr Bitsilli makes a strong case for Chekhov's recurrent use of the same words within the context of a given story. Chekhov's avoidance of synonyms restores to the word its original meaning or endows it with a new meaning which it previously possessed only in potentiality.[40] My own experience with reading Chekhov's stories confirms Bitsilli's analysis but also extends it to Nabokov's poetics.[41]

The littérateur Chorb is obsessed with a maniacal quest: recreation of his dead wife's perfect image. The nature of this quest and its teleology in the story might explain Nabokov's fixation—Chekhovian in its genesis—upon several single objects in the text. For example, when Chorb is already asleep, the prostitute wanders around his room "naked, but in her stockings" (Stories, 153). Just before that, she examines the contents of Chorb's trunk: "Blinking and cautiously stretching out her bare arm, she palpitated a woman's dress, a stocking, scraps of silk—all this stuffed in anyhow and smelling so nice that it made her feel sad" (Stories, 153). This is happening while Chorb, the modern Orpheus, descends into the Hades of his sleep to rescue his dead wife. In the context of the scene, the references to stockings—the prostitute's and those belonging to Chorb's wife—become a source of bitter contextual irony. After Chorb and his wife have eloped right after the wedding, they laugh at "a lovely blond hair" ("chudesnyi svetlyi volos"; VCh, 9/Stories, 149), a signature that a previous guest left in the wash basin. Later, when Chorb glances at the prostitute, he notices that "her bobbed hair was blond" ("volosy u neë svetlye, strizhennye"; Stories, 152/VCh, 13).

I spoke earlier of the narrator's focus on various attributes of electricity as the source of his wife's death ("a death, caused by the impact of an electric stream, the same stream which . . . yields the purest and brightest light"; Stories, 148). Consider one more curious fixation. Leaves first appear at the beginning of the story in the form of "loopy shadows" on the night sidewalk. Later, as Chorb walks through the town where "he had met and married" his wife, a flashback returns him to their blissful times together, to a walk they took "on the eve of the wedding":

> How good was the earthy, damp, somewhat violety smell of the dead *leaves* strewing the sidewalk! On those enchanting overcast days the sky would be of a dull white, and the small twig-reflecting puddle in the middle of the black pavement resembled an insufficiently developed photograph. The gray-stone villas were separated by the mellow and motionless *foliage* of yellowing trees, and in front of the Kellers' house the *leaves* of a withering poplar had acquired the tone of transparent grapes. One glimpsed, too, a few birches behind the bars of the gate; ivy solidly muffled some of their boles, and Chorb made a point of telling her that ivy never grew on birches in Russia, and she remarked that the foxy tints of their minute *leaves* reminded her of spots of tender rust upon ironed linen. Oaks and chestnuts lined the sidewalks; their black bark was velveted with green rot; every now and then a *leaf* broke away to fly athwart the street like a scrap of wrapping paper. She attempted to catch it on the wing by means of a child's spade found near a heap of pink bricks at a spot where the street was under repair. A little way off the funnel of a workers' van emitted gray-blue smoke which drifted aslant and dissolved between the branches—and a resting workman, one hand on his hip, contemplated the young lady, as light as a dead *leaf,* dancing about with that little spade in her raised hand. She skipped, she laughed. Chorb, hunching his back a bit, walked behind her—and it seemed to him that happiness itself had that smell, the smell of dead *leaves.* (*Stories,* 151; italics added)

This is early Nabokov at his greatest. Nothing evokes the sense of Chorb's irreparable loss better than this cinematic depiction of autumn. Close-ups are followed by long- and extra-long shots that put individual objects in perspective. Colorful pastoral motifs (grapes, ivy) intertwine with signs of relentless modernity (black and white photography). Shadows and reflections neighbor full-blown objects. Russia—gleaming in Chorb's remote past—is contrasted with Germany. As a result, the reader is given insights into the protagonist's nostalgia. The sense of the imminence of death permeates the passage. Retroactively, death taints even Chorb's most blissful memories of his wife. The English text enhances the omnipresence of death and dying by translating the Russian adjective *vialyi* (literally, faded) as "dead." Twice, where the Russian has *vialye list'ia,*

Nabokov opts for "dead leaves" in the Englished text. He also renders the Russian *blëklyi list* (literally, pale or discolored leaf) as "dead leaf." By emphasizing the metonymic link between leaves and death, Nabokov thereby enhances the associations between Chorb's wife and death, which reach a crescendo by the end of the passage: "that lady, as light as a dead leaf" (cf. earlier "she attempted to catch [a leaf] on the wing"). The passage points to the young woman's innocence and childishness ("child's spade"; "dancing about"; "skip[ping]"). The references to blissful love, foliage, and death come together in the last sentence: ". . . i emu kazalos', chto vot tak, kak pakhnut vialye list'ia, pakhnet samo schast'e" (. . . it seemed to him that happiness itself had that smell, the smell of dead leaves; *VCh*, 11/ *Stories*, 151).

When, having returned to the initial point of the honeymoon, Chorb walks at night toward the Kellers' house, he is said to "hardly recognize the streets" where some of the happiest times in his life had occurred. In a smooth transition, his idealized memories—evoked in the earlier long passage—here join his present. Again, the reader stumbles across a reference to leaves. "Saturated with light," several leaves appear "quite translucent" (*Stories*, 151). Although it is springtime, the description of the leaves as "translucent" recalls the earlier "leaves of a withering poplar [which] has acquired the tone of transparent grapes" (*Stories*, 151). In both cases, light and shadows suggest Hadean parallels between Chorb's wife and Eurydice. Another echo of classical mythopoetics becomes evident when one compares the lists of trees and vines in Nabokov's story and in the pastoral part of the Orpheus chapter of *Metamorphoses*. Both texts mention firs, oaks, poplars, ivy, and, grapes.

The last form of markedness to be considered is Nabokov's particular forte, prosodic structures that stress privileged meaning. In the passage quoted above, the last three sentences employ metrical markedness to enhance their artistic effect. The motions of the smoke, the falling leaves, the dancing young lady, and Chorb's own gait find rhythmical correlatives: *"Poódal' iz trubý / rabóchego furgóna / struílsia sízyi . . .* [iambic trimeter Ia3, last foot truncated] dymok, *naklóniálsia, táial mezhdu vétok* [trochaic pentameter T5], *i otdykhávshii kámenshchik smotrél* [iambic pentameter Ia5] podbochenias', na lëgkuiu, kak blëklyi list, *báryshniu, pliasávshuiu s lopátkoi / v pódniatoi ruké* [T5; second verse truncated]. *Ona prýgala i smeiálas'. / Chorb, slegka górbias', / shagál za néiu, /—i emú kazálos', / chtó vot ták, / kak pákhnut viálye líst'ia, / pákhnet samó schást'e* [the classical binary meters metamorphose first into two-stress accentual verse (dol'nik 2) and then perfect three-stress dol'niks (dol'nik 3) which crown the pas-

107

sage]." In the corresponding Englished passage, one also finds certain elements of a prosodic organization of prose: "A little way off *the fúnnel of a wórker's van / emítted gráy blue smóke* [Ia 4/3; or *gray-blue smóke which drífted aslánt and dissólved.* . . ; anapaestic tetrameter An4; other ternary units may be identified within this segment]. . . which drifted aslant and dissolved *betwéen the bránches and a résting wórkman* [Ia5] . . . one hand on his hip, contemplated *the young lády as líght as a déad leaf* [anapaestic trimeter An3], . . . dancing about with that little spade in her raised hand. *She skípped, she láughed* [trochaic dimeter T2]. Chorb, hunching his back a bit, walked behind her—*and it séemed to him that háppiness itsélf / had the smell, the sméll of déad leaves* [T6/5; fourth foot of second verse truncated]." Thus, both the Russian and the English versions contain units of metricized prose in which prosodic markedness signals the privileged nature of the protagonist's memories.

The mid- to late 1920s were the years of Nabokov's formal quest, paralleled by his evolving sui generis metaphysics. Blending religious mythopoetics, cultural history, and the author's personal past, the story testifies to his growing mastery and control over the material of fiction. The structure of the narrative in "The Return of Chorb" exhibits genetic ties to short stories by both of his Russian masters, Chekhov and Bunin. Nabokov's story is Buninesque in its fixation upon a maniacal protagonist and in its striking culmination, typical of Bunin's crime narratives. However, instead of a closed ending, which would follow in Bunin's crime stories like "Loopy Ears," Nabokov opts for a Chekhovian open ending which corresponds to the ambiguous project of the protagonist. On the basis of various forms of characterization and authorial markedness (color, euphony, prosodic markers, etc.), the reader should draw his or her own conclusion about the ethics and psychology of the protagonist.

Like Chorb, one of the first protagonists privy to his author's world view, Nabokov is engaged in a painstaking quest. Chorb sets out to recreate his wife's perfect image. Nabokov undertakes to retrace and reclaim (and, later, eclipse) the best achievements of Chekhov and Bunin, his predecessors in the art of short story writing.

Memory, Pilgrimage, and Death in "The Aurelian" (1930)

The protagonist of "Pil'gram" (The Aurelian, 1930), a German shopkeeper and entomologist, dies of a stroke at the threshold of his perfect dream. The fifty-year-old owner of a butterfly store in Weimar Berlin, Pilgram spends his entire adult life attempting to undertake a collecting trip to one of the regions renowned for its rich butterfly population. All of his attempts fail for various reasons: his poor health disqualifies him from being sent to the colonies during World War I; the postwar crisis destroys his hard-earned savings; his business deteriorates, plunging him into debt. Finally, when Pilgram has all but given up on his obsessive plan, good fortune brings him a rich collector, one Sommer, who buys a major collection of lepidoptera. The sum would only allow Pilgram several months of economical travel, but he embraces the salutory opportunity without hesitation. Leaving his pitiful wife, Eleanor, behind without a source of income, Pilgram sets out to go to Spain. A fatal stroke (he has suffered one before) halts his journey. In the morning, Eleanor finds him dead, sitting on the floor of his shop.

Such is the outline of this fascinating story, the first since December 1928, which Nabokov wrote in ten days in March 1930 in Berlin.[42] In 1930 "The Aurelian" appeared in issue 43 of *Contemporary Annals,* to become Nabokov's second short story featured in the best journal of the Russian emigration. "The Aurelian" elicited numerous responses in émigré reviews, including a separate essay in a Parisian newspaper, *Rossiia i slavianstvo* (Russia and Slavdom).[43] In his milestone study of Russian émigré literature, Gleb Struve referred to "The Aurelian" as one of Nabokov's best and most emblematic stories.[44] Georgii Adamovich praised the story for its "economy of means" and absence of gratuitous ornamentation—the qualities he valued most.[45] Nabokov included "The Aurelian" in his second collection of short stories, *The Eye* (1938), and chose it as one of the first to be translated into English. The translation was published in *The Atlantic Monthly* in 1941 and thereafter reprinted in his English-language collections.

"The Aurelian" opens Nabokov's Middle period and represents a turning point in terms of its relationship between formal composition and projected metaphysical outlook. In the final paragraph of "The Aurelian," a textual opening invites the reader to follow the protagonist on his otherworldly journey. Although the otherworldly vistas in such early texts as "Christmas" and "Details of a Sunset" anticipate the textual opening in "The Aurelian," only in the latter do we see a critical dichotomy between the metaphysical opening through which Pilgram enters the otherworld, and the closed physical ending that tells of Pilgram's death:

> Yes, Pilgram had gone far, very far. Most probably he visited Granada and Murcia and Albarracin, and then traveled farther still, to Surinam or Taprobane; and one can hardly doubt that he saw all the glorious bugs he had longed to see—velvety black butterflies soaring

over the jungles, and a tiny moth in Tasmania, and that Chinese "skipper" said to smell of crushed roses when alive, and the short-clubbed beauty that a Mr. Baron had just discovered in Mexico. So, in a certain sense, it is quite irrelevant that some time later, upon wandering into the shop, Eleanor saw the chequered suitcase, and then her husband, sprawling on the floor with his back to the counter, among scattered coins, his livid face knocked out of shape by death. (*Stories*, 258)

The paradox of "The Aurelian," its mesmerizing power, lies in the fact that the plot is over when the reader learns of Pilgram's death. At the same time, the text of Pilgram's otherworldly travels continues in the reader's memory. A narrative split occurs at the story's physical ending. Along with Pilgram's dead body—here symbolizing the end of the plot—the reader leaves behind a near-linear narrative of a Buninesque type. On the one hand, like many a Bunin short story with a closed ending, "The Aurelian" ends on a striking death. On the other hand, Nabokov's metaphysical text continues beyond its closed physical ending. The narrative split between the closed ending and the textual opening in "The Aurelian" corresponds to a complex inner split within Pilgram's own existence between his mundane "dreary" Berlin life ("berlinskim proziabaniem") and the "phantom of perfect happiness" ("prizrakom pronzitel'nogo schast'ia"; *Stories*, 252/ *S*, 193). After the initial act of reading, Pilgram's death records itself in the reader's memory as a distant recollection, while the text of Pilgram's otherworldly dream goes on as he continues his longed-for expedition across Spain, South America, Ceylon, or eternity. In "The Aurelian" Nabokov foregrounds a new model of a short story which—from the point of view of the ideal reader, the author's double in Nabokov's terms— *never ends.*

My purpose in this section is to inquire into the motif and design of entering the otherworld by considering the ways the protagonist's characterization supports the story's acute dichotomy between the idealized otherworldly dimension that underwrites the structure of a textual opening and the oppressive quotidian reality that warrants a closed ending. I will then explore pilgrimage not only as an allegory and a structural embodiment of Pilgram's dream, but also as a recurrent motif in Nabokov's life and oeuvre. My next concern will be the Russian text's transformation from the draft to the fair copy to the final version, as well as the latter's revamping into an English-language short story. I will evaluate the extent to which the changes in the surviving Russian versions, but also the translators' decisions in the English, shape the sui generis nature of the story's metaphysics. Finally, I will assess the connections between the story and Nabokov's experience as an exile as well as his career as a lepidopterist.

The two-world architecture of Pilgram's existence is signaled to the reader as early as the first paragraph. Inscribed into the otherwise inconspicuous cityscape of a Berlin residential street, Pilgram's butterfly store stands apart from the other shops surrounding it, "a fruiterer's . . . a tobacconist's . . . a delicatessen" (*Stories*, 248). The passersby—noticing the bright colors of the butterflies on display—would "stop for a second before that symbol of fair weather" (*Stories*, 248). They "would say to themselves, 'What colors—amazing!' and plod on through the drizzle. Eyed wings wide-open in wonder, shimmering blue satin, black magic—these lingered for a while floating in one's vision ["zaderzhivalis' u nego v pamiati," literally, lingered for a while in one's memory] until one boarded the trolley or bought a newspaper" (*S*, 185/*Stories*, 248). The centrality of memory in fixating the opposition between the radiant otherworld of butterflies and the mundane world of city routine is underscored in both the Russian and English versions. The opening passage suggests that although beatitude may be only one step off the everyday route, very few individuals allow it to remain as part of their memory.

The protagonist enters the space of the narrative through the door to his neighborhood pub, where the street's other shopkeepers imbibe their daily dose of alcohol while also playing cards. Pilgram, a "flabby elderly man with a florid face, lank hair, and a greyish mustache" (*Stories*, 249), enters the pub on Saturdays and follows his weekly routine of ordering rum, smoking his pipe, and watching the game. He is a familiar presence at the pub, where no one suspects his otherworldly dreams. Although Pilgram may not blend completely with the other frequenters of the pub, he appears to be an integral part of their established existence. He is "Herr Professor," a more learned burgher, but a good old burgher all the same. He emblematizes a shopkeeper's sensibility: hard work during the week and a weekend's rest at the pub. He makes sure not to miss a chance at having "a go at [the owner's daughter's] elusive hip"; his jokes are rude and devoid of humor. He is mindful of clock time and checks his "thick silver watch" against the cuckoo clock. His Saturday pub ritual ends "punctually at eleven" (*Stories*, 249), after which he proceeds to his apartment, where a brass plate on the door announces his name.

The reader follows Pilgram into his apartment, discovering more about his mundane existence. He resides in a "tiny dingy" apartment ("malen'-kaia, tusklaia"; *Stories*, 249/*S*, 188) with a wife to whom he has been married for twenty-five years. Very little seems to connect Pilgram and his wife. In fact, the only word he ever says to her in the story is "that guttural 'Ruhe!' [Be quiet!] several times, more and more fiercely" (*Stories,* 249). Even his wife, faceless, loyal, and all-enduring, misreads his character. In fact, Nabokov's narrator stresses Pilgram's singularity vis-à-vis his "butterfly" dream. The first authorial statement regarding Pilgram's existing in two worlds appears precisely during a description of his sleep, the time—as some metaphysical systems believe—when the soul joins the transcendent source:

> He slept on his back with an old-fashioned night-cap coming down on his forehead; it was to all appearances the solid and sonorous sleep that might be expected in an elderly German shopkeeper, and one could readily suppose that his quilted torpor was entirely devoid of visions; but actually this churlish, heavy man, who fed mainly on *Erbswurst* and boiled potatoes, placidly believing in his newspaper and quite ignorant of the world (in so far as his secret passion was not involved), dreamed of things that would have seemed utterly unintelligible to his wife or his neighbors. . . . (*Stories,* 250)

Set against the gray, oppressive background of all this, Pilgram's inner life not only gives him, an otherworldly daydreamer, strength to lead a shopkeeper's existence, but also redeems him in the eyes of the reader. If it had not been for Pilgram's love for butterflies, one would find it hard to identify with this grim and gruesome character, who even sacrifices having children to realize his passionate and obsessive dream.

For Nabokov, the otherworld conflates love, the transcendent, and perfect memories in an open moment of blissful eternity. In keeping with his paradigmatic formulation of an otherworldly state in the poem "Being in Love," it seems fruitful to inquire into the meaning of Pilgram's dream in terms of love, passion, and happiness. Indeed, his plan for a butterfly-collecting expedition is characterized as "strastnaia mechta" (passionate daydream) and "liubov'" (love) and referred to as "schastie" (happiness) nine times in the Russian text. The story's omniscient narrator presents the history of Pilgram's private otherworldly dream as originating in his childhood. Butterflies figure in Pilgram's earliest childhood memories: "[Pilgram] liubil babochek s tekh por, kak sushchestvuet" (literally, "Pilgram has loved butterflies since he has existed"; *S,* 101; note that Nabokov's use of the verb "to exist" cements the opposition between Pilgram's otherworldly love for butterflies and his mundane existence). Pilgram might have inherited a thirst for travel from his father, a "sailor, a rover, a bit of a rogue" (*Stories,* 251), and his mother, a Dutch woman from

Indonesia. After his father's death, Pilgram converted their colonial souvenir shop into a butterfly store with rich holdings and collections. He had several opportunities to start a more lucrative business, but clung to his butterfly trade as "the only symbolic link between his dreary existence and the phantom of perfect happiness" (*Stories,* 252). Very few outside the closed circuit of entomologists, and none within his shopkeeper's circle, know that Pilgram is a "first-class entomologist" (*Stories,* 251–252) with several discoveries and contributions to his credit. Remarkably, given Pilgram's status as a butterfly expert, he has never left his native Prussia. His only experiences in butterfly collecting were limited to Sunday summer trips to the outskirts of Berlin. Waves of nostalgic childhood memories overcome Pilgram during his little trips:

> ... вспоминал детство, поимки, казавшиеся ему тогда такими необыкновенными, и с грустью смотрел на бабочек, все виды которых ему были давным-давно известны, прочно, безнадёжно соответствовали пейзажу, — или же на ивовом кусте отыскивал большую, голубовато-зелёную, шероховатую на ощупь гусеницу с маленьким фарфоровым рогом на задке. Он держал её, оцепеневшую, на ладони, вспоминал такую же находку в детстве, — замирание, приговорки восторга, — и, как вещь, ставил её обратно на сучок. (*S,* 192)

(. . . and he would be reminded of captures that had seemed to him so miraculous in his boyhood as he melancholically gazed at the familiar fauna about him, limited by a familiar landscape, to which it corresponded as hopelessly as he to his street [Nabokov added this last clause in the English version; it recalls the opening description of Pilgram's shop amidst the other ones on his street and augments the note of hopelessness]. From a roadside shrub he would pick up a large turquoise-green caterpillar with a china-blue horn on the last ring; there it lay on the palm of his hand, and [*] presently, with a sigh, he would put it back on its twig as if it were some dead trinket"; *Stories,* 252)

In the English, Nabokov decided to tone down the Russian version's deeply lyrical recollection of Pilgram's childhood discovery of a caterpillar, marked above with an asterisk. In a literal translation, the omission would read as follows: "he recalled finding the same caterpillar in his childhood,—feeling numb, mumbling words of rapture." Perfect childhood memories charge Pilgram's lifelong anticipations of a real collecting trip with ideal characteristics. His dream of perfect happiness consists in netting "the rarest butterflies of distant countries, to see them in flight with his own eyes . . . and feel the follow-through of the swishing net and then the furious throbbing of wings through a clutched fold of the gauze" (*Stories*, 252). Pilgram longs to regain the lost paradise of his childhood— a leitmotif of Nabokov's works from the earliest stories to the latest, from the novels *Glory* and *The Gift* to *Lolita* and *Ada*.

Pilgram refers to the possibility of a real trip as nothing other than "schast'e" (happiness). Like Germann in Aleksandr Pushkin's "Pikovaia dama" (The Queen of Spades, 1833), whose inflamed mind endows surrounding objects with signs of "three, seven, ace," Pilgram also sees everything in terms of the way it relates to his "phantom" of happiness. At one point, when he fails yet again to set out on a lepidopterological expedition, Pilgram's savings, turned into worthless paper by inflation, are described as "real'naia sgushchënnaia vozmozhnost' schast'ia" (*S*, 194; literally, real concentrated possibility of happiness).

Pilgram cognizes and maps the world outside Prussia in terms of its butterfly population and relationship to his dream. Completely oblivious to anything except lepidoptera, he creates in his memory an esoteric map of the world, a guidebook to the space of his dream trips. In surveying his representative butterfly and moth collections, he revisits the native region(s) of certain species. The English version omits two seminal sentences describing Pilgram's "longing/yearning" ("tomlenie," in the Russian, frequently used with sensuous connotations) for the places he has visited only in his mind:

> Всякая чужая страна представлялась ему исключительно как родина той или иной бабочки, — и томление, которое он при этом испытывал, можно только сравнить с тоской по родине. Мир он знал совершенно по-своему, в особом разрезе, удивительно отчётливом и другим недоступном. (*S*, 196)

> (He envisioned any foreign country exclusively as the homeland of one butterfly or another—and his yearning can only be compared to a longing for one's homeland. He knew the world in his peculiar way, from a unique perspective, surprisingly clear and yet unattainable for the others.)

The importance of the notion of "longing for one's homeland" could not be overestimated given Nabokov's status as a Russian émigré in the 1930s and the story's appearances in émigré publications. In the Russian text, the word "rodina" (homeland) figures in two different contexts. First it refers to Pilgram's real homeland, Prussia ("vsiu zhizn' on prozhil na rodine"; *S*,

192), the territory which he tries to leave behind. Later "rodina" refers to his ideal homeland, an enchanting movable dreamscape inhabited by perfectly beautiful butterflies.

Although Pilgram never "traveled farther than Peacock Island on a neighboring lake" (*Stories*, 251), he seems very much aware of the tremendous, almost prohibitive, differences between the dull familiar look of Prussian landscapes and the otherworldly landscapes of his "journeys." The atlas of his private trips via memory and imagination includes a variety of territories with such famous sites for butterfly collecting as Digne in southern France, Ragusa (Dubrovnik) in Dalmatia, and Sarepta on the Volga. Pilgram has mastered the space of his projected journeys to the point of knowing their most intricate details. In his mind, he visits the Canary Islands, Corsica, Lapland, Italy, Spain, the Ussurian region in the Far East, Congo, Indonesia, and many other lands. In his visions, the butterfly collecting sites are marked with signs of exceptionality, singularity, mysteriousness, and blissfulness. To him there is "no greater delight" (*Stories*, 254) than lifting a stone to find "a plump sleepy moth of a still undescribed species." Gravel in Italian gardens crunches "invitingly" ("tainstvenno," literally, mysteriously). The Ussurian region is referred to as "volshebnyi" (magic, enchanted). Thus, Pilgram's unparalleled atlas of world lepidoptera actually becomes a map of his own private otherworld created and preserved in his memory. It should be noted that although Nabokov often invents his details, like the names of the exotic locales, most of the details in the story are informed by genuine facts. In the case of the geography of Pilgram's dream-travels, Nabokov at times creates the illusion of strangeness by using names that are obsolete or less known to the Russian and/or American reader. Thus, for instance, he uses the ancient Sanskrit name of Ceylon, "Taprobane," and the pre-1913 name of Kangting, "Tatsienlu." He adopts "Heligoland" ("Helgoland" in *The Atlantic Monthly*), the slightly misspelled Old Norse version of Hálogaland, a region in Norway's Nordland country, the homeland of Knut Hamsun.

Also noteworthy is the language that Nabokov employs to map the dreamscape of Pilgram's travels. Each ecological niche that he visits, Corsica and Sumatra alike, centers upon a particular species of butterfly or moth: ". . . the Islands of the Blessed, where in the hot ravines that cut the lower slopes . . . there occurs a weird local race of the cabbage white; and also that other island, those railway banks near Vizzanova and the pine woods farther up, which are the haunts of the squat and dusky Corsican swallowtail" (*Stories*, 254).

The lepidoptera color their native landscape (or cityscape as in the case of mothing in Seville) with ethereal beauty and transfer to the surroundings their own phenomenal features. In the case of Pilgram's lepidoptera, the very language that he uses charges the butterflies with anthropomorphic details. The Corsican swallowtail ("korsikanskii makhaon") is described in the Russian as "smuglyi" (literally, dark-complexioned), used exclusively in reference to human skin, as in "smugloe litso" (dark-complexioned or dark-skinned face). Grass on an Alpine meadow is called "koltunnaia," which the Englished text renders as "matted" for the lack of an appropriate English adjective; in the Russian, "koltunnyi" derives from "koltun" (plica, a human hair disease) and can mean "tousled" (as in "tousled hair"). Another species, a moth, is characterized as "tolsten'kaia" and "sonnaia" (plump and sleepy); both adjectives in the Russian are normally used in reference to people, not fauna. The English is of course not equipped with diminutives to the extent that Russian is; "tolsten'kaia" (plump), from "tolstaia" (fat), adds a great deal of affection to the description of the moth.

The anthropomorphic characterization of Pilgram's butterflies lays ground for a key statement regarding his communication with the lepidopterological otherworld. When the rich collector Sommer expresses interest in purchasing a large collection, Pilgram negotiates the price while also contemplating the particulars of his would-be journey:

> И теперь, тонко торгуясь с Зоммером, он ощущал волнение, тяжесть в висках, чёрные пятна плыли перед глазами, — и предчувствие счастья, предчувствие отъезда было едва выносимо. Он знал отлично, что это безумие, знал, что оставляет нищую жену, долги, магазин, который и продать нельзя, знал, что две-три тысячи, которые он выручит за коллекцию, позволят ему странствовать не больше года, — и всё же он шёл на это, как человек, чувствующий, что завтра — старость, и что счастие, пославшее за ним, уже больше никогда не повторит приглашения. (*S*, 201–202)

> ([And now, as he skillfully negotiated the price with Sommer, he felt excitement, heaviness in his temples, black spots floating before his eyes—and a foretaste of happiness, foretaste of departure, was almost unbearable (this sentence, omitted in the English version, is provided in a literal translation).] He knew it was madness; he knew he was leaving a helpless Eleanor, debts, unpaid taxes, a store at which only trash was bought; he knew that the 950 marks he might get would permit him to travel for no longer than a few months; and

still he accepted it all as a man who felt that tomorrow would bring dreary old age and that the good fortune [literally, happiness] which now beckoned would never again repeat its invitation; *Stories,* 256)

Pilgram feels that the otherworld—the haven of perfect happiness—communicates with him, calls for him, summons him to undertake an expedition. As with many of Nabokov's privileged characters, Pilgram's contacts with the otherworld affect him physically. Earlier in the story, the reader learns about the liminal fainting spells that he would go through when trying to imagine the tropics: ". . . popytka tuda proniknut' mechtoi vyzyvala serdtsebienie i chuvstvo, pochti nesterpimoe, sladkoe, obmorochnoe . . ." (S, 198).[46] Pilgram's "pangs," his heart pains, link him with the otherworldly experiences of such characters as Ivanov in "Perfection," Vasiliy Ivanovich in "Cloud, Castle, Lake," and Pnin in the eponymous novel.

Nabokov's description of Pilgram's imminent happiness points to another butterfly story, the early masterpiece "Christmas." In both texts, an otherworldly experience is presented as a butterfly imago coming out of a cocoon. Here is a comment by the protagonist of "The Aurelian": "When finally Sommer said that on the fourth he would give a definite answer, Pilgram decided that the dream of his life was about to break at last from its old crinkly cocoon" (*Stories,* 256). In "Christmas" the metamorphosis occurs at the end of the story, amounts to a textual opening, and offers its protagonist a modicum of consolation. In "The Aurelian," whose English title derives from the now obsolete "aurelia," a pupa or chrysalis, the metaphor of Pilgram's lifetime dream—"about to break at last from its old crinkly cocoon"—provides a foretaste of his liberation at the end of the story. The "old crinkly cocoon" stands for Pilgram's mundane existence, while he himself is that aurelia trapped and dormant inside the boundaries of its dark and narrow world. Coming out of the cocoon to become a beautiful butterfly allegorizes Pilgram's dream of exiting the constraints of this world and entering the otherworld.

The motif of pilgrimage is central in the signification of the protagonist's otherworldly journey. The name of the protagonist draws immediate attention due to its foreign sound to a Russian ear. As in the case of "The Return of Chorb," Nabokov's passion for dictionary research might have yielded a fitting name for his protagonist. "Pilgram" (or "pilgrame") is the Scots-English word for "pilgrim."[47] In Russian, two different words are used, the native Slavic *palomnik* and the Latin-derived *piligrim.* While an English speaker seems quite likely to apprehend the "pilgram"-"pilgrim" connection, fewer Russian speakers might be able to sense that the name Pilgram encodes pilgrimage. Since the story's commentators have not noticed the highly meaningful link, the evolution of the protagonist's name deserves a closer look. In the first, heavily marked draft of the story, Nabokov uses the name Karl Gruber.[48] On the first few pages of the fair copy, he refers to his protagonist as Alfred Zommer (Sommer) but then decides to change it to Pilgram, without any first name. The fair copy has preserved Nabokov's changes: he heavily crossed out the name Sommer and corrected it to Pilgram. The name Sommer was given to the rich amateur sent by destiny to buy a collection of "those small clear-winged moths that mimic wasps or mosquitoes" (*Stories*, 255); the collector's name was originally Krechmar (Kretschmar)—the name of the German protagonist of the novel *Kamera obskura* (1932–1933). In the fair copy, the story also bears a different title, "Palomnik," precisely the native Russian term for "pilgrim." Nabokov must have put much stock into the title and its special relationship to the protagonist's name. The first draft contains no title whatsoever. In the fair copy, from which a typescript was presumably made and sent to *Contemporary Annals*, two alternative titles (or two words of a single earlier title) are so heavily crossed out that it is difficult to make out what lies underneath the heavy layer of ink.[49] The final title, "Palomnik" (The Pilgrim), was written above the two crossed-out words. Beneath the titles Nabokov wrote "rasskaz" (short story)—something he did not usually do in other manuscripts. Perhaps the ecclesiastically charged title did not quite agree with his authorial and fictional intentions; by adding a clear genre label he must have hoped to avoid his piece being taken for an essay on pilgrimage.[50] Unfortunately, neither the typescript of the story nor the corrected proofs seem to have survived. My guess is that Nabokov changed the title to "Pil'gram" either at the stage of a typescript or in the galley proofs.[51] In the English version, Nabokov changed the title from "Pil'gram" to "The Aurelian." The fact that he opted for such a rare word as "aurelian" bespeaks his authorial wish to maintain an aura of mystery about the story's title.

In the English version of the story, Nabokov also added the first name "Paul" to the name "Pilgram" on the brass plate of the protagonist's door, thereby converting "Pilgram" into a last name. This may have had something to do with the fact that such a last name does exist in Germany and Great Britain. Several dictionaries of British surnames list "Pilgram" as a possible variant of the name "Pilgrim," originally given to someone who has made a pilgrimage to Rome or the Holy Land. A German *Deutsches Namenlexicon* also lists "Pilgram" as a possible variant of a last name. Consequently, at least for English and German readers, the last name

"Pilgram" is a speaking name that also preserves an outlandish aura. For Russian readers, the name "Пильграм" is virtually unreadable, while such a title as "Паломник," which Nabokov rejected, would have obviated the meaning of the story. It was not surprising to discover therefore that the English version is missing a passage that suggests pilgrimage, but not as directly as would the Russian word *palomnik* had it remained the title of the story.

The following long sentence—omitted in the English text—occurs as part of the narrator's lengthy explication of how Pilgram maps the dreamspace of his journeys:

> Если бы он побывал в какой-нибудь прославленной местности, Пильграм заметил бы только то, что относилось к его добыче, служило для неё естественным фоном, — и только тогда запомнил бы Эректеон, если бы с листа оливы, растущей в глубине святилища, слетела и была подхвачена свистящим сачком греческая достопримечательность, которую лишь он, специалист, мог оценить. (*S,* 196)

> (If he were to visit some renowned place, Pilgram would only notice what relates to the objects of his collecting and serves as its natural background; he would only remember the Erechtheum if a Greek rarity—which he alone could appreciate as a specialist—were to fall off an olive branch growing in the depth of the sanctuary and be caught by a whistling net.)

The Erechtheum is an ancient Greek sanctuary, the original temple of tutelary deities, situated on the north side of the Acropolis of Athens.[52] As a holy place in ancient Greek cults, the Erechtheum symbolizes a site of pilgrimage. The notion of pilgrimage is organic to the otherworldly dreams of Paul Pilgram, the story's modern pilgrim. Pilgrimage implies a visit to a place with which one is already familiar through cultural memory. A trip to a holy place, be it Jerusalem, Rome, or Mecca, promises a pilgrim liberation from various burdens of everyday existence. The goal of any pilgrimage, whether a sinful monarch's or a pious nun's, is to reach a space that is charged with the timeless presence of holiness. During a pilgrimage, a pilgrim matches a set of expectations based on the information obtained via various sources (oral history, books, sermons, etc.) with the actual holy place he or she visits. Pilgrimages are said to have a purifying effect upon those who undertake them because they offer cognitive keys to one's existence. In the case of Nabokov's protagonist, the reader observes a kindred relationship between Pilgram's earlier knowledge of the otherworldly spaces that he strives to visit and the physical realities of the actual locales. In the Russian version, the narrator explains that Pilgram possesses a brilliant memory that stores a great deal of information about world lepidoptera. Owing to his vast knowledge and his fine memory, Pilgram has compiled in his mind a matchless map of his would-be pilgrimages. In anticipation of a real pilgrimage after Sommer's visit, Pilgram begins to examine a real map on the wall of his shop, "choosing a route, estimating the time of appearances of this or that species" (*Stories,* 256). Suddenly, we are told, "something black and blinding welled before his eyes" (*Stories,* 256)—a prefiguration of his fatal stroke. An anticipation of a real pilgrimage has a profound impact upon Pilgram. At this point, since the reader does not know the end of the story, he or she can wonder about the shock of recognition that Pilgram would experience during his pilgrimage.

The larger context of Nabokov's oeuvre yields at least one more major exploration of the motif of pilgrimage (*palomnichestvo* in Russian). The 1927 poem "Palomnik" (The Pilgrim), originally published in *The Rudder* and later included in the collection *The Return of Chorb,* bears a dedication to the critic Iulii Aikhenval'd, a friend of Nabokov's and a fellow émigré. In the poem the lyrical persona, probably an exile, travels in his mind to the country estate ("usad'ba") of his childhood, where he stays amidst perfect memories. At one point, the Nabokovian protagonist of the poem hears a summoning signal:

> И я тогда услышу: вспомни-ка
> рыдающий вагон
> и счастье странного паломника,
> чья Мекка там, где он.
>
> Он рад бывал, скитаясь по миру,
> озёрам под луной,
> вокзалам громовым и номеру
> в гостинице ночной.
> (*VCh,* 232/*Stikhi,* 197–198)

> And then I will hear: recall
> the sobbing train car
> and the happiness of a strange pilgrim
> whose Mecca is where he is.
>
> He used to rejoice, wandering around the world,
> in lakes beneath the moon,

in thundering train stations and a room
   in a night hotel at night.

One notices several parallels between the pilgrim's experiences in the poem and Pilgram's in the story. I have spoken earlier about the marked use of the word "happiness" in "The Aurelian" to refer to Pilgram's other-worldly expectations. The adjective "strannyi"—in reference to a pilgrim—also surfaces in the story: "strannye liudi, priekhavshie izdaleka" (*S,* 196; literally, strange people who have come from afar). Finally, the image of a pilgrim in a hotel at night also enters into the text of the story: "Pilgram saw himself troubling the sleep of a little hotel" (*Stories,* 254). In the story Pilgram's otherworld fills his room with its presence when a gray moth flies in through an open window. In the poem the lyrical pilgrim walks to the window (heavily, like Pilgram himself) through which some "bright foreign country" beckons him to enter its space:

О, как потянет вдруг на яркую
   чужбину, в дальний путь...
Как тяжело к окну прошаркаю,
   как захочу вернуть

всё то, дрожащее, весеннее,
   что плакало во мне,
и — всякой яви совершеннее —
   — сон о родной стране
(*VCh,* 232/*Stikhi,* 198)

Oh, how suddenly I would be drawn to the bright
   foreign country, to take a long trip . . .
How heavily I would shuffle to the window,
   how I would wish to bring back

all those trembling, springtime things
   which wept inside me,
and more perfect than any reality—
   is a dream about one's homeland.

This poem says that an exile's perfect dream of a distant homeland eclipses the real experiences ("iav'") of visiting such a homeland. Traveling to one's homeland, charged with holy memories and thus akin to a site of pilgrimage, allows the poem's protagonist to realize the superiority of a movable pilgrimage, the kind he used to undertake in his dreams, over a physical journey. The poem uses the noun "iav'" (wide-awake reality), which would later figure in the poem "Being in Love," in Nabokov's primary opposition between this world "iav'" and the otherworld ("potustoronnost'"). This, in turn, links the motif of pilgrimage in "The Pilgrim" and "The Aurelian" with Nabokov's larger project of writing the otherworld. A pilgrim, the space of whose holy land is always with him or her—etched in memory—does not need to set out on an actual physical pilgrimage.[53] This is why the story of Pilgram's pilgrimage to a perfect idealized homeland of his beloved butterflies ends the way it does at the narrative's culmination, with the closed end of Pilgram's death and open journey across the reader's memory.

Nabokov's short fiction makes a leap between the loose texture of "Rozhdestvenskii rasskaz" (A Christmas Story, 1928) and the astounding power of "The Aurelian" (1930). Such an artistic transformation took a great deal of searching. Prior to "The Aurelian," Nabokov had not written any short stories for one and a half years. The hiatus, separating the Early and Middle periods, gave him time to capitalize on the achievements of such stories as "Christmas" and "The Return of Chorb" and leave behind the emblematic shortcomings of "Kartofel'nyi El'f " (The Potato Elf, 1924) and "Skazka" (A Nursery Tale, 1926). Although the story took just ten days to write, the surviving manuscripts tell an extraordinary story of the shaping of Nabokov's poetics.

A comparison of the densely edited first draft with the clean fair copy yields the first level of changes. I would like to concentrate on Nabokov's artistic decisions that alter Pilgram's characterization and the story's narrative structure. I have already written of Nabokov's decision to change his protagonist's name from Karl Gruber to Alfred Sommer to Pilgram. Several changes—both large- and small-scale—emphasize Pilgram's fixation upon his dream and enhance the motif of pilgrimage.

In the first draft Pilgram and his wife are said to have tried to have children. Eleanor first had a stillborn baby, then a miscarriage, then another serious medical problem. Only then is Pilgram reported to have "left her alone" ("ostavil eë v pokoe"); for a while he betrayed his wife with an old seamstress. Such a cluster of prosaic details—had it indeed remained in the final Russian version—would take the reader's attention away from Pilgram's otherwise monomaniacal nature. To use a different example, the first draft allows an insight into the shaping of the seminal formulation about Pilgram's butterfly store as the only link between his "dreary" mundane existence and the otherworldly "phantom of perfect happiness" (*Stories,* 252). Originally, Nabokov described the space of Pilgram's longed-for pilgrimage as "zhiv[oi] éntomologicheski[i] ra[i]" (literally, live entomological paradise). As Nabokov's otherworld was becoming more and more sui generis, he experienced a growing need to write it without relying on readily available formulas. A reference to an "entomological paradise" would have simplified and literalized Nabokov's metaphorical private codes. Hence his decision to leave out a reference to paradise, a traditional religious concept.

One more important editorial decision is related to the entomological sign system in the story. The first draft contained an epigraph from the second stanza of Anafasii Fet's often-anthologized poem "Babochka" (The Butterfly, 1884): "Ne sprashivai: otkuda poiavilas'? / Kuda speshu?" (Don't ask: whence I come? / Whither I haste?).[54] Apparently, Nabokov originally intended to keep the epigraph in the fair copy but then changed his mind—after writing out the first verse—and marked it out diligently. He knew Fet's heritage intimately and would later translate three poems by Fet into English.[55] In *The Gift*, during the first "imagined" conversation between Godunov-Cherdyntsev and Koncheyev, the former claims that he "forgives [Fet] everything for . . . the wing-fanning, 'breathing' butterfly" ("za dyshashuiu babochku"; *Gift*, 73/*SSoch*, 3:67). The reference is to the second and third stanzas of Fet's "The Butterfly"; the last two verses of the second stanza read: "Zdes' na tsvetok ia lëgkii opustilas' / I vot—dyshu" (Here I descended onto a light flower / And here I am—breathing). Although Nabokov omitted the epigraph from Fet in his final version, he did leave a covert trace of the poem. While not disrupting the unity of the text, the following Russian sentence uses Fet's motif of a breathing butterfly as a subtext. The sentence is omitted in the English text:

> ... Пильграм ясно почувствовал, что он никогда никуда не уедет, подумал, что ему скоро пятьдесят, что он должен всем соседям, что нечем платить налог, — и ему показалось дикой выдумкой, невозможным ьредом, что сейчас, вот в этот миг, садится южная бабочка на базальтовый осколок и дышит крыльями. (*S*, 199)

> (Pilgram felt it clearly that he would never go anywhere; he thought that he was going to be fifty soon, that he owed to all the neighbors, that there was no money to pay taxes,—and it seemed a wild fantasy, an impossible delirium that right now, at that very moment, a southern butterfly descended onto a basalt rock and breathed with her wings.)[56]

Two important changes signal the growing perfection of Nabokov's poetics. In the first draft one finds a passage—omitted in the fair copy—

which describes the logical steps Pilgram undertakes in preparation for his departure. He purchases a convenient suitcase (in the final version he ends up using his father's old one). He goes to the local precinct to "sign out." He goes to the consulates of the countries he hopes to visit (France, Spain, etc.). Although such preparations may indeed be necessary, the focus on the minute details of Pilgram's preparations make his trip look like one of the tourist excursions that he vehemently resents.

Reading the final Russian version, the reader is never completely sure whether Pilgram is indeed planning a real trip. The reader wonders whether he is capable of separating the reality of his otherworldly dreams and the actuality of a butterfly-collecting expedition. In this connection, the following paragraph, which Nabokov chose to omit in the fair copy, appears especially gratifying and illuminating. In the first draft it is found on the last page, right after the sentence in which Pilgram drops a money-pot and bends to pick up the coins:

> Никто не видел, как он вышел из дома. Вечерняя, ещё солнечная улица была полна народа — соседи запирали лавки, шорник напротив играл со своей собакой, две девушки высокими голосами о чём-то оживлённо разговаривали. И у всех были прилежные глаза, все знали свою улицу, знали кто когда проходит мимо, готовы были потом обсуждать всякую необыкновенную мелочь, — и всё таки никто ничего не увидел.[57]

> (No one saw him leave the house. The evening street, still sunny, was crowded; the neighbors locked up their shops, the harness-maker across the street played with his dog, two young women discussed something animatedly in their high voices. And everyone had diligent eyes, they all knew their street, knew who passes by where, and were prepared afterward to discuss any conspicuous trifle; but still no one saw anything.)

In the first draft, Nabokov must still have felt compelled to justify his decision to create a narrative split between the textual opening of Pilgram's departure and his death that engenders a closed ending. The quoted passage reads like a section of a detective story and prompts the readers to investigate the hidden possibilities of Pilgram's disappearance. Conversely, the effect of the last split paragraph in the printed version is to launch the reader on an endless journey along with the protagonist and across the textual otherworldly opening. By leaving the explanatory passage out of the final version, Nabokov decided not to "cater" to what he would later label "commonsense"—the enemy of artistic creation (and of reading by the same token). Just as he ends his seminal lecture "The Art of Literature and Commonsense" with a call to "shoot [commonsense] dead" (*LL*, 380), he concludes "The Aurelian" with Pilgram's death. The philistine in Pilgram remains on the floor of his shop with his face "knocked out of shape" not by death, but by a burgher's commonsense, by a commonsensical cause. One notices a Chekhovian principle at work in the story. Chekhov insisted that a rifle hanging on the wall ought to have fired by the end of the play.[58] In "The Aurelian" the money-pot into which Pilgram puts small change plays the role of Chekhov's rifle and kills the protagonist. However, by killing his privileged protagonist with such a mundane item as a money-pot, Nabokov not only economizes his artistic means, but also awards his protagonist the best prize, textual eternity in the reader's memory. Although "death" is the last word of the physical text, the otherworldly textual opening transcends the meaning of the story. The idealist dreamer in Pilgram defies the constraints of philistine commonsense and sets out on an endless journey across the memory of the reader (provided, of course, that the reader realizes that commonsense could never justify genuine artistic imagination).

Finally, there is one change which I find regrettable. In both the first draft and the final Russian version, Eleanor sees Pilgram's note ("Off to Spain"; *Stories*, 254) and bursts into tears. In the first draft, the narrator offers the following remark: "Mysl', chto muzh deistvitel'no uekhal [i uekhal v takuiu nevedomuiu stranu, kotoruiu mozhno uvidet' tol'ko v kinematografe, dolgo] ne umeshchalas' u neë v mozgu" (The thought that her husband has really left [and has left for some incomprehensible country which one can only see in the movies] could not fit in her brain; *S*, 206–207; the brackets indicate the omitted phrase).

Nabokov's decision to omit this clause is understandable: he was trying to avoid clichés and easily accessible metaphors, like the one comparing Spain to a movie. For Eleanor, Spain is at best an exotic country of bullfights and castanets which she knows from newsreels and not the home of remarkable lepidoptera. Still, ironically, Eleanor's cinematic perception of where her husband went (she has just learned it from his note and still does not know that he is dead) would enhance the story's dramatization of the prohibitive gap between Pilgram and his wife. As the émigré critic A. Savel'ev aptly remarked in his review of issue 43 of *Contemporary Annals*, Pilgram's wife also dreams ("tozhe mechtaet"), but her dreams are quite innocuous and do not threaten to destroy their philistine routine.[59]

The revisions that Nabokov undertook while translating the story are among the most radical, comparable only to the transformation of the Russian novel *Kamera obskura* into the Anglo-American novel *Laughter in the Dark*. I have already identified several passages that Nabokov chose to exclude from the translation as well as his additions to the English text. Jane Grayson, in a study of Nabokov's poetics of self-translation, noticed several structural changes that he made in the English version. In addition to the fact that the story was now divided into four parts marked with Roman numerals, Grayson also mentions that Nabokov tightened the plot and added dates to provide a temporal framework.[60] The American version of "The Aurelian" reads quite differently from its Russian counterpart, almost like a new story. Nabokov translated it in 1941 together with Peter A. Pertzoff; it was the second translation of a short story that he supervised to be published in the United States.[61] I would venture to propose that Nabokov was Englishing his Russian story with the American reader, if not with a specific magazine audience (*The Atlantic Monthly*), in mind. This might explain his insistence on contextualizing, historicizing, and overexplaining the details of the story's European milieu.

A number of examples of the ways Nabokov Americanized certain European cultural concepts may be found in the text. The "skinny" and unappealing owner of Pilgram's neighborhood pub becomes a good American "bartender, a dashing fellow in a . . . green sweater" (*Stories*, 248); while the German pub owner has a knack for pouring cheap cognac into the snifters, his American coeval "was deft at shaving off with one stroke the foam topping the glass under the beer tap" (*Stories*, 248). The pub owner's ample daughter ("krupnaia devitsa") metamorphoses into the bartender's "pretty girl" who is now wearing a "polka-dotted frock" (*Stories*, 249) rather than a plaid wool dress. Pilgram's dingy apartment is now equipped with a palm tree "that looked as bleak as if it were growing on Heligoland" (*Stories*, 249). Several additions specify the time and the amounts of money involved in the story. The American reader is told that Pilgram and Eleanor were married in 1905, which, along with the length of time they have been married, yields the exact year when the story takes place: 1930. The day on which Sommer walks into Pilgram's shop to change his fortune is specified to be "a certain first of April, of all dates" (*Stories*, 255). The pupae Pilgram sells are assigned a price, one mark, instead of the Russian "nedorogo" (inexpensively). A female species of a rare butterfly which Pilgram discusses with a colleague is said to have cost fourteen pounds at an auction. The sum of money that Pilgram hopes to get from Sommer has been lowered from "two–three thousand" to 950 marks. Certain other details must have been deemed insignificant for the American audience and dropped or revamped. The Ussurian region does not figure in the English version. Pilgram's 8:29 train is no longer referred to as the Cologne train. The English version excludes the important reference to the Erechtheum, the ancient Greek sanctuary, but adds another one roughly in the same part of the text. The symbolic weight of a holy site is now assigned to Tatsienlu, East Tibet; Tatsienlu, better known as Kangting, is located in the Tibetan Autonomous District, a center of Buddhism. Nabokov adds a long sentence explaining the meaning of the term "aurelian" and its relationship to Pilgram's occupation. Finally, he introduces a very American distinction between professional entomologists (like Pilgram) and amateurs (like the rich collector Sommer); in the Russian version, the distinction is not in their professionalism but in their means.

The above additions attune the story to the wavelength of the American reader in the 1940s. They do not affect the meaning of Pilgram's otherworldly dream. Conversely, the second group of changes does address the story's central cluster of motifs. On the whole, the English version downplays the focus of the Russian text upon the absolute happiness which Pilgram hopes to achieve during his expedition. The very word "dream" ("mechta" in the Russian) is translated as "plan." In the Russian, the seminal formulation qualifies Pilgram's dream as "blazhennaia" (literally, blissful). Also, the Englished version adds a dark side to Pilgram's dream, which is presented as pure and perfect in the Russian story: ". . . the realization of what had been in his youth a delightfully exciting plan but had now gradually become a dark, passionate obsession" (*Stories*, 250). At the end of the story, Pilgram looks at the map of his would-be journey and sees, in the Russian, "something *green* and blinding" and, in the English, "something *black* and blinding" (italics added).

The English version also leaves out the childhood flashback Pilgram experiences when he picks up a caterpillar from a tree. Nabokov's change alters the history of Pilgram's otherworldly dream, which in the Russian text is grounded in the protagonist's earliest perfect memories; the Russian story depicts Pilgram's first caterpillar as a boy's first love. To offer one more example, the very word "schast'e" (happiness) occurs nine times in the Russian text and only twice in the translation. Where the Russian has "happiness" twice within a single sentence, the English has it only once; in the next instance the Russian "schast'e" has no equivalent at all; later it is rendered as "good fortune," and even "great thing." While Nabokov might have been trying to avoid redundancy, the Russian text's insistence upon using the same term over and over again supports the idea of Pilgram's fixation upon his dream. The English text depolarizes the original's crucial opposition between the world of Pilgram's everyday existence and the perfect otherworld mapped in his memory. In the end, the American story with its "dashing" bartender and Pilgram's savior, the rich amateur Sommer ("a sunburned, bespectacled man in an old macintosh and without any hat"; *Stories*, 255) appears to be less of a tragedy and more of a tale with a mysterious ending than its Russian ancestor.

In the 1960–1970s, when most of his Russian works were being translated, Nabokov considered the English versions of his Russian works as textually definitive for non-Russian readers.[62] He preferred that translations into other languages be made from the English rather than the Russian versions. Indeed, several English versions of the Russian short stories contain definite improvements, both structural and linguistic. In this respect, both the translations of "The Return of Chorb" and "Terra Incognita" would qualify as definitive versions. However, I find it difficult to understand why Nabokov would choose to downplay some of the best artistic discoveries of "The Aurelian." As a tentative explanation, I suggest that because "The Aurelian" was translated quite early in Nabokov's career in Anglo-American letters, he had not yet elaborated a full-fledged poetics of Englishing. Also, Nabokov's collaboration with Pertzoff did not prove to be a lasting one, and it was not until Dmitri Nabokov became his permanent co-translator that most of the Russian stories were given new lives on American soil.

I have spoken in Chapter 1 of the way Nabokov shares with his privileged characters a capacity to partake in otherworldly experiences. "The Aurelian" enjoys a special status, since both Pilgram and his creator are entomologists, living in Berlin in the 1930s. One finds numerous connections between Pilgram's and Nabokov's own lifelong passions for butterflies exhibited through their professional activities as lepidopterists, as well as in Nabokov's discursive statements in *Speak, Memory* and elsewhere.

Characteristic is Nabokov's utilization of his entomological expertise. First, every name of an entomologist in the story corresponds to the name of a real scientist. Dr. Rebel, the Viennese entomologist who names a species after Pilgram, refers to Hans Rebel (1861–1940). Dr. Staudinger, whom Pilgram praises for his learning, points to a major German entomologist, Otto Staudinger (1830–1900). A reference to a certain Eisner, who is said to have purchased a rare butterfly at an auction, recalls the name of Nabokov's (and Pilgram's) fellow entomologist Gustavus August Eisen (1847–1940). Even Father Dejean, mentioned in the English version as an explorer of Tibet, appears to have been a historical personage, Pierre François Marie August Dejean (1780–1845). Finally, "a Mr. Baron," a discoverer of a Mexican butterfly, probably refers to Oscar Theodor Baron (1847–1926). Even more fascinating are the entomological transformations of the names of the story's characters. Pilgram's name was originally Gruber; a Fritz Gruber is listed in the biographical dictionary of entomologists.[63] Additionally, the name suggests the word "grub," a synonym of "larva." In the final version, Nabokov opted for the name Sommer; two entomologists with this name lived in the nineteenth century. This name—related as it is to the summer season when butterflies are transformed and live—was later assigned to the rich collector. Finally, the English version adds the name of "a certain rare moth" that Dr. Rebel named after Pilgram, *Agrotis pilgrami. Agrotis* is in fact a representative genus in the subfamily Noctuinae.[64] Thus, Nabokov the scientist incorporates precise information into the story's geographical and entomological dimensions. Nabokov the poet balances the scientific slant with the story's otherworldly radiance.

In the English version, Nabokov adds a clause in the paragraph describing Pilgram's mind trips to the territories of his dream: "And *as clearly as if it were a reminiscence* Pilgram saw himself troubling the sleep of a little hotel by stamping and jumping about a room through the wide-open window of which . . . a whitish moth had dashed in . . ." (*Stories*, 254; italics added). The notion of one's future reminiscence, also prominent in other short stories (cf. "A Guide to Berlin"), points directly to Nabokov's *Speak, Memory*. Chapter 6 of the autobiography-and-memoir presents the history of Nabokov's passion for butterflies as going back to his childhood. Like Pilgram, who loved butterflies literally since he "began to exist" ("liubil babochek s tekh por, kak sushchestvuet"; *S*, 190), Nabokov's existence "from the age of seven . . . was dominated by a single passion" (*SM*, 119). "If my first glance of the morning was for the sun," he reports, "my first thought was for the butterflies it would engender" (*SM*, 119–120). Both Pilgram and Nabokov experience recurrent flashbacks to the "original event," the formative moment of their careers in lepidopterology. During his Sunday trips to the outskirts of Berlin, Pilgram recalls the rapture of finding "a large turquoise-green caterpillar" (*Stories*, 252). Nabokov reminisces about locating "a rare visitor, a splendid, pale-yellow creature with black blotches, blue crenels, and a cinnabar eyespot above each chrome-rimmed black tail. As it probed the inclined flower from which it hung . . . , my desire for it was one of the most intense I have ever experienced" (*SM*, 120). Nabokov's dream butterfly, his first swallowtail ("makhaon"), also figures in "The Aurelian." The memories of Nabokov's and Pilgram's growing interest in butterflies are rendered in a markedly romantic language, employing such words as "love," "passion," "desire," and "ecstasy." The fifty-year-old Pilgram sighs as he envisions himself as a child enamored with butterflies; Nabokov, "as a grown man . . . under ether during appendectomy . . . saw [his own self] in a sailor suit mounting a freshly emerged Emperor moth . . ." (SM, 121). As a researcher at Harvard's Museum of Comparative Zoology, the forty-five-year-old Nabokov experienced joys of discovery that were comparable to the blissful memories of his "Russian boyhood" (SM, 125).

Pilgram and his creator also share the highly private and individual nature of their passion. Nabokov recalls the "acute desire to be alone, since any companion, no matter how quiet, interfered with the concentrated enjoyment of my mania" (SM, 126; cf. Pilgram's "obsession"). At times, both Pilgram and Nabokov despair over "how little the ordinary person notices butterflies" (SM, 129). A Swiss hiker replies to Nabokov that he saw "none" while descending the same trail. In the first draft of "The Aurelian" Pilgram experiences an attack of bile when his acquaintance, a doctor, insists that there are no butterflies in Greece, for it is too hot ("slishkom zharko"). At best, people notice the most obvious features of the butterflies, their bright colors. Pilgram's customers predominantly go for "popular stars among butterflies, some of them set on plaster and framed—intended merely for ornamenting the home" (Stories, 251). Nabokov's Mademoiselle buys for him ("something better than your cabbage butterflies") a "banal Urania moth mounted on plaster" (SM, 128). The fact that for the most part people understand nothing about butterflies' beauty only enhances Pilgram's—and Nabokov's own—sense of being privileged vis-à-vis their perfect and private lepidopterological otherworld.[65]

In places, the "butterfly" chapter of Nabokov's memoir reads as a post-textual commentary on those details that the genre of "The Aurelian" did not allow him to elaborate. In fact, the term "Aurelian" figures directly in the text of the memoir as if pointing back to the short story; Nabokov recalls a particular subspecies that preoccupied him in Russia: "Those were the dung-loving males of what the old Aurelians used to call the Poplar Admirable" (SM, 133; italics added). Given the fact that Nabokov's consciousness to some extent informs that of Pilgram, one expects to find the same names of the butterfly and moth species in both texts. Moreover, Nabokov provides the names of entomological treatises that he read in his childhood; they give one an idea of where Pilgram might have obtained his encyclopedic knowledge. Several names of entomologists, mentioned only in passing in the story, are reintroduced in the memoir. For instance, Nabokov provides the background on the name of Dr. Staudinger, of whom Pilgram speaks with awe. One also finds a reference to the Grand Duke Nikolai Mikhailovich's *Mémoires* of Asiatic lepidoptera, which might have informed Pilgram's maps of the Far East; in the first draft of the story Pilgram frets over the fact that only rich collectors, like the Grand Duke Nikolai Mikhailovich, get a chance to travel. And those readers curious about the source of the name Kretschmar, which Nabokov originally intended for his protagonist, learn from the memoir that an entomologist with such a name had described a butterfly, *Plusia excelsa*, which Nabokov rediscovered as a Russian teenager.

Finally, in *Speak, Memory* Nabokov quotes a stanza from Fet's "soliloquizing" poem "The Butterfly" (in Nabokov's translation): "Whence have I come and whither am I hasting / Do not inquire; / Now on a graceful flower I have settled / And now respire" (*SM*, 129). What used to flutter over the surface of "The Aurelian" has descended—some fifteen years later—on a page of Nabokov's memoir. Thus, "The Aurelian" may be considered a "future recollection" ("budushchee vospominanie"), as Nabokov put it in both the 1925 "A Guide to Berlin" and the 1935 "Torpid Smoke" (*Stories*, 160; *Stories*, 400).

In *Speak, Memory* Nabokov also alludes to several butterfly collecting trips that illumine Pilgram's plans in the story. "In the summer of 1929," Nabokov reminisces, "every time I walked through a village in the Eastern Pyrénees, and happened to look back, I would see in my wake the villagers frozen in the various attitudes my passage had caught them in, as if I were Sodom and they Lot's wife" (*SM*, 131). In the Russian version of "The Aurelian" one finds a similar description of the locals' reaction ("udivlenie i strakh aborigenov"; literally, the aborigines' surprise and fear) to the "strange people who have come from afar" (*S*, 196). Nabokov's 1929 trip to the eastern Pyrénees near the Spanish border is also important, because several of Pilgram's plans concern an expedition to southern France and to Spain. His final trip into eternity is also camouflaged as a trip to Spain, during which "he visited Granada, Murcia, and Albarracin" (*Stories*, 258). Two more references to Nabokov's life may elucidate the poetics of "The Aurelian." One has to do with his recurrent dream of undertaking a tropical expedition that he never realized, much like his privileged character Pilgram. Nikolai Raevskii, a writer who knew Nabokov in the 1920s in Prague and shared his professional interest in lepidoptera, recalled how an excited Nabokov told him about his dream of an expedition to New Guinea, French Equatorial Africa, and the Solomon Islands: "The climate there is wretched everywhere, but I am young, healthy, physically trained, so I would hope to survive and bring back remarkable collections."[66] Raevskii also recalled warning Nabokov in the 1920s against undertaking a long expedition to exotic lands because "the writer Nabokov could die an untimely death" in a dangerous climate. Raevskii's memoir contains insightful remarks about the relationship between Pilgram and his creator. Raevskii suggests that "The Aurelian" tells a story of Nabokov's own "unrealized entomological dream." He speaks of the strength and irresistibility of Pilgram's (and Nabokov's) passion, which preserved for life "the pure child's perception of nature."[67]

A former émigré who was repatriated to the USSR after World War II, Raevskii wrote his memoir in the 1980s. Despite the fact that he corresponded with Nabokov until the latter's death, his knowledge of Nabokov's American years was sporadic. Perhaps this lack of information explains his insistence that "The Aurelian"'s central motif of an unrequited and deferred dream underlies Nabokov's career in entomology. Raevskii apparently did not know that coming to America gave Nabokov a chance to go on the kinds of collecting trips that he had dreamed about as an émigré in Europe—to the American West and Southwest—during which he reexperienced the joys of his childhood.[68]

One experience catching butterflies in the United States, a visit to the Grand Canyon in 1941, during which Nabokov discovered a new species of the *Neonympha* genus, inspired an English poem, "On Discovering a Butterfly."[69] Written in 1943 and anticipating an equally rewarding trip to Utah, the poem appeared in *The New Yorker* and ended with the following stanza:

> Dark pictures, thrones, the stones that pilgrims kiss,
> poems that take a thousand years to die
> but ape the immortality of this
> red label on a little butterfly.
> (*PP*, 156)[70]

The motif of pilgrimage bridges—yet from another angle—Nabokov's biography and poetics. Chronologically, "The Aurelian" (1930) follows Nabokov's Russian poem "The Pilgrim" (1927) and precedes "On Discovering a Butterfly" (1943). Although his artistic aspirations did not remain unchanged over these years, all three texts share a unique feature: the perfect dream—uniting Pilgram and the lyrical personae of the two poems—awards a taste of timelessness, a window into otherworldly eternity. The three variants of the same human type, the optimistic young pilgrim of the

Russian poem, the middle-aged deferred pilgrim of the story, and the clairvoyant ex-pilgrim of the English poem, may not see the meaning of their pilgrimages in the same terms. But they would all agree with what their creator writes at the end of Chapter 6 of *Speak, Memory*, the chapter bringing his lifelong experiences of butterfly collecting to a common artistic denominator. In this remarkable passage, the teenage Nabokov pursues a butterfly on a northern bog outside Petersburg (cf. Pilgram's bogs in Lapland) and sees that miraculously, "in the distance, fleeting cloud shadows dappled the dull green of slopes above timber line, and the gray and white of Longs Peak" (*SM*, 139). Having transcended both the time and the space separating Russia of the 1910s from the Colorado of the 1940s, Nabokov continues:

> I confess I do not believe in time, I like to fold my magic carpet, after use, in such a way as to superimpose one part of the pattern upon another. Let visitors trip. And the highest enjoyment of *timelessness*— in a landscape selected at random—is when I stand among rare butterflies and their food plants. This is *ecstasy*, and behind the *ecstasy* is *something else, which is hard to explain*. It is like a momentary vacuum into which rushes *all that I love*. A sense of oneness with sun and stone. A *thrill* of gratitude to whom it may concern—to the contrapuntal genius of human fate or to tender ghosts humoring a lucky human. (*SM*, 139; italics added)

Chapter 6 of the autobiography stands as a monument to Nabokov's lifelong passions, writing and butterflies. As in "The Aurelian," he places a major textual opening right at the end of his chapter, printed in *The New Yorker* as a separate piece under the title "Butterflies."[71] The textual openings at the end of both the story and the autobiography allow the reader access to eternity by alluding to what Nabokov identified as the otherworldly source of his art in the 1942 poem "Fame":

> But one day while disrupting the strata of sense
>   and descending deep down to my wellspring
> I saw mirrored, besides my own self and the world
>   something else, something else, something else.
> (*PP*, 113)

Exhibiting intimate connections with Nabokov's biographic and literary contexts, "The Aurelian" celebrates the success of a new poetics. Artistically speaking, the beauty, grace, and magnetism of the "The Aurelian" lie in reaffirming what Aristotle favored in his *Poetics*, the impossible but plausible: "Yes, Pilgram had gone far, very far" (*Stories*, 258). This narrative split between the story's otherworldly textual opening and its commonsensical closure, rendered in such convincing and penetrating language, highlights Nabokov at his best. Possibly Nabokov's most idealistic short story, "The Aurelian" typifies his Middle period, when Germany was still a relatively safe haven for the Russian exile, when there was hope for a Russian writer in Europe, when he still felt as a happy "pilgrim whose Mecca is where he is."

Entering the Otherworld in "Cloud, Castle, Lake" (1937)

An emblematic text for the poetics of Nabokov's High period, the short story "Oblako, ozero, bashnia" (Cloud, Castle, Lake, 1937) always remained one of his favorites.[72] The protagonist, Vasiliy Ivanovich, a Russian émigré living in Berlin in the 1930s, wins a "pleasure trip" at a charity ball. He is very reluctant to go, and, indeed, the trip fulfills his worst expectations. On the train, as both a foreigner and an *intelligent*, Vasiliy Ivanovich immediately falls victim to the collective brutality of his German philistine sojourners. At some point during the trip, Vasiliy Ivanovich encounters an otherworldly landscape—a castle, a lake, and a cloud—and decides to stay there for the rest of his life. His plan fails as his companions drag him to the train and force him to go back with them. Broken and devastated, Vasiliy Ivanovich returns to Berlin.[73]

The story was written in June 1937, in Marienbad (Mariánské Lázně), Czechoslovakia, at Villa Busch, where the Nabokovs stayed during the summer. The rapid growth of German fascism in the mid-1930s, the semivoluntary surrender of the Weimar Democracy to National-Socialist totalitarianism, open state-sponsored anti-Semitism with the Holocaust already in the works, the decline of the Berlin emigration—all of this and much more could not but trouble Nabokov. To quote Jürgen Bodenstein, "especially in some works written [in the middle to late 1930s] (e.g. "Cloud, Castle, Lake," "Tyrants Destroyed," *Invitation to a Beheading* . . .), Nabokov shows that he can react strongly to the threats of totalitarian regimes, brutality, and vulgarity to freedom and individuality."[74] Consider also Alfred Appel Jr.'s description of the Nabokovs' memories of Nazi Germany: "One evening on her way back to their apartment, Véra Nabokova witnessed one of the first of the Berlin book-burnings, and the passage of time has not dulled her or her husband's memories. They have not revisited Germany since their return to Europe ten years ago; they cannot forget the crimes, or forgive a criminal. . . ."[75] But nothing reflects the cause of Nabokov's despair, anger, and fear better than the Russian Fascist newspaper *Novoe slovo* (*The New Word*) published in Berlin in the late 1930s. An examination of its issues for 1937–1938 presents yet another layer of evidence regarding both Nabokov's evident anti-Nazism and his fears not only for his family's safety but for his own as well. Of special interest is a repugnant anti-Semitic piece by one Andrei Garf entitled "Literaturnye pelënki" (Literary Diapers). In the article Nabokov (who was obviously not Jewish) was grouped with Russian-Jewish émigré artists, the painter Marc Chagall and the poet Dovid Knut (plus the poet David Burliuk, who was frequently mistaken for a Jew), and subjected to Nazi excoriation. The following quotation from Garf's opus is sobering: "There, in the boiling pots, all those 'exercises' by the sirins, the chagals [*sic*], the knuts, the burliuks, and hundreds of others will be cleansed entirely. And all those 'works of genius' will flow where flows all filth, opening passage to fresh, national art."[76]

According to Boyd, Nabokov began to "turn a cold eye . . . on Germany," and "Cloud, Castle, Lake" was his "first attack," a "direct assault."[77] The story was published in *Russkie zapiski* (Russian Annals) in Paris soon after it was written.[78] It serves as one of the best examples disproving the numerous accusations of Nabokov's *nerusskost'* (non-Russianness). The story not only deals with existential issues by depicting "the hostile German community . . . as psychologically destroying a mild Russian bachelor named Vasiliy Ivanovich,"[79] but on a larger scale can be read as Nabokov's prophetic pronouncement upon the destiny of the first wave of the Russian emigration in Europe; Nabokov, who was part of it, was already at the time making plans to escape Europe for the New World. The English translation of the story—the first to be translated by Nabokov after his arrival in the United States—appeared in *The Atlantic Monthly* in 1941 and contained several alterations that he must have made to enhance the anti-Fascist message.[80]

In his draft of the translation—made from the text published in *Russian Annals*—Nabokov's co-translator, Peter A. Pertzoff, rendered the tourist song literally: "Say farewell to empty fears, / Take a walking stick, / And march along the highway / With your fellow-men. // In the hills of your country / With your fellow-men, / Without empty fears / Without doubts, the devil take it. // Mile after mile, / With the sun, with the wind, / With your fellow-men."[81] Although devoid of prosodic features, Pertzoff's rendition of the song corresponded closely to the Russian original:

Распростись с пустой тревогой,
палку толстую возьми
и шагай большой дорогой
вместе с добрыми людьми.

По холмам страны родимой
вместе с добрыми людьми,
без тревоги нелюдимой,
без сомнений, чорт возьми.

Километр за километром
Вместе с солнцем, вместе с ветром,
вместе с добрыми людьми. [82]

Nabokov was not satisfied with Pertzoff's work and retranslated the song, restoring the original's meter (trochaic tetrameter, T4) but also making radical changes. The (anti)lyrics of the German tourist song were refocused from politically neutral and signifying *poshlost'* and philistinism to encoding Nazi slogans: "Tramp your country's grass and stubble, / With the good, the hearty guys / Kill the hermit and his trouble / And to hell with doubts and sighs!" (the facsimile of Nabokov's translation is reproduced in Figure 3).[83]

When preparing the story for the 1958 collection *Nabokov's Dozen*, Nabokov further historicized the context of "Cloud, Castle, Lake," which was now set in a concrete time, "1936 or 37." He also rewrote the last stanza of the song, now a perfect quatrain, and included a characteristic image of Nazi youths marching:

In a paradise of heather
Where the field mouse screams and dies,
Let us march and sweat together
With the steel-and-leather guys!
(*Stories*, 433) [84]

"Cloud, Castle, Lake" is a story about a failed attempt by its protagonist, Vasiliy Ivanovich, to escape the oppressive reality of the world he lives in, enter the otherworld, and stay there. Given the historical/sociopolitical context of the story, the central opposition is the world of Nazi Germany of 1936–1937, alien to the protagonist and negatively depicted, versus the otherworld, charged with a number of idealized characteristics. Vasiliy Ivanovich takes the excursion, "thrust upon" him by a "feminine Fate in a low-cut gown" ("naviazannaia emu sluchainoi sud'boi v otkrytom plat'e"; *Stories*, 430/*VF*, 236), almost against his will, under the pressure of the

Song
from "Cloud, Castle, Lake."

Stop that moping and moping,
take a knotted stick and rise,
come a-tramping in the open
with the good, the hearty guys!

Tramp your country's grass and stubble,
with the good, the hearty guys,
kill the hermit and his trouble
and to hell with doubts and sighs!

One mile, two miles, five and twenty,
sunny skies and wind in plenty ...
Come a-tramping with the gays!

3. Facsimile of Vladimir Nabokov's song from "Cloud, Castle, Lake." Washington, D.C. Library of Congress, Division of Manuscripts and Archives, Vladimir Nabokov Collection. Reproduced by permission.

totalitarian bureaucratic machine.[85] At the same time, the idealized realm of the otherworld surfaces in the protagonist's state of mind as early in the story as the night before the departure:

... а потому что в ту ночь ни с того, ни с сего ему начало мниться, что эта поездка ... на которую он решился так неохотно, принесёт ему вдруг чудное, дрожащее счастье, чем-то схоже и с его детством, и с волнением, возбуждаемым в нём лучшими произведениями русской поэзии, и с каким-то когда-то виденным во сне вечерним горизонтом, и с тою чужою женой, которую он восьмой год безвыходно любил (но ещё полнее и значительнее всего этого). И кроме того он думал о том, что всякая настоящая хорошая жизнь должна быть обращением к чему-то, к кому-то. (*VF*, 236)

(. . . because that very night, for no reason at all, he began to imagine that this trip . . . would bring him some wonderful, tremulous happiness. This happiness would have something in common with his childhood, and with the excitement aroused in him by Russian lyrical poetry, and with some evening sky line once seen in a dream, and with that lady, another man's wife, whom he had hopelessly loved for seven years—but it would be even fuller and more significant than that. And besides, he felt that the really good life must be oriented toward something or someone; *Stories*, 426–427)

It is remarkable that "(i) s tóiu chuzhóiu zhenói" is an amphibrachic (Am3)/dactylic (D3) line—depending on whether or not one counts the conjunction "i"; the choices of the obsolete instrumental endings of the pronoun (*ta-toi*/**toiu**), adjective (*chuzhaia-chuzhoi/chuzh**oiu***) render a ternary metrical pattern, while the modern ending of the noun (*zhena-zhen**oi***) makes sure that the meter is not "forced."[86] It is my suggestion that ternary metrical patterns function as markers of the privileged, otherworldly meaning in the text of the story. In fact, one may claim a functional opposition between binary and ternary meters in "Cloud, Castle, Lake." The German tourist song is written in a trochaic tetrameter, as might be expected for its purpose; in Russian versification trochaic tetrameter is a common meter of song lyrics.[87] The English translation preserves the meter of the Russian ("Stóp that wórrying and móping"), as well as the ternary meter of the line about Vasiliy Ivanovich's beloved ("[with] that lády, anóther man's wífe"; anapest An3/amphibrach Am3). Also compare "k chemú-to, k komú-to" and "towards sómething or sómeone."[88]

The otherworld already manifests itself to Vasiliy Ivanovich on the train,[89] although his German fellow travelers do their best to invade his privacy. While Vasiliy Ivanovich's communication with the otherworld becomes severed, the crucial opposition of the story's two worlds is maintained. Trying not to think about the "absurdity and horror" (*Stories*, 432) of his position, Vasiliy Ivanovich turns to the landscape. Three points deserve special attention. First, he is the only one in the group who takes an interest in contemplating the world outside the train car. The word "world" in "kakuiu prelest' priobretaet *mir*, kogda zavedën i dvizhetsia karusel'iu" (what charm the *world* acquires when it is wound up and moving like a merry-go-round; italics added; *VF,* 238/*Stories,* 432) signifies the space that is opposed to the space of the train car wherein Vasiliy Ivanovich is a captive. The landscape encodes special meaning for the protagonist. A meadow is charged with memories of his beloved: "Vospominanie liubvi, pereodetoe lugom" (A memory of love, disguised as a meadow; *VF,* 238–239/*Stories,* 432). Vasiliy Ivanovich reads signs of the landscape as prefigurations of the otherworld, an opening which he will encounter later on. Particularly important are the clouds, both indices and icons of the otherworld in the context of the story. Both in Russian and in English the sentences that describe the clouds have a ternary metrical pattern, dactylic in Russian ("Péristye oblaká, vróde nebésnykh borzýkh"; *VF,* 239) and anapestic in English ("Wispy clóuds—greyhóunds of héaven"; *Stories,* 432).[90] The metrical markedness of the signs of the otherworld in "Cloud, Castle, Lake" is not coincidental, but is interwoven with the central cluster of images in the story.[91]

Second, the protagonist notices a number of otherworldly clues in the landscape. These openings and paths into the otherworld lure Vasiliy Ivanovich. Perhaps the fact that he is watching the landscape through the window of a moving train can explain the remark about "the anonymity of all the parts of a landscape": "nevozmozhnost' nikogda uznat', kuda vedët von ta tropinka,—a ved' kakaia soblaznitel'naia glush'!" (the impossibility of ever finding out where that path you see leads—and look, what a tempting thicket!; *VF,* 239/*Stories,* 432). Because the protagonist can never fix an eye on any part of the landscape, he is unable to experience the kind of epiphanic moment that he will experience at the culmination of the story. An intimation of such an epiphanic moment, the beginning of a communication with the otherworld, is described in the following passage:

> Бывало, на дальнем склоне или в лесном просвете появится и как бы замрёт на мгновенье, как задержанный в груди воздух, место до того очаровательное, — полянка, терраса, — такое полное выражение нежной, благожелательной красоты, — что, кажется, вот бы остановить поезд и — туда, навсегда, к тебе, моя любовь... но уже бешено заскакали, вертясь в солнечном кипятке, тысячи буковых стволов, и опять прозевал счастье. (*VF,* 239)

> (It happened that on a distant slope or in a gap in the trees there would appear and, as it were, stop for an instant, like air retained in the lungs, a spot so enchanting—a lawn, a terrace—such perfect ex-

pression of tender well-meaning beauty—that it seemed that if one could stop the train and go thither, forever, to you, my love . . . But a thousand beech trunks were already madly leaping by, whirling in a sizzling sun pool, and again the chance for happiness was gone; *Stories*, 432)

Thus the train moves on, taking Vasiliy Ivanovich away from what could have been an opening to the otherworld, colored by the presence of his beloved. "Byvalo" (it happened) signals the possibility of Vasiliy Ivanovich's having already experienced such intimations. But he had never been able to enter the otherworld, the impact of which is described at the climax of the story: "vlecheniiu, pravda kotorogo zakliuchalas' v ego zhe sile, nikogda eshchë ne ispytannoi" (an attraction the truth of which consisted in its own strength, a strength which he had never experienced before; *VF*, 245/*Stories*, 435).

Finally, Vasiliy Ivanovich recognizes patterns in the structure of the objects he contemplates through the train window. Patterning plays a major role in Nabokov's aesthetics, which are inseparable from his ethics and metaphysics. Alexandrov writes about the role of patterning in his oeuvre that "the key to answering this question lies in recognizing that Nabokov's view of the world of nature as 'made' is an extension of his conception of human life as filled with fatidic patterning that implies a transcendent maker." [92] It is remarkable that the recognition of patterning occurs at the stations, when the protagonist achieves a static position with respect to the world outside the train car:

> А на остановках Василий Иванович смотрел иногда на сочетание каких-нибудь совсем ничтожных предметов — пятно на платформе, вишнёвая косточка, окурок, — и говорил себе, что никогда-никогда не запомнит более вот этих трёх штучек в таком расположении, этого узора, который однако сейчас он видит до бессмертности ясно. (*VF*, 239)

> (At the stations, Vasiliy Ivanovich would look at the configuration of some entirely insignificant objects—a smear on the platform, a cherry stone, a cigarette butt—and would say to himself that never, never would he remember these three little things here in that particular interrelation, this pattern, which he now could see with such deathless precision; *Stories*, 432)

The English text translates "uzor" as "pattern," in keeping with Nabokov's own discursive writings of the American period, where the notion of patterning in the equation nature = artifice finds full development (*Speak, Memory*). Moreover, from uncovering patterns of inanimate objects on the platforms, Vasiliy Ivanovich shifts to reading the faces of rural schoolchildren and finding in them imprints of fatidic patterns. As a result of his intense "gazing into" the faces of the children, Vasiliy Ivanovich fuses one of the boys' faces with a recollection of his own face as a child: "and would gaze until the whole party of village schoolboys appeared as on an old photograph, now reproduced with a little white cross above the face of the last boy on the right: the hero's childhood [detstvo geroia]" (*Stories*, 432). "Détstvo geróia," a ternary line (dactylic in Russian and amphibrachic in English: the héro's chíldhood), signals its privileged meaning to the reader.[93] This photographic superimposition of the protagonist's fate upon that of a chance schoolboy comes close to the state of cosmic synchronization that Nabokov shared with his favorite characters (Godunov-Cherdyntsev, Pnin, Krug, and others). During this moment of fatidic superimposition, Vasiliy Ivanovich seems to experience a kind of fusion of the past and future, shaped by the intuition of the otherworld. This recalls his expectations the night before the departure and the role his childhood memories play there.

Vasiliy Ivanovich can only communicate with the world outside the train window "by snatches" ("uryvkami"). The collective activities in which the Germans on the train force him to participate (singing totalitarian songs, playing vapid games, etc.) are fundamentally opposed to the personal nature of his otherworldly experiences. Eventually, and in conjunction with the story's central opposition, Vasiliy Ivanovich comes to perceive all his fellow travelers as one "collective . . . many-handed being, from which one could not escape" ("sbornoe . . . mnogorukoe sushchestvo, ot kotorogo nekuda bylo devat'sia"; *Stories*, 433/VF, 241).[94] It is immediately after this realization that the final prefiguration of the otherworld manifests itself to the protagonist, again at a train station:

> Но вдруг на какой-то станции все повылезли, и это было уже в темноте, хотя на западе ещё стояло длиннейшее, розовейшее облако, и пронзая душу, подальше на пути, горел дрожащей звездой фонарь сквозь медленный дым паровоза, и во мраке цыкали сверчки, и откуда-то пахло жасмином и сеном, моя любовь. (*VF*, 241)

> (But suddenly at some station all climbed out, and it was already dark, although in the west there still hung a very long, very pink cloud, and farther along the track, with a soul-piercing light, the star

of a lamp trembled through the slow smoke of the engine, and crickets chirped in the dark, and from somewhere there came the odor of jasmine and hay, my love; *Stories*, 433–434)

The "natural" objects (cloud, crickets, jasmine, hay) and the "artificial" attributes (lamp, smoke of the engine) complement each other in a harmonious vista. "Skvoz' médlennyi dým parovóza" is congruent with "otkúda-to pákhlo zhasmínom i sénom"—both being amphibrachic (A3 and A4) lines.[95] The "star of a lamp" pierces the soul of Vasiliy Ivanovich and evokes other intimations of the otherworldly in the story, also rendered in ternary lines for that matter—the "trémulous háppiness," the "ínstant, like áir retáined in the lúngs." And it is on the afternoon of the second day of his trip that Vasiliy Ivanovich faces the opening to the otherworld: "otkrylos' emu to samoe shchast'e, *o kotórom on kak-to vpolgrëzy podúmal*" (that very happiness of which he had once half dreamt was suddenly discovered; *VF*, 243/*Stories*, 435; the italicized phrase is anapestic, An 4).

The architecture of the opening to the otherworld deserves consideration in some detail. Three main structural elements constitute the otherworldly landscape that reveals itself to the protagonist: a lake, a large cloud, and an ancient castle. In the context of Vasiliy Ivanovich's epiphanic experience, the "unusual expression" of the lake's water ("ozero s neobyknovennym vyrazheniem vody"; *Stories*, 435/*VF*, 243) calls for the most literal reading and signifies a bilateral act of communication between the protagonist and the otherworld. Later in the same passage, the "inexpressible . . . harmoniousness" of the three principal parts of the opening is characterized as a smile ("po ulybke ego"). It is precisely the interrelation of the formative elements of the opening's idyllic space and timeless temporality—the chronotope of the otherworld—that the passage emphasizes. In addition to space and time, the opening to the otherworld is a function of a third, crucial characteristic: the beholder, Vasiliy Ivanovich himself. This is why the text stresses the abundance of "such views in Central Europe" (*Stories*, 435). Since this phrase has been a subject of scholarly speculation, I would like to make a digression and offer some information that might help to understand the meaning of the reference.

Suggestions have been made concerning the possible location of the landscape described in the story. Natal'a Tolstaia and Mikhail Meilakh have hypothesized that Nabokov actually had in mind a certain view of a Bohemian medieval castle that he had observed while staying in Marienbad, where he wrote the story.[96] The text of the story contains only one specific reference to the itinerary of Vasiliy Ivanovich's trip. At the end of the story, one of Vasiliy Ivanovich's fellow travelers, Schramm, points to the attractions of the last day of the excursion: "There will be beer at Ewald . . . Five hours by train. Hikes. A hunting lodge" (*Stories*, 436). In the Russian text, the name of the town is spelled "Эвальд"; thus the "Ewald" of the English text appears to be a near-transliteration of the Russian, rather than a correct rendition of a Russianized German word. A thorough inquiry into the atlases and geographical/population indices of Germany, as well as Czechoslovakia and Austria, from the 1930s–1940s revealed nothing spelled "Ewald." There is, however, a resort in Austria by the name of Ehrwald, situated near the German-Austrian border. A major tourist attraction located at the foot of Zugspitze, Ehrwald was likely to become part of the trip's itinerary, especially in light of Schramm's reference to hikes. Nabokov, who had hiked through the Schwarzwald in 1925, had a very good idea of the area. In the Russian, depending on whether one does a phonetic transcription or a transliteration (both are common), Ehrwald could be rendered as both "Эвальд" and "Эрвальд." That Nabokov opted for an English transliteration of a Russianized spelling of an Austrian town is in tune with his fondness for devising language codes. My decoding of "Ewald" as "Ehrwald" does not contradict the Tolstaia/Meilakh hypothesis about the location of the cloud/castle/lake landscape in western Bohemia. A five-hour train ride from a place in western Bohemia to Ehrwald in Austria sounds about right; it is also plausible that tourists would make it from Ehrwald back to Berlin in one day ("Tomorrow, according to the appointed itinerary . . . we are all returning to Berlin").

In fact, during a "Prague spring" of research at Slovanská knihovna (Slavonic Library) in Prague in April–May 1993, I undertook a trip to the famous spa triangle in western Bohemia to investigate the details of the story's inception. Nabokov arrived in Prague on May 22, 1937, to join his wife and son and see his mother.[97] A few days later the Nabokovs moved to Franzensbad (Františkovy Lázně), a picturesque spa town renowned for its baths and mineral springs. Entry no. 1997 in the town Kurliste for 1937 shows "Nabokoff Véra mit Kind" arriving from Berlin and staying in Café Egerländer in accommodations for two persons.[98] In the middle of June Nabokov had to go to Prague to give a reading. On June 23 he rejoined Véra in an even more renowned and beautiful spa resort, Marienbad (Mariánské Lázně), a favorite of Russian writers and European aristocracy in the nineteenth and early twentieth centuries. An entry (no. 5599) in Marienbad's registry of guests shows "Nabokoff Véra, Private, usually residing in Nice" registering at Villa Busch on June 26.[99] Villa Busch is no longer to be found in modern Marienbad under the pre–

4. View of a "lake" and "castle." Zámek Kynžvart, Mariánské Lázně, The Czech Republic. Photo by the author.

World War II name. Built in 1880 and named after one Major Franz Busch, it is situated only a few minutes from the center of Marienbad with its gorgeous colonnade and drinking sources. In 1945 the Villa was renamed Credo; its current address is Ibsenova ulice, 185. The Nabokovs stayed in Marienbad until the end of June; "Cloud, Castle, Lake," dated in manuscript June 25–26, 1937, was written during their stay there.[100] The central landscape metaphor of the story, its perfect combination of a castle, a cloud, and a lake, might have been informed by a series of real landscapes and buildings that Nabokov observed during the weeks spent at the Bohemian spas. My first impulse was to search for a castle in the vicinity of Marienbad. A detailed inquiry into Marienbad's historic attractions yielded a castle a few miles (a day's trip on foot) away from town. Zámek Kynžvart, formerly a royal residence, and currently an ill-kept museum, is located in a typical Central European forest (oaks, elms, firs) beside a lake. However, its architecture (see Figure 4) and size do not have much in common with the towered castle Vasiliy Ivanovich encounters in the story.

My next stop was Franzensbad, where I examined the site of Hotel Egerländer, located outside the main part of town in an overgrown park. Also renamed during the Soviet era, presently Hotel Zátiší, the hotel consists of two buildings, the main part, an inconspicuous 1920s building, and a smaller building, currently serving as a restaurant and formerly known as Cafe Egerländer. To my surprise, the small hotel building where the Nabokovs stayed in 1937 turned out to be a miniature castle built in the 1920s in the kind of Romantic pseudomedieval style that was popular at the turn of the nineteenth and early twentieth century both in Europe and in the United States (a well-known American example would be San Simeon in California; some of these pseudo-castles are one step short of Disneyland fairy-tale architecture; the Bohemian pseudo-castles also bear some kinship to the Arts and Crafts Movement in England and the Jugendstil of the 1920s). Cafe Egerländer corresponds to Nabokov's description of Vasiliy Ivanovich's castle with an upstairs room right in the tower. In the photographs I tried to capture the castle's diminishing proportions as Vasiliy Ivanovich might have seen it through thick verdure while being dragged away by his violent German companions (see Figures 5 and 6). I visited Franzensbad on May 8, which roughly corresponds to the time of year in the story as well as the season when Nabokov stayed in the "castle." Later, I also explored Franzensbad's architecture looking for buildings in a similar fairy-tale style. I found another building from the same period (Figure 7) incorporating the same pseudo-medieval features of structure and decor as Cafe Egerländer. The building, also now a restaurant, has a tower with a room upstairs and even overlooks a pond overgrown with thick verdure.

Finally, upon returning to Prague, I visited the village of Dobřichovice southwest of the city, where Nabokov had stayed with his mother in 1924 at a "good hotel."[101] The only good hotel in the village proved to be Pension Stejskal, a large and interesting building erected in the 1900s (Figure 8). The most remarkable of all prototypes in terms of its architecture (it transcends the medieval type rather than merely copying it in fairy-tale proportions), Pension Stejskal also has a tower with guest rooms in it. Additionally, in the area adjacent to the pension, I located another pseudo-medieval tower that even shows the crenellations alluded to in Nabokov's text (Figure 9). That pseudo-medieval castles/towers were indeed a noticeable feature of Bohemian architecture in the early twentieth century is also evident from a Czech postcard (Figure 10); another Czech postcard from the turn of the century illustrates a landscape with a castle's otherworldly reflection in the water (Figure 11).

This information, of course, elucidates only one facet of the complex creative process behind the text of "Cloud, Castle, Lake." I do not pretend to have uncovered the real iconographic subtext for Vasiliy Ivanovich's

5. View of a "castle." Františkovy Lázně, The Czech Republic. Photo by the author.

6. View of a "castle" and "verdure." Františkovy Lázně, The Czech Republic. Photo by the author.

7. View of a "castle" and "lake." Františkovy Lázně, The Czech Republic. Photo by the author.

8. View of a "castle." Dobřichovice, The Czech Republic. Photo by the author.

9. View of a "tower." Dobřichovice, The Czech Republic. Photo by the author.

10. Czech postcard with a view of a "tower." N.p., 1900–1920s. Author's collection.

otherworldly castle. Only the protagonist's memory and imagination, informed by those of Nabokov, possessed the gift of transforming a naïvely designed pseudo-medieval hotel into a perfect embodiment of timeless happiness.[102]

To return to the imminence of Vasiliy Ivanovich's otherworldly revelation, one may recall that the protagonist encountered several potential

11. Czech postcard with a view of a "castle," a "lake," and "clouds." Mailed 1915. On the back: Castle Vaňáč, Nechanice (Nechanice is a town some 40 miles east of Prague). Author's collection.

openings to the otherworld along the way. However, only at the story's culmination does he reach a state that fully corresponds to Nabokov's own intuitive metaphysics of the otherworld:

> ... но именно, именно этот, по *невыразимой и неповторимой* согласованности его трёх главных частей ... по какой-то *таинственной невинности* ... был чем-то таким единственным, и родным, и давно *обещанным,* так *понимал созерцателя,* что Василий Иванович даже прижал руку к сердцу, словно смотрел тут ли оно, чтоб его отдать. (*VF*, 243–244; italics added)[103]

> (... but just this one—in the inexpressible and unique harmoniousness of its three principal parts, ... in some mysterious innocence it had, ... was something so unique, and so familiar, and so long-promised, and it so *understood* the beholder that Vasiliy Ivanovich even pressed his hand to his heart, as if to see whether his heart was there in order to give it away; *Stories,* 431)[104]

In the English, Nabokov italicized *understood,* undoubtedly to stress the bilateral communication between the beholder and the otherworld. Moreover, the description of the protagonist's heart during the epiphanic moment is reminiscent of the heart pains experienced by Pnin in the later, eponymous novel. During moments of intense heart pain Pnin is able to communicate with the past, which appears to be ruled by beneficent committees of the dead and charged with memories of Mira Belochkin—his first love, killed in a Nazi concentration camp. Likewise, Vasiliy Ivanovich communicates with the otherworld, filled with the presence of his beloved or even somehow generally feminized, and colored by the happiest memories of his childhood and his favorite Russian poetry.

The correspondences between the architecture of the opening to the otherworld and the architectonics of its verbal signs in "Cloud, Castle, Lake" reflect the relationship between metaphysics and aesthetics in the larger context of Nabokov's writings. In the cloud/castle/lake episode, the narrator's recognition of the poeticity of the otherworldly landscape precedes a line that signifies the castle, the central part of this landscape:

На той стороне, на холме, густо облепленном древесной зеленью (которая тем поэтичнее, чем темнее), *высилась прямо из дактиля в дактиль старинная чёрная башня.*

(On the other side, on a hill thickly covered with verdure [and the darker the verdure, the more poetic it is], *towered, arising from dactyl to dactyl, an ancient black castle*"; *VF*, 243/*Stories*, 435; italics added)

The italicized clause, dactylic in both Russian and English, simultaneously encodes three dimensions—the metric, the iconic, and the transcendental: dactyl, a ternary meter, in addition to its being sheer verse (dimension one) also represents the physical space, the architecture of the otherworld's opening (dimension two) by lending itself to a graphical depiction that echoes the structure of a tower wall with its crenellations:

Because the opening to the otherworld is a transitional and privileged zone, a boundary between the physical and the metaphysical, this adds a transcendental component (dimension three) to the triple signification of the dactylic line.[105]

This scheme of the complex signification of the metaphysical via the metaliterary may suggest the presence of a major textual opening, coinciding with the culmination of the story. By the signification of the metaphysical via the metaliterary I mean not only the metricized patterning that represents a glimpse of the otherworld, but the whole cluster of self-reflecting imagery throughout the text that both encodes the otherworld (sections of the text serve as models of the otherworld) and positions the reader to enter into a (meta)textual communication with the otherworld which this signification (re)creates. The reader who identifies with Vasiliy Ivanovich thus partakes in his epiphanic experience. Through reading about the metaphysical vista that manifests itself to Vasiliy Ivanovich, the reader faces a textual opening, a window into textual eternity in the reader's memory.

It is also noteworthy that none of the participants of the excursion suspect the nearness of the otherworld's opening: "At some distance, Schramm, poking into the air with the leader's alpenstock, was calling the attention of the excursionists to something or other; they had settled themselves around on the grass in poses seen in amateur snapshots, while the leader sat on a stump, his behind to the lake, and was having a snack" (*Stories*, 435). Schramm, the ideologue of collectivism (read: totalitarianism), the "special stimulator" of the group, senses no signs of the otherworld. The group's leader and chief disciplinarian is even sitting with "his behind [*zadom*] to the lake" (*Stories*, 435/*VF*, 244). The Germans' characteristic poses further solidify the story's opposition between the totalitarian world of Nazi Germany and the perfect otherworld. Totalitarianism is opposed by its nature to the unique, individual, deeply personal experiences of the otherworld. Unaware of the actual nature of Vasiliy Ivanovich's experience, the totalitarian forces in the story do their best to sever his communications with the metaphysical realm and physically remove him from the threshold of the mundane and the transcendent.[106]

When Vasiliy Ivanovich heads toward the boundary of the otherworld, he is described as "concealing his own shadow" ("priachas' za sobstvennuiu spinu"; *Stories*, 435/*VF*, 244). As mentioned at the beginning of the analysis, Vasiliy Ivanovich's attempt to enter the otherworld is also his escape from the world where he feels like a captive alien.[107] When dealing with the otherworldly experiences of Nabokov's art, one is inclined to operate within the esoteric context of semi-intuitive terms. In Chapter 1 I have outlined the model of entering the otherworld as the pinnacle of Nabokov's development as the writer of short stories. Below, I would like to elucidate what I mean by entering the otherworld in the context of "Cloud, Castle, Lake."

Following the lake's shore, Vasiliy Ivanovich crosses the boundary of this world and the otherworld, encountering various manifestations of it on his way. Some sort of otherworldly magnetism (and this might be the only causality that one infers from the structure of the scene) brings him to an inn, where he encounters its owner. Vasiliy Ivanovich switches to Russian, but, remarkably, the owner understands him "as in a dream and continue[s] in the language of his environment, his family" (*Stories*, 435).[108] The room for travelers is upstairs, and Vasiliy Ivanovich decides to take it for the rest of his life ("ia snimu eë na vsiu zhizn'"; *VF*, 244). What is it about this room, described as "most ordinary" (*Stories*, 435), that attracts him so? The passage following the room's description is pivotal for the story and contains clues for answering our question:

... но из окошка было ясно видно озеро с облаком и башней, в неподвижном и совершенном сочетании счастья. Не рассуждая, не вникая ни во что, лишь бесприкословно отдаваясь влечению, правда которого заключалась в его же силе, никогда ещё неиспытанной, Василий Иванович в одну солнечную секунду понял, что здесь, в этой комнатке с прелестным до слёз видом в окне, наконец-то так пойдёт жизнь, как он всегда этого желал. Как именно пойдёт, что именно здесь случится, он этого не знал, конечно, но всё кругом было помощью, обещанием и отрадой, так что не могло быть никакого сомнения в том, что он должен тут поселиться. Мигом он сообразил, как это исполнить, как сделать, чтобы в Берлин не возвращаться более, как выписать сюда своё небольшое имущество — книги, синий костюм, её фотографию. Всё выходило так просто! (*VF*, 244–245)

(... but from the window one could clearly see the lake with its cloud and its castle, in a motionless and perfect correlation of happiness. Without reasoning, without considering, only entirely surrendering to an attraction the truth of which consisted in its own strength, a strength which he had never experienced before, Vasiliy Ivanovich in one radiant second realized that here in this room with that view, beautiful to the verge of tears, life would at last be what he had always wished it to be. What exactly it would be like, what would take place here, that of course he did not know, but all around him were help, promise, and consolation—so that there could not be any doubt that he must live here. In a moment he figured out how he would manage it so as not to have to return to Berlin again, how to get the few possessions that he had—books, the blue suit, her photograph. How simple it was all turning out; *Stories*, 436)[109]

The most important thing about the room is the sight of the three major signs of the otherworld, their constant presence in the "motionless and perfect correlation of happiness" (*Stories*, 435). By staying in the room, Vasiliy Ivanovich would be able to communicate with the otherworld that holds all that is most dear to him, the living memories of his distant beloved above all. Because of the metaphysical nature of the otherworld, the problem of entering it is not so much the problem of placing oneself into a specific physical space (a room, a castle, the other shore), but rather the problem of entering a state of the beyond, of being both physically and spiritually separated from the routine of the mundane world. Therefore, the chronotope of the otherworld may be defined as a singular combination of three components: a specifically architectured space, a timeless temporality = eternity, and a personal spiritual dimension.[110] The experience of being inside the otherworld is one of fatidic fusion when the protagonist's future and past merge in his present and generate an outburst of energy ("sile, nikogda eshchë ne ispytannoi"; *VF*, 245) and happiness ("nepodvizhnom i sovershennom sochetanii schast'ia"; *VF*, 244).

Vasiliy Ivanovich's German companions physically remove him from the boundary of the otherworld. While being carried away from the cloud/lake/castle scene, he cannot even turn back. Nonetheless, the protagonist is described as feeling "how the radiance behind his back receded" (*Stories*, 436)—such is the last emanation of the otherworld. The otherworld closes behind the protagonist's back: "and then it was no longer there, and all around the dark firs fretted but could not interfere" (*Stories*, 436). The protagonist is back on a train, reenclosed in the totalitarian space where he undergoes torture and humiliation.

Andrew Field comments on the end of "Cloud, Castle, Lake": "At his urgent request, the narrator lets his 'representative' go, and though one assumes he will go back to the perfect and dream-like lake, Nabokov has explained to me: 'He will never find it again. If I let him go, it is in the hope that he might find a less dangerous job than that of my agent.'"[111] Alan C. Elms, rejecting a relatively widespread reading of the final paragraph as implying an "ultimately happy ending," arrives at a similar conclusion regarding the story's teleology, although from a psychoanalytical standpoint.[112] In accordance with my interpretation of the story, the final paragraph dealing with Vasiliy Ivanovich's visit with the narrator after returning to Berlin may be read as follows. Although Vasiliy Ivanovich comes close to the otherworld, he is unable to stay within its boundaries. A broken man, devastated physically and spiritually, he "begs" his employer to allow him to resign from his position. His employer, the narrator, lets him go ("Ia ego otpustil, razumeetsia"; *Stories,* 437/*VF,* 247). Only in that sense, and not as a result of a murder by the Germans on the train, can Vasiliy Ivanovich be considered "dead" at the end of the story.[113]

In the remaining brief remarks I will link the story's central thematic cluster with its narrative structure. Two features of the narrative are especially striking: the notion of the narrator's representative ("predstavitel'") and the protagonist's/narrator's addresses to a beloved.

In the first sentence of the Russian text, Vasiliy Ivanovich is referred to as "odin iz moikh predstavitelei" (one of my representatives; *VF,* 235/*Stories,* 430). The English translation adds another reference to the narrator's representative by converting the Russian "u menia on zarabatyval" (literally, as my employee, he was earning) into the more specific and unambiguous "as my representative, he was earning" (*VF,* 245; *Stories,* 430). What is the meaning and function of "my representative"? Does Vasiliy Ivanovich merely serve as a source of factual information that he conveys to his employer, the narrator, upon returning to Berlin and that this narrator thereafter conveys to the reader? If we are dealing with something more than a mere renarration of Vasiliy Ivanovich's account, does "representative" in fact characterize a significant element of Nabokov's poetics?

"Representative" figures can be found in several other fictions by Nabokov, including *The Gift* (1937–1938), "A Busy Man" (1931), "Recruiting" (1935), and "Torpid Smoke" (1935). The notion also figures in the Russian version of "Mademoiselle O" (Chapter 5 of *Other Shores*).[114] In *The Gift,* while envisioning or recalling an episode for his father's biography that he undertakes to write, Godunov-Cherdyntsev speaks of his representative as being part of his father's expedition and witnessing its events: "ili eshchë tot predstavitel' moi, kotorogo v techenie vsego moego otrochestva ia posylal vdogonku ottsu" (or else that representative of mine whom I sent in the wake of my father throughout my boyhood; *SSoch,* 3:106/*Gift,* 112). At the very end of "Recruiting," at first glance a plotless meditation on the methods of story-writing, the narrator refers to himself as "moi predstavitel'" (my representative) and thereby literally separates the *narrator-I* and the *narrator-agent* ("my representative . . . was now alone on the bench"; *VF,* 126/*Stories,* 405).[115] According to Pekka Tammi, both the novel (*The Gift*) and the short story ("Recruiting") have autobiographical narrators who are aware of their scribal art. A detail in the text of "Recruiting" points to the fact that the narrator *is* a writer: ". . . at all costs I had to have somebody like him for an episode in a novel with which I have been struggling for more than two years" (*Stories,* 404).[116] At the same time, "Cloud, Castle, Lake" contains no evidence of the narrator's awareness of scribal art, of being a writer. The reader possesses virtually no specific information about the narrator in "Cloud, Castle, Lake" beyond his being Vasiliy Ivanovich's employer of some sort. While in all three works "representative" stands for the narrator's temporal and spatial extension that allows him to obtain information about various events without necessarily having to witness them,[117] Vasiliy Ivanovich of "Cloud, Castle, Lake" exemplifies a different kind of representation from that in "Recruiting." Vasiliy Ivanovich and the narrator of "Cloud, Castle, Lake," share a capacity to partake of epiphanic experiences, to communicate with the otherworld. This, perhaps, explains the quasinarrative lyrical digression, the address to a beloved, occurring at the first instance of the otherworld's manifestation to the protagonist. In the English text, the digression even opens a new paragraph:

> We both, Vasiliy Ivanovich and I, have always been impressed by the anonymity of all the parts of a landscape, so dangerous for the soul, the impossibility of ever finding out where that path you see leads—and look, what a tempting thicket! It happened that on a distant slope or in a gap in the trees there would appear and, as it were, stop for an instant, like air retained in the lungs, a spot so enchanting—a lawn, a terrace—such perfect expression of tender meaning beauty—that it seemed that if one could stop the train and go thither, *forever, to you, my love* . . . But a thousand beech trunks were already madly leaping by, whirling in a sizzling sun pool, and again the chance for happiness was gone. (*Stories*, 432; italics added)

Throughout the story, the I-narrator identifies himself at five separate narrative moments. The notion of the narrator's "representative" figures directly in four of the five, two in the beginning ("one of *my* representatives," "*I* cannot remember his name at the moment"), one at the culmination ("as *my* representative, he was earning enough"), and one in the final paragraph ("he called on *me* . . . begged *me* to let him go . . . *I* let him go"; italics added). The fifth instance, the collective "we both, Vasiliy Ivanovich and I," deserves closer scrutiny. Here we have a marked shift from a narration with a heretofore distinct hierarchy of narrative perspectives to a fusion of narrative perspectives. By the hierarchy of narrative perspectives I mean, in simpler terms, an awareness of who is speaking in the story and who is reporting the speech. Until the introduction of "we both," the narrative develops in the third person with occasional and covert signals of free indirect discourse, as in the instance where Vasiliy Ivanovich's remark about insects seems to be backed up by the narrator's consciousness: "They spent the night in a tumble-down inn. A mature bedbug is awful, but there is a certain grace in the motions of silky silver-fish" (*Stories,* 434). In the last paragraph of the story, the third-person na-ture of the narrative is reaffirmed when Vasiliy Ivanovich is described as telling the story of his fatal trip to the I-narrator: "After returning to Berlin, he called on me . . . told his story . . ." (*Stories,* 437). By implication, everything that precedes the last paragraph of the story is the narrator's retelling of Vasiliy Ivanovich's account. In this case, all the more revealing is the disruption of the hierarchy of narrative perspectives that the collec-tive "we both" creates. In the description of one of the intimations of the otherworld following the sentence with "we both," it is impossible to iden-tify who is speaking. Vasiliy Ivanovich and the I-narrator have now merged their voices and are speaking in a new, collective mode precisely because they share a capacity to partake in a communication with the otherworld.

I have suggested that for Vasiliy Ivanovich the otherworld hosts ideal-ized memories of his unattainable beloved, "that lady, another man's wife, whom he had hopelessly loved for seven years" (*Stories,* 430–431). One of the main reasons for entering the otherworld is to enable Vasiliy Ivanovich to communicate with his beloved, to remain in a place where "life would at last be what he had always wished it to be" (*Stories,* 431). If "my love" exemplifies an act of Vasiliy Ivanovich's addressing his distant beloved, could it also signal that the narrator has joined Vasiliy Ivanovich's com-munication in order to address his own beloved? I suggest that "my love" refers not only to Vasiliy Ivanovich's beloved, but also to the narrator's beloved, with whom the narrator communicates in the course of the nar-rative. Since the narrator is retelling Vasiliy Ivanovich's narrative to his (the narrator's) beloved, she is more than a mere narratee, a purely textual construct of any narrative: she is also the narrator's addressee, the receiver of the narration.[118]

All three instances of the fusion of voices—the narrator's and Vasiliy Ivanovich's—in the act of addressing their beloved women signal a grow-ing complexity of the narrative mode. The second instance of addressing a beloved occurs without any warning, without any indication of a change in narrative perspective like the one performed by "we both" in the first instance: "But suddenly at some station all climbed out, and it was already dark, although in the west there still hung a very long, very pink cloud, and farther along the track, with a soul-piercing light, the star of a lamp trembled through the slow smoke of the engine, and crickets chirped in the dark, and from somewhere there came the odor of jasmine and hay, *my love"* (*Stories,* 433–434; italics added). "My love" here stands for both Vasiliy Ivanovich's beloved within the story and the narrator's beloved, who is the immediate receiver of his narrative. The third, and the most telling, instance occurs at the heart of the scene describing the opening to the otherworld: "Of course, there are plenty of such views in Central Europe, but just this one—in the inexpressible and unique harmoniousness of its three principal parts, in its smile, in some mysterious innocence it had, *my love! my obedient one! . . .*" (*Stories,* 435; italics added). Situated in a most epiphanic narrative moment, this final address to a beloved undercuts completely the hierarchy of narrative perspectives and narrative voices in "Cloud, Castle, Lake." Here not only the perspectives and the voices of Vasiliy Ivanovich and the narrator but also the consciousness behind them merge in one overwhelming act of addressing, ultimately aimed at the feminized otherworld.[119] All three instances of such gradual fusion of the two voices occur at the moments when the otherworld— charged with the feminine presences in the story—manifests itself: the first two during the prefigurations and the third upon beholding the opening of the otherworld.

The notion of address(ing)—*obrashchenie*—figures in the text of "Cloud, Castle, Lake," in Vasiliy Ivanovich's thoughts of the forthcoming contact with the otherworld: "I krome togo on dumal o tom, chto nastoiashchaia khoroshaia zhizn' dolzhna byt' obrashcheniem *k chemú-to, k komú-to*" (And besides, he felt that the really good and true life must be oriented *toward sómething or sómeone; VF,* 236; *Stories,* 431; italics added). The italicized phrase is amphibrachic; moreover, the addressees are classified as living entities (*komu-to*) and otherworlds (*chemu-to*). While "someone" stands for the feminine addressee, "something" represents the otherworld that hosts her. Animacy and gender as grammatical categories of Russian here support both the story's ground-breaking narrative structure and the underlying motif of entering a dimension which overturns the laws of mundane living. Thus, the feminized otherworld can also be understood as the ultimate addressee of the entire narrative, the ultimate addressee of both the narrator and his representative. The feminine presence whom both the narrator and the protagonist address in the story is not only a distant beloved, but, ultimately, an inspiring otherworldly Muse.

Stories of entering the otherworld represent a major topos of Nabokov's oeuvre. Nabokov seems to set up hypotheses of what the otherworld and communications with it might be like. Examining the Nabokov canon reveals a number of texts related to "Cloud, Castle, Lake" (1937). The end of "Cloud, Castle, Lake" points to the novel *Invitation to a Beheading* (1935).[120] When Vasiliy Ivanovich is being dragged away from the otherworldly landscape, he says, "Oh, but this is nothing less than an invitation to a beheading" ("da ved' èto kakoe-to priglashenie na kazn'"; *Stories*, 436/*VF*, 246). The Russian poet Vladislav Khodasevich referred to "Cloud, Castle, Lake" as an "afterword, or, perhaps, foreword" to *Invitation to a Beheading*.[121] The protagonist of *Glory* (1930) plans and undertakes an expedition to Zoorland, the otherworldly idealized Russia of his memories and dreams.

Nabokov is one of the few twentieth-century writers whose texts offer a harmony of meaning—structure, theme, and metaphysics. "Cloud, Castle, Lake" is characteristic of his modernist practice, which may be defined as writing (other)world(s) in (other)word(s).

Poetry, Exile, and Prophetic Mystification in "Vasiliy Shishkov" (1939)

Друг друга отражают зеркала
Взаимно искажая отраженья
(The mirrors reflect each other
Mutually distorting the reflections.)[122]
—*Georgii Ivanov, "Portret bez skhodstv" (A Portrait without Resemblance)*

Всякий истинный сочинитель эмигрирует [sic] в своё искусство и пребывает в нём.
(Every true author emigrates to his art and stays therein.)[123]—*Vladimir Nabokov,*
"Opredeleniia" (Definitions)

Like his Russian master Ivan Bunin, Nabokov belongs to a rare category of literary practitioners who write poetry and prose simultaneously throughout most of their careers. Although Nabokov gained recognition chiefly as a Russian writer of fiction, and later as an American novelist, the importance of his Russian and English poems cannot be overestimated. As a poet, he had a manifest formal agenda and was particularly preoccupied with versification (rhyme, sound orchestration). His Russian poems of the two European decades before World War II are especially interesting to a student of his stories for several reasons. They serve as dictionaries of Nabokov's nascent motifs and tropes, often having preexisted his fictions as poetic studies in theme and imagery. Additionally, the poems sometimes provide more insight into Nabokov's consciousness than does his fiction.

Written in Paris in 1939, "Vasiliy Shishkov" (1939) was Nabokov's last

Russian short story, fashioning the author's fictional representative as a Russian émigré poet. Through the fictional persona of his alter ego, Nabokov examined the impact of exile upon creativity and questioned his own aesthetic preferences in the late 1930s. Written and published less than a year before his departure for the New World, the story emerged as a twofold testament. On the one hand, Nabokov makes a pronouncement regarding the future of Russian poetry in exile. On the other, the story prompts a model of its own reading in which the author informs and creates the text insofar as the text witnesses, documents, and unmakes the author.

In most cases, Nabokov further historicized and contextualized the English texts of his short stories as compared to their Russian twins. It is not surprising that the Englished version sets the story in a concrete historical time, spring of 1939. The Englished text also supplies an additional layer of authorial information by identifying the narrator, who is nameless in the Russian text, directly with the author, Vladimir Nabokov: " . . . and to you, Gospodin Nabokov, I must show this—a cahier of verse" (*Stories*, 495). One should not overlook the fact that the story's protagonist, the poet Vasiliy Shishkov, addresses its autobiographical narrator as Mr. Nabokov (the Russian "Gospodin": Mister), and not as Mr. Sirin, although Sirin was Nabokov's constant pen name in the Russian émigré literary world. As if to compensate for the lack of unequivocal authorial presence (in the Russian version, Shishkov simply says, "And to you, I must show . . ."), the Russian text links itself with the genre of memoirs: "Moi vospominaniia o nëm sosredotocheny v predelakh vesny sego goda" (literally, my reminiscences of him are confined to the spring of this year; *VF*, 205). The memoiristic vein is downplayed in the Englished text: "The little I remember about him is centered within the confines of last spring: the spring of 1939" (*Stories*, 494).[124] In this short fictional memoir, Englished in the early 1970s, Gospodin Nabokov becomes a source that radiates the presence of the author.

The narrator of the story, a Russian writer living in Paris, is approached by a young poet by the name of Vasiliy Shishkov. Shishkov seeks advice in a literary matter, and during their next meeting he shows the narrator a notebook with some thirty poems. The poems testify that he is an untalented graphomaniac:

> Стихи были ужасные, — плоские, пёстрые, зловеще претенциозные. Из совершенная бездарность подчёркивалась шулерским шиком аллитераций, базарной роскошью и малограмотностью рифм ..., а о темах лучше вовсе умолчать:

автор с одинаковым удальством воспевал всё, что ему попадалось под лиру. (*VF*, 206–207)

(The poetry was dreadful—flat, flashy, ominously pretentious. Its utter mediocrity was stressed by the fraudulent chic of alliterations and the meretricious richness of illiterate rhymes. . . . As to the themes, they were best left alone: the author sang with unvarying gusto anything that his lyre came across; *Stories*, 495)

The disappointed maître, "not spoiled by such desires" as the request of the young poet, answers him with perfect honesty that the poems were "hopelessly bad" (*Stories*, 495). Shishkov then confesses that the "bad" poems were a hoax produced in a single sweep only to determine the extent of the narrator's honesty: "Those credentials are not mine. I mean, I did write that stuff myself, and yet it is all forged. The entire lot of thirty poems was composed this morning, and to tell the truth, I found rather nasty the task of parodying the product of metromania. In return, I now have learned that you are merciless—which means that you can be trusted" (*Stories*, 495). Shishkov presents another notebook with the "real" poems by which he is to be judged. This time the narrator finds the poems "very good" (*Stories*, 496). Shishkov goes on to share some of his turbulent emotions with his new interlocutor. Shishkov lacks a direction and a place in life: he fluctuates between some of the most extreme solutions, which include going to Africa or to Russia, entering a monastery, and committing suicide. He also alludes to some other way of interrupting his routine: disappearance. In fact, Shishkov does actually disappear before long after undertaking to publish a monthly review, *A Survey of Pain and Vulgarity*. Neither the narrator himself nor anyone else ever hears of Vasiliy Shishkov again. The notebook with poems remains in the hands of the narrator, who wonders whether Shishkov "did not overestimate /

The transparence and soundness
Of such an unusual coffin."
(*Stories*, 499)

A protagonist with the last name Shishkov also figures in two other short stories, both from the Middle period, "A Bad Day" and "Orache." Set in the 1910s and structured as fragments of a larger semiautobiographical narrative, both stories feature a boy, Putya Shishkov, who suffers from being unable to reconcile his rich emotional life with the indifferent or threatening façades of the public world.[125] Anticipating the dilemma of his later namesake, the young Putya Shishkov also seeks an escape into a world of his own in which the colors and shapes of people and objects would change according to his imagination. Sitting in a carriage on his way to a country birthday party (in the company of a moody older sister) Putya considers plans of escape: "Plead sickness? Topple down from the box?" (*Stories*, 269).

The first name Vasiliy also figures prominently in several of Nabokov's short stories. "Spring in Fialta" features the expatriate Vasen'ka, a diminutive of Vasiliy, and "Cloud, Castle, Lake" and "Recruiting" portray the Russian émigré, Vasiliy Ivanovich. He, although not a poet like Vasiliy Shishkov, is a poetry lover who feels threatened by the oppressive vulgarity of the world around him and seeks refuge in another world. In addition, scholars have pointed to the fact that the name Vasiliy derives etymologically from the Greek $\beta\alpha\sigma\iota\lambda\epsilon\upsilon\sigma$ (king), suggesting a mark of being privileged that Nabokov often grants his favorite characters, Vasiliy Shishkov being one of them.[126] At the same time, Nabokov points out in "Recruiting" that the name Vasiliy Ivanovich emblematizes a typical Russian combination of a first name and a patronymic; Vasiliy Ivanovich thus stands for an "X," a Russian "Mr. Smith." One is compelled to compare the characteristics that Nabokov's narrators give their privileged characters in the related stories; Vasiliy Shishkov is a "neobyknovenno simpatichnyi, chistyi, grustnyi chelovek" (an extraordinary attractive, pure, melancholy human being" *VF*, 213; *Stories*, 495); Vasiliy Ivanovich in "Cloud, Castle, Lake" is described as "ètomu milomu korotkovatomu cheloveku s umnymi i dobrymi glazami" (that likable little man, . . . his eyes so intelligent and kind; *VF*, 236/*Stories*, 426). Finally, Nabokov's geneological tree is germane, for Vasiliy Ivanovich Rukavishnikov was the name of Nabokov's uncle and Shishkov, a prominent name in Russian literature, the maiden name of his great-grandmother.[127]

The next layer of information concerns Nabokov's place in the Russian émigré literary context of the 1930s. Such an inquiry is necessary to decode the reasons for his decision to mystify critics by adopting a pen-name, "Vasiliy Shishkov," and subsequently to demystify his pen-name through the eponymous short story. By the mid-1930s Nabokov had become the leading émigré prose writer of the younger generation (for details of his critical reception, see Chapter 4). Between 1930 and 1939 six of Nabokov's novels were serialized in *Contemporary Annals*, the leading émigré review and one of the best ever in Russian cultural history. From 1921 to 1939 his short stories appeared regularly in eight major émigré newspapers and magazines. In the 1930s, due to the decline in Berlin's Russian emigration and also because he was planning to move to Paris, Nabokov began to print his short stories exclusively in Paris, chiefly in the leading newspaper, *The Latest News,* but also in *Contemporary Annals* and the short-lived albeit excellent *Russkie zapiski* (Russian Annals). By the mid-1930s only a handful of enemies would dare deny Nabokov his peerless position in Russian prose. His poetry, published almost weekly in *The Rudder* in Berlin in the 1920s then occasionally in Parisian periodicals in the early 1930s was never hailed in the same way as his prose fiction.[128] In most cases, with the exception of the personally hostile Georgii Adamovich/Georgii Ivanov and Zinaida Gippius/Dmitrii Merezhkovskii circles, the reasons for the lukewarm reception of Nabokov's poetry had to do with its actual quality. Rhythmically old-fashioned, stylistically conservative, and at times marred by formal incongruities, his Russian verse could never claim praise equal to that granted his prose. Nor could it compete with the poetry of the leading émigré poets of the older generations, such as Georgii Adamovich, Ivan Bunin, Zinaida Gippius, Georgii Ivanov, Viacheslav Ivanov, Vladislav Khodasevich, and Marina Tsvetaeva. As for the best Russian émigré poets of the younger generation, Nabokov may arguably be placed in the same category with Igor' Chinnov, Vladimir Korvin-Piotrovskii, Antonin Ladinskii, Irina Odoevtseva, Boris Poplavskii, and Anna Prismanova. (I say this less for the sake of classification and more to signal that the entire "Vasiliy Shishkov" controversy was not simply a vengeful act of desperation on the part of the ostracized Nabokov, but more importantly a matter of healthy poetic competition in which he was hoping to prove his poetic merits even to those who would deny them a priori. The three poems that I will identify below as "the Vasiliy Shishkov cycle"—produced in conjunction with the eponymous 1939 short story—may well be among Nabokov's very best.)

The younger generation of émigré poets also included a number of lesser lights like Dovid Knut, Iurii Mandel'shtam, Anatolii Shteiger, Vladimir Smolenskii, Ekaterina Tauber, and Iurii Terapiano. Several of the younger poets belonged to the so-called Parisian Note school of Russian poetry (Parizhskaia nota) with Georgii Adamovich as their aesthetic leader and mentor.[129] The followers of Adamovich tended to be negatively disposed toward Nabokov throughout the 1930s and even as late as the 1950s–1970s, when Adamovich himself had tried to make amends with Nabokov.[130] The opinions of the Parisian Russian poets as regards Nabokov were also shaped by one of Adamovich's closest literary associates of the time, Georgii Ivanov, and by the Gippius/Merezhkovskii enclave.[131] The enmity on the part of Georgii Ivanov is usually explained on purely personal grounds: in 1929 Nabokov published a very negative review of the novel *Izol'da* (1929) by Ivanov's wife, Irina Odoevtseva.[132] In response, Ivanov rejected Nabokov's poetry outright in one short sentence which oozes hostility: "Stikhi prosto poshly" (The verses are simply vulgar—what could have been worse to Nabokov than an accusation of *poshlost'/poshlust?*).[133] This must have angered Nabokov so much that he subsequently refused to give Ivanov any credit whatsoever, even for his outstanding short novel *Raspad atoma* (Splitting of the Atom, 1938), which he dismissed as "poshlen'kii, sentimental'nyi, zhemannyi" (tacky, sentimental, affected).[134] In the preface to *Poems and Problems,* Nabokov spoke of the "dreary drone of the anemic 'Paris school'" (*PP,* 14).

Whether it was for personal reasons or for reasons of professional loyalty, it is still difficult to explain why such a fine critic as Adamovich, both passionate and rational about poetry, was ill-disposed to Nabokov's verse while he favored some of the lesser poets. Throughout the 1930s Adamovich's responses to Nabokov's fiction were overall becoming more and more enthusiastic although still filled with sour-grape reservations. In 1934 he published a long essay on Nabokov. While claiming to be the first overview of Nabokov's writings (which it was not), the essay said remarkably little about his verse: ". . . v stikhakh . . . on rassudochno-trezv i bezmuzykalen" (. . . in verses he is cerebral and devoid of music).[135] Adamovich is off-target in this short verdict. Nabokov's poetry is much less "cerebral" than his prose. As to the musicality, his poems suffer from an excess of musicality and sonority, from a narcissistic exploitation of the melodiousness of Russian classical prosody. What I think disturbed Adamovich in most of Nabokov's verse was its failure, despite a seeming sincerity and openness, to communicate with the reader, to speak to his reader as a friend, an interlocutor, a confidant.[136] Additionally, Adamovich must have found irksome a certain overcrowding of phenomenal details in Nabokov's poems. Adamovich preached to his disciples, the poets of Parisian Note, to speak of specific direct feelings and immediate reflections with little reference to the phenomenal world.[137]

All in all, with the exception of Godunov-Cherdyntsev's verse in *The Gift,* Nabokov apparently published no poetry under his name from 1936 until his departure for the United States in 1940. However, he continued to seek recognition for his poetry. Nabokov certainly had axes to grind with Adamovich as the leading tutor of the younger Parisian writers, with G. Ivanov as his single most vicious critic, and with Gippius and Merezhkovskii, who had been skeptical of his talent from its earliest manifestations. "Vasiliy Shishkov" was not Nabokov's first attempt to settle matters with his literary enemies. The blow would have been successful had the

1931 story "Lips to Lips" indeed been printed by *The Latest News* as the newspaper originally intended.[138] A second *coup de plume* would have been more triumphant had the poem "Iz Kalmbrudovoi poèmy 'Nochnoe puteshestvie'" (From Calmbrood's long poem "Night Journey," 1931) been published in Paris instead of in Berlin's *The Rudder*.[139] (*The Rudder* ceased publication several months later; by the early 1930s the days of Russian émigré literature were numbered in Berlin, and Paris became the major literary center of the Russian emigration.) Camouflaged as an installment in Nabokov's translation from an invented English poet Vivian Calmbrood (actually Nabokov's anagram), the excerpt abounded with references to the literary climate of émigré Paris, especially the polemic between Adamovich and Khodasevich.[140] Nabokov's pastiche was directed against a critic disguised as the bearer of "адамова голова" (adamic head), a double pun on Adamovich, whose prerevolutionary verse was associated with the Acmeist search for the transparent Adamic language.[141] The next brilliant, if covert blow, was dealt to Nabokov's literary foes in *The Gift*, where the Adamovich–"adamic head" association probably gave rise to the name Christopher Mortus.[142] In the novel, Mortus is the penname of an influential Parisian émigré critic, whose satirized image is informed by both Adamovich and Gippius. Following *The Gift*, another opportunity for Nabokov to wage an elegant attack against his opponents did not present itself until the eve of World War II.

Vladislav Khodasevich, a major Russian poet and Nabokov's literary comrade-in-arms, died on June 14, 1939.[143] Living in Paris and mourning the loss of Khodasevich, Nabokov composed "Poèty" (The Poets), part of a cycle of three programmatic poems he wrote in the summer and early fall of 1939. This poem, one of his best, albeit not devoid of formal shortcomings, centers on the destiny of Russian émigré poets who were shaped in exile (cf. Vasiliy Shishkov in the story) and typifies his recurring motif of exiting this world and entering another:

Пора, мы уходим: ещё молодые
со списком ещё не приснившихся снов,
с последним, чуть зримым сияньем России
на фосфорных рифмах последних стихов.

А мы ведь, поди, вдохновение знали,
нам жить бы, казалось, и книгам расти,
но музы безродные нас доконали, —
и ныне пора нам из мира уйти.

(*PP*, 92; cf. *Stikhi*, 260)

It is time, we are going away: still youthful,
with a list of dreams not yet dreamt,
with the last, hardly visible radiance of Russia
on the phosphorent rhymes of our last verse.

And yet we did know—didn't we—inspiration,
we would live, it seemed, and our books would grow
but the kithless muses at last have destroyed us,
and it is time now for us to go.
(PP, 93) [144]

The first four of the nine quatrains identify with the plight of the younger generation of émigré poets to which Nabokov himself belonged and do not equate "exiting the world" directly with death; the Englished variant downplays this even further by replacing "pora nam iz mira uiti" (literally, it is time for us to leave the world) with "time for us to go." However, the next three quatrains build up a Khodasevich-specific tension between the beauty and grace of the world, on the one hand, and its horror and ugliness, on the other: "ne videt' vsei muki, vsei prelesti mira" (not to see all this world's enchantment and torment); "detei maloletnikh, / igraiushchikh v priatki vokrug i vnutri / ubornoi" (the young children / who play hide-and-seek inside and around / the latrine). [145] Like the Khodasevich of his tragic cycle "Evropeiskaia noch'" (The European Night, 1922–1929), Nabokov draws on the realia of modern Western civilization, such as an advertisement for aspirin: "rydan'ia reklamy na tom beregu" (an electric sign's tears on the opposite bank). The last two quatrains concentrate—presumably—on the death of Khodasevich. Note the way Nabokov uses ellipses in the Russian text to indicate a threshold for something that words cannot communicate:

Сейчас переходим с порога мирского
в ту область... как хочешь её назови:
пустыня ли, смерть, отрешенье от слова, —
а может быть проще: молчанье любви...

In a moment we'll pass across the world's threshold
into a region [ellipses in the Russian]—name it as you please:
wilderness, death, disavowal of language,
or maybe simpler: the silence of love. . .
(*PP*, 94–95; cf. *Stikhi*, 261)

The last quatrain points directly to the title poem of Khodasevich's third pre-émigré verse collection, *Putëm zerna* (Grain's Way, 1920). Below are the last three couplets of "Grain's Way" and the last quatrain of "The Poets":

Так и душа моя идёт путём зерна:
Сойдя во мрак, умрёт — и оживёт она.

И ты, моя страна, и ты, её народ,
Умрёшь и оживёшь, пройдя сквозь этот год, —

Затем, что мудрость нам единая дана:
Всему живущему идти путём зерна.
(Grain's Way, 1917) [146]

Молчанье далёкой дороги тележной,
где в пене цветов колея не видна,
молчанье отчизны (любви безнадежной),
молчанье зарницы, молчанье зерна.
(The Poets, 1939; *PP*, 94; cf. *Stikhi*, 261)

(A literal translation of the excerpt from Khodasevich's poem: Thus my soul goes by grain's way: / Having descended into darkness it then returns to life. // And you, my country, and you, her people, / Will die and return to life, having lived through this year— // For we share the same wisdom: / All that lives will go by grain's way; Nabokov's translation of his quatrain: the silence of a distant cartway, its furrow, / beneath the foam of flowers concealed; / my silent country (the love that is hopeless); / the silent sheet lightning, the silent seed; *PP*, 95)

Both poems refer to homeland ("moia strana," "otchizna"). Moreover, Nabokov ends his *tombeau* with a key word from Khodasevich's lexicon, *zerna* (grain) in the genitive singular, exactly as Khodasevich ends his. The poems also share an underlying mythopoetics: the motif of a grain of wheat dying into the ground in order to be reborn: "In very truth I tell you, unless a grain falls into the ground and dies, it remains that and nothing more; but if it dies, it bears a rich harvest" (John 12:24).

Sometime in June 1939 Nabokov also wrote a Khodasevich obituary that sums up the deceased poet's achievement. In the obituary the poet's death is described in the same terms as in "The Poets," as a departure. In both texts, Nabokov employs forms of the verb *ukhodit'/uiti* (to leave, to depart). At the end of his Khodasevich obituary, he writes:

Как бы то ни было, теперь всё кончено: завещанное сокро-
вище стоит на полке, у будущего на виду, а добытчик *ушёл*
туда, откуда *быть может* кое-что долетает до слуха больших
поэтов, пронзая наше бытие своей *потусторонней свеже-
стью* — и придавая искусству как раз то *таинственное*, что
составляет его невыделимый признак [italics added].[147]

(Be it [*sic*] as it may, all is finished now: the bequeathed gold shines
on a shelf in full view of the future, whilst the goldminer *has left* for
the region from where, *perhaps,* a faint something reaches the ears of
good poets, penetrating our being with *the beyond's fresh breath* [lit-
erally, otherworldly freshness] and conferring upon art that *mystery*
which more than anything characterizes its essence; *SO,* 227; italics
added)

I have italicized four key notions shared by "The Poets" and "On Khodasevich," two related to the main secret and two to the recurrent motif of
entering the otherworld. Both tributes to Khodasevich, in prose and in
verse, appeared in the July (69) issue of *Contemporary Annals* for 1939. The
obituary was signed with Nabokov's usual pen-name, V. Sirin, while the
poem bore a different signature: Vasiliy Shishkov. Nabokov's plans for an
elegant revenge against his foes became a tour de force of literary
mystification.

All the technical circumstances behind the hoax have not been uncovered. Nabokov shared his plot with a few friends. Among the editors of
Contemporary Annals, his accomplices were Il'ia Fondaminskii-Bunakov
and Vadim Rudnev.[148] At the same time, in 1957 another former editor,
Mark Vishniak, referred to Vasiliy Shishkov as if he were a real poet, and
not Nabokov's mystification.[149] A two-page manuscript with two other
poems, dated "X. 39" and signed "Vas. Shishkov," has survived among
some sixty letters that Nabokov sent the émigré littérateur Zinaida Shakhovskaia in the 1930s.[150] Of the two poems preserved by Shakhovskaia,
the second, "Otviazhis'—ia tebia umoliaiu!" (Will you leave me alone? I
implore you!), was published in the April (70) issue of *Contemporary Annals* in 1940 under the title "Obrashchenie" (The Appeal) and also signed
"Vas. Shishkov"—half a year after the "Vasiliy Shishkov" mystification
had been unveiled by Nabokov himself. In the manuscript two poems—
"My s toboiu tak verili v sviaz' bytiia . . ." (We so firmly believed in the
linkage of life . . .) and "Will you leave me alone? . . ."—are united by a
title, "Obrashcheniia" (Appeals), and assigned roman numbers I and II.
The three poems (We so firmly believed in the linkage of life . . . ," "The

Poets," and "Will you leave me alone? I implore you!" [also known as "The Appeal"] form a three-part lyrical cycle that exhibits numerous connections with the short story "Vasiliy Shishkov" as well as with the circumstances behind its inception, production, and reception. My reconstruction of the "Vasiliy Shishkov" poetic cycle is supported among other facts by Nabokov's consecutive arrangement of the three poems in the 1953 collection *Stikhotvoreniia* (Poems).[151] In addition to their textological connections, all three poems of the "Vasiliy Shishkov" cycle display organic ties in their versification (ternary meters, rhyming practices; see below) and also share several central clusters of images and motifs, including nostalgia and entering the otherworld.

For instance, the poems speak of refusing oneself the privilege of seeing Russia in dreams: "ukhodim: eshchë molodye, / so spiskom eshchë ne prisnivshikhsia snov" (we are going away: still youthful, / with a list of dreams not yet dreamt"; "The Poets") and "chtob s toboi i vo snakh ne skhodit'sia / otkazat'sia ot vsiacheskikh snov" (lest we only in dreams come together, / all conceivable dreams to foreswear; "Will you leave me alone? . . ."); in both cases "snov" (genitive plural of the Russian "son": dream) is in the rhyming position.

"The Poets" was printed in *Contemporary Annals* in July 1939 and attracted the attention of émigré critics. Before discussing the possible reasons why Adamovich allowed himself to be deceived by Nabokov's mystifying scheme—and hailed the birth of a new poet—I would like to outline another motive for Nabokov's choice of the name "Vasiliy Shishkov." It goes back to Khodasevich, who had a number of reasons to dislike both G. Ivanov and Adamovich.

Khodasevich's fondness for literary mystifications has been a subject of critical discussions, including those in his own memoirs.[152] During a joint evening of poetry in 1936 in Paris, Nabokov heard Khodasevich read "Zhizn' Vasiliia Travnikova" (The Life of Vasilii Travnikov), a fictional account of the life and works of Aleksandr Pushkin's elder contemporary, whom Khodasevich invented not only to trap his literary enemies but also to reaffirm his own place in what he saw as the kernel tradition in Russian poetry.[153] The Khodasevich piece on Travnikov contained several quotations from the fictitious poet's oeuvre. Khodasevich composed and stylized some, while he borrowed at least one from his late friend the poet Muni (S. V. Kissin). A brilliant performance, "The Life of Vasilii Travnikov" beguiled the audience and elicited much praise from Adamovich, who was generally reluctant to pay Khodasevich his due.[154] As the Khodasevich scholar A. L. Zorin has pointed out, the blindness and gullibility of the public—led by Adamovich himself in being taken in by this obvious hoax—defies rational explanation. Khodasevich's mystification worked perfectly, which not only created a precedent for Nabokov's invented poet, Vasiliy Shishkov, but also offered concrete tips.

Nabokov's biographer has suggested that the names Shishkov and Travnikov share an etymological pattern: both derive from general botanical terms, the former from *shishka* (pine cone), the latter from *trava* (grass).[155] There is another possible antecedent for Nabokov's choice of an alternative nom de plume and the name of his fictitious character. In 1926 he started a short story about a young émigré who crosses the Russian border illegally to undertake an expedition to his old manor-house.[156] The story was left unfinished, but Nabokov signed the manuscript with the name "Vasiliy Shalfeev." The last name Shalfeev, although less common than either Shishkov or Travnikov, is also of botanical origin, from *shalfei,* a medicinal herb familiar to most Russians for its soothing effect upon the respiratory system (Nabokov suffered from frequent throat ailments) and known in English as garden sage (*Salvia officinalis*). Someone as fond of dictionaries as Nabokov was (he used to read the Dal' dictionary and later *Webster's* in bed) may have considered this pseudonym with a double etymological twist as a possibility. In addition, the risky expedition that the protagonist of the 1926 "Shalfeev" story undertakes to Russia across the Polish border seems akin in spirit and design to what Martin plots in *Podvig* (Glory, 1931) and Vasiliy Shishkov contemplates and then rejects in 1939: "Try making my way back to Russia? No, the frying pan is enough" ("èto polymia"; *Stories,* 499/*VF,* 213).

Just as the inception of these two mystifications reveals many affinities, their reception also follows a similar pattern, especially when in both cases the herald of the two "new" poets—Travnikov and Shishkov—was Adamovich. "Rejecting hope and consolation in life, in poetry [Travnikov] strove to repudiate any use of ornamentation"—thus Khodasevich assessed his invented protagonist's contribution.[157] Having subscribed to Khodasevich's mystification, Adamovich praised the discovered poet for writing the kind of verse that had been unknown in Russia before Aleksandr Pushkin and Evgenii Baratynskii: "impeccable, sober, devoid of any sentimentality, any stylistic excesses."[158] Three years later, Adamovich gave an enthusiastic endorsement to another "discovered" poet, Vasiliy Shishkov, in his regular column in *The Latest News:*

> Who is Vasiliy Shishkov? Have other poems signed with his name appeared before? I cannot be sure of it, but I do not seem to recall

seeing this name in print. In any event, the name did not stick to my memory, although judging by the poem published in *Contemporary Annals,* it should have. In Shishkov's "The Poets" every line, every word exhibits talent [Adamovich quotes the first two quatrains of "The Poets"]. I regret being unable to quote this marvelous poem in full for lack of space; I will however ask again: Who is Vasiliy Shishkov? Where does he come from? It is very possible that in a year or two this name will be familiar to all who care about Russian poetry.[159]

Scholars of Nabokov's versification have commented on the choice of a meter not common in his versification, amphibrachic tetrameter (Am 4), for "The Poets." An argument has been made that the choice of a meter that only occurs once in Nabokov's verse after 1925 was the main reason why Adamovich did not suspect a Nabokovian presence behind the text of the poem signed "Vas. Shishkov."[160] However, it seems highly unlikely that Adamovich would have remembered Nabokov's metrical repertoire in such detail in 1939, especially given that Nabokov had not published verse under his name since 1935. The "Vasiliy Shishkov" cycle not only contains less ornamentation than just about any other of Nabokov's pre–World War II Russian poems, but also addresses the issues that were most vital for the entire émigré literary community with utmost precision and sobriety. If Nabokov in his earlier mystification, "Night Journey," and Khodasevich in "The Life of Vasilii Travnikov" seem to partake of a playful and witty sensibility of the Pushkinian Golden Age, then Nabokov of the "Vasiliy Shishkov" cycle employs literary mystification to communicate with the readers directly and without any mediating stylization. Constructing a new authorial persona for himself and lurking behind the semitransparent veil of mystification, Nabokov created a genuine voice which is unparalleled by his other poems. In the poems of the "Vasiliy Shishkov" cycle, thoughts on love, language/silence, and death are intoned by a relentless and at times clairvoyant poet. The death of Khodasevich was not the only one standing behind the several deaths in the cycle. There is something of the poet Boris Poplavskii (1903–1935), Nabokov's junior by some three years and a dapper darling of Russian Paris, in the image of Vasiliy Shishkov in the eponymous story. Poplavskii's death in 1935 startled the émigré literary community and signaled that something was amiss in the lives of its younger poets. Additionally, "Will you leave me alone? . . . " (printed in 1940 when the Shishkov mystification was subsiding into history) speaks of Russia gleaming through the grass of two "far-parted tombs" ("skvoz' travu dvukh nesmezhnykh mogil"). The two nonadjacent graves refer to Nabokov's father, V. D. Nabokov, killed on March 28, 1922 and buried in Tegel outside Berlin, and mother, E. I. Nabokova, who died on May 2, 1939, and was buried at the Russian section of Olšánske Hřbitovy in Prague (see Figure 12).[161]

One cannot resist reading Shishkov's/Nabokov's poem, as well as the comments that it elicited from Adamovich, in a postfactum light of somber irony: on August 17, 1939, when Adamovich's review was printed, Russia Abroad had but ten months remaining. The Nazis would march into Paris on July 13, 1940, thereby shutting down the era of the First Russian Emigration. Rather than noting the meter of "The Poets," which is not at all unusual for twentieth-century Russian prosody, Adamovich probably saw in the poem a sober, direct, naked voice prophesying the end of Russian culture in European exile.

The short story "Vasiliy Shishkov" comments not only on the verse of the invented poet and his inventor, but also on its reception by Russian émigré critics. In the brief remarks prepared by Nabokov for the 1979 edition of his poetry, only half a sentence deals with the "Vasiliy Shishkov" controversy: " . . . that I could not help prolonging the joke and described my meetings with the non-existent Shishkov in a short story which, among other treats [*sredi prochego iziuma*], contained a critical reading of the poem itself and Adamovich's praises" (*Stikhi*, 320).

No one thus far has attempted to take Nabokov's remark seriously and literally. In "Vasiliy Shishkov" the young poet Shishkov and his interlocutor, the narrator Nabokov, offer critical commentaries on each other's work. Since the character is a literary personification of his creator, it is only to be expected that the poetic material and the critical commentaries it elicited would be homologous with Nabokov's poetic and critical oeuvre. To narrow the circle, I propose to examine the critical exchange between Shishkov and Nabokov—the metaliterary centerpiece of the story—in light of Nabokov's verse and criticism and critical observations on Nabokov by Adamovich and Khodasevich.

When Nabokov reads the first notebook containing what Shishkov would subsequently label as his parodies of "the product of metromania," he is outraged by three defects: the tasteless sound orchestration, the poor rhyming practices, and the omnivorousness of the poems' themes. He offers examples of atrocious rhymes from Shishkov's "bad" poems: " . . . dostatochno skazat', chto sochetalis' takie pary, kak 'zhasmina-vyrazhala uzhas mina', 'besedki' i 'bes edkii', 'noktiurna'-brat dvoiurnyi" (for example, *teatr-gladiator, mustang-tank, Madonna-belladonna; VF, 207/Stories, 495*); the rhymes in the Englished text are somewhat better

12. The grave of Nabokov's mother, Elena (Helena) Nabokova. Prague, Olšánske Hřbitovy. Photo by the author.

than in the original. In comparing these examples with several examples of Nabokov's own "chic" alliterations and unfortunate rhymes, I will draw from the entire corpus of Nabokov's verse as selected by him for the 1979 edition, but a certain emphasis will be placed on his poetic output of the 1930s, particularly the seven poems published in Paris under the pen-name "Sirin" between 1931 and 1935.[162]

Nabokov's poetic output exhibits a number of alliterations of the sort that he criticized in the story: "v Nazarete na zare" ("Lastochki," 1920), "zdravstvui, o zdravstvui, grëza berëzovoi severnoi roshchi" ("Babochka," 1917–1922), "za potselui Tseilon" ("Ia Indiei nevidimoi vladeiu . . . ," 1923), "baluiu balladoi" ("Bezumets," 1933, originally published in *The Latest News*). These alliterations smack of the excesses of Igor' Severianin and Konstantin Bal'mont and are much inferior to some of Nabokov's own like "gaer grubyi" ("Ten'," 1925) or "charuiushchemy chapparaliu" ("K kn. S. M. Kachurinu," 1947).[163]

The next layer of comparison involves Shishkov's and Nabokov's rhymes. There are striking resemblances between the examples criticized in the story and the following compound rhymes in Nabokov's poetry: "apostolu—po stolu" ("Tainaia vecheria," 1918), "uglovatyi—voshla ty" ("Ia pomniu v pliushevoi oprave . . . ," 1923), "iz raia—vybiraia" ("Pu-stiak—nazvan'e machty . . . ," 1926), "pripomnish' son—na pamiat' on" ("Snovidenie," 1927). His poetic corpus also includes such trite and "meretricious" (as the narrator of the story puts it) rhymes as "lazur'iu—glazur'iu" (1923), "vetra—metra" (1925), "nashe—krashe" (1927), "pro-stiraiu—osiazaiu" (1928), "schastlivo—opaslivo" (1930), "rabami—oblakami" (1934), "sidit—gliadit" (1934), "Kachurin—lazuri" (1947) and such cacophonic rhymes as "sëla—dolgii" (1926) and "besposhchaden—radi" (1932).

In a study of Nabokov's versification, G. S. Smith proposes that "depar-tures from exactitude" have a marked function in his verse.[164] Smith finds it noteworthy that Nabokov employs cacophonous compound rhymes like "besedki—bes edkii" to demonstrate the poor quality of Shishkov's "bad" poems. He also points out that in "serious" poems like "Fame," Na-bokov uses "outlandish" compound rhymes as an ideologically or aes-thetically marked category. Such practice reaches a climax in the most di-rectly political of his poems, "O praviteliakh" (On Rulers, 1944), where both the compound rhymes and a reference to "my deceased name-sake" point to the great Futurist poet Vladimir Maiakovskii (incidentally, Na-bokov considered Maiakovskii a "paltry Soviet poet not devoid of some glamour and knack but fatally corrupted by the regime he served with loyalty"; *Stikhi*, 320).[165] In contrast to Smith's data, my own analysis of Nabokov's versification shows experimentation with inexact and compound rhyming—with varying degree of success—to be a consistent feature of his poetry. In fact, as early as 1919 we find such Maiakovskian signature rhymes as "mogli vy—netoroplivyi" ("Football"; cf. Maiakovskii's famous poem "A vy mogli by" [Would You Dare, 1913], where "ryby" is rhymed with "mogli by"). Moreover, in the 1930s Nabokov was trying to work out a signature rhyme of his own—most likely challenged by the exhilarating experimentation in Soviet Russia by such poets as Nikolai Aseev, Semën Kirsanov, Il'ia Sel'vinskii, and Nikolai Tikhonov and certainly by Marina Tsvetaeva in emigration. Two important long poems of the 1930s—both published in *The Latest News*—display a peculiar rhyming of a feminine clausula with a dactylic one or vice versa. In "Vecher na pustyre" (An Evening on a Vacant Lot, 1932) we find seven rhymes of this sort: "proshche—zanoschivoi," "odinochestvo—nochi," "baloven'—nebyvaloi," "pamiat'iu—plamia," "schastiia—chashchu," "otnialo—neplotno," "oko—krivobokuiu." Another poem, the confessional "Kak ia liubliu tebia" (How I love you, 1934) contains four more rhymes of this type: "oprometchivo—trudnoi rechi," "snova—osnovano," "stvolami—plamenem," "rastsvetshei—vechnoe." The experimentation with inexact rhyming—both Nabokov's (author) and Shishkov's (text)—signals again that Nabokov might have reached a plateau in poetry and that he tried to revitalize his poetic form.

To go a step further, a comparison of the rhyming practices in the three poems of the "Vasiliy Shishkov" cycle (presumably drawn from Shishkov's "good" poems in the second notebook) with the rest of Nabokov's poetry of the 1930s also reveals much affinity. In the cycle we find such bleak and feeble rhymes as "molodye—Rossii," "glazakh—vetviakh," "pokinul—dolinu"; such parodic rhymes as "maloletnikh—letnikh," "slëzy—berëzy," "udivitel'no—nedeistvitel'noi"; such purely grammatical rhymes as "obidet'—videt'" (cf. also "byt'—zabyt'" in the 1923 poem "Sankt-Peterburg—uzornyi inei . . ."). Adamovich must have been so taken by the prophetic message of "The Poets" that he overlooked some of its obvious formal weaknesses, several of which are emblematic of Nabokov's versification overall. On the one hand, while Nabokov's metrical conservatism is not atypical of the versification of Russian émigrés (classical meters were often employed as a protective armor against what many émigré poets saw as the ideologically charged avant-gardism of Russian Soviet poetry), his rhyming practices bespeak a certain indifference to the semantic function of rhyme. On the other hand, in his émigré criticism Nabokov did display an understanding of what constitutes a quality rhyme. For instance, in a 1931 review, he wrote: "I think that if one were to tune one's lyre to Pushkin's or Derzhavin's prosody, one ought to avoid inexact rhymes (ravnina—edinyi, veter—vstretit', lirnik—kumirni)." [166] He also advised his younger brother, Kirill Nabokov, in 1930 to pay closer attention to rhyming perfection:

> More than once I have written in *The Rudder* about ungraceful rhymes, which torture one's ears and create a comical effect due to one's ear's habitual associations. For instance, you rhyme "mozg" and "roz"; having reached the word "roz," where one's ear awaits a rhyme, one involuntarily makes "rozg" from "roz," and this "rozg" [i.e., "birch rods" instead of "roses"] is laughable. "Zhadnyi" and "sada" or "pozharishch" and "lapishch" do not rhyme at all, while "rastsvet" and "tsvet" or "kogti" and "nogti" rhyme too obviously, being cognates, and this is bad. A rhyme ought to make the reader both amazed and satisfied, amazed by how unusual it is, and satisfied with its preciseness and musicality. (*PSS*, 118)

Thus, in the discursive writings, as well as in the story, Nabokov criticizes rhymes that are akin to his own inexact rhymes, including those of the "Vasiliy Shishkov" cycle.

What are we to make of such a seeming double standard? A case of not seeing a beam in one's own eye? Perhaps a blindness to the limitations of one's own verse would be too one-dimensional for Nabokov. What do "phosphorescent rhymes of our last verse" signify in "The Poets"? Are they gleaming with formal brilliance? Or are they, perhaps, dim and moldy? Or do they in fact signal the imminence of the poetic death and "disappearance" of Vasiliy Shishkov, along with his creator Vladimir Nabokov, then still Sirin, and their colleagues, other Russian émigré poets? It is probably all of the above if one concludes that Nabokov provides a double-edged commentary in "Vasiliy Shishkov" on his own poetic practices. Thus, his analysis of first Shishkov's "bad" poems and now his "good" ones also sends an important self-critical message regarding his poetic crisis of the 1930s.

Before shifting to the matter of Shishkov's disappearance within his own verse, I will sum up my comparisons of Shishkov's and Nabokov's versification. Atypical of Nabokov's prosody as the meter of "The Poets" may be, its rhyming connects the "Vasiliy Shishkov" cycle with his poetic output in general and with the other poems of the 1930s in particular. For Nabokov, rhyme seems to have been a structural/structuring and grammatical device, and only occasionally a paronomastic device.[167] In the poems of the "Vasiliy Shishkov" cycle, the oracular poetic persona makes up for the unremarkable versification.

When offering Nabokov the second, "much more tattered," notebook with "good" poems ("Here's my real passport. . . . Read just one poem at random, it will be enough for both you and me"; *Stories*, 495), Shishkov also confronts him with an unexpected and unwanted critical judgment of his work:

> By the way, to avoid any misapprehension, let me warn you that I do not care for your novels [note that Nabokov renders *knigi* as "novels" and not literally as "books," thereby narrowing the circle of Shishkov's response to fiction only; the Russian "books" could refer to both poetry and prose; by 1939 Nabokov had published in emigration two separate volumes of poetry plus the collection *The Return of Chorb* with fifteen stories and twenty-four poems], they irritate me as would a harsh light or the loud conversation of strangers when one longs not to talk, but to think. Yet, at the same time, in a purely physiological way—if I may put it like that—you possess some secret of writing, the secret of certain basic colors, something exceptionally rare and important, which, alas, you apply to little purpose, within the narrow limits of your general abilities—driving about, so to speak, all over the place in a powerful racing car for which you have absolutely no use, but which keeps you thinking where could one thunder off next. (*Stories*, 495–496)

Shishkov's comments sum up a view of Nabokov as a metaliterary writer that goes back to the 1930s and was later embraced by a pleiad of Western critics and postmodernist writers. This formulation, "in a purely physiological way," suggests that Nabokov possesses an inherently golden pen that ensures the brilliance of his style and the effectiveness of his devices. Such physiological writing—so one is compelled to assume from Shishkov's critique—does not open any metaphysical horizons. The "metaliterary" view prevailed in the pre–World War II émigré criticism, only to experience a second upsurge in Western academia in the 1960s–1980s. By the end of the 1930s, depending on whether the émigré critics were well disposed toward Nabokov (Khodasevich, Bitsilli, Struve, N. Andreev) or against him (Gippius / Merezhkovskii, Adamovich), they would either hail or belittle him on quite similar grounds. Compare, for instance Khodasevich's seminal formulation from his essay "O Sirine" (On Sirin, 1937) with Adamovich's from the aforementioned "Sirin."

For Khodasevich,

> . . . Sirin becomes predominantly the artist of form, of literary device, and not only in the sense—now common and widely recognized—that the formal side of his writings stands out for its exceptional diversity, complexity, brilliance, and novelty. . . . Sirin not only masks or hides his devices, . . . but rather reveals them like a conjurer. . . . Here, I feel, lies the key to Sirin. His works are inhabited not only by dramatis personae, but also countless devices which—like elves or gnomes—. . . carry out enormous tasks. . . . They create the world of a work of art and become its indispensable characters. This is why Sirin does not hide them: his main goal is to show how devices live and work . . . I actually think, or am almost sure that Sirin . . . will one day open up and present us with a ruthless satirical portrayal of a writer. Such a portrayal would be a natural stage in the development of this central theme which possesses him.[168]

And now Adamovich:

> Sirin's prose resembles Chinese shadows: a perfectly white background which nothing can disturb or stir up. And against this background weaving the most quaint patterns are what seem to be people or passions or fates. Try looking through the chinks into what's gaping in between: there is nothing there, one loses vision in milky-white emptiness. . . . Could it be that he would prefer the rubber smoothness of style over everything else? It is suffocating, cold, and strange to read Sirin's prose. And it matters not whether we look inside it or glance at its surface. But let me repeat it, he is a remarkable writer, a most original figure. . . . The remaining doubts concern only what he does with his gift.[169]

While Adamovich wrote three years earlier than Khodasevich, both claim—the former with skepticism, the latter with optimism—that Nabokov's potential is still to reach fruition in the future. The critics expect different things from Nabokov, although both fashion him as a metaliterary gamesman. For Adamovich, who makes the mistake of separating artistry from ethics in Nabokov's indivisible world, "a moral criterion is inapplicable" to Nabokov. Apparently oblivious to the fact that in most of his pre-1934 mature works (especially *Kamera obskura* and *The Defense*) Nabokov makes ethical judgments about his characters, Adamovich challenges him to become a writer concerned with the human condition. Between January 1934 and March 1936 *Despair* and *Invitation to a Beheading* were published, as it were, in response to Adamovich's requests. Khodase-vich's wish also came true in several works of the late 1930s that feature writers as their major characters. Already in "Spring in Fialta," which Khodesevich does not discuss in his essay, we encounter a successful Hungarian-French writer, Ferdinand, the story's "salamander of fate." The protagonist of "Spring in Fialta," the Russian émigré Vasen'ka, makes the following comment about Ferdinand's writing:

> At the beginning of his career it had been possible to distinguish some human landscape, some old garden, some dream-familiar dis-position of trees through the stained glass of his prodigious prose . . . but with every new book the tints grew still more dense, the gules and purpure still more ominous and today one can no longer see any-thing at all through that blazoned, ghastly rich glass, and it seems that were one to break it, nothing but a perfectly black void would face one's shivering soul. (*Stories*, 420)

Notice how close this comes to both Adamovich's and Khodasevich's remarks on Nabokov. The complexity here lies in the fact that although Vasen'ka (Victor), the narrator of "Spring in Fialta," and not his rival, Fer-dinand, happens to be Nabokov's privileged character in the story, Ferdi-nand also shares much with his creator. Note the narrator's comment re-garding Ferdinand's responses to unwilling critics: "But how dangerous he was in his prime [Nabokov was reaching his prime in the late 1930s], what venom he squirted, with what whips he lashed when provoked! The tor-nado of his passing satire left a barren waste where felled oaks lay in a row, and the dust still twisted, and the unfortunate author of some adverse re-view, howling with pain, spun like a top in the dust" (*Stories*, 420 – 421). I have demonstrated above that the 1930s witnessed precisely a "tornado" of Nabokov's counterattacks, overt at times, covert at others, but always ele-gantly hitting the target. In "Vasiliy Shishkov" Nabokov's duel with the critics reached a high point: the short story finalized what the novel *The Gift*, and the story "Spring in Fialta" had done with such elegance and poignancy.

The Gift—focusing on the writer Godunov-Cherdyntsev and thereby granting Khodasevich's wish—began to appear serially in April 1937, some three months after the Khodasevich essay. Godunov-Cherdyntsev's imag-ined conversations with his literary ally, the poet and critic Koncheyev (whose image is informed by Nabokov's vision of Khodasevich), bridge Nabokov's one-dimensional reception by most émigré critics and the criti-cal responses to the "Vasiliy Shishkov" controversy. In the second conversation, which takes place in the Grünewald in Berlin, Koncheyev lists five shortcomings in Godunov-Cherdyntsev's writing. Here is Koncheyev's third comment: ". . . you sometimes bring up parody to such a degree of naturalness that it actually becomes a genuine serious thought, but on this level it suddenly falters, lapsing into a mannerism that is yours and not a parody of a mannerism, although it is precisely the kind of thing you are ridiculing—as if somebody parodying an actor's slovenly reading of Shakespeare had been carried away, had started to thunder in earnest, but had accidentally garbled a line" (*Gift,* 339). Nabokov used his skill in creating literary personae to demystify the authorship of "The Poets." After the story "Vasiliy Shishkov" had appeared in *The Latest News,* Adamovich had no choice but to respond publicly to Nabokov's short story. In a concluding section of his regular literary column, Adamovich discussed the chances that Vasiliy Shishkov was fictional:

> I must confess that a suspicion had crossed my mind: could it be that Sirin made it all up, that he created both Vasiliy Shishkov and his verse? Sirin's own poetry is certainly of a much different sort. But if it is at all possible to compose something for another consciousness and to intuit the other's themes, such a possibility is twice as likely for Sirin with his talent and inventiveness. In parodies and pastiches inspiration sometimes loses restraint and even forgets about the acting like an actor who lives his part.[170]

One gets an almost uncanny feeling from reading this last sentence, so closely does it recall the message of Koncheyev's critical comment about Godunov-Cherdyntsev's art of parody in *The Gift!*

Adamovich reiterated his reasons for having welcomed Shishkov with much enthusiasm. He insisted that the entire text of "The Poets" was written "on such a compositional level that ornamentation [*ukrashenie*] [was] not needed or [was] inseparable from the poem's whole."[171] Adamovich was still unwilling to fall victim to Nabokov's mystification. He labeled "Vasiliy Shishkov" a "feuilleton," thereby downplaying the fictionality of Nabokov's short story.[172] Adamovich also called Shishkov a "Russian Rimbaud," which not only testified to his continuing admiration for "The Poets" but also ipso facto identified the teleology of Shishkov's career with that of the mythologized French poet and adventurer.[173] In the story, Shishkov relays to Nabokov that he considered going to "Africa, to the colonies" (*Stories,* 499) but then decided against it.[174] Despite that, Adamovich assumed that Shishkov ended up "running away from literature to Africa," [175] again betraying his tendency to treat the story as a piece of journalism or as a memoiristic account and not as a work of fiction.

Adamovich plots his review of the story with great caution: he wants to consider every possibility and yet shield himself from a possible next round of Nabokov's mystification. Having insured himself against the "fictional" outcome of Nabokov's story, Adamovich goes on to suggest the Khodasevich hoax "The Life of Vasilii Travnikov" as a precedent for "Vasiliy Shishkov" in case Nabokov's creation indeed turned out to be a "quaint mystification." Adamovich seems torn at the end of his review. He is right in identifying the genesis of Nabokov's invented poet with Khodasevich's earlier mystification. He is, however, unwilling to be Nabokov's fool. Thence comes his most important comment, which he utters as though unaware of the depth of its meaning: "It would be a great pity if Shishkov the fugitive turned out to be 'a metaphysical being' [*sushchestvom metafizicheskim*]: it would be a great joy to know his other works and to discover that his silence is not final." [176] For Adamovich, the poet Shishkov's "metaphysical" nature (Adamovich uses "metaphysical" in the sense of "fictional") is a disappointment; among other things it would prove that Adamovich had no reason to deny Nabokov's poetry its due. But for Nabokov, the metaphysical disappearance of Shishkov is the story's ultimate triumph over time and the shrinking émigré cultural context! Incidentally, in a rather long preface to the English text of the story, printed in *Tyrants Destroyed* (1975) three years after Adamovich died, Nabokov elucidated several circumstances behind the Vasiliy Shishkov controversy. He quoted "The Poets" in full and also made this comment on Adamovich:

> Adamovich refused at first to believe eager friends and foes who drew his attention to my having invented Shishkov; finally, he gave in and explained in his next essay that I "was a sufficiently skillful parodist to mimic genius." I fervently wish all critics to be as generous as he. I met him briefly, only twice; but many old literati have spoken a lot, on the occasion of his recent death, about his kindness and penetrativeness. He had really only two passions in life: Russian poetry and French sailors. (*Stories*, 657)

It remains to explain the last three sentences of "Vasiliy Shishkov." Since this was Nabokov's last Russian short story, its ending could also signal a guide to the poetics of his short fiction. The narrator, Gospodin Nabokov, analyzes the nature of Shishkov's disappearance as follows:

Что вообще значили эти его слова — „исчезнуть“, „раствориться“? Неужели же он в каком-то невыносимом для рассудка, дико буквальном смысле имел в виду исчезнуть в своём творчестве, раствориться в своих стихах, оставить от своей личности только стихи? Не переоценил ли он „прозрачность и прочность такой необычной гробницы“? (*VF*, 213–214)

(And, generally speaking, what did he have in mind when he said he intended "to disappear, to dissolve"? Cannot it actually be that in a wildly literal sense, unacceptable to one's reason, he meant disappearing in his art, dissolving in his verse, thus leaving of himself, of his nebulous person, nothing but verse? One wonders if he did not overestimate

> The transparence and soundness
> Of such an unusual coffin; *Stories*, 499)

The English text represents the last bit of the story as a two-line quotation from a poem. In fact, metrically speaking, it is a single line of an anapestic pentameter (An5) broken into two demistiches by a caesura after the first unstressed syllable of the third foot: "*the transpárence and sóundness of súch an unúsual cóffin.*" In the Russian text, the line is rendered graphically as prose, while metrically it is a verse of an amphibrachic pentameter (Am5) with a caesura falling after the second foot: "prozráchnost' i próchnost' takói neobýchnoi grobnítsy." In both cases, the verse quoted by Nabokov points—if covertly—to the ternary meters of the "Vasiliy Shishkov" cycle, the English to the anapests of "We so firmly believed . . ." (An4) and "Will you leave me alone? . . ." (An3), the Russian to the amphibrach of "The Poets" (Am4). At the same time, not a single complete poem in Nabokov's 1979 collection creates a precedent for an Am5, while only two lines—the beginning of Koncheyev's poem quoted in *The Gift*—are known to have been written in An5.[177] What is the exact connection between the poems of the "Vasiliy Shishkov" cycle and the poem from which Nabokov quotes in the end of the story? Were the Russian émigrés who read the story in 1939 supposed to infer from it—given the critical repercussions of the earlier publication of "The Poets"—that Nabokov was quoting yet another poem from the notebook Shishkov had entrusted to him before "disappearing"? Or were they to take this as another instance of his use of prosodic structures in prose as markers of privileged meaning, here the motif of disappearance? In the final analysis, is the line of verse at the end of the story Nabokov's or Shishkov's? Are we after all supposed to separate Nabokov the author of the story and Shishkov the literary persona that this text creates?

In the 1970s Nabokov was compelled to provide an extensive background in the preface to the English version of the story—the most extensive preface in all of the short stories—and include the entire "The Poets" (*Stories*, 656–657). After the publication of the Russian version of the story in 1939, émigré readers did not need any such preface: the poems, as well as reviews in the émigré press, were easily accessible; those readers were steeped in the émigré context and partook of much the same information as Nabokov himself. He was rightly concerned that the context of the story be made available to the English-language reader in the 1970s. The preface to his Englished story provides the reader with the missing information about the author-text continuum. Nabokov's efforts were aimed at restoring the sparkle of his time-dimmed mirrors.

Finally, what is "Vasiliy Shishkov" about? Here the text tells about the author's intention to abandon his cultural milieu. Nabokov's biographers have demonstrated at length how by the end of the 1930s he was "searching for an exit" from the narrowing and thinning context of Russia Abroad.[178] The late 1930s were a time when Nabokov searched for a new literary persona that would allow him to speak/write in a foreign language. He tried French—the short story "Mademoiselle O" (1936) was the fruit of this—but opted for English. For a short period in 1938–1939 he worked simultaneously in both English and Russian. Anticipating Nabokov's move from the Old World to the New World, "Vasiliy Shishkov" was his harmonious, perfect exit from the world of the Russian emigration. While Adamovich suspected that Shishkov had left for Africa, there are transparent hints in the story about Shishkov's possible move to America. There are German-Jewish refugees discussing visa intricacies on the fringes of the story. The gently comical portrayals of a group of refugees—both preceding Nabokov's conversations with Shishkov—contain remarkable parallels with the portrayal of German-Jewish refugees in the film *Casablanca* (directed by Michael Curtiz, 1943). In the film, much as in the story, the refugees practice conversing in a foreign language with no sense of proper usage.

Nabokov's postface "On a Book Entitled *Lolita*" (1956) offers an insight into his post-émigré assessment of his search for a new language in which to write: "My private tragedy, which cannot, and indeed should not, be anybody's concern, is that I had to abandon my natural idiom, my untrammeled, rich, and infinitely docile Russian tongue for a second-rate brand of English, devoid of any of those apparatuses—the baffling mirror, the black velvet backdrop, the implied associations and traditions—which the native illusionist, frac-tails flying, can magically use to transcend the heritage in his own way" (*L*, 316–317). Look at how precisely Nabokov puts it. The "baffling mirror" transforms him into Shishkov against the contextual "backdrop" of "associations and traditions"—the native Russian heritage preserved yet transformed in exile. This is exactly what Nabokov says and does in "Vasiliy Shishkov." He rescues the heritage of Russian émigré culture. He preserves its texts—Shishkov's poems. But insofar as Nabokov as a quintessential Russian émigré author creates Vasiliy Shishkov in his text, this very text decreates Nabokov as émigré author by pronouncing his own verdict: to disappear in "his art," to dissolve in "his poetry." There is after all inexplicable illusionism in Shishkov's disappearance. To quote the narrator's remark in the story, "Where the deuce did he go?" (*Stories,* 499). Still, Shishkov's otherworldly disappearance into the "transparent and sound" world of his liminal poems is not the worst alternative for the culture of the Russian emigration.

It is revealing to compare Nabokov's skepticism regarding the future of the Russian emigration in 1939 with his optimistic and inspirational jubilee remarks on the tenth anniversary of the Bolshevik Revolution in 1927:

> We are the wave of Russia gone out of its shores; we have been spilled all over the world. . . . We celebrate ten years of freedom. Perhaps no other people has known the freedom we know. In this invisible Russia that surrounds us, nourishes our lives, fills our souls, and colors our dreams there is no law other than our love for her, and no other authority than our own conscience. . . . Nowadays, when they celebrate the USSR-gray anniversary [*otmechaetsia seryi, èsèsèsèrnyi iubilei*], we celebrate ten years of contempt, faithfulness, and freedom. Let us not blame our exile. Today let us repeat the words of the ancient warrior of whom Plutarch wrote: "At night, in tents, amidst a desert far away from Rome, I put up my tent, and my tent was Rome for me." [179]

Some twelve years later Nabokov's creation, the émigré poet Shishkov, "implored" his homeland to leave him alone:

> Will you leave me alone? I implore you!
> Dusk is ghastly. Life's noises subside.
> I am helpless. And I am dying
> Of the blind touch of your whelming tide.

One stanza later, the poet is ready to sacrifice so much—his name, his native tongue—only for his homeland to let go of him:

> I'm prepared to lie hidden forever
> and to live without name. I'm prepared,
> lest we only in dreams come together,
> all conceivable dreams to foreswear;
>
> to be drained of my blood, to be crippled,
> to have done with the books I must love,
> for the first available idiom
> to exchange all I have: my own tongue.
>
> (*PP*, 96; *Stikhi*, 262)

The latter stanza anticipates what Nabokov would say twenty years later in "On a Book Entitled *Lolita*." When "Will you leave me alone? . . ." came out in the last issue of *Contemporary Annals* under the name "Vas. Shishkov," Nabokov had less than two months left to enjoy his ambivalent status as a Russian émigré with an unwanted Nansen refugee passport. On May 19, 1940, he would sail to America, no longer Vladimir Sirin, but Vladimir Nabokov the would-be Russian-American writer. The cultural climate in the United States was not conducive to preserving and developing the émigré heritage. In America, as Nabokov put it in his foreword to *The Gift*, the rich world of Russian émigré culture "remained unknown to American intellectuals (who, bewitched by Communist propaganda, saw [Russian émigrés] merely as villainous generals, oil magnates, and gaunt ladies with lorgnettes)." Incidentally, one of his foes, Zinaida Gippius, did in fact look like a "gaunt lady" with a lorgnette and is disguised in "Vasiliy Shishkov" as "an ample female (a translatress . . . or perhaps a theosophist) with a gloomy little husband resembling a black breloque" (*Stories*, 498)—one pictures Dmitrii Merezhkovskii right away!

Nabokov needed his last Russian short story not only to triumph over his émigré literary foes before exiting gracefully. He needed to make a closing statement regarding the destiny of Russian emigration. In fact, while he parted with his Russian voice, which he would never quite regain thereafter ("Vasiliy Shishkov" is both a valediction and a last testament), the creation of a new English-language persona was in the works. The name of the narrator in *The Real Life of Sebastian Knight* (1938, 1941) is "V," suggesting that the English-speaking voice in the novel was not yet ready for a full-fledged (named) narrator.

The move to America placed the Russian Nabokov in a "transparent and sound coffin." While in the United States, and especially after the success of *Lolita*, he hardly participated in the cultural life of the Russian émigré community.[180] His literary name in Russian underwent transformations from Vladimir Sirin to Vladimir Nabokov-Sirin to Vladimir Nabokov. The "coffin" or the "sepulcher" of Vasiliy Shishkov's verse benefits from a very literal reading, especially since the narrator uses the expression "bukval'no . . . ischeznut'" (to disappear literally). Additionally, Vasiliy Shishkov—however much he is constructed as Nabokov's literary persona—emblematizes the destinies of other émigré poets during World War II. Many émigré writers died between 1939 and 1945. A number of them (both Jewish and non-Jewish)—Raisa Blokh, Iurii Fel'zen, Il'ia Fondaminskii-Bunakov, Iurii Mandel'shtam, Elizaveta Kuz'mina-Karavaeva (Mother Maria), and others—perished in Nazi concentration camps.[181]

Via his artistic practices, laid bare in "Vasiliy Shishkov" and central to the poetics of his other short stories, Nabokov validated the workings and products of artistic imagination as ontologically equivalent to the "objective" world informing his fiction. This feature of Nabokov's poetics is related to his conception of artistic cognition, where all is a function of the perceiver, who "authors" the world of his text.

From the vantage point of the 1990s, "Vasiliy Shishkov" stands as both the author's guide to his own text and the text's immortalization of the author.[182] Shishkov's disappearance is Nabokov's window onto textual eternity, a perfect textual opening. As a footnote to Nabokov's lifetime of equating the author and the text, the prominent Russian émigré scholar Vladimir Veidle called his 1977 obituary "Nabokov's Disappearance." One could not think of a more Nabokov-specific formulation.[183]

In 1955 Georgii Adamovich, one of the key players in the Vasiliy Shishkov controversy, published a volume of memoiristic essays entitled *Odinochestvo i svoboda* (Solitude and Freedom). As if attempting to correct postfactum his earlier reservations about Nabokov's poetry, Adamovich devoted an extensive section to analysis of it. He was right to point out that Nabokov the poet had "studied and learned something from Pasternak."[184] Other critics would later identify a number of parallels between the two great writers.[185] It is not impossible that while Nabokov had been influenced by Boris Pasternak's poetry in the 1920s-1930s, Pasternak had considered Nabokov's experience of writing a novelistic biography of a poet (*The Gift*, 1937–1938) and including his verses in the text of his novel in writing *Doctor Zhivago* (1958). The relationship between Nabokov the novelist and poet and, Pasternak the poet and novelist, is possibly reciprocal. However, if there is one major feature that these disparate writers share, it is their organic understanding of the mirroring relationship between the author and the text.

The last issue of Mark Slonim's short-lived but absolutely first-rate Parisian biweekly newspaper *Novaia gazeta* (The New Paper) featured an essay by Pasternak, "Vstrechi s Maiakovskim" (Meetings with Maiakovskii).[186] The same issue also featured Nabokov's essay, an anti-Freudian lampoon, "Chto vsiakii dolzhen znat'?" (What Everyone Has to Know?).[187] Pasternak's essay ends by describing his reaction to Maiakovskii's tragedy *Vladimir Maiakovskii* (1914):

> И так просто было это всё. Искусство называлось трагедией. Так и следует ему называться. Трагедия называлась „Владимир Маяковский". Заглавие скрывало гениально простое открытие, что поэт не автор, — но предмет лирики, от первого лица обращающийся к миру. Заглавие было не именем сочинителя, а фамилией содержания.[188]

> (And all this was so simple. Art was called tragedy, as art should be called. The name of the tragedy was *Vladimir Maiakovskii*. The title concealed a brilliantly simple discovery, that the poet is not the author, but the subject of the lyrical verse who addresses the world in first person. The title was not the first name of the author, but the last name of the content.)

Nabokov's dazzling and prophetic short story "Vasiliy Shishkov" proves the same point. He creates a textual opening by giving the ending the shape of two lines of verse that communicate to the reader the mystery of the poet's death and art's immortality. Here Nabokov sums up all the achievements of his Russian short stories. The privileged protagonist, the poet Vasiliy Shishkov, fashions and writes his Russia as the ultimate otherworld within him, thereby creating his valediction and exile's "Exegi monumentum."

3   Nabokov's Dialogue with Chekhov: From "Lady with a Lap Dog" to "Spring in Fialta"

. . . .

"Began reading Chekhov yesterday," John said to him, wriggling his eyebrows. "Very grateful to you for the advice. Appealing, humane writer."

"Oh, he certainly is," said Martin, and quickly thought to himself, "Is there going to be a fight?"[1]*—Vladimir Nabokov,* Glory

Thanks for my predecessor's book. I am sure his ghost is appalled by the boners in the dreadful translation you have graced with your preface. You can well imagine how strongly I disapprove of your preface. Do you really think that Chehov [sic] is Chehov because he wrote about "social phenomena," "readjustments of a now industrial middle class"? . . . I thought he wrote of the kind of things that gentle King Lear proposed to discuss in prison with his daughter.[2]*—Vladimir Nabokov to Edmund Wilson, February 29, 1956*

Nabokov's admission that he continued Chekhov's tradition in Russian prose into the second half of the twentieth century says a great deal. This is the same Nabokov who denied genetic connections between his oeuvre and the works of such great modernist masters as Marcel Proust and Franz Kafka and who was generally reluctant to discuss his literary genealogy. Rating Russian writers for a student audience at Cornell in 1947, Nabokov assigned only Pushkin and Chekhov a solid *A;* half a point below Tolstoi but significantly higher than Gogol' (*B−*) and Dostoevskii (*C−*).[3] In his Cornell lectures Nabokov referred to Chekhov and Pushkin as "the purest writers that Russia has produced in the sense of the complete harmony that their writings convey" (*LRL,* 250). Later, in Switzerland, responding to a growing flow of criticism elicited by his works, and Simon Karlinsky's article "Nabokov and Chekhov: The Lesser Tradition" in particular,

Nabokov reflected in "Anniversary Notes" (1970): "I do love Chekhov dearly. I fail, however, to rationalize my feelings for him. I can easily do so in regard to the greater artist, Tolsto[i], with the flash of this or that unforgettable passage . . . , but when I imagine Chekhov with the same detachment all I can make out is a medley of dreadful prosaisms, ready-made epithets, repetitions, doctors, unconvincing vamps, and so forth; yet it is his works which I would take on a trip to another planet" (SO, 286–287).

A student of Russian literature is likely to disagree with some of Nabokov's assessments of Chekhov's achievement, such as the claim that Chekhov exemplifies that "a writer may be a perfect artist without being exceptionally vivid in his verbal technique or exceptionally preoccupied with the way his sentences curve" (LRL, 252). At the same time, a student of Nabokov cannot afford merely to rely on his admission of his Chekhovian lineage without a detailed comparative inquiry into Nabokov's response to Chekhov. Such a task is indeed challenging, for despite the voluminous scholarship on Chekhov, few critics have pinpointed what exactly constitutes Chekhov's unique achievement in Russian prose, particularly his status vis-à-vis both the nineteenth-century classics and the twentieth-century modernists (the situation is somewhat better with his plays).[4]

The groundwork for the Nabokov-Chekhov comparison has been done singlehandedly by Simon Karlinsky.[5] He deems meaningful Chekhov's and Nabokov's training and professional careers in biological sciences. In two articles Karlinsky demonstrates that both Chekhov and Nabokov represent the alternative tradition of biological humanitarianism as opposed to that of ideological humanitarianism prevalent in Russian culture.[6] Karlinsky insists that one cannot find in Chekhov's and Nabokov's writings any easily paraphrasable philosophical, sociological, or theological theories or viewpoints. More specifically, he indicates that Nabokov's short stories reveal numerous Chekhovian elements, on the level of both single plot stratagems and motifs or details of characterization.[7] Nabokov is said to have learned from Chekhov to end his stories at unconventional moments, as in "Podlets" (An Affair of Honor, 1927), in which he uses as a subtext Chekhov's "Duèl" (The Duel, 1891).[8]

In his Russian stories Nabokov went through a many-sided Chekhovian apprenticeship, and a number of his stories suggest Chekhovian subtexts. For instance, the early "Christmas" subtextualizes both "Toska" (Longing, 1886) and "Vragi" (The Enemies, 1887) with their abysses of a father's grief for his dead son, while the narrative tone of the early "Govoriat po-russki" (Russian Spoken Here, 1923) recalls a number of Chekhov's stories in which the first-person narrator discloses a protagonist's secret and speaks to the reader as a trusted friend ("Agaf'ia," 1886; "Moi razgovor s pochtmeisterom" [My Conversation with the Postmaster], 1886; "Son" [A Dream], 1885; "Shutochka" [A Little Joke], 1886). The opening passages of Chekhov's "Liubov'" (Love, 1886) may have suggested the style of Nabokov's "Beneficence" and especially "A Letter That Never Reached Russia," which is an address to the narrator's beloved. The highest number of allusions to Chekhov can be found in the feuilletonistic pieces from Nabokov's transitional Middle period. For instance, a failed "reunion" of former close friends in the famous "Tolstyi i tonkii" (Fat and Thin; 1883) is mirrored in Nabokov's "Reunion," where two brothers, an obese, successful Soviet engineer and a poor desolate Russian émigré, fail to communicate after many years of not seeing each other. A child's terror and bewilderment, presented with such psychological verisimilitude in the Putya Shishkov stories, "A Bad Day" and "Orache," has an antecedent in Chekhov's extraordinary short piece "Ustritsy" (The Oysters, 1884). "Breaking the News" echoes the Chekhovian irony of noncommunication at moments of extreme grief or joy; Chekhov's "The Enemies," among other stories, offers a likely structural model. Even "Terra Incognita," possibly a parody of a turn-of-the-century pulp-adventure story unique among Nabokov's works, seems to have a Chekhovian parallel. Like "Terra Incognita," Chekhov's "V more" (At Sea, 1883; rev. 1901) is also singular in his immense oeuvre: it reads like a Russian stylization of a Western thriller narrative. Finally, brief mention should be made of Nabokov's numerous variations on Chekhov's Russian *intelligent;* Nabokov said in the Cornell lectures that he "combined the deepest human decency of which man is capable with an almost ridiculous inability to put his ideals and principles into action; . . . frittering away his provincial existence in a haze of utopian dreams; knowing exactly what is good, what is worth while living for, but at the same time sinking lower and lower in the mud of a humdrum existence, unhappy in love, hopelessly inefficient in everything—a good man who cannot make good" (*LRL*, 253).

How well this applies to the protagonists of "Perfection," "Cloud, Castle, Lake" or "Vasiliy Shishkov"! Both Ivanov and Vasiliy Ivanovich are very close to Chekhov's Alëkhin from the short story "O liubvi" (About Love, 1898). Like Ivanov and Vasiliy Ivanovich, Alëkhin hopelessly loves a married woman he cannot have; both protagonists suffer and dwell on idealized memories.

As a way of demonstrating the "rather divine bond" between Chekhov and Nabokov (a quotation from Godunov-Cherdyntsev's imagined conversation with Koncheyev in *The Gift*), Karlinsky examines Chekhov's and Nabokov's critical reception and outlines a telling scheme.[9] Chekhov and Nabokov were viewed negatively and at times with hostility by the prevalent critical trends of their times and milieux, Chekhov by the radical critics of the 1880s (N. Mikhailovskii, A. Skabichevskii) and then by the turn-of-the century symbolists (Z. Gippius, D. Merezhkovskii); Nabokov by the postradical and postsymbolist Russian émigré critics of the 1920s and 1930s. Such parallel negative receptions occurred against the background of the writers' strong endorsements by their leading senior contemporaries: Lev Tolstoi, Nikolai Leskov, and Vladimir Korolenko for Chekhov and Aleksandr Kuprin, Mark Aldanov, and Evgenii Zamiatin for Nabokov.

Why did Chekhov and Nabokov fall prey to such similar criticisms, both in tone and in substance, from radical and conservative critics, from atheists and spiritualists? Both Chekhov and Nabokov were independent and nonpartisan. Both chose to profess the principle that a writer's politics should be his literature, and not vice versa. Chekhov and Nabokov both undermined the traditional Russian myths of the writer as an oracle and as a suffering subject. They opposed social and cultural collectivism, or what in Russian is called *gruppovshchina* (group action) on the part of an artist, and favored individual response. Both rejected organized religion and made their metaphysical beliefs private. Finally, in questioning the status quo of their contemporary societies and cultures, both Chekhov and Nabokov shared a common artistic nemesis, bourgeois *poshlost'* and self-satisfaction, the mortal enemies of artistic creation. Chekhov's lifelong desire to fight the philistine within oneself ("squeeze out the slave within thyself drop by drop") and Nabokov's appeal that "commonsense must be shot dead" (*LL*, 380) were two expressions of the same artistic credo.[10] Consider some parallels between Nabokov's and Chekhov's views of art and life as illustrated by their epistolary and discursive writings.

From Chekhov's letters: "'The City of the Future' will turn out a work of art only under the following conditions: 1. absence of unending word-eruptions on political, social, and economic subjects. . . ."[11] "All of our reviews are dominated by literary groups, by partisan boredom. It's suffocating!"[12] "I understand solidarity and some such things at the stock market, in politics, in religious affairs (a sect), etc., but solidarity among young littérateurs is impossible and unnecessary. . . . Let us be ordinary people, let us treat *everyone* the same, then we won't need the artificially inflated solidarity. At the same time, the insistence on private, professional, group solidarity, the kind that your people want, will create inevitable spying after each other, suspicion, control. . . ." [13] "I think that it is not for belletrists to solve such problems as God, pessimism, etc. The task of a belletrist is only to depict who, how, and under which circumstances, talked or thought of God and pessimism. An artist should be not a judge of his characters and what they say, but only an dispassionate witness." [14] "I am afraid of those who seek tendencies between the lines and who certainly want to see me as either liberal or conservative. I am neither liberal nor conservative. . . . I would like to be a free artist and only regret that God did not give me strength to be that. I hate lies and violence in all its forms. . . . This is why I feel no special sympathy for the police, the butchers, the scientists, the writers, the young people. I consider brand names and labels a prejudice. My most sacred things are the human body, health, intelligence, talent, inspiration, love and absolute freedom, being free of power and lies, whatever the latter two are represented by. This is a program which I would follow if I were a great artist." [15] "In my childhood I had a religious education . . . with choir singing, readings in church from the Gospels and Psalter, with punctual attendance at matins, with the obligation to help at the altar and to ring the bells. And the result? When I recall my childhood it appears rather gloomy to me. I have no religion now." [16] "Sometimes, you would be passing a concession stand in the third class, see cold fried fish cooked a while ago, and think to yourself: who needs such unappetizing fish? In the meantime there are people who need this fish and find it tasty. The same with Barantsevich's writings [K. Barantsevich, a belletrist popular in Chekhov's time]. He is a bourgeois writer, writing for a clean public which rides in the third class. For this public Tolstoi and Turgenev are too luxurious, aristocratic, a bit alien and hard to digest. . . . He is false . . . because bourgeois writers cannot help being false." [17]

From Nabokov's letters: "Zina, Zina [Zinaida Shakhovskaia], I am still afraid that you are on the wrong track, that you do not realize that kind human feelings, turbines, religion, 'spiritual demands,' 'responses to contemporary life' have nothing to do with writing prose and poetry. Let us be creators of fiction [*sochiniteliami*] first and foremost, Zina! I assure you that only one thing matters: it is, if you will excuse me, art. . . . Have you noticed the stinking Dobroliubovism [*dobroliubovshchina*, after N. A. Dobroliubov, Russian radical critic of the 1850s] and unctuousness [*eleinost'*] of our émigré criticism? This, of course, is only a poor anachronism in respect to the wild, triumphant philistinism (or 'learned Marxism') into which the ripe apple of Russian thought has deteriorated in Russia. . . . Likewise, when I read in French, I never touch anything that has even a drop of Catholicism (hence both Claudel and Mauriac are poisoned for me)."[18] "I want to repeat by way of self-vindication, that the only important thing is whether the book is well-written or not, and as to whether its author a rogue or a righteous chum is completely beside the point."[19] "I read in *Vozrozhdenie* [*The Rebirth*, a Parisian Russian newspaper] the Spanish impressions of Father Ioann [Father Ioann Shakhovskoi, Z. Shakhovskaia's brother, later the Russian Orthodox archbishop of San Francisco], and I must say that they disappointed me. I could not care less who is going to win in Spain, but the ease with which Russian pilots convert to Christianity makes me doubt the whole thing strongly [Nabokov is presumably talking about the Russian émigré pilots who fought on Franco's side during the Spanish Civil War]."[20]

Nabokov's views on philistinism and *poshlost'* are summed up in his lecture "Philistines and Philistinism" (*LRL*, 309–314). Chekhov is known to have remarked that a well-mannered person is not the one who notices that the person next to him has spilled gravy on the tablecloth, but the one who pretends not to notice it. Compare Chekhov's dictum with the following words of Nabokov: "I may use the terms *genteel* and *bourgeois*. Genteel implies the lace-curtain refined vulgarity which is worse than simple coarseness. To burp in company may be rude, but to say 'excuse me' after a burp is genteel and thus worse than vulgar" (*LRL*, 309). Nabokov understood the term "bourgeois" "following Flaubert, not Marx. *Bourgeois* in Flaubert is a state of mind, not a state of pocket." A bourgeois for him is a "smug philistine, a dignified vulgarian" (*LRL*, 309), and his use of the term is very close to Chekhov's own.

The parallels between Nabokov's and Chekhov's beliefs might explain some of the reasons why critics have reacted to the two writers in such similar fashions. Rather than continue the list of parallels, I would like to pause and examine one case of Chekhov's and Nabokov's reception, which is emblematic of the entire spectrum of accusations leveled against them. Students of Nabokov and Chekhov are likely to benefit from the fact that one critic managed to attack both writers singlehandedly. Zinaida Gippius (1869–1945), also a prominent poet and prosaist, launched a "crusade" against Chekhov soon after his death in 1904 and continued to criticize his writings throughout her émigré years.[21] Following the publication of Nabokov's works in the 1920s, Gippius, frequently writing criticism under her pen-name Anton Krainii (Anton the Extreme, possibly a pun on Anton Chekhov, whom Gippius saw as devoid of extremes, too "normal" a person and a writer, and an embodiment of "stasis"), assumed a similarly inimical stance toward Nabokov.[22] Her attempts at belittling Chekhov and Nabokov were as congruent as they were ill-grounded. Although a symbolist and a Christian metaphysician, she sided with Chekhov's earlier utilitarian materialist critics of the 1880s in voicing accusations against his writings as spiritually barren and therefore somehow alien to Russian letters.[23] As Karlinsky puts it, "Dostoevskii and Chekhov were for Gippius the opposing polarities of Russian literature, Dostoevskii representing its warmth, spirituality and humanity and Chekhov the cold of death, emptiness and indifference."[24] In fact, Gippius's criticism, along with an influential critique by Lev Shestov and Dmitrii Merezhkovskii's brochure *Chekhov and Gor'kii* (1906), continued to shape Chekhov's reception by a large share of the Russian intelligentsia into the second half of this century. Anna Akhmatova resented Chekhov's writings and reiterated Gippius's unfair accusations.[25] A characteristic statement along the same lines was made by Joseph Brodsky, one of "Akhmatova's orphans," in an American interview: "I'm just punning here, but he's not a metaphysician; he is a physician, in every sense of the word. . . . What Chekhov lacks is mental aggression, for me, I don't like him as a prose writer."[26] Of course, Brodsky is not "just punning" when he speaks of the alleged absence of a metaphysical dimension in Chekhov's prose. He has chosen to deny it. And it seems difficult to presuppose a lack of "mental aggression" in stories like "Palata No. 6" (Ward 6, 1892), "Step'" (The Steppe, 1888) and "Gusev."

The story of Gippius's negative reception of Nabokov is a fascinating one, for it begins in the decade when she was still actively involved in anti-Chekhovian activities. Upon reading Nabokov's first collection of verse, privately printed in 1916, Gippius told the writer's father that his son would "never be a writer."[27] Wrong though she was — each of Nabokov's subsequent publications earned him a higher place on the literary Olympus — Gippius persisted in denying the writer his due. Throughout the 1920s and 1930s she made occasional negative remarks about Nabokov. She and her husband, Dmitrii Merezhkovskii, were also the ideological center of a circle of Parisian littérateurs known as "Zelënaia lampa" (Green Lamp), several of whose members recoiled at the mere mention of Nabokov's name.[28]

The most embarrassing instance of Gippius's blind hostility toward Nabokov took place in 1930 in an article entitled "Literaturnye razmyshleniia" (Thoughts on Literary Topics). Published in the second issue of the Paris émigré review *The Numbers* — throughout its short history a bastion of anti-Nabokovians — Gippius's article contained a defense of Georgii Ivanov's vengeful and offensive critique of Nabokov.[29] In her "defense" of

Ivanov—brought about by the indignation of many émigré writers at his hostile and insulting review of Nabokov's works—Gippius drew a direct parallel between her own attacks on Chekhov and G. Ivanov's attack on Nabokov:

> In previous times such (and much more extreme) "opinions" would easily appear in all journals . . . and newspapers. Freedom of opinion was accepted, and even if the matter concerned not some Sirin [*ne o kakom-to Sirine*] but L. Andreev or Chekhov. And it . . . was objectionable to no one to state that, let's say, *Rech'* [The Speech] has "spilled mud on its pages" by printing X's opinion of L. Andreev as a "not very skillful conjurer," and *Den'* [The Day] has "disgraced itself" with Y's opinion of Chekhov, "this embodiment of stasis" [taken verbatim from Gippius's earlier essay "Fragrant Gray Hair"].
>
> Different times, different places, and look: a comparatively soft-spoken, if direct, article by G. Ivanov, written about no one else but such a mediocre writer as Sirin [*o takom posredstvennom pisatele, kak Sirin*], causes a storm of indignation. . . . Even Khodasevich could not help it, and he, with his fine literary sensibility, could not have been enchanted by such a poorly "made" novel as *The Defense*.[30]

Gippius managed to inject a very large dose of venom into two short paragraphs. She applied to Chekhov Ivanov's very dismissive and grave judgments of Nabokov, while implying ipso facto that Chekhov and Nabokov constitute an ongoing tradition in Russian letters, or an anti-tradition, as she would have it. Gippius was naturally not alone; she voiced an opinion prevalent in her cultural milieu, first the Russian decadent circles of the turn of the century whom Chekhov described as "zdoroven-neishie muzhiki" (here: burly peasants) because he thought their aestheticized psychic malaise was artificial,[31] later her own Parisian émigré literary circle, whose members Nabokov portrayed as "mystagogues [who] combined intellectual talent and moral mediocrity [and thirsted] for a creed as a jailed drug addict thirsts for his pet heaven" (*SM*, 284).

Gippius was not the only important literary figure to reject Chekhov. At least three of her major contemporaries—all of whom would later become émigrés—the existential philosopher Lev Shestov, the poet and critic Georgii Adamovich, and the writer-philosopher Dmitrii Merezhkovskii—also misconstrued the literary tradition which Chekhov started and Nabokov continued. In fact, it is hard to find any explanation other than some sort of collective critical stampede, an eclipse of critical sensibility, to account for such statements as Shestov's formula "singer of hopelessness" ("pevets beznadëzhnosti") in the essay "Tvorchestvo iz nichego" (Creation from the Void, 1904) and Adamovich's "all our traditions are severed in him" in the essay "Sirin" (1930).[32]

How could the "anti-Chekhovians"—turned anti-Nabokovians—not see that Chekhov connects the classical tradition of Gogol', Tolstoi, Turgenev, Saltykov-Shchedrin, and even Dostoevskii with the Russian twentieth century?[33] How could Gippius or Adamovich in the 1920s and 1930s fail to see that Nabokov's prose is the highest synthesis rather than an artistic and spiritual dead-end of Russian literary culture?

The critics of Chekhov and Nabokov perceived the two writers as alien bodies outside the great tradition of Russian letters, Chekhov as a "twilight" writer devoid of human verve and spirituality, Nabokov as a cynical Westerner merely writing in Russian. The anti-Chekhovians refused to recognize that Chekhov laid a foundation for a trend in Russian prose that, to borrow a term that John Burt Foster Jr. recently applied to Nabokov, may be called covert modernism.[34] As opposed to the overt modernism of Andrei Belyi or Fëdor Sologub, the innovators who broke away from the traditional structures of language and narrative to seek new artistic means to convey cataclysmic changes in Russian society, the Chekhov of the 1890s–1900s maintained the semblance of relying upon linguistic and some narrative conventions of Russian nineteenth-century prose.

Chekhov's double status as a bridge between Russian realist fiction of the 1850s–1880s and the fiction of early Russian modernism has not been emphasized enough in scholarship. On the one hand, as an heir to (and late contemporary of) the classics, Chekhov continued to construct his narratives upon the fundamental psycho-structural principle that René Girard calls "triangular desire."[35] This principle, exemplified by such works as Tolstoi's "Kreitserova sonata" (The Kreutzer Sonata, 1889) or Turgenev's "Stepnoi korol' Lir" (King Lear of the Steppe, 1870), demanded a three-corner conflict (be it adultery, rivalry, or war) which is conceived by the author in such a way as to give the narrative its movement and direction. Structures of nineteenth-century triangular desire shaped Chekhov's poetics throughout his career. This is true of most of his short fiction, from the early short novel "Drama na okhote" (The Shooting Party, 1885) to the late novella "Dom s mezoninom" (The House with the Mezzanine, 1896), and from the early story "Zhivoi tovar" (Live Goods, 1882) to the late "Anna na shee" (Anna on the Neck, 1895, continuing the adultery theme of Tolstoi's *Anna Karenina*, 1877). On the other hand, Chekhov's major narrative innovation in the genre of the Russian short story was to fling the plot open, to introduce the open ending. The open ending of a typical Chekhov story embodied his covert modernist attack on classical literary conventions that imposed a narrative structure upon the raw material of fiction. Instead, Chekhov let the material of art suggest the structure of the finished product. Defying narrative closure and allowing the reader to project her or his own resolution was a radical artistic move on Chekhov's part. Open-endedness reflected Chekhov's view that art, like life, does not require any plots and mixes everything, the profound with the quotidian, the tragic with the ludicrous.[36]

Several major literary figures among the modernists, including Aleksandr Blok and Andrei Belyi, stressed Chekhov's centrality in the history of Russian modernism.[37] In his brilliant obituary Belyi emphasized Chekhov's place as a continuous link between "fathers" and "sons."[38] Belyi wrote that Chekhov combined Tolstoian precise architecture of images ("otchëtlivost' i lepka obrazov") with symbolist ephemeral breath of Doom ("Rok") as it appears in Maurice Maeterlinck's works. He also likened Chekhov to another major Western modernist, Knut Hamsun: "[there is in Chekhov] gentle sadness and quiet joy as if even Doom were an illusion."[39] Belyi not only posited Chekhov as a bridge between the nineteenth-century classical tradition ("fathers") and twentieth-century modernism ("sons"), but also argued that Chekhov, like any great artist, transcended the boundaries of movements and trends. In connection with Chekhov's place vis-à-vis symbolism and realism, Belyi wrote: "Genuine symbolism coincides with genuine realism. Both are about the actual. Actuality is the deepest and primary quality of life. Relatively recently the realism of symbolism and the symbolism of realism were revealed [otkrylsia]. A truly deep artist can no longer be called either symbolist or realist in the old sense."[40] The Chekhovian synthesis of the classical and the modern continued in Nabokov's art. Therein lies the main difficulty for Nabokov's (and Chekhov's) critics. The anti-Nabokovians, Gippius and Adamovich alike, were perplexed and irritated because they could not put their finger on the precise nature of Nabokov's artistic and spiritual quest just as they had failed to do so with Chekhov. As a consequence, the critics could not pinpoint the shape of the relationship between humankind and the transcendent in the works of both the master and the disciple.[41]

Nabokov's covert modernism would be unthinkable without Chekhov as his predecessor. One of the major figures among the "sons," Nabokov continued Chekhov's quest for new forms that both enter into dialogue with and transform the Russian classical tradition.[42] In Chekhov's play *Chaika* (The Seagull, 1896), one of the main characters, the aspiring young writer Treplev, speaks of a need to create *novye formy* (new forms): "We need new forms. New forms are what we need, and if there are none, then it's better to have nothing" (Chekhov 12–13:8).[43] Despite the failure of Treplev's play-within-a-play, his metaliterary remarks are to be taken seriously as representing one side of a complex *fin de siècle* literary polemic occurring on the Russian literary stage. Treplev's mother, the famous actress Arkadina, whose only aesthetic credo is talent, qualifies her son's play as "something decadent," by no means a gratuitous remark. Also present on the stage is Arkadina's lover, the popular and successful belletrist Trigorin, a master of naturalist fiction. In the play Trigorin becomes the lover of the female protagonist, Nina Zarechnaia, a young actress and Treplev's beloved. On an allegorical level, the play's triangle of desire represents a competition between symbolism (as the new, modernist art) and naturalism (as the passing albeit still mighty tradition). At the end of the play, Treplev does succeed as a modernist writer but fails as a human being. One would like to believe that he has found in his art what another of *The Seagull*'s dramatis personae, Dr. Dorn, wishes Treplev to find after the failure of his early "decadent" play:

> . . . depict only the important and the eternal . . . if I were to experience the kind of spiritual loftiness that artists feel during creation, then, I think, I would despise my material shell and all that it entails, and rush high up and away from the Earth [*ot zemli podal'she v vysotu*]. . . . And one other thing. In a work of art there ought to be a clear, definite idea. You should know what you write for, or otherwise if you follow this artistic road without a definite goal, you will get lost and your talent will destroy you. (Chekhov 13:18–19)

Dr. Dorn belongs to the cohort of Chekhovian doctors who are privileged to share the authorial perspective. The ideal course in the challenging quest for new forms is a "golden mean," to use the expression of Chekhov's most recent Russian biographer, between Treplev's experimental modernist leanings and Trigorin's realism of a professional belletrist, between art's metaphysical "height" ("vysota") and representational and popular goals of fiction.[44] In different ways, Chekhov and Nabokov both found this golden mean in their covertly modernist prose.

For today's student of Nabokov's art, the task of delineating his cosmology is somewhat easier than for his contemporaries in the 1930s. We can now turn to Nabokov's authorial statements, including the ones he made in *Speak, Memory* and other discursive writings and interviews: "since in my metaphysics, I am a confirmed non-unionist and have no use for organized tours through anthropomorphic paradises, I am left to my own, not negligible devices when I think of the best things in life . . ." (*SM*, 297); ". . . I know more than I can express in words, and the little I can express would not have been expressed, had I not known more" (*SO*, 45). We also have at our disposal Véra Nabokov's seminal remarks on Nabokov's other-world (*potustoronnost*') in the introduction to the 1979 collected Russian poems. We may consult Vadim Vadimych's emblematic poem "Being in Love" from *Look at the Harlequins!* Finally, the research of the past decade has significantly advanced our understanding of the complex phenomenon of Nabokov's metaphysics.

Students of Nabokov know that metaphysics do not always lie on the surface of the writer's works and are not spoken about in transparent terms. Chekhov's metaphysics are subtle and require an effort to be detected. First and foremost they are manifest in the characters' quest for liberation from the routine of their mundane existence, their search for an ideal love, and the intimations of immortality which they experience in the course of their fiascoes. Metaphysics are hardly manifest in Chekhov's works to the same degree as in Nabokov's. The intimations of the otherworld—rarely exceeding the level of suggestion and symbol—are predicated upon Chekhov's ongoing exploration of the miracle of memory's transcendental powers. A number of stories and plays also reveal Chekhov's vision of death as a culmination of life's cognitive moments. Here is an excerpt from the middle of "Lady with a Lap Dog":

> In Oreanda they sat on a bench, not far from the church, looking silently at the sea down below. Yalta was hardly visible through the morning fog; white clouds stood motionless upon the mountain peaks. Leaves didn't stir on the trees, crickets screamed, and the monotonous, hollow sound of the sea coming up from below spoke of quietude, of the eternal sleep awaiting us all. The same sound could be heard from down below when there was no Yalta or Oreanda, and it was still heard now and would continue with the same indifference and hollowness when we were no longer around. And in this permanence, this sheer indifference to the life and death of each one of us, there lies, perhaps, the promise of our eternal salvation, of life's uninterrupted stride on earth, of continuous movement towards perfection. (Chekhov, 10:133)

The two people listening to the noise of the universe are Anna and Gurov soon after they have become lovers. The church in the foggy background signals Chekhov's connections with traditional Christian metaphysical beliefs and, simultaneously, his distance from institutions of Russian Orthodoxy. The concern with that concealed realm of "eternal sleep" betrays Chekhov's own unorthodox metaphysical quest. Much like the otherworldly experiences of Nabokov's characters, Chekhovian otherworldly intimations offer his characters a foretaste of idealized dreams and a chance to communicate with unattainable loved ones, among both the living and the dead. Consider the following examples.

In "Gusev" (1890), one of Chekhov's most memorable stories, the protagonist dies on board a vessel returning to Russia from the Far East by way of the Indian Ocean. According to the custom, Gusev's lifeless body is placed into a canvas sack and thrown overboard. The story ends with a magnificent description of the body's descent into the ocean, which, on a mythopoetic plane, breaks down the oppositions between life and death. As Gusev's body sinks deeper and deeper, the consciousness of the third-person narrator is joined with the eye and mind of Gusev, who is supposed to be dead: "He is rapidly sinking to the bottom. Will he ever reach it? They say it's four versts [1 verst equals 1.06 km] to the bottom. Having covered eight to ten sazhens [1 *sazhen'* amounts to 2.13 meters], he slows down, rocks back and forth, as if he is thinking of something, and then, drawn by the current, rushes to the side faster than downward" (Chekhov 7:338).

Then follows a passage describing Gusev's (Chekhov consistently refers to him as "Gusev" and not as "Gusev's body") encounter with tropical fish and with a "lazy" shark. In the story's final paragraph I see a perfect example of Chekhov's otherworld, a dimension that transcends mundane existence and resists translation into conventional terms:

> And above, at this very time, on the side where the sun sets, clouds roll themselves into various shapes; one cloud looks like Arc de Triomphe, another like a lion, a third like scissors. . . . From the clouds appears a broad green ray which stretches all the way to the middle of the sky; a little later falls a violet ray, a golden next to it, then a pink one. . . . The sky becomes a tender purple. Looking at this majestic, this enchanting sky, the ocean frowns at first, but soon it gains colors so tender, joyful, and passionate that the human tongue probably doesn't have the words to name them. (Chekhov 7:339)

In his deathbed delirium, Gusev sees serene clouds and visits his native Russian village. Given Chekhov's suggestive depiction of Gusev's descent into the element of the ocean, the reader is likely to wonder about the realm which Gusev has entered. A textual opening very similar to the one in "Gusev" is found in the ending of Nabokov's "Perfection," where

Ivanov also descends into the sea (death, closed ending) and enters a perfect otherworld (eternity, textual opening). In both cases, a textual opening compels the reader to ponder metaphysical issues.

A number of Chekhov's characters exhibit otherworldly linkages. These are often mentioned in passing, as in "Poprygun'ia" (The Grasshopper, 1892), where a momentary intimation of immortality ("dumala o tom, chto ona bessmertna i nikogda ne umrët" [she was thinking that she was immortal and she would never die]; Chekhov 8:15) serves as a sharp contrast to the otherwise philistine aura of the heroine. In several stories, including "Ionych" (1898), metaphysical undertones weigh heavily in the central scene. The male protagonist, the provincial physician Dr. Startsev, becomes privy to the otherworld only once, in the middle of the story, during the well-known cemetery scene.[45] The female protagonist, Ekaterina Ivanovna (Kotik), plays a joke on Dr. Startsev and asks him to meet her at eleven P.M. at the town cemetery. Startsev is torn between his bourgeois commonsense and his love for Kotik. Chekhov describes Startsev's experience at the cemetery:

> At first Startsev was struck by what he was seeing for the first time and would probably never see again: a world which was unlike anything else, a world where the moonlight was as fine and soft as though its cradle were right there, where there was no life, none at all, but where in every dark poplar, in every grave one felt the presence of a mystery promising a quiet, beautiful, and eternal life. From the gravestones and the withered flowers, mixing with the autumnal scent of leaves, there wafted forgiveness, sadness, and quietude. (Chekhov 10:31)

Initially, Startsev is deeply affected by his vision of the transcendent. Yet, as he starts thinking about it in the rational terms of a physician and businessman, the otherworld ceases to communicate with him. Instead, Startsev imagines himself dead, and "oblivion and quietude" are replaced by "the deaf longing of the beyond, the suppressed despair" (Chekhov 10:31). The complexity of the metamorphoses which occur in Startsev's consciousness can only be measured by the consequences of the cemetery scene. Fearing death, Startsev somehow comes to equate the intimation of a beautiful ethereal otherworld with the omens of an ugly anthropomorphic afterlife; he also desires Kotik and senses a feminine spectral presence at the cemetery. On the next day he proposes to Kotik, is rejected, and thereafter shuts off his feelings; he is soon transformed into a callous, greedy, and indifferent money-making machine. Startsev is unable to strike a balance between love's alluring indeterminacy, on the one hand,

and Mammon and the promise of a bourgeois status quo, on the other. At the end of this deeply felt Chekhovian drama, the occasional influxes of otherworldly memories remind the protagonist not of the beatitude and harmony to which he could have remained privy, but of a fatal mistake which he almost committed by succumbing to love.

Chekhov's experience with relating to the reader of short fiction a soul-to-soul, tete-à-tete human perception of the otherworld was emblematic for Nabokov, who saw a kindred spirit in Chekhov. To recall Belyi's essay, "Chekhov did not try to explain anything: he *looked and saw. His symbols are more refined, transparent, less deliberate."[46] The assessment of one of Russia's greatest modernists anticipates Nabokov's comment in the Cornell lectures about Chekhov's paradoxical literary achievement, particularly paradoxical for a Russian writer who is traditionally more concerned than a Western coeval with dotting the religious *is* and crossing the ethical *ts*. As a covert modernist, Chekhov betrays a tendency, growing ever stronger in his late works, that Nabokov described as reliance upon "the undercurrents of suggestion to convey a definite meaning" (*LRL*, 251). Chekhov's inferential, allusive communication with the reader is especially visible in his stories when a character undergoes a metaphysical experience.

Chekhovian traces are omnipresent in Nabokov's oeuvre. Throughout his bilingual and bicultural career, the shapes of his responses to Chekhov vary, assuming hypertextual forms of admiration, gentle mockery, polemics.[47] We find Chekhov in Nabokov's discursive writings, not only the American lectures but an unpublished Russian essay entitled "Chelovek i veshchi" (Man and Things, 1928), read in Berlin in the 1920s.[48] Chekhov preoccupied Nabokov throughout his long career in Russian and American letters (see Chekhov's photograph in Figure 13). From the 1920s to the 1970s, at various points and through different artistic mediums, Nabokov kept returning to his great predecessor. For instance, in *Mary* the old émigré poet Podtiagin has Chekhov's first name, Anton, and Pushkin's patronymic, Sergeevich. In *Glory* Martin "felt flattered by the infatuation of the English with Chekhov" (*Glory*, 162), while the protagonist of *The Eye* reads to his charges Chekhov's "Roman s kontrabasom" (A Romance with a Double Bass, 1886). The image of the jailer Rodion in *Invitation to a Beheading* recalls Nikitich in Chekhov's "Ward 6." In *The Real Life of Sebastian Knight* Sebastian hallucinates about "a black-robed monk moving swiftly toward him from the sky" (*RLSK*, 62)—a reference to Chekhov's short story "Chërnyi monakh" (The Black Monk, 1894). References to Chekhov are even found in the American fiction, including *Lolita,* where

13. Anton Chekhov, Melikhovo outside Moscow, 1897.

the nymphet studies *The Cherry Orchard* (*L*, 229), *Ada* ("consumptive Anton"; *Ada*, 498), and "That in Aleppo Once . . ." ("I come to you like that gushing lady in Chekhov who was dying to be described"; *Stories*, 560).

Nabokov's dialogue with Chekhov focused on the form of the short story. An open-ended short story, for which Chekhov is perhaps best known, did not satisfy Nabokov completely. He entered into a full-scale dialogue with a text that represented the height of Chekhov's own literary achievement in the genre of the short story, with an open ending and glimpses of the otherworld in the middle. "Lady with a Lap Dog" (1899), an icon of Chekhov's poetics and easily one of the world's ten most read short stories, elicits a long section in *Lectures on Russian Literature*, where it receives as much attention as "The Greatcoat" by Gogol' but more than Dostoevskii's *Crime and Punishment* or *The Idiot*. Nabokov contended that "in the typical Chekhov way the tale fades out with no definite full-stop but with the natural motion of life" (*LRL*, 262). He concluded that "all the traditional rules of story-telling have been broken in this wonderful story" (*LRL*, 262). Additionally, two of Nabokov's privileged protagonists, Martin of *Glory* and Sebastian of *The Real Life of Sebastian Knight*, love "Lady with a Lap Dog."

For accuracy's sake, I should say that Nabokov's first attempt at a large-scale dialogue with Chekhov came in 1927 when he wrote "An Affair of Honor." At the end of "An Affair of Honor" the protagonist, Anton Petrovich, who has Chekhov's first name, fails to appear at his own duel and sits in his room devouring a ham sandwich; no resolution follows in the story, and the ending is an open one in a Chekhovian fashion. Later, in a 1966 preface to the English text in *Nabokov's Quartet*, Nabokov confessed that " 'An Affair of Honor' renders, in a drab expatriate setting, the degradation of a romantic theme whose decline had started with Chekhov's magnificent story 'The Duel'" (*NQ*, 9; cf. *Stories*, 645). "A degradation of a decline" did not provide sufficient motivation for Nabokov to create a masterpiece. "An Affair of Honor" abounds in fine Chekhovian details and adopts an open-ended structure, but it lacks both the psychological depth of "The Duel" and the ephemeral suggestiveness of Chekhov's modern tragedy-in-passing. Nabokov had to wait another decade before engaging in a challenging dialogue with Chekhov, which constituted an act of creative rereading and rewriting of "Lady with a Lap Dog."

Composed in Berlin in April 1936 and published soon thereafter in *Contemporary Annals*, "Spring in Fialta" belonged—by Nabokov's own admission—to "the leading troika" of his short stories (the other two being "Cloud, Castle, Lake" and "The Vane Sisters").[49] Nabokov also referred to it as an "exemplary" short story such as "Lady with a Lap Dog" and Kafka's "The Metamorphosis."[50] After exploring the significance of Yalta and the Riviera in Chekhov's and Nabokov's lives and in informing the setting and events of the two stories, I will discuss the remarkable structural parallels but also some differences indicative of Nabokov's dialogue with Chekhov's story. My next step will be to trace a series of key verbal motifs originating in the text of "Lady with a Lap Dog" and then resurfacing in "Spring in Fialta." Following some brief comments about the narrators in both stories, I will concentrate on the core of Nabokov's dialogue with Chekhov: their different understanding of the nature of love. Nabokov's vision of love as otherworldly and fatidic compelled him to offer an alternative to the ending in "Lady with a Lap Dog," the ending that corresponds to Chekhov's own view of love as earthly and open-ended.

Yalta, the Crimean resort which provides a setting for "Lady with a Lap Dog," helps to reconstruct the biographical background for Nabokov's dialogue with Chekhov. "Spring in Fialta" is set in a fictitious resort whose name Boyd decoded as Crimean Yalta plus Adriatic Fiume (*Fi-* + *-alta*).[51] In the Russian text, Nabokov's narrator is willing to offer a clue to Fialta's fictional status:

> Я этот городок люблю; потому-ли, что во впадине его названия мне слышится сахаристо-сырой запах мелкого, тёмного, самого мятого из цветов, [the Russian word for "violet" is *fialka*] и не в тон, хотя внятное, звучание Ялты.... (*VF*, 8)

(the English version, published in *Harper's Bazaar* in 1947, changes Yalta into "lovely Crimean town": I am fond of Fialta; I am fond of it because I feel in the hollow of those violaceous syllables the sweet dark dampness of the most rumpled of small flowers, and because the alto-name of a lovely Crimean town is echoed by its viola . . . ; *Stories*, 413)

Fiume (now Rijeka), a city on the Dalmatian Riviera (currently part of Croatia), was among the earliest memories recorded by Nabokov. In the summer of 1904 the Nabokovs stayed in the resort town of Abbazia (Opatija), a short distance from Fiume, in a villa with a "crenellated, cream-colored tower" (*SM*, 75).[52] During the same summer the Nabokovs also stayed in Beaulieu on the French Riviera, which may have resulted in a superimposition of two sets of childhood memories, of the Adriatic and of the French Riviera. Prior to 1937, when Nabokov moved to the Côte d'Azur for almost two years, he had not seen much of the French Riviera. There were the even earlier memories of seeing Nice in 1903, the 1904 summer stay in Beaulieu, and then a short stop in Nice in 1923 en route back to Berlin after a summer in Solliès-Pont in Provence.[53] Thus, when Nabokov was writing "Spring in Fialta" in Berlin in 1936, he had to rely on his imagination interacting with a palimpsest of memories in which the Adriatic Fiume is conflated with those parts of the French Riviera (Nice) which he had seen by that point. Conversely, in 1942, when Nabokov was editing and improving on Peter A. Pertzoff's literal translation from the Russian, he had already seen most of the French Riviera—including Cannes, Cap d'Antibes, and Menton—during the long stay there in 1937–1938.[54] The Russian text never mentions the word "Riviera"; nor does it give any other overt geographic or ethnographic references, thereby maintaining Fialta as first and foremost a fictional resort composed of blended memories. Conversely, the English text adds a number of specific references, such as the adjective "Dalmatian" to refer to a local shopkeeper or the word "Riviera" itself, which launches a series of more or less specific associations. The word "Riviera" appears twice in the English text where it is absent in the original. The female protagonist is said to surface outside Fialta on "a Riviera beach" (*Stories*, 424); later Fialta is divided into two parts, one of which is called "the Riviera part of Fialta" (*Stories*, 426). In English the term "Riviera" is customarily used to describe the Côte d'Azur in France. However, "Riviera" also means a warm coastal resort area and could, therefore, refer to the Adriatic coast of Dalmatia and even the Crimean coast.

Other geographical references in the English text heighten the fictional ambiguity of Fialta's locale. In the Russian text the protagonist/narrator learns of the death of his beloved at a train station in Milan, which becomes "Mlech" in translation. No such place as Mlech is found in any world gazetteers. At the same time, Mlech could be Nabokov's variant of Mletci (Mleci), the Croatian word for Venice.[55] Elsewhere, the protagonist sees his brother off to Vienna, which in the English text becomes Posen, the German name of the Polish city of Poznan. The night express which the protagonist takes to Fialta becomes "Capparabella express" (*Stories*, 413), Capparabella being Nabokov's invention. Thus, the English text increases the Russian version's ambiguity of setting. Fialta could be understood as a fictitious resort somewhere in southern Europe on the Mediterranean coast. Certain archetypal features of any Mediterranean resort town—Nice, Menton, Ospedalotti, or Abbazia—are blended to create a sense of unrecognizable familiarity, warranted in part by the fact that any two coastal resorts in southern Europe should have something in common.

Like Nabokov, Chekhov also enjoyed a special relationship with the Mediterranean coast. He was on the Riviera four times, in March–April 1891, in September 1894, in the winter of 1897–1898, and in December 1900. While each of the trips involved a stay in Nice, the most important trip for the Nabokov-Chekhov dialogue came in 1894, when Chekhov went from Vienna to Abbazia, Trieste, Fiume, Venice, Milan, Genoa, and Nice (Fiume, Venice, and Milan figure in the Russian and English versions of "Spring in Fialta").[56] The ambiance of the Riviera resort towns found its way into Chekhov's fiction in 1895 in the short story "Ariadna" and four years later in "Lady with a Lap Dog."

Nabokov had insufficient firsthand experience of the Riviera when creating his recognizably fictional resort and utilized his predecessor's experience of conflating attributes of the Crimean and the Mediterranean coasts in the language and setting of a Russian short story. Chekhov's artistic method blended his own recollections with layers of collective memory stored in the language. In July 1888 the twenty-eight-year-old Chekhov went to Yalta to stay at the dacha of his publisher, Aleksei Suvorin. In a letter to his sister, M. P. Chekhova, Chekhov describes his fresh impressions of the Crimea:

> Looking at the shore from aboard the ship, I realized why it hasn't yet inspired a single poet or given a plot to any decent artist-belletrist. Doctors and wealthy ladies advertise it, and that's its main strength. Yalta is a cross of something European, resembling pictures of Nice, with something tacky and country-fairish. Box-like hotels full of miserable withering consumptives, insolent Tartar mugs, bustles with shameless expressions of something vile, those faces of lazy rich men seeking three-penny adventures, the smell of perfume instead of cedar and the sea, a pitiful, seedy pier, melancholy lights far away in the sea, the chatter of young ladies and their suitors who came here from all over the place to enjoy nature but about which they know nothing, all this makes such a dull impression and affects you so strongly that you begin to accuse yourself of preconceived notions and partiality.[57]

Chekhov's social criticism aside, the most remarkable detail in the letter is that it had been written before he actually saw Nice, to which he compares Yalta. Chekhov's artistic intuition prompted him to conclude that Yalta as an emblem of Crimean resorts and Nice as a paradigm of the tourist's French Riviera must have a great deal in common. Nabokov's decision to conflate Yalta and Fiume by creating Fialta, a fictional southern seaside resort par excellence, is genetically related to Chekhov's Riviera-like Yalta. As the reader is bound to notice, both space and time in Fialta conflate the past and the present; we have two towns within one as well as two "interlaced" times, the linear historical time and the spiral time of memory. Mindful of Chekhov's earlier experience, Nabokov created a fictional resort that hosted exiles whose lives conflated lofty memories of Russia and the quotidian realia of Europe.[58]

The composition of the plot in "Spring in Fialta" mirrors that of "Lady with a Lap Dog" and enters into dialogue with it. Set in a popular seaside resort, conflating fiction and fact, both stories contain parallel triangles of desire, each involving a married couple and a lover, who is also married. Gurov and Vasen'ka (Victor), the male adulterers in the stories, share a great deal. They are middle-aged, educated, and financially comfortable, and their lifestyles involve traveling. Both have an artistic streak: Gurov is said to have studied operatic singing, and Vasen'ka works for a film company and deals with artists. They even share a connection to writing. Gurov studied philology at the university; Vasen'ka is well versed in literature and expresses strong opinions about contemporary authors. Both are married and have children. Vasen'ka's family is said always to be present "in the clear north of [his] being" ("na iasnom severe moego estestva"; *Stories*, 414/VF, 8). After Gurov sees Anna off, he thinks to himself: "Pora i mne na sever" (It's time for me to go back north too; Chekhov 10:135). Later, when Gurov returns to Moscow, it is already winter in his hometown ("uzhe vsë bylo po-zimnemu"; Chekhov 10:135).

Gurov and Vasen'ka also share a spectrum of associations and perceptions. One phenomenon of their shared vision is the motif of pity/pitifulness ("zhalost'," "zhalkii" in the Russian), which colors Gurov's and Vasen'ka's meetings with Anna and Nina. In "Lady with a Lap Dog" Gurov recollects the details of his first day with Anna while thinking to himself: "Chto-to v nei est' zhalkoe vsë-taki" (There is something pitiful about her; Chekhov 10:130). While the term never recurs in the story, Anna's inner struggle, her unhappiness with adultery, upsets Gurov: "he was irritated by this naïve tone, by repentance, so unexpected and out of place" (Chekhov 10:133). Vasen'ka writes about his state of mind right after he and Nina have made love for the first time: "i tak kak ia eshchë ne umel chuvstvovat' tu boleznennuiu *zhalost'*, kotoraia otravliala moi vstrechi s Ninoi, ia byl, veroiatno, sovershenno vesel (uzh ona-to navernoe byla vesela) [italics added]"; cf. the English: "and as I did not yet realize the presence of that growing morbid pathos which was to embitter so my subsequent meetings with Nina, I was probably quite as collected and carefree as she was" (*VF,* 18/*Stories,* 420). While editing a draft of the translation, Nabokov corrected Pertzoff's literal "that morbid pity which later poisoned my meetings with Nina."[59]

Although Nabokov's heroine, Nina, in effect takes her affair the opposite way, is too light and carefree, the reader is reminded of her underlying structural connection to Chekhov's Anna. First of all, their first names, Anna and Nina, are phonetically similar since they share three out of four letters. Second, the two women have no children in their marriages. Third, they look a little bit alike: both narrators mention their being small and slender.

Both Chekhov and Nabokov offer very detailed characteristics of the deceived husbands, Anna's von Driderits and Nina's Ferdinand. Ferdinand might be a partial Nabokovian anagram of Driderits (*erd . . . d* cf. *d . . . der*). Driderits is a Russian civil servant of German extraction, a recurrent motif in Chekhov's text (cf. the officer Tuzenbakh in *The Three Sisters* or the zoologist von Koren in "The Duel," both texts well known to Nabokov). Ferdinand is a "Franco-Hungarian writer" (*Stories,* 420). However, given the historical time frame of the story's events (1917 plus fifteen years that have passed since the Bolshevik Revolution = 1932), Ferdinand must have been born at the turn of the century as a subject of the Austro-Hungarian Empire, hence his sharing the "royal" name of the assassinated Archduke Ferdinand. Thus, we have two deceived husbands who exhibit traits of foreignness (German, Austro-Hungarian) vis-à-vis their Russian wives (Anna, Nina) and their Russian lovers (Gurov, Vasen'ka).

Despite these parallels, however, one notices a partial reversal of narrative functions between Gurov of "Lady with a Lap Dog" and Nina of "Spring in Fialta." *Mutatis mutandis,* in Nabokov's story Nina's character recalls that of Gurov and Vasen'ka's that of Anna. Gurov and Nina take the lead in the affairs with Anna and Vasen'ka, who are passive lovers. Nina seduces Vasen'ka during one of their chance meetings arranged by fate or doom: "'Ferdinand has gone fencing,' she said conversationally; her eyes rested on the lower part of my face as if she were lip-reading, and after a moment of reflection (her amatory comprehension was matchless), she turned and rapidly swaying on slender ankles led me along the sea-blue carpeted passage" (*Stories,* 419). In "Lady with a Lap Dog" Gurov and Anna also consummate their affair in Anna's hotel room, although it is Gurov who takes the initiative: "'Let's go to your room,' he uttered quickly, and they began to walk fast. Her room was stuffy and smelled of perfume . . ." (Chekhov 10:131). Both Gurov and Nina have a long history of adulteries which began soon after each was married/engaged, Gurov as a second-year university student, Nina as a seventeen-year-old Russian *baryshnia*. She has had a number of lovers and, at least on the surface, experiences no pangs of conscience over her infidelities. Nina and Gurov are both sociable and lively in the company of the opposite sex. Chekhov's narrator makes an explicit comment about Gurov's interactions with men and women: "Men bored him and made him weary; he was reserved and cold around them; however, when he was with women, he felt free and knew what to talk about and how to carry himself, and even being quiet was easy in women's company. There was something in his appearance, character, his entire demeanor, something attractive and fleeting, which attracted women to him, made them want him; he, too, knew it, and some force drew him to women" (Chekhov 10:128–129).

Nina is also charged with this evanescent attractiveness, which lures men to her wherever she may be. Here is Vasen'ka's assessment of the circle of people who surrounded Ferdinand and Nina: "Among these I recall: an artist with an impeccably bald though slightly chipped head, . . . a poet . . . a humble business man who financed surrealist ventures (and paid for the *apéritifs*) . . . a pianist . . . a jaunty but linguistically impotent Soviet writer . . . ; there were several other gentlemen present who have become confused in my memory, and doubtless two or three of the lot had been intimate with Nina. She was the only woman at the table . . ." (*Stories,* 421–422). Except for the two brief scenes where Nina is shown with Vasen'ka's wife, Elena, no other women at all appear on the narrative stage together with Nina. Very telling is the composition of the scene in Ferdinand's favorite Parisian café. Soon after they have become lovers, Nina and Vasen'ka enter the café, where Ferdinand and his crowd are already drinking. This affords Vasen'ka, who is the narrator, a cinematic perspective of the scene which is both that of an insider (point-of-view shots) and an outsider (the sense of spatial totality):

> An orchestra of women was playing when we entered the café; first I noted the ostrich thigh of a harp reflected in one of the mirror-faced pillars, and then I saw the composite table . . . at which, with his back to the plush wall, Ferdinand was presiding. . . . Having forsaken the two or three obvious haunts where naive amateurs of Montparnassian life would have expected to find him, he had started patronizing this perfectly bourgeois establishment because of his peculiar sense of humor, which made him derive ghoulish fun from the pitiful *spécialité de la maison*—this orchestra composed of half a dozen weary-looking, self-conscious ladies interlacing mild harmonies on a crammed platform and not knowing, as he put it, what to do with

their motherly bosoms, quite superfluous in the world of music. (*Stories*, 421)

The all-female band performing for a group of Ferdinand's cohorts, among whom Nina was the "only woman at the table," enhances the sense of Nina's singularity in the world of men. In addition, the café scene may contain an allusion to Chekhov's scene in the provincial opera house where Gurov comes to seek Anna. There, too, we find mentions of a poor orchestra ("pod zvuki plokhogo orkestra") with its philistine violins ("obyvatel'skikh skripok"; Chekhov 10:139). But most importantly, in both scenes we find the spatial actualization of the basic triangular intrigue. Gurov, Anna, and Driderits on the one hand and Nina, Vasen'ka, and Ferdinand on the other are placed within the same enclosed physical space with solid lines of desire stretching, respectively, between Gurov and Anna and Nina and Vasen'ka, and dotted lines of matrimony between Anna and Driderits and Nina and Ferdinand.

Vasen'ka, who is made to be a little like Anna, presents himself as fairly timid and reserved. Living his life "in a kind of a continuous stumble," he experiences some moral qualms and a vague sense of loyalty to his wife and children.[60] Although Vasen'ka does not make it explicit, it seems likely that the affair with Nina is his first and only one. As for Anna, she confesses to Gurov right after they have become lovers that it is her first affair. In fact, in Anna's initial perception of what happened, she stands as a "durnaia zhenshchina" (fallen woman; Chekhov 10:132–133). The "morbid pathos" ("boleznennaia zhalost'") which embitters Vasen'ka's meetings with Nina might have been inherited not only from Gurov's perception of Anna as having "something pitiful about her" ("chto-to zhalkoe"), but also directly from Anna, who cannot reconcile her love for Gurov with a morbid sense of guilt for her "fall." Vasen'ka's perception of his relationship with Nina as a priori doomed and hopeless ("and our romance was even more hopeless than it had ever been"; *Stories*, 429) echoes Anna's own belief that the affair with Gurov should never have happened ("We are saying goodbye forever, because that's the way it ought to be, since we shouldn't have met in the first place"; Chekhov 10:135).

In addition to the parallels and differences between the main characters of the two short stories, the nuanced depth of the dialogue between "Spring in Fialta" and "Lady with a Lap Dog" can be traced if one follows a number of parallel verbal motifs in both stories (see Table 1).

In addition to verbal motifs, a number of situation rhymes (hotel room scenes; theater/music hall scenes, etc.) connect "Spring in Fialta" with

Table 1: Parallel in Verbal Motifs
"Lady with a Lap Dog" and "Spring in Fialta"

Motif	"Lady with a Lap Dog"	"Spring in Fialta"
1. pity	что-то в ней есть жалкое (there is something pitiful about her)	болезненн[ая] жалость, которая отравляла мои встречи с Ниной (that growing morbid pathos which was to embitter my subsequent meetings with Nina)
2. boredom	а между тем здесь такая скука (by the way it's so boring here)	весна в Фиальте облачна и скучна (spring in Fialta is cloudy and dull)
3. fate	это хорошо, что я уезжаю, — говорила Анна Гурову. — это сама судьба (it's good that I am leaving, Anna said to Gurov, this is fate)	ещё меньше понимаю, чего от нас хотела судьба (and still less do I understand what was the purpose of fate in bringing us constantly together)
4. staircases/ ascending and descending stairs	и они оба шли бестолково, по коридорам, по лестницам, то поднимаясь, то спускаясь (and they both walked in some frenzy down corridors, now ascending, now descending stairs)	и у поворота лестницы в гостинице ...: собиралась вниз, держа ключ в руке ... и меня повела (on the landing of a hotel . . . waiting for the elevator to take her down, a key dangling from her fingers . . . led me along)
		нам понравилась старая каменная лестница, и мы полезли вверх, и я смотрел на острый угол Нининого восходящего шага (we were attracted by an old stone stairway, and we climbed up and I kept looking at the sharp angle of Nina's step as she ascended)
5. humidity/ flowers	его обдало запахом и влагой цветов (he felt a humid scent of flowers)	всё мокро ... сахаристо-сырой запах ... самого мелкого из цветов (everything is damp . . . the sweet dark dampness of the most rumpled of small flowers)

(continued)

Motif	"Lady with a Lap Dog"	"Spring in Fialta"
6. north/ northerners	пора и мне на север (it's time for me to head back north too)	дома ... на ясном севере моего естества (at home ... in the clear north of my being)
7. inkwells	и была на столе чернильница серая, от пыли, со всадником на лошади, у которого была поднята рука со шляпой, а голова отбита (on the desk there stood an inkwell, gray with dust, with a horseman mounted on a horse, his raised hand holding a hat and his head broken off)	каменное подобие горы св. Георгия с чёрным туннелем у подножия, оказавшимся отверстием чернильницы, и со сработанным в виде железнодороаных рельсов жолобом для перьев (a dreadful marble imitation of Mount St. George showing a black tunnel at its base, which turned out to be the mouth of an inkwell, and with a compartment for pens in the semblance of railroad tracks)
8. playbills	ему бросилась в глаза афиша с очень крупными буквами: шла в первый раз „Гейша" (a playbill with very big letters caught his eye: "Geisha" was playing for the first time)	к афишной доске, на которую были наклеены гусар, укротитель в усах и оранжевый тигр (their backs against a circus billboard, which depicted a red hussar and an orange tiger of sorts)
9. lilac color	вода была сиреневого цвета (water was the color of lilac)	пахнуло ... сиреневатой сизостью (to inhale ... the dregs of the hazy blue morning street)[сиреневый literally means color of lilac]
10. bodily warmth	плечи, на которых лежали его руки, были теплы (the shoulders whereupon his hands rested were warm)	но камень был, как тело, тёплый (but the stone was as warm as flesh) от неё шло знакомое тепло (she diffused a familiar warmth)

Note: Capitalization and markers of direct speech have been omitted.

"Lady with a Lap Dog" paradigmatically. Even the change of seasons in "Spring in Fialta" involves both partial reversal and recollection of Chekhov's story. In "Lady with a Lap Dog" the lovers first meet in the fall, the so-called velvet season both in the Crimea and on the Mediterranean coast. At the train station in the Crimea Gurov senses the imminence of the cold season and his return to Moscow, where it is already winter: "uzhe pakhlo osen'iu, vecher byl prokhladnyi" (fall was in the air, the evening was chilly; Chekhov 10:135). All the other meetings between Gurov and Anna in the story occur in winter in European Russia. However, memories of the warm Yalta climate and its semitropical flora create a contrast with a decidedly winter landscape of Moscow: "Old limes and birches, white with rime, look so dear, they are closer to one's heart than cypresses and palms, and around them one doesn't feel like thinking of the mountains and sea" (Chekhov 10:135–136). In Nabokov's story the time of the central episode is, of course, spring in the synthetic Mediterranean Fialta with its cypresses, mountains (Mount St. George), and sea. There are, however, signals which suggest, time and again, that Nabokov is continuing his dialogue with Chekhov. Nabokov wants to maintain the recognizable presence of "Lady with a Lap Dog" in his own text and yet keep a certain distance from it. When Vasen'ka steps out on the balcony after making love with Nina for the first (and possibly last) time, he feels "a combined smell of dry maple leaves and gasoline" ("pakhnulo . . . benzinom, osennim klenovym listom"; *Stories*, 419–420/ *VF*, 18; the English text omits the word "autumn" in "autumn maple leaves," which mirrors and mimics Chekhov's "pakhlo osen'iu" [fall was in the air]. Nabokov's dialogue with his predecessor over the perfect form of a short story extended to all the dimensions of writing: tropes, rhythm, plot, structure of closure, and narrative mode.[61]

While "Spring in Fialta" maintains the same fundamental triangle of desire as "Lady with a Lap Dog," the mode of narration in Nabokov's story is much more complex and fascinating for a narratologist. Chekhov's clear-cut linear narrative time gives way to Nabokov's spiral time.[62] Vasen'ka, Nabokov's first-person autobiographical narrator in "Spring in Fialta," creates a spiral mode of narrating the story of his relationship with Nina.[63] In this spiral narrative the composite resort of Fialta serves as the cumulative span of the coil to which the narrative returns after each round of recollections of the past. One notices the presence of such structures in other works by Nabokov, both novels (*Mary, The Defense*) and short stories ("The Return of Chorb," "The Circle"). Several of his works with spiral structures exhibit a common denominator: the characters' attempts to come to terms with their memories. "Lady with a Lap Dog" starts in Yalta, where it reaches its first climax, continues in Moscow with a second culmination in S. (the provincial city where Anna lives with her husband), and then returns to Moscow again, where it comes to an open ending. Yalta, as the only locale where Anna and Gurov were perfectly alone, fills their subsequent meetings and times apart with idealized memories. Yalta figures in their dreams, but not in the actual events following their departures for the north. Conversely, "Spring in Fialta" opens in Fialta, where Vasen'ka and Nina have their last meeting, which becomes the spatial final point of Nina's and Vasen'ka's prolonged affair; Nina dies in a car crash in the vicinity of Fialta. The largest portion of the narrative unravels in Fialta within the course of one day, while the rest of Nina's and Vasen'ka's history is narrated in framed inserts or digressing flashbacks.[64] One notices that all of the meetings between Nina and Vasen'ka are chance ones, "zaslugi sud'by" (fate's . . . services; *VF*, 10–11/*Stories*, 415). While the map of Anna and Gurov's love affair only includes three points, Vasen'ka and Nina meet all over Europe: first in Russia, then in France, Germany, on the Riviera, and so forth. Vasen'ka and Nina never try to arrange their meetings, never plan them, but the meetings recur with chance regularity. On the contrary, after Gurov's visit to S., the lovers' meetings acquire a design of planned regularity: Anna visits Moscow once every two to three months and stays in the same hotel (the famous Slavianskii Bazar in the center of Moscow). Anna and Gurov even employ a special private message code: upon checking into the hotel, Anna "sent a man in a red hat to summon Gurov. Gurov saw her in the hotel, and no one in Moscow knew about it" (Chekhov 10:141).

Chekhov employs a transparent third-person omniscient narrator with occasional moments of free indirect discourse at culminative points when the narrator's consciousness leaps out to merge with Gurov's. Nabokov admired Chekhov's unobliging and suggestive narrator and even quoted the famous ending in his Cornell lectures (*LRL*, 262). Still, in the case of "Spring in Fialta," he set out to create an unmistakably Nabokovian narrator whose complexity exceeds, perhaps, even that of *The Gift*, with which the story exhibits several connections. My primary concerns here are with the ways Chekhov's and Nabokov's narrators obtain the information and with the relationship between the implied author and the narrator. In "Lady with a Lap Dog" Chekhov's narrator does not make any pretense of not being omniscient. He offers no explanation about the way he obtains the information which he offers to the reader. At times, he joins with Gurov and presents the events as observed through Gurov's eyes, from Gurov's vantage point. An example of such a presentation of events is found in the scene where Gurov and Anna first meet. Dining outside, Gurov observes that "a woman wearing a beret was walking unhurriedly towards the next table. Her face, her gait, dress, hairdo told him that she came from good society, was married . . ." (Chekhov 10:129). Another example where the narrator's visual perspective merges with Gurov's is the scene at the opera house, where Gurov eyes the crowd hoping to find Anna. At other times, and naturally when the narrator recounts the history of Gurov's love life, the visual perspective, overarching and omniscient, is devoid of a vantage point. Chekhov's omniscient narrator claims to know all and yet retains the services of his protagonist. Additionally, the narrator tends to lose sight of a visual vantage point only to restore it at the end of a passage. In sum, Gurov is *not* the only eye of Chekhov's narrator.

The exquisite opening paragraph of "Spring in Fialta" creates an overarching narrative perspective whereby the reader is offered a panoramic aerial view of Fialta and its environs (no wonder a reference is made to tourist postcards of Mount St. George) along with information about the weather. In the opening paragraph the narrator is still in the making: his vantage point has not been established. However, as early as the first line of the second paragraph, Nabokov gives the reader a clue to understanding his first-person narrator: "Imenno v odin iz takikh dnei raskryvaius', kak glaz, posredi goroda na krutoi ulitse . . ." (*VF*, 7). A literal rendition of this clause reads: "On just such a day, I open like an eye in the midst of a town on a steep street." [65] Nabokov opted for a different translation: "It was on such a day in the early thirties that I found myself, all my senses wide open, on one of Fialta's steep little streets" (*Stories*, 413). The word *glaz* (eye) is the focus here. While artistically superior, Nabokov's English obliterates somewhat the emphasis of the original Russian on Vasen'ka's being the perceiving (eyeing) narrator. Three words in the Russian establish the narrative perspective: "raskryvaius' kak glaz." "Raskryvaius'" (I open, I unfold), an imperfective verb in the first personal singular present tense, tells the reader that a first-person narrator is taking over the narration. "Kak glaz" (like an eye) signals the importance of the narrator's ocular, point-of-view, perspective. From this point on the reader perceives the narrated events, both present (unfolding in Fialta) and past (the history of Vasen'ka and Nina), from Vasen'ka's visual vantage point, the way Vasen'ka has witnessed them.

In "Spring in Fialta" Nabokov's narrator functions as an authorial representative, with whom the author shares his own world-vision and innermost experiences. [66] A diminutive form of Vasiliy, Vasen'ka's name signals his genetic connection with Vasiliy Ivanovich of "Cloud, Castle, Lake" and Vasiliy Shishkov of the eponymous short story. In "Cloud, Castle, Lake" Nabokov and his representative, Vasiliy Ivanovich, are capable of recognizing otherworldly patterns in the landscape. Likewise, Vasiliy Shishkov partakes of his narrator's (creator's) view of exile as a metaphysical condition. For a number of Nabokov's representatives, love is an otherworldly state in harmony with Vadim Vadimych's emblematic poem "Being in Love" from *Look at the Harlequins!* The otherworld, in whatever shape it reveals itself to Nabokov's representatives—be it Vasiliy Ivanovich's triad of a cloud, a lake, and a castle or Martin's Zoorland in *Glory*—offers them a chance to be with their distant beloved women. In order to understand Vasen'ka's status as both Nabokov's representative and first-person narrator, let us examine how the otherworldly vision of love influences the structures of desire in the story.

Nabokov wrote "Spring in Fialta" as a breather from working on his penultimate Russian novel, *The Gift.* Fyodor Godunov-Cherdyntsev, the protagonist of *The Gift,* and Vasen'ka of "Spring in Fialta" exhibit several connections. Also partially congruent, as signaled by their name patterns, are the women Vasen'ka and Fyodor love, Nina and Zina. In *The Gift* fatidic otherworldly love becomes the source of blissful happiness, bringing the two lovers together in marriage and allowing Fyodor to become a great writer and create his first masterpiece, the novel *The Gift.* Conversely, in "Spring in Fialta" Nabokov tests a tragic possibility: although the relationship with Nina allows Vasen'ka to realize his artistic potential, the two *innamorati,* unlike Fyodor and Zina at the end of *The Gift,* can never be permanently together in this world.[67]

Vasen'ka's meetings with Nina occur in a dimension which is dissimilar to the reality of his mundane existence and marked by a set of disparate spatial and temporal characteristics. As the center of the narrative spring in the story, Fialta organizes Vasen'ka's recollections of his previous meetings with Nina. The last fatal meeting in Fialta helps him to "understand" the nature of his love for Nina and gives him the perfect artistic form to immortalize his memories of her: ". . . and suddenly I understood something I had been seeing without understanding—why a piece of tin-foil had sparkled so on the pavement, why the gleam of a glass had trembled on a tablecloth, why the sea was a-shimmer: somehow, by imperceptible degrees, the white sky above Fialta had got saturated with sunshine, and now it was sun-pervaded throughout, and this brimming white radiance grew broader and broader, all dissolved in it, all vanished, all passed . . ." (*Stories,* 429). What exactly does Vasen'ka understand? To answer this question, one needs to compare Vasen'ka's last meeting with Nina with the other meetings which he describes in his narrative.

Vasen'ka exists in two different worlds. There is the world of solid bourgeois existence, the world of his successful career, his "wife and children at home, . . . an island of happiness always present in the clear north of [his] being, always floating beside [him], and even through [him], but yet keeping on the outside most of the time" (*Stories*, 414). And there is the other-world, which is filled with meetings with Nina and their reverberating memories which are stirred up by each subsequent occasion.[68] Also significant is the fact that their first meeting occurred in Russia, which both left as young people to become expatriates in Europe. Virtually nothing is said in the story about Vasen'ka's nostalgia or even his Russian cultural milieu in emigration. Nina, who is married to a non-Russian and cosmopolitan product of interwar Europe, seems even less attached to anything native (cf. Sonia in *Glory*). However, Vasen'ka and Nina do share a private Russian connection, which might explain the exaltation with which Vasen'ka recollects their meeting in the Russian countryside on the eve of 1917. Just like Ganin in *Mary* and Martin in *Glory*, Vasen'ka equates his unattainable and bygone Russia with the birth of a perfect love.

Despite the idealized perception of Nina, Vasen'ka stresses that his family life with its acquired status quo, Western European and bourgeois, was never endangered by his involvement with Nina, however strong his love and longing for her may have been. For instance, he recounts an episode when he stayed in the same house with Nina and Ferdinand in the Pyrenées and desired her: ". . . how I waited, how certain I was that without my having to tell her she would steal to my room, how she did not come, . . . and my struggle between blissful southern fatigue . . . and the wild thirst for her stealthy coming" (*Stories*, 424). Endowed with a rare plasticity of character, Vasen'ka is able to switch codes from mundane to otherworldly when he sees Nina and back when he is not with her:

> And regardless of what happened to me or to her, in between, we never discussed anything, as we never thought of each other during the intervals in our destiny, so that when we met the pace of life altered at once, all its atoms were re-combined, and we lived in another, lighted time-medium, which was measured not by the lengthy separations but by those few meetings of which a short, supposedly frivolous life was thus artificially formed. And with each new meeting I grew more and more apprehensive; no—I did not experience any inner emotional lapse, the shadow of tragedy did not haunt our revels, my married life remained unimpaired. . . . I grew apprehen-

sive because something lovely, delicate, and unrepeatable was being wasted, something which I abused by snapping off poor bright bits in gross haste while neglecting the modest but true core which perhaps it kept offering me in a pitiful whisper. (*Stories*, 425)

The motif of two lives, the mundane outer life and the idealized inner as structuring the protagonist's being, takes form in Chekhov's "Lady with a Lap Dog." When Gurov and Anna sit on the bench in Oreanda, Chekhov's narrator creates a sense of an otherworldly intimation which symbolizes their love in all its intensity, vulnerability, and indeterminacy. At that point, the story might go in two different directions, the Chekhovian and the Nabokovian. At first, Gurov treats his Yalta experience as a pleasant adventure, a source of special memories. However, soon after his return to Moscow he realizes that the memories not only have not faded away, but "are clear in his mind as if he parted with Anna Sergeevna only yesterday" (Chekhov 10:136):

> Whether the voices of his children . . . would resound through a quiet evening, or a love song would be heard, or an organ playing in a restaurant, . . . , suddenly everything would be resurrected in his memory: what happened at the pier, early morning with fog on mountain peaks, a steamship from Feodossia, and the kisses. . . . With his eyes shut, he envisioned her live image, and she appeared more beautiful, young, and tender than she was; and he also seemed to himself to be better than back in Yalta. In the evenings she would glance at him from a bookcase, or a fireplace, or a corner; he sensed her breath and the gentle rustle of her dress. (Chekhov 10:136)

Note that Gurov's memories of Anna, which descend upon him like an avalanche, embellish reality and idealize it. The description of Gurov's memories of Anna may in fact anticipate Vasen'ka's account of the chance regularity of his encounters with Nina: "Once I was shown her photograph in a fashion magazine full of autumn leaves and gloves and windswept golf links. . . . On a Riviera beach she almost escaped my notice behind her dark glasses and terracotta tan. . . . In a bookshop she nodded to me from a page of one of her husband's stories . . ." (*Stories*, 424).

Gurov, unlike Vasen'ka, is an active person who takes destiny in his hands. He goes to S. and seeks out Anna. They begin to meet secretly. Idealized, otherworldly memories of Anna give way to Gurov's painstakingly double life. At the end of the story the reader encounters Chekhov's famous statement about Gurov's two parallel lives, which is amazingly similar to Nabokov's description of Vasen'ka's own two worlds. The American writer Jim Shepard suggested that "Spring in Fialta" "owe[d]" to "Lady with a Lap Dog" "some of its thematic heart: that pervasive and disorienting sense that the false part of one's life is happening openly while the real and interesting part remains hidden."[69] Vasen'ka's monologue to the reader is written from the vantage point of knowing that Nina would die after their meeting in Fialta. This awareness might explain his carefully weighted, relentless, and unequivocal statement about not being able to choose between Nina and everything else: "Even in the absence of my sentimental discord [*otsutsevie razlada*], I felt myself bound to seek for a rational, if not moral, interpretation of my existence, and this meant choosing between the world in which I sat for my portrait, with my wife, my young daughters, the Doberman pinscher . . . , between that happy, wise, and good world . . . and what? Was there any practical chance of life together with Nina, life I could barely imagine . . ." (*Stories,* 425). Thereafter Vasen'ka tries to imagine living with Nina as husband and wife, replacing Ferdinand, and the prospect of having to deal with Nina's "past, teeming with protean partners" (*Stories,* 425) terrifies him. He also speculates that she would never leave Ferdinand. Such postfactum speculation is, of course, quite understandable. No less understandable is Vasen'ka's attempt to put his relationship with Nina in rational, transparent, and conventional terms. It is not until the very end of his narrative, when he has related the entire history of his relationship with Nina and given it the artistic form of a short story, that Vasen'ka understands—like Vasiliy Ivanovich of "Cloud, Castle, Lake," in "one radiant second" (*Stories,* 435)—what it is that Nina means to him.

Compare Vasen'ka's monologue and Gurov's thoughts on the way to a secret date with Anna. Gurov is walking his daughter to school:

> As he was talking he thought that there he was going to a rendezvous about which not a single soul knew anything, and probably never would. He had two lives: one apparent [*iavnaia,* cf. Vadim Vadimych's *iav'* (apparent reality) vs. *potustoronnost'* (otherworld)], which everyone who cared saw and knew of, full of conventional truth and conventional deceit, perfectly resembling the lives of his acquaintances and friends; and yet another life which flowed in secrecy. And due to some strange concurrence of circumstances, perhaps coincidental, everything that was important, interesting, necessary to him, everything he was sincere about and didn't lie to himself, that which constituted the core of his existence, occurred secretly from others,

whereas his lies, the shell behind which he would hide to conceal the truth . . . going to receptions with his wife, that was all on the surface. (Chekhov 10:141)

Gurov wants to change his predicament: he loves Anna like "a husband . . . , like a gentle friend." He and Anna both know that "their love has changed them" (Chekhov 10:143). Herein lies one of the fundamental differences between Chekhov's and Nabokov's stories. Even though Gurov and Anna do not know just how to "free themselves of the unbearable obstacles" (Chekhov 10:143) such as their marriages, they both take active steps to overcome them rather than surrender to fate. This is why "Lady with a Lap Dog" has an open ending which compels the reader to speculate about the future of the characters. This is also why the otherworld, showing through the chinks of mundane reality during the Oreanda episode, is no longer needed in Chekhov's story once Anna and Gurov have joined their lives in this world, which for them is vibrant with hopes.

Unlike Gurov, Vasen'ka is neither able to alter anything nor willing to try. A passive subject, he surrenders himself to fate even though he may apprehend its overarching designs. It is paradoxical that Vasen'ka feels both increasing sadness and "morbid pathos" and yet does not attempt to change his life. He realizes that in this world he and Nina will never be together. In "Spring in Fialta" Nabokov creates a drama of a growing conflict between the stable mundane world and the evanescent otherworld. Only at the end of the story, a few hours before Nina's death, does Vasen'ka venture to confess his love and change his life. Several motifs that recur in Nabokov's stories culminate here:

У ног наших валялся ржавый ключ, и на стене полуразрушенного дома, к которой площадка примыкала, остались висеть концы какой-то проволоки... я подумал о том, что некогда тут была жизнь, семья вкушала по вечерам прохладу, неумелые дети при свете лампы раскрашивали картинки. Мы стояли, как будто слушая что-то; Нина, стоявшая выше, положила руку ко мне на плечо, улыбясь и осторожно, так чтобы не разбить улыбки, целуя меня. С невыносимой силой я пережил (или так мне кажется теперь) всё, что когда-либо было между нами, начиная вот с такого же поцелуя, как этот; и я сказал, наше дешёвое, официальное *ты* заменяя тем одухотворённым, выразительным *вы*, к которому кругосветный пловец возвращается, обогащённый кругом: „А что, если я вас люблю?" (*VF*, 34)

(At our feet lay a rusty old key, and on the wall of the half-ruined house adjoining the terrace, the ends of some wire still remained hanging . . . I reflected that formerly there had been life there, a family had enjoyed the coolness at nightfall, clumsy children had colored pictures by the light of a lamp . . . We lingered there as if listening to something; Nina, who stood on higher ground, put a hand on my shoulder and smiled, and carefully, so as not to crumple her smile, kissed me. With an unbearable force, I relived (or so it now seemed to me) all that had ever been between us beginning with a similar kiss; and I said (substituting for our cheap, formal "thou" that strangely full and expressive "you" to which the circumnavigator, enriched all around, returns), "Look here—what if I love you?"; *Stories*, 429)

The rusty keys are the keys to the lovers' impossible happiness. The decrepit house and the memories of a family which lived there once symbolize the chance phantom of a mundane existence which Vasen'ka and Nina could share together. Vasen'ka's account of his declaration of love incorporates famous lines from two oft-quoted poems by Aleksandr Pushkin. The first is "Ty i vy" (Thou and You, 1828), in which a woman accidentally switches from the second-person formal pronoun *vy* to the informal *ty*.[70] The switch of language codes creates an entirely new spectrum of communication between the man who is in love and his beloved:

Пустое *вы* сердечным *ты*
Она, обмолвясь, заменила
И все счастливые мечты
В душе влюблённой возбудила.
Пред ней задумчиво стою,
Свести очей с неё нет силы;
И говорю ей: как вы милы!
И мыслю: как тебя люблю.[71]

She slipped and substituted
a heartfelt *thou* for the empty *you*
And all the happy dreams
Have been stirred up in the enamored soul.
I stand before her pensively,
I cannot take my eyes off her;
And I say to her: how lovely *you* are!
And I think to myself: how much I love *thee*.

In Vasen'ka's account we have a reversal of Pushkin's poem. The usually informal and more intimate *ty,* which Vasen'ka here calls "our cheap, formal 'thou,'" takes the place of the formal *vy,* which is here described as "that strangely full and expressive 'you.'" Vasen'ka's reversal can only be understood in the context of his relationship with Nina and his previous remarks on the nature of their communication in the presence of Ferdinand and his friends. Earlier in the Russian text of the story Vasen'ka mentions that over the ten years of their acquaintance he and Ferdinand even began to address each other as thou ("i na ty pereshli"). He also speaks about his impaired communications with others in Nina's presence: "Segur complained to me about the weather, and at first I did not understand what he was talking about; . . . it was just as much outside of anything that could serve us to be a topic of conversation as was, for instance, Nina's slender elbow . . ." (*Stories,* 423). Thus, Vasen'ka wishes to break out of the routine of communication in which he is accustomed to addressing his beloved Nina with the same informal pronoun with which he refers to Ferdinand and his cohort Segur, both of whom he despises. He also wants to establish a tone which would allow him to channel that "unbearable force" of which he speaks earlier in the passage.

Vasen'ka's confession, both desperate and timorous, recalls Pushkin's poem which most Russians know by heart, the 1829 "Ia vas liubil . . ." (I loved you . . .):

Я вас любил: любовь ещё, быть может,
В душе моей угасла не совсем;
Но пусть она вас больше не тревожит;
Я не хочу печалить вас ничем.
Я вас любил безмолвно, безнадежно,
То робостью, то ревностью томим;
Я вас любил так искренно, так нежно,
Как дай вам бог любимой быть другим.[72]

I loved you: perhaps my love
Hasn't died out completely in my soul;
But let it not disturb you any longer;
I don't want to sadden you with anything.
I loved you silently, hopelessly,
Tormented now by timidness, now by jealousy;
I loved you so sincerely, so tenderly,
As I wish you to be loved by someone else.

The words of Pushkin's lyrical hero reverberate in Vasen'ka's confession. Moreover, the fifth verse of Pushkin's poem contains a clue to understanding what is about to follow Vasen'ka's confession: "Nina glanced at me, I repeated those words, I wanted to add . . . but something like a bat passed swiftly across her face, a quick, queer, almost ugly expression, and she . . . became embarrassed; I also felt awkward . . . and before she returned to her husband and car, we stood for a little longer by the stone parapet, and our romance was even more hopeless [*beznadezhno*] than it had ever been" (*Stories*, 429/*VF*, 34). "Beznadezhno" (hopelessly) is one of the crucial motifs in Vasen'ka's account of his relationship with Nina; Vasen'ka insists that their "seemingly carefree" meetings were "really hopeless" (*Stories*, 425). Now, when for the first and last time he tries to reverse things by communicating to Nina what is in his heart, he ends up disrupting their fragile emotional equilibrium. How could it happen after all those years of their "kind of relationship" (*Stories*, 414)?

The artistic task of finding adequate poetic means to render and communicate to the reader of a fictional narrative what both the narrator and the characters perceive as lying outside their mundane reality and its linguistic medium has been at stake throughout the entire history of literature, from ancient myths to modernity. The Romantics enjoyed a special place among Chekhov's and Nabokov's literary models. Writers of the Romantic period conflated human experiences of love and the transcendent. They elevated to a major topos the discussion of language's inadequacy to connote certain absolute spheres of being. William Blake wrote about this in 1793:

> Never seek to tell thy love
> Love that never told can be;
> For the gentle wind does move
> Silently, invisibly.[73]

Blake's and Pushkin's "silently" ("bezmolvno") paves the way for a late Russian Romantic recension, Fëdor Tiutchev's programmatic poem "Silentium" (written ca. 1830). Tiutchev's poem has a direct bearing on the artistic problem which Nabokov explores in "Spring in Fialta." Tiutchev's poetic dictum about a private otherworld within one's soul was a major point of reference for the Russian artists of subsequent generations and schools. References to "Silentium" surface in several stories by Chekhov and Nabokov.[74] Tiutchev postulates two main principles. The first is the impossibility of communicating to the other one's intimate thoughts and feelings, for such a communication is doomed to result in mis-communication:

> Как сердцу высказать себя?
> Другому как понять тебя?
> Поймёт ли он, чем ты живёшь?
> Мысль изречённая есть ложь[75]

> How can a heart express itself?
> How can the other understand you?
> Will he understand by what you live?
> An uttered thought is a lie

The second principle is about one's soul being a private otherworld—the only dimension where one can communicate completely:

> Лишь жить в себе самом умей —
> Есть целый мир в душе твоей
> Таинственно-волшебных дум;
> Не оглушит их жизни шум,
> Дневные разгонят лучи, —
> Внимай их пенью — и молчи!..[76]

> Just know how to live within yourself
> A whole world is within your soul
> Of hidden and majestic thoughts;
> The outside noise will not deafen them,
> The daytime rays will not disperse them,
> Perceive their songs but do not speak!

Nabokov was well aware of the verbal limitations of communicating love, or any desire for that matter. He was also very interested in the way Chekhov conveyed "definite meaning" via "suggestive" verbal means. When Vasen'ka confesses his love to Nina, he tries to translate his private, otherworldly love into conventional terms. He senses a need to alter a linguistic code—hence the *ty-vy* metamorphosis. Alas, it does not help him. A disaster is now imminent because Vasen'ka has disrupted the private and secret world in which he and Nina dwelt when they were together. Might the "rusty key" ("rzhavyi kliuch") at the lovers' footsteps be a warning which Vasen'ka failed to apprehend, an evocation of Tiutchev's "Vzryvaia, vozmutish' kliuchi, / Pitaisia imi — i molchi" (By delving you will muddy the springs, / Partake of them and be silent"; note that *kliuch* in Russian means both spring and key). Might Nabokov be literalizing Tiutchev's *kliuchi:* "springs" but also "keys"? The key to Vasen'ka's and Nina's happiness in this world is rusty; the locks are broken; the doors are missing. A terrified "ugly" expression runs across Nina's face as though Vasen'ka's clear-cut declaration of love has touched the wrong strings in her soul (cf. Blake's "Never seek to tell thy love / Love that never told can be" and Tiutchev's "How can the other understand you?"). Nina is embarrassed for Vasen'ka and herself. They cannot communicate, despite Vasen'ka's attempt to turn everything into a joke ("'Never mind, I was only joking,' I hastened to say, lightly circling her waist"; *Stories,* 429). Nina has to return to her "husband and car." She has only a few hours to live in their world.

Here Nabokov creates a detail which signals that he continues a dialogue with Chekhov during the "confession scene." Vasen'ka and Nina are seeing each other for the last time. Vasen'ka's hand encircles Nina's waist, touching her body. This hand is the last link they seem to have left. Vasen'ka remarks that "the stone was as warm as flesh, and suddenly I understood something I had been seeing without understanding" ("no kamen' byl, kak telo, tëplyi, i vnezapno ia ponial to, chego, vidia, ne ponimal dotole"; *VF,* 35/*Stories,* 429). In the final episode of "Lady with a Lap Dog," Gurov comes up to Anna, who is in tears, and puts his hands on her shoulders. Then he looks at himself in the mirror: "The shoulders upon which his hands rested were warm and trembling. He felt compassion for this life, still so warm and beautiful, but probably about to start loosing its luster and to wither, like his own life. . . . And only now, when his hair had turned gray, he fell in love as one should, genuinely, for the first time in his life" (Chekhov 10:142–143). All of Chekhov is in Gurov's "compassion for this life"! Gurov's silent self-awareness, posing the "overwhelming questions" ("'How? How?' he asked, squeezing his head between his hands, 'How?'") and letting the reader answer them, bespeaks, to quote Robert L. Jackson, Chekhov's view "of ourselves and of the unknown world which continually lies before us and into which, at critical moments, we too step, 'gay and full of spirits,' leaving the past behind us, as we suppose, forever." [77]

Vasen'ka's *ty-vy* code switching in the culminative scene echoes Gurov's own in Chekhov's story. Gurov first addresses Anna as "thou" after they make love in Anna's hotel room in Yalta (Chekhov 10:132). At that point Anna is still a pleasant seaside adventure, one of the many representatives of the "inferior race" as Gurov used to refer to women. Anna continues to say "you" to Gurov. Then, during the climactic scene in the opera house, Gurov comes up to Anna and says "zdravstvuite" (the formal "hello").

Throughout the scene, he continues to use the formal "you" while addressing Anna, which gives his words a more solemn intonation.[78] Finally, in the last episode, both Gurov and Anna say "thou" to each other. They are now intimates. They understand each other perfectly and defy the prohibitive dictums of Tiutchev's "Silentium." Quite a different destiny awaits Vasen'ka and Nina in "Spring in Fialta." What, then, was the reason for Nabokov's decision to end the story with Vasen'ka's failed declaration of love, followed by his revelation on the eve of Nina's death in a car crash? And what is the meaning of this artistic decision in light of Nabokov's dialogue with Chekhov, which one finds on many levels of the story's structure, language, and metaphysics? To answer these questions, I will consider Nina's death against the background of the otherworldly motifs in the story.

The instrument of Nina's death, a "truck of a traveling circus," belongs to a series of recurrent images in the story.[79] In fact, there are seven references to the circus in "Spring in Fialta." One of the first things Vasen'ka's unfolding movie-eye notices is a "dejected poster of a visiting circus" (*Stories,* 413).[80] In the opening of the story springtime Fialta emerges as a town of perfect visual and aromatic harmony which "especially anoints one's soul" (*Stories,* 413). Fialta prepares Vasen'ka—who has just arrived on the fictional Capparabella express—for his last meeting with Nina. Obviously, Vasen'ka does not know it yet, as he never knows when to expect a fate-arranged meeting with his evanescent beloved. After a sleepless night on the train, Vasen'ka describes his state:

> What a luscious elation I felt rippling through my veins, how gratefully my whole being responded to the flutters and effluvia of that grey day saturated with a vernal essence which itself it seemed slow in perceiving! My nerves were unusually receptive . . . ; I assimilated everything [*ia vsё ponimal;* literally, I understood everything]; the whistling of a thrush in the almond trees beyond the chapel, the peace of the crumbling house, the pulse of the distant sea, panting in the mist, all this together with the jealous green of bottle glass bristling along the top of a wall and the fast colors of a circus advertisement featuring a feathered Indian on a rearing horse in the act of lassoing a boldly endemic zebra, while some thoroughly fooled elephants sat brooding upon their star-spangled thrones. (*Stories,* 414)

It is not by chance that this long passage is crowned with images of a traveling circus: right after it Vasen'ka runs into Nina. The circus recurs again as soon as Vasen'ka finishes reviewing his previous meetings with

Nina over the span of fifteen years. This time it is Ferdinand who notices the circus poster: "'God, what an Indian!' Ferdinand suddenly exclaimed with fierce relish, violently nudging me and pointing at a poster" (*Stories*, 423). This happens right after Vasen'ka's remark that he is unable to comprehend signs of the quotidian, like the small talk of Ferdinand's friend about the weather, when Nina is around him. Among the examples of what lies outside the mundane reality represented by Ferdinand and Segur, Vasen'ka lists "Nina's slender elbow" and "a bit of tin-foil someone had dropped" (*Stories*, 423).[81] The reader next encounters the circus at the beginning of a crucial passage which contrasts the two worlds in Vasen'ka's being, the stable bourgeois world and the ephemeral otherworld charged with Nina's presence. In this passage the narrator describes Fialta's two parts: "Fialta consists of the old town and of the new one; here and there, past and present are interlaced, struggling either to disentangle themselves or to thrust each other out . . ." (*Stories*, 426). Fialta's division into two parts, each with its "own method," temporality, and spatial characteristics, corresponds to the division of Vasen'ka's being into two worlds, which exists simultaneously and which he identifies earlier in the story. Now comes the next circus poster:

> On our way to the hotel, we [Vasen'ka and Nina, who are now alone] passed a half-built white villa [cf. the later image of a decrepit building where a family once lived], full of litter within, on a wall of which again the same elephants, their monstrous baby knees wide apart, sat on huge, gaudy drums; in ethereal bundles the equestrienne (already with a penciled mustache) was resting on a broad-backed steed; and a tomato-nosed clown was walking a tight-rope, balancing an umbrella ornamented with those recurrent starts—a vague symbolic recollection of the heavenly fatherland of circus performance. (*Stories*, 426)

I suggest taking this description as literally as possible. The circus as a performing art usually involves a strong dose of risk and liminality. This liminality, often performed rather than real, is nevertheless an effective means of keeping the onlooker in suspense, as when a gymnast walks on a thin rope under the dome of the circus or when an animal trainer puts her head inside a lion's mouth, or when a magician hypnotizes his victim. Of all the performing arts, the circus possesses to the greatest extent the aura of magic, of supernatural effects. Under the dome of the circus, and especially an itinerant circus, an exile of circuses without a permanent residence, mundane reality undergoes metamorphoses. What is impossible in the real world becomes possible in the circus. The circus as a space where commonsensical laws cease to exist has become the subject of several memorable scenes in Russian literature, including the famous circus scene in Mikhail Bulgakov's *Master and Margarita* (1940; publ. 1967) and Nikolai Zabolotskii's remarkable poem "Tsirk" (The Circus, 1928). The motif of a circus as a threshold between the mundane and the otherworldly enters Nabokov's arsenal as early as 1924, in the story "Kartofel'nyi Ėl'f " (The Potato Elf). Shock, the teetering conjurer, "always appeared unreal and shifty, thinking about something else when talking about trivialities, but keenly observing everything around him when immersed in astral fancies" (*Stories*, 231). Vasen'ka's reference to the "heavenly fatherland of circus performers" ("nebesna[ia] rodin[a] tsirkachei"; *Stories*, 426/*VF*, 29) means that there is a link between the otherworldly nature of Vasen'ka's relationship with Nina and the recurrent circus imagery in the story. Also noteworthy is the fact that only a few sentences after the latter circus description Nina draws Vasen'ka's attention to Segur's automobile, a "yellow long-bodied Icarus."[82] Nina died, as Vasen'ka would later find out from a newspaper, when the automobile of Ferdinand's friend Segur "ran at full speed into the truck of a traveling circus" (*Stories*, 429). In retrospect, the presence of the circus poster and Segur's vehicle at such proximity to each other in time and space means that their further rapprochement is imminent. During his epiphanic moment at the end of the story, Vasen'ka is able to perceive all the out-of-time connections between different objects which he had not apprehended before. His narrative in "Spring in Fialta" is constructed in such a way as to allow the reader to follow it in its making. The last appearance of the circus before Nina's death—the last one Vasen'ka eyewitnesses—occurs as soon as Nina and Vasen'ka have been left alone by Ferdinand and Segur. This time they run across live circus performers rather than another playbill: "the circus on its way to Fialta had apparently sent out runners" (*Stories*, 428). Soon thereafter, the lovers climb a staircase and find themselves at the terrace where Vasen'ka tries and fails to communicate his love to Nina.

I suggest that the recurrent circus images that accompany Vasen'ka and Nina throughout their meeting in Fialta are the esoteric signs of the otherworld which claims Nina at the end of the story. Recall a crucial comment Vasen'ka makes after he runs into Nina in the morning: "This time we had met in warm and misty Fialta, and I could not have celebrated the occasion with greater art, could not have adorned with bright vignettes the list of fate's former services, even if I had known that this was to be the last one; the last one, I maintain, for I cannot imagine any heavenly firm of brokers [*nikakuiu potustoronniuiu organizatsiiu;* literally, any other-worldly organization] that might consent to arrange me a meeting with her beyond the grave" (*Stories*, 415/*VF*, 10–11).

What is Nabokov warning us against? He must be warning the reader against equating his sui generis otherworld with the afterlife as the traditional domain of the dead, especially since later in the story the same adjective, "heavenly," refers to the "fatherland" of circus performers. Nina dies as result of a collision between the circus truck (a marked sign of the otherworld) and Segur's automobile (a marked sign of the mundane world). She dies as result of a conflict, germinating throughout Vasen'ka's narrative, between the blissful otherworld of their hopeless and incommunicable private love and the wide-awake world in which she is a faithful imitator of her protean husband and Vasen'ka a successful business and family man. The story's last sentence offers yet another clue to understanding Nina's death: " . . . Ferdinand and his friend, those invulnerable rogues, those salamanders of fate, those basilisks of good fortune, had escaped with local and temporary injury to their scales, while Nina, in spite of her long-standing, faithful imitation of them, had turned out after all to be mortal" (*Stories*, 429). Nina's physical death, much like the prospect of Vasen'ka's and Nina's afterlife meetings, is not of interest to Nabokov, who would later admit to having "no use for organized tours through anthropomorphic paradises" (*SM*, 297). Her physical death serves as a means of closing the narrative. However, Nina's "mortality" can only be understood in contrast to the "immortality" of her husband, a belletrist and Vasen'ka's rival. Resulting from a collision of two worlds which compete for her, a collision both literal and metaphorical, Nina's death demonstrates that she can no longer exist in two worlds as disparate as Ferdinand's world and the otherworld. In fact, Ferdinand's "mortality"—quite different from Nina's—is alluded to right after the evocation of the "heavenly fatherland of circus performers": "In the back yard of the hotel, a kitchen boy armed with a knife was pursuing a hen which was clucking madly as it raced for its life" (*Stories*, 426). One sentence later, Vasen'ka describes the mythological vehicle which will bring Nina to her physical death, a "yellow long-bodied Icarus." The hen trying to escape its death points toward one of Ferdinand's metaphors in the story: a basilisk, a mythological half-rooster, half-snake representing death, the devil, and sin. At the very end of the story Ferdinand, a "basilisk of good fortune," escapes death in a car crash. He manages to deceive death. In the physical world where Ferdinand is a best-selling author who wishes to drink "pigeon's blood" (*Stories*, 427) as a potion for immortality, Nina is doomed to be a mortal. By the same token, Ferdinand and his cohort are never to be able to enter the otherworld, and that is their "immortality" and punishment. Ultimately, to quote Alexander Zholkovsky's essay on the philosophy of Nabokov's composition, "the event [of Nina's death seems] as if [it] does not occur, but only reveals some timeless, otherworldly, Platonic dimension." [83]

In the seminal lecture "The Art of Literature and Commonsense," Nabokov stated that ". . . in one way or another the process [of artistic creation] may still be reduced to the most natural form of creative thrill—a sudden live image constructed in a flash out of dissimilar units which are apprehended all at once in a stellar explosion of the mind" (*LRL*, 379). On the eve of Nina's physical death, Vasen'ka undergoes a vatic experience whose account corresponds to this definition of literary creation, as well as to the description of cosmic synchronization offered in *Speak, Memory*: "the capacity of thinking several things at a time" (*SM*, 218). Vasen'ka's exalted state also anticipates his otherworldly experience of "suddenly under[standing] something" at the end of the story right before Nina's death. In Nabokov's autobiography the fruitful moment of cosmic synchronization is presented in a series of images and ideas which he registers simultaneously while "richly, serenely aware of [his] own manifold awareness" (*SM*, 219). Here, again, is Vasen'ka's account of his moment of complete clarity:

> . . . and suddenly I understood something I had been seeing without understanding—why a piece of tin-foil had sparkled so on the pavement, why the gleam of a glass had trembled on a tablecloth [a reference to the Englishman's glass with what Ferdinand calls "pigeon's blood"], why the sea was a-shimmer: somehow, by imperceptible degrees, the white sky above Fialta had got saturated with sunshine, and now it was sun-pervaded throughout, and this brimming white radiance grew broader and broader, all dissolved in it, all vanished, all passed. . . . (*Stories*, 429)

Vasen'ka understands that the only domain where he and Nina will always be together is his memory, an otherworldly narrative sustained by language and love. In the course of his own narrative of chance meetings with Nina, culminating in spring in Fialta, Vasen'ka becomes a writer. Unable to subject his perfect memories to silence, he creates instead a work of art through writing "Spring in Fialta" (cf. Vasen'ka's "This time we had met in warm and misty Fialta, and I could not have celebrated the occasion with greater art . . ."; *Stories*, 415).[84] This work of art appears to Vasen'ka almost in its entirety and definitely in all the blinding and cathartic purity of its architectonics, of all its structures of mundane and other-worldly love. The news of Nina's death, which Vasen'ka learns from a newspaper in Mlech, a station which is nowhere to be found in this world, only gives his story its final shape with a closed ending that is simultaneously a textual opening onto art's metaphysics. Ultimately, Vasen'ka's rivalry with the writer Ferdinand, and Nabokov's competition with Chekhov, is not only over Nina, but also over a better form of literary work. Earlier, Vasen'ka intuitively disapproves of Ferdinand's suffocating narratives: "At the beginning of his career, it had been possible perhaps to distinguish some human landscape, some old garden, some dream-familiar disposition of trees through the stained glass of his prodigious prose . . . but with every new book the tints grew still more dense, the gules and purpure still more ominous; and today one can no longer see anything at all through that blazoned, ghastly rich glass, and it seems that were one to break it, nothing but a perfectly black void would face one's shivering soul" (*Stories*, 420).

Nabokov's and Vasen'ka's "Spring in Fialta" is metafiction par excellence, a union of the metaliterary and the metaphysical. It is a narrative about the making of a short story which tells about the nature and workings of the otherworld. As a self-conscious artist, Vasen'ka creates a work which possesses a dimension lacking in Ferdinand's glamorous books, an otherworldly textual opening. Vasen'ka has immortalized Nina in his short story, and the otherworldly opening makes sure that she will always be with him. This, to borrow Humbert Humbert's expression from *Lolita*, is the only immortality that Vasen'ka and Nina may share: "I am thinking of aurochs and angels, the secret of durable pigments, prophetic sonnets, the refuge of art. And this is the only immortality you and I may share, my Lolita" (*L*, 309).[85]

"Do you realize what it is you are doing? You are killing realism," Maksim Gor'kii wrote in a letter to Chekhov soon after the publication of "Lady with a Lap Dog" in 1899. "And you will soon shoot it to death," Gor'kii continued. "This form has outlived its time, no one can write so simply of such simple matters . . . you will definitely do realism in. I am extremely happy about it. . . . Truly, our times need the heroic stuff: everyone wants something exhilarating, bright, something that, you know, would not look like life, but would be higher than life, better, more beautiful."[86]

In "Lady with a Lap Dog" Gurov's meeting with Anna in Yalta moves him to dwell on real life and its choices. This suggested to Chekhov a form for his work, an open-ended short story with an omniscient narrator without any awareness of the art of writing. He wrote his story in keeping with his own artistic principle of letting the material suggest the shape of the future story. The "higher, more beautiful" life that so excited Gor'kii is the distant prospect of Gurov's and Anna's happiness, which is alluded to at the end of the story. One could almost suggest that the distant future, which so many Chekhovian characters, be they Sasha in "The Betrothed" or Petia Trofimov in *The Cherry Orchard,* idealize and glorify, is Chekhov's *unwritten otherworld.* But, to quote another one of the Chekhovian dreamers about the future, Ol'ga from *The Three Sisters,* "Esli by znat', esli by znat'!" (If we could only know, if we could only know!; Chekhov 13:188).

"Spring in Fialta" not only firmly establishes Nabokov as Chekhov's successor in modern Russian letters, but also allows us to see Nabokov's innovation against the backdrop of Chekhov's short story. In his twentieth-century hypertext of "Lady with a Lap Dog," written by a Russian exile and set in a cosmopolitan fictional resort on the Mediterranean coast, Nabokov closed Chekhov's open-ended structure but endowed it with a textual opening. "The moment of greatest sadness," Shepard writes about the effect of the ending, "becomes the moment when we suddenly understand something we had been seeing without understanding: a radiance that had been present throughout the story, in Fialta, in Nina, and in what both engender in [Vasen'ka]." [87] The reader knows that Nina will die at the end, and the plot confirms the reader's expectations. However, Nina is immortal in the reader's memory. When we revisit the text via memory—and "one cannot *read* a book: one can only reread it" (*LL,* 3)—we are awarded the pleasure and harmony of recollection akin to Nabokov's own cosmic synchronization. We see Nina with a bouquet of "small dark, unselfishly smelling violets" under the Fialta sky "brimming white radiance." Nina's evanescent otherworldly beatitude conquers her physical mortality, first in the narrator's memory, then in his writing, and then in the reader's grateful palimpsestic memory.

Nabokov's "long-drawn" dialogue with Chekhov—reaching its Russian climax in "Spring in Fialta"—focuses on two different models of the use and pleasure of reading. Although Chekhov and Nabokov belong to the same tradition, identified here as covert modernism, they represent its two alternative trajectories. Chekhov's stories make readers question themselves vis-à-vis the open-ended characters and try to perfect this world both poetically and prosaically. Nabokov's stories make readers forget themselves and surrender to memory only to find themselves again. By making "Spring in Fialta" a text of dialogue with "Lady with a Lap Dog,"

Nabokov created his version of the Chekhov who links the "fathers" and the "sons," Russian classical literature and Russian modernism. This brings us back to the epigraph, to Nabokov's objection to Edmund Wilson's sociological view of Chekhov.

Writing to his dearest American literary interlocutor about one of the foremost poets in his native Russian literature, Nabokov draws on Shakespeare, a literary giant of his adopted Anglo-American tradition. In Shakespeare's poetry Nabokov was able to seek out a passage which would speak in Wilson's native terms about the kind of Chekhov whom Nabokov glorified in "Spring in Fialta" and brought with him to America, his new literary home. The episode of which he writes in his letter to Wilson is found in act 5, scene 3, of *King Lear*. After King Lear and his daughter Cordelia have been taken prisoner and brought to the British Camp near Dover, the King pronounces a majestic, soul-piercing monologue. Containing several parallels with "Spring in Fialta," the monologue expresses, miraculously, the core of Nabokov's own vision of Chekhov's art:

No, no, no, no! Come, let's away to prison:
We two alone will sing like birds i' the cage:
When thou dost ask me blessing I'll kneel down
And pray, and sing, and tell old tales, and laugh
At gilded butterflies, and hear poor rogues
Talk of court news; and we'll talk with them too,—
Who loses and who wins; who's in, who's out;—
And take upon the mystery of things
As if we were God's spies: and we'll wear out
In a wall'd prison packs and sects of great ones
That ebb and flow by the moon.[88]

4   Nabokov and Bunin: The Poetics of Rivalry

The Cold Heaven

Suddenly I saw the cold and rook-delighting heaven
That seemed as though ice burned and was but more ice,
And thereupon imagination and heart were driven
So wild that every casual thought of that and this
Vanished, and left but memories, that should be out of season
With the hot blood of youth, of love crossed long ago;
And I took all the blame out of all sense and reason,
Until I cried and trembled and rocked to and fro,
Riddled with light. Ah! when the ghost begins to quicken,
Confusion of the death-bed over, is it sent
Out naked on the roads, as the books say, and stricken
By the injustice of the skies for punishment?[1]
—*W. B. Yeats, from* Responsibilities *(1914)*

. . . that melody, the pain, the offense, the link between
hymen and death . . .[2]—*Nabokov, "Spring in Fialta"*

On November 9, 1929, Kirill Zaitsev, a Russian critic, a law professor, and a monk later in his life, published an article entitled "'Bunin's' World and 'Sirin's' World" in the Paris newspaper *Rossiia i slavianstvo* (Russia and Slavdom).[3] Although Zaitsev appeared to be familiar with Nabokov's output of the 1920s, both in poetry and in prose, his article was an immediate response to the first installment of *The Defense*, published in 1929 in *Contemporary Annals* in the same issue with a section of Bunin's novel *Zhizn' Arsen'eva* (The Life of Arseniev, 1928–1933; complete text 1952). "There are very few books," Zaitsev wrote, "which bring joy to the reader." He likened reading Bunin's novel to having a gulp of oxygen and suggested that "from the heights of Bunin's poetry one falls into the sheer darkness of Sirin's spiritual underground." Zaitsev went on to praise Nabokov's artistic brilliance, yet concluded that one finished his novel with a sigh of relief: "Thank God, one does not need to read this depressing and most talented description of people who have nothing to live by, to strive for.... How terrifying it is to see life as Sirin sees it! What a joy it is to see life as Bunin sees it!"[4]

However wrong or blind Zaitsev may have been in his assessment of Nabokov's achievement, the very appearance of such a comparative article as early as 1929 signals that the émigré critics were ready to regard (and attack) Nabokov as Bunin's literary rival. By November 1929, when Zaitsev's article was published, the émigré Nabokov (Sirin) had to his credit two poetry collections and two novels, published in Berlin, as well as numerous periodical appearances, predominantly in the Berlin newspaper *The Rudder.* Nabokov's first collection of short stories and poems, *The Return of Chorb,* was very soon to come out. Although he had had several poems and a short story published in the leading Paris review *Contemporary Annals* by 1929, Nabokov was not well known in Paris, then the literary center of the Russian emigration, before the serialization of *The Defense* in 1929 and its book publication in 1930. Indeed, it was the appearance of Nabokov's third novel that startled émigré literary circles. To quote Nina Berberova, "a great Russian writer, like a phoenix, was born from the fire and ashes of revolution and exile. Our existence from now on acquired a meaning. All my generation were justified. We were saved."[5]

The critic and poet Mikhail Tsetlin (Amari) was probably the first to point out the connections between Nabokov's and Bunin's art in a 1928 review of *King, Queen, Knave.*[6] In 1930, in a literary questionnaire published in *Numbers,* Georgii Fedotov spoke of Bunin's and Nabokov's texts as the major works of their time.[7] By the mid-1930s the number of articles, interviews, and questionnaires in which Bunin and Nabokov were compared, juxtaposed, or merely listed side by side as the authors of the best contemporary works increased steadily as Nabokov's literary star shone brighter and brighter over the dimming horizons of Russia Abroad.[8] In a 1931 questionnaire, "Best Work of Russian Literature of the Last Decade" (conducted by the Paris weekly *The New Paper*), two masters of the older generation named works by Bunin and Nabokov. Aleksandr Kuprin chose Bunin's "Solnechnyi udar" (The Sunstroke, 1925), Valentin Kataev's *Rastratchiki* (The Embezzlers, 1927) and Nabokov's *The Defense,* while

Vladislav Khodasevich picked *The Life of Arseniev* from the works of the older generation of writers and *The Defense* and Iurii Olesha's *Zavist'* (Envy, 1927) from those of the younger.[9]

The Nabokov-Bunin opposition even made its way into Western criticism as part of the larger juxtaposition between the older and younger émigré authors. In a survey of Russian émigré letters the American Slavicist Albert Parry complimented Nabokov while dismissing Bunin as one of the figures of the literary past: "There is no hope, perhaps, for such fossils as Bunin, Shmelev, or Ossorgin [*sic*] to do fine, creative work about their *milieu* in exile—they are too sunk in their Russian past and traditions—but Sirin, Aldanov, Berberova and other youngsters . . . can, and do, produce fine work on non-Russian themes."[10] Parry was short-sighted in respect to Bunin: his article came out in July 1933, only a few months before the announcement of Bunin's Nobel Prize, which finally recognized his contribution, made him into a worldwide literary celebrity, and boosted his popularity among fellow exiles. Students of the period know of the catalytic impact that Bunin's award had on the cultural climate of Russia Abroad. His prize came after a wave of critical discussions and polemics that had swept across Russian émigré publications from Paris to Riga, from Kharbin to Chicago. The polemics focused on the future of Russian literature in exile. Is it possible to maintain a literary culture apart from its organic linguistic substratum? What distinguishes Russian émigré literature from its Soviet counterpart? What will happen to the literature of Russia Abroad within the next several decades? Who will be the heirs of the great Russian literary tradition that the older generation of writers in exile was believed to have rescued from Bolshevik disfigurement? Such were the questions the émigré critics and writers mulled over in the late 1920s—early 1930s.[11] Bunin's Nobel Prize refocused critical attention. The vehemently anti-Soviet Bunin became the first Russian writer to be awarded the world's highest distinction. Therefore, the emphasis was shifting away from the justification of the present of Russian literature in exile to prognoses about its future.[12] Because Nabokov had become a leading émigré writer by the mid-1930s, critics both well- and ill-disposed toward him were naturally inclined to contrast him with Bunin.[13] Nabokov's name came up more and more frequently, both in print and in Montparnasse café discussions, as the new master of Russian literature in exile and, ipso facto, both an heir and a rival to the Nobel-crowned old master.

The notion of the poetics of rivalry which I would like to explore in this chapter suggests that I read the literary and personal relationship between Nabokov and Bunin as a dialogic text in which the two masters challenge each other to greater artistic achievements. Beyond mere mentions of Bunin as one of Nabokov's literary models, virtually nothing has been done in post–World War II criticism to explore the relationship between the two writers.[14] In the Soviet Union, until the late 1980s, literary critics were not free to discuss Nabokov; nor did Bunin scholars have access to Western archives. In the vast body of Bunin criticism produced in the Soviet Union, one finds two principal references to Nabokov. The first was made by the poet Aleksandr Tvardovskii, a Soviet cultural eminence, who labeled Nabokov Bunin's "epigone" in his 1965 preface to the nine-volume edition of Bunin's works published in Moscow.[15] Tvardovskii's words were reiterated by the ranking Bunin specialist, Oleg Mikhailov, who called Nabokov "the Peter Schlemihl of [Russian] émigré literature."[16] In the West many critics have been misled by Nabokov's scarce references to his émigré years. In his memoir *Speak, Memory,* as well as in the interviews and letters published during his American period, Nabokov downplayed and obfuscated the role of the émigré cultural contexts, and specifically of Bunin, in his artistic development. Moreover, he was able to foist this view not only upon his first biographer, Andrew Field, but also upon the author of the more recent monumental biography, Brian Boyd. Boyd, for instance, does not seem curious about the possibility that Nabokov corresponded with Bunin for many years and that the two writers left major imprints in each other's lives and texts.

I have studied what remains from an extremely interesting correspondence between Nabokov and Bunin spanning almost twenty years. I have also perused the complete diaries of Bunin and his wife, currently known in their edited version. Finally, I have searched for possible cross-references in the letters as well as the recollections of those littérateurs who knew both Bunin and Nabokov: Adamovich, Aldanov, Berberova, Roman Gul', Odoevtseva, Andrei Sedykh, Boris Zaitsev, and others. Archival and testimonial research and a comparative analysis of Nabokov's and Bunin's oeuvres have allowed me to reconstruct the peripeties of the writers' escalating relationship, a friendship turned rivalry.

The story of the Nabokov-Bunin relationship is one of love and jealousy, of opposites that attract and affinities that repel, of admiration, irony, and bitterness, and, in the end, of a literary duel. Chronologically, their relationship falls into three phases. The first lasted from the 1920s until 1933, when Bunin received the Nobel Prize and the two writers finally met in person. The second continued roughly until Nabokov's departure for the New World in 1940; this was the period of his rapid ascent to first-rate literary stardom which eclipsed Bunin's own fame. The third centered on Bunin's composition of *Tëmnye allei* (Dark Avenues) and lasted until his death in 1953.

As a young writer in the 1920s, Nabokov capitalized on several landmark stylistic achievements of Bunin, his senior contemporary (Bunin was thirty years older and already famous in the Russia of Nabokov's childhood). By the middle of the 1930s Nabokov had developed into the most original émigré author of the younger generation. He continued the stylistic and narrative traditions of Chekhov's and Bunin's short stories, yet "opened," in Bunin's own words, a "whole new world" ("otkryl tselyi mir") in Russian literature.[17] Regarding Nabokov as his rival, and haunted by his fame, Bunin decided to reclaim his literary status as the foremost living Russian writer by creating his masterpiece and his testament, *Dark Avenues*. In the latter part of this chapter, I will inquire into the principal aesthetic, ethical, and metaphysical issues which shaped the dialogue between Bunin's *Dark Avenues* and Nabokov's stories of the late 1930s. I will also consider the theoretical implications of their literary rivalry for an understanding of the motor that drives literary evolution, particularly the Russian Formalists' idea that writers reach back to grandfathers or great-uncles.[18] While Bunin did to some extent reach back to Lev Tostoi and Ivan Turgenev, he also reached forward, in *Dark Avenues* and elsewhere, to his literary "nephew" Vladimir Nabokov.

In order to unravel the complex bundle of authorial and textual interconnections between the two giants of modern Russian literature, it is best to start at the very beginning. Nabokov's father, a leading Constitutional Democrat, and Bunin, who in Russia belonged to the camp of liberal writers, became acquainted in Berlin in 1920.[19] In a letter of December 12, 1920, V. D. Nabokov mentioned his son's poetry and referred to the long poem "Les" (The Forest), published in *The Rudder* under a provisional *nom de plume*, "Cantab": "If you saw in *The Rudder* my son's poetry (signed 'Cantab'), would you drop me a few lines with your opinion of it?"[20] Bunin sent V. D. Nabokov a copy of his recently published collection *Gospodin iz San Frantsisko* (The Gentleman from San Francisco, 1920), which included some of his best pre-1917 stories and poems. In the accompanying letter he evidently complimented Nabokov's poem.[21] This, in turn, encouraged V. D. Nabokov to enclose in his next letter to Bunin a clipping from the 1921 Christmas issue of *The Rudder* with three poems and a short story ("The Woodsprite"), signed with the now permanent "Vlad. Sirin."[22] He asked permission to send Bunin a batch of his son's poems.[23]

On March 18, 1921, Nabokov sent Bunin his first letter along with a number of poems. In the letter, suffused with the pathos of admiration and gratitude, he thanked the master for his encouragement: ". . . the kind words are coming from you, the only writer in our blasphemous and graceless age [*v nash koshchunstvennyi i kosnoiazychnyi vek*] who serves beauty apprehending it in everything. . . . Forgive my clumsy expressions, but this is as hard as confessing love—an old love." Nabokov treated Bunin as a mentor, someone he could "turn to in the days of great loneliness."[24] In the next letter, written in Berlin in November 1922, Nabokov spoke of how happy he was to know Bunin's poetry by heart. "I only want you to understand," he wrote, "with what strict admiration [*s kakim strogim vostorgom*] I look from my hill at the shining mountain peak where you have carved in the rock your eternal, incomparable words."[25] Nabokov enclosed a poem with a dedication to Bunin. The poem, "Kak vody gor, tvoi golos gord i chist . . ." (Like mountain streams, your voice is proud and clear . . .), was printed in *The Rudder* under the title "I. A. Buninu" (To I. A. Bunin) and later included in Nabokov's third collection, *Grozd'* (The Cluster, 1923).[26] Of special interest for our discussion is the final, fifth stanza of the poem:

Безвестен я и молод, в мире новом,
кощунственном, — но светит всё ясней
мой строгий путь: ни помыслом, ни словом
не согрешу пред музою твоей.[27]

I am unknown and young in the new
blasphemous world, but my demanding path
shines brighter and brighter: neither in thought nor in word
will I sin before your muse.

In the poem, Nabokov reiterates several ideas expressed in his first two letters to Bunin. A case in point is his use of the word *koshchunstvennyi* (blasphemous). In the first letter to Bunin, Nabokov described his time as a "blasphemous age." In the poem "blasphemous" refers to the world surrounding Nabokov. Both the letter and the poem regard Bunin's poetry as an aesthetic beacon guiding the young poet. This, in turn, raises the first crucial question about the nature of the Nabokov-Bunin dialogue spanning over thirty years. What formative role, if any, did Bunin's poetry play in Nabokov's development? What did Nabokov learn from Bunin the poet?

Nabokov's exposure to Bunin's poetry was most intense in the 1900s–1910s. Later, in a well-known 1949 letter to Edmund Wilson, he claimed that "Blok, Bely, Bunin . . . wrote their best stuff in those days" (*Wilson Letters*, 220). Throughout the 1920s–1950s Nabokov revisited Bunin's poetic oeuvre, as a reviewer of Bunin's 1929 *Selected Poems, 1900–1925*, as a co-contributor to various émigré periodicals in the 1920s and 1930s, and as a teacher of Russian literature in the 1940s and 1950s. In a postcard to Bunin, sent from Ariège in the Pyrenees in 1929, Nabokov wrote that he had known many of Bunin's verses since childhood and noticed some changes he had made in the new volume: "I read them, think of them, and—of course—this is the most beautiful creation of the Russian muse over the past thirty years."[28] The review of Bunin's *Selected Poems*, the only piece of criticism that Nabokov ever wrote solely on Bunin, helps to understand what he saw in his older contemporary:

> Bunin's poems are the best the Russian muse has created over several decades. In the past, during the loud Petersburg years, the glamorous clanking of the modish lyres deafened [Bunin's poetry]; but this poetic noise is gone without a trace, the "masters of blasphemous words" have been forgotten, only cold air wafts from the dead conglomerates of Briusov's verses; once deceiving one with its musicality, Bal'mont's poetry now seems out of key; and only the trembling of one lyre, a trembling unique only to deathless poetry, moves us just as it used to, no, stronger than before, and it now seems strange that in those Petersburg years, not everyone hearkened to it, not every soul was struck by the voice of a poet who had no peers since Tiutchev.[29]

Nabokov's assessment of Bunin's place in Russian poetry reflects his own biases circa 1929. One notices in the review a negative reaction to much of the poetry of Russian symbolism. While Nabokov named two of its leaders, Briusov and Bal'mont, the third reference is to Blok's poem "Za grobom" (Following the Coffin, 1908), which describes the funeral of a young author: "Byl on tol'ko literator modnyi / Slov koshchunstvennykh tvorets" (He was only a fashionable littérateur / Only a master of blasphemous words).[30]

Nothing could have pleased Bunin more than a comparison with the symbolists, specifically with Blok, in which he emerges as the winner! Nabokov's review contributed to the growing rapprochement between him and Bunin during the first phase of their relationship and culminated in 1933 when they finally met. Nabokov continued to regard Bunin's poetry highly throughout his career. In fact, he had several independent occasions in the late 1930s–1950s to voice his opinion. In a 1938 letter to an American Slavicist, Elizabeth Malozemoff, at the time working on a Bunin dissertation, Nabokov named Khodasevich and Bunin as the foremost poets of their time.[31]

The variety and eclecticism of Nabokov's poetic influences make it difficult to identify distinct traces of Bunin in his verse. In the initial period of Nabokov's versemaking, one finds echoes of Bunin's first collection, *Listopad* (Foliage, 1901). Nabokov's period of "private curatorship," when he explored biblical and "Byzantine" motifs in his poetry (*PP*, 13), yielded a number of poems with religious thematics, modeled in part after Bunin's ingenious treatment of biblical motifs. Nabokov adopted two specific elements of Bunin's poetic technique. The first is the recurrent device of repeating a word or cluster of words for rhythmic and/or emphatic purposes. Naturally, the device was not invented by Bunin. However, Nabokov praised this device in his review as Bunin's particular forte and armed himself with it. One finds a number of poems in which Nabokov employs Bunin's stylistic hallmark:

И на земле мы многое забыли:
лишь изредка воспомнится во сне
и трепет наш, и трепет звёздной пыли,
и чудный гул, дрожавший в вышине

And on earth we have forgotten much:
only rarely we recall in a dream
our *tremble,* the *tremble* of stardust,
and wondrous hum, trembling in the sky
(*Stikhi,* 11; italics added)

The second borrowing has to do with what Nabokov described (in a letter to the Bunin scholar Malozemoff) as Bunin's powerful gift for "color distinguishing." Nabokov called Bunin *tsvetovidets* (literally, color perceiver). He was especially enthusiastic about Bunin's use of the color purple, which he associated with "the growth and maturity of literature": "Bunin saw purple keenly as an extreme degree of density in the blueness of the sky and sea."[32] Nabokov was perfectly right about Bunin's effective use of the hues of purple. Shades of purple (*lilovyi, sirenevyi,* etc.) are also omnipresent in Nabokov's own verse: "Vsia ulitsa blestit i kazhetsia *lilovoi*" (1916); "tucha belaia iz-za *lilovoi* tuchi" (1921), "Na pliazhe v polden' *lilovatyi*" (1927; italics added). In the 1922 poem Nabokov wrote for Bunin, he used the epithet "purple" both as a Bunin-specific device and as a sign of his admiration for Bunin's craft:

Ты любишь змей, тяжёлых злых узлов
лиловый лоск на дне сухой ложбины.

(*Stikhi*, 38)

You like snakes, the purple luster
of their vile weighty knots on the bottom of a dry ravine.

Finally, Nabokov adopted a feature that distinguished Bunin's original collections from books by his contemporaries. As early as the 1910s Bunin began to publish his short stories under the same covers as his poems.[33] Nabokov did the same in the collection *The Return of Chorb*, which signaled, among other things, a transition to the stage when he "illustrate[d] the principle of making a short poem contain a plot and tell a story" (*PP*, 15).[34]

In sum, Nabokov regarded Bunin as one of his poetic predecessors, while taking little from the older master. While Nabokov's poetic orientation oscillated throughout the 1920s and early 1930s among various poetic schools, Bunin himself remained remarkably consistent in his poetic direction. Having coined his own unmistakable and unique poetic intonation as early as the 1900s, he continued to produce first-rate verse throughout the 1910s and in emigration, although his output did decrease drastically. To a student of Russian poetry, Bunin sounds mostly like Bunin, while Nabokov often sounds like a potpourri of the nineteenth- and twentieth-century poetic repertoire, a Pushkin, a Fet, a Bunin, a Blok, and a Pasternak all at once. To quote David M. Bethea's ruthless comment, "despite its occasional charm and 'neo-[a]cmeist' specificity of detail, [Nabokov] was at best a 'Blokian' and at worst a 'Balmontian.'"[35] Iurii Tynianov wrote in 1924 that "each *new* appearance in poetry is marked first and foremost by a *novelty of intonation*."[36] Although a profusely gifted poet, Nabokov did not find an original intonation. In this respect, he was never, and could never be, either an heir or a rival to Bunin. Bunin knew it very well; not until the almost simultaneous appearance of Nabokov's collection *The Return of Chorb*, the short story "The Aurelian," and *The Defense* did he begin to sense that Nabokov might represent real competition.

In May 1926 Nabokov sent Bunin a copy of his first novel, *Mary*, garnished with an endearing inscription (see Figure 14): "Most respected and cherished Ivan Alekseevich, I am both happy and terrified at sending you my first book. Please do not judge me too harshly. Very truly yours, V. Nabokov."[37] *Mary* has been called the most Buninesque of all Nabokov's prose.[38] Bunin's wife, Vera Muromtseva-Bunina, who preferred *Mary* to

14. Facsimile of Nabokov's inscription to Bunin on a copy of *Mary* (1926). Beinecke Rare Book and Manuscript Library, Yale University, New Haven, Conn. Reproduced by permission.

all of Nabokov's later novels, reported that Bunin also liked Nabokov's first novel.[39] Only one comment in Bunin's hand has survived in his copy of *Mary:* "Akh, kak plokho!" (Oh, how awful!).[40] It was made in reference to the following passage in Chapter 8:

> Это было не просто воспоминание, а жизнь, гораздо действительнее, гораздо „интенсивнее" — как пишут в газетах, — чем жизнь его берлинской тени. Это был удивительный роман, развивающийся с подлинной, нежной осторожностью.
>
> (It was not simply reminiscence but a life that was much more real, much more "intense"—as they say in newspapers—than the life lived by his shadow in Berlin. It was a marvelous romance that developed with genuine, tender care; *SSoch,* 1:73/*Mary,* 55–56.)

Bunin frequently judged literature solely on the basis of verbal style, which he considered the test of a writer's mastery of his craft. The negative comment was probably caused by Nabokov's use of the adjectives *intensivnee* (more intense) and *udivitel'nyi* (marvelous). While both adjectives are employed ironically in the passage, they could have struck Bunin as stylistically unfortunate choices. *Mary* did not alarm him as much as did *The Defense, Glory,* and Nabokov's short stories published in Paris in the 1930s. Throughout the initial, "enchanted" phase of the Nabokov-Bunin relationship, Bunin's interest in Nabokov increased proportionally with Nabokov's growing presence in émigré letters.[41]

Nabokov's letters to Bunin of 1929–1931 are gentle and caring. In 1931 he thanked Bunin for sending two new books (*Bozh'e drevo* [God's Tree] and *Ten' ptitsy* [The Bird's Shadow], both 1931): "I read the first with that pleasure—unique and eluding definition—which you alone know how to give the reader with such generosity. . . . Let me only complain that neither one had an inscription, the living trace of your hand." [42] Bunin invited the Nabokovs to visit him in Grasse.[43] In 1930 Nabokov and Bunin exchanged photographs.[44] The same year, Bunin sent Nabokov the first four parts of his novel published as *Zhizn' Arsen'eva. Istoki dnei* (The Life of Arseniev: The Well of Days) with an inscribed recognition of Nabokov's talent (see Figure 15): "Dear Vladimir Vladimirovich, from the bottom of my heart and with much love for your wonderful talent I wish you a long, happy, and glorious career. Iv. Bunin. 6. II. 1930. Paris." [45] Bunin showed more and more signs of interest in Nabokov in the early 1930s. Vera Muromtseva-Bunina's diaries help reconstruct the dialectic of Bunin's evolving attitudes to the younger master. In January 1930 she recorded a conversation about her husband's prospects of winning a Nobel Prize,

15. Facsimile of Bunin's inscription to Nabokov on a copy of *The Life of Arsen'ev* (1930). Private collection, Orël, Russia. Courtesy of the Leeds Russian Archive, Leeds, England.

which tormented him at the time. "One can nominate Sirin, but how can one nominate Merezhkovskii," was Bunin's remark. The littérateur and Maecenas I. I. Fondaminskii, who had recently returned from Berlin, shared with Bunin his impressions of Nabokov, whom he had just met: "He wants to move to Paris. . . . He adores you, Ivan Alekseevich." Bunin's questions to Fondaminskii were: "And what does he look like? What did he say about literature?" [46]

Bunin and Nabokov planned to meet for the first time in Paris. In a letter sent to Bunin on October 30, 1931, Nabokov wrote that it would be "terrifying and marvelous" ("strashno i veselo") to meet him.[47] Nabokov's trip was delayed until the fall of 1932, and the two writers did not get a chance to see each other in Paris. News of Nabokov's triumph, of the great impression that his reading in November 1932 produced upon both his Parisian fans and numerous nay-sayers, reached Bunin in Grasse before long—in letters and newspapers. Three years had elapsed since the fall of 1929, when the writer Galina Kuznetsova, Bunin's intimate friend, recorded in her diary that after reading Nabokov Bunin told her that the critics and public had "overlooked a writer": "He has been writing for ten years, and neither [Parisian] critics nor readers know him." [48] Now, in the fall of 1932, the émigré public was intrigued, enchanted, and mesmerized by Nabokov. In the words of the Paris daily *The Latest News*, "Rarely is a literary evening as successful as the past reading of V. Sirin. Russian Paris showed exceptional attention to a young writer who has made a big name in a short time." [49] Indeed, between 1929 and 1932, Nabokov became the new star of the Paris-based leading émigré literary review *Contemporary Annals*.[50] As a prose writer, he debuted there with a short story, "Terror," in 1927. Then followed *The Defense* (1929), another short story, "The Aurelian" (1930), the short novel *The Eye* (1930), *Glory* (1931–1932), and, finally, *Kamera obskura* (1932–1933). In 1931 he also debuted as a short story writer in the most influential émigré newspaper, *The Latest News*. Nabokov's literary legend was being shaped in all centers of Russia Abroad: Paris, Prague, Berlin, Shanghai, Warsaw, Riga, Belgrade. He was at the center of critical attention.[51]

A close examination of the diaries, letters, and memoirs of those close to Bunin reveals that the first notes of resentment against Nabokov were heard in the Bunin household around 1931–1932, following Nabokov's rapid success. Some anti-Nabokovian notes were sounded by Bunin's close friends, who were a priori negatively predisposed toward Nabokov. Thus, in November 1932, Bunin's wife records a letter from "the other Vera," the wife of the writer Boris Zaitsev: "[Vera Zaitseva] gave a very talented account of Sirin. I also perceive him this way, but, of course, never say everything. Everyone is now a diplomat. She writes that he is 'Novyi grad' without religion. . . . Looking at him one would not say: 'Fellow writers, there is something doomed in your fate' [Brat'ia pisateli, v vashei sud'be chto-to lezhit rokovoe]."[52] Zaitseva is referring to the religious-philosophical journal *Novyi grad* (The New City), published in Paris by Il'ia Fondaminskii, Fëdor Stepun, and Georgii Fedotov in 1931–1936. Translated from private terms into accessible terms, Zaitseva's letter levels charges which are familiar to students of Nabokov: the seeming absence in his work of faith and humanism, which are supposedly inherent in great Russian writers, and, therefore, Nabokov's presumed "non-Russianness." Bunin's wife grows apprehensive of Nabokov's "Westernness." On October 10, 1931, she records in her diary: "I read Sirin. What lightness and how modern he is. He is more modern than many foreign authors. Here is somebody with an 'ironic attitude to life.' Soon he will be a candidate for the Nobel Prize."[53] What had seemed like a pleasantry back in 1930 was suddenly being regarded as a real possibility, especially in light of Bunin's own failed nominations.[54] Finally, one member of Bunin's household, his "disciple" Leonid Zurov, was openly hostile to Nabokov and envious of his success. Nabokov's coeval, Zurov originally fashioned himself as a fiction writer in Bunin's vein but then began to react to what he saw as Bunin's stylistic exuberance by writing in a different literary mode, purposely impoverished metaphorically and rarely successful stylistically. Bunin's wife recorded several lengthy conversations with Zurov—whose opinions she tended to value with maternal zeal—about the Nabokov phenomenon. On December 30, 1932, she wrote in her diary:

> [Zurov] told me: 'I do not want to go around flashing and shining [*razblëstyvat'sia*], like Sirin, I even cross out very successful similes; just as I keep my room free of decorations, I want to write simply. In this I also differ from [Bunin]. Although this glamor [*ètot blesk*— here used derisively] only happens occasionally in [Bunin's] works, there is always something serious behind it. And Sirin only has glamor. He took this feature from Bunin and went around shining. Now they even compare Sirin with [Bunin]. This might be unpleasant to [Bunin]. In the past, he was the only one who could do it, and now Sirin also does it, and even more frequently.[55]

Such comments, which surely surfaced more and more in Bunin's household, prepared the way for Bunin's disenchantment with Nabokov in the late 1930s. Still, despite the gossip and backbiting in his own household, in 1932–1933 Bunin was still fond of Nabokov. After all, there were Nabokov's friendly and loyal letters as well as his highly favorable review of Bunin's poetry, in which younger émigré poets displayed little interest.[56] In fact, on two other occasions Nabokov polemicized with the critics of Bunin's poetry on the pages of *The Rudder,* fiercely defending Bunin from the attacks of the dismissive younger radicals.[57] And of course there were Nabokov's short stories, now appearing in Paris and displaying certain features of style and composition that distinguished them from virtually everything else in émigré fiction. Of all readers, Bunin certainly knew that Nabokov was pursuing in short fiction the tradition which Chekhov had established and he himself had enriched and perfected in the 1910s–1920s (I have previously referred to this tradition as covert modernism). But Bunin also discerned the innovations, both in structure and in metaphysical thematics, that put Nabokov much ahead of his contemporaries in Russia Abroad. As Bunin followed the qualitative growth of Nabokov's short fiction from the early stories, some of them collected in *The Return of Chorb* (a copy of which he owned), to the stories of the early 1930s, he reflected upon the formative role his own short stories might have played in Nabokov's artistic career.[58]

In July 1931 Nabokov's short story "A Bad Day" appeared in the Paris daily *The Latest News,* now the leading émigré newspaper. The story bore a dedication to Ivan Bunin. "A Bad Day," Nabokov's first story to be published in *The Latest News,* where Bunin was a regular contributor, would be followed by fourteen more during Nabokov's Middle period (1930–1935) alone.

A question immediately comes to mind: what were the reasons behind Nabokov's dedication? Clearly, he had had numerous prior opportunities to acknowledge his gratitude to one of the greatest masters of short fiction. By 1931 Nabokov had published a collection of fifteen short stories with visible Bunin traces. Some of them had appeared in émigré periodicals, including the Parisian review *Contemporary Annals,* which had featured Bunin's finest works of the 1920s ("Mitia's Love," "The Sunstroke"). Why did Nabokov not dedicate to Bunin his first appearance in *Contemporary Annals,* the story "Terror"? And what about "The Aurelian," whose protagonist echoes the hero of Bunin's "The Gentleman from San Francisco"? I think that Nabokov was deeply concerned with Bunin's stylistic traces and that his dedication constituted a carefully weighed and precise recognition of what he perceived as Buninesque features in his own early short stories.

Thematically, "A Bad Day" shows connections with a series of Bunin's stories, mostly dating back to the 1890s–1900s, which depict the anxieties of a young adolescent against the background of the Russian countryside in summer. As I have suggested in Chapter 2, "A Bad Day," along with another story from the Middle period, "Orache," might have been two installments of Nabokov's unrealized Bildungsroman. In "A Bad Day," the protagonist, Putya (Peter) Shishkov, a painfully self-conscious teenager with an acute awareness of falseness, has to attend a children's party at a neighboring country estate. Alienated from his pedantic older sister, and possibly encumbered by his budding sexuality (to which Nabokov points only very covertly), Putya perceives the world in private terms which he alone can understand. He is uncomfortable around his peers, which they notice right away and use to boycott his presence. Putya is also fascinated by Tanya, a "pretty girl of eleven or twelve with an ivory pale skin, bluish shadows under the eyes, and a black braid caught by a white bow above her delicate neck" (*Stories*, 270). He tries to win her attention, but, alas, another teenager, the robust and insolent Vasya Tuchkov, is more successful. The story ends anticlimactically after Putya's rival pronounces what amounts to the boy's verdict in the eyes of his peers: "And here comes the poseur" ("A vot idët lomaka"; *Stories*, 276/*S*, 103).

At least five short stories and a novella by Bunin constitute a thematic and stylistic background for "A Bad Day." In "Pervaia liubov'" (First Love, 1890), the earliest, we find three teenage boys in the country who also represent, much like Putya, Vasya, and Volodya in "A Bad Day," their author's "remembered self which is really split here among three lads" (*Stories*, 651). Mitia, the protagonist, is in love with his friend's cousin Sasha and terribly ashamed to admit it to the other boys. Like Nabokov's Putya, he is dreamy and torn by complexes, at times offended by his friends' teenage bravado. At the end of "A Bad Day" one senses echoes of Mitia's despair in the culminating scene of "First Love," where the boy's uncle embarrasses him in front of Sasha and her girlfriends. "First Love" points to a later short text, "Kukushka" (Cuckoo, 1898), in which we also encounter three teenagers in the country; one of them is named Mitia. Much as Putya Shishkov may be seen as a teenage predecessor of one of Nabokov's most memorable protagonists, Vasiliy Shishkov, Mitia of "First Love" and "Cuckoo" exhibits some nascent features of the protagonist of "Mitia's Love" (1924), one of Bunin's finest novellas of the émigré period. Partly set on a Russian country estate, "Mitia's Love" attracted a great deal of critical attention because of the novelty of its treatment of a young man's sexuality. Linda Saputelli Zimmermann has drawn several parallels between "A Bad Day" and Bunin's masterpiece. She compares the composition of desire in the two stories: Putya's attraction to Tanya in "A Bad Day" and

Mitia's to Katia in "Mitia's Love." She also suggests curious reflections of Bunin's color palette in Putya's avidly colorful vision of the world.[59] One can also notice some traces of Bunin's "Na dache" (In the Country, 1895)—a *dachnyi rasskaz* (Russian country house short story) with a Chekhovian narrative flow—in the setting of "A Bad Day." Finally, a little story by Bunin written in 1930 and also entitled "First Love" might have left an imprint in Nabokov's creative practice and informed "A Bad Day."[60] In it Bunin draws a sketch of a young adolescent's love for a proud and fastidious teenage girl. Like Putya, Bunin's protagonist plays with his peers while actually being on the verge of desperate tears. The parallels between Nabokov's "A Bad Day" and Bunin's "In the Country," "First Love" (1890), "Cuckoo," "Mitia's Love," and "First Love" (1930) may be due not so much to the younger writer's conscious effort to dialogize with the older master but to the shared setting of the Russian countryside gentry topos.[61] However, there is a marvelous short work from Bunin's pre-1917 period which lends Nabokov's story some of its concrete verbal motifs.

Bunin reworked "Dalëkoe" (Distant Dreams, 1903) twice and published it at least three times during the émigré years. In its 1937 version, it reads like a draft for his autobiographical novel *The Life of Arseniev*.[62] "Distant Dreams" depicts one day in the life of a nine-year-old protagonist, Il'ia. Unlike Putya, Il'ia is having a wonderful day as his father takes him hunting. The first half of the story describes a ride to the swamp, while the second climaxes in the hunting scene and Il'ia's excitement. The verbal echoes of Bunin's story in "A Bad Day" center on the description of the carriage, the horse, and the hunting dog, as well as certain elements of nature. Both stories abound with references to summer flowers and insects, grasshoppers in particular, with images of summer sky and clouds and instances of effective chiaroscuro interplay of sun and shade ("Shine and shade speckled the depths of the forest: one could not separate the pattern of tree trunks from that of their interspaces"; *Stories*, 269). Given what Nabokov said in the 1938 letter to Malozemoff, one also finds Bunin's signature color, purple (*lilovyi*), resurfacing in Nabokov's story. Bunin's young protagonist sees "blue cornflowers, purple cockles [*lilovye kukoli*] and yellow charlock flowers" (Bunin 2:286). Nabokov's Putya picks bilberries, "big, with a bloom dimming their blue, which revealed a bright [purple] luster" (*lilovym bleskom; S*, 94/*Stories*, 271). Such parallels, as well as Nabokov's dressing the coachman in the same item of clothing, a "sleeveless vest" (*bezrukavka*), as Bunin's coachman in "Distant Dreams," create a sense of recognition for a Bunin reader encountering Nabokov's story. Nabokov's evocation of Bunin's image of a dog chasing after a moving carriage or the tarry smell wafting from the carriage also works in a similar fashion. Such evocations might be partially coincidental and are not necessarily subtextual. However, when Nabokov transfers Bunin's image of a hunting dog's "sleek coat" (*atlasnaia sherst'*) to a horse's coat (*S*, 88) without any alterations, this comes close to being a direct link with its textual antecedent.

Graceful and rhythmically elegant, stylistically near-perfect, "A Bad Day" is nevertheless one of the least Nabokovian among his stories. In some respects, Nabokov's project of reproducing some of Bunin's emblematic achievements was successful. "A Bad Day" proved Nabokov capable of writing with brilliance in Bunin's celebrated medium: a psychological short story in which sections of distanced narrative in medias res alternate with instances of free indirect discourse. Like Bunin in the overall majority of his short stories, Nabokov in "A Bad Day" also paid special attention to descriptions, sometimes excessively exuberant but always authentic-sounding.

And yet there is something about "A Bad Day" that strikes a student of Nabokov as alien to the very spirit of his art. First, we find virtually nothing of the kind of two-dimensionality, the opposition between the mundane and the otherworldly, that had evolved in his stories by the early 1930s (see Chapter 1). Second, despite the perceived drama of a boy's loneliness, the story is too serene and devoid of tension in comparison to most of Nabokov's other short fictions, or Bunin's stories for that matter. Even as compared to its immediate sequel, "Orache," "A Bad Day" exhibits fewer moments of absolute despair in which wordplay (pun, anagram, homonym, etc.) and human tragedy are as inseparable as are the metaliterary and metaphysical categories in Nabokov's fiction. Only a few instances of a characteristically Nabokovian urge "to do things with words," to borrow J. L. Austin's expression, figure in the story. In the episode where Putya encounters an old French governess, a literary cousin of Mademoiselle O from the eponymous story/memoir, Nabokov creates an estranged perspective by rendering the old French lady's heavily accented Russian via hybrid Russian-French words written in the Latin alphabet: "*Priate-qui? Priate-qui?* [from the Russian *priatki,* hide-and-seek] . . . *Sichasse pocajou caroche messt* [from *seichas pokazhu khoroshee mesto:* now I'll show you a good place]" (*Stories,* 275). Such wordplay hardly ever occurs in Bunin's stories. The funny speech of the old governess, recorded with an absurd logic, shows Putya's despair and alienation during the name-day party. (Incidentally, this kind of Russian-French wordplay goes back to Tolstoi's *War and Peace,* where Nikolai Rostov—in a moment of acute emotional exaltation—reads the French spelling of his sister's name, "Natache," as encoding the French word "une tache" [spot], which is semantically charged in the episode.)

Thus, in the end, "A Bad Day"—dedicated to Bunin and evoking several of his stories—sent a professional message to the old master. On a symbolic plane, Nabokov honored Bunin's contribution to the genre of the Russian short story, which Chekhov revolutionized and Bunin brought to perfection. "A Bad Day" summed up a number of features which Nabokov was willing to admit having learned from Bunin during the Early period. A number of his works from the 1920s–early 1930s— both short stories and novels—reveal a continuous dialogue with Bunin occurring simultaneously on several levels of the text, from plot composition to minuscule if always fortuitous details.

The first example comes from Nabokov's "In Memory of L. I. Shigaev," written in Berlin in 1934 and published in Paris the same year. The story is structured as an obituary for the narrator's deceased friend, a Russian *intelligent*. As an account of the narrator's friendship with this gentle and pure soul, the story recalls and/or anticipates several of the real obituaries Nabokov wrote and published in the 1920s–1930s, especially those for his friends, the critic Iulii Aikhenval'd, the poet Sasha Chërnyi, and the wife of Il'ia Fondaminskii.[63] There is a plausible antecedent for Nabokov's fictional obituary among Bunin's works of the émigré period, the short story "Aleksei Alekseevich," originally published in Paris in 1927.[64] Both open point-blank, by stating the irreversible facts: Nabokov's "Umer Leonid Ivanovich Shigaev" (Leonid Ivanovich Shigaev is dead; *VF*, 87/*Stories*, 368), and Bunin's "Nelepaia, nepravdopodobnaia vest': Aleksei Alekseevich umer!" (The senseless, unbelievable news: Aleksei Alekseevich is dead!; Bunin 5:367). This opening statement is followed in both short texts by a series of recollections—some of them anecdotal—which are very loosely connected with one another. Bunin's Aleksei Alekseevich and Nabokov's Leonid Ivanovich are very different people, the former a jovial theater buff, the latter a shy academic. The narrators' attitudes to their deceased friends also differ drastically: Nabokov's narrator expresses love for his older fatherly friend, while Bunin's memoirist treats the deceased with slightly cynical condescension. However, in both stories, the dead subjects come out remarkably alive because their invented histories are presented as live recollections.

"Christmas," one of Nabokov's finest stories of the Early period, points to Bunin's "Snezhnyi byk" (Snow Bull, 1911). Set on a country estate in winter, Bunin's short story is outstanding in its compassionate depiction of a father's love for a young son. The boy in "Snow Bull" is not dead, as in Nabokov's "Christmas," but he is terrified. The boy cries in his sleep for several nights in a row. His father, a landlord by the name of Khrushchëv—also the name of the family of substeppe landowners in Bunin's "Sukhodol" (Dry Valley, 1911)—gets up to comfort him. I know very few texts in all of Russian literature which create such a moving and believable sense of a father's pain and fear for his son's young life, a father's pure tenderness and care, as in Bunin's "Snow Bull" and Nabokov's "Christmas." Despite the affinities between the setting of the two stories and their focus on fatherly love, one also notices intrinsic differences between Bunin's and Nabokov's artistic worlds. Khrushchëv goes out into the winter night to eliminate what he thinks is the cause of his son's pain: an ugly snow sculpture of a bull casting macabre shadows into the boy's room. Having destroyed the cause of pain, both his son's and his own, he walks about his yard marveling at the pacifying earthly harmony of the winter surroundings. Nabokov offers his privileged character, Sleptsov, different means of dealing with his pain: an otherworldly metaphor, a giant Indian moth, transcends his pain of loss and helps him to preserve idealized memories of his dead teenage son.

Another example of Nabokov's dialogue with his older contemporary, this time on the level of characterization, occurs in "The Aurelian," the finest story of the Middle period. Pilgram, the protagonist, a philistine on the surface and an otherworldly dreamer on the inside, lives his entire life in preparation for a journey he hopes to undertake one day (see Chapter 2). From behind the counter of his dismal shop, Pilgram undertakes regular journeys in his mind, and his destinations include the Islands of the Blessed, Corsica, Andalusia, Dalmatia, and other exotic regions. Pilgram resembles the hero of Bunin's "The Gentleman from San Francisco" (1915)—one of the highest points of Bunin's pre-1917 creativity. Like Pilgram, the gentleman from San Francisco has never lived to his heart's content despite being in his late fifties (Pilgram is almost fifty). He works hard making money and hopes to take a trip to "Europe, India, Egypt," where "people of his sort were accustomed to begin enjoying life" (Bunin 4:308). As it turns out, Bunin's protagonist dies on the paradisal island of Capri at the height of his earthly and sensuous dream's consummation, while Nabokov's Pilgram suffers a fatal stroke on the verge of his otherworldly obsession becoming a reality.[65]

Nabokov, who is known to have devised dazzling traps for many of his literary colleagues, conjured up a parodic evocation of Bunin's melodramatic novella "Syn" (The Son, 1916). In "Syn," which Nabokov was not very likely to have valued as highly as Bunin's other works, a woman falls in love with a young man half her age. For a while she tries to block the growing attraction or, rather, to channel it into maternal feelings for a young man (her own children are female). At one point in the story, her young lover kneels before her in the garden and presses himself against her lap: "And looking at his hair, his white thin neck, she thought with pain and delight: 'Oh, yes, yes, I could have had a son just like that!'" [66] In Nabokov's "The Potato Elf," one of the longest stories of the Early period, we find a mise en scène whose structure parodies the one in "The Son." Fred Dobson, a circus dwarf, sits at the feet of Nora Shock, the wife of his colleague, and narrates his life. His "black jacket, inclined face, fleshy little nose, tawny hair, and that middle parting reaching the back of his head vaguely moved Nora's heart": "As she looked at him through her lashes she tried to imagine that it was not an adult dwarf sitting there, but her non-existing little son in the act of telling her how his schoolmates bullied him" (*VCh*, 174/*Stories*, 234; in "The Son" the young man also appears miserable and lonely).

While the list of evocations of Bunin's stories could go on, I will stop here to offer a more generalized view of what Nabokov learned from Bunin during the Early and Middle periods.

First, I think that Nabokov learned from Bunin—one of the foremost stylists of Russian prose in the twentieth century—the art of intonation and rhythm. Every major writer is recognizable by the intonation of his or her prose, a function of both the syntax and semantics of a given textual unit. The rhythm of Bunin's prose has been the subject of previous critical inquiry. Both Èmma Polotskaia and Elizabeth Malozemoff have stressed the role of Bunin's poetry in the formation of the intonational contours of his prose.[67] Nabokov's simultaneous preoccupation with both poetry and prose is analogous. Two passages illustrate what I mean by "Bunin's intonations" in Nabokov's short stories: one from "The Gentleman from San Francisco," the other from "The Aurelian," both dealing with the protagonists' projected journeys leading to death. Bunin writes of the trip the American gentleman hopes to undertake:

> В декабре и январе он надеялся наслаждаться солнцем Южной Италии, памятниками древности, тарантеллой, серенадами бродячих певцов и тем, что люди в его годы чувствуют особенно тонко, — любовью молоденьких неаполитанок, пусть даже и не совсем бескорыстной; карнавал он думал провести в Ницце, в Монте-Карло, куда в эту пору стекается самое отборное общество, где одни с азартом предаются

автомобильным и парусным гонкам, другие рулетке, третьи тому, что принято называть флиртом, а четвёртые — стрельбе в голубей, которые очень красиво взвиваются из садков над изумрудным газоном, на фоне моря цвета незабудок, и тотчас же опускаются белыми комочками о землю; начало марта он хотел посвятить Флоренции, к страстям господним приехать в Рим.... (Bunin 4:309)

(In December and January he hoped to enjoy the sun of Southern Italy, the monuments of antiquity, the tarantella, the serenades of strolling singers, and that which men of his age relish with the utmost finesse: the love of little, youthful Neapolitaines, even though it be given not entirely without ulterior motives; he contemplated spending the Carnival in Nice, in Monte Carlo, whither the very pick of society gravitates at that time,—Monte Carlo, where some give themselves up with passion to automobile and sail races; others to roulette; a third group to that which it is the custom to call flirting; a fourth, to trap-shooting, in which the pigeons, released from their cotes, soar up most gracefully above emerald-green swards, against the background of a sea that is the color of forget-me-nots,— only, in some minute, to strike against the ground as little, crumpled clods of white; the beginning of March he wanted to devote to Florence; about the time of the Passion of Our Lord to arrive at Rome. . . .) [68]

In Nabokov's story, one of Pilgram's dream-trips is described as follows:

Он посещал Тенериффу, окрестности Оротавы, где в жарких, цветущих овражках, которыми изрезаны нижние склоны гор, поросших каштаном и лавром, летает диковинная разновидность капустницы, и тот, другой остров — давнюю любовь охотников, — где на железнодорожном скате, около Виццавоны, и повыше, в сосновых лесах, водится смуглый, коренастый корсиканский махаон. Он посещал и север — болота Лапландии, где мох, гонобобель и карликовая ива, богатый мохнатыми бабочками полярный край, — и высокие альпийские пастбища, с плоскими камнями, лежащими там и сям среди старой, скользкой, колтунной травы, — и, кажется, нет большего наслаждения, чем приподнять такой камень, под которым и муравьи, и синий скарабей, и толстенькая сонная ночница, ещё, быть может, никем не названная; и там же, в горах, он видел полупрозрачных, красноглазых аполлонов, которые плывут по ветру через горный тракт, идущий вдоль отвесной скалы и отделённый широкой каменной оградой от пропасти, где бурно белеет вода. (*S*, 197)

(In these impossible dreams of his he had visited the Islands of the Blessed, where in the hot ravines that cut the lower slopes of the chestnut- and laurel-clad mountains there occurs a weird local race of the cabbage white; and also that other island, those railway banks near Vizzavona and the pine woods farther up, which are the haunts of the squat and dusky Corsican swallow-tail. He visited the far North, the Arctic bogs that produced such delicate downy butterflies. He knew the high Alpine pastures, with those flat stones lying here and there among the slippery matted grass; for there is no greater delight than to lift such a stone and find beneath it a plump sleepy moth of a still undescribed species. He saw glazed Apollo butterflies, ocellated with red, float in the mountain draught across the mule track that ran between a steep cliff and an abyss of wild waters; *Stories*, 254; the translation departs significantly from the original.)

In both cases, we have extremely long passages consisting of long sentence units, separated by semicolons and held together semantically, rather than syntactically. In each of these sentence units within the long passages, the intonation is cemented by a series of subordinate or participial clauses, some short, some much longer, woven together with or without conjunctions (cf. Bunin's "Monte-Karlo, kuda . . . obshchestvo, gde . . . golubei, kotorye . . ." and Nabokov's "apollonov, kotorye . . . trakt, idushchii . . . propasti, gde . . ."). The long syntactic contours in both passages entail several long independent clauses, each of which is a complex-complex or complex-compound sentence.[69]

Malozemoff has pointed to the prominence of "Biblical syntax" in Bunin's prose.[70] Bunin uses the Russian conjunctions equivalent to the English "and" (*i, a, da*) in order to open a sentence as well as connect a series of sentences within a passage or a sequence of independent clauses within a single long sentence. Such a syntactic structure creates a flow of prose with a prosodic organization, a succession of speech units of relatively similar length, each of which, in this case, starts with an "and" conjunction.[71] Examples of such a syntactic structure are omnipresent in Bunin's prose. For instance, the very end of "The Gentleman from San Francisco" consists of three very long sentences each starting with "and." In Nabokov's case, one example strikes me as a particularly extreme demonstration of Bunin's intonational forte. The magnificent last sentence from "Perfection," one of the longest in Russian short fiction, comprises a sequence of eleven (!) independent clauses, all beginning with the Russian conjunction *i* (and). Such a long series of units of similar length, all opening with the same conjunction, creates an incantational intonation which here enhances the sense of an otherworldly opening in the text of the story.[72]

As for the narrative structure of Nabokov's short stories from the Early and Middle periods, at least one significant feature may be attributed to Bunin's influence. Seven of Nabokov's stories from the Early period ("The Revenge," "The Potato Elf," "A Matter of Chance," "Details of a Sunset," "Bachmann," "The Dragon," "Terror"), and five from the Middle period ("The Aurelian," "Terra Incognita," "Perfection," "The Leonardo," "A Russian Beauty") follow Bunin's favorite narrative recipe of employing death to create narrative closure (cf. "The Gentleman from San Francisco," "Kazimir Stanislavovich," "Loopy Ears," "Mitia's Love," "The Affair of Cornet Elagin"). Among Nabokov's early stories, two utilize death in the most Buninesque fashion, a mixture of tragic and melodramatic. In "Revenge" an English professor's young and chaste wife finds a skeleton in her bed and suffers a massive fright-induced heart attack. In "The Potato Elf" Nora reveals the fact of her son's death right after Dobson's heart attack at the train station.

During the Middle period Nabokov continues to employ death as a means of ending a narrative, although in stories like "The Aurelian" and "Perfection" one can already distinguish the shape of his argument with Bunin that reaches a crescendo in the mid to late 1930s. The argument concerns the artists' understanding of the phenomenon of death. During the Middle period rapid changes in Nabokov's aesthetics, ethics, and metaphysics are especially manifest. In "The Leonardo" the proto-Nazi thugs murder their Russian neighbor only because he is beyond their understanding. Death there is an instrument of human conflict, a reflection of the historical condition, and the artist's way of bridging his aesthetics and his view of society's eroded ethics. In "The Leonardo" Nabokov shares Bunin's overwhelming concern with violence in society and death as its ultimate consequence. Nabokov's narrative structure mirrors German society on the verge of Nazism. He follows Bunin's view that artistic form reflects the shape of modernity. To recall a tirade by Sokolovich in "Loopy Ears," Bunin's serial killer with "ideas," "Every boy is crazy about [James Fenimore] Cooper where all they do is scalp people, . . . every pastor knows that in the Bible the word 'kill' is used more than a thousand times and in most cases with incredible praise of and gratitude for these acts of divine will. . . . Soon Europe will become nothing but a kingdom of killers" (Bunin 4:390–391). Conversely, in "A Russian Beauty," and especially in "The Aurelian" and "Perfection," the shift away from Bunin's view of death is evident. Some twenty years later, in a 1963 introduction to *Bend Sinister*, Nabokov would write: "there is nothing to fear, death is but a question of style, a mere literary device, a musical resolution" (*BS*, xviii–xix). The focus of the endings in "The Aurelian" or "Perfection" is not on the protagonist's death as we are accustomed to seeing it in our mundane lives, but on entering the otherworld. The protagonist's otherworldly experience reverberates in the reader's memory even after "the clouded glasses" (*Stories*, 347) have been removed and the character is pronounced dead by his creator.

On November 10, 1933, soon after the announcement of Bunin's Nobel Prize, Nabokov sent a letter of congratulations. He described the jubilant state of their fellow exiles, "everybody greeting each other as during a holiday."[73] And after several failed attempts, Nabokov and Bunin finally met in person. The Russian community in Berlin organized a gala to honor Bunin. It was scheduled for December 30, chaired by Iosif Gessen, with speeches and readings from Bunin's works. Although Bunin was not expected, he arrived at the last moment.[74] Nabokov gave a lyrical speech about Bunin's poetry, in which he reiterated some of the main points made earlier in his 1929 review of Bunin's *Selected Poems*. He also recited his favorite poems by Bunin. The two were photographed standing on the stage together. Émigré papers furnished the photographs with characteristic captions:

> The Russian colony in Berlin celebrated the arrival of the Nobel Prize laureate in literature, I. A. Bunin, with a gala-event. On stage the famous Russian writer was greeted by I. V. Gessen, the former leader of the Constitutional-Democratic Party. . . . Applauding, from the right, the poet Sergei Krechetov [well-known Silver Age publisher and poet], from the left, the most talented of the young Russian writers, V. V. Sirin.[75]

Bunin and Nabokov, who had never met personally before, stood next to each other as the two stars of Russian literature. A correspondence spanning more than twelve years preceded this meeting. It began in 1921 when Nabokov was a virtually unknown poet and Bunin the literary king of the emigration, the last classic, who did not have to write anything more to maintain his literary reputation (a 1934 photograph of Bunin is reproduced in Figure 16). During the first phase of the Nabokov-Bunin

16. Ivan Bunin, Cannes, France, 1934. Courtesy of the Leeds Russian Archive, Leeds, England.

dialogue, ending in their 1933 meeting, Chekhov remained for Nabokov a stable point of reference, while Bunin served as a live representative of the great Russian tradition, both a classic and a contemporary who continued to evolve and thereby challenge him to new achievements. By the end of 1933 Nabokov's fame and legend had spread all around Russia Abroad. He was no longer in the position to regard Bunin as his literary mentor. Little is known of the content of Nabokov's conversation with Bunin early in January 1934, when they met again, for lunch (some recollections of this lunch made their way into *Speak, Memory,* into the episode describing a Paris meeting between the two writers, discussed later in the chapter). Their relationship entered its second phase, from 1933 until 1939, a literary race in which Nabokov would always be several steps ahead of Bunin.

The middle to late 1930s were an extremely difficult time for the aging Bunin. He was devastated by the breakup with the writer Galina Kuznetsova; the reasons for their estrangement were incomprehensible to him (Kuznetsova became a companion of the singer Marga Stepun).[76] In his diaries Bunin wrote of the years 1934–1936 as some sort of madness, which resulted in a series of mistakes, financial recklessness, giving up royalties from his eleven-volume *Works;* Bunin also spoke of approaching old age, of sinking to a profound low, of his complete lack of willpower, of a senseless existence.[77]

Such was the background against which Nabokov's meetings with Bunin took place in France in 1936–1939. After 1933–1934 the two writers saw each other once more in Berlin, in October 1936, but not much is known about their meeting.[78] In January 1936, when Nabokov arrived in Paris for a series of readings, his fame had grown enormously in Russian literary circles. He was also gaining an international reputation. Nabokov, who had been called "Bunin's heir," was beginning to eclipse Bunin.[79] Critics spoke of Bunin's influence on Nabokov's language, but emphasized how different Nabokov's "art of composition" was from that of Bunin.[80] An article from a Russian-language newspaper in San Francisco with a characteristic title, "V. V. Sirin—the New Star in Literature," illustrates the reception of Nabokov's works in the mid-1930s:

> Over the past years we have witnessed the rapid ascent of a new star in literature, Vladimir Vladimirovich Sirin-Nabokov. . . . Sirin is one of those happy exceptions when one can set aside cautious reservations, since, despite his youth, this Russian émigré is no longer an apprentice, but a perfectly mature writer. There is no doubt that he is a

star of great magnitude, the most distinguished of the new writers to come out of Russia (both Soviet and émigré) over the past 6–7 years.[81]

Nabokov's presence in Russian letters began to haunt the already troubled Bunin. Their stories in English translations appeared in the same magazine in London.[82] Their books came out in the same publishing houses as the Russian book market steadily shrank. The leading émigré critics, including Adamovich, Bitsilli, Khodasevich, Struve, and Veidle, now discussed Nabokov's works regularly in Paris periodicals. Pëtr Bitsilli a professor of Russian literature at the University of Sofia, wrote in a provocative 1936 essay that Nabokov's "gift is so mighty and his formal perfection so high" that he would "remain part of [Russian literature] so long as it still exists."[83] The same year Bitsilli opened his long essay "Vozrozhdenie allegorii" (The Rebirth of Allegory) with a reference to Bunin's remark on Tolstoi.[84] Bunin was becoming a historical point of departure in critical discussions of Nabokov's thriving art.

Separate mention should be made of Nabokov's place in the Russian periodicals of the 1930s. I have already discussed Nabokov's regular appearances in the leading émigré newspaper, *The Latest News*. His contributions to the foremost émigré quarterly, *Contemporary Annals,* might have been the source of Bunin's greatest distress. Between 1930 and 1940 (when the review ended its existence with its seventieth issue) works by and about Nabokov appeared in twenty-eight out of thirty issues (including six novels, one short novel, and four short stories), while works by and about Bunin appeared in only ten issues.[85] In contrast, from 1920 to 1930 (forty issues) seven works by and about Nabokov were featured in comparison with twenty by and about Bunin. Students of Bunin know that after 1930 his output of fiction and poetry went down drastically, not to recover until 1937, when he began working on his last testament, the book of love stories entitled *Dark Avenues*.[86] Bunin's sense of his own creative crisis in the mid-1930s (most of the stories in *Dark Avenues* were not written until 1940–1944; the only other book he wrote and published before the war was the 1937 *Osvobozhdenie Tolstogo* [Tolstoi's Liberation], about half of which consisted of quotations) might explain the change in his attitude to Nabokov from interest and cautious appreciation in the late 1920s–early 1930s to growing animosity in the late 1930s.[87] The surviving accounts of their meetings between 1936 and 1939 help to explain some of the reasons behind Bunin's decision to prove his worth in Russian letters by creating a masterpiece, one of the finest works in Russian literature, *Dark Avenues*.

Nabokov arrived in Paris on January 28, 1936.[88] As he described his day in a letter, half an hour later he was already sitting in a café with a "tipsy Bunin" ("s podvypivshim Buninym").[89] In a letter to his wife, sent on January 30, Nabokov gave a journalistic account of the meeting with his literary colleague:

> At first our conversation flagged, mainly I think because of me. I was tired and cross. Everything irritated me: his manner of ordering hazel-grouse, and every intonation, and his bawdy little jokes, and the deliberate servility of the waiter, so that he later complained to Aldanov I was thinking about something else all the time. I haven't been so angry in a long time as over going to dine with him. But toward the end and later, when we went out in the street, sparks of mutuality began to flash here and there, and when we went into the Café de la Paix, where plump Aldanov was waiting for us, it was quite cheery.[90]

In *Speak, Memory,* written some fifteen years after their meeting in Paris and revised thereafter, Nabokov devoted a long passage to Bunin. This account stems from his discussion of Russian émigré literature in the 1930s. Nabokov adumbrates his mention of Bunin before speaking directly of him: "And there was the old *cher maître* dropping pearl by pearl an admirable tale he had read innumerable times, and always in the same manner, wearing the expression of fastidious distaste that his nobly furrowed face had in the frontispiece of his collected works" (*SM,* 282).[91] The actual account of their meetings follows a few pages later:

> Another independent writer was Ivan Bunin. . . . At the time I found him tremendously perturbed by the personal problem of aging. The first thing he said to me was to remark with satisfaction that his posture was better than mine, despite his being some thirty years older than I [Bunin was born in 1870, Nabokov in 1899]. He was basking in the Nobel prize he had just received and invited me to some kind of expensive and fashionable eating place in Paris for a heart-to-heart talk. Unfortunately, I happen to have a morbid dislike for restaurants and cafés, especially Parisian ones—I detest crowds, harried waiters, Bohemians, vermouth concoctions, coffee, *zakuski* [Russian *hors d'oeuvres*], floor shows and so forth. . . . Heart-to-heart talks, confessions in the Dostoevskian manner [actually Bunin detested Dostoevskii as much as Nabokov did], are also not in my line. Bunin, a spry old gentleman, with a rich and unchaste vocabulary, was puzzled by my irresponsiveness to the hazel grouse of which I had had enough in my childhood and exasperated by my refusal to discuss eschatological matters. Toward the end of the meal we were utterly bored

with each other. "You will die in dreadful pain and complete iso-
lation," remarked Bunin bitterly as we went toward the cloak-
room. . . . I wanted to help Bunin into his raglan but he stopped me
with a proud gesture of his open hand. Still struggling perfunc-
torily—*he* was now trying to help *me*—we emerged into the pallid
bleakness of a Paris winter day. My companion was about to button
his collar when a look of surprise and distress twisted his handsome
features. Gingerly opening his overcoat, he began tugging at something under his armpit. I came to his assistance and together we
finally dragged out of his sleeve my long woolen scarf . . . stuffed into
the wrong coat. The thing came out inch by inch; it was like unwrap-
ping a mummy and we kept slowly revolving around each other in
the process, to the ribald amusement of three sidewalk whores. Then,
when the operation was over, we walked on without a word to a street
corner where we shook hands and separated. (*SM*, 285–286)

The historical novelist Mark Aldanov, who witnessed part of the meeting, said that "when Bunin and [Nabokov] talked to each other and
looked at each other it felt all the time as if two movie cameras were
rolling."[92] The 1936 Paris meeting finally made it clear to both Nabokov
and Bunin that as human beings they had nothing to say to each other. As
artists, they had already grown too far apart. On an allegorical level, "un-
wrapping a mummy" during a ritual dance the two writers performed in
a Parisian street before "amused" prostitutes signified Nabokov's imminent "separation" not only from Bunin as the best living Russian prose
writer of the older generation, but also from the boundaries of Russian
culture, which Bunin could never conceive of traversing. *Invitation to a
Beheading* was being serialized in *Contemporary Annals* as the two writers
faced each other on a Parisian street, and *The Gift* was on its way. As we
know from Bunin's letters of the late 1930s–1950s, he never fully came to
terms with the Nabokov phenomenon: here was a writer whose art exhibited much stylistic kinship with Bunin's own fiction and yet shared very
little with his underlying world view.

The émigré author Nina Berberova wrote about Bunin in *Kursiv moi*
(The Italics Are Mine, 1969) that he was "an absolute and inveterate athe-
ist" (["byl] absoliutnym i zakorenelym ateistom"). She also said that he
never concerned himself with religious issues and had no capacity for abstract thinking. Berberova, who knew both Nabokov and Bunin well,
called Bunin a "completely *earthly* person" ("*zemnoi* chelovek"), a "concrete wholesome animal" with a talent to "create the beautiful in primitive
forms, ready and preexisting him."[93] To see Bunin as Berberova did is to

miss the point. I will not pursue here the biographical details of Bunin's upbringing and adult life and the role organized religion played there. I will say, however, that the world view which Bunin's fiction projects—let alone his travels to the Holy Land documented in *Bird's Shadow* or his biblical poetry—strikes me as remarkably Judeo-Christian, with an emphasis on the mythopoetics of the Old Testament. Indeed, Bunin's mind was characteristically Cartesian in some respects. As for Descartes of the Third Meditation, the existence of God and divine order was for Bunin ultimately a notion that required no proof. He did not probe the cosmology of the universe in his writings. Bunin's concerns as a philosopher of human existence were with the fundamental issues an average human mind can fathom, mainly with the limits and powers of desires. His covert modernism and his world view as a modern subject derive from his keen interest in the extremities and crises of desire in the twentieth century. Bunin's artistic preoccupation with death, manifest in the stories of the 1910s and culminating in *Dark Avenues,* reflected not his interest in the postmortem survival of consciousness but rather his awareness that death ends the joy of earthly living celebrated in his writings. Beyond Bunin's meditations on the evanescence of life (e.g., "Light Breathing"), largely inherited from Ecclesiastes or such poets of antiquity as Horace, his modern metaphysical concerns are few.

To return to my reconstruction of the 1936 Paris meeting between the two writers, Bunin saw in Nabokov a writer who was no longer inside the artistic territory that Bunin claimed as his own. Prior to that, while reading Nabokov's short stories such as "The Aurelian" or "Perfection" and the novels *The Defense* or *Invitation to a Beheading,* and in fact as early as 1929, Bunin saw a writer who, as he put it, "opened a whole world" ("otrkyl tselyi mir") of his own in Russian literature.[94] But Bunin probably realized that as the last representative of Russian literature which starts with "Zhukovskii and Karamzin," includes Tolstoi and Turgenev, and "ends with Ivan Bunin" he could not discern the nature of Nabokov's discovered metaphysical world.[95]

The Nabokov that Bunin saw in January 1936 was no longer the exalted young author of confessional letters, nor the brilliant admirer of Bunin's verse whom Bunin perceived in the reflected light of his Nobel fame, but Nabokov the mature writer who knew his worth full well and no longer needed to be part of a literary tradition, school, or even a culture besides "that of talent."[96] Bunin's reaction to Nabokov was a mixture of disappointment, bile, jealousy—and continuing admiration of his talent. These components would define the nature of his responses until Nabokov's move to America in 1940. As for Nabokov, he described the character of his subsequent meetings with Bunin as "a bantering and rather depressing mode of conversation, a Russian variety of American 'kidding,' and this precluded any real commerce between [them]" (*SM*, 287).

Nabokov and Bunin continued to see each other in Paris. On February 8, 1936, Bunin attended the evening of readings by Nabokov and Khodasevich held under the aegis of *Contemporary Annals*. Nabokov read three short stories, "A Russian Beauty," "Terra Incognita," and "Breaking the News."[97] On February 15, 1936, Bunin and Nabokov participated in a poets' evening along with Adamovich, Berberova, Tsvetaeva, and others. At the end of February Nabokov returned to Berlin, leaving Bunin with uneasy memories of their encounters. A delicate spring broke in the complex mechanism of their relationship. Witnesses of the émigré literary scene, some of whom knew both writers, reported Bunin's divided remarks about Nabokov. For instance, Zinaida Shakhovskaia began her 1937 article on Nabokov—printed in *La cité chrétienne*—with a reference to a conversation she had had with Bunin about young émigré authors. She claimed that the conversation had taken place "exactly" a year prior to the publication of the article (i.e., in July 1936) and thus after Nabokov's January meeting with Bunin later described in *Speak, Memory*. Shakhovskaia reported Bunin's remark that young writers "do not know their craft" ("les jeunes ne connaissent pas leur métier"). "And what about Nabokov?" the journalist asked. "Celui là appartient déjà à l'histoire de la littérature russe. Un monstre, mais quel écrivain" (He has already established himself a place in the history of Russian literature. A monster, but what a writer).[98] After Bunin's 1938 trip to the Baltic countries, his Estonian correspondent V. V. Shmidt recorded that, to her surprise, he spoke with complete indifference of Nabokov.[99] Berberova, who knew Bunin for over twenty years in France, recalled that "Nabokov's name made Bunin furious" ("privodilo v iarost'") in the late 1930s.[100]

When Nabokov returned to Paris in 1937, his meetings with Bunin, if devoid of "chemistry," still continued. Bunin attended Nabokov's readings. Later, during Nabokov's long stay on the French Riviera, Bunin visited him twice. The first visit was in Cannes, where the Nabokovs lived in July–October 1937. Nabokov sent the Bunins holiday greetings in December 1937.[101] Bunin wrote back from Paris in February 1938. His postcard is one of the few surviving pieces of correspondence addressed to Nabokov: "Dear Writer, I am planning to join you (and, possibly, for a long time). They say that the Riviera is all full up, that even finding a little room is a problem. And what about Menton, where you are staying? Please drop a line, I will be much obliged. I send greetings to you and your wife, and in my mind I give your heir a whipping. Yours, Iv. Bunin."[102] Bunin did not end up staying in Menton (a photograph of Nabokov in Menton is reproduced in Figure 17). In 1938, when Bunin was living in Beausoleil, he went up to the mountains to visit Nabokov in the village of Moulinet, Nabokov's picturesque abode in the Alpes Maritimes.[103] To quote Nabokov's letter, "Nakanune ot"ezda, sredi eralasha ukladki iavilsia k nam Lekseich, nobelevskii" (On the eve of your departure, amid the confusion of packing, Lekseich the Nobel man [Lekseich from Bunin's patronymic, Alekseevich] showed up).[104] As Boyd put it, "their meetings seemed destined for disjunction."[105] A note of condescending irony, heretofore undetectable on Nabokov's side of the relationship, suddenly voiced itself in a postcard written after Bunin's visit. Nabokov had gone a long way from confessing love to Bunin as his aesthetic ideal circa 1921 to treating him as some sort of comical figure in 1938 (even if Bunin with his delusion of grandeur did appear grotesque to Nabokov at the height of the latter's Russian career). In November 1938 Nabokov presented Bunin with a copy of *Invitation to a Beheading* with a sober inscription compared to the one he had made in a copy of *Mary* in 1926: "To Dear Ivan Alekseevich Bunin with the very best regards from the author. XI. 1938."[106] Bunin did not leave a single mark in the text of his copy.

Bunin and Nabokov exchanged several letters in the spring–summer of 1939, including a letter of recommendation for Nabokov that Bunin signed "Ivan Bunin, Prix Nobel 1933" and dated, ironically, April 1, 1939.[107] Nabokov and Bunin saw each other again in Paris in the fall of 1939. Bunin's wife noted in her diary: "We see [*vidaemsia*] the Vishniaks, Zenzinov, Fondaminskii, Sirin, the Zaitsevs."[108] Their last meeting occurred at the apartment of the politician and historian Aleksandr Kerenskii on May 15, 1940, the day before the Nabokovs' departure for the United States.[109] As Nabokov sailed for the New World after having literally crossed the boundaries of Russian émigré literature—like his dear protagonist Vasiliy Shishkov had in the story of the same name—Bunin stayed behind in France with vexing memories of this "greenhorn who pulled out a pistol and killed all the older writers with one shot."[110] To quote Nabokov himself, "across the dark sky of exile, Sirin passed . . . like a meteor, and disappeared, leaving nothing much else behind him than a vague sense of uneasiness" (*SM*, 288). Bunin's anxiety over Nabokov's dazzling achievement gave him the creative impetus to work again. In the wake of their friendship turned rivalry, and probably under the impact of having witnessed Nabokov's triumph in Paris, Bunin conceived of a book

17. Vladimir Nabokov, Menton, France, 1937–1938. Courtesy of Ardis Publishers.

which would settle the score between them. When the first Russian edition of *Dark Avenues* came out in New York in 1943, Nabokov was teaching Russian at Wellesley, Bunin had ten more years left to live, and Russian prose gained a masterpiece.

Bunin wrote these jealous words to an American Slavicist before World War II: "I think that I influenced many. But how can that be established, how determined? I think that probably had I not existed, there would have been no Sirin (even though, at first glance, he seems so original)."[111] In preparation for her excellent 1938 study, Malozemoff asked Nabokov to comment on Bunin's role in his development. Nabokov, writing back in January 1938, said that he did not consider himself a follower of Bunin.[112] Judging solely on the basis of Bunin's and Nabokov's works which had been published by 1938, as well as the letters which both writers had sent her, Malozemoff concluded that "Sirin's tricky stylistic novelties, his bold experiments . . . will probably soon begin to appall Bunin. Sirin audaciously approaches the mysteries of life, dualities of conscience, the depths of a criminal's soul. He is as far from Bunin as Dostoevsky is from Tolstoy."[113] Forty years later, curiously echoing both Bunin's own words and Malozemoff's remarks, a Third Wave émigré critic suggested that Bunin's style had paved the way to Nabokov's anti-Bunin poetics ("Buninskaia stilistika posluzhila anti-buninskoi poètike").[114]

Memories of Nabokov's literary stardom infuriated the seventy-year-old Bunin after Nabokov's departure in 1940. During and after the war Bunin reread Nabokov's works in his personal library. He even returned to his earlier notes concerning the reviews of Nabokov's fiction in prewar émigré periodicals. Sometime in the early to middle 1930s Bunin marked with a vertical pencil line the opening passage in the margins of V. S. Varshavskii's 1933 review of *Glory*:

> The critics often place Sirin next to Bunin. Bunin is, doubtless, connected with the end of the classical period of Russian literature. . . . [Bunin's] is the creation of a person from a dying-out race that has been unable to adjust itself. The last of the Mohicans.
>
> The race that is winning is of a pettier sort [*bolee melkaia*], but more flexible and tenacious of life. This very—rather tiring—exuberance of physiological vitality strikes one first of all in Sirin. Everything is extremely rich [*sochno*] and colorful, and somehow exceedingly lush [*zhirno*]. But behind this flooded plane—flooded far and wide—lies an emptiness, not an abyss, but a flat emptiness, an emptiness that is a shoal, whose danger is precisely in the absence of depth.[115] (italics added)

In his postwar rereading, Bunin underlined with red ballpoint pen the first two sentences in the review of Nabokov's novel, in which the critic links Bunin with the decline of the Russian classical tradition.

Traces of Bunin's reactions have also survived in his letters. On September 3, 1945, he wrote to Aldanov that he had gone through some old issues of *Contemporary Annals:* "How many interesting works! How much horrible stuff! [*skol'ko chudovishchnogo!*]. For instance, Sirin's *The Gift.* At times this is like Ippolit from *War and Peace.*"[116] It goes without saying that a parallel between Tolstoi's Ippolit—gibbering and devoid of any real substance—and Nabokov's splendidly controlled and intellectually saturated writing in *The Gift* is simply a product of the bilious old man that Bunin frequently appeared to be in his letters of the 1940s–1950s. One needs, however, to go beyond these intemperate responses to Nabokov and to recognize in them the late repercussions of that enormous shock which Nabokov's works of the 1930s produced on Bunin, thereby compelling him to accept the challenge of the younger rival.

In *Dark Avenues,* one of the most polemical masterpieces ever written, Bunin was settling a threefold score. First, he wanted to bring to an end his lifelong argument with modernism and modernists. From the earliest steps of his career, Bunin had never considered himself a modernist. The reasons for that are many and have to do with his origins and youth, his first encounters with the symbolists in Moscow and Petersburg at the turn of the century, and his close ties with the Sreda (Wednesday) group of writers (Leonid Andreev, Maksim Gor'kii, Nikolai Teleshov, Skitalets, Evgenii Chirikov), who appropriated the realistic traditions of Russian nineteenth-century prose.[117] Additionally, he inherited his disdain toward the Russian modernists, the "other camp" ("drugoi lager'"; Bunin 9:296) as he labeled it, from Chekhov, to whom he was personally close and who resented decadence in art and in life ("What sort of decadents are they," Bunin reported Chekhov saying; "they are burly peasants [*zdorovenneishie muzhiki*]").[118]

From the outset of his artistic career, Bunin associated modernism(s) not with a quest for new form but with a new decadent style of behavior, with Aleksandr Blok's gypsy lyrics and Carmen, with the Stray Dog (Brodiachaia sobaka) Cabaret, with the theosophical movement, with Viacheslav Ivanov's Tower (Bashnia), with ethical and aesthetic "perversions" of various kinds.[119] He detested such major modernists as Belyi and Sologub on personal and on literary grounds. This is evident not only from his letters and diaries, but also from his memoirs, where the fallacies of the Russian modernists, especially the symbolists, are a leitmotif. In view of what Bunin perceived as a threat from Blok, Belyi, Sologub, and other Russian modernists, he also came to regard himself as the carrier of the flame of the great Russian nineteenth-century tradition of Pushkin, Tolstoi, Turgenev, and Chekhov. As a result, Bunin's militant antimodernism and self-awareness as a keeper of traditions made him blind to the covert modernism of his own art.[120] Overt Russian modernists sought to create their own innovative stylistic methods in order to keep up with the cataclysmic changes of their time (e.g., Belyi) or to preserve Russia's disappearing cultural past (e.g., Remizov). As a covert modernist, Bunin brought the stylistic conventions of Russian classical prose to the point of absolute (and at times obsessive) linguistic and narrative perfection, while also contesting such nineteenth-century Russian thematic taboos as sex and the depiction of the female body.

However, Bunin was not blind to Nabokov's covert modernism, which was especially manifest in the short stories of the High period and *The Gift*, where Nabokov negotiates between his nineteenth-century narrative leanings and his sui generis metaphysics.[121] In fact, I would argue that Bunin perceived Nabokov's works of the middle to late 1930s, which included *Invitation to a Beheading, The Gift,* "Spring in Fialta," "The Visit to the Museum," and "Cloud, Castle, Lake," as a betrayal of the Russian classical tradition which Bunin served to preserve in exile. He initially viewed Nabokov as a poet working in the classical vein and a fiction writer with marked affinities with Chekhov's stories and Bunin's own prose of the 1910s. To an extent, in the 1920s Nabokov did fashion himself as a follower and defended Bunin from attacks by the younger Parisian poets. His stories of the Early and Middle periods exhibit numerous traces of a stylistic apprenticeship with Bunin, especially in vocabulary and imagery as well as rhythm and intonation. Nabokov's late Russian novels and stories of the High period emblematize a fusion of the Russian classical tradition with modernist trends, both Russian and European. In "Cloud, Castle, Lake" Vasiliy Ivanovich, a Chekhovian *intelligent,* encounters a window into eternity, an otherworldly domain with antecedents in the mythopoetics of Russian symbolism. This fusion probably signaled to Bunin that Nabokov was no longer on his side of the artistic barricade, in his "camp."[122] He reacted to Nabokov's writings as vehemently as he did because he saw in them a son who looks more like the neighbor across the hall than like his own father.

Finally, in *Dark Avenues* Bunin was settling a score with his personal past, with his failed love for Galina Kuznetsova. This prompted the subject matter of his book: love and its tragic consequences. A number of female protagonists in *Dark Avenues,* including those of "Genrikh" and "Chistyi ponedel'nik" (Ash Wednesday), were modeled after his beloved. Bunin had to prove himself the best living Russian writer. This demanded a form which would typify and crown his entire career in fiction, as well as address the issues which are at the core of his world vision. Bunin found such a form: a book of short stories, unified by a focus on writing love, death, and the female body—all three inseparable in his perception. In *Dark Avenues,* he actualized a notion which figures as early as his 1915 story "Grammatika liubvi" (Grammar of Love). In his project to create a grammar of the Russian love story—both a summation of the best thematic achievements of the century and a half of the Russian short story and a compendium of its narrative repertoire—Bunin anticipated the notion of narrative grammar which literary scholars began to explore in the 1960s.[123] He began his future collection in 1937 and even managed to publish five stories in *The Latest News* before the outbreak of World War II. The majority of the stories were written in Grasse during the war. The first edition of *Dark Avenues* appeared in New York in 1943 and consisted of eleven short stories. The second, authoritative edition came out in Paris in 1946 with thirty-eight stories. In his literary will Bunin requested that two more postwar stories be added to the 1946 edition. In its final form *Dark Avenues* is a text of forty short stories, divided into three uneven parts. Most important for Bunin's duel with Nabokov and the modernists is its second part, thirteen of whose fourteen stories were composed between September and November 1940, in a titanic creative effort which may be likened to Pushkin's Boldino autumn of 1830.

In the middle section of *Dark Avenues* we find some of Bunin's best-known stories, "Rusia," "Vizitnye kartochki" (Calling Cards), "V Parizhe" (In Paris), "Genrikh," "Natali." This is Bunin at his absolute best. The stories are perfect stylistically and display a superb economy of means and judicious balance of description and dialogue. Almost every story points to earlier texts by Bunin as well as stories by major Russian authors. For instance, "Muza" (Muse) revisits several motifs from Tolstoi's "The Kreutzer Sonata"; "Calling Cards" goes back to Bunin's earlier "The Sunstroke" and sharpens its argument with Chekhov's "Lady with a Lap Dog"; "Natali" polemicizes with Nabokov's "A Russian Beauty." [124] Bunin himself considered *Dark Avenues* his best work, in terms of style and subject matter. He was convinced that he had said a "new word" in art, created a "new approach" to life.[125]

One could easily devote an entire study to a comparison of *Dark Avenues,* the middle part in particular, and Nabokov's stories of the High period.[126] Here I would like to concentrate on one story, to my mind the best in Bunin's collection, as the centerpiece of his answer to Nabokov's artistic challenge. I have chosen to focus on "Genrikh" (a male name, the Russian equivalent of the German "Heinrich" and the English "Henry") for two reasons. First, "Genrikh" polemicizes with the structure and subject matter of Nabokov's best short story of the High period, "Spring in Fialta," discussed in Chapter 3. Second, it emblematizes Bunin's argument with the modernists, especially with Russian symbolists.

Set in the atmosphere of the Russian Silver Age, "Genrikh" tells the story of the Russian poet Glebov (an invented writer) and his lover, the Russian journalist Elena Genrikhovna, who published her work under a male pen name, Genrikh, derived from her patronymic. Glebov, a successful writer and a very handsome man, is simultaneously involved in three affairs. One is with a sixteen-year old Nadia, his poetic disciple, another with an exotic fin-de-siècle woman by the name of Li (from the English "Lee" or the Chinese "Li"). The third affair, culminating in the story, is with Genrikh. In the middle of a Russian winter, Glebov and Genrikh take a train to Vienna together, after which Glebov goes to Nice, intending to meet Genrikh on the French Riviera. Genrikh has important business in Vienna. She intends to break off her long-term sexual relations with an Austrian author and publisher, Arthur Spiegler, while hoping to continue their professional relationship. Genrikh translates Spiegler's works into Russian and supplies his magazine with news of Russia's bohemian circles. On the train, Glebov and Genrikh experience an outburst of passion—genuine albeit stimulated by their secret escape. Genrikh promises to give a brief explanation to her Austrian employer and join Glebov the following morning. Glebov spends several days alone waiting for Genrikh, drinking and gambling to dim his emotional pain. Finally, in Venice, Glebov learns from a newspaper that Genrikh has been shot by Spiegler. Such is the summary of the narrative, which does little justice to its artistic perfection. What are the main issues of Russian cultural history that the story addresses?

I have already spoken of Bunin's unceasing polemics with Russian modernists. Aleksandr Blok, the foremost poet of the Russian Silver Age, remained, to use Berberova's expression, an "open wound" (*rana*) for Bunin throughout his life.[127] In 1922 Bunin recorded in his diary: "I read Blok—what tiresome, droning, monotonous nonsense, vapid in its pompousness and somehow blasphemous [*koshchunstvennyi*]."[128] "Blasphemous" would become the key word in Bunin's perception of the great poet. Perhaps most revealing of all was his long 1950 letter to his former secretary, the writer and publisher Andrei Sedykh: "You must not be upset about Blok. He was a perverted actor, pathologically inclined to blasphemy."[129] Bunin linked mysticism—an integral part of Blok's symbolist mythopoetics—with moral corruption, madness, and roguery. In his diary for 1922, he noted after reading Blok: "Yes, mysteriousness, all sorts of 'secret hints to that which no one can get' [*namëki tëmnye na to, chego ne vedaet nikto*]—the mysteriousness of a rogue or madman."[130] In her long vivid memoir of Bunin, the émigré poet Irina Odoevtseva quotes a series of his contemptuous remarks about Blok. She reports that Bunin called Blok a "stage poseur" (*èstradnyi figliar*), a "circus clown" (*ryzhii iz tsirka*), a "country-fair jester" (*shut balagannyi*).[131] It is not hard to notice that Bunin's attitudes to Blok are rather similar to his attitudes to Nabokov during and after his work on *Dark Avenues*. Much as in Blok, Bunin resented in Nabokov what he perceived as literary games, tricks played behind the reader's back, designed to create a sense of mystery, presumably to cover up the emptiness of the soul. In 1939, in a letter to an émigré admirer, Bunin wrote: "All the same, Sirin is intolerable: a driver of a smart cab [*likhach vozle nochnogo kabaka; likhach* also has the connotation of a frisky daredevil] waiting outside a nightclub; although he is remarkable."[132] Writing to Aldanov in 1951, Bunin referred to Nabokov as *"shut gorokhovyi"* (buffoon, clown).[133]

In "Genrikh" Bunin's negative literary and personal attitudes—rational and irrational—toward Blok, Nabokov, and modernism form a dense polemical text. By creating a protagonist who embodies what he saw around 1940 as the quintessence of a modernist artist, combining Blok and Nabokov, he sought to resolve, once and for all, his lifelong conflict with modernism as both art and vision. By writing a story which polemicizes with Nabokov's best Russian short story, "Spring in Fialta," Bunin was determined to demonstrate his artistic superiority over the younger master. By choosing this story as the main aim of his polemics with Nabokov, he also directed this polemic at the question of Chekhov's legacy. Bunin was sure to sense Chekhov's artistic presence in Nabokov's story. In fact, he alludes to "Lady with a Lap Dog" as Glebov imitates the mannered speech of a Russian provincial describing Italian attractions: "'In Florence I like only Trecento. . . .' And he was actually born in Belëv and only spent one week in Florence in all his life" (Bunin 7:136). In Chekhov's story Gurov amuses Anna during their first encounter by imitating a philistine also from Belëv, a provincial Russian town, complaining of boredom in Yalta. "Genrikh" finalizes a three-corner dialogue involving Nabokov, Chekhov, and Bunin himself. In "Spring in Fialta," as I have argued in Chapter 3, Nabokov disagrees with Chekhov's view of the earthly nature of love, the view that informs the open-ended structure of his short fiction as exemplified by "Lady with a Lap Dog." Bunin's "Genrikh" also concerns itself with creating the kind of narrative closure that produces the strongest effect upon the reader. In contrast with the otherworldly opening which transcends death at the end of Nabokov's "Spring in Fialta," Bunin offers an ending in which death is introduced to resolve a crisis of desire.

One finds a number of typological parallels between the themes, characters, and plot structures in "Genrikh" and "Spring in Fialta." Both stories are about desire and deceit. Glebov in Bunin's story is deceiving two lovers (Nadia, Li) by claiming that he is going to Nice "alone." Vasen'ka in "Spring in Fialta" also takes a trip to a Riviera town to get away from his wife and family routine. During the course of their last meetings with Nina and Genrikh, Vasen'ka and Glebov experience surges of love and attempt to make their relationships with the women permanent. In both stories the triangles consist of a Russian man in Europe, a Russian woman in Europe, and a European man. Finally, both Russian female protagonists die at the hands of foreign modernist authors. In "Spring in Fialta" Nina is killed in a crash while riding in the car with the protean Ferdinand and his androgynous friend Segur. In "Genrikh" the jealous Spiegler shoots the female protagonist dead with a pistol. The stories open with cityscapes presented through the eyes of the male protagonists (Glebov's wintry Moscow, Vasen'ka's springtime Fialta) and end with news of the death of Nina and Genrikh. In both cases, the male protagonists learn the news of their lovers' deaths from newspapers, Glebov in Venice, Vasen'ka at the train station in Milan. These are some generally similar contours to both plots, although one finds the center of Bunin's dialogue with Nabokov's "Spring in Fialta" in the character of Genrikh's employer and lover, the Austrian modernist Arthur Spiegler ("Артур Шпиглер" in the Russian original).

One needs to recall that in "Spring in Fialta" Nina is married to a very successful Hungarian-French author, Ferdinand. She does not love him, but feels connected to him and, in part, has surrendered to his powers. Genrikh's affiliation with the Austrian writer Spiegler is different. On the train Genrikh tells Glebov how much she detests Spiegler. She promises to end her liaison with him during the forthcoming meeting in Vienna. Genrikh is frightened of having to go through the breakup with Spiegler, a manipulative and possessive person. During their previous meeting she has attempted to talk to him. "You cannot imagine," she tells Glebov on the train, "the hatred that was written across his face!" (Bunin 7:137). Miserable at the prospect of the meeting in Vienna, Genrikh complains to Glebov: "In a few hours you are going to leave, and I will stay there alone, go to the café to wait for my Austrian. . . . And in the evening the café again and a Hungarian orchestra, those soul-maiming violins" (Bunin 7:137).

The "Hungarian orchestra" (a literary cliché) in the Viennese café may point to Ferdinand's national origins (born a subject of the Austro-Hungarian Empire) and his bohemian fondness for cafés. Genrikh's description also recalls the scene in "Spring in Fialta" where Vasen'ka and Nina join Ferdinand and his cohorts in a "perfectly bourgeois" café with an "orchestra . . . of half a dozen weary-looking self-conscious ladies" (*Stories,* 421). Like Genrikh, Nabokov's protagonist recoils at the vapid atmosphere of the café.

Another dimension which links Spiegler to Ferdinand, and Bunin's story to "Spring in Fialta," is Glebov's and Vasen'ka's perception of the literary merits of their rivals. The reader learns a great deal from Vasen'ka about Ferdinand's writings. His main accusation is that Ferdinand tricks the reader by covering the missing "truth" with layers of dazzling but barren ornamentation. Vasen'ka writes of Ferdinand:

> Having mastered the art of verbal invention to perfection, he particularly prided himself on being a weaver of words, a title he valued higher than that of a writer; personally, I never could understand what was the good of thinking up books, of penning things that had not really happened in some way or other; and I remember once saying to him . . . that, were I a writer, I should allow only my heart to have imagination, and for the rest rely upon memory. . . . (*Stories,* 420)

Vasen'ka's accusations against Ferdinand—who is at the height of his popularity right before Nina's death—come very close to Bunin's own view of modernist writing as roguish mysteriousness and literary games and tricks behind the reader's back. In "Genrikh" Glebov associates his rival Spiegler with the kind of belles-lettres that were fashionable in Europe in the 1900s. He likens the Austrian writer to Stanisław Przybyszewski (1868–1927), a Polish modernist whose writings enjoyed an enormous but short-lived success in Europe, including Russia, in the 1900s. Przybyszewski's works captured the minds of readers with their depiction of mysticism and ambivalent sexuality. In "Spring in Fialta" Nabokov's first-person narrator tells the reader that Ferdinand enjoyed a rapid success and then went quickly out of fashion. It is also not difficult to notice that Bunin's Arthur Spiegler suggests the name of a real Austrian modernist, Arthur Schnitzler (1882–1931), a playwright and novelist who made a big name for himself with fictions and dramas portraying the subliminal atmosphere of fin-de-siècle Vienna. The names of Przybyszewski and Schnitzler also figure in other stories of *Dark Avenues,* including "Chistyi ponedel'nik" (Ash Wednesday), set in Silver Age Moscow, where the protagonist brings her beloved new books to read, including those of "Hofmannsthal, Schnitzler, . . . , Przybyszewski" (Bunin 7:239).

To understand the depth of Bunin's polemics with the modernist ethos, one needs to examine the connections between the characters of Glebov and Nadia and the cultural mythology of the Russian Silver Age. In Glebov's character Bunin captured some features of Aleksandr Blok. Glebov, like Blok of the 1900s, is a young poet approaching fame. We see a number of biographical echoes, such as strong interest in gypsy songs and trips to Italy.[134] Glebov's last name might be a palindromic anagram of Blok: *bleg-blok;* in the final position the voiced *g* and the devoiced *k* are the same sound. Taken out of the context of Bunin's cultural polemics in "Genrikh," such echoes seem coincidental. However, in their correlation with other traces of Silver Age and specifically Blokian mythology, such details add up to a dense text of dialogue. Nadia, Glebov's sixteen-year-old lover, may point to the popular myth of Blok's involvement with very young female admirers, of whom Bunin knew firsthand but also heard in emigration. For instance, he certainly knew of the remarkable 1936 memoir by Mother Maria (Elizaveta Kuz'mina-Karavaeva, née Pilenko, 1891–1945), describing her visit to Blok in 1906 when she was only fourteen.[135] Another real actor on the Silver Age scene, the poet Nadezhda L'vova (1891–1913), might have stood behind Nadia (diminutive form of Nadezhda). Aleksandr Bakhrakh reported that while working on "Genrikh" in 1940, Bunin could not fall asleep, thinking of the kind of verse Nadia would compose in the story.[136] In 1913 L'vova shot herself with a revolver given her by the symbolist poet Valerii Briusov, with whom she had been involved and who influenced her life and writing (cf. Nadia and Glebov; Genrikh and Spiegler).[137]

As we have seen, all the characters in "Genrikh" personify various traits of the modernist ethos as Bunin understood it. Why is it then that Bunin, who resented modernism, made the protagonists, Glebov and especially Genrikh, so appealing to readers and so easy to identify with? In fact, the entire scene in the train compartment where Glebov and Genrikh realize that they are in love and cannot live without each other is one of the most moving and psychologically powerful scenes in Russian literature. It combines Turgenev's perfectly intoned dialogue and Chekhovian detail. Moreover, the description of Genrikh presents Bunin's classical ideal of female beauty: "ample breasts . . . thin waist, full hips, narrow, light, chiseled ankles" (Bunin 7:134–135). In contrast to Li's small breasts, thin figure, dark eyes, and black-velvet beret, Genrikh in her plain gray dress and with a "Greek hairdo of lemony-red hair" is made to look like a heroine of Russian classical prose, an Anna Odintsova from Turgenev's *Ottsy i deti* (Fathers and Sons, 1861). Dressed like a femme fatale, the dark and sardonically sensuous Li embodies a decadent woman full of extremities, a modernist female character as Bunin perceived one.

Bunin's art in "Genrikh," as well as the other stories in *Dark Avenues,* again bears witness to his covert modernism. This is the paradoxical duality of *Dark Avenues* and the source of its artistic triumph. On the one hand, his couples who live in the modern age, be they Glebov and Genrikh or a Russian general and his younger beloved in the story "In Paris," attempt to revitalize codes of love typical of Russian classical literature. Glebov, who seems to have forgotten that only the day before he was leading a bohemian and promiscuous existence in Moscow, suddenly demands that Genrikh give up the Austrian completely and go with him to Nice or somewhere in Italy. He does not want to let Genrikh go, and rightly so: the modernist Spiegler kills Genrikh when she tries to break away from him. Bunin wanted to show that the modernist ethos kills love, distorts human fates, perverts human relations. On the other hand, as we know from his diaries, Bunin also wanted *Dark Avenues* to be a hymn to the female body and to human sexuality. Bunin's diary entry of February 3, 1941, reveals his artistic self-awareness and self-doubt in the process of writing *Dark Avenues:* "That miraculous something beautiful beyond words, entirely matchless in all of earthly experience, which is the female body has *never* been written by *anyone.* And not only the body. I must try it, I must. I have tried—it comes out vulgar. I need to find some other words." [138] Bunin's diaries from the 1940s testify to his anxiety as he faced a simultaneous need to parse the narrative grammar of love in classical prose and to create a new language—previously unknown in Russian literature—to express the sexuality of a modern subject. His desire to write about the female body clashed with his insistence on adhering to the laws of "chaste" Russian classical literature. Bunin's masters and senior contemporaries, Turgenev, Tolstoi, and Chekhov, skipped scenes where characters have sex (Tolstoi's late work "Father Sergius" is one notable exception; overall, dealing with sexual problems, as Tolstoi does in "The Kreutzer Sonata," and describing sex are two entirely different matters). In Chekhov's "Lady with a Lap Dog" the act of sexual intercourse is omitted from the scene where Gurov and Anna become lovers in Anna's hotel room. While such Western authors as Gustave Flaubert and later Guy de Maupassant, both of whom Bunin valued a great deal and reread frequently, had revolutionized the literary treatment of the human body and sex, Bunin's Russian predecessors had refused to depict sex. [139]

In "Genrikh" Bunin goes much further than his Russian predecessors by describing a naked female body, as well as the lovers' passionate foreplay. Yet, fearful of vulgarizing perfection and experiencing the mighty pressure of the nineteenth-century Russian tradition, he cuts his description short as Glebov and Genrikh start making love in their train compartment. The last sentence of the following passage relies on a perfectly architectured suggestion of sexual intercourse:

> She pulled him close and began to kiss so strongly, that he was short of breath. "Genrikh, I do not recognize you."—"I don't either. But come here, come to me."—"Wait. . . ." "No, no, right now!"—"Just one word: tell me definitely, when will you leave Vienna?"—"Tonight, this very evening!" The train was already moving: the spurs of the border guards walked gently along the carpet past the door, clinking [*mimo dveri miagko shli i zveneli po kovru shpory pogranichnikov*]. (Bunin 7:137–138)

In his development as the last and late representative of the Russian classical prose tradition, Bunin was conditioned by narratives in which "triangular desire" operates in the plot while the underlying sexuality of such desire is suppressed. The principle of triangular desire—culminating in nineteenth-century fiction—demanded that Spiegler, the third party in "Genrikh" (cf. Rogozhin in Dostoevskii's *The Idiot* or Laevskii in Chekhov's "The Duel"), attempt to reclaim his lost or threatened status.[140] To take the example of Tolstoi's "The Kreutzer Sonata," the enraged cuckold Pozdnyshev commits murder to punish his wife and her lover for their adultery. Tolstoi brings the reader to Pozdenyshev's house, where the lovers die under his dagger. Death as the result of the triangular desire is the focus of the narrative, while the deeply sexual behavior of the characters is virtually left out of the picture. In fact, the bedroom figures not as a place where the adulterers consummate their affair, but as the place where Pozdnyshev's wife dies of an open wound on their marital bed.

Bunin faced a double challenge in writing *Dark Avenues*. He rejected modernist experimentation, both with narrative structure and with language, and resented it in Nabokov's late Russian prose. He wanted to remain with the classics. However, from the vantage point of the late 1930s–1940s, he also saw that an artistic solution was needed to make his collection absolutely peerless in Russian letters and to meet the challenge of his modernist rivals.

Bunin's linguistic solution was to steer clear of sexual expressions, which are either vulgar or strictly scientific in Russian, while bringing the chaste language of classical literature to its furthest limits in writing about sex, as in the train scene in "Genrikh." His narrative solution was to treat sex as somehow inseparable from death. In stories like "Genrikh," "Natali" or "In Paris" death as a means of narrative closure was Bunin's way of keeping a balance between his covert modernism and his overt classical leanings. The death of Genrikh, as it was enacted and timed in the narrative, reflected both Bunin's split aesthetics and his integral world vision. In fact, the view of sexual love and death as organically connected goes back to his earlier works, especially to his refashioning of biblical narratives. Equating woman with death is certainly a theme of modernist literature and art as, for instance, in the works of August Strindberg and Edvard Munch. In Bunin's "Chang's Dreams" (1916) the dog's master, a former sea captain, philosophizes about the way women are somehow linked to death. The captain's words echo the wisdom of Solomon: "Oh, woman! 'Her house leads to death and her ways to the dead'" (Bunin 4:383). In stories like "Mitia's Love" or "The Son" the internal causality of the narrative is that of love inevitably bringing about a fatal resolution. Odoevtseva, who knew Bunin well, especially in the 1940s, recorded his statement on the subject: "Haven't you figured out that love and death are linked inseparably? Each time, when I was going through a catastrophe of love . . . I was close to suicide." [141]

The connection of death and sexual desire in structuring a fictional narrative was at the heart of Bunin's argument with Nabokov.[142] Nabokov may have polemicized with Chekhov about many things, including the structure of an ending and the nature of love, but he is distinctly Chekhovian in the treatment of sex. Like Chekhov in "Lady with a Lap Dog" Nabokov suppresses the bedroom scene in "Spring in Fialta": "and only when the door had been locked did [the two halves of the French window] let go that curtain with something like a blissful sigh; and a little later I stepped out on the diminutive cast-iron balcony . . . [two slight erotic signs]" (*Stories,* 419). In fact, Nabokov's focus in "Spring in Fialta" is not on the sexual dimensions of love, but rather on its otherworldly nature, which cannot be expressed in any conventional terms, be they erotic or psychological. His Russian works, with the possible exceptions of *Kamera obskura* and *The Enchanter,* are chaste in the spirit of Russian classical prose.[143]

For Nabokov, as for both of his Russian masters, Chekhov and Bunin, treatment of sexual love was simultaneously a narrative and a linguistic problem. According to the world view expressed in his Russian fictions and culminating in "Spring in Fialta," love as the experience beyond any words was incommensurate with human linguistic powers. This idea was central to Blake's "Never seek to tell thy love . . ." and Tiutchev's "Silentium," to take two Romantic texts which shed light on the meaning of the story. Nabokov had to invent a poetics which would adequately convey his view of love as an otherworldly state of being, a view which is prominent throughout the history of human thought. To quote the Babylonian Talmud, "three things afford a foretaste in miniature of the bliss of the World to Come: the sabbath, sexual intercourse and a sunny day." [144]

Nabokov's linguistic decision in "Spring in Fialta," as well as elsewhere in his Russian short stories, was to allude metaphorically to the sexual dimension of love without actually describing it. In fact, it was not until much later, in the 1950s–1960s, in *Lolita* and *Ada,* that Nabokov was able to create a harmonious language of sexuality. This invention was in part possible because of his switch to a new linguistic medium not only with a very different history and sensibility behind it, but also with the previous experiences of such modernist innovators in the English language as D. H. Lawrence and James Joyce. Nabokov's narrative choice in "Spring in Fialta" was to create a textual opening—a textual zone in which the protagonist realizes that he and his beloved exist as lovers in an entirely different unearthly dimension and that human language is not fit to describe it. In the final passage of the story Vasen'ka is awarded a foretaste of the otherworld, signified by sunlight over Fialta, blinding and transcendent: "white sky above Fialta had got saturated with sunshine, and now it was sun-pervaded throughout, and this brimming radiance grew broader and broader, all dissolved in it, all vanished, all passed" (*Stories,* 429).

In "Spring in Fialta" the conflict is not between two male rivals, Vasen'ka and Ferdinand, competing for Nina, but between two worlds, each claiming Nina as its own. We can only speculate about Bunin's intuition of the otherworldly nature of love in "Spring in Fialta." Most likely, he apprehended something mysterious in the causality of Nabokov's story, a causality that lay beyond the limits of his own Cartesian world view. The parallels between the typological narrative schemes of Bunin's and Nabokov's stories augmented the striking differences in the way the two writers viewed the role which death and sex play in fiction.

In "Spring in Fialta," where Nina and Vasen'ka are caught in a clash between the mundane world and the otherworld, death is assigned a role quite similar to the role Nabokov described in his 1950 English poem "The Room." [145] The penultimate stanza in this versified account of a poet's death in a hotel room reads as follows:

Perhaps my text is incomplete.
A poet's death is, after all,

a question of technique, a neat
enjambment, a melodic fall.

(*PP*, 165)

In "Spring in Fialta" Nabokov employs death as a technique of creating narrative closure. However, despite the death of the female protagonist, the reader leaves the text not with a sense of despair over Nina's death, but with a sense of cathartic lightness, of sadness and joy both recorded in the reader's memory under the impact of the textual opening. The textual opening presents Nina's narrative "death" as thinkable only in contrast to her husband's "immortality." Growing "broader and broader" over the sky of Fialta, the "brimming white radiance" symbolizes the reader's expanding consciousness, pondering the aesthetic, ethical, and metaphysical dilemma conjured up by Nabokov. Conversely, as Bunin's readers leave his story, they feel devastated by the draining sense of textual closure, a brick wall of death, an end of impossible love:

> Он сел на скамью и при гаснущем свете зари стал рассеянно развёртывать и просматривать ещё свежие страницы газеты. И вдруг вскочил, оглушённый и ослеплённый как бы взрывом магния: „Вена. 17 декабря. Сегодня, в ресторане 'Franzensring' известный австрийский писатель Артур Шпиглер убил выстрелом из револьвера русскую журналистку и переводчицу многих современных австрийских и немецких новеллистов, работавшую под псевдонимом 'Генрих'". (Bunin 7:142)

> (He sat down on a bench, and in sunset's dimming light unfolded and glanced obliviously through the newspaper's fresh pages. And suddenly he jumped up, deafened and blinded as though by an explosion of magnesium: "Vienna. 17 December. Today, in the restaurant Franzensring, the well-known Austrian author Arthur Spiegler shot with a revolver a Russian journalist and translator of many contemporary Austrian and German novelists who worked under the pseudonym 'Genrikh.'")

Bunin's stories from *Dark Avenues* reached Nabokov in America during World War II. Both Bunin and Nabokov contributed to the first issues of *Novyi zhurnal* (The New Review), the American heir of the Parisian *Contemporary Annals*, started in 1942 in New York by their mutual friends Tsetlin and Aldanov. The first issue of *The New Review* included Bunin's short story "Rusia," one of the finest in *Dark Avenues*, as well as Nabokov's last publication of original Russian fiction, a chapter from an abandoned novel, *Solus Rex*.[146] Bunin's "Natali" appeared in the second issue of *The New Review*, to which Nabokov contributed a conclusion to Pushkin's unfinished drama *Rusalka* (The Mermaid, 1829–1832). "Genrikh" was featured in the third issue of *The New Review* along with Nabokov's poem "Fame," containing one of the most explicit admissions of his "main secret." The simultaneous appearance of "Fame" with its keys to Nabokov's otherworldly aesthetics and of "Genrikh" as a condensed statement of Bunin's artistic credo can be seen as the finale of the literary duel between the two great masters.

In sum, the literary rivalry between Bunin and Nabokov centered on four principal issues. The first concerned the role of death in the narrative. For Bunin, death as a means of closure was an embodiment of his philosophy of life, according to which love and death are organically inseparable: the stronger the passions, the more likely they are to result in the death of the character(s). To take the example of "Natali," Bunin closed the story—as well as the entire middle part of *Dark Avenues*—with one short sentence: "V dekabre ona umerla na Zhenevskom ozere v prezhdevremennykh rodakh" (In December she died on Lake Geneva during premature childbirth; Bunin 7:172). Bunin's closure works in exactly the opposite fashion than that of "A Russian Beauty" by Nabokov, with which it plots a dialogue. In the latter, written some ten years earlier than "Natali," the female protagonist, Ol'ga Alekseevna, finally meets a future husband at the end of the story. The dispassionate and even gently ironic narrator makes but one comment about what awaits his heroine: ". . . i Ol'ga Alekseevna laskovo protianula: 'Vot khamy', — a sleduiushchim letom ona umerla ot rodov" (. . . and Olga drawled out in an affectionate voice "What boors!" and next summer she died in childbirth; *S*, 242/*Stories*, 389). In the following closing passage nothing happens in terms of the plot, although something crucial does take place in terms of closure: "That's all. Of course, there may be some sort of sequel, but it is not known to me. In such cases, instead of getting bogged down in guesswork, I repeat the words of the merry king in my favorite fairy tale: Which arrow flies for ever? The arrow that has hit its mark" (*Stories*, 389). Writing to Aldanov in 1942, Nabokov criticized Bunin's ending: "Cannot you agree with me, that 'Natali' . . . is a completely helpless thing in terms of composition? . . . It is characteristic that they [Bunin's female protagonists] all die, for it does not matter [to Bunin] how to end the story, but one must end it anyhow."[147]

For Bunin, "hitting the mark" meant closing the story with death at the height of the protagonists' happiness. "Forever" was hardly an option in his universe. For Nabokov, whose ending creates its own fairy-tale mythology, death amounted to hanging "The End" on the story. To quote the poem which closes or, rather, opens the ending of *The Gift*, "and no obstruction for the sage exists where I have put The End: the shadows of my world extend beyond the skyline of the page, blue as tomorrow's morning haze—nor does this terminate the phrase" (*Gift*, 366). The reader has already parted with the characters, while the story's music still sounds in one's ears.[148]

The second issue concerns the metaphysics of Nabokov's and Bunin's fictions. Bunin's fiction absorbed much of Judeo-Christian metaphysics. Endowed with a Cartesian mind and a richly sensual imagination, he was not interested in creating alternative models of the universe in his fiction, nor keen on challenging traditional Judeo-Christian beliefs. His concern was with documenting, with the utmost precision and power, the progress of a human life in *this* world, which is the only world, he believed, that a writer and characters were capable of capturing. Nabokov, on the other hand, created both a "new world" and a corresponding mythopoetics of his own. His stories create different models of what the otherworld might be like: an idyllic landscape in "Cloud, Castle, Lake," the "brimming white radiance" over the Fialta sky, the overturned and sinking beach front in "Perfection." In *Dark Avenues*, which was written in response to Nabokov's short stories of the 1930s, Bunin focused just on one model: desire bringing about tragedy. To Bunin, this model described the core of earthly existence.

This brings us to the third major point of difference. In Bunin's world, fate is incomprehensible to a human mind. Much like love, fate is irrational, and it overturns our habitual and instinctive striving for an open-ended future. In the incomprehensible and devastating intrusion of fate, he insists, lies the source of short fiction. In his short stories, tragedy follows a time of perfect happiness and harmony. It is a tragedy of freedom undercut by senseless death which is unfathomable to a human mind. Genrikh is shot by her Austrian lover; Natali dies in childbirth; Galia Ganskaia of the eponymous story commits suicide. Instead of fatidic patterns, which may exist beyond human reach, a human mind faces but the chaos of chance. For Nabokov, as he put it in *Other Shores*, a human life is the "recurrence of secret themes in wide awake fate" (*SSoch*, 4:133). His privileged characters, be it Sleptsov in "Christmas" or Vasen'ka in "Spring in Fialta," can and do apprehend the schemes and themes of their own existence. Their creator, Nabokov, allows his characters to fathom the designs of their fictional existence. In a world where otherworldly patterns show through the "chinks" of a mundane reality (*iav'*), fate, like death, becomes a question of literary technique, a "melodic fall." "[Nabokov] is remarkably successful," Alexandrov points out, "in demonstrating how both he and his characters are trapped in fatidic webs that abut a transcendent realm."[149]

Finally, there is the status of memory in Bunin's and Nabokov's works. Critics have pointed out parallels between the functioning of memory in the works of Marcel Proust, a paradigmatic European artist of memory, and the works of Bunin and Nabokov.[150] Yet there is at least one major difference in the way memory works in Nabokov's and in Bunin's poetics. In Bunin's fiction, including *The Life of Arseniev* and *Dark Avenues,* memory is unstructured, and the shape of recollections is often determined by a chance concurrence of narrative circumstances as well as by the idiosyncrasies of the one who is doing the recollecting. In addition, memory in his poetics is firmly linked to orality, with its sources in Russian folk mythology. In "Rusia" the train carrying the protagonist/narrator and his wife makes an unscheduled stop at a small junction. The protagonist mentions that he once spent a summer in the area and recalls a summer romance. Having completed the oral narrative cycle, triggered by a chance association, the narrator returns to his daily routine. The shape of the recollected narrative in the short story mirrors the shape of unstructured memory. The artist records and frames a recollection in all its raw authenticity. Conversely, in Nabokov's works, memory is always controlled and structured. At the end of "Spring in Fialta" Vasen'ka becomes a writer because he learns how to channel his memories of Nina into the perfect shape of a short story. The shape of his short story is given to him in its entirety and complexity in a moment of cosmic synchronization, when his memories of Nina, spanning more than fifteen years, are all interconnected and structured.

Was the Bunin-Nabokov rivalry finalized with the publication of *Dark Avenues* in its complete form in 1946? Since Nabokov wrote no prose fiction in Russian after his arrival in the United States, and Bunin only wrote a few stories between 1946 and his death in 1953, the only other major instance of their dialogue was the publication of Bunin's volume entitled *Vesnoi, v Iudee. Roza Ierikhona* (In Judea, in Spring: The Rose of Jericho) by Chekhov Publishing House in New York in 1953. This was the penultimate collection Bunin put together, and it included stories written before and after *Dark Avenues.*[151] Bunin's title, *In Judea, in Spring,* borrowed from a story in *Dark Avenues,* evoked the title of Nabokov's short story "Spring in Fialta." Three years later the same émigré publishing house put out Nabokov's third collection of Russian short stories, which should have appeared in Paris before the war but never did.[152] Nabokov gave the 1956 collection the title *Vesna v Fial'te* (Spring in Fialta).[153]

Nabokov and Bunin continued to wonder about each other for the rest of their lives. Odoevtseva recorded a conversation with Bunin in October 1947, in which he complained of the poor quality of writing by younger authors: "Of course, not all the young authors write this way. There are remarkable young authors. Take Sirin, for instance. He also plays tricks [*Tozhe shtukarit*]. But how can you argue with it—it is good. They do not judge winners."[154] Did Bunin truly consider Nabokov a winner of their literary duel? Four years later, writing to Aldanov with recommendations for a literary event being planned in his honor in New York, he asked that Nabokov read his 1916 short story "Tret'i petukhi" (The Third Cock-Crow) at the event and sent Nabokov his "cordial regards."[155] Bunin still remembered the 1933 Berlin evening in his honor where he first met Nabokov, who recited Bunin's poems. However, the past did not repeat itself. Nabokov chose not to read Bunin's works in 1951.[156] He honored Bunin in a different way, by devoting to him a long passage in *Conclusive Evidence*. In the first version of his autobiography he ended the passage differently than in the later *Speak, Memory*. He said nothing about the absence of "real commerce" between them. Instead, he talked about the "bantering and rather depressing give-and-take sort of double talk, which [he regretted] now when there [was] so little chance of his ever visiting [Bunin] in remote France" (*CE*, 216). When Bunin read *Conclusive Evidence*, he rushed an angry letter to Aldanov:

> ... развратна[я] книжк[а] Набокова с царской короной на обложке над его фамилией, в которой есть дикая брехня про меня — будто я затащил его в какой-то ресторан, чтобы поговорить с ним „по душам" — очень на меня это похоже! Шут гороховый, которым Вы меня когда-то пугали, что он забил меня и что я ему ужасно завидую.[157]

> (. . . the perverse book by Nabokov, with the tsar's crown above his name on the cover, with wild lying about me, how I dragged him into some restaurant for a "heart-to-heart" conversation—would I ever do that! An awful clown; you used to scare me by saying that he had beat me and that I envied him terribly.)

In his American career as a teacher and critic of Russian literature, Nabokov did not devote much attention to Bunin's literary contribution.[158] In a lecture at Wellesley College in 1941 he spoke of Bunin and other émigré authors, contrasting them with Soviet Russian writers.[159] At Cornell he taught Bunin's poetry, but not his prose.[160] In 1951 he turned down a request by the *New York Times* to review Bunin's *Reminiscences:* "If I undertook to write an article on this book, I would certainly do so in a destructive vein. However, the author, whom I used to know well, is a very old man, and I do not feel that I should demolish his book. As I cannot praise it, I would rather not review it at all."[161]

There were two more instances when Bunin left an imprint in Nabokov's text. In *Other Shores,* the Russian version of the autobiography, the passage describing Nabokov's encounters with Bunin ends with an imitation of Bunin's prose. In the English text it would follow the words "Bunin and I adopted a bantering and rather depressing mode of conversation" (*SM,* 287):

> — и в общем до искусства мы с ним никогда и не договорились, а теперь поздно, и герой выходит в очередной сад, и полыхают зарницы, а потом он едет на станцию, и звёзды грозно и дивно горят на гробовом бархате, и чем-то горьковатым пахнет с полей, и в бесконечно отзывчивом отдалении нашей молодости опевают ночь петухи. (*SSoch,* 4:288)

> (—in a word, he and I never got to the matter of art, and now it is too late, and the hero comes out into the next garden, and summer lightning flashes, and then he rides to the train station, and the stars shine ominously and miraculously on casket velvet, and some bittery smell wafts in from the fields, and in the endlessly responsive remoteness of our youth cocks crow the night away.)

Nabokov's imitation picks up several recurrent motifs of Bunin's writing. The image of crowing cocks occurs in his fiction and poetry several dozen times. The "hero" going out into the garden and riding to the station points, among other works, to the narrative rhythm of *The Life of Arseniev,* where the young protagonist returns to his home estate several times only to leave it for a new chapter in his biography. Finally, the "cocks crowing the night away" is an inverted quote from Bunin's vignette "Petukhi" (Cocks), originally published in 1930 in *The Latest News* and later included in the collection *God's Tree* (1931), of which Nabokov owned a copy. In Bunin's vignette the last sentence ends with "petukhi opevaiut noch'" instead of Nabokov's "opevaiut noch' petukhi" (Bunin 5:426).[162]

My findings and inferences here, based on the letters and texts of Nabokov and Bunin, suggest an unusual wrinkle not only in the classical

Formalist view, but also in more recent conceptions of literary dynamics. I am thinking of Harold Bloom's captivating notion of "the anxiety of influence." Both scenarios of literary history, the Formalist and the Bloomian, work well on Nabokov's side of the Nabokov-Bunin relationship. As a young author, Nabokov adopted some of the stylistic devices that had been perfected by his literary "uncle" Bunin (Nabokov's literary "fathers" being the Russian symbolists and, to an extent, acmeists). Later, during the American period, Nabokov made obfuscatory statements about Bunin and Russian émigré culture. In *Speak, Memory* he stated that he had "always preferred [Bunin's] little known verse to his celebrated prose" (*SM*, 285); in the Russian version the adjective describing Bunin's prose becomes *parchovyi*, from *parcha*, brocade ("parchovaia proza"; *SSoch*, 4:288), which suggests ornate style and excessive exuberance. Elsewhere Nabokov wrote about Bunin: "A poetic genius, but a writer of prose almost as bad as Turgenev." [163] Given the enormous significance of Bunin's prose for Nabokov's development, the comment can be seen as what Bloom calls "an act of creative correction that is actually and necessarily a misinterpretation." [164] However, the situation becomes problematic on Bunin's side of the issue. In the course of his rivalry with Nabokov, he agonized over the dazzling achievements of the younger master who defied artistic schools and literary "camps." Driven by a desire to reclaim his status as the foremost Russian writer, Bunin created his finest work, *Dark Avenues*. His last creative decade offers the case of a literary anxiety so complex and polyvalent that a term for it is yet to be invented. Bunin of the 1940s and 1950s was not anxious that others might have influenced him, but rather that those whom he had influenced would not acknowledge it.

Coda

· ·

A Man's life of any worth is a continual allegory—and very few eyes can see the Mystery of his life—a life like the scriptures, figurative—which such people can no more make out than they can the hebrew [sic] Bible. Lord Byron cuts a figure—but he is not figurative—Shakespeare led a life of Allegory: his work are comments on it.[1]
—*John Keats, letter to George and Georgina Keats,*
February 14–May 3, 1819

"Yes, I know that I had sworn, in my previous letter to you, not to mention the past, especially the trifles in our shared past" (*Stories,* 137): so opens the second paragraph of Nabokov's short story "Pis'mo v Rossiiu" (literally, A Letter to Russia), written in Berlin in 1925 and translated into English as "A Letter That Never Reached Russia."[2] In a short preface to the English translation, Nabokov explained the changes in the translated title as his means of minimizing ambiguity. Even if this text of roughly a thousand words might have been originally intended as a letter by a historical Russian exile in Berlin to his historical if distant beloved living in Russia, it never reached the addressee in a postal envelope. Thus, Nabokov seems to be saying to his American reader, it is she or he who is now the addressee of the historical-letter-turned-fiction. The irony of the Englished title is, of course, that "the letter" indeed "never reached Russia," either in a canvas sack with other items of foreign mail or as a short story printed there. In the 1970s Nabokov could only dream of his writings reaching the mass audience in Russia.[3] Now that his works, including "A Letter That Never Reached Russia," have found their addressees in the Russia of the 1990s, it seems fitting to use this epistolary short story in my closing remarks about Nabokov's artistic development.

Breaking his earlier promise not to dwell on the past, Nabokov's epistolary narrator continues: "For we authors in exile are supposed to possess a lofty pudicity of expression, and yet, here I am, from the very first lines, disdaining that right to sublime imperfection, and deafening with epithets the recollection on which you touched with such lightness and grace. Not of the past, my love, do I wish to speak to you" (*Stories,* 137). It is true that nowhere else in the letter except its opening paragraph does the narrator speak of the past, of his shared past with his Russian beloved. As he explains in his metafictional digression, his opening paragraph of reminiscences was triggered by the letter in which his beloved evoked their secret wintry dates in prerevolutionary St. Petersburg. Her playful evocation hit home, and the writer's memory sent him on a journey to the eight-year-old past, and then something unpredictable happened. Through writing, memory built a chain of artistic recollections of ardent "kiss[ing] behind a waxen grenadier's back" in the "glorified snuffbox" of the Suvorov museum, of the dazzling "silvery blaze of the Tavricheski Park," of a Russian soldier's bayonet being plunged "into the straw-bellied German-helmeted dummy in the middle of a Petersburg street" (*Stories,* 137). The rest of the story, describing one unforgettable night in the Russian émigré's interwar Berlin, is in fact a prolonged justification of the writer's preference for sublime perfection over sublime imperfection. What does it mean when a writer chooses to "deafen with epithets" an idealized recollection which does not seem to need literary ornamentation to survive the trials of time? In the second paragraph of "A Letter That Never Reached Russia" Nabokov posits a problem which pertains to his entire oeuvre. This problem, the relationship between the raw material of fiction sustained by memory and the form of the aestheticized final product, lies at the heart of my inquiry into the poetics of Nabokov's short stories.

A student of Nabokov's short fiction is confronted, among other things, with three fundamental issues. The first issue concerns the autobiographical nature of his short stories. Most of Nabokov's fifty-eight Russian and ten English stories (plus the originally French "Mademoiselle O") abound in autobiographical references of varying density and depth. The short stories record such disparate information as the unconsummated 1911 duel between his father and the newspaperman Mikhail Suvorin ("Orache"), his own butterfly-collecting trips ("The Aurelian"), and his literary feuds with émigré litterateurs ("Vasiliy Shishkov").

The second, metafictional issue has two dimensions, the metaliterary and the metaphysical. On the one hand, Nabokov's stories both conceal and reveal guides to their own poetics. On the other hand, the vertiginous devices which the stories employ are never self-sufficient but rather allow the author, his privileged characters, and the reader—if she or he happens to be Nabokov's ideal reader—to gain access to the otherworld. Nabokov's otherworld is a dimension that cannot be accessed effortlessly. In fact, as in the case of the story "Oblako, ozero, bashnia" (Cloud, Castle, Lake, 1937), only the privileged protagonist, the gentle Vasiliy Ivanovich, apprehends the otherworldly opening and surrenders to "an attraction the truth of which consisted in its own strength, a strength which he had never experienced before" (*Stories*, 435). The rest of his companions, described as "the collective, wobbly, many-handed being" ("sbornoe, miagkoe, mnogorukoe sushchestvo"; *Stories*, 433/VF, 241), sit with their behinds to the perfect otherworldly landscape, completely unaware, as it were, of its existence.

In "Slava" (Fame, 1942)—one of Nabokov's most important poems—the lyrical voice records a state of bliss:

> И я счастлив. Я счастлив, что совесть моя,
> сонных мыслей и умыслов сводня,
> не затронула самого тайного. Я
> удивительно счастлив сегодня.

> And I'm happy. I'm happy that Conscience, the pimp
> of my sleepy reflections and projects,
> did not get at the critical secret. Today
> I am really remarkably happy.
>
> (*PP*, 110–111)

In "A Letter That Never Reached Russia," the epistolary narrator concludes his letter on a nearly identical note of happiness: "Listen: I am ideally happy [*Slushai, ia sovershenno schastliv*]. My happiness is a kind of challenge. As I wander along the streets . . . , absently sensing the lips of dampness through my worn soles, I carry proudly my ineffable happiness. The centuries will roll by, . . . everything will pass, but my happiness, dear, my happiness will remain . . ." (*VCh*, 48/*Stories*, 140). The parallels between the way Nabokov writes the otherworld in an epistolary short story from the Russian period and a poem from the American period point to a third fundamental issue of his short stories, the problem of addressing.

Nabokov's epistolary narrator, a Russian émigré writer, addresses a beloved woman whom he has not seen for eight years. Using an estranged perspective, he tells her of things she will never see, things which fill a single night of his existence: a brightly lit train's "marvelous clatter," a "front of a cinema rippl[ing] in diamonds," a "blissful, melancholy sensation" of exile. At the end of his act of addressing, the narrator achieves a state of otherworldly happiness. The double paradox of this happiness is that writing not only creates but also records and immortalizes it. This is what the narrator means when he tells his beloved that his "happiness will remain." Nabokov wants the reader to know that the narrator's beloved, however distant and conjured up, serves as the addressee rather than a mere narratological figure, a narratee.[4] As a fictional act of addressing, "A Letter That Never Reached Russia" stands in line with a number of his other stories whose protagonists address their unattainable beloved women. As the author's "representative" in Nabokov's own terms, the narrator of "A Letter That Never Reached Russia" shares his capacity to communicate with the otherworld with Vasiliy Ivanovich of "Cloud, Castle, Lake" or Vasiliy Shishkov of the eponymous story. Through different acts of addressing, the epistolary narrator of the early "A Letter That Never Reached Russia" and Vasiliy Ivanovich of the late "Cloud, Castle, Lake" speak with distant women they love and long for, while the poet Vasiliy Shishkov gives his confessional verses to the Russian Muse of exile. In the end, the otherworld, usually somehow feminized, serves as the ultimate addressee of many short stories.

The intensely autobiographical nature, the twofold metafictionality, and the prominence of literary acts of addressing all make it very difficult to apply generic terms to Nabokov's prose fiction. Indeed, what is "A Letter That Never Reached Russia"? A short story with an epistolary façade? Or an actual unmailed (or returned) letter which now reads like a short story? Or perhaps an essay in the genre of creative nonfiction about the epistemological act which allows the writer to achieve a state of otherworldly bliss? To complicate the matter further, the scene at the Suvorov museum in St. Petersburg where the two lovers meet on cold winter mornings is repeated in both versions of Nabokov's English autobiography, *Conclusive Evidence* (1951) and *Speak, Memory* (1966), and the Russian autobiography, *Drugie berega* (Other Shores, 1954): "So from these great museums we graduated to smaller ones, such as the Suvorov, for instance, where I recall a most silent room full of old armor and tapestries, and torn silk banners, with several bewigged, heavily booted dummies in green uniforms standing guard over us" (*SM*, 236/*SSoch*, 4:262).

Is "A Letter That Never Reached Russia" an excerpt from a future autobiography, a dress rehearsal of the play which Nabokov would not actually stage for another quarter of a century?

The generic status of Nabokov's short stories is even more mutable than that of the novels; Charles Newman aptly terms their author "the protean novelist of our time—not merely because he has spanned several cultures, or turned traditional formulae to contemporary uses—but because he has succeeded in developing structures in which once disparate poetic, philosophical, theatrical, and documentary voices are enjoyed under the name of the novel."[5] Among Nabokov's short stories, one finds numerous forms of writing: letters ("The Admiralty Spire"), obituaries ("In Memory of L. I. Shigaev"), literary polemics ("Vasiliy Shishkov"), meditations ("The Word"), travel guides ("A Guide to Berlin"), essays on literary subjects ("Recruiting"), political satire ("Tyrants Destroyed"), feuilletons ("A Dashing Fellow"), memoirs ("Mademoiselle O"), etc. How does one make sense of such a generic variety? While it would take a separate study to investigate all generic connections between Nabokov's short stories and his other forms of writing, I would like to propose a model that elucidates the relationship between his short stories and his epistolary and autobiographical heritage.

I see Nabokov's short stories as the middle, fictional, stage of a three-stage development in which autobiographical information had been first processed in his letters (also diaries) and given a semblance of historicity, then recoded in his short stories and recorded as fictional, and, finally, defictionalized again and presented as remembered historical past in his autobiographies. Chronologically, Nabokov's short stories were created during the middle phase of his life, in the 1920s–1940s, and he did not complete a single short story in Russian or in English after 1951, the year when the original version of the autobiography *Conclusive Evidence* came out in the United States.[6]

I will trace three stages—the epistolary, the short-fictional, and the autobiographical—of three themes which permeate Nabokov's works: the theme of first love, the theme of artistic creation, and the theme of memory. Before considering specific examples, I would like to make two more distinctions with regard to Nabokov's letters.

Nabokov left a large epistolary legacy. His Russian letters of the 1920s–1940s, only some of which have been published or analyzed, can be divided into two groups.[7] The first group consists of conventional business letters with a purely communicative function, such as his correspondence with editors or his appeals for help with obtaining entrance visas. The other group, however, exhibits features which link it to the genre of the "familiar letter," a codified post-Neoclassical literary genre specific to its time and associated in the Russian Golden Age with a group of literary practitioners, the Arzamas circle (1808–1825).[8] Nabokov's literary letters, as opposed to the familiar letters in the Age of Pushkin, were never intended for circulation or subsequent publication, and in fact he always guarded his personal privacy. Still, and probably because Nabokov's aesthetics are rooted so firmly in the Pushkinian Golden Age, his literary letters share with the familiar letter of the 1800s–1820s their aesthetic *ustanovka*, to use the term of Iurii Tynianov, who took a serious interest in letters as a writer's laboratory.[9] Both Nabokov's literary letters and the Arzamasian familiar letter privilege the aesthetic function over the communicative one, which dominates in business correspondence.[10] For Nabokov, as for the Arzamasians, literary letters are works of art and exhibit a high degree of artistic structuredness.

The literary letters of the 1920s gave Nabokov a chance to test some of his original designs, on the level of both individual tropes and the overall narrative structure of a short story. As William Mills Todd III has observed, the familiar letter gave Pushkin "much exercise in this casual, yet subtly ordered, creativity. When Pushkin became a professional writer in the 1820s, he put his accomplishments in correspondence to use in the creation of the larger, more public work, *Eugene Onegin*."[11] For Nabokov, who was exactly a hundred years younger than Pushkin, the literary letters of the 1920s represent an epistolary stage of a complex three-stage artistic development leading ultimately to his autobiographies.

The shape of Nabokov's three-stage artistic development has virtually no equivalents among other Russian writers. To establish the points of reference, I will now look briefly at the careers of his chief Russian masters, Chekhov and Bunin. Chekhov was Nabokov's predecessor in his treatment of letters as drafts and notebooks for future works, many of them never realized. He consistently treated his letters as drafts or notebooks for future stories and plays. An example of such a letter is the 1888 letter to his sister where Chekhov outlines a number of details and images of a southern coastal resort, both a Yalta and a Nice (see Chapter 3). Some of his notes toward a future story surfaced in 1895 in "Ariadna"; others were later utilized in 1899 in "Lady with a Lap Dog." Similarities aside, one finds two principal differences between Chekhov's and Nabokov's treatment of letters as artistic testing grounds of the future projects. For Chekhov, who was one of the most prolific letter writers ever, virtually every epistolary act involves some conscious gestures toward a future work of fiction, some elements of a creative laboratory. Conversely, Nabokov's letters of the Russian period exhibit a division into two groups, the strictly "business" letters and "literary" letters. The second difference has to do with the fact that for Chekhov literary letters were not just a stage of his artistic development, but rather a major part of his activities as a writer. He would recycle the same motifs or tropes many times, and they were as likely to originate in his stories and plays as in his letters. In Nabokov's case, the Russian literary letters were a distinct first stage of a three-part development. We therefore have a situation where a linguistic discovery—an epithet, a metaphor, a pun—is born during an epistolary act, later given a sec-ond fictional life in a short story, and, finally, born again as a recollected memory.

Because Chekhov died at the age of forty-four, we can only speculate on what might have been the connections between his letters, his fiction, and his memoirs if he had left memoirs. At the same time, the epistolary, the fictional, and the memoiristic components are all well represented in Bunin's oeuvre. In fact, Bunin produced a variety of memoirs, from the autobiographical recollections written in the mid-1930s to his late *Vospominaniia* (Reminiscences, 1950). As opposed to Chekhov's and Nabokov's letters, Bunin's letters are markedly devoid of artistry and verbal experimentation. Bunin treated letters as strictly communicative and not as creative acts. They are businesslike and to the point.[12] In his will of 1942 he spoke unequivocally about the prospects of publishing his letters: "All my letters (to all my addressees) are not to be published. . . . I almost always wrote my letters poorly, carelessly, hurriedly and not always in accordance with how I was feeling . . ." (Bunin 9 : 480). A major exception, both stylistically and generically, is his correspondence with O'lga Zhirova, for whom he composed endearing letters in the form of masterful limericks:

Пишу тебе два mots,
Спасибо за письмо,
За чудную картинку,
Где Ваня кормит свинку.[13]

I send you a couple of words,
And thank you for your letter.
For a marvelous picture,
Where Vania [Bunin himself] is feeding a pig.

Otherwise, one finds in Bunin's letters an attitude to the epistolary act as a priori below the act of writing artistic prose. As to his memoirs, they too are the exact opposite of Nabokov's. Devoted chiefly to specific recollections of meetings with other artists, Bunin's memoirs were written first and foremost to settle scores with the past, as polemical diatribes. One does not find in them traces of his style as the writer of short stories or discussions of such cosmological issues as the nature of time, love, or memory that are central to Nabokov's memoirs.

Two letters that Nabokov sent in the summer of 1923 from Soliès-Pont, Provence, illustrate how he treats his literary letters as a test site for future short fictions, many of which were never written. Nabokov went to Provence to work as a farmhand, to get away from Berlin in the aftermath of a broken engagement. In the first letter, written to his ex-fiancée on May 25, 1923, he tries to negotiate his uncertain status in the eyes of the woman he still loves and longs for. It is difficult, he admits, to alienate himself from the memories of great happiness. And then follows a most fascinating epistolary twist which elevates the letter to the level of a literary text. Earlier in the letter Nabokov admits to being too exhausted after a day of toiling to write "with style" (*literaturno*). However, he still chooses sublime perfection. He describes the extraordinary heat of the southern night, the cypresses and the palm trees, the frogs that croak and gasp, deafening the orchard where a large nightingale with disheveled feathers [*rastrepannyi*] sits in the high branches against the contour of the moon.[14]

Just as the frog "deafens" the nightingale's song in Nabokov's letter, its writer chooses, to use an expression from "A Letter That Never Reached Russia," to "deafen with epithets" (*zaglushat' èpitetami*) the seething memories of his unattainable beloved. Why? Most likely, this is a case of a rapidly growing writer's literary imperative to exercise his looming aesthetics. A different letter, written from Soliès-Pont to Nabokov's mother some three weeks later, adds another literary level to the description of a Provençal summer night:

Сейчас — вечер, трогательные тучки. Я гулял по плантации, за пробковой рощей, ел персики и абрикосы, смотрел на закат, слушал как чмокал и свистел соловей — и у песни его и у заката был вкус абрикосов и персиков. (*SL*, 6)

(It is evening now, with lovely cloudlets in the sky. I took a walk around the plantation, behind the grove of cork oaks, ate peaches and apricots, admired the sunset, listened to a nightingale's tweets and whistles, and both its song and the sunset tasted of apricot and peach; *SL*, 3)

The literary nightingale in the two letters must have had a historical antecedent. Although Nabokov's second letter strikes quite a different note, it continues to elaborate on a series of interconnected images to be used later in a work of fiction. The nightingale's song and the sunset—tasting of apricot and peach—demonstrate the verbal perfection and economy of poetic means that distinguish Nabokov's best writing. It is not surprising that the cluster of images which he collected and recorded in letters during the summer of 1923 would make its way to his fiction, in this case the 1931 novel *Glory*. The protagonist, a Russian exile like his creator, goes to work at a farm in southern France. In the passage describing Martin's evenings at the farm, a student of Nabokov's letters encounters several familiar images: ". . . before turning in, he would walk over to the cork woods beyond the farm, and smoke and muse. Overhead the nightingales whistled in short rich phrases, from the pond came the rubbery croaking of frogs" (*Glory*, 164). Moreover, the same chapter mentions a letter Martin wrote to his beloved in London, "testing fate." Sonia's answer did not leave much hope: "Enough, for Christ's sake. I will never marry you. Moreover, I loathe vineyards, the heat, snakes, and, especially, garlic. Cross me out, do me that favor, darling" (*Glory*, 165).

The two letters from Provence are emblematic of Nabokov's epistolary art, through which he discovered himself as a writer of fiction. They might have materialized in a short story but instead ended up in an episode of his novel. Nabokov's other literary letters of the 1920s did serve as textual testing grounds for single tropes and whole descriptions that later resurfaced in his short stories. In this connection, Nabokov's letters to Bunin are of special interest. The letters span over eighteen years and testify to the changing literary and personal relationship between the two writers. Nabokov's first letter to Bunin, written in 1921, sets the tone for the initial stage of the correspondence. Nabokov, then a virtually unknown young Russian poet, structures the letter as a declaration of love.[15] The confessional tone and the motifs of love are crucial because he incorporates parts of his letters to Bunin into his short stories written in the form of addresses to beloved women. In his second letter to Bunin, written in 1922, Nabokov describes the moment when he composed "Kak vody gor, tvoi golos gord i chist . . ." (Like water from the mountains, your voice is proud and pure . . .), the poem later published with a dedication to Bunin:

Это было в дождливую ночь. Я возвращался к себе. Ветер трепал деревья вдоль чёрной улицы, блестевшей местами, как мокрая резина, и с коротким плотным звуком падали каштаны.[16]

(It was on a rainy night. I was walking back home. Along the black street which glistened here and there like wet rubber, the wind shook the trees, and chestnuts fell on the ground with short heavy knocks.)

With some emendations, the description reappears as fiction in a 1924 story, "Blagost'" (Beneficence). The story is structured as an address by its protagonist, a sculptor, to his girlfriend, who has left him and most likely will never come back. The protagonist waits for his beloved near the Brandenburg Gate. She never shows up, and as the evening progresses into a rainy night, the story comes to its closure, a masterful sketch of Berlin's disjointed harmony:

> Чёрные стёкла были в мелких, частых каплях дождя, будто сплошь подёрнутое бисером звёзд ночное небо. Гремели мы вдоль улицы, обсаженной шумными каштанами, и мне всё казалось, что влажные ветви хлещут по окнам. А когда трамвай останавливался, то слышно было, как стукались наверху об крышу срываемые ветром каштаны: ток — и опять, упруго и нежно: ток... ток... Трамвай трезвонил и трогался, и в мокрых стёклах дробился блеск фонарей, и я ждал с чувством пронзительного счастья повторения тех высоких и кротких звуков. (*VCh*, 164)

> (The black windowpanes were specked with a multitude of minute raindrops, like a night sky overcast with a beadwork of stars. We were clattering along a street lined with noisy chestnut trees, and I kept imagining that the humid boughs were lashing the windows. And when the tram halted one could hear, overhead, the chestnuts plucked by the wind knocking against the roof. Knock—then again, resiliently, gently: knock, knock. The tram would chime and start, the gleam of the streetlamps shattered in wet glass, and, with a sensation of poignant happiness I awaited the repetition of those meek, lofty sounds; *Stories*, 78)

A number of motifs and tropes from the 1922 letter to Bunin echo in the short story. We find the same colors (black street, black windows), the same glitter of street lamps, the artist's happiness at seeing the universe in its unending bifurcation.[17] In "Beneficence" the central image of falling chestnuts acquires yet another level of signification. The sound of falling chestnuts, mapping the beat of a young heart, initiates a series of recurrent motifs. Moments of intense happiness, during which Nabokov's privileged protagonists (Ivanov of "Perfection," Pnin of the eponymous novel, and others) experience what he called cosmic synchronization, are frequently marked by heart pains. The heart expands rapidly as it feels the pangs of the otherworld.

The narrator's beloved in "Beneficence" will never receive his passionate address. This connects her with the distant Russian addressee in "A Letter That Never Reached Russia." Written less than a year after "Beneficence," the epistolary story also draws on Nabokov's second letter to Bunin as it describes the colors, lights, and sounds of nighttime Berlin. I am thinking in particular about the note of sheer happiness on which the narrator ends his letter: "Listen: I am ideally happy. My happiness is a kind of challenge" (*Stories*, 140). One thing I might add is that "A Letter That Never Reached Russia" was originally printed in the émigré newspaper *Rul'* (*The Rudder*), with a subtitle, "From the second chapter of the novel *Shchast'e* [Happiness]." Nabokov contemplated an autobiographical novel, "some important elements of which were to be reslanted in [*Mary*]" (*Stories*, 647). He never wrote it, but insofar as I can judge, the novel was supposed to contain a major epistolary dimension which is lacking in *Mary*.[18]

Finally, here is an example of a single image which originates in the letter to Bunin and finds its way to another one of the early short stories, "Port" (The Seaport, 1924). In the 1921 letter to Bunin Nabokov speaks of the "black street which glistened here and there like wet rubber." In "The Seaport" the lonesome Russian émigré Nikitin comes to a seaport in southern France. As he wanders around the docks looking for work, he encounters a black soldier wearing a colonial uniform ("negr v kolonial'noi forme"). The soldier's face, glittering with drops of sweat, is likened to a wet rubber shoe: "litso, kak mokraia galosha" (*VCh*, 18). The image of a night street in Berlin has traveled a long way and undergone quite a metamorphosis!

Nabokov's letters to Bunin provide a foretaste of Nabokov's three-stage development, in which autobiographical information proceeds from literary letters via fictional texts into autobiography. Of course, it would be absurd to assume that only the information recorded in his literary letters would later find its way to the autobiographies. The business letters—and several of Nabokov's letters to Bunin from the 1930s deal exclusively with dry professional matters—naturally carry a residue of biographical information (names, dates, places, prices, etc.). However, the literary letters are indispensable here because in them factual information is given an artistic verbal shape. Consider, for instance, Nabokov's postcard to Bunin sent from London in 1939. He describes an English spring: "Tut vesna,— gazon i sizost'—vo vsiu tsvetut aniutiny glazki, zhëltye s chërnym, lichikami neobyknovenno pokhozhi na Gitlera,— obratite vnimanie pri sluchae."[19] (Spring's here—lawns and dampness—pansies are everywhere in bloom, yellow and black, their little faces bearing a terrible resemblance to Hitler—take a look when you get a chance.)

In *Speak, Memory* Nabokov describes a "breezy day in Berlin" when he and his son "stood before a bed of pallid pansies, each of their upturned faces showing a dark mustache-like smudge, and had great fun, at [Nabokov's] rather silly prompting, commenting on their resemblance to a crowd of bobbing little Hitlers" (*SM*, 305). Or take an incident he mentions in the autobiographies: "In the summer of 1929, every time I walked through a village in the Eastern Pyrenees, and happened to look back, I would see in my wake the villagers frozen in the various attitudes my passage had caught them in, as if I were Sodom and they Lot's wife" (*SM*, 131). We find the starting point for Nabokov's evocation of the Old Testament (Genesis 19:26) in a letter written to Bunin from a Pyrenean village in 1929: "We are living in a lovely remote corner; we are the only 'aliens' in this village and as we proceed down the main street, the locals turn into pillars of salt."[20] This motif of the perplexed "local inhabitants" (*Stories*, 254) staring with surprise at the butterfly collectors, "strange people who have come from afar" ("strannye liudi, priekhavshie izdaleka"; *S*, 196) to their remote corner of the world, is echoed during the middle, fictional stage of Nabokov's three-stage development, in the short story "The Aurelian." What an incredible artistic memory! Clearly without access to his 1929 letter, Nabokov repeated almost verbatim a mythic image which he had mailed off twenty years before writing the autobiography. There is more than a perfect memory at work here. There is also his conviction that once conjured up, an artistic discovery will always be at the artist's fingertips.

"Admiralteiskaia igla" (The Admiralty Spire), created in one sweep of inspiration on May 23, 1933, in Berlin, is crucial for understanding the epistolary past and the autobiographical future of Nabokov's short stories. Written in the form of a letter, the story is long and rich in cultural and historical allusions. Unlike "A Letter That Never Reached Russia," with which it shares autobiographical information, "The Admiralty Spire" possesses a complex plot that evolves simultaneously on two levels. The subject matter is the relationship of autobiographical fiction to the events which inform it. The *Vorgeschichte* is a Russian novel by an unknown author published in one of the Baltic countries. The novel's title, *The Admiralty Spire*, borrowed from the prologue to Pushkin's long poem *The Bronze Horseman*, catches the eye of the protagonist, who is a professional émigré writer. He picks up a copy, reads it, and then dashes off an indignant response to the author. Although the name printed on the cover is a male one, Sergei Solntsev, the epistolary protagonist/narrator opens his letter with an address to a woman: "You will pardon me, dear Madam, but I am a rude and straightforward person, so I'll come right out with it: do not labor under any delusion: this is far from being a fan letter" (*Stories*, 348). The protagonist conjectures that the author of the novel is a female who obtained a lot of private information from his first love, a Russian by the name of Katya. Sixteen years have elapsed since the protagonist's last meeting with Katya, "the age of a bride, an old dog, or the Soviet republic" (*Stories*, 349), as he puts it. Now, as the middle-aged caustic émigré writer reads a mediocre and overwritten tale of his own first love, the maimed memories call for literary revenge. And avenge himself he does!

The two thematic levels of Nabokov's story are the theme of first love, one of the most central for his entire oeuvre, and the theme of poor art degrading treasured memories of an idealized past. Halfway through his critique, the protagonist tears down the cynical mask, deflates "the arrogant rubber fatman who . . . clowned around at the beginning of [the] letter," and addresses his first love directly rather than via the façade of a "corpulent lady novelist in her novelistic hammock" (*Stories*, 356). In a different tone, suffused with gentle bitterness and self-irony, the protagonist writes: "Katya, why have you made such a mess of it now [*napakostila*]? Come, let us have a calm, heart-to-heart talk. . . . How intensely I must have loved you if I still see you as you were sixteen years ago, make agonizing efforts to free our past from its humiliating captivity, and save your image from the rack and disgrace of your own pen!" (*Stories*, 356–357).

If one translates into biographical terms the situation recreated with such moving verisimilitude in the protagonist's recollections, and with such vapid disregard for the indeterminacy and suggestiveness of the language of Russian romantic love in Solntsev's eponymous novel, it would amount to the following. What would happen if Nabokov's historical first love, Liusia Shul'gina, the Tamara of *Speak, Memory* and in part the Mashen'ka (Mary) of his first novel, were indeed to produce a subjective, politicized, and ill-written account of their love which "perpetrates" (*Stories*, 357) and violates Nabokov's own perfect memories?[21] This is only a supposition, but it serves to illustrate his polemical task as an autobiographer in *Speak, Memory*/*Other Shores*. One of the finest in the entire book, the "Tamara" chapter (12 in *Speak, Memory;* 11 in *Other Shores*) reads like a short story that polemicizes—some twenty years later—with its own protobiographical past distorted in Katya's novel, which, of course, is also Nabokov's creation. This paradigmatically Nabokovian predicament corresponds to the three-stage model of his artistic career which I have proposed. What remains is to identify and examine the correspondences between "The Admiralty Spire" and the autobiographies.

In *Speak, Memory* Nabokov spoke about his correspondence with Tamara: "Happy is the novelist who manages to preserve an actual love letter that he received when he was young within a work of fiction, embedded in it like a clean bullet in flabby flesh and quite secure there, among spurious lives" (*SM,* 249). In "The Admiralty Spire" the protagonist summarizes the way Katya distorted their shared past: "the trimmings are yours, I'll concede, and so are the stuffing and the sauce, but the game ... is not yours but mine, with my buckshot in its wing" (*Stories,* 349). The hunting imagery, rehearsed in the story and brought out again in *Speak, Memory,* signals the importance Nabokov attributes to the epistolary past of his fiction and autobiographies. He regrets that he did not "keep the whole of" his correspondence with Tamara within works of fiction. That would have created more of a literary background, like the one in "The Admiralty Spire," against which to construct an autobiography. I will not deal here with the novel *Mary* and its autobiographical dimension. It is clearly very important as Nabokov's first large-scale attempt at fictionalizing his past and the story of his first love. In *Speak, Memory* Nabokov makes several statements about the way the writing of *Mary* "relieved [him] of that fertile emotion" (*SM,* 244–245). But he is most specific in *Other Shores:* "vposledstvii, v poluavtobiograficheskoi povesti, ia pochuvstvoval sebia vprave sviazat' èto [the extraordinary sunsets in 1917 which Aleksandr Blok records in his diary] s vospominaniem of Tamare" (later, in a semiautobiographical short novel, I felt that I was entitled to link this with my recollections of Tamara; *SSoch,* 4:266). Finally, in a preface to the English translation of *Mary,* Nabokov makes a very interesting admission:

> Readers of my *Speak, Memory* (begun in the Nineteen-Forties) cannot fail to notice certain similarities between my recollections and Ganin's. His Mary is a twin sister of my Tamara. . . . I had not consulted [*Mary*] when writing Chapter Twelve of the autobiography a quarter of a century later; and now that I have, I am fascinated by the fact that despite the superimposed inventions . . . a headier extract of personal reality is contained in the romantization than in the autobiographer's scrupulously faithful account. (*Mary,* xiv)

Nabokov's letters to Liusia Shul'gina would have been of enormous interest to my project, had they been available. Still, his references to the correspondence with his first beloved, both in "The Admiralty Spire" and in the autobiographies, may be supplemented with some of his other literary letters.

Two letters to Nabokov's sister Elena (Helene) Sikorski, née Nabokov, after they had resumed their correspondence, severed by World War II, contain clues for decoding "The Admiralty Spire" and the autobiographies. In the first, dated November 26, 1945, Nabokov informs his sister that he has "gained a huge amount of weight" and now looks like the Russian poet Aleksei Apukhtin (1840–1893): "zdorovo rastolstel, stal pokhozh na Apukhtina" (*SL*, 61/*PSS*, 26). In "The Admiralty Spire" the protagonist refers to himself as corpulent, although he contrasts his "piquant" and "zesty" corpulence with the flabbiness of "the poet Apukhtin, the fat pet of ladies" (*Stories*, 348). Just how much self-irony is contained in this statement becomes evident toward the end of the story, when Nabokov's narrator invokes two oft-quoted poems by Apukhtin, soon after he has broken down and deflated his relentless rubber dummy. He now begins to doubt his own efforts to "free [their] past from its humiliating captivity, and save [Katya's] image from the rack and disgrace of [her] own pen!" (*Stories*, 357). The narrator is not sure if he is succeeding, because "[his] letter smacks strangely of those rhymed epistles" that Katya used to "rattle off by heart" (*Stories*, 357). The Russian text makes two references to Apukhtin's verse without identifying their sources. The first is a slightly altered opening line from "Pis'mo" (The Letter, 1882), which should read: "Uvidia pocherk moi, Vy, verno, udivites'." [22] The second is from "Otvet na pis'mo" (A Response to a Letter, 1885): "Zdes' more zhdët tebia, shirokoe, kak strast', / I strast', shirokaia, kak more." [23] The Englished version of the story, produced in the 1970s, identifies the author of the two quotes: "'The sight of my handwriting may surprise you'—but I shall refrain from closing, as Apukhtin does, with the invitation: 'The sea awaits you here, as vast as love / And love, vast as the sea!'—I shall refrain, because, in the first place, there is no sea here, and, in the second, I have not the least desire to see you" (*Stories*, 357).

When Nabokov wrote the original version of "The Admiralty Spire" in 1933, he was the opposite of corpulent. The photographs of the time, as well as memoirs of the 1930s, present him as a very skinny and athletic individual. Why the Apukhtin association? Is it because Nabokov did not want the reader to look for resemblances between his narrator and himself? But why then did he not fictionalize his historical past in the story completely beyond recognition? His letters to his sister Elena might offer some clues. Apukhtin, whose obesity usually comes to mind along with a few passionate stylized poems like "Nochi bezumnye, nochi bessonnye . . ." (Mad nights, sleepless nights . . . , 1876), represented for Nabokov the direct opposite of his own physique and mature verse. In *Speak, Memory* he recoils at the "shameful gleanings from Apukhtin's and Grand Duke Konstantin's lyrics of the *tsïganski* type" (*SM,* 225) present in his own first poem. Conversely, in 1945, when Nabokov likened himself to Apukhtin in a letter, he was already contemplating writing his autobiography. He had also just gained a lot of weight as a result of quitting smoking.[24] The associations with Apukhtin and his verse are tested in a familiar letter to his sister before being incorporated into an autobiography. With the Apukhtin references we observe a complex transformation. First, they make a fatidic intrusion in "The Admiralty Spire." Then Nabokov's biographical circumstances solidify a double-ironic identification in a post–World War II letter.[25] Later yet, in *Speak, Memory,* Nabokov discusses Apukhtin in connection with his own early attempts at poetry. Finally, in the 1970s he enhances the Apukhtin motif while Englishing his 1933 story.

In the late 1940s, already brimming with his autobiography, Nabokov revisited the material he had earlier channeled through fiction. One such visit to the past is documented in a letter he sent his sister on December 6, 1949. He describes riding a bicycle to his uncle's estate to fetch a book: "It was at the end of the summer, a cold dark evening, carbide in a bicycle lamp, probably in the middle of August, definitely in 1914" (*PSS,* 58). In all versions of Nabokov's story of first love—"The Admiralty Spire," the novel *Mary,* the "Tamara" chapter of the autobiographies—the reader finds the young lovers riding bicycles along park alleys. In *Speak, Memory* he recalls how "on dark rainy evenings [he] would load the lamp of [his] bicycle with magical lumps of calcium carbide, and . . . ride cautiously into the darkness" (*SM,* 233).[26]

Had we possessed the letters Nabokov wrote to Tamara before the Revolution and from the Crimea in 1917–1918, the postepistolary past and the protobiographical future of his Russian short stories would no doubt have been even more explicit. Still, it is a rewarding experience to compare the figurations of certain key motifs and separate images in "The Admiralty Spire" and Nabokov's autobiographies. Much attention is given in the story to the depiction and critique of a literary milieu which surrounded Katya. In Solntsev's novel Olga and Leonid, whose names disguise those of Katya and the protagonist, are placed in the middle of an "exquisitely cultured beau monde." The protagonist hurries to correct the distorted memories:

That upperclass milieu—the fashionable set, if you will—to which Katya belonged, had backward tastes, to put it mildly. Chekhov was considered an "impressionist," the society rhymester Grand-Duke Constantine [Konstantin Romanov], a major poet, and the arch-Christian Alexander Blok a wicked Jew who wrote futuristic sonnets about dying swans and lilac liqueurs. Handwritten copies of album verse, French and English, made the rounds . . . the darling among them was a piece by poor Louis Bouilhet, who wrote in the middle of last century. . . . Reveling in his cadences, Katya would declaim his alexandrines. . . . (*Stories*, 351)

Nabokov's narrator also corrects the author of the irksome novel about the songs which Katya would sing at gatherings; not operatic repertoire, but gypsy songs, so "modish" in their society. The protagonist admits that "*tsï-ganshchina*" even inclined him to composing verse (*Stories*, 351).

Tamara in *Speak, Memory*, like Katya in the story, also knew a "vast store of minor poetry" (*SM*, 231). At the same time, Nabokov's relationship with Tamara was not as "literary" as the one Katya and the narrator enjoy in the story. This might explain the fact that he plants a recollection of the pseudo-gypsy cult and the popular poetry of the 1910s not in the "Tamara" chapter, but in the chapter right before it (Chapter 11 in *Speak, Memory*). Nabokov reconstructs for the reader the extended moment of composing his first poem, created, just as in "The Admiralty Spire," under the spell of first love and gypsy songs. Compare the following autobiographical description with the one from the story quoted above:

On the veranda where our relatives and friends assembled, [the gramophone] emitted from its brass mouthpiece the so-called *tsï-ganskie romansï* beloved of my generation. These were more or less anonymous imitations of gypsy songs—or imitations of imitations. . . . When silence returned, my first poem was ready. . . . It was indeed a miserable concoction, containing many borrowings besides its pseudo-Pushkinian modulations. . . . Worst of all were the shameful gleanings from Apukhtin's and Grand Duke Konstantin's lyrics of the *tsïganski* type. They used to be persistently pressed upon me by a youngish and rather attractive aunt, who could also spout Louis Bouilhet's famous piece. . . . (*SM*, 225)

The multiple parallels and the differences between the two passages testify again to the extent to which Nabokov's short stories fictionalize his biographical past and yet prepare for its subsequent restoration to the level of autobiographical prose. At times, however, an image travels from a short story to the autobiography almost unchanged after so many years as fiction. Such is the case with one remarkably vivid and naturalistic detail in Katya's portrait. The protagonist reminisces about picking strawberries: "Zharko nalivalos' solntse, — i èto solntse, i zemlianika, i katino chesuchëvoe plat'e, potemnevshee podmyshkami . . ." (The hot sun bore down, and that sun, and the strawberries, and Katya's frock of tussore silk with darkening blotches under the arms . . ."; *VF*, 224/*Stories*, 352–353). In the "Tamara" chapter Nabokov revisits the summer of first love: " . . . and there she was, my happy Tamara, on the points of her toes, trying to pull down a racemosa branch in order to pick its puckered fruit, with all the world and its trees wheeling in the orb of her laughing eye, and a dark patch from her exertions in the sun forming under her raised arm on the raw shantung of her yellow frock" (*SM*, 239–240); in the Russian version of the memoir:

> ... и вот — вижу её, привставшую на цыпочки, чтобы потянуть книзу ветку черёмухи со сморщенными ягодами, и дерево и небо и жизнь играют у неё в смеющемся взоре, и от её весёлых усилий на жарком солнце расплывается тёмное пятно по жёлтой чесуче платья под её поднятой рукой. (*SSoch*, 4:265)

It is, of course, both nearly impossible and fruitless to speculate whether or not this penetrating detail was actually remembered and brought into exile as part of Nabokov's baggage or was conjured up only later. It might be helpful, however, to consult his 1967 interview, where he revamps and applies a Platonic idea to the art of memory. The interviewer, Alfred Appel Jr., asked Nabokov to "comment on the significance of autobiographical hints in works of art that are literally *not* autobiographical." He replied that "imagination is a form of memory. An image depends on the power of associations, and association is supplied and prompted by memory" (*SO*, 77–78). Thus, the autobiographical detail, the dark blotch in the armpit of Katya or Tamara, undergoes the same metamorphic cycle in which it first stands as fiction, presumably a product of imagination, and then as a recollection, presumably a product of memory. To quote Nabokov, "when we speak of a vivid individual recollection we are paying a compliment not to our capacity of retention but to Mnemosyne's mysterious foresight in having stored up this or that element which creative imagination may want to use when combining it with later recollections and inventions. In this sense, both memory and imagination are a negation of time" (*SO*, 78).

"The Admiralty Spire" continues to shape a metafictional motif which passes from the short stories to the autobiography. The epistolary protagonist stresses that he and his beloved were structuring their fresh memories as future recollections: "we were preparing in advance for certain things, training ourselves to remember, imagining a distant past and practicing nostalgia, so that subsequently, when that past really existed for us, we would know how to cope with it, and not perish under its burden" (*Stories*, 352). "The Admiralty Spire" in effect charts two fictional trajectories of the same cluster of memories now turned into two protoautobiographies, one put together by a graphomaniac, the other by an artist of memory. The motif of the present as a series of would-be recollections plays a prominent part in such stories as "A Guide to Berlin" and "Torpid Smoke."[27] In "A Guide to Berlin" Nabokov suggests that the "sense of literary creation" is to "portray ordinary objects as they will be reflected in the kindly mirrors of future times" (*Stories*, 157). He speaks of a little boy eyeing objects and people inside a beer hall. The boy's memory is still flung open to the world, and "whatever happens to him in life, he will always remember" the raw and splendid details in their unstructured interrelation. The details only seem unstructured, while in fact they have already been given the shape of a "future recollection" (*Stories*, 160). In "Torpid Smoke," which records the pains of a new poem being delivered into this world, the protagonist also speaks of glimpsing "a future recollection" ("budushchee vospominanie"; *Stories*, 400/*VF*, 82) which he receives in a moment of "terrifying clarity" akin to what Nabokov would later term "cosmic synchronization": "it dawned upon me that exactly as I recalled such images of the past as the way my dead mother had of making a weepy face . . . so one day I would have to recall, with merciless, irreparable sharpness, the hurt look of my father's shoulders as he leaned over that torn map . . . ; and all this mingled creatively with the recent vision of blue smoke clinging to dead leaves on a wet roof" (*Stories*, 400).

Speak, Memory is very much a guide to its own making, and the transformations of future recollections into autobiographical material are a leitmotif in the book. Consider, for instance, a game Nabokov describes playing with a friend in the Crimea: "The idea consisted of parodying a biographic approach projected, as it were, into the future and thus transforming the very specious present into a kind of paralyzed past as perceived by a doddering memoirist" (*SM*, 248). With the help of irony, playful and yet clairvoyant, the passage crystallizes a seminal point. Nabokov's autobiography is iconoclastic in its structure, theme, and metaphysics and does indeed elevate facts and details, both historical and imagined, to the level of art.[28] Biographical method, which he parodied as a young poet, is naturally a part of any autobiography. However, his autobiography is exceptional in its insistence upon what he called "secret themes in a wide-awake fate" ("tainye temy v iavnoi sud'be"; *SSoch,* 4:133) in the preface to the Russian version. This is why when the same motif receives a lifelong treatment in letters, short stories, and autobiography it blurs beyond distinction the conventional boundary between the fictional nature of art and the biographical shape of life.

In "Vstrecha" (The Reunion, 1931), a story from Nabokov's Middle period, the protagonist tries to recall the name of a poodle which belonged to a little girl he used to know as a child: "Somewhere in his memory there was a hint of motion, as if something very small had awakened and begun to stir. . . . Everything vanished, but, at an instant his brain ceased straining, the thing stirred again, more perceptibly this time, and like a mouse emerging from a crack when the room is quiet, the live corpuscle of a word. . . . 'Give me your paw, Joker.' Joker! How simple it was. Joker. . . ." (*Stories,* 311).

Almost twenty years later, in 1948, Nabokov wrote Chapter 7 of his autobiography, which he published as a short story, entitled "Colette," in *The New Yorker* in 1948 and later included in *Nabokov's Dozen* (1958) under a different title, "First Love." At the end of the chapter, he describes the anatomy of one miraculous recollection:

> And now a delightful thing happens. The process of recreating that penholder and the microcosm in its eyelet stimulates my memory to a last effort. I try to recall the name of Colette's dog [Colette is the name of a French girl he met on the beach in Biarritz]—and triumphantly, along those remote beaches, over the glossy evening sands of the past, where each footprint slowly fills up with sunset water, here it comes, here it comes, echoing and vibrating: Floss, Floss, Floss! (*SM,* 152/*Stories,* 610)

On April 15, 1937, on the day of their twelfth wedding anniversary, Nabokov sent his wife a letter of exceptional artistic beauty and tenderness. It was April in Paris. Véra Nabokov was still in Berlin with their son Dmitri, hoping to join her husband before long.[29] Nabokov wrote his letter in Russian, but at places he inserted French and English phrases and private codes—a common practice in his letters to his wife. A few sentences illustrate the letter's deeply affectionate tone:

> My life, my love, *it is twelve years today* [the italicized words were originally written in English]. And on this very day *Despair* has been published, and *The Gift* appears. . . . My darling, I love you. . . . *My*

love, my life, how long it's been since you've stood before me, and God, how many new things there will be about my little one, and how many births I have missed (of words, of games, of all sorts of things).... Poor Ilf [Il'ia Il'f, a Soviet Russian writer, co-authored his books with Evgenii Petrov] has died. And, somehow, one visualizes the Siamese twins being separated. I love you, I love you. . . . I embrace you, my joy, my tired little thing.... (*SL,* 22–24)

Two months later, when Nabokov was working on one of his finest short stories, he shared with his "representative," the Russian émigré protagonist Vasiliy Ivanovich, the experience of addressing a distant beloved. There are, of course, structural and generic differences between his epistolary address to his wife and Vasiliy Ivanovich's interrupted and renarrated monologue to "that lady, another man's wife, whom he had hopelessly loved for seven years" (*Stories,* 430–431). However, the similarities are striking. One of the unique features of "Cloud, Castle, Lake" lies in its fusion of voices, the protagonist's and the narrator's, at several culminative points where the opening of the otherworld shows through chinks in mundane reality. They join their voices in a double-voiced address to their beloved women, one being Vasiliy Ivanovich's unattainable love, the other his "employer's" beloved, who is also the story's immediate addressee. Here is an example: "It happened that on a distant slope or in a gap in the trees there would appear and, as it were, stop for an instant, like air retained in the lungs, a spot so enchanting—a lawn, a terrace—such perfect expression of tender well-meaning beauty—that it seemed that if one could stop the train and go thither, forever, to you, my love . . ." (*Stories,* 432). Elsewhere, the reader also finds forms of passionate address recalling the ones Nabokov used in the letter to Véra: "my love" (*Stories,* 434); "my love! my obedient one!" (*Stories,* 435). The connections between his letters to his wife and "Cloud, Castle, Lake" present yet another perspective on the postepistolary trace in his short stories. They also point to the proto-autobiographical status of his epistolary and short-fictional addresses to his wife.

In the penultimate chapter of both *Speak, Memory* and *Other Shores* Nabokov makes a dazzling artistic move which will always distinguish him as an innovative autobiographer. In a rather neutral, almost detached tone, he recalls his growing literary success in the late 1920s. Then, suddenly, a magical intrusion of three words changes the course of his entire autobiographical narrative: "By 1928, my novels were beginning to bring a little money in German translations, and in the spring of 1929, *you and I* went butterfly hunting in the Pyrenees" (*SM,* 281; italics added). This "you

18. Vladimir, Véra, and Dmitri Nabokov, Berlin, 1935. Courtesy of Ardis Publishers.

and I" cluster, two shifters put together, initiates a series of addresses reaching a crescendo in the final chapter where Nabokov's son is born and the family leaves Europe for the New World (a photograph of Vladimir, Véra, and Dmitri Nabokov is reproduced in Figure 18).[30] The final chapter begins and ends as an address to Nabokov's wife, either a long familiar letter or a literary monologue put down on paper—one cannot really tell:

They are passing, posthaste, posthaste, the gliding years—to use a soul-rending Horatian inflection. The years are passing, my dear, and presently nobody will know what you and I know. Our child is growing; the roses of Paestum, of misty Paestum, are gone. . . . We shall go still further back, to a morning in May, 1934. . . . There I was walking home, at 5 A.M., from the maternity hospital near Bayerischer Platz, to which I had taken you a couple of hours earlier. (*SM,* 295)

In this chapter, Nabokov touches on almost all of his most important aesthetic, ethical, and metaphysical beliefs. He describes thinking of love for a person in terms of "drawing radii from [his] love—from [his] heart, from the tender nucleus of personal matter—to monstrously remote points of the universe" (*SM,* 296). He stresses being a "confirmed nonunionist" in questions of faith. And, what is central for this discussion, he talks about the omnipotence of memory versus the speediness of time. In this connection, Nabokov's invocation of a Horatian ode in the first sentence of the chapter is far from gratuitous. He paraphrases the opening of Horace's Ode to Postumus (Ode 14, Book 2), in which the ancient poet addresses his friend with bitterness and solemnity: "Eheu fugaces, Postume, Postume, / labuntur anni . . ." (Alas, my Postumus, our years / glide away silently . . .).[31] The subject of the Horatian ode is the brevity of life, the nearness of crossing over, the inevitability of death. At the end of the poem Horace envisions an heir who would spill the best wine on the floor during a luxurious feast. Nabokov also speaks of an heir in his final chapter, about his son, whose development was a source of many "discoveries" for his parents (*SM,* 297). In fact, he crowns the chapter and thus his entire autobiography with a now famous description of the parents marveling at their son's discovery of a liner which would take them across the Atlantic: "a splendid ship's funnel, showing from behind the clothesline as something in a scrambled picture—Find What the Sailor Has Hidden—that the finder cannot unsee once it has been seen" (*SM,* 310). The finder here is not only his five-year-old son, but also Nabokov himself and the reader. And the ultimate discovery is the unique shape of an autobiography, the perfect vessel of art emerging into sight from life's chaotic clotheslines. The invocation of both Horace and Virgil (roses of Paestum from *Georgics,* Book 4) as shapers of the Western literary tradition might also signal that Nabokov is fully aware of a complex literary synthesis which resulted in the text of his autobiography. Indeed, in *Speak, Memory,* as nowhere else, we can see Nabokov's artistic quest in all its unity and diversity. Here everything comes together in his protean art. The prominence of addressing connects the autobiography with the genre of epistolary novel, not only in its history

(Jean-Jacques Rousseau's *La nouvelle Héloïse,* Wolfgang von Goethe's *The Suffering of Young Werther,* Pushkin's unfinished *Novel in Letters*), but also its revitalization by Nabokov's contemporaries (Viktor Shklovskii's *Zoo: Letters Not about Love or the Third Héloïse*).[32] Several chapters of the auto-biography ("Mademoiselle O," "First Love") were written as separate short stories, and nearly all were published in periodicals in the form of short stories ("Tamara," "Lodgings in Trinity Lane").[33] The fact that a number of chapters of the autobiography stand as short stories in their own right suggests that as a covert modernist Nabokov understood quite clearly that the meaning of genre is not only in its Neoclassical rigidness, but also in its constant openness to encompass innovations. In other words, his experiments with conflating the autobiographical and the epistolary in such short stories as "Beneficence," "A Letter That Never Reached Russia," "The Admiralty Spire," and the American "That in Aleppo Once . . ." (1943) created a foundation upon which the writer constructed his autobiography. Before embarking on an autobiography in the 1940s (his first attempts, of which little survives, go back to 1935),[34] Nabokov had rehearsed acts of addressing a beloved in several short stories, including "Cloud, Castle, Lake" and even "Spring in Fialta," where the protagonist exclaims in the midst of a first-person narrative: "But then what should I have done with you, Nina, how should I have disposed of the store of sadness that had gradually accumulated as a result of our seemingly carefree, but really hopeless meetings?" (*Stories,* 425).

At the end of *Speak, Memory* and *Other Shores,* the most explicit among Nabokov's autobiographies,[35] the author confesses his love to his wife and mother of his child, his lifelong Muse: his Russia, his Mnemosyne, and his Lorelei. Heinrich Heine's celebrated poem "Die Lorelei" (1823) is not only relevant here as a paradigmatic Romantic statement about love and memory, but also because in "The Admiralty Spire" Nabokov's narrator recalls the last verse from Osip Mandel'shtam's prophetic poem "Dekabrist" (The Decembrist, 1917), which refers to Heine's lyric. Nabokov uses Mandel'-shtam's verse doubly ironically when he rips apart Solntsev's falsifying novel: "And at the end of the book you have me join the White Army and get caught by the Reds during a reconnaissance, and, with the names of two traitresses—Russia, Olga—on my lips, die valiantly . . ." (*Stories,* 356). The last two verses of Mandel'shtam's poem read:

Всё перепуталось и сладко повторять:
Россия, Лета, Лорелея

Everything has been all mixed up and it is sweet to repeat:
Russia, Lethe, Lorelei.[36]

The study of the poetics of Nabokov's short stories helps to visualize not only the anatomy of his art, but also its genesis and evolution. A passage in the Russian version of his autobiography makes a profound if concealed statement about his understanding of a writer's development. In Chapter 1 of *Other Shores* Nabokov speaks of his development as a child. He claims to have learned words and numbers simultaneously, to have realized all at once that he is he and his parents are his parents, whose age relates to his in a certain way. This, he says, "corresponds to the theory of ontogenetic repetition of the previous stages of development. From a phylogenetic standpoint, the moment when the first human being started to reflect about himself coincided with the dawning of the sense of time" (*SSoch*, 137; cf. *SM*, 21).[37] *Mutatis mutandis,* Ernst Heinrich Haeckel's evolutionary law, to which Nabokov refers, applies to Nabokov's life in literature. Short stories are a stage through which a writer like Nabokov goes in order to embrace larger and more protean forms, and his autobiography is structured as an analysis of his artistic development. The fact that Nabokov wrote his last short story, "Lance," the same year his autobiography was published (1951) might suggest that he had finalized his own achievement by finding a literary form which would be not only a personal history of its author, an autobiography, but also a literary history of its text in the making, a textobiography.

As I prepare to take leave of this study, I am reminded of Nabokov's early Russian story, "Passazhir" (The Passenger, 1927), where a critic makes a recommendation to an ambitious author: "The Word is given the sublime right to enhance chance and to make of the transcendental something that is not accidental" (*Stories*, 187). The span of Nabokov's career in letters (1916–1977) coincided with a period of ruthless challenges by literary critics to fundamental notions of the author and of authorship. Throughout the six decades of Nabokov's prolific life in letters, several major schools of critical thought, both Continental and American, subjected to intensive inquiry and defied the traditional assumptions of so-called humanist criticism. Nabokov began his professional literary career in the early 1920s in Berlin, when the Formalist attack against biographical criticism was reaching a crescendo in his native Russia. Between 1923 and 1937, he made six visits to Prague, where aesthetics and literary evolution were being redefined by the Czech Structuralists. Nabokov continued to write in the 1930s, in Germany and then in France, steadily becoming the new star of Russian émigré fiction. The Russian Formalist School had already been suppressed in Soviet Russia by the time of his move to the United States, while the center of inquiry into the nature of authorship had moved from Europe to America. Conditioned in part by T. S. Eliot's seminal essays of the 1920s, the New Critics not only denounced the tenets of humanist criticism, but also introduced their thinking into American university teaching in the 1940s–1950s. These, of course, were the decades of Nabokov's tenure as a college professor, where he could not but encounter New Criticism. The success of *Lolita,* Nabokov's increasing fame and acclaim in the 1960s, and his move to Europe coincided with the Poststructuralist assault against traditional mythologizations of the author.[38] Poststructuralism— particularly its French wing—had a tremendous impact upon the critical thought of our time and affected the prevalent critical reception of Nabokov in the 1970s and 1980s as a metafictional writer.

In a number of discursive writings and interviews, and specifically in "The Art of Literature and Commonsense" (written ca. 1941, published 1980), Nabokov advocated a humanist and specifically neo-Romantic view that places the author at the center of literary creation. He assigns three main components to artistic creation. It is irrational in defiance of commonsense as the mortal enemy of fiction. It is transcendental, and in the "divinely absurd world of the [artist's] mind, mathematical symbols do not thrive" (*LL,* 374). Finally, artistic creation is inspirational, and Nabokov is a firm believer in the centrality of those "radiant seconds" in the life of the artist when "the past and the present *and* the future [the work of art] come together in a sudden flash; thus the entire circle of time is perceived, which is another way of saying that time ceases to exist" (*LL,* 378). The artist's memory functions as a bridge between the two stages of inspiration, "rapture" (*vostorg*) and "recapture" (*vdokhnovenie*), in Nabokov's (originally Pushkinian) respective English and Russian terms (*LL,* 378–379).

The author in Nabokov's conception occupies a position vis-à-vis her or his creative world which is ontologically similar to the one held by the Creator in the universe. Nabokov's artistic experience, both bilingual and bicultural, puts into question the validity of the Poststructuralist views of the author and authorship, especially the influential ideas of the French philosophers of culture Roland Barthes and Michel Foucault. Barthes and Foucault were the culmination of the twentieth-century offensive against the humanist notion of the author as an individual endowed with exceptional linguistic and cognitive powers. Barthes's "The Death of the Author" (1968) and Foucault's "What Is an Author?" (1970) constitute a two-part desperate and brilliant attempt to remove the author from the domain of literary criticism. In their writings the role of the author was downgraded to that of a modern *scriptor,* an author-function, a mere device to record myriad information units that surround the author. Such a schematic and reductionist view of the author left no room for irrational components of creativity—first and foremost for inspiration. On the whole, the Poststructuralist critical enterprise attributed little significance to the author's talent, world vision, and individuality and applied identical hermeneutic strategies to all writers across the board. In the case of Nabokov, the critics' reluctance to recognize the centrality of a metaphysical quest in his works apparently came as a consequence of Poststructuralist doubt that meaningful and interpretable vectors may oscillate between an author's personal cosmology and that projected by the author's text.

In Nabokov's 1971 interview he advocated a critical approach that considers the author in his or her own terms: "[the] main favor I ask of the serious critic is sufficient perceptiveness to understand that whatever term or trope I use, my purpose is not to be facetiously flashy or grotesquely obscure but to express what I feel and think with the utmost truthfulness and perception" (*SO,* 179). Through examining the world of Nabokov's short stories, I have tried to elaborate approaches to his poetics that stem directly from his text, are unique to it, and are sustained by it at every point of analysis. The short stories are an ideal subject for such an inquiry into the shaping of Nabokov's career: there are almost seventy of them, spanning many years and several countries and even continents. The very form of the short story, of the Russian short story particularly, is more rigid, conservative, and palimpsestic than that of the novel. Thus, every innovation, however small, registers more tangibly against the backdrop of the entire tradition, in this study chiefly against the works of Nabokov's two great Russian masters, Anton Chekhov and Ivan Bunin.

I think that much more remains to be done in the field of Nabokov's short stories, not only on such promising topics as his relationship with Russian symbolist, ornamentalist, and neorealist prose (Zinaida Gippius, Fëdor Sologub, Aleksei Remizov, Leonid Andreev), early Soviet prose (Isaak Babel', Vsevolod Ivanov, Leonid Leonov, Boris Pil'niak), and the traces of the Anglo-American short story (James Joyce, F. Scott Fitzgerald) in his fictions. This also touches on the theoretical issues in reading his short stories. By bridging poetics and biography, by viewing the text and the author as subject and name headings of the same creative entity, we may be able to explain what makes Nabokov in some ways always absolutely unlike any other—never a Barthesque *scriptor,* but always a lyrical visionary, a modern version of the prophet in Pushkin's programmatic poem "Prorok" (1826):

> Arise, prophet, and see, and hearken,
> Be filled with my will,
> And go around seas and lands
> Searing the people's hearts with the Word.[39]

In closing, I would like to draw on the work of a major American poet and a senior contemporary of Nabokov, Wallace Stevens (1879–1955). The penultimate section of Stevens's "Notes toward a Supreme Fiction" (1942, 1947) contains a passionate outcry of an author who wants his fictions to be understood in their own terms, as a mixture of the irrational, the divine, and the inspirational:

> That's it: the more than rational distortion,
> The fiction that results from feeling. Yes, that.
>
> They will get it straight one day at the Sorbonne.
> We shall return at twilight from the lecture
> Pleased that the irrational is rational
>
> Until flicked by feeling, in a gildered street,
> I call you by name, my green, my fluent mundo.
> You will have stopped revolving except in crystal.[40]

The words of Wallace Stevens resound in the opening passage from Nabokov's unpublished lecture on the philosophy of fiction. This passage, offered in the 1940s to future American writers by an ex-Russian writer, Vladimir Nabokov, supports the view of his poetics that I hold in this book. The brackets probably indicate what Nabokov intended to expand in his lecture:

> Man found out that he argued with his fellows that the sky was blue; he called this "true" and as soon as he had called it that it ceased to interest him. But as he looked up at the blueness it gave him a peculiar tingle. The tingle was much more real to him [no: as real] than the lovely color that apparently caused the thrill. [The communication of this perception or emotion is a beginning of art inasmuch as the tingling man's neighbor did not at first understand what he was being told. For the beginning and end of art is esoteric].[41]

Appendix: A Complete Annotated List of Nabokov's Short Stories

Data from Liudmila Foster, *Bibliografiia russkoi zarubezhnoi literatury, 1918–1968;* Michael Juliar, *Vladimir Nabokov;* Boyd, *RY;* Boyd, *AY;* Iurii Abyzov, *Russkoe pechatnoe slovo v Latvii;* and Nabokov's collections, periodical appearances, and manuscripts. In cases where the English title differs drastically from a literal translation of the Russian title, the literal translation is listed first.

Alphabetical List

RUSSIAN, FRENCH, AND ENGLISH

Admiralteiskaia igla (The Admiralty Spire)
The Assistant Producer
Bakhman (Bachmann)
Blagost' (Beneficence)
Bogi (Gods)
Britva (Razor)
Conversation Piece, 1945 (originally Double Talk)
Draka (The Fight)
Drakon (The Dragon)
First Love (originally Colette, cf. Chapter 7 of *SM*)
A Forgotten Poet
Govoriat po-russki (Russian Spoken Here)
Groza (The Thunderstorm)
Istreblenie tiranov (Tyrants Destroyed)
Ivan Vernykh (Ivan Vernykh)
Kartofel'nyi Èl'f (The Potato Elf)
Katastrofa (The Catastrophe; Details of a Sunset)
Khvat (A Dashing Fellow)

Korolëk (The Leonardo)
Krasavitsa (A Russian Beauty)
Krug (The Circle; originally Rasskaz = A Story)
Lance
Lebeda (Goosefoot; Orache)
Lik (Lik)
Mademoiselle O (originally in French; cf. Chapter 5 of *SM*)
Mest' (Revenge)
Muzyka (Music)
Nabor (Recruiting)
Natasha (Natasha)
Nezhit' (The Woodsprite)
Obida (The Offense; A Bad Day)
Oblako, ozero, bashnia (Cloud, Lake, Castle; Cloud, Castle, Lake)
Opoveshchenie (Breaking the News)
Pamiati L. I. Shigaeva (In Memory of L. I. Shigaev)

Paskhal'nyi dozhd' (Easter Rain)
Passazhir (The Passenger)
Pil'gram (The Aurelian)
Pis'mo v Rossiiu (A Letter to Russia; A Letter That Never Reached Russia)
Podlets (The Scoundrel; An Affair of Honor)
Port (The Seaport)
Poryv (The Outburst)
Poseshchenie muzeia (The Visit to the Museum)
Putevoditel' po Berlinu (A Guide to Berlin)
Rozhdestvenskii rasskaz (The Christmas Story)
Rozhdestvo (Christmas)
Scenes from the Life of a Double Monster
Signs and Symbols (originally Symbols and Signs)
Skazka (A Nursery Tale)
Slovo (The Word)
Sluchai iz zhizni (A Slice of Life)
Sluchainost' (A Matter of Chance)
Sovershenstvo (Perfection)
Terra Incognita (Terra Incognita)
That in Aleppo Once . . .
Tiazhëlyi dym (Torpid Smoke)
Time and Ebb
Udar kryla (Wingstroke)
Untitled/Unfinished Russian Story, 1926
Usta k ustam (Lips to Lips)
Uzhas (Terror)

The Vane Sisters
Vasilii Shishkov (Vasiliy Shishkov)
Venetsianka (The Venetian Woman; La Veneziana)
Vesna v Fial'te (Spring in Fialta)
Vozvrashchenie Chorba (The Return of Chorb)
Vstrecha (The Reunion)
Zaniatoi chelovek (A Busy Man)
Zvonok (The Doorbell)
Zvuki (Sounds)
(total of 69 stories: 58 Russian, 1 French, 10 English)

ENGLISH ONLY

The Assistant Producer
Conversation Piece, 1945 (originally Double Talk)
First Love (originally Colette; cf. Chapter 7 of *SM*)
A Forgotten Poet
Lance
Scenes from the Life of a Double Monster
Signs and Symbols (originally Symbols and Signs)
That in Aleppo Once . . .
Time and Ebb
The Vane Sisters
(total of 10 stories)

Chronological List in Order of Completion (with Information on the Stories' Inception and Publication in Periodicals and Collections)

The first set of data for each story refers to the time and place of creation (if known); the next set of data indicates the original periodical appearance in Nabokov's lifetime (if any; for complete bibliographic information on each story, see Works Cited); the next set of data indicates if the story ever appeared in Nabokov's lifetime Russian collections (*VCh, S, VF*); the last set of data indicates the appearance of the story in one of Nabokov's lifetime English-language collections (*NS, ND, NQ, RB, TD, DS*) or the location of the manuscript if the story remains unpublished. With the exception of "Slovo," "Paskhal'nyi dozhd'," "Natasha," "Ivan Vernykh," and "Untitled/Unfinished Russian Story 1926," all other short stories appeared in English in *Stories*. I have examined *de visu* all the known original periodical appearances of the short stories except "Kartofel'nyi Èl'f," "Paskhal'nyi dozhd'," "Mest'," "Pamiati L. I. Shigaeva," and "Udar kryla." I have not been able to examine the manuscripts of the three unpublished stories: "Natasha," "Ivan Vernykh," and "Untitled/Unfinished Russian Story 1926."

THE EARLY PERIOD (33 STORIES)

"Nezhit'." *Rul'*, 1921.

"Slovo." January 1923, Berlin. *Rul'*, 1923.

"Zvuki." September 1923, Berlin.

"Udar kryla." October 1923, Berlin. *Russkoe èkho*, 1924.

"Bogi." October 1923, Berlin.

"Govoriat po-russki." About 1923, Berlin.

"Port." Early 1924, Berlin. *Rul'*, 1924. *VCh*.

"Mest'." Spring 1924, Berlin. *Russkoe èkho*, 1924.

"Blagost'." March 1924, Berlin. *Rul'*, 1924. *VCh*.

"Kartofel'nyi Èl'f." April 1924, Berlin. *Russkoe èkho*, 1924. *VCh, RB*.

"Paskhal'nyi dozhd'." Spring 1924, Berlin. *Russkoe èkho*, 1925.

"Sluchainost'." Spring 1924, ?Berlin. *Segodnia*, 1924. *TD*.

"Katastrofa." Second week of June, 1924, ?Berlin. *Segodnia*, 1924. *VCh, DS*.

"Groza." July 22–25, 1924, Berlin. *Segodnia*, 1924. *VCh, DS*.

"Natasha." August 1924, Dobřichovice, Czechoslovakia. Unfinished and unpublished. *VN, LC*.

"Venetsianka." September 1924, Berlin.

"Bakhman." October 1924, Berlin. *Rul'*, 1924. *VCh, TD*.

"Drakon." November 1924, Berlin.

"Rozhdestvo." End of 1924, Berlin. *Rul'*, 1925. *VCh, DS*.

"Poryv." About 1924. Lost in the papers of *Sovremennye zapiski*.

"Pis'mo v Rossiiu." January 1925, Berlin. *Rul'*, 1925. *VCh*.

"Draka." Late June–early July 1925, Berlin. *Rul'*, 1925.

"Vozvrashchenie Chorba." October 1925, Berlin. *Rul'*, 1925. *VCh, DS*.

"Putevoditel' po Berlinu." December 1925, Berlin. *Rul'*, 1925. *VCh, DS*.

"Britva." February 11–12, 1926, Berlin. *Rul'*, 1926.

"Ivan Vernykh." April 26, 1926. Berlin. Unpublished, VN Berg.

"Skazka." About late May or early June 1926, Berlin. *Rul'*, 1926. *VCh, TD*.

"Untitled/Unfinished Russian Story 1926." 1926, Berlin. Unpublished, VN LC.

"Uzhas." July 1926, Berlin. *Sovremennye zapiski*, 1927. *VCh, TD*.

"Passazhir." February 1927, Berlin. *Rul'*, 1927. *VCh, DS*.

"Zvonok." April or May 1927, Berlin. *Rul'*, 1927. *VCh, DS*.

"Podlets." Late August–early September 1927. *VCh, NQ, RB*.

"Rozhdestvenskii rasskaz." First half of December 1928, Berlin. *Rul'*, 1928.

THE MIDDLE PERIOD (19 STORIES)

"Pil'gram." Late March 1930, Berlin. *Sovremennye zapiski*, 1930. *S, NS, ND*.

"Obida." End of June 1931, Berlin. *Poslednie novosti*, 1931. *S, DS*.

"Zaniatoi chelovek." September 17–26, 1931, Berlin. *Poslednie novosti*, 1931. *S, DS*.

"Terra Incognita." Late October–early November 1931, Berlin. *Poslednie novosti*, 1931. *S, RB*.

"Usta k ustam." November–December 6, 1931. *VF, RB*.

"Vstrecha." Mid-December 1931, Berlin. *Poslednie novosti*, 1932. *S, DS*.

"Lebeda." December 30, 1931–January 14, 1932, Berlin. *Poslednie novosti*, 1932. *S, DS*.

"Muzyka." About early 1932, Berlin. *Poslednie novosti*, 1932. *S, TD*.

"Khvat." April 21–May 5, 1932, Berlin. *Segodnia*, 1932. *S, RB*.

"Sovershenstvo." June 1932, Berlin. *Poslednie novosti*, 1932. *S, TD*.

"Admiralteiskaia igla." May 23, 1933, Berlin. *Poslednie novosti*, 1933. *VF, TD*.

"Korolëk." July 1933, Berlin. *Poslednie novosti*, 1933. *VF, RB*.

"Krug." Finished by mid-February 1934, Berlin. Published under the title "Rasskaz" in *Poslednie novosti*, 1934. *VF, RB*.

"Opoveshchenie." March 1934, Berlin. *Poslednie novosti*, 1934. *S, RB*.

"Pamiati L. I. Shigaeva." April 1934, Berlin. *Illiustrirovannaia zhizn'*, 1934. *VF, TD.*

"Krasavitsa." July 1934, Berlin. *Poslednie novosti*, 1934. *S, RB.*

"Tiazhëlyi dym." Sent by mid-February 1935, Berlin. *Poslednie novosti*, 1935. *VF, RB.*

"Nabor." July 1935, Berlin. *Poslednie novosti*, 1935. *VF, TD.*

"Sluchai iz zhizni." Early September 1935, Berlin. *Poslednie novosti*, 1935. *S, DS.*

THE HIGH PERIOD (7 STORIES)

"Mademoiselle O." Early January 1936, Berlin. *Mèsures*, 1936. Chapter 5 of *SM, NS, ND.*

"Vesna v Fial'te." April 1936, Berlin. *Sovremennye zapiski*, 1936. *VF, NS, ND.*

"Oblako, ozero, bashnia." June 25–26, 1937, Marienbad, Czechoslovakia. Published under the title "Ozero, oblako, bashnia" in *Russkie zapiski*, 1937. *VF, NS, ND.*

"Istreblenie tiranov." Second half of May–June 1938, Menton, France. *Russkie zapiski*, 1938. *VF, TD.*

"Poseshchenie muzeia." About October 1938, Paris. *Sovremennye zapiski*, 1939. *VF, NQ, RB.*

"Lik." November 1938, Paris. *Russkie zapiski*, 1939. *VF, NQ, TD.*

"Vasilii Shishkov." Late August 1939, Paris. *Poslednie novosti*, 1939. *VF, TD.*

THE AMERICAN PERIOD (10 STORIES)

"The Assistant Producer." January 1943, Cambridge. *The Atlantic Monthly*, 1943. *NS, ND.*

"That in Aleppo Once. . . ." May 1943, Cambridge. *The Atlantic Monthly*, 1943. *NS, ND.*

"A Forgotten Poet." Finished by May 1944, Cambridge. *The Atlantic Monthly*, 1944. *NS, ND.*

"Time and Ebb." End of August 1944, Wellesley. *The Atlantic Monthly*, 1945. *NS, ND.*

"Double Talk." Late March–early April 1945, Cambridge. *The New Yorker*, 1945. *NS.* Retitled "Conversation Piece, 1945" in *ND.*

"Signs and Symbols." May 1947, Cambridge. Published under the title "Symbols and Signs" in *The New Yorker*, 1948. *ND.*

"Colette." Finished spring 1948, Cambridge. *The New Yorker*, 1948. Chapter 7 in *SM.* Retitled "First Love" in *ND.*

"Scenes from the Life of a Double Monster." September–October 1950, Ithaca. *The Reporter*, 1958. One part out of projected three was finished. Complete manuscript VN LC. *ND.*

"The Vane Sisters." Finished on March 5, 1951, Ithaca. *Hudson Review*, winter 1958–1959. *NQ, TD.*

"Lance." Beginning of November 1951, Ithaca. *The New Yorker*, 1952. *ND.*

Notes

· ·

Introduction

1 Actually, Nabokov's first non-Russian short story was written in French and appeared in 1936 as "Mademoiselle O." "Englishing" is Nabokov's own term; see *Stories,* 662.

2 See, for instance, three recent anthologies: "Spring in Fialta" was the choice of Ron Hansen and Jim Shepard (*You've Got to Read This*); "The Vane Sisters" of Charles Neider (*Great Short Fiction from the Masters of World Literature*); "The Circle" of Roger Angell (*Nothing But You*). *Nabokov's Dozen* appeared in paperback as *Spring in Fialta* (New York: Popular Library, 1959).

3 See an advertisement in the back of the 1938 original edition of *Sogliadatai* which lists *Vesna v Fial'te* as forthcoming from the émigré publishing house Russkie zapiski (Paris-Shanghai). It planned to put out two volumes of Nabokov's short stories, *Sogliadatai* in 1938 and *Vesna v Fial'te* in 1939. The outbreak of World War II postponed the publication of *Vesna v Fial'te* for over fifteen years; it was published in New York by Chekhov Publishing House. For Nabokov's correspondence with Russkie zapiski regarding the publication of *Sogliadatai* and *Vesna v Fial'te,* see VN LC, container 8, folder 16.

4 The term "disappearance" (*ischeznovenie*) belongs to the fine émigré critic and scholar Vladimir Veidle (Weidle), who entitled his obituary "Ischeznovenie Nabokova" (The Disappearance of Nabokov). Comparative references to Sirin—Nabokov's prewar Russian pen-name—appear in P. Bitsilli's *Tvorchestvo Chekhova* (The Art of Chekhov, 1942; 104, 135), a major émigré scholarly contribution to the study of the poetics of prose fiction. The notion of Russia Abroad as a Russian émigré society within the societies of interwar Europe, Asia, and the Americas was foregrounded by the historian Marc Raeff in his seminal book *Russia Abroad.*

5 A good example of a major Russian émigré collection which had literally been buried for over forty years is the case of the rich periodical holdings of the Russian Historical Archive Abroad (RZIA) at the Slovanská knihovna (Slavonic Library) in Prague. When I arrived in Prague in April 1993 for two months of research, the remaining parts of the RZIA collection (the archives had been taken to the Soviet Union in 1945) were being re-

opened to scholars. They had been kept in a vault in a deep cellar (Klimentinum is a former Greek Orthodox monastery), covered with a quarter-inch layer of dust. On the history of the RZIA collection, see Richard J. Kneeley and Edward Kasinec, "The Slovanská knihovna in Prague and Its RZIA Collection," *Slavic Review* 51:1 (Spring 1992): 122–130.

6   See Marina Turkevich Naumann, *Blue Evenings in Berlin;* Ljubo Dragoljub Majhanovich, "The Early Prose of Vladimir Nabokov-Sirin"; Linda Saputelli Zimmermann, "The Russian Short Stories of Vladimir Nabokov"; Julian W. Connolly, *Nabokov's Early Fiction;* Douglas Fowler, *Reading Nabokov,* 62–90; John Burt Foster Jr., *Nabokov's Art of Memory and European Modernism,* 110–129, 131–145; Pekka Tammi, *Problems of Nabokov's Poetics.*

7   Charles Nicol and Gennady Barabtarlo, eds., *A Small Alpine Form,* xiv.

8   See two recent encyclopedic overviews: Natal'ia I. Tolstaia and Mikhail Meilakh's "Russian Short Stories," in Vladimir E. Alexandrov, ed., *The Garland Companion to Vladimir Nabokov;* Gennady Barabtarlo's "English Short Stories," in Alexandrov, ed., *The Garland Companion;* see also A. S. Muliarchik, *Russkaia proza Vladimira Nabokova,* 92–122.

9   Isaac Bashevis Singer, *The Collected Stories,* vii.

10 Studies of Russian emigration include Robert C. Williams's *Culture in Exile;* Robert H. Johnston's *New Mecca, New Babylon;* Hans-Erich Volkman, *Die Russische Emigrationen in Deutschland;* Marc Raeff, *Russia Abroad.* For a study of Russian publishing culture in Berlin in the 1920s, see Thomas R. Beyer, Gottfried Kratz, and Xenia Werner, *Russische Autoren und Verlage in Berlin nach dem Ersten Weltkrieg.*

11 Alexandrov has rooted Nabokov's art in the aesthetics of the Russian Silver Age (*Nabokov's Otherworld,* 213–234). Other comparative inquiries into the Nabokov–Silver Age connections include D. Barton Johnson's "Belyj and Nabokov: A Comparative Overview," *Russian Literature* 9 (1981): 379–402.

12 See, for instance, Nabokov's lectures on Chekhov in *LRL,* 245–282.

13 Among the various models of textual interaction and transmission, I feel most comfortable with a modified model of Gérard Genette's subtextualization/hypertextualization as expressed in *Palimpsestes: La littérature au second degré.*

14 Harold Bloom's theory of the anxiety of influence originally appeared in 1973 in his book *The Anxiety of Influence.*

15 For a series of useful analyses of exemplary Russian short stories, see L. Michael O'Toole, *Structure, Style, and Interpretation in the Russian Short Story.* For a discussion of the generic development of the Russian short story, see Charles A. Moser, ed., *The Russian Short Story,* xi–xxiv. For an overview of theoretical perspectives on the short story, see Charles E. May, ed., *Short Story Theories.* For a short theoretical discussion of the generic nature of the short story, see Mary Rohrberger and Dan E. Burns, "Short Story and the Numinous Realm," *Modern Fiction Studies* 28:1 (Spring 1982): 5–12.

16 Singer, *Collected Stories,* vii.

17 William Maxwell, *All the Days and Nights,* x.

18 Quoted in Stephen Jan Parker, "Vladimir Nabokov and the Short Story," *Russian Literature Triquarterly* 24 (1991): 69.

19 See introduction in Nicol and Barabtarlo, *A Small Alpine Form.*

20 Quoted in Parker, "Vladimir Nabokov and the Short Story," 69.

21 See Nabokov, "Solux Rex"; "Ultima Thule." For analyses of the two chapters of Na-

bokov's unfinished novel, see D. Barton Johnson, "Vladimir Nabokov's *Solus Rex* and the 'Ultima Thule' Theme," *Slavic Review* 40:4 (1981): 544–556; Strother B. Purdy, "Solux Rex: Nabokov and the Chess Novel," *Modern Fiction Studies* 14:4 (Winter 1968–69): 379–385. Although in the 1920s and 1930s Nabokov routinely published excerpts of his Russian novels in émigré newspapers, assigning them short story–like titles, this does not qualify such excerpts to be considered short stories. For examples of Nabokov's excerpts that resemble short stories, see "Ot"ezd Ardaliona" and "Still ist die nacht," both from *Despair;* "Zoorlandiia," from *Glory;* "Smert' Aleksandra Iakovlevicha," "Progulka v Griuneval'd," and "Odinochestvo," all three from *The Gift.* Also noteworthy is Nabokov's serialization of his autobiography/memoir in American periodicals after World War II. Another telling example of a short story–like title is "Triangle within Circle," a section of *The Gift* that appeared in *The New Yorker* in 1963.

22 Gerald Prince, *Dictionary of Narratology,* 26.

23 Nicol and Barabtarlo, *A Small Alpine Form,* xi.

24 The following works have helped me formulate my view of the structure of narrative closure: Frank Kermode, *The Sense of an Ending;* Barbara Herrnstein Smith, *Poetic Closure.*

25 See Nicol and Barabtarlo, *A Small Alpine Form.* See especially introduction and contributions by D. Barton Johnson, Stephen Matterson, John Burt Foster Jr., Galina L. De Roeck, Leona Toker, and Susan Elisabeth Sweeney. See also Foster, *Nabokov's Art of Memory and European Modernism.*

26 Wolfgang Iser, "Interaction between Text and Reader," in *The Reader in the Text,* ed. S. Suleiman and I. Grossman, 106.

27 Wolfgang Iser, *The Act of Reading,* 69.

28 Iser suggests that "what has been read shrinks in the memory to a foreshortened background, but it is being constantly evoked in a new context and so modified by new correlates that instigate a restructuring of past syntheses" (*The Act of Reading,* 111).

29 See E. D. Hirsch Jr., *Validity in Interpretation,* especially Chapter 2. See also Umberto Eco, *The Open Work.*

30 Brian Boyd mentions two courses which Stanford chose from a list of four Nabokov offered. The courses Nabokov taught at Stanford summer school were "The Art of Writing" and "Modern Russian Literature" (Boyd, *AY,* 22–23, 29–30). Two manuscripts at VN LC contain lectures for a course in creative writing: eleven pages of notes on style and ten pages of notes on short stories, both deposited in container 8, folder 11.

31 Nabokov, "Lectures," MS, VN LC, container 8, folder 11.

32 See Barabtarlo, "English Short Stories."

33 In 1996, Svetlana Pol'skaia (Polsky), a Swedish Slavicist, located a surviving copy of *Russkoe ėkho* (The Russian Echo), the Berlin newspaper in which Nabokov published "Easter Rain" in 1925; see *The Nabokovian* 37 (Fall 1996): 4.

34 Jane Grayson's book contains a brief section on the short stories; see *Nabokov Translated,* 134–136.

1   *Writing and Reading the Otherworld*

1 *LL,* 1.

2 This seminal passage was translated by Dmitri Nabokov and cited in his "Translating with Nabokov," see George Gibian and Stephen Jan Parker, eds., *The Achievements of Vladimir Nabokov,* 174.

3   V. S. Varshavskii, *Nezamechennoe pokolenie*, 214.

4   Jonathan Borden Sisson, "Cosmic Synchronization and Other Worlds," 10. A condensed version of Sisson's views is found in his article "Nabokov's Cosmic Synchronization and 'Something Else,'" *Nabokov Studies* 1 (1994): 155–177.

5   D. Barton Johnson, *Worlds in Regression*, 1–2.

6   Ellen Pifer, "Shades of Love," *Kenyon Review* 11:2 (Spring 1989): 78.

7   This is only a brief summary of Alexandrov's position in *Nabokov's Otherworld*; the introduction to the book ("Nabokov's Metaphysics, Ethics, and Aesthetics," 2–22) contains his principal statements on the metaphysical issues in Nabokov's writings. Note also that numerous philosophical and aesthetic roots of Nabokov's otherworldly aesthetics may be found in the culture of the Russian Silver Age. For an investigation of his links to the Silver Age, see "Conclusion: Nabokov and the Silver Age of Russian Culture" in Alexandrov's *Nabokov's Otherworld*.

8   Alexandrov, *Nabokov's Otherworld*, 5.

9   Boyd, *RY* and Boyd, *AY*. See also his "Nabokov's Philosophical World," *Southern Review* 14:3 (1981): 260–301, and *Nabokov's Ada: The Place of Consciousness*, which anticipate the approach taken in the biography. A number of other scholars have made contributions to the study of metaphysical issues in Nabokov's works.

10 See Johnette Rodriguez, "Iconoclastic Icons," *The New Paper* (April 13–20, 1988).

11 Richard Rorty, rev. of *Nabokov's Otherworld*, *Common Knowledge* 1:2 (Fall 1922): 126.

12 The Russian text has been retransliterated back into Russian and quoted from *LATH*. The poem was reprinted in 1979 in *Stikhi* (317–318) in the section "Poems from Short Stories and Novels" with minor changes. Notice that "I luchshe nedogovoryonnost'" recalls Fëdor Tiutchev's programmatic poem "Silentium" (1830s), with its plea for verbal reticence ("Mysl' izrechënnaia est' lozh'"): An uttered thought is a lie). Also note that Vadim Vadimych's prose translation and commentary follow Nabokov's own strategy as translator of *Eugene Onegin*.

13 There is also in Russian the term *zagrobnyi mir* (literally, world beyond the coffin, afterlife, hereafter) and the term *mir inoi* (another world, sometimes employed in science fiction and fantasy, as, for instance, in G. N. Grebnev's sci-fi novel *Mir inoi* [1961]; literally, The Other World).

14 Alexandrov, *Nabokov's Otherworld*, 3.

15 In 1923 Nabokov translated *Alice in Wonderland* into Russian as *Ania v strane chudes*. In an 1971 interview Paul Sufrin confronted Nabokov with a question about Carroll's book: "In many of your writings, you have conceived what I consider to be an Alice-in-Wonderland world of unreality and illusion. What is the connection with your real struggle with the world?" Here is Nabokov's answer: "*Alice in Wonderland* is a specific book by a definite author with its own quaintness, its own quirks, its own quiddity. If read carefully, it will be seen to imply, by humorous juxtaposition, the presence of a quite solid, and rather sentimental, world, behind the semi-detached dream" (*SO*, 184–185). Cf. also Nabokov's remark about *Alice in Wonderland* in *LL*, 373–374.

16 Pifer, "Shades of Love," 76.

17 Johnson, *Worlds in Regression*, 2.

18 For a helpful discussion of Nabokov's angels, predominantly in his poetry, see Natal'ia I. Tolstaia, "Sputnik iasnokrylyi," *Russkaia literatura* 1 (1992): 188–192. See also Nabokov's own remarks on the evolution of his poetry, where he identifies a period "reaching well into the 1920s" with "a kind of private curatorship, aimed at preserving

nostalgic retrospections and developing Byzantine imagery," which, as he claims, " has been mistaken by some readers for an interest in 'religion,' which beyond literary stylization, never meant anything to me" (*PP*, 13–14).

19 For details of the trip, see Boyd, *RY*, 188.

20 Vladimir Nabokov, "Udar kryla," MS, VN Berg.

21 Vladimir Nabokov, "Bogi," MS, VN Berg.

22 For previous discussions of the story, see Boyd, *RY*, 232; Naumann, *Blue Evenings in Berlin*, 181–192; Connolly, *Nabokov's Early Fiction*, 16–20; and Zimmermann, "The Russian Short Stories," Chapter 3.

23 Vladimir Nabokov, "Drakon," MS, VN Berg.

24 For discussions of "The Seaport," see Zimmermann, "The Russian Short Stories," Chapter 5; Majhanovich, "The Early Prose," 31–33; Naumann, *Blue Evenings in Berlin*, 35–43; Boyd, *RY*, 210–211.

25 Vladimir Nabokov, "Venetsianka," MS, VN Berg.

26 Del Piombo's painting appears on the cover of the French edition of Nabokov's early stories to which "The Venetian Woman" gave its title; see *Vén*. For a description of the painting by Sebastiano del Piombo which probably informed *The Portrait of a Venetian Woman* in the story, see Mauro Lucco and Carlo Volpe, eds., *L'opera completa di Sebastiano del Piombo*, 103.

27 H. W. Janson, *History of Art*, 377–387; the painting is found on 383.

28 Johnson, *Worlds in Regression*, 1; see also 5, fn. 2.

29 Cf. also Nabokov's statement in the lecture "The Art of Literature and Commonsense": "If the mind were constructed on optional lines and if a book could be read in the same way as a painting is taken in by the eye, that is without the bother of working from left to right and without the absurdity of beginnings and ends, thus would be the ideal way of appreciating a novel, for thus the author saw it at the moment of its conception" (*LL*, 380); this statement is close to Joseph Frank's influential notion of the spatial form in literature.

30 Important discussions of "Christmas" may be found in Boyd, *RY*, 71–72, 236, 272; Majhanovich, "The Early Prose," 27–31; Naumann, *Blue Evenings in Berlin*, 193–203; Zimmermann, "The Russian Short Stories," Chapter 1. See also David M. Bethea, "Izgnanie kak ukhod v kokon," *Russkaia literatura* 3 (1991): 167–175. Alexandrov makes an important remark in *Nabokov's Otherworld*, 244, fn. 9.

31 See David M. Bethea, *Joseph Brodsky*, 237; see also Priscilla Meyer, "The German Theme in Nabokov's Work of the 1920s," in Nicol and Barabtarlo, eds., *A Small Alpine Form*.

32 For discussions of Nabokov's anti-Darwinism, see *SM*, 25; Boyd, *RY*, 280–281; Alexandrov, *Nabokov's Otherworld*, 227–230, and "A Note on Nabokov's Anti-Darwinism, or Why Apes Feed on Butterflies in *The Gift*," in G. S. Morson and E. C. Allen, eds., *Freedom and Responsibility in Russian Literature*.

33 I have consulted Ken Pimentel and Kevin Teixeira's *Virtual Reality: Through a New Looking Glass* and Howard Rheingold's *Virtual Reality*.

34 On the history of *The Rudder* and Russian émigré journalism, see I. V. Gessen, *Gody izgnaniia*.

35 The "Nabokov brothers" motif in "Scene from the Life of a Double Monster" is discussed in Sweeney, "The Small Furious Devil," 216.

36 See Ellendea Proffer, ed., *Vladimir Nabokov*, 31.

37 See Nabokov, "Pamiati Iu. I. Aikhenval'da," "Pamiati A. M. Chërnogo," "Pamiati Amalii Osipovny Fondaminskoi."

38 See Sergej Davydov, *Teksty-Matrëški Vladimira Nabokova*, 10–51.

39 Sisson, "Cosmic Synchronization," 30.

40 Ibid.

41 Alexandrov, *Nabokov's Otherworld*, 129.

42 Vladimir Nabokov, "Muzyka," MS, VN LC, container 7, folder gg.

43 Some aspects of the story are discussed in Natal'ia I. Tolstaia, "V. V. Nabokov Stages a Play: 'A Busy Man,'" in Nicol and Barabtarlo, eds., *A Small Alpine Form;* Svetlana Pol'skaia [Polsky], "Death and Immortality in Nabokov's 'A Busy Man,'" *Nabokov Studies* 2 (1995): 213–232.

44 The following discussions of "Terra Incognita" are noteworthy: Boyd, *RY*, 373; Julian W. Connolly, "Nabokov's 'Terra Incognita' and 'Invitation to a Beheading,'" *Wiener Slawistischer Almanach* 12 (1983): 55–65; Connolly, *Nabokov's Early Fiction*, 131–136; Sisson, "Cosmic Synchronization," 95–133.

45 See Kniga, 486, for A. A. Dolinin's and R. D. Timenchik's speculations regarding Nabokov's coinage of plant names.

46 Sisson, "Cosmic Synchronization," 95–96, 97, 106; the expression "aesthetic bliss" is Nabokov's and appears in the essay "On a Book Entitled *Lolita*"; see *L*, 314. Sisson offers a very compelling analysis of the meaning of "aesthetic bliss" in Nabokov's oeuvre in Chapter 1 of his dissertation; see Sisson, "Cosmic Synchronization," 1–24.

47 See Chapter 4 of ibid., "Alternative Realities in 'Terra Incognita,'" especially 95–96, 98–101.

48 The original is at the Metropolitan Museum of Art in New York.

49 Quoted in Sisson, "Cosmic Synchronization," 108; for a discussion of Rousseau's painting, see ibid., 107–108.

50 See Sisson, "Cosmic Synchronization," 97–106, 131.

51 See Georgii Adamovich, *Odinochestvo i svoboda*, 226.

52 Sisson, "Cosmic Synchronization," 11.

53 I. A. Richards, *Principles of Literary Criticism*, 107.

54 On Turgenev's and Chekhov's use of rhythmical contours, see P. Bitsilli, *Tvorchestvo Chekhova*, 55–62. For discussions of Belyi and Nabokov, see Alexandrov, *Nabokov's Otherworld*, 218–223; and Johnson, "Belyj and Nabokov." An analysis of the interrelation between Bunin's poetry and prose—also relevant for Nabokov's career—is found in È. A. Polotskaia, "Vzaimootnoshenie poèzii i prozy u rannego Bunina," *Izvestiia AN SSSR* 29:5 (September–October 1970): 412–418. I will discuss traces of Bunin's rhythmical contours in Nabokov's prose in Chapter 4.

55 Andrei Belyi, *Maski*, 11.

56 Vladimir Nabokov, "Lik," MS, VN LC, container 7, folder t.

57 Important analyses of the story are found in Boyd, *RY*, 493–494; Sergei Davydov, "Poseshchenie kladbishcha i muzeia," *Diapazon* 1 (1993): 36–39; de Roeck, "'The Visit to the Museum': A Tour of Hell"; and Liudmila A. Foster, "'Poseshchenie muzeia' Nabokova v svete traditsii modernizma," *Grani* 85 (1972): 176–187; Iurii I. Levin, "Bispatsial'nost'' kak invariant poèticheskogo mira V. Nabokova," *Russian Literature* 28:1 (1990): 64–65. Levin's article contains highly illuminating observations concerning the problem of exiting one space and entering another in Nabokov's works; on the short stories, see also ibid., 85–88, 93–94.

58 On surrealism, oneiric processes, and the Nikolai Gogol' connection in the story, see Foster, "'Poseshchenie muzeia.'"

59 Foster, "'Poseshchenie muzeia,'" 179.

60 De Roeck has analyzed the echoes of the Greek myth suggested by the statue of Orpheus and read the story as Nabokov's polemic with Jean-Paul Sartre's 1938 novel *La nausée.*

61 "To Mark Aldanov." February 3, 1938. Letter quoted in Boyd, *RY*, 493.

62 Boyd, *RY*, 493.

63 Davydov, "Poseshchenie kladbishcha i muzeia," 38.

64 For details of the Bolshevik uprising, see, for instance, Alexander Rabinowitch, *The Bolsheviks Come to Power,* 273–304.

65 Slava Paperno and John V. Hagopian, "Official and Unofficial Responses to Nabokov in the Soviet Union," in George Gibian and Stephen Jan Parker, eds., *The Achievements of Vladimir Nabokov,* 100–103.

66 See also Gennady Barabtarlo's archival findings in "To Prince Kachurin—for Edmund Wilson," *The Nabokovian* 29 (Fall 1992): 30–34.

67 See Parker, "Vladimir Nabokov and the Short Story," 72. For a lengthy comparison of "Lady with a Lap Dog" and Nabokov's "Spring in Fialta," see Chapter 3.

68 For a classic study of the psychology of the act of reading "Light Breathing," see L. S. Vygotskii, *Psikhologiia iskusstva,* 140–156.

69 Andrei Belyi, *Simvolizm kak miroponimanie,* 249.

70 See Alexandrov, *Nabokov's Otherworld,* 213–234, especially 218–223; Johnson, "Belyj and Nabokov."

71 Cf. Georgii Adamovich, "Sirin," *Poslednie novosti* 4670 (January 4, 1934): 3.

72 Sisson, "Cosmic Synchronization," 1.

Interlude: Mapping Narrative Space in Nabokov's Stories

1 See Joseph Frank, *The Idea of Spatial Form;* Frank's influential essay "Spatial Form in Modern Literature" originally appeared in 1945 and was subsequently reprinted in his volume of essays *The Widening Gyre* (1963).

2 I am following Bakhtin's definition of chronotope as given in the essay "Formy vremeni i khronotopa v romane" (Forms of Time and Chronotope in the Novel); see M. M. Bakhtin, *Literaturno-kriticheskie stat'i,* 121; the bulk of Bakhtin's essay was written in 1937–1938; it originally appeared in 1975.

3 Nabokov's preoccupation with maps and spatial illustration is evident from the maps on the inside covers of the original hardback edition of *Speak, Memory,* Nabokov's illustrations used in his Cornell lectures and reproduced in *LL* and *LRL,* and the detailed map of the Montreux apartment that he drew for his sister Elena; see *PSS,* 112.

4 For other discussions of "A Guide to Berlin," see Johnson, "A Guide to Nabokov's 'A Guide to Berlin'"; Boyd, *RY,* 249–252. The kind of literary form which Nabokov adopts in "A Guide to Berlin" left a trace in the Russian émigré literary milieu. A sequence of short vignettes entitled "Putevye zametki" (Travel Notes) appeared in the Parisian newspaper *Zveno* (The Link) in 1925. It was signed "Cave" (in the Latin alphabet), which was probably the pseudonym of the émigré poet Leonid Kavetskii. The piece consisted of five vignettes with a prologue and epilogue; their titles resemble Nabokov's: "The Streetcar," "The Bus," "The Metro," "The Taxi," "The Fiacres." Cave's

"Travel Notes" may have influenced Nabokov's "A Guide to Berlin" which appeared during the same year; see Cave, "Putevye zametki."

5   SSoch, 1:121.

6   Peter Gay's splendid book *Weimar Culture: The Outsider as Insider* depicts the atmosphere that affected Nabokov during his Berlin years.

7   See Omry Ronen [Omri Ronen], "Zaum' za predelami avangarda," *Literaturnoe obozrenie* 12 (1991): 42. In addition to the trace of *Zoo* in "A Guide to Berlin," one also finds dialogic references in *Glory*; Sonia and Martyn visit the Berlin Zoo, and Sonia's rejection of Martyn echoes Alia's treatment of the narrator in Shklovsky's epistolary novel. Finally, one might investigate the fruitful links between *Zoo*, the novel by Shklovskii; Zoo the Berlin attraction; and Zoorlandiia (Zoorland), the otherworldly Russia of Martyn's dreams.

8   Shklovskii arrived in Berlin in the summer of 1922 and left in the fall of 1923. On Shklovskii's Berlin period and the background for *Zoo*, see Richard Sheldon, "Introduction," in Viktor Shklovsky, *Zoo or Letters Not about Love*. In addition to *Zoo*, Shklovskii's appearances in Berlin's Russian publications included *Literatura i kinematograf* (1923), *Chaplin: sbornik statei* (1923), and others; see Sheldon, ed., *Viktor Shklovsky: An International Bibliography*. Useful background on Soviet writers in Berlin is also found in Joshua Rubenstein, *Tangled Loyalties*. Williams offers very important observations about the blurred lines between the Soviet and émigré writers in the early 1920s, as well as Berlin's pro-Soviet daily *Nakanune* (On the Eve) and the short-lived review *Beseda* (Conversation), co-edited by Maksim Gor'kii and Vladislav Khodasevich in 1923–1925 in Berlin; see Williams, *Culture in Exile: Russian Emigrés in Germany*. While living in Berlin in the 1920s, Nabokov encountered several Soviet Russian writers, including Aleksandr Tarasov-Rodionov, the author of *Shokolad* (Chocolate, 1925), who tried to talk him into repatriating; see Boyd, *RY*, 375. For a discussion of Nabokov's attitudes to Soviet Russian writers, see Boyd, *RY*, 198–199. The issue of his relationship with Soviet Russian literature awaits its explorer. Nabokov dedicated an entire story, entitled "Rozhdestvenskii rasskaz" (A Christmas Story, 1928), to the trepidations of a Soviet Russian writer; see Zoran Kuzmanovich, "'A Christmas Story': A Polemic with Ghosts," in Nicol and Barabtarlo, eds., *A Small Alpine Form*. Several of Nabokov's short stories, including "Govoriat po-russki" (Russian Spoken Here, 1923), "Britva" (The Razor, 1926), and "Vstrecha" (The Reunion, 1931), depict contacts between Russian émigrés and Soviet visitors to the West.

9   Viktor Shklovskii, *O teorii prozy*, 15.

10 The notion of a "future recollection" recurs elsewhere in Nabokov's works, including the story "Tiazhëlyi dym" (Torpid Smoke, 1935); see *VF*, 82/*Stories*, 400. Also, a reference to the would-be "A Guide to Berlin" is found in the earlier "Blagost'" (Grace), where a German lady is selling postcards and a book entitled "A Guidebook to Berlin"; see *VCh*, 160.

11 In 1925 Nabokov took his pupil Aleksandr Zak to the then German and now Polish seaside resort of Zoppot, now Sopot; see Boyd, *RY*, 243.

12 Several important aspects of the story, including the Ivanov-Pnin parallels, are discussed in Robert Grossmith, "Perfection," in Nicol and Barabtarlo, eds., *A Small Alpine Form*. Alexandrov mentions the Gnostic aspects of "Perfection" in *Nabokov's Otherworld*, 35, 85; also see Boyd's remarks in *RY*, 379–380.

13 Vladimir Nabokov, "Lik," MS, VN LC, container 7, folder t.

14 Nabokov's longest critical discussion of Dostoevskii is found in *LRL,* 97–136.

2   Testing Nabokov's Paradigms

1   See Boyd, *RY,* 249–250. Other critical discussions of the story include Naumann, *Blue Evenings in Berlin,* 20–35; Connolly, *Nabokov's Early Fiction,* 11–16; Majhanovich, "The Early Prose," 14–21; Zimmermann, "The Russian Short Stories," Chapter V; Tammi, *Problems of Nabokov's Poetics,* 54; Philip T. Sicker, "Practicing Nostalgia: Time and Memory in Nabokov's Early Russian Fiction," *Studies in Twentieth-Century Literature* 11:2 (Spring 1987): 253–270; and Gleb Struve, "Current Russian Literature: II. Vladimir Sirin," *The Slavonic and East European Review* 12:35 (January 1934): 440.

2   This is Andrew Field's expression; he calls the story an "open form"; see *Nabokov: His Life in Art,* 147.

3   Boyd, *RY,* 180–181. In a letter sent by V. D. Nabokov to Ivan Bunin, he mentions his son's poems published in *The Rudder* and signed "Cantab"; see "To Ivan Bunin," June 15, 1920, letter in Bunin Leeds. The third sentence of the story signals Nabokov's intention to employ various forms of verbal play. Herr Keller is said to have taken his wife to a "smart nightclub," in the Russian *nariadnyi kabachëk, kabachëk* literally meaning "little tavern." In German *der Keller* among other things can mean "restaurant/bar," *die Kellerei* meaning "wine/champagne cellar."

4   On some linguistic and cultural background of the word *chërt,* see Maks Fasmer, *Ètimologicheskii slovar' russkogo iazyka,* 4:347–348; V. I. Dal', *Tolkovyi slovar',* 4:615–616.

5   See Zimmermann, "The Russian Short Stories," 178.

6   On Nabokov's use of the chiaroscuro technique, see Julian W. Connolly, "The Play of Light and Shadow in 'The Fight,'" in Nicol and Barabtarlo, eds., *A Small Alpine Form,* 25–37.

7   *SM,* 265; see also Boyd, *RY,* 171. Later, during the American years, *Webster's* became Nabokov's favorite bedtime read; see Boyd, *AY,* 461.

8   In the scheme elaborated in a treatise entitled *Celestial Hierarchies* and attributed falsely to Dionysius the Areopagite, the cherubim are given the second rank in the first angelic triad: seraphs, cherubim, thrones. In preparation for this section, I have consulted numerous sources on the subject of the complex etymology, meaning, and mythopoetic significance of the word "cherub." See under "Kheruvim," "Cherub," "Cherubim," "Chorbe," "Angel," "Chorob," "Uriel," "Oriel," "Cherubino," "Putto," and "Zacchai" in the following dictionaries and encyclopedias: *Slovar' sovremennogo . . . iazyka* 17: 119–121; *Oxford English Dictionary* 3:91–92; *The Encyclopedia of the Jewish Religion,* 85; *The Interpreter's Dictionary of the Bible* 1:557, 563; James Hastings, ed., *A Dictionary of the Bible,* 1:377–380, 384; James Hastings, ed., *Encyclopedia of Religion and Ethics* 3:508–513; *The Century Dictionary,* 949–950; *The Encyclopaedia Britannica* (11th Ed.) 6:86–87; David Noel Freedman, ed., *The Anchor Bible Dictionary,* 1:899–900, 912; Harold Osborne, ed., *The Oxford Companion to Art,* 45–46, 945; *Polnyi pravoslavnyi bogoslovskii èntsiklopedicheskii slovar'* 2:2276–2278; Hustav Davidson, *A Dictionary of Angels, including the Fallen Angels,* 88, 215; Nicolò Tommaseo, *Dizionario della lingua italiana,* 1375. I have tried to consult some of the sources which Nabokov might have been able to use during the 1920s. I have also consulted *Bibliia, The Revised English Bible,* and the English translation of the Jewish Bible, *Tannakh: The Holy Scriptures.*

9   Cherub has also been used as a proper name of an individual angel, particularly of Uriel (Oriel). Incidentally, the name of one of the angels serving under Oriel is Chorob, even closer to Chorb graphically than Cherub. Nabokov was well aware of the biblical stature of the cherubim and of the Christian classification of the angels. In 1918, possibly under the influence of the poet Maksimilian Voloshin (1877–1932), he wrote a cycle of poems entitled "Angely" (Angels), which included a poem "Kheruvimy" (Cherubim), published in *The Rudder* in 1921. For a discussion of the angels in Nabokov's oeuvre, see Tolstaia, "Sputnik iasnokrylyi." Nabokov was well versed in the Bible and ecclesiastical history; see Boyd, *AY*, 291.

10 The austere connotations of the biblical supreme angels have been downplayed by Western art and literature, where "cherub" came to mean angelic youth or child (Italian *putto*) with specific iconographic representations in sculpture and painting, especially that of the Baroque. In classical Russian literature, the diminutive "kheruvim-chik" (little cherub) often connotes pretty child and even serves as an affectionate term. In Part 3 of *The Brothers Karamazov* Dostoevskii employs the ambiguous interplay of austere biblical and playful diminutive connotations when he has Grushen'ka, the novel's holy harlot, call the young Alësha Karamazov "kheruvim": " 'I don't know, I don't understand, I don't understand anything of what he told me, but my heart heard it, he turned my heart around. . . . He took pity on me, the first one to, the only one, that's what it is! Why, cherub, didn't you come before?' She fell on her knees before him in some kind of ecstasy. 'All my life I have waited for someone like you, I knew that someone like you will come and forgive me. I believed that someone will love me, the vile thing, not just for my shame!' " (Dostoevskii, *Sobranie sochinenii*, 9:445). Grushen'ka reenacts Mary Magdalene's pleas, and Dostoevskii has also charged the young monk, truth-seeker, and future revolutionary Alësha with features of Christ.

11 See Maxim D. Shrayer, "Conflation of Christmas and Paschal Motifs in Čechov's 'V roždestvenskuju noč,' " *Russian Literature* 35:7 (February 15, 1994); Robert Louis Jackson, " 'If I Forget Thee, O Jerusalem': An Essay on Chekhov's 'Rothschild's Fiddle,' " in Savely Senderovich and Munir Sendich, eds., *Anton Chekhov Rediscovered;* Savely Senderovich, "Anton Chekhov and St. George the Dragonslayer (An Introduction to the Theme)," in Senderovich and Sendich, eds., *Anton Chekhov Rediscovered.*

12 Connolly, *Nabokov's Early Fiction*, 11–16; Zimmermann, "The Russian Short Stories," Chapter V.

13 Ovid, *Metamorphoses*, 234–237.

14 Ibid., 324–325.

15 Ibid., 237.

16 For readings of "Loopy Ears," see Thomas Gaiton Marullo, "Crime without Punishment: Ivan Bunin's 'Loopy Ears,' " *Slavic Review* 40:4 (Winter 1981): 614–624; Albert J. Wehrle, "Bunin's Story 'Petlistye ushi' ('Loopy Ears')," *Russian Literature Triquarterly* 11 (Winter 1975): 442–454; Julian W. Connolly, "Bunin's 'Petlistye ushi': The Deformation of a Byronic Rebel," *Canadian-American Slavic Studies* 14:1 (Spring 1980): 52–61. Another possible subtext here might be *Bruges-la-Morte*, the famous novel by the Belgian modernist Georges Rodenbach (1855–1898).

17 See V. D. Nabokov, "To Ivan Bunin," February 19, 1921, letter in Bunin Leeds; "To Ivan Bunin," n.d., postcard in Bunin Leeds; Vladimir Nabokov, "To Ivan Bunin," n.d. (circa 1931), letter in Bunin Leeds.

18 Ivan Bunin, *Roza Ierikhona*, 30. A slightly different version of the text of the story is

found in Bunin 4:386–398. I am intentionally referring to the edition which Nabokov was likely to use in the 1920s.

19 Bunin, *Roza Ierikhona*, 29.
20 Ibid., 31.
21 Ibid., 38.
22 Ibid., 39.
23 Ibid., 40.
24 Ibid., 42.
25 Ibid., 44.
26 Ibid.
27 One finds several examples of a small-scale dialogue between Nabokov and Bunin throughout the texts of two stories; see, for instance, the references to cathedrals, cabmen (in the 1910s Sokolovich rides in a cab to the hotel; in the 1920s, Chorb also rides a cab [*izvochick*] from the station to the hotel), black velvet (*barkhat*), etc.
28 The expression belongs to Thomas Gaiton Marullo; Marullo's fine article "Crime without Punishment" discusses Dostoevskian repercussions in Bunin's story.
29 Tammi, *Problems of Nabokov's Poetics*, 54.
30 Boyd, *RY*, 250.
31 See Zinaida Shakhovskaia's typed notes in ZSh LC.
32 See Boyd, *RY*, 183–209; also see Zinaida Shakhovskaia, *V poiskakh Nabokova*, 55. See photos in Boyd, *RY*; and Ellendea Proffer, *Vladimir Nabokov*, 40, 42.
33 Boyd, *RY*, 183.
34 Ibid., 158–159.
35 Ibid., 197.
36 Unlike his paternal ancestors, who went back to pre-Petrine aristocracy, Nabokov's own mother came from wealthy merchants, the Rukavishnikovs, with a telling "merchant" name.
37 Boyd, *RY*, 202.
38 See "To Svetlana Zivert," May 25, 1923, letter quoted in Mikhail Gol'denberg, "Budem prezhde vsego sochiniteliami . . . ," *Vestnik* (August 8, 1995): 44–45.
39 See Boyd, *RY*, 239–244.
40 See Bitsilli, *Tvorchestvo Chekhova*, 29–44, especially 29.
41 I have observed, for instance, the way Chekhov uses the word "smekh" (laughter) recurrently in the short text of "On the Night of Christmas Eve"; see Shrayer, "Conflation of Christmas and Paschal Motifs in Čechov's 'V roždestvenskuju noč.'"
42 Boyd, *RY*, 351–352.
43 Lollii L'vov, " 'Pil'gram V. Sirina," *Rossiia i slavianstvo* (September 6, 1930): 3–4.
44 Gleb Struve, *Russkaia literatura v izgnanii*, 283. Useful discussions of the story are found in Boyd, *RY*, 351–352; Zimmermann, "The Russian Short Stories," 311–317; Tammi, *Problems of Nabokov's Poetics*, 54; Jane Grayson, *Nabokov Translated*, 134; Carol T. Williams, "Nabokov's Dozen Short Stories," *Studies in Short Fiction* 12:3 (Summer 1975): 220–221; Georgii Adamovich, " 'Sovremennye zapiski' kn. 43-ia," *Poslednie novosti* 3424 (August 7, 1930): 3; A. Savel'ev, " 'Sovremennye zapiski' kniga 43-ia," *Rul'* (August 15, 1930): 2–3; Andrew Field, *VN: The Life and Art*, 145; Christopher Hüllen, *Der Tod in Werk Vladimir Nabokovs Terra Incognita*, 119; 125.
45 Adamovich, " 'Sovremennye zapiski' kn. 43-aia."
46 Hüllen, *Der Tod*, 115, discusses Pilgram's and Ivanov's heartaches as well as the motif of

living on the threshold of being and nonbeing, the motif originally noted by Vladislav Khodasevich in "O Sirine"; see his *Literaturnye stat'i i vospominaniia*, 125.

47 Several sources were consulted in preparation for this discussion; see *Oxford English Dictionary*, 7:858–859; *Slovar' sovremennogo russkogo literaturnogo iazyka*, vol. 9; Hans Bahlow, *Deutsches Nameslexicon*, 378; P. H. Reaney, *A Dictionary of British Surnames*, 273–274; Patrick Hanks and Flavia Hodges, *A Dictionary of Surnames*, 420.

48 See Vladimir Nabokov, "Pilgram" ("Palomnik"), MS, TS, and tear copy of the *Sovremennye zapiski* publication with Nabokov's notes toward an English translation, VN LC, container 7, folders dd, ee, ff.

49 The second word is "babochek," genitive plural of "babochka" (butterfly); the first word appears to be "liubitel'" (lover). The original title might have been "Liubitel' babochek" (A Lover of Butterflies).

50 In 1925, following the publication of "Bachman" in *The Rudder*, Nabokov received a peculiar request from Dr. Bernhard Hirschberg of Frankfurt a/M. Taking Nabokov's short story to be a memoiristic essay, Hirschberg asked for permission to translate it into German to be published in "one of the local newspapers." See "To Vladimir Nabokov," letter, March 8, 1925, VN LC, container 8, folder 13.

51 It is also possible that Nabokov did not want to have two texts under the same title; in 1927 he wrote and published a poem also entitled "Palomnik."

52 Sir Paul Harvey, *The Oxford Companion to Classical Literature*, 4–5.

53 Alexandrov discusses a similar problem of Nabokov's "escape from emigration" with examples from Nabokov's discursive writings, *Speak, Memory*, *The Defense*, *The Gift*, and *Lolita*; see his "Spasenie ot èmigratsii u Nabokova."

54 See Afanasii Fet, *Polnoe sobranie stikhotvorenii*, 303.

55 The poems by Fet which Nabokov translated are "Alter Ego" (1878), "Izmuchen zhizn'iu, kovarstvom nadezhdy . . ." (When life is torture, when hope is a traitor . . . , 1864), and "Lastochki" (The Swallows, 1884). For a discussion of Fet's "The Butterfly" in Nabokov's oeuvre, see Bethea, "Izgnanie kak ukhod v konon: obraz babochki u Nabokova i Brodskogo," 175, fn. 6.

56 "The Butterfly" also points to Fet's earlier poem "Ne sprashivai, nad chem zadumyvaius' ia . . ." (Don't ask me what occupies my thoughts . . . , 1854), which might have informed the image of Pilgram the dreamer. In Fet's poem the lyrical voice confesses that "his soul is filled with an insane dream" ("Mechtoi bezumnoiu polna dusha moia"); see Fet, *Polnoe sobranie*, 262.

57 Vladimir Nabokov, "Pilgram" ("Palomnik"), MS, VN LC, container 7, folder dd.

58 For a relevant discussion of the shotgun principle, see Tammi, "Chekhov's Shot Gun and Nabokov."

59 Savel'ev, "'Sovremennye zapiski' kniga 43-ia."

60 Grayson, *Nabokov Translated*, 34. Only a few minor changes were made in the *Contemporary Annals* version, which was virtually identical with the text that appeared in Nabokov's second collection, *The Eye*. Since neither the authorized typescript nor the galley proofs have survived, one has to rely on the existing manuscript of Nabokov's fair copy as the final version of the story. The editors of *Contemporary Annals* and/or Nabokov himself did make a few insignificant changes on the atomistic level. For instance, the adjective "Siberian" (*sibirskii*) in reference to Lepidoptera was replaced with "foreign" (*inostrannyi*) in the description of Pilgram's previous attempts at undertaking a collecting trip; the reference to Siberia might have confused the Russian reader.

61 Virtually nothing has been written about the translator of three of Nabokov's best short stories, "Cloud, Castle, Lake," "The Aurelian," and "Spring in Fialta." Nabokov's relationship with Peter A. Pertzoff (1908–1967) goes back as far as 1933, when M. Karpovich recommended Pertzoff to Nabokov as a skillful translator, originally in regard to translating Nabokov's novels to be published in the United States. In 1938 Nabokov and Pertzoff discussed the possibility of translating the entire collection of short stories, *The Eye.* In 1940 Pertzoff tried to help Nabokov to find a job; there was a possibility of a library job at a university library. In 1941 Nabokov suggested that Pertzoff take on a translation of *The Gift*, but the project was never consummated. The first short story which Pertzoff and Nabokov translated and placed in an American magazine was "Cloud, Castle, Lake," printed in *The Atlantic Monthly* in July 1941. It was followed by "The Aurelian," which appeared in *The Atlantic Monthly* in November 1941. As one can see from the surviving manuscripts and the correspondence, the co-translators followed the same procedure. First, Pertzoff would prepare a more or less literal translation of the Russian original. Then, Nabokov would go over it and edit it very thoroughly, rewriting up to 70 percent of Pertzoff's English. Nabokov called the process "drakonit'" (to dragonize). Despite the number of emendations, he was very pleased with Pertzoff's work and hoped to continue their collaboration, which was beginning to turn into friendship after Nabokov visited Pertzoff in Ithaca in 1944. In August 1941 Nabokov suggested that Pertzoff start working on "Spring in Fialta." The translation underwent several revisions by Nabokov and was finished by March 1943. *The Atlantic Monthly* rejected the story, claiming that it was too long, and in 1947 the story was printed in *Harper's Bazaar*, predominantly a high-fashion magazine. No correspondence with Pertzoff past 1944 has survived among Nabokov's papers. His eleven letters to Pertzoff are deposited in VN LC, container 8, folder 21. See also the Official Personnel File of Peter Pertzoff, Library of Congress. I am grateful to Alice L. Birney, American Literature manuscript historian, for assistance in locating Pertzoff's file.

62 See Boyd, *AY,* 484.

63 I have consulted Pamela Gilbert, *A Compendium of the Biographical Literature on Deceased Entomologists.*

64 See Charles V. Covell Jr., *A Field Guide to the Moths of Eastern North America,* 181–182.

65 For a discussion of the links between insect mimicry and Nabokov's otherworld, see Alexandrov, "Nabokov's Metaphysics of Artifice."

66 Nikolai Raevskii, "Vospominaniia o Vladimire Nabokove," *Prostor* 2 (1989): 115.

67 See ibid., 112–117. Also see Boyd's quote from Nabokov's letter to Véra Nabokova about being "drawn to Africa and Asia," in Boyd, *RY,* 210.

68 On Nabokov's trips, see Boyd, *AY,* 467–468, 644–646.

69 See Boyd, *AY,* 28–29.

70 Nabokov, "On Discovering a Butterfly."

71 Nabokov, "Butterflies."

72 See Boyd, *RY,* 439.

73 Although "Cloud, Castle, Lake" received a larger share of the critics' attention as compared to many other short stories by Nabokov, virtually nothing has been said about the motif and the design of the otherworld in the story. Svetlana Pol'skaia's two-part essay "Kommentarii k rasskazu V. Nabokova 'Oblako, ozero, bashnia'" and "Voskreshenie korolia Ofiokha," *Scando-Slavica* 35 (1989) and 36 (1990), leaves undeveloped its most promising suggestion. Pol'skaia points out, correctly in my view, that the problem

of leaving this world for an alternative reality is central to "Cloud, Castle, Lake." At the same time, her reading of the story as a modern hypertext of the Gospels demonstrates the danger of a departure from the context of Nabokov's sui generis metaphysics. Douglas Fowler briefly discusses the connection between the protagonist's experience in the story and the Platonic idea of a "superworld behind ours" (*Reading Nabokov*, 65). Also noteworthy are Max Duperray's brief remarks about the displacement of the protagonist, Vasiliy Ivanovich, and the Kafkaesque tones in the story ("Au-dela du fantastique," in *Du fantastique en littérature*, 161–165).

74　Jürgen Bodenstein, "*The Excitement of Verbal Adventure*," 342, 336.

75　Alfred Appel Jr., "Nabokov: A Portrait"; in Rivers and Nicol, eds., *Nabokov's Fifth Arc*, 6.

76　See Andrei Garf, "Literaturnye pelënki," *Novoe slovo* (March 20, 1938): 6–7.

77　Boyd, *RY*, 489.

78　The story was reprinted in the 1956 Russian-language collection *Spring in Fialta* with only a few minor changes, some due to a switch to new orthography, others merely stylistic, involving a change of a participle from past to present ("tikavshikh" in *Russkie zapiski* vs. "tikaiushchikh" in *Vesna v Fial'te*) or a noun from singular to plural ("tysiacha" vs. "tysiachi"). The only significant change concerned an added verse to the last quatrain of a German song; the meaning of the song will be discussed below.

79　Naumann, *Blue Evenings in Berlin*, 7.

80　See Nabokov, "Cloud, Castle, Lake." As he acknowledges in his "Foreword" to *DS*, the story was "translated by Peter Pertzoff in collaboration with the author"; see *Stories*, 662. In *The Atlantic Monthly* publication, there is no indication that this is a translation; the name of the translator does not appear.

81　Vladimir Nabokov, "Cloud, Castle, Lake," corrected TS, VN LC, container 8, folder 20.

82　Nabokov, "Ozero, oblako, bashnia," 36–37.

83　Nabokov, "Cloud, Castle, Lake," 739. In *The Atlantic Monthly* version, the song's last stanza still had three lines as in the Russian original.

84　In the 1956 Russian version Nabokov added a fourth verse to make the last stanza a perfect quatrain but did not enhance the anti-Fascist message as he did in the English text. In an earlier story, "The Leonardo," the atmosphere of violent, self-satisfied collective philistinism anticipates that of "Cloud, Castle, Lake." Romantovskii, the protagonist of "The Leonardo," shares several features with Vasiliy Ivanovich. See also Nabokov's remarks in the preface to "The Leonardo" (*Stories*, 653). The MS of the English text of the song in Nabokov's hand is in container 8, folder 20.

85　For a discussion of totalitarian bureaucratism, see Fowler, *Reading Nabokov*, 63.

86　The motif of loving a distant woman, someone else's wife, also figures prominently in "Perfection," where Ivanov is said to have loved only one woman, "edinstvennaia zhenshchina, kotoruiu on v zhizni liubil, chuzhaia zhena" (*S*, 216). The same motif earlier appears in *Mary* in a slightly different version.

87　The Russian text of the story contains covert references to two poems by Tiutchev, one—encoded as a pun—to the 1830 poem "Silentium" ("My sliz'. Rechënnaia est' lozh'," roughly: We are slime. That which is uttered is a lie; cf. Tiutchev's "Mysl' izrechënnaia est' lozh'," roughly: An uttered thought is a lie) and the other to "Vchera, v mechtakh obvorozhënnykh . . ." (Yesterday, in enchanted dreams . . . , written ca. 1830s). Nabokov's "divnoe o rumianom vosklitsanii" refers to Tiutchev's line "Rumianym, gromkim vosklitsan'em" (see Tolstaia's commentary in *Krug*, 538). Tiutchev's poems, all three in iambic tetrameter (Ia4), are only alluded to in the story and may not be considered a part of any structural opposition in the text of "Cloud, Castle, Lake." The English text omits any specific textual allusions and merely refers to "a volume of Tiutchev, whom he had long intended to reread" (*Stories*, 431).

88 The manuscript of the draft provides a taste of Nabokov's creative laboratory. Especially telling are those instances where he introduced or enhanced the metrical markedness of his prose. In the particular case of "k komu-to, k chemu-to" (*VF*, 236), Nabokov added "k chemu-to" thereby introducing an amphibrachic beat.

89 Bodenstein talks about the train in the story in connection with the so-called "transcendent designs" in Nabokov's writings; see Bodenstein, "'The Excitement of Verbal Adventure,'" 350.

90 The first of the two dactylic lines, "péristye oblaká," presents us with a marginal case of a dactylic trimeter (D3) with masculine rhymes. In Russian ternary meters "the arrangement of strong syllables constitutes the permanent framework of the line" and "the threat of a hiatus of five syllables ensures the preservation of stress" (Boris Unbegaun, *Russian Versification*, 51–53). At the same time, no analysis of versification can ever go against the natural properties of a language: first and foremost, its accentuation. Although "péristye oblaká," if taken out of its context in Nabokov's story, might be classified as a line of trochaic tetrameter (Tr4) with pyrrhics in the second and third feet, the second line of his metrical cluster prohibits a trochee. In order for us to read the two lines as indeed trochaic, we would have to misstress the word "nebésnykh" and pronounce it as "nébesnykh," i.e., "péristye oblaká / téni nébesnykh borzýkh," which is, of course, inadmissible. Therefore, the metrical cluster in question *is* dactylic and contains a rare (in ternary meters) omission of stress in the nonfirst position.

91 In the Russian manuscript Nabokov inserted the metricized bit about the "greyhounds" between the lines. Remarkably, when correcting the typescript of Peter Pertzoff's translation, he changed what Pertzoff had already made into a dactylic line; Pertzoff had "fleecy clouds, like heavenly borzois," which is fine, but Nabokov changed that into "wispy clouds,—greyhounds of heaven," which is even better. See Vladimir Nabokov, "Ozero, oblako, bashnia," MS, VN LC, container 7, folder r; Vladimir Nabokov, "Cloud, Castle, Lake," corrected TS, VN LC, container 8, folder 20.

92 Alexandrov, "Nabokov's Metaphysics of Artifice," 133.

93 Nabokov tried several variants before arriving at the simple and yet metrically perfect "detstvo geroia." He corrected Pertzoff's rhythmically drab "the childhood of hero" to "the hero's childhood." See Vladimir Nabokov, "Cloud, Castle, Lake," corrected TS, VN LC, container 8, folder 20.

94 In "The Visit to the Museum" Nabokov also creates a sense of an individual's paralysis when facing a collective that invades his or her privacy; compare the protagonist's comments about the group of student visitors in "The Visit to the Museum" with Vasiliy Ivanovich's terror at the end of "Cloud, Castle, Lake."

95 In the English text "the ódor of jásmine and háy" is amphibrachic.

96 See Tolstaia and Meilakh, "Russian Short Stories," 656.

97 For some background on Nabokov's 1937 visit to Czechoslovakia, see Boyd, *RY*, 438–439.

98 See *Beilage zur Franzenbader Kurliste für die Saison 1937* (Franzenbad: n.p., 1937).

99 See *Beilage zur Marienbader Kurliste für die Saison 1937* (Marienbad: Herausgegeben vom Stadtrat, 1937). I gratefully acknowledge the help of Dr. Peter Bouše, Director, Mariánské Lázně Museum.

100 Vladimir Nabokov, "Ozero, oblako, bashnia," MS, VN LC, container 7, folder r.

101 Boyd, *RY*, 233.

102 Special thanks to Professor Alexander Parves of the Yale School of Architecture for expert information.

103 Cf. Fowler's discussion of the Platonic superworld in the story: "The fairytale atmosphere of the story is not only a matter of setting and simplified oppositions, it resides also in the miraculousness of Vasiliy's discovery—or his recovery, for the revelation of cloud, castle, and lake is Platonic; the vision seems to have existed before, in a dimension that now penetrates into Vasiliy's and that he seems to recognize from prior knowledge or intuition" (Fowler, *Reading Nabokov*, 66).

104 The Russian manuscript contains a curious clause that Nabokov crossed out; it follows the word "nevyrazimoi" (inexpressible, unique) and reads as follows: "ezheli ne trebovat' ot slov nekoi bozhestvennoi matematiki" (literally, if one does not demand from words some divine mathematics). Apparently, the clause refers to the moment of perfect and timeless harmony between Vasiliy Ivanovich and the otherworld that defies logic and introduces transverbal sense.

105 The opening to the otherworld is glimpsed in the text as early as the story's title, "Oblako, ozero, bashnia." "Óblako ózero báshnia" is, of course, a truncated dactylic (D3) line. The fact that the story originally appeared in *Russkie zapiski* as "Ozero, oblako, bashnia" (just as in the surviving manuscript) and was renamed "Oblako, ozero, bashnia" in the Russian collection *Spring in Fialta* testifies to Nabokov's apparent concern with the function of the title in the story's complex system of signification. After all, the title is one of the elements of the text most likely to be remembered by the reader. In the case of the English title, a ternary pattern must have been impossible to recreate.

106 See Fowler, *Reading Nabokov*, 65–66.

107 A gnostic interpretation might be relevant to the story but will not be entertained in this analysis. For gnostic readings of Nabokov's works, see Johnson, *Worlds in Regression* (Chapter 6), and Davydov, *Teksty-Matrëški* (Chapter 3).

108 The English adds the adjective "Russian" to the noun "veteran" and thereby further charges the space of the boundary with Vasiliy Ivanovich's memories. In the draft the innkeeper appears first as an "old widower, former Russian soldier" ("vdovets, byvshii russkii soldat"); Vladimir Nabokov, "Cloud, Castle, Lake," corrected TS, VN LC, container 7, folder r.

109 Cf. the identical function of the verb "zakliuchat'sia" (to consist in) in describing Pilgram's otherworldly dream in "The Aurelian": "schast'e zakliuchalos' v tom, chtoby . . ." (literally, the happiness consisted in . . .).

110 The proposed chronotope of the otherworld entails a set of characteristics that are essentially Nabokov's own characteristics of cosmic synchronization.

111 Field, *Nabokov: His Life in Art*, 197.

112 Alan C. Elms, "Cloud, Castle, Claustrum," in Daniel Rancour-Laferriere, ed., *Russian Literature and Psychoanalysis*, 360.

113 It is crucial for Pol'skaia's reading of the story that Vasiliy Ivanovich is killed at the end

of the story. See Pol'skaia, "Kommentarii k rasskazu V. Nabokova 'Oblako, ozero, bashnia,'" 116 and passim.

114 In "A Busy Man" the angelic Engel is referred to as "representative" of a celestial firm. In "Torpid Smoke" the reader encounters a distant cousin of other Nabokovian representatives, a "solitary blind toiler." In *Drugie berega* (Other Shores) the following sentence in Chapter 5 describes the arrival of the Mademoiselle: "Ia ne poekhal vstrechat' eë na Siverskuiu, zheleznodorozhnuiu ostanovku v deviati verstakh ot nas, no teper' vysylaiu tuda prizrachnogo predstavitelia i cherez nego vizhu iasno . . ." (I didn't go to meet her in Siverskaia, the train station ten versts away from our house, but now I am dispatching my spectral representative and though him can clearly see . . . ; *SSoch*, 4:185). In both the original French version and the Englished version the word "representative" is missing, while his role is played by the verb "to imagine."

115 Tammi describes the split as an "effort to step from a lower plane of observation to a superior one—an attempt to 'peer beyond [one's] own limits'" (*Problems of Nabokov's Poetics*, 127).

116 See ibid., 55.

117 This is not to be confused with the case of a traditional omniscient narrator, who knows more about the events that he narrates than anyone else in the narrative and does not need to justify the sources of the information. In "Cloud, Castle, Lake" the function of the final paragraph is to explain where and under which circumstances the narrator obtains the information about Vasiliy Ivanovich's amusement trip.

118 Prince, *Dictionary of Narratology*, 57 and 3.

119 Just how gradual this fusion of voices really is can be observed in a curious statement appearing between the second and the last addresses to the beloved in the story. I have in mind the instance when Vasiliy Ivanovich is given a loaf of bread to carry: "Vasiliy Ivanovich, as the least burdened, was given an enormous round of bread to carry under his arm. How I hate you, our daily!" Here the narrator and Vasiliy Ivanovich share an existential perspective, but not a narrative one, since the bread—the object of Vasiliy Ivanovich's address—is clearly on the same diegetic plane as Vasiliy Ivanovich, who is carrying it, and not on the same plane as the narrator.

120 Although written two years prior to "Cloud, Castle, Lake," *Invitation to a Beheading* was published in book form in 1938, less than a year after the publication of the story in *Russkie zapiski*.

121 See Vladislav Khodasevich, "Knigi i liudi: 'Russkie zapiski' kniga 2-ia," *Vozrozhdenie* (August 8, 1936): 7.

122 Georgii Ivanov, *1943–1958: Stikhi*, 22.

123 Vladimir Nabokov, "Opredeleniia," TS, VN LC, container 8, folder 7.

124 In fact, Nabokov did plan to write a separate chapter of his memoir dedicated to the émigré contexts of his Russian years, see Boyd, *RY*; bits and pieces of this chapter must have entered Chapter 14 of *Speak, Memory*.

125 In the collection *The Eye*, "Orache" follows "A Bad Day" and they literally form a textual continuum. For the authorial background of V. D. Nabokov's 1911 called-off duel which informed the events of "Orache," see Boyd, *RY*, 98–99.

126 See Pol'skaia, "Kommentarii k rasskazu V. Nabokova 'Oblako, ozero, bashnia.'" An illuminating discussion of the name Vasiliy Ivanovich is found in the story "Recruiting."

127 In the nineteenth century the name of Admiral Aleksandr Semënovich Shishkov (1754–1841) was associated with a literary group whose members sought to defend the purity of the Russian language against the invasion of Western syntax and vocabulary; in the twentieth century the novelist Viacheslav Iakovlevich Shishkov (1873–1945) left an impressive body of work including a well-known novel, *Peipus-ozero* (Peipus-Lake).

128 From 1931 to 1934 at least seven poems by Nabokov were featured in Parisian Russian periodicals, two in *Sovremennye zapiski* (September 1931) and five in *Poslednie novosti* (July 31, 1932; September 8, 1932; January 29, 1933; May 3, 1934; June 28, 1934). Between 1934 and 1939 not a single poem by Nabokov seems to have appeared in Paris, while only one was published elsewhere, in no. 8 (1935) of the Estonian-based magazine *Nov'* (The Virgin Soil). Boyd (*RY*, 509) has speculated that Nabokov ceased publishing his poetry because he was being denied his due by the Parisian critics of the Adamovich circle. However, Nabokov's known poetic output of the 1930s is quite small compared to the hundreds composed in the 1920s: only about a dozen original poems plus those incorporated into *The Gift*. Most likely, the decline of his poetic output in the 1930s signals an internal dissatisfaction with his own poetic achievement. For Nabokov's own remarks on the distribution of his poetic output, see *PP*, 13–15; see also Véra Nabokova's introduction in the 1979 *Stikhi*.

129 See Nabokov's somewhat eccentric and elusive comments on the aesthetics of the Parisian Note in *SM*, 284–285; an earlier version of the chapter of Nabokov's autobiography where he mentions Adamovich and Merezhkovskii by name was published as "Exile" in *The Russian Review* in 1951. The earlier passage is also found in *CE*, 212–213.

130 In *Odinochestvo i svoboda* (222–228), Georgii Adamovich devoted a large and insightful section to Nabokov's poetry. Several other memoirs by the Parisian Russian littérateurs carried hostility to Nabokov into the 1970s; see, for instance, Iurii Terapiano, *Literaturnaia zhizn' russkogo Parizha za polveka*, 92 and passim; Aleksandr Bakhrakh, *Po pamiati, po zapisiam*, 99–104 and passim; V. S. Ianovskii, *Polia eliseiskie*, 20, 128, 247–248, 257. Many Parisian poets did have reasons to be irritated by Nabokov's consistent épatage of their poetry; a typical example may be found in his very favorable review (and exceptional for that matter) of Antonin Ladinskii's poetry collection, *Chërnoe i goluboe* (Black and Blue); in the review, in passing, Nabokov manages to "kill" Terapiano, Nikolai Otsup, Iu. Mandel'shtam, Adamovich, and even Boris Poplavskii with a few caustic remarks; see Kniga, 389.

131 G. Ivanov and Adamovich clashed after World War II, which is evident from Ivanov's very interesting and controversial article "Konets Adamovicha" (The End of Adamovich), *Vozrozhdenie* 11 (September–October 1959): 179–186.

132 See Nabokov, "Irina Odoevtseva. 'Izol'da,'" rev. of *Izol'da*, by Irina Odoevtseva.

133 Georgii Ivanov, rev. of *Mashen'ka: Korol', dama, valet, Chisla* 1 (1930): 235.

134 "To Zinaida Shakhovskaia," n.d. (stamped April 1939), letter in ZSh LC.

135 Adamovich, "Sirin," 3. Two overviews of Nabokov's writings, both published in 1930, preceded the article by Adamovich. See Gleb Struve, "Tvorchestvo Sirina"; and Nikolai Andreev, "Sirin," *Nov'* 3 (October 1930): 3.

136 The longest statement on Nabokov's poetry by Adamovich appeared in *Odinochestvo i svoboda*, 222–228.

137 Igor' Chinnov, personal interview. 15 March 1994. Daytona Beach, Florida.

138 See Davydov's analysis of the "Lips to Lips" controversy in Chapter 1 of his *Teksty-Matrëški Vladimira Nabokova;* see also Boyd, *RY,* 373–374.

139 Nabokov, "Iz Kalmbrudovoi poèmy 'Nochnoe puteshestvie.'" See also *Stikhi,* 238–242.

140 On the Adamovich-Khodasevich polemic, see Roger Hagglund, "The Russian Emigré Debate of 1928 on Criticism," *Slavic Review* 32:3 (September 1973): 515–526, and "The Adamovič-Xodasevič Polemics," *The Slavic and East European Journal* 20:3 (1976): 239–252.

141 On Nabokov and Adamovich and some origins of "adamic head," see Field, *VN: The Life and Art of Vladimir Nabokov,* 132–135; Boyd, *RY,* 370–371, 569, fn. 22. Nabokov's pastiche was reprinted in the 1979 posthumous edition of his verse; see Nabokov, *Stikhi,* 238–242.

142 See John Malmstad, [Dzhon Malmsted], "Iz perepiski V. F. Khodasevicha (1925–1938)," *Minuvshee* 3 (1987): 286; see also Aleksandr Dolinin, "Dve zametki o romane 'Dar,'" *Zvezda* 11 (1996): 173–176, 179–180.

143 On Nabokov and Khodasevich, see [Nikita] Struve, "V. Khodasevichi; V. Nabokov," *Vestnik R. Kh. D.* 148:3 (1986): 123–128.

144 For Nabokov's commentary to the poem, see *Stikhi,* 319–320.

145 Nabokov's use of the word "ubornaia" (latrine; in the genitive case, "ubornoi") in a lyrical poem was probably informed by Vladimir Korvin-Piotrovskii's poem "Iz nochnykh progulok" (From Nighttime Walks), *Rul'* 2458 (December 25, 1928): 2, where this word also appears in a description of a cityscape; the poem was published in *Rul'* on the same page with Nabokov's own "A Christmas Story."

146 Vladislav Khodasevich, *Sobranie stikhov,* 94–95.

147 Nabokov, "O Khodaseviche," 264.

148 See Vladimir Nabokov, "Notes for the Russian Recital in New York City (early 1950s)," corr. MS and TS, VN LC, container 8, folder 5.

149 M. N. Vishniak, *"Sovremennye zapiski,"* 123.

150 Vladimir Nabokov, "Obrashcheniia," MS, ZSh LC.

151 See *Stikhotvoreniia,* 19–23; "We so firmly believed . . ." is dated 1938, "The Poets" and "Will you leave me alone? . . ." 1939. In *Stikhi* only one short poem separates "We so firmly believed . . ." from "The Poets" and "Will you leave me alone? . . . ," which follow each other consecutively. In *PP* and *Stikhi* Nabokov assigned a different title to "Will you leave me alone? . . .": "K Rossii" (To Russia); cf. "Obrashchenie" (The Appeal) in the *Contemporary Annals* publication. The poems "Oko" (Oculus) and "Chto za noch' s pamiat'iu sluchilos'" (What happened overnight) may also be related to this cycle. "Oculus" is the fourth known poem by Nabokov written in 1939; see *PP,* 100–101, and *Stikhi,* 264. Dated 1939 and written in Paris, it mentions the "disappeared boundary between eternity and matter": ". . . ischezla granitsa / mezhdu vechnost'iu i veshchestvom"; compare in "We so firmly believed . . .": ". . . dymka volny / mezhdu mnoi i toboi, mezhdu mel'iu i tonushchim" (a wave's haze / between me and you, between shallow and sinking). "What happened overnight . . ." is dated 1938 in *Stikhotvoreniia* (18), *PP* (90–91), and *Stikhi* (259); *PP* and *Stikhi* indicate that it was written in Menton.

152 See A. L. Zorin, "Nachalo," in Vladislav Khodasevich, *Derzhavin,* 30–36; also see Zorin's fine commentary on the subject of the Vasilii Travnikov controversy in Kho-

dasevich, *Derzhavin*, 382–383. About Muni (S. V. Kissin), see Vladislav Khodasevich, *Nekropol'*.

153 For details of the reading, see Boyd, *RY*, 424–425.

154 See Zorin, "Nachalo"; Boyd, *RY*, 509. Adamovich devoted a section of his literary column in *The Latest News* to Khodasevich's "discovery." In a recent interview (March 15, 1994, Daytona Beach, Florida), one of the very last living émigré poets of the first wave, Igor' Chinnov (1908–1996), pointed out to me that although Adamovich was a very sensitive critic and wonderful stylist, his general knowledge of literature was more limited than it appears from reading his prose. For instance, in the 1940s Adamovich admitted to Chinnov that he had never read Dante's *The Divine Comedy*. Adamovich's willingness to "buy into" the Khodasevich scheme may have resulted from his insufficient knowledge of late eighteenth-century Russian literary culture; even more ludicrous is the readiness of Adamovich to believe the story about Travnikov's surviving archive, which Khodasevich claimed to have found.

155 Boyd, *RY*, 509.

156 Ibid., 261.

157 Khodasevich, *Derzhavin*, 340.

158 Ibid., 31.

159 Georgii Adamovich, "'Sovremennye zapiski'—kniga 69-aia. Chast' literaturnaia," *Poslednie novosti* 6716 (August 17, 1939): 3.

160 Gerald S. Smith, "Nabokov and Russian Verse Form," *Russian Literature Triquarterly* 24 (Spring 1990): 285.

161 Tolstaia suggested this in her useful commentary in Nabokov, *Krug*, 521.

162 Note that the poem "Probuzhdenie" (The Awakening) appeared in vol. 47 (1931) of *Sovremennye zapiski*, never to be reprinted again; see "Probuzhdenie." "We so firmly believed . . ." was reprinted in Iurii Ivask, ed., *Na zapade*, 290; both "We so firmly believed . . ." and "The Poets" were featured in Iurii Terapiano's selection of émigré poetry in 1959 in the review *Grani*. "The Poets" also appeared in both English and Russian in 1970 in the Nabokov issue of *TriQuarterly*, subsequently published as Appel and Newman, eds., *Nabokov*.

163 Unless otherwise indicated, all quotations from Nabokov's poetry are from *Stikhi*, his self-selected and largest volume of Russian poetry, published posthumously in 1979.

164 See Smith, "Nabokov and Russian Verse Form."

165 *Stikhi*, 320.

166 See *Kniga*, 392.

167 A rare exception is the poem "Vliublënnost'" (Being in Love), composed by the last of Nabokov's literary personae, Vadim in *Look at the Harlequins!* (1973). In Vadim's poem, "vliublënnost'" (literally, being in love) is rhymed with "potustoronnost'" (literally, otherworldliness), thereby making a point about the connections between love and the otherworld.

168 Khodasevich, *Literaturnye stat'i i vospominaniia*, 249–250; the essay originally appeared in *Vozrozhdenie* 4065 (February 13, 1937): 9.

169 Adamovich, "Sirin," 3.

170 Adamovich, "Literaturnye zametki," *Poslednie novosti* 6552 (September 22, 1939): 3.

171 Ibid.

172 "Vasiliy Shishkov" appeared on September 12, 1939, on page 3 of *The Latest News*,

where they usually placed literary columns (e.g., the regular column by Adamovich), short stories, and feuilletons.

173 For an illuminating discussion of the cultural mythology of Rimbaud's disappearance from the literary scene, see Chapter 1 in Svetlana Boym's *Death in Quotation Marks*.

174 Nabokov himself had considered undertaking an expedition to the tropics, as reported by Nikolai Raevskii, "Vospominaniia," 115.

175 Adamovich, "Literaturnye zametki."

176 Ibid.

177 The two lines in *The Gift* are quoted in Linyov's review of Koncheyev's poetry collection; see *SSoch*, 3:152.

178 "Searching for an Exit: France, 1939–1940" is the title of Chapter 22 in Boyd, *RY*.

179 Vladimir Nabokov, "Iubilei," *Rul'* 2120 (November 19, 1927): 2.

180 He did continue to publish in Russian in the leading New York émigré periodicals, *Novyi zhurnal* and *Vozdushnye puti;* several of his Russian books also appeared after World War II, including the first complete edition of *The Gift* (1952) and the first edition of the Russian collection *Spring in Fialta* (1956). Those publications, as well as the Russian versions of *Lolita* and *Speak, Memory* and the translated excerpts from the *Eugene Onegin* commentary, were tributes to Nabokov's Russian years. In America Nabokov wrote no fiction in his original Russian. He also "disappeared" from émigré cultural life and gave very few readings in Russian. He did continue to write occasional poems in Russian.

181 Dovid Knut (1900–1955) immigrated to Israel after World War II and virtually "disappeared" from the Russian émigré literary life.

182 See Grayson, *Nabokov Translated*, 116–118. Grayson calls Nabokov's creation of Vasiliy Shishkov's persona "bidding farewell to [his] identity as a Russian writer, and to the Russian language."

183 Veidle, "Ischeznovenie Nabokova," *Novyi zhurnal* 129 (1977): 271–274.

184 Adamovich, *Odinochestvo i svoboda*, 222.

185 See Bakhrakh, *Po pamiati, po zapisiam*, 103–104. Bakhrakh compares Pasternak's poem "Chto zhe sdelal ia za pakost'. . ." (What a nasty thing I did . . .) and Nabokov's polemical "Kakoe sdelal ia durnoe delo . . ." (What is the evil deed . . .).

186 See Boris Pasternak, "Vstrechi s Maiakovskim," *Novaia gazeta* 5 (May 1, 1931): 12. The essay was excerpted from Pasternak's memoiristic work *Okhrannaia gramota* (Safe Conduct, 1929–1931). The excerpt was probably reprinted from its publication as "Pervye vstrechi s Maiakovskim" (First Meetings with Maiakovskii) in *Literaturnaia gazeta* 20 (April 14, 1931). In the complete text of *Safe Conduct* it appears as Chapters 3–5 of Part 3.

187 Nabokov, "Chto vsiakii dolzhen znat'," *Novaia gazeta* 5 (May 1, 1931): 3.

188 Pasternak, "Vstrechi."

3 Nabokov's Dialogue with Chekhov: From *"Lady with a Lap Dog"* to *"Spring in Fialta"*

1 *Glory*, 122.

2 "To Edmund Wilson." February 29, 1956, in *Wilson Letters*, 297–298.

3 Boyd, *AY*, 115. In the published lectures on Tolstoi, Nabokov offered a different scale: "first, Tolstoy; second, Gogol; third, Chekhov"; see *LRL*, 137.

4 Studies of Chekhov's poetics that have proven invaluable in my comparative research on Nabokov and Chekhov include Bitsilli, *Tvorchestvo Chekhova;* A. P. Chudakov, *Poètika Chekhova;* and Robert Louis Jackson's numerous works on Chekhov. For an excellent recent discussion of Chekhov's achievement and problems in reading Chekhov, see Jackson, "Introduction," in *Reading Chekhov's Text.* The role of memory in the Nabokov-Chekhov comparative poetics demands a separate forum. I will only point out here that both Chekhov's and Nabokov's texts exhibit numerous connections with Marcel Proust. Jackson considers the Chekhov-Proust parallels in "Chekhov i Prust: postanovka problemy," in *Chekhoviana: Chekhov i Frantsiia,* 129–140. Nabokov's connections with Proust are explored in Foster's *Nabokov's Art of Memory and European Modernism.*

5 See Simon Karlinsky, "Nabokov and Chekhov," in Alexandrov, ed., *The Garland Companion;* "Nabokov and Chekhov: The Lesser Tradition," in Alfred Appel Jr. and Charles Newman, eds., *Nabokov.* Some remarks on Chekhov's trace in Nabokov are found in John A. Barnstead, "Nabokov, Kuzmin, Chekhov and Gogol'," in Julian W. Connolly and S. I. Ketchian, eds., *Studies in Honor of Vsevolod Setschkarëv.*

6 For this opposition, see Karlinsky, "Nabokov and Chekhov: The Lesser Tradition," 16.

7 Karlinsky has discussed some Chekhovian elements in Nabokov's novels and plays, including the structure of *Mary* (which Karlinsky labels the "most Chekhovian of Nabokov's novels"; "Nabokov and Chekhov," 395) with its last-minute "switch away" from the expected ending to a surprising one; the egomaniac Herman Karlovich in *Despair;* the failure of the protagonists to accomplish their plans in *King, Queen, Knave* and *The Defense;* a gallery of "unconvincing vamps" such as Magda/Margot in *Kamera obskura/Laughter in the Dark;* the impossibility of the central event of the play *Sobytie* (The Event, 1938); and various Chekhovian motifs in *The Gift.*

8 See Karlinsky, "Nabokov and Chekhov: The Lesser Tradition"; and Zimmermann, "The Russian Short Stories," 136. Tammi ("Chekhov's Shot Gun," 3–5) has demonstrated that Nabokov draws on Chekhov's "shotgun principle" of the economy of narrative means in "Lik," by having the protagonist's boorish schoolmate, Koldunov, shoot himself with the gun which he earlier tried to sell to him. I have also observed that while the shotgun principle literally underlies Lik's encounters with Koldunov and structures the story, it is figuratively echoed when Lik leaves his new shoes at the site of Koldunov's imminent suicide and later returns for them.

9 Karlinsky, "Nabokov and Chekhov," 397.

10 "To A. S. Suvorin," January 7, 1889, letter in Chekhov, *Pis'ma,* in *Polnoe sobranie sochinenii i pisem,* 3:133.

11 "To Al. P. Chekhov," May 10, 1886, letter 176 in Chekhov, *Pis'ma,* 1:241.

12 "To A. N. Pleshcheev," January 23, 1888, letter 362 in ibid., 2:183.

13 "To I. L. Leont'ev (Shcheglov)," May 3, 1888, letter 431 in ibid., 2:261.

14 "To A. S. Suvorin," May 30, 1888, letter 447 in ibid., 2:280.

15 "To A. N. Pleshcheev," October 4, 1888, letter 491 in ibid., 3:11.

16 "To I. L. Leont'ev (Shcheglov)," March 9, 1892, letter 1135 in ibid., 5:20; English translation quoted from Jackson, "Introduction," 8.

17 "To A. S. Suvorin," August 15, 1894, letter in Chekhov, *Pis'ma,* 5:311.

18 "To Zinaida Shakhovskaia," September 15, 1934, letter quoted in Gol'denberg, "Budem prezhde vsego sochiniteliami," 47.

19 "To Zinaida Shakhovskaia," undated, circa 1936, letter quoted in ibid.

20 "To Zinaida Shakhovskaia," November 12, 1937, letter quoted in ibid.

21 Simon Karlinsky, "Russian Anti-Chekhovians," *Russian Literature* 15:2 (1984): 187. Gippius's pre-émigré essays on Chekhov appeared originally in the journal *Novyi put'* (The New Way) and thereafter were collected in her book *Literaturnyi dnevnik (1899–1907)* (A Literary Diary, 1908), published under the pen-name "Anton Krainii." In *A Literary Diary* see especially the essay "Byt i sobytiia" (Mores and Events); see *Literaturnyi dnevnik*, 285–308. In 1925 Gippius published an essay, "Blagoukhanie sedin: o mnogikh" (Fragrant Gray Hair: About Many), as part of a remarkable memoir entitled *Zhivye litsa* (Living Faces, 1925). The essay contains a section about a meeting with Chekhov and Suvorin in Europe in 1891. Gippius labeled Chekhov a "genius of immobility" (*genii nepodvizhnosti*). With tongue-in-cheek irony, she branded Chekhov "a remarkably wholesome person," "close to and needed by those souls who strive for a 'norm' and immobility but have no voice." See "Blagoukhanie sedin," 133–136.

22 Ibid., 133–134.

23 For a detailed consideration of Gippius's views of Chekhov, see Karlinsky, "Russian Anti-Chekhovians." A personal note may be detected in Gippius's deprecations of Chekhov. Chekhov's own antipathy for Gippius is evident from his letter to A. S. Suvorin; see "To A. S. Suvorin," March 1, 1892, letter 1123 in Chekhov, *Pis'ma* 5:8.

24 Karlinsky, "Russian Anti-Chekhovians," 186.

25 Ibid., 194.

26 Joseph Brodsky, "Poetry in the Theater," *Theater* 20:1 (Winter 1988): 51–54. On "Akhmatova's orphans," see Shrayer, "Two Poems on the Death of Akhmatova."

27 Boyd, *RY*, 121.

28 On the Parisian Zelënaia lampa (Green Lamp), see Iurii Terapiano, *Literaturnaia zhizn' russkogo Parizha za polveka*, who even provides several protocols of the meetings. The anti-Nabokovians attending the Sunday meetings of the Green Lamp included G. Adamovich, G. Ivanov, N. Otsup, S. Sharshun, Iu. Terapiano, and others.

29 In his article, published in the inaugural issue of *The Numbers*, G. Ivanov likened Nabokov, among other things, to Boris Lazarevskii, a minor writer and a friend and epigone of Chekhov. See Georgii Ivanov, rev. of *Mashen'ka; Korol', dama, valet; Zashchita Luzhina; Vozvrashchenie Chorba* by V. Sirin, *Chisla* 1 (1930): 233–236.

30 Anton Krainii, "Literaturnye razmyshleniia," *Chisla* 2–3 (1930): 148.

31 Bunin offers this testimony in the memoir part of his *O Chekhove* (220): "Kakie oni dekadenty! — govoril on, — oni zdorovenneishie muzhiki, ikh by v arestantskie roty otdat'. . ." ("What sort of decadents they are!" he would say. "They are burly peasants; it would serve them right to send them to penal companies.").

32 Shestov's essay enjoyed a great deal of popularity even among those writers and critics who considered Chekhov one of Russia's great writers, including Bunin, who thought it "one of the best essays on Chekhov" (Bunin, *O Chekhove*, 116). Shestov's essay, much like Dmitrii Merezhkovskii's *Chekhov and Gor'kii* (1906), cannot be placed in the same line with the ungrounded negative remarks of Gippius or Adamovich. Shestov rates Chekhov very highly, a much higher virtuoso than Maupassant—a very high rating indeed for a Russian critic of the 1900s (Lev Shestov, "Tvorchestvo iz nichego," in *Nachala i kontsy*, 6). However, Shestov's main goal was that of an existential philosopher and cultural critic rather than a literary critic per se. This might explain the lack of any professional methodology of literary analysis and a consideration exclusively of those

Chekhov texts which fit Shestov's thesis. Unfortunately, Shestov's essay has had a lasting impact on Chekhov's reception. Russian (and Western) anti-Chekhovians continued to reiterate several of Shestov's points into the second half of the twentieth century: ". . . Chekhov, being himself a writer and an educated person, had a priori rejected all consolations, both metaphysical and positive" (12); ". . . Chekhov real, only hero is a hopeless person" (39); ". . . Chekhov is an irreconcilable enemy of every sort of philosophy" (50). Chekhov makes a fleeting appearance in the 1930 Adamovich essay, in the context of Nabokov's Gogolian leanings. Without any reservations, Adamovich ("Sirin") refers to Chekhov as a writer of an "immeasurably smaller caliber" than Gogol'. In fact, as late as 1960, Adamovich reprinted Shestov's essay on Chekhov in the émigré review *Mosty* (Bridges) and praised it in his preface (see Adamovich, "Po povodu stat'i Shestova 'Tvorchestvo iz nichego,'" *Mosty* 5 (1960): 117–120).

33 Bitsilli was a rare exception among émigré critics; his 1942 monograph (*Tvorchestvo Chekhova*) considers Chekhov's lineage in Russian classical literature. Shestov does speak of the influence of late Tolstoi upon Chekhov; however, he contrasts the Tolstoi of "The Death of Ivan Il'ich" with the Tolstoi of both *War and Peace* and *Anna Karenina*; see Shestov, "Tvorchestvo iz nichego," 10–11. For a concise discussion of Chekhov's place in the Russian tradition, see Mikhail Gromov, *Chekhov*, 315–323.

34 See Foster, *Nabokov's Art of Memory and European Modernism*, 146–155.

35 With some adjustments, I am following René Girard's very important notion of triangles of desire as expressed in his 1965 book *Desire, Deceit, and the Novel*, especially 2–3.

36 See Bunin's commentaries in Bunin, *O Chekhove*, 211–212.

37 See Blok's 1907 essay "O realistakh" (On Realists), and Andrei Belyi, "Chekhov," in *Simvolizm kak miroponimanie*, 371–375.

38 See Belyi, *Simvolizm kak miroponimanie*, 372.

39 Ibid., 374.

40 Ibid., 372.

41 Very telling about Chekhov's status among émigré writers of the older generation is a questionnaire, "Nashi pisateli o Chekhove," published in the Parisian weekly *Illiustrirovannaia zhizn'* (Illustrated Life) 18 (July 12, 1934). It contained comments by A. Kuprin, M. Aldanov, Don-Aminado, B. Zaitsev, M. Osorgin, A. Remizov, N. Tèffi, and I. Shmelëv. Remizov, while confessing his love for Chekhov's writings, placed him in the third rank of writers along with Vasilii Sleptsov, who was clearly a much less significant writer than Chekhov. Osorgin suggested that while Chekhov left many disciples, no one seemed to be a worthy heir to Chekhov's art.

42 For a very illuminating discussion of Chekhov and Russian classical literature, see Bitsilli, *Tvorchestvo Chekhova*. Very little has been written on Nabokov and Russian classical literature. For a very useful discussion of Nabokov and Gogol', see Victor Terras, "Nabokov and Gogol," in J. Douglas Clayton, ed., *Poetica Slavica*. Some aspects of Nabokov's relationship with Pushkin are considered in Sergej Davydov, "Nabokov and Pushkin," in Alexandrov, ed., *The Garland Companion*.

43 For a discussion of the theme of art in *The Seagull*, see Robert Louis Jackson, "The Seagull: The Empty Well, the Dry Lake, and the Cold Cave," in *Chekhov*. "Art is at the center of *The Seagull*," writes Jackson. ". . . everybody talks about art. Everybody embodies or lives out a concept of art" (99).

44 Gromov, *Chekhov*, 323.

45 For an analysis of the story, and the cemetery scene in particular, in light of the Gospels

and the Eastern Calendar, see Alexander Mihailovic, "Eschatology and Entombment in 'Ionych,'" in Jackson, *Reading Chekhov's Text.*

46 Belyi, *Simvolizm kak miroponimanie,* 374.

47 Here I apply a modified model of textual interaction which adds to Genette's a distinction between subtextualization and hypertextualization. I see the former as the creation of a text which relies (in some way, not necessarily in terms of a direct textual or authorial contact) upon an established literary source. I see the latter as a textual debate which shapes a text in view of the existence of a point of controversy within an earlier text. These are working definitions and do not represent final conclusions.

48 Vladimir Nabokov, "Chelovek i veshchi," MS, VN Berg. Nabokov discusses Chekhov's Dr. Chebutykin from *The Three Sisters,* who keeps repeating "veshch'" (thing) as a sign of appreciation.

49 Parker, "Vladimir Nabokov," 68.

50 Ibid., 69.

51 Boyd, *RY,* 426. Relevant discussions of the story are found in Matterson, "Sprung from the Music Box of Memory"; Barbara Heldt Monter, "'Spring in Fialta': The Choice That Mimics Chance," in Appel and Newman, eds., *Nabokov;* Linda Nadine Saputelli, "The Long-Drawn Sunset in Fialta," in Connolly and Ketchian, eds., *Studies in Honor of Vsevolod Setschkarëv;* Jim Shepard, "'Spring in Fialta' by Vladimir Nabokov," in Hansen and Shepard, eds., *You've Got to Read This;* Tolstaia and Meilakh, "Russian Short Stories"; Alekandr Zholkovskii, "Philosophy of Composition," in Ronald Vroon and John E. Malmstad, eds., *Readings in Russian Modernism;* and Chapter 7 of Foster's *Nabokov's Art of Memory and European Modernism.*

52 A photograph of Villa Neptune where the Nabokovs stayed in Abbazia in 1904 was printed in Ellendea Proffer, *Vladimir Nabokov,* 21.

53 See Boyd, *RY,* 54–58; 208–211.

54 "Spring in Fialta" was the third story whose translation Nabokov co-authored with Pertzoff. See "Spring in Fialta," corrected TS, VN LC, container 8, folder 20; Boyd, *RY,* 440–446.

55 I am grateful to the curator of the Slavic Collection, Sterling Memorial Library (Yale University), Ms. Tatiana Lorković, for pointing this out.

56 For the details of Chekhov's travels, see Gromov, *Chekhov;* and G. Berdnikov, *Chekhov;* also see N. I. Gitovich, *Letopis' tvorchestva A. P. Chekhova.* A useful survey of Chekhov's connections with France, including the French Riviera, is found in V. B. Kataev, "Frantsiia v sud'be Chekhova," in *Chekhoviana: Chekhov i Frantsiia.* The image of Lika Mizinova hangs over Chekhov's Riviera sojourn of 1894. On Chekhov and Mizinova, see, for instance, Berdnikov, *Chekhov,* 343–364; critics have written about Lika Mizinova as a prototype for the female protagonist of "Ariadna." A case could be made for the presence of Chekhov's "Ariadna" in the background of the dialogue between "Spring in Fialta" and "Lady with a Lap Dog." "Ariadna" (1895) is an imbroglio narrated by its protagonist and partly set in Abbazia on the Dalmatian Riviera. The female protagonist, a slender brunette, tender and sensuous and never fully comprehended by the autobiographical narrator, has something in common with the heroine of "Spring in Fialta." In this chapter, I will limit myself to Nabokov's dialogue with "Lady with a Lap Dog."

57 "To M. P. Chekhova," July 14, 1988, letter in Chekhov, *Pis'ma,* 2:295–296.

58 Also noteworthy is the place of Yalta in Chekhov's and Nabokov's lives. "Lady with a Lap

Dog," written and published in 1899, the year Nabokov was born, records Chekhov's aesthetic aspirations at the time of his increasing rapprochement and intimacy with Ol'ga Knipper, his future wife. Chekhov wrote "Lady with a Lap Dog" in October, and the fresh memories of their time together in Yalta, their walks on the pier and trips to Oreanda, inform the plot of the story (see Gromov, *Chekhov*, 302–308; Berdnikov, *Chekhov*, 455–460). Nabokov might have heard about Chekhov in Yalta directly from Ol'ga Knipper-Chekhova, who was a guest of the Nabokovs during her visit to Berlin in 1921 (Boyd, *RY*, 184); for a memoir of the Nabokovs' Berlin Salon, and specifically of Ol'ga Knipper-Chekhova, see Nicolas Nabokov, *Bagázh*, 109–110. Earlier, in 1917–1919, after fleeing from European Russia to the Crimea, the Nabokovs lived on Countess Panina's estate in Gaspra outside Yalta (on Nabokov in the Crimea, see Boyd, *RY*, 136–160; *SM*, 244–251). Gaspra is famous in literary history because Tolstoi stayed there for almost a year during his illness in 1901. During this illness Chekhov visited him in Gaspra, and Nabokov most certainly knew about this. In the Russian text of his memoir, *Drugie berega*, Nabokov adds a sentence about Chekhov and Tolstoi in Gaspra; see *SSoch*, 4:269. Finally, as Nabokov would later describe it in *Speak, Memory*, Yalta was a place where he longed for his first love, Liusia Shul'gina, from whom he had been separated by the Civil War: "There was I, holding a letter from Tamara. I looked at the abrupt Yayla Mountains, covered up to their rocky brows with the karakul of the dark Tauric pine; at the maquis-like stretch of evergreen vegetation between mountain and sea.... Suddenly I felt all the pangs of exile.... Thenceforth for several years, until the writing of a novel [*Mary*] relieved me of that fertile emotion, the loss of my country was equated for me with the loss of my love" (*SM*, 244–245). In the same episode of the autobiography, Nabokov describes the "white Yalta pier (where, as you remember, the lady of Chekhov's 'Lady with a Lapdog' lost her lorgnette among the vacational crowd)," thereby acknowledging that the story had shaped his perception of Yalta. Nabokov's Yalta is charged with motifs of exile, longing, and first love. As scholars have indicated, "Spring in Fialta" reveals a number of parallels with the "Tamara" chapter of *Speak, Memory* (Matterson, "Sprung from the Music Box of Memory," 104). The Yalta motifs play an important part in *Glory*, which precedes "Spring in Fialta" chronologically. Thus, the reflected and refracted rays of the Yalta motifs, originally Chekhovian, are continuously transformed and shaped betwixt mirrors of Nabokov's poetics and biography.

59 Vladimir Nabokov, "Spring in Fialta," TS with Nabokov's corrections, VN LC, container 8, folder 20.

60 Shepard, "'Spring in Fialta,'" 402.

61 On rhythm in Chekhov's prose, see Bitsilli, *Tvorchestvo Chekhova*, 54–61. Some useful observations on the prosodic structure of the Russian text of "Spring in Fialta" are found in Vasil'ev, "Stranitsa iz rasskaza Nabokova 'Vesna v Fial'te,'" *Filologicheskie nauki* 3 (1991): 33–40, although he never attempts to trace the semantic functions of the prosodic contours of Nabokov's prose. My tentative conclusion is that Nabokov continues to employ the kind of metrical markedness that he uses in both "The Return of Chorb" and "Cloud, Castle, Lake." Consider, for instance, the passage describing Vasen'ka's meeting with Nina in Russia, beginning "Zazhigaiutsia okna i lozhatsia ..." (*VF*, 11) where metrical markedness enhances the exalted sense of privileged if distant memories.

62 On Nabokov's spiral structures in "Spring in Fialta" and elsewhere, see Charles Nicol, "'Ghastly Rich Glass,'" *Russian Literature Triquarterly* 24 (1991): 174–178; Nicol terms the plot of "Spring in Fialta" "a retrograde plot." See also Nabokov's own seminal remarks on the spiral ("The spiral is a spiritualized circle") in *SM,* 275–288.

63 See Tammi, *Problems of Nabokov's Poetics,* 55; Foster, *Nabokov's Art of Memory,* 130–131.

64 Foster provides a scheme of the "large-scale temporal structure" of the story in *Nabokov's Art of Memory,* 246, fn. 5.

65 Vladimir Nabokov, "Spring in Fialta," TS, VN LC, container 8, folder 20.

66 Saputelli, "The Long-Drawn Sunset," 234.

67 For a short lucid discussion of "Spring in Fialta" vs. *The Gift,* see Boyd, *RY,* 427. For an analysis of the otherworld in *The Gift,* see Alexandrov, *Nabokov's Otherworld,* 108–136.

68 Nicol calculated eleven such meetings; see "'Ghastly Rich Glass,'" 175.

69 Shepard, "'Spring in Fialta,'" 402.

70 Zholkovskii pointed this out; see Zholkovskii, "Philosophy of Composition," 393.

71 A. S. Pushkin, *Stikhotvoreniia i poèmy,* 105.

72 Ibid., 122–123.

73 William Blake, *A Selection of Poems and Letters,* 60.

74 To recall Nabokov's "Cloud, Castle, Lake," Vasiliy Ivanovich attempts to read "Silentium" on the train, among his philistine sojourners, en route to an encounter with the otherworld. It is, therefore, not at all suprising that Tiutchev's incantational "Mysl' izrechënnaia est' lozh'" (An uttered thought is a lie) is distorted in Nabokov's short story written some one hundred years later: "My sliz'. Rechënnaia est' lozh'" (*VF,* 337; literally, We are slime. That which is uttered is a lie). Chekhov employs quotations from Tiutchev's poems in several stories. For instance, in *Drama na okhote* (A Shooting Party, 1884) Olen'ka sings a verse from "Vesenniaia groza" (A Springtime Rainstorm, 1829); see Chekhov, 3:270.

75 Fëdor Tiutchev, *Stikhotvoreniia. Pis'ma. Vospominaniia sovremennikov,* 45.

76 Ibid., 45.

77 Robert Louis Jackson, "'The Betrothed': Chekhov's Last Testament," in Savely Senderovich and Munir Sendich, eds., *Anton Chekhov Rediscovered,* 60.

78 For a discussion of some intricacies of Gurov's use of *ty* and *vy,* see Berdnikov, *Chekhov,* 429.

79 See Zholkovskii, "Philosophy of Composition," 397.

80 Movie-eye is a reference to Kino-Eye, the innovative Constructivist approach to filmmaking represented in the theories and films of the Russian cinematographer Dziga Vertov. For a brief summation of Vertov's innovations, see Jay Leyda, *Kino,* 176–179. It would of course be farfetched to suggest any direct parallels with Vertov's narrative technique. However, the metaphor of a movie-eye conveniently describes how Nabokov constructs Vasen'ka as his narrator at the beginning of the story.

81 Zholkovskii ("Philosophy of Composition," 393) labels the sparkle of tin-foil "Chekhovian."

82 The word "Icarus" was added in English. Its mythological connotations are apparent. Tammi offers extremely interesting observations on the recurrence of this fictional car make in Nabokov's artistic universe in *King, Queen, Knave, Despair, Lolita,* and *Look at the Harlequins!;* see Tammi, *Problems of Nabokov's Poetics,* 352.

83 Zholkovskii, "Philosophy of Composition," 398.

84 See Zholkovskii's seminal remarks about the way Vasen'ka as the narrator who loses Nina wishes to compensate his loss by making her part of his narrative ("Philosophy of Composition," 394).

85 Also consider Fowler's important remarks on reading "Spring in Fialta" backward from *Lolita*; see Fowler, *Reading Nabokov*, 67–80.

86 Quoted in L. Maliugin and I. Gitovich, *Chekhov*, 470.

87 Shepard, "'Spring in Fialta,'" 404.

88 William Shakespeare, *The Complete Works*, 889. The long section devoted in *Lectures on Russian Literature* to Chekhov's "V ovrage" (In the Gully, 1900) ends with a reference to King Lear: "Old Grigori dissolves in tears—a weak and silent King Lear" (*LRL*, 280).

4 Nabokov and Bunin: The Poetics of Rivalry

1 W. B. Yeats, "The Cold Heaven," in *The Collected Poems of W. B. Yeats*, ed. Richard J. Finneran, 125.

2 *Stories*, 419.

3 Kirill Zaitsev, "'Buninskii' mir i 'Sirinskii' mir," *Rossiia i slavianstvo* (November 9, 1929): 3. Kirill Zaitsev should not be confused with the well-known writer Boris Zaitsev. After Bunin had been awarded the Nobel Prize in 1933, K. Zaitsev published a book-length interpretation of Bunin's life and art, *I. A. Bunin. zhizn' i tvorchestvo*, the only pre–World War II Russian monograph about Bunin.

4 Zaitsev, "'Buninskii' mir i 'Sirinskii' mir."

5 Nina Berberova, "Nabokov in the Thirties," in Appel and Newman, eds., *Nabokov*, 225.

6 Mikhail Tsetlin, rev. of *Korol', dama, valet* by V. Sirin, *Sovremennye zapiski* 37 (1928): 536–538.

7 "Literaturnaia anketa" (*Chisla*), 322.

8 See, for instance, V. S. Varshavskii, rev. of *Podvig*, by V. Sirin, *Chisla*, 7–8 (1933): 266–267.

9 "Samoe luchshee proizvedenie russkoi literatury poslednego desiatiletiia," *Novaia gazeta* 3 (April 1, 1931): 1–2.

10 Albert Parry, "Belles Lettres among Russian Emigrés," *American Mercury* 29 (July 1933): 317. In 1920s émigré criticism Mark Slonim held a similar position toward Bunin and other writers of his generation, favoring younger émigré writers and the new writing in Soviet Russia. In "Literatura èmigratsii," (*Volia Rossii* 2 [1925]) he spoke of the inertia and stasis among the writers of the older generation in Russia Abroad (176), about Bunin's repeating himself "a thousand times" in his poetry (177); he also punned that Bunin's title of the Russian Academician "fits his writing best" (179). In the sequel to his 1925 article ("Literatura èmigratsii," *Volia Rossii* 3 [1926]), he openly referred to Bunin, Merezhkovskii, and Chirikov—all three actively working in the 1920s—as history rather than contemporaneity, as the literary past (183). In "Molodye pisateli za rubezhom" (*Volia Rossii* 10–11 [1929]), Slonim reiterated his earlier points about Bunin and the writers of the older generations (101); he also awarded, with some reservations, compliments to Nabokov as a fiction writer (115–116), mainly praising Nabokov's handling of "non-Russian" themes.

11 Consider, for instance, the heated polemics that unfolded on the pages of Mark Slonim's short-lived *Novaia gazeta* in 1931, with contributions by Slonim, Aldanov, Terapiano, Gaito Gazdanov, and N. Andreev. For an example of Bunin's reception in the

mid-1920s as the literary bastion of "truth," see T. Tamanin, "Pravda Bunina," *Zveno* (March 30, 1925): 3. For a very fine overview of the émigré cultural climate circa late 1920s, see Roger Hagglund, "The Russian Emigré Debate of 1928 on Criticism," *Slavic Review* 32:3 (September 1973): 515–526.

12   In 1934 the Warsaw weekly review *Mech* 1–14 (The Sword) printed a series of very symptomatic articles devoted to the ideological and cultural rebirth of Russian emigration. The authors included D. Filosofov, V. Zlobin, V. Fëdorov, Dm. Merezhkovskii, and Iu. Fel'zen. Another way of getting into the core of the polemics about the future of émigré literature is to peruse the influential Prague review *Volia Rossii* (The Will of Russia) for 1925 to 1930. See especially Slonim's long two-part essay "Literatura èmigratsii" (1925–1926); his "Molodye pisateli za rubezhom" (1929); and Sergei Postnikov's "Russkaia zarubezhnaia literatura v 1925 godu," *Volia Rossii* 2 (1926): 182–192. See also Georgii Adamovich, "O literature v èmigratsii. I," *Poslednie novosti* (June 11, 1931): 2. Gleb Struve (*Russkaia literatura v izgnanii*) and Raeff (*Russia Abroad*) provide invaluable overviews of the ideological and cultural debates surrounding Russian émigré literature. See also Struve, "Russian Writers in Exile: Problems of an Emigré Literature," in Werner P. Friedrich, ed., *Proceedings of the Second Congress of the International Comparative Literature Association,* 2:592–606.

13   Gleb Struve, one of the shapers of Nabokov's literary legend in the 1930s, spoke of Nabokov's stylistic apprenticeship with Bunin and yet suggested that one could not imagine two writers more dissimilar ("O V. Sirine"). On the other hand, Vladimir Zlobin, who was the secretary of Gippius and Merezhkovskii, also juxtaposed Nabokov and Bunin in a mock-essay "O nashem 'tolstom' zhurnale," *Mech* 8 (1934): 13–14: "Do you know Sirin's hand? One of a master! Bunin has long been outdone. And again, as usual, 'I don't know why my hand wrote this.'"

14   I am grateful to a handful of critics who touched upon the subject of the Nabokov-Bunin relationship in their works. Connolly (*Ivan Bunin,* 31) mentions affinities between the figurations of memory in Bunin, Nabokov, and Proust. Connolly (135) also speaks of Buninesque echoes in Nabokov's works, although he does not specify them. Tammi (*Problems of Nabokov's Poetics,* 12, fn. 34) points out the Nabokov-Bunin opposition as a commonplace in émigré criticism. Bethea (*Joseph Brodsky,* 221) and Zholkovsky ("Philosophy of Composition," 333; *Text Counter Text,* 88–113) mention Bunin's influence. To the best of my knowledge, the only study of Bunin's traces in Nabokov is by Maia Kaganskaia ("Otrechenie," published in the Paris émigré review *Sintaksis* 1 [Syntax] in 1978). In her somewhat tendentious essay, which reflects a number of inherited Russian émigré biases against Nabokov's English works, and especially *Lolita,* Kaganskaia considers his career from *Mary* to *Lolita* as his disavowal of the Turgenev-Bunin tradition. Naumann (*Blue Evenings in Berlin,* 7) lists Bunin among Nabokov's major Russian influences. Zimmermann ("The Russian Short Stories of Vladimir Nabokov," 66–69, 193) discusses the connections between Nabokov's and Bunin's short stories. Several émigré critics, including Struve, Iurii Ivask, Aleksandr Savel'ev, Tsetlin, and Veidle, pointed out affinities between the two writers. Their comments will be considered later in the chapter. Finally, Shakhovskaia included a brief chapter on Bunin and Nabokov in her 1979 book (*V poiskakh Nabokova,* 115–116); she denies Bunin's influence on Nabokov.

15   See Bunin 1:30. See also Paperno and Hagopian, "Official and Unofficial Responses," on Nabokov's reception in the Soviet Union; Tvardovskii's remarks are discussed on 104–106.

16 In *Literaturnoe nasledstvo. Ivan Bunin,* 84, pt. 1:50. The name of a man who sold his shadow to the devil (from Adelbert von Chamisso's tale), Peter Schlemihl has come to mean a person who makes a desperate bargain. In Mikhailov's retrograde view, Nabokov's bargain was supposedly giving up the noble calling and identity of a Russian writer after switching to English.

17 Quoted in Galina Kuznetsova, *Grasskii dnevnik,* 184.

18 This idea is a leitmotif of several articles by Iu. N. Tynianov, including "O literaturnoi èvoliutstii" (On Literary Evolution), "Oda kak oratorskii zhanr" (Ode as an Oratorical Genre), "O parodii" (On Parody), and "Dostoevskii i Gogol' (k teorii parodii)" (Dostoevskii and Gogol' [Toward a Theory of Parody]), all in *Poètika. Istoriia literatury. Kino.*

19 See Militsa Grin, *Ustami Buninykh,* 2:10, 78. Four letters from V. D. Nabokov have survived among Bunin's papers. See "To Ivan Bunin," June 15, 1920, postcard in Bunin Leeds; August 3, 1920, postcard in Bunin Leeds; December 12, 1920, letter in Bunin Leeds; February 19, 1921, letter in Bunin Leeds. Bunin's letters to V. D. Nabokov do not appear to have survived. See also Vera Muromtseva-Bunina's accounts of seeing V. D. Nabokov in Berlin in spring 1920 in Grin, *Ustami Buninykh,* 2:10; see also ibid., 2:83.

20 "To Ivan Bunin," December 12, 1920, postcard in Bunin Leeds. See *Rul'* 10 (November 27, 1920): 3. The poem appeared in Nabokov's collection *Gornii Put'* (The Empyrean Path); see *GP,* 134–135.

21 This can be deduced from V. D. Nabokov's letter of February 19, 1921.

22 The three poems were "Videnie Iosifa" (The Apparition to Joseph), "Krestonostsy" (The Crusaders), and "Pavliny" (Peacocks).

23 V. D. Nabokov suggested that his son's poems be published in Paris in a new literary weekly with Bunin's and Kuprin's participation. It is unclear what edition he refers to in his letter to Bunin of February 19, 1921. In any event, the only two poems that Nabokov published in Paris throughout 1921 were the ones printed in *Contemporary Annals,* "Kto menia povezët . . ." (Who will be driving me . . .) and "Poka v tumane strannykh dnei . . ." (While in the mist of dubious days . . .); see *Sovremennye zapiski* 7 (Oct. 1921): 107–108. It is not impossible, although it is unlikely, that Bunin facilitated the publication of the then virtually unknown Nabokov in the leading émigré review.

24 "To Ivan Bunin," March 18, 1921, letter in Bunin Leeds. A total of eleven letters and seven postcards from Nabokov to Bunin, plus a letter from Nabokov to Vera Muromtseva-Bunina, have survived. At least five books with inscriptions by Nabokov to Bunin have survived.

25 "To Ivan Bunin," November 26, 1922, letter in Bunin Leeds.

26 Ibid.

27 Nabokov, "I. A. Buninu"; *Grozd',* 22; see also *Stikhi,* 38. In *Stikhi* the poem appears under the title "I. A. Buninu" and is dated 1920, not 1922 as in the manuscript.

28 "To Ivan Bunin" [May 11, 1929], postcard in Bunin Leeds.

29 Nabokov, "Iv. Bunin. 'Izbrannye stikhi.'"

30 See A. Dolinin's and R. Timenchik's commentary in Kniga, 520. In a 1966 interview Nabokov assessed Blok's role in his life: "Ever since [my boyhood] I remained passionately fond of Blok's lyrics. His long pieces are weak, and the famous *The Twelve* is dreadful, self-consciously couched in a phony 'primitive' tone, with a pink cardboard Jesus Christ glued on at the end" (*SO,* 97). See also Andrei Chernyshev, ed., "Kak redko . . . ," *Oktiabr'* 1 (1996): 134.

31 Large portions of Nabokov's unpublished letter to Elizabeth Malozemoff, dated Janu-

ary 22, 1938, are quoted in her excellent dissertation. See Malozemoff, "Ivan Bunin, as a Writer of Prose," 67, 78–79.

32 Malozemoff (ibid., 271) quotes from Nabokov's unpublished letter to her dated January 22, 1938.

33 A number of Bunin's books of the émigré period combine poetry and prose under the same cover; see, for instance, *Nachal'naia liubov'*, *Roza Ierikhona*, and *Mitina liubov'*.

34 Brian Boyd (*RY*, 291) is right in calling this decision "deliberate" on Nabokov's part.

35 Bethea, *Joseph Brodsky*, 221. See also Irina Rodnianskaia's comments on the introduction to Nabokov's poetry by the poet Andrei Voznesenskii (*Literaturnoe semiletie*, 88).

36 The formulation is taken from Tynianov's seminal article "Promezhutok" (The Interval, 1924) in *Poètika*, 179.

37 Presentation copy, Vladimir Nabokov, *Mashen'ka* (Berlin: Slovo, 1926), Beinecke Rare Book and Manuscript Library, Yale University.

38 See Kaganskaia, "Otrechenie." Struve also speaks of Bunin's influence upon the descriptions in *Mary*; (*Russkaia literatura v izgnanii*, 284).

39 See "To N. P. Smirnov," January 14, 1961, letter in N. P. Smirnov, ed., "Pis'ma V. N. Buninoi N. P. Smirnovu," *Novyi mir* 3 (1969): 228.

40 Presentation copy, Vladimir Nabokov, *Mashen'ka* (Berlin: Slovo, 1926), 86, Beinecke Rare Book and Manuscript Library, Yale University.

41 A number of times throughout the 1920s works by Nabokov and Bunin appeared next to each other in various publications. See, for instance, *Vestnik glavnogo pravleniia obshchestva gallipoliitsev* (Belgrad: Russkaia tipografiia, 1924), where Bunin contributed an essay (6) and Nabokov a poem (7). See also *Rul'* (April 27, 1924): 6–7 (two poems by Bunin and Nabokov's "Beneficence"); *Sovremennye zapiski* 33 (Dec. 1927) (Bunin's story and Nabokov's *The University Poem*); *Sovremennye zapiski* 40 (installment of Bunin's *The Life of Arseniev* and first installment of Nabokov's *The Defense*).

42 "To Ivan Bunin," n.d. (1931), letter in Bunin Leeds.

43 See Nabokov's reference to Bunin's earlier invitation in "To Ivan Bunin," May 18, 1929, letter in Bunin Leeds.

44 "To Ivan Bunin," October 8, 1930, letter in Bunin Leeds.

45 Presentation copy of Iv. Bunin, *Zhizn' Arsen'eva. Istoki dnei* (Paris: Sovremennye zapiski, 1930), private collection, Orël, Russia. I am grateful to Dr. Richard D. Davies (Leeds Russian Archive) for providing me with a photocopy of the presentation page.

46 Vera Muromtseva-Bunina, diary TS, Bunin Leeds. See also Grin, *Ustami Buninykh*, 2:236.

47 "To Ivan Bunin," October 30, 1931, letter in Bunin Leeds.

48 Kuznetsova, *Grasskii dnevnik*, 124, 184.

49 "Vecher V. V. Sirina," *Poslednie novosti* (November 17, 1932): 3. On Nabokov's 1932 trip to Paris, see Boyd, *RY*, 390–397.

50 Prior to the publication of "Terror," Nabokov appeared in *Contemporary Annals* twice as a poet, in nos. 7 (1921) and 11 (1922).

51 For a passionate account of Nabokov's visit to Paris in 1932, see Nina Berberova, *Kursiv moi*, 2:367–374; the English variant, adopted from *The Italics Are Mine*, is found in her "Nabokov in the Thirties."

52 Vera Muromtseva-Bunina, diary, TS, November 30, 1932, Bunin Leeds. An abridged version was published in Grin, *Ustami Buninykh*, 2:278. In his *Povest' o Vere* (The

Story of Vera, 1967) Boris Zaitsev quotes from Muromtseva-Bunina's letter to his wife, which repeats the diary entry; see Zaitsev, *Zolotoi uzor*, 318. Zaitsev also published Muromtseva-Bunina's letters to his wife in his 1968 *Drugaia Vera. Povest' vremennykh let* (The Other Vera: A Tale of Bygone Years); see Zaitsev, *Zolotoi uzor*, 394–395. In her letter, dated November 14, 1932, Zaitsev's wife speaks of the "great enthusiasm for Sirin" (*uvlechenie Sirinym*) in Russian Paris.

53 Grin, *Ustami Buninykh*, 2:253.

54 In 1931–1932 the general opinion was that Bunin's chance for getting the Nobel Prize was nil. Such was also the sense in Bunin's household; see Grin, *Ustami Buninykh*, 2:252.

55 Vera Muromtseva-Bunina, diary, TS, December 30, 1932, Bunin Leeds. In a letter to N. P. Smirnov written in the 1960s, she repeats Zurov's earlier formulations almost verbatim: "blesk, sverkanie i polnoe otsutstvie dushi" (glamor, shining, and complete absence of soul); see "To N. P. Smirnov," January 14, 1961, letter in Smirnov, "Pis'ma V. N. Buninoi N. P. Smirnovu."

56 Terapiano recalls that the younger poets were cold to Bunin's poetry (*Literaturnaia zhizn' russkogo Parizha*, 278). V. S. Ianovskii (*Polia eliseiskie*, 248) suggests that the poets of the Parisian Note viewed Nabokov's poetry negatively in the light of Bunin's verse.

57 On January 29, 1930, Nabokov published an essay entitled "Na krasnykh lapkakh" (On Little Red Feet) in *The Rudder* next to A. Savel'ev's very favorable analysis of Bunin's love stories of the 1910s–1920s. Nabokov's essay was aimed against a harshly negative and insolent review of Bunin's *Selected Poems* by Aleksei Èisner, published in the Prague journal *Volia Rossii* (The Will of Russia). On October 15, 1930, Nabokov returned to the polemics with Bunin's critics in another essay, "O vosstavshikh angelakh" (On the Rebellious Angels), which was a caustic analysis of the aesthetics of the Prague journal and its radical authors. He was compelled to write the second polemical essay by the appearance of a defense of Èisner by a fellow Prague poet, Viacheslav Lebedev, published in no. 7/8 of *Volia Rossii.*

58 In a 1930 letter to Bunin Nabokov wrote: "Some time ago Gessen [Iosif Gessen] told me about your reaction to [*The Return of Chorb*]—I always feel your kind disposition toward me. See "To Ivan Bunin," n.d. (written after February 6, 1930), letter in Bunin Leeds.

59 Zimmermann, "The Russian Short Stories," 67–68.

60 Cf. Nabokov's English-language short story entitled "First Love."

61 One should also consider the availability of certain texts by Bunin to Nabokov in the 1930s. It is possible to speculate with a fair amount of certainty what émigré collections by Bunin Nabokov owned or could have read. The pre-1917 editions of Bunin's works, especially the separate collections, must have been harder to come by in emigration. To the best of my knowledge, Bunin did not republish either "First Love" (1890) or "Cuckoo" during his émigré years.

62 See Bunin 2:519. The story was included in Bunin's 1924 collection *Roza Ierikhona* (Rose of Jericho). In 1925 a modified version appeared in the Parisian *Vozrozhdenie* (Renaissance). Finally, in 1937 Bunin published a third version, "Vosem' let" (Eight Years), in *The Latest News* as a variant of a draft of *The Life of Arseniev;* see Bunin 6:299–305.

63 See "Pamiati Iu. I. Aikhenval'da," "Pamiati A. M. Chërnogo," and "Pamiati Amalii Osipovny Fondaminskoi."

64 See Bunin 5:531.

65 I should also mention another of Bunin's pre-émigré stories, "Otto Shtein" (1916),

which might have informed "The Aurelian." The protagonist, a young natural scientist who, like Pilgram, lives in Berlin, prepares and undertakes an expedition to tropical countries.

66 Bunin 4:333.

67 See È. A. Polotskaia, "Vzaimootnoshenie poèzii i prozy rannego Bunina," *Izvestiia AN SSSR* 29:5 (September–October 1970): 412–418; Malozemoff, "Ivan Bunin," 269, 279–280.

68 Bunin, *The Gentleman from San Francisco*, 281–282.

69 I am using the most linguistically unloaded terms as they are applied to English-language syntax and sentence structure. John B. Opdycke (*Harper's English Grammar*, 227) defines a complex-complex sentence as a "complex sentence in which a dependent clause is subordinate to another dependent clause" and a complex-compound sentence as consisting "of two or more independent clauses and one or more subordinate or dependent clauses."

70 Malozemoff, "Ivan Bunin," 266.

71 In the text of the Bible, especially the Old Testament, the role of the "and" conjunctions in organizing the syntax can only be discovered by English speakers via reading the King James Bible rather than modern translations such as the Oxford/Cambridge edition, to which I generally refer throughout this study. A student of the Russian Orthodox Bible, which Bunin actually knew very well and drew upon on numerous occasions, will immediately recognize the "i . . . i . . . i" structure.

72 A special case is Nabokov's use of actual units of ternary and binary meters such as the ones in "Cloud, Castle, Lake"; see my discussion in Chapter 2.

73 "To Ivan Bunin," November 10, 1933, letter in Bunin Leeds.

74 See "Vecher v chest' Bunina v Berline," *Vozrozhdenie* (January 11, 1934): 4; Boyd, *RY*, 403–404; Field, *VN*, 157–158. See also Vera Muromtseva-Bunina's diary entry for December 31, 1933, in Grin, *Ustami Buninykh*, 2:299: "Sirin understands [Bunin's] poetry much better than others and recites it with proper sound."

75 Photo and caption from the Kharbin newspaper *Rubezh* (The Border) for December 30, 1933, reproduced in Boyd, *RY*.

76 In August, 1935 Bunin's wife noted in her diary: "Marga [Stepun] is staying until 10 Sept., and Galia [Kuznetsova] is leaving for Goettingen early in October. I think, or, rather, am sure, that for good. They are joining their lives [*oni slivaiut svoi zhizni*]. . . . Galia's staying in our house was uncanny [*ot lukavogo*]." (Grin, *Ustami Buninykh*, 3:15.)

77 Diary entry for May 10, 1936; Grin, *Ustami Buninykh*, 3:18–19, 20.

78 See "To Zinaida Shakhovskaia," October 24, 1936, postcard in ZSh LC. The meeting occurred during Bunin's journey through Germany, after which he became a confirmed anti-Hitlerite. He was humiliated by the German customs officers, which made big news in the Russian émigré community; see Grin, *Ustami Buninykh*, 3:21–22.

79 See Nikolai Andreev, "'Sovremennye zapiski' (Kniga 49, 1932 g.—Chast' literaturnaia)," *Volia Rossii* 4–6 (1932): 183.

80 See Struve, "Current Russian Literature: II. Vladimir Sirin," 440. See also his "O V. Sirine" (*Ruskii v Anglii* [May 15, 1936]: 3), where Struve wrote, somewhat too categorically, "As a stylist, Nabokov learned something from Bunin, but it is difficult to imagine two writers more different in spirit and essence." In 1930 ("Tvorchestvo Sirina") Struve spoke of parts of *The Defense* as being Buninesque, although he stressed that Nabokov's concept of the novel had nothing to do with Bunin's art. Also consider a Ger-

man overview of Russian émigré letters by Arthur Luther, "Russische Emigrantendich-tung," *Die Literatur* 36 (October 1933–September 1934): 146–150, who focuses on Bunin, Nabokov, and Sergei Gornyi.

81   Al. Nazarov, "V. V. Sirin—novaia zvezda v literature," *Novaia zaria* (August 11, 1934): 5.

82   See Bunin's "In the Forest" and Nabokov's "The Passenger," both published in *Lovat Dickson's Magazine* in the mid-1930s.

83   Bitsilli, "Neskol'ko zamechanii o sovremennoi zarubezhnoi literature," 132.

84   Pëtr Bitsilli, "Vozrozhdenie allegorii," *Sovremennye zapiski* 61 (1936): 191.

85   Some patterns in Nabokov's appearances in *Contemporary Annals* are considered by Danièle Beaune, "La publication de Nabokov," *Cahiers de l'émigration russe* 2 (1993): 57–65, who does not attempt any statistics and does not discuss the Nabokov-Bunin re-lationship.

86   See Malozemoff's useful statistics and diagram, "Ivan Bunin," 257[a–c].

87   Bunin was also busy editing his eleven-volume prewar *Works*.

88   See Boyd, *RY*, 422–423.

89   "To Zinaida Shakhovskaia," letter of February 2, 1936, ZSh LC. See also Boyd, *RY*, 423–425; Field, *VN*, 162.

90   "To Véra Nabokova," January 30, 1936, letter quoted in Boyd, *RY*, 423.

91   I am grateful to Dr. Robert Bowie (Miami University, Ohio) for pointing out this detail.

92   "To Véra Nabokova," January 30, 1936, letter quoted in Boyd, *RY*, 423.

93   Berberova, *Kursiv moi*, 292. By the way, in connection with Berberova's reference to Bunin's *Memoirs*, the expression "the italics are mine," which gave its title to Berberova's own memoir, appears on the first page of Bunin's text; see Ivan Bunin, *Vospominaniia*, 7.

94   Quoted in Kuznetsova, *Grasskii dnevnik*, 184.

95   The quotation is from Bunin's letter to Roman Gul'; see "To Roman Gul'," Septem-ber 10, 1952, letter in Roman Gul' Papers, Beinecke Rare Book Library, box 2, fol-der 40.

96   The expression is Nabokov's and appears in his 1966 interview with Herbert Gold: "I note incidentally that professors of literature still assign [Blok and Mandel'shtam] to different schools. There is only one school: that of talent" (*SO*, 97).

97   Nina Berberova, "Nabokov i ego 'Lolita,'" *Novyi zhurnal* 57 (1958): 114–115. See Boyd, *RY*, 424–425; Aleksandr Bakhrakh, *Bunin v khalate*, 78; Bakhrakh, *Po pamiati, po za-pisiam*, 99–104.

98   Zinaida Shakhovskaia [Schakhowskoij], "Un maitre de la jeune littérature russe Wladimir Nabokoff-Sirin," *La cité chrétienne* (July 20, 1937). Shakhovskaia also referred to the same conversation with Bunin in her 1959 article: Jacques Croisé, "Les cas Nabokov ou la blessure de l'exil," *La revue des deux mondes* (August 15, 1959): 663. In *V poiskakh Nabokova* Shakhovskaia provides Russian versions of both articles.

99   See *Literaturnoe nasledstvo. Ivan Bunin*, vol. 84, book 2:335.

100   Berberova, *Kursiv moi*, 298. During a telephone interview on March 20, 1992, Ber-berova told me how much Bunin disliked Nabokov in the later years: "On ego terpet' ne mog, nazyval 'durakom'" (He could not stand him, called him a "fool").

101   "To Vera Muromtseva-Bunina and Ivan Bunin," December 24, 1937, postcard in Bunin Leeds.

102   "To Vladimir Nabokov," February 8, 1938, postcard in VN LC, container 8, folder 17.

103   See Boyd, *RY*, 486–488.

104 "To Zinaida Shakhovskaia," n.d. (1938), postcard in ZSh LC.

105 Boyd, *RY*, 487.

106 Presentation copy of Vladimir Nabokov, *Priglashenie na kazn'* (Paris: Dom knigi, 1938), Beinecke Rare Book Library, Yale University.

107 See "To Ivan Bunin," March 27, 1939, postcard in Bunin Leeds; "To Ivan Bunin," March 29, 1939, postcard in Bunin Leeds; "To Ivan Bunin," n.d. (1939), letter in Bunin Leeds; "To Ivan Bunin," April 2, 1939, letter in Bunin Leeds. Bunin's letter of recommendation (the original is in VN LC, container 8, folder 18) was published by Dmitri Nabokov; see *SL*, 30. See also "To Vladimir Nabokov," April 3, 1939, letter in VN Berg.

108 Grin, *Ustami Buninykh*, 3:34.

109 Andrew Field (*Nabokov: His Life in Part*, 227–228) mixed up many details of the meeting; he described it as taking place at Bunin's apartment and confused Bunin with Kerenskii; see Boyd's corrected version in *RY*, 522.

110 These words of Bunin were reported by Lev Liubimov, an émigré who was repatriated to Russia after World War II and wrote a tendentious and retrograde memoir, "Na chuzhbine" (In a Foreign Land), *Novyi mir* 3 (1957): 167.

111 "To Elizabeth Malozemoff," December 7, 1937, unpublished letter quoted in Malozemoff, "Ivan Bunin," 228.

112 Malozemoff, "Ivan Bunin," 236.

113 Ibid.

114 Kaganskaia, "Otrechenie," 74.

115 Varshavskii, rev. of *Podvig*. I am grateful to Richard D. Davies for providing me with a copy of Varshavskii's review with Bunin's notes and underlinings from the Leeds Russian Archive.

116 "To Mark Aldanov," September 3, 1945, letter in A. F. Zweers, "Perepiska I. Bunina s M. Aldanovym," *Novyi zhurnal* 150 (1983): 179.

117 See the famous photo of the group in *Literaturnoe nasledstvo. Ivan Bunin*, 1:29.

118 Bunin, *O Chekhove*, 220.

119 A survey of Bunin's antimodernist statements would take too much space. Among his representative attacks on Russian modernism, see the 1927 "Iz zapisei" (From the Notes [Bunin 9:279–298]); the 1950 *Vospominaniia*, and his diaries collected in Grin, *Ustami Buninykh*.

120 Bunin was certainly aware that some critics regarded him as one of the major modernists of his time. For instance, one of the most learned émigré critics, Vladimir Veidle, listed Bunin's name along with those of Marcel Proust, André Gide, Thomas Mann, Miguel de Unamuno, W. B. Yeats, Stefan George, and Rainer Maria Rilke in a 1939 article, "Dvadtsat' let evropeiskoi literatury," *Poslednie novosti* (February 10, 1939): 3.

121 For a discussion of Nabokov's "covert modernism," see the section "The Covert Modernism of *The Gift*" in Chapter 7 of Foster's *Nabokov's Art of Memory*. Foster's concern is mainly with the status of memory in Nabokov's fiction vis-à-vis the writings of European modernists.

122 On Nabokov's roots in the Russian Silver Age, especially in the works of Blok, Belyi, and Nikolai Gumilëv, see Alexandrov, *Nabokov's Otherworld*, 213–234.

123 I am thinking in particular about Tzvetan Todorov's *Grammaire du "Décaméron"* (1969). A Russian émigré thinker, I. A. Il'in, discussed the "grammar" of Bunin's "love" in his 1959 book on Bunin, Remizov, and Shmelëv. He emphasized the "mys-

terious" connections between love and death (suicide) in Bunin's stories (*O t'me i prosvetlenii*, 75–76).

124 In his commentary, Mikhailov discussed *Dark Avenues* as Bunin's polemics with "the flagmen of Russian realism"; see Bunin 7:357–358.

125 See, for instance, Irina Odoevtseva, *Na beregakh Seny*, 294, 318, 366.

126 No one thus far has attempted a comparative poetics of Nabokov's short stories and Bunin's *Dark Avenues*. Several works have dealt with the poetics of *Dark Avenues;* see Serge Kryzytski, "Dark Alleys," in *The Works of Ivan Bunin*, 204–213; Adamovich, "Po povodu 'Tëmnykh allei,'" in *Odinochestvo i svododa*, 115–117; Liudmila A. Foster, "O kompozitsii 'Tëmnykh allei' Bunina," *Russian Literature* 9 (1978): 55–65; Mikhail Kreps, "Elementy modernizma v rasskazakh Bunina o liubvi," *Novyi zhurnal* 137 (1979): 54–67 (discusses love stories in general but also several stories from *Dark Avenues*); and A. Baboreko, "Zlatoe drevo zhizni," in *Al'manakh bibliofila*.

127 Berberova, *Kursiv moi*, 293.

128 Grin, *Ustami Buninykh*, 2:95.

129 "To Andrei Sedykh," February 1, 1950, letter in the Papers of Andrei Sedykh, box 1, folder 14, Beinecke Rare Book Library, Yale University. Cf. Nabokov's negative judgment of *The Twelve* in *SO*, 96.

130 Grin, *Ustami Buninykh*, 2:95; Bunin slightly misquotes Mikhail Lermontov's poem "Zhurnalist, chitatel' i pisatel'" (The Journalist, the Reader and the Writer, 1840).

131 Odoevtseva, *Na beregakh Seny*, 309–310.

132 "To M. V. Karamzina," March 29, 1939, letter in A. K. Baboreko, "Pis'ma [I. A. Bunina] k M. V. Karamzinoi," in *Literaturnoe nasledstvo: Ivan Bunin*, 680.

133 "To Mark Aldanov," June 10, 1951, letter in A. F. Zweers, "Perepiska I. A. Bunina s M. A. Aldanovym," *Novyi zhurnal* 155 (1984): 132. See also Andrei Chernyshev, ed., "Ètomu cheloveku . . . ," *Oktiabr'* (1996): 145–146.

134 On Blok's 1909 trip to Italy, see Vl. Orlov, *Gamaiun*, 405–416.

135 See Maria, mon[akhinia] [Mother Maria], "Vstrechi s Blokom," *Sovremennye zapiski* 62 (October 1936): 211–228.

136 See Bakhrakh, *Bunin v khalate*, 96; Bunin did not end up quoting any of Nadia's poems, but I find Bakhrakh's suggestion of the allusion to Nadezhda L'vova very helpful.

137 See Vadim Kreyd, "L'vova, Nadezhda Grigor'evna," in Marina Ledkovsky et al., eds., *Dictionary of Russian Women Writers*. Bunin personally knew Briusov best of all the symbolists and was certainly fully aware of the details surrounding L'vova's death.

138 Grin, *Ustami Buninykh*, 3:81.

139 See, for instance, ibid., 2:66, where Bunin speaks of his quest to create "something new," to "start a book of which Flaubert dreamed, *A Book about Nothing.*" See ibid., 2:185, for a reference to Bunin's reading Maupassant in 1928. See also ibid., 3:94, 97, 100: Bunin reread *Madame Bovary* in 1941. As for the works of Fëdor Sologub, who did dwell at length on erotic topics, Bunin saw them as artistically inferior and stylistically out of the classical mainstream. For his negative remarks about Sologub's *The Petty Demon*, see ibid., 1:157.

140 Once again, I am referring to Girard's seminal theory of "triangular desire" in nineteenth-century literature, as outlined in his *Deceit, Desire, and the Novel*.

141 Odoevtseva, *Na beregakh Seny*, 295.

142 The scene in the train compartment alludes, very gently, to intimate encounters be-

tween Nina and Vasen'ka in "Spring in Fialta." Standing in front of the mirror in a nightgown, Genrikh is described as wearing "night slippers, trimmed with polar fox fur" ("v nochnykh tufliakh, otorochennykh pestsom"). Compare, in "Spring in Fialta," Vasen'ka imagining Nina's late night visit to his room: her "pink ankles above the swan's-down trimming of high-heeled slippers" ("rozovykh shchikolok nad lebiazh'ei opushkoi tufelek"; *Stories,* 420/*VF,* 26).

143 Kaganskaia ("Otrechenie") insists that Nabokov's English works exhibit a rapid shift from the "chaste" (*tselomudrennyi*) to the sexually explicit. Unlike Kaganskaia, I do not see this transition as any sort of "betrayal" by Nabokov of his Russian past.

144 Louis Jacobs, "The Hereafter," in *A Jewish Theology,* 309.

145 Death in fictions by Beckett and Nabokov (his English novels) became the subject of the final chapter of Garrett Stewart's *Death Sentences: Styles of Dying in British Fiction.* I am not sure, however, why the author includes Nabokov in British fiction.

146 On *Solux Rex,* see Johnson's article, "Nabokov's *Solux Rex* and the 'Ultima Thule' Theme."

147 "To M. A. Aldanov," May 6, 1942, letter in Chernyshev, "Kak redko," 132.

148 Toker offers very interesting remarks on the role of death in the closure of Nabokov's "Signs and Symbols" in "'Signs and Symbols' in and out of Contexts."

149 Vladimir E. Alexandrov, "The Pleasures of Fate, or Why Free Will and Chance Are Incompatible with Nabokov's Artistic Form," in Michael S. Flier and Robert P. Hughes, eds., *For SK,* 41.

150 See, for instance, A. F. Zweers's very interesting article "Proustian Passages in Ivan Bunin's *The Life of Arsen'ev,*" *Canadian Slavonic Papers* 30:1 (March 1988): 17–33. Bunin himself admitted in a 1936 letter to Bitsilli that upon reading Proust he "was frightened" (*ispugalsia*) by the "Proustian passages" (*prustovskie mesta*) in his own *The Life of Arseniev. The Well of Days,* which, he insisted, had been written before he finally got around to reading Proust; see A. Meshcherskii, "Neizvestnye pis'ma I. Bunina," *Russkaia literatura* 4 (1961): 154. Foster investigates the comparative functions of memory in works by Proust and Nabokov in his *Nabokov's Art of Memory.* The poetics of memory in Bunin's and Nabokov's short stories have not been explored in separate studies. Nabokov's dialogue with Bunin's *The Life of Arseniev,* occurring in *The Gift* simultaneously on several thematic and structural levels, calls for a separate investigation. Of special interest would be a comparative analysis of the "father" theme, the childhood recollections, and the "literary" theme in both autobiographical novels.

151 The last collection, for which Bunin himself made the selection, was the 1954 *Petlistye ushi i drugie rasskazy* (Loopy Ears and Other Stories).

152 The collection was supposed to have been published in 1939 by the publishing house Russkie zapiski (Russian Annals). See Nabokov's correspondence with Russkie zapiski, VN LC, container 8, folder 16.

153 It is also worth considering that the complete texts of *The Life of Arsen'ev* and *The Gift* both were published in 1952 by Chekhov Publishing House.

154 Odoevtseva, *Na beregakh Seny,* 290.

155 "To Mark Aldanov," February 9, 1951, letter in A. F. Zweers, "Perepiska I. A. Bunina s M. A. Aldanovym," *Novyi zhurnal* 154 (1984): 101–102. See also Chernyshev, "Ètomu cheloveku," 144.

156 See "To Mark Aldanov," February 2, 1951, letter in Chernyshev, "Kak redko," 140.

157 "To Mark Aldanov," June 10, 1951, letter in Zweers, "Perepiska I. A. Bunina s M. A.

Aldanovym," *Novyi zhurnal* 155 (1984): 131. See also Chernyshev, "Ètomu cheloveku," 145–146.

158 Nabokov also mentioned Bunin in the forewords to *SO* (xvii) and *The Gift* ("gone are Bunin, Aldanov, Remizov"). In a 1971 interview with Parker ("Vladimir Nabokov," 72) he named "Light Breathing" as his favorite short story by Bunin.

159 Boyd, *AY*, 25; Chernyshev, "Kak redko," 128.

160 Boyd, *AY*, 137. Nabokov mentioned Bunin's "The Gentleman from San Francisco" as suggested reading for Harvard students. See "To M. Karpovich," October 12, 1951, letter in *SL*, 127.

161 "To Francis Brown," April 19, 1951, letter in *SL*, 119.

162 Commentary in Bunin 5:536; Ivan Bunin, *Bozh'e drevo*, 94.

163 "To Mark Aldanov," May 6, 1942, letter in Chernyshev, "Kak redko," 132.

164 Bloom, *The Anxiety of Influence*, 30. Nabokov's *Ada* may also encode a reference to Bunin. Considering that Van Veen's Russian name is Ivan and that he, like Bunin, was born in 1870 (Ivan Veen—Ivan Bunin; anagramatism)—and given the significance of Russian gentry culture, Bunin's native substratum, in the framework of the novel— Nabokov's protagonist, whom he both loved and "loathed" (*SO*, 120) could be the last tribute to Bunin's dual function in his Russian career.

Coda

1 John Keats, *The Letters of John Keats*, 305.

2 Julian Connolly provides a compelling reading of the story in "Nabokov and the Narrative Point of View," *Nabokov Studies* 1 (1994): 9–20.

3 For an examination of Nabokov's readership in pre-perestroika Russia, see Paperno and Hagopian, "Official and Unofficial Responses." Their article supplements Ellendea Proffer's pioneering essay, "Nabokov's Russian Readers." Distribution of *tamizdat* and *samizdat* literature in the Soviet Union was an abnormal process which exalted the reader's expectations and made the act of reading both unnecessarily rushed and perfunctory. Only after the wave of post-1987 Russian editions did Nabokov gain a proper massive audience in Russia; see Aleksei Zverev, "Literary Return to Russia," in Alexandrov, ed., *The Garland Companion*, 291–305.

4 I have discussed this issue in more detail in Chapter 2.

5 Charles Newman, "Beyond Omniscience," *TriQuarterly* 10 (Fall 1967): 37–52.

6 In 1959–1966 Nabokov worked—off and on—on a short story entitled "The Admirable Anglewing"; he never brought the project to fruition; see Boyd, *AY*, 379, 385, 508. In his 1971 interview ("Vladimir Nabokov," 70), Stephen Jan Parker asked Nabokov whether he was contemplating any new short stories. Nabokov responded that "now and then a very complete image flashes before [him], quivers for a moment and is firmly dismissed." He admitted "conserving" his energy for "ampler tasks."

7 See *SL*, "Letters Written in Germany and France, 1923–1939," and *PSS*. Parts of Nabokov's Russian correspondence are deposited at the Berg Collection, New York Public Library; the Library of Congress; Leeds Russian Archive, Brotherton Library, University of Leeds; Bakhmeteff Archive, Columbia University Library; Beinecke Library, Yale University; Hoover Institution, Stanford University; and other archives. I have examined parts of his literary correspondence of the 1920s–1930s, including that with Nina Berberova, Ivan Bunin, Vladislav Khodasevich, Zinaida Shakhovskaia, and others.

8 See William Mills Todd III, *The Familiar Letter as a Literary Genre in the Age of Pushkin.* For a concise overview to the problem of familiar letter in the Age of Pushkin, see the introduction, 3–18.

9 For an overview of the Formalists' studies of the Russian familiar letter, see ibid., 13–16. The term *ustanovka* was defined by Tynianov in a seminal article, "Oda kak oratorskii zhanr" (Ode as an Oratorical Genre, 1922): "*Ustanovka* is not only the dominant of a literary work (or genre) which charges the subordinate factors with their functions, but also the function of a literary work (or genre) with respect to the closest non-literary speech series [*rechevoi riad*]" (*Poètika,* 228). Nabokov's business letters are precisely such a nonliterary speech series vis-à-vis his literary letters. Tynianov discusses the Russian familiar letter in another important article, "Literaturnyi fakt" (Literary Fact, 1924); see Tynianov, *Poètika,* 265–267.

10 My use of the term "aesthetic function" is close to Jan Mukařovský's and to Roman Jakobson's "poetic function." By the prevalence of the aesthetic function over the communicative in Nabokov's literary letters I mean that while they do deliver a given amount of information to the addressee (i.e., they communicate information), their foremost function is to reflect upon their own poetics. Mukařovský deals with the aesthetic function in several works, including the 1936 monograph translated into English as *Aesthetic Function, Norm and Value as Social Facts.* Mukařovský speaks, among other things, of "the competition between the aesthetic and the communicative functions in literature" (9).

11 Todd, *The Familiar Letter,* 192.

12 See Bunin's literary wills in Bunin 9:480–483.

13 Quoted in Bunin's diary entry for July 8, 1941; see Grin, *Ustami Buninykh,* 3:103; see also 30, 99, 103, 112, 130, 156–157, 175.

14 "To Svetlana Siewert," May 25, 1923, letter quoted in Gol'denberg, "Budem," 44–45. A typewritten copy of the letter is in ZShLC.

15 "To Ivan Bunin," March 18, 1921, letter in Bunin Leeds.

16 "To Ivan Bunin," November 26, 1922, letter in Bunin Leeds.

17 The transformation of images and motifs from the letter to the short story was a gradual one, as becomes apparent if one compares the newspaper version of "Beneficence" with the book version. The style of the newspaper version, more in line with a spontaneous emotional letter than controlled fictional prose, is improved significantly in the book version. For instance, compare the following sentence from *The Rudder* version with the one quoted in the main text: "Chërnye stëkla byli v melkikh, chastykh kapliakh dozhdia, chto napomnilo nochnoe nebo, splosh' podërnutoe biserom zvëzd."

18 See Parker, "Vladimir Nabokov," 71.

19 "To Ivan Bunin," April 8, 1939, postcard in Bunin Leeds.

20 "To Ivan Bunin," May 18, 1929, letter in Bunin Leeds.

21 On Liusia Shul'gina, see Boyd, *RY,* 110–160.

22 A. N. Apukhtin, *Polnoe sobranie stikhotvorenii,* 223.

23 Ibid., 241. Zimmermann identifies Apukhtin's poems in her very illuminating discussion of "The Admiralty Spire" ("The Russian Short Stories," 87–90). She also makes very good observations on the Russian cultural milieu right before the Revolution, especially the gypsy songs, of which Nabokov's narrator speaks at considerable length.

24 Boyd, *AY,* 87.

25 In a different letter to his sister Elena, Nabokov recalls having mistakenly attributed Afanasii Fet's poem to Apukhtin in 1914; see *PSS,* 58.

26 In *Mary* (67), Ganin "would plunge into the black, bubbling darkness and ignite the soft flame of his bicycle lamp; and now, when he inhaled the smell of carbide, it brought back everything else. . . ."

27 Zimmermann notes that in *Speak, Memory* Nabokov's account of composing verse is "taken almost verbatim" from "Torpid Smoke" ("The Russian Short Stories," 225).

28 I am indebted to Alexandrov's analysis of the relationship between aesthetics, ethics, and metaphysics in *Speak, Memory;* see Chapter 2 in *Nabokov's Otherworld,* 23–57. Alexandrov also makes a case for Nabokov's use in *Speak, Memory* of devices "that one normally associates with works of fiction" (*Nabokov's Otherworld,* 46–50).

29 I am not interested in all facets of Nabokov's career; for details of Nabokov's life in 1937, see Boyd, *RY,* 432–446.

30 On shifters, see Roman Jakobson, "Shifters, Verbal Categories, and the Russian Verb," in his *Selected Writings,* 2:130–147.

31 Henry D. Wild et. al., eds., *A Selection of Latin Verses with Notes,* 49.

32 Both Shklovskii's *Zoo* and Nabokov's *Lolita* are examined in Linda S. Kauffman, *Special Delivery.*

33 I have not dealt here with the short-fictional and autobiographical status of "Mademoiselle O" because it has already received detailed consideration in Foster, "An Archeology of 'Mademoiselle O,'" in Nicol and Barabtarlo, eds., *A Small Alpine Form,* 111–135, and *Nabokov's Art of Memory,* 110–129. In *Nabokov's Art of Memory* Foster speaks of Nabokov's "fascination with the uncertain boundaries between fiction and autobiography"; see also Hal H. Rennert, "Literary Revenge," *Germano-Slavica* 4:6 (1984): 331–338. "Tamara" was published in *The New Yorker* in 1949; "Lodgings in Trinity Lane" (which corresponds to Chapter 13 of *Speak, Memory*), appeared in *Harper's Magazine* in 1951. I anticipate that some readers might object to my not having engaged the subject of *Pnin*'s serialization in *The New Yorker* prior to its publication in a book form. *Pnin* was conceived as a novel, and the fact that Nabokov had four of its seven chapters published as separate magazine pieces testifies to his keen sense of the literary market. However, the serial publication of four chapters of *Pnin* is drastically different from the publication of "Mademoiselle O," which was conceived as a short story/memoiristic essay to be published in the French periodical *Mèsures.* In the 1920s and 1930s Nabokov published a number of excerpts from his Russian novels in émigré newspapers, usually assigning them storylike titles, but this does not qualify such excerpts to be considered short stories.

34 See Boyd, *RY,* 420–421.

35 In this discussion I have not touched upon the subject of Nabokov's fictional pseudo-autobiography (*Look at the Harlequins!*), in which the epistolary dimension plays a very significant part. This subject still awaits its investigator. One should always keep in mind that "Being in Love," a key poem for understanding Nabokov's otherworld, appears in this novel. Also pertinent here is V's re(w)righting of his brother's biography in *The Real Life of Sebastian Knight.*

36 O. E. Mandel'shtam, *Sobranie sochinenii,* 66.

37 In the Russian, the end of the passage reads as follows: "Vsë èto sootvetstvuet teorii ontogeneticheskogo povtoreniia proidennogo. Filogeneticheski zhe, v pervom cheloveke osoznanie sebia ne moglo ne sovpast' s zarozhdeniem chuvstva vremeni" (*SSoch,* 4:137). In the English, Nabokov replaced the biological terms with less specific ones: "All this is as it should be according to the theory of recapitulation; the beginning of

reflexive consciousness in the brain of our remotest ancestor must surely have coincided with the dawning of the sense of time" (*SM*, 21). In the last chapter of *Speak, Memory* Nabokov speaks of the "phylogenetic passion" boys have for "things on wheels" (*SM*, 300).

38 In Chapter 1 of *The Magician's Doubts*, Michael Ward considers the applicability of Poststructuralist theory to Nabokov's œuvre.

39 Pushkin, *Stikhotvoreniia*, 95.

40 Wallace Stevens, *The Collected Poems*, 406–407.

41 Vladimir Nabokov, "Grand Overture. The Philosophy of Fiction," MS, VN LC, container 8, folder 11.

Works Cited

. . . .

Works by Vladimir Nabokov

The list below contains only Nabokov's periodical publications and contributions to anthologies. For separate book editions, consult the List of Abbreviations. Unless otherwise indicated, the works appeared under Nabokov's regular pre–World War II pen-name, "V[ladimir] Sirin," or under his real name, "Vladimir Nabokov."

"Admiralteiskaia igla." *Poslednie novosti* 4456 (June 4, 1933): 3; 4457 (June 5, 1933): 2.
"Alter Ego." Tr. from the Russian of Afanasii Fet. *The Russian Review* 3:1 (Autumn 1943): 31.
"The Assistant Producer." *The Atlantic Monthly* 171:5 (May 1943): 68–74.
"The Aurelian." *The Atlantic Monthly* 168:5 (November 1941): 618–625.
"Bakhman." *Rul'* 1192 (November 2, 1924): 2–3; 1193 (November 4, 1924): 2–3.
"'Beatriche' V. I. Piotrovskogo." Rev. of *Beatriche,* by V. I. Piotrovskii. *Rossiia i slavianstvo* 98 (October 11, 1930): 4.
"Blagost'." *Rul'* 1032 (April 27, 1924): 6–7.
"Britva." *Rul'* 1586 (February 19, 1926): 2–3.
"Butterflies." *The New Yorker* 24:16 (June 1948): 25–28.
"Chto vsiakii dolzhen znat'?" *Novaia gazeta* 5 (May 1, 1931): 3.
"Cloud, Castle, Lake." *The Atlantic Monthly* 167:6 (June 1941): 737–741.
"Colette." *The New Yorker* 24:23 (July 31, 1948): 19–22.
"Davno-l'—po naberezhnoi snezhnoi. . . ." *Sovremennye zapiski* 7 (October 1921): 108.
"Double Talk." *The New Yorker* 21:19 (June 23, 1945): 20–25.
"Draka." *Rul'* 1465 (September 26, 1925): 2–3.
"Exile." *Partisan Review* 18:1 (January–February 1951): 45–58.
"A Forgotten Poet." *The Atlantic Monthly* 174:4 (October 1944): 60–65.
"Groza." *Segodnia* 221 (September 28, 1924): 6.
"I. A. Bunin. 'Izbrannye stikhi.'" Rev. of *Izbrannye stikhi,* by Ivan Bunin. *Rul'* 2577 (May 22, 1929): 2–3.
"I. A. Buninu." *Rul'* 560 (October 1, 1922): 2.

"Irina Odoevtseva. 'Izol'da.'" Rev. of *Izol'da*, by Irina Odoevtseva. *Rul'* 2715 (October 30, 1929): 5.

"Istreblenie tiranov." *Russkie zapiski* 8–9 (August–September 1938): 3–29.

"Iz Kalmbrudovoi poèmy 'Nochnoe puteshestvie.'" *Rul'* 3223 (July 5, 1931): 2.

"Iubilei." *Rul'* 2120 (November 19, 1927): 2.

"Kartofel'nyi Èl'f." *Russkoe èkho*. 5 parts in 24:44 (June 8, 1924): 6–7; 24:45 (June 15, 1924): 5–7; 24:46 (June 22, 1924): 8; 24:47 (June 29, 1924): 6–7; 24:48 (July 6, 1924): 12. Rpt. *Rul'* 2754 (December 15, 1929): 2–3; 2755 (December 17, 1929): 2–3; 2756 (December 18, 1929): 2–3; 2757 (December 19, 1929): 2.

"Katastrofa." *Segodnia* 155 (July 13, 1924): 5–6.

"Kèmbridzh." *Rul'* 288 (October 28, 1921): 2.

"Khvat." *Segodnia* 273 (October 2, 1932): 4; 275 (October 4, 1932): 2.

"Korolëk." *Poslednie novosti* 4505 (July 23, 1933): 6; 4506 (July 24, 1933): 2.

"Kostër." In *Vestnik glavnogo pravleniia obshchestva gallipoliitsev*, 7. Berlgrad: n.p., 1924.

Kto menia povezët . . ." *Sovremennye zapiski* 7 (October 1921): 107–108.

"Krasavitsa." *Poslednie novosti* 4895 (August 18, 1934): 3.

"Krestonostsy." *Rul'* 43 (January 7, 1921): 3.

"Lance." *The New Yorker* 27:51 (February 2, 1952): 21–25.

"Lebeda." *Poslednie novosti* 3966 (January 31, 1932): 2–3.

"Les." *Rul'* 10 (November 27, 1920): 3. Signed "Cantab."

"Lik." *Russkie zapiski* 14 (February 1939): 3–27.

"Lodgings in Trinity Lane." *Harper's Magazine* 202:1208 (January 1951): 84–91.

"Mademoiselle O." *Mèsures* 2:2 (April 15, 1936): 145–172. Signed "V. Nabokoff-Sirine."

"Mademoiselle O." Tr. Vladimir Nabokov and Hilda Ward. *The Atlantic Monthly* 171:1 (January 1943): 66–73.

"Mest'." *Russkoe èkho*, April 20, 1924: 6–8. Rpt. *Zvezda* 11 (1996): 22–25.

"Muzyka." *Poslednie novosti* 4022 (March 27, 1932): 3.

"My s toboiu tak verili v sviaz' bytiia. . . ." *Grani* 44 (1959): 62–63. Signed "Vl. Nabokov-Sirin."

"Nabor." *Poslednie novosti* 5260 (August 18, 1935): 3.

"Na krasnykh lapkakh." *Rul'* 2789 (January 29, 1930): 2–3.

"Nezhit'." *Rul'* 43 (January 7, 1921): 3.

"Obida." *Poslednie novosti* 3763 (July 12, 1931): 2–3.

"Obrashchenie." *Sovremennye zapiski* 70 (April 1940): 128–129. Signed "Vas. Shishkov."

"Odinochestvo." *Poslednie novosti* 5881 (May 2, 1937): 3–4.

"O Khodaseviche." *Sovremennye zapiski* 69 (July 1939): 262–264.

"On Discovering a Butterfly." *The New Yorker* 19:13 (May 15, 1943): 26.

"Opoveshchenie." *Poslednie novosti* 4763 (April 8, 1934): 2.

"Ot"ezd Ardaliona." *Poslednie novosti* 4610 (November 5, 1933): 3.

"O vosstavshikh angelakh." *Rul'* 3006 (October 15, 1930): 2.

"Ozero, oblako, bashnia." *Russkie zapiski* 2 (1937): 33–42.

"Pamiati Amalii Osipovny Fondaminskoi." In *Pamiati Amalii Osipovny Fondaminskoi*, 69–72. Paris: n.p., 1937.

"Pamiati A. M. Chërnogo." *Poslednie novosti* 4161 (August 13, 1932): 3.

"Pamiati Iu. I. Aikhenval'da" ("Uznavat' cheloveka znachit . . ."). *Rul'* 2457 (December 23, 1928): 5.

"Pamiati L. I. Shigaeva." *Illiustrirovannaia zhizn'*, September 27, 1934.

"Paskhal'nyi dozhd'." *Russkoe èkho,* April 12, 1925. Rpt. *Zvezda* 4 (1999): 57–61.

"Passazhir." *Rul'* 1905 (March 6, 1927): 2–3.

"The Passenger." Tr. Gleb Struve. *Lovat Dickson's Magazine* 2 (1934): 719–725.

"Pavliny." *Rul'* 43 (January 7, 1921): 3.

"Pil'gram." *Sovremennye zapiski* 43 (July 1930): 191–207.

"Pis'mo v Rossiiu." Subtitled "Iz vtoroi glavy romana 'Schast'e.'" *Rul'* 1263 (January 29, 1925): 2–3.

"The Poets." *TriQuarterly* 17 (Winter 1970): 5.

"Poèty." *Grani* 44 (1959): 63. Signed "Vl. Nabokov-Sirin."

"Poèty." *Sovremennye zapiski* 69 (1939): 214–215. Signed "Vas. Shishkov."

"Poèty." *TriQuarterly* 17 (Winter 1970): 4.

"Poka v tumane strannykh dnei. . . ." *Sovremennye zapiski* 7 (October 1921): 107–108.

"Pomplimusu." *Sovremennye zapiski* 47 (1931): 233.

"Port." *Rul'* 1055 (May 24, 1924): 2–3.

"Poseshchenie muzeia." *Sovremennye zapiski* 68 (March 1939): 76–87.

"Probuzhdenie." *Sovremennye zapiski* 47 (1931): 232–233.

"Progulka v Gruneval'd." *Poslednie novosti* 6170 (February 15, 1938): 3.

"Putevoditel' po Berlinu." *Rul'* 1540 (December 24, 1925): 2–3.

"Rasskaz." *Poslednie novosti* 4735 (March 11, 1934): 3; 4736 (March 12, 1934): 3.

"The Return of Tchorb." Tr. Gleb Struve. *This Quarter* 4:4 (June 1932): 592–602.

"Rozhdestvenskii rasskaz." *Rul'* 2458 (December 25, 1928): 2–3.

"Rozhdestvo." *Rul'* 1243 (January 6, 1925): 2–3; 1245 (January 8, 1925): 2.

"Scenes from the Life of a Double Monster." *The Reporter* 18:6 (March 20, 1958): 34–37.

"Skazka." *Rul'* 1691 (June 27, 1926): 2–3; 1692 (June 29, 1926): 2–3.

"Slava." *Novyi zhurnal* 3 (1942): 157–161.

"Slovo." *Rul'* 640 (January 7, 1923): 9–10.

"Sluchai iz zhizni." *Poslednie novosti* 5295 (September 22, 1935): 3.

"Sluchainost'." *Segodnia* 139 (June 22, 1924): 7–8.

"Smert' Aleksandra Iakovlevicha." *Poslednie novosti* 6238 (April 24, 1938): 3.

"Solus Rex." *Sovremennye zapiski* 70 (1940): 5–36.

"Sovershenstvo." *Poslednie novosti* 4120 (July 3, 1932): 2–3.

"Spring in Fialta." *Harper's Bazaar* 81 (May 19, 1947): 138, 190, 192, 194, 203, 204, 206, 208, 219.

"Still ist die nacht" (*sic*). *Poslednie novosti* 4582 (October 8, 1933): 3.

"The Swallow." Tr. from the Russian of Afanasii Fet. *The Russian Review* 3:1 (Autumn 1943): 32.

"Symbols and Signs." *The New Yorker* 24:12 (May 15, 1948): 31–33.

"Tamara." *The New Yorker* 25:42 (December 10, 1949): 35–39.

"Terra Incognita." *Poslednie novosti* 3896 (November 22, 1931): 2–3.

"That in Aleppo Once. . . ." *The Atlantic Monthly* 172:5 (November 1943): 88–92.

"Tiazhëlyi dym." *Poslednie novosti* 5092 (March 3, 1935): 3.

"Time and Ebb." *The Atlantic Monthly* 175:1 (January 1945): 81–84.

"Torzhestvo dobrodeteli." *Rul'* 2819 (March 5, 1930): 2–3.

"Triangle within Circle." *The New Yorker* 139:5 (May 23, 1963): 37–41.

"Udar kryla." *Russkoe èkho* 1 (January 1924). Rpt. *Zvezda* 11 (1996): 10–21.

"Ultima Thule." *Novyi zhurnal* 1 (1942): 49–77.

"Universitetskaia poèma." *Sovremennye zapiski* 33 (December 1927): 223–254.

"Uzhas." *Sovremennye zapiski* 30 (1927): 214–220.

"The Vane Sisters." *Hudson Review* 11:4 (Winter 1958–1959): 491–503.
"Vasilii Shishkov." *Poslednie novosti* 6742 (September 12, 1939): 3.
"Venetsianka." *Zvezda* 11 (1996): 26–41.
"Vesna v Fial'te." *Sovremennye zapiski* 61 (July 1936): 91–113.
"Videnie Iosifa." *Rul'* 43 (January 7, 1921): 3.
"Vozvrashchenie Chorba." *Rul'* 1505 (November 12, 1925): 2–3; 1506 (November 13, 1925): 2–3.
"Vstrecha." *Poslednie novosti* 3936 (January 1, 1932): 2–3.
"When life is a torture, when hope is a traitor. . . ." Tr. from the Russian of Afanasii Fet. *The Russian Review* 3:1 (Autumn 1943): 31.
"Zaniatoi chelovek." *Poslednie novosti* 3863 (October 20, 1931): 2–3.
"Zoorlandiia." *Rossiia i slavianstvo* 149 (October 30, 1931): 3–4.
"Zvonok." *Rul'* 1969 (May 22, 1927): 2–4. Reprint *Libavskoe russkoe slovo* 126 (1927): 2; 127 (1927): 2; 128 (1927): 2.

Other Works

Abyzov, Iurii. *Russkoe pechatnoe slovo v Latvii: 1917–1940. Bio-bibliograficheskii spravochnik.* 4 vols. Stanford: Stanford Slavic Studies, 1991.

Adamovich, Georgii. "Bunin. Vospominaniia." *Novyi zhurnal* 105 (1971): 115–137.

———. "Literatura v 'Russkikh zapiskakh.'" *Poslednie novosti* 6534 (February 16, 1939): 3.

———. "Literaturnye zametki." *Poslednie novosti* 6752 (September 22, 1939): 3.

———. "Litsa i knigi." *Sovremennye zapiski* 52 (1933): 324–334.

———. *Odinochestvo i svoboda.* New York: Izdatel'stvo imeni Chekhova, 1955.

———. "O literature v èmigratsii. I." *Poslednie novosti* 3732 (June 11, 1931): 2.

———. "Po povodu stat'i Shestova 'Tvorchestvo iz nichego.'" *Mosty* 5 (1960): 117–120.

———. "'Russkie zapiski.' Chast' literaturnaia." *Poslednie novosti* (September 15, 1938): 3.

———. "Sirin." *Poslednie novosti* 4670 (January 4, 1934): 3.

———. "'Sovremennye zapiski' kn. 43-ia." *Poslednie novosti* 3424 (August 7, 1930): 3.

———. "'Sovremennye zapiski' kn. 45-ia. Chast' literaturnaia." *Poslednie novosti* 3536 (November 27, 1930): 2.

———. "'Sovremennye zapiski.' Kniga 61.—Chast' literaturnaia." *Poslednie novosti* 5606 (June 30, 1936): 3.

———. "'Sovremennye zapiski'—kniga 69-aia. Chast' literaturnaia." *Poslednie novosti* 6716 (August 17, 1939): 3.

Aikhenval'd, Iu[lii]. "Literaturnye zametki." *Rul'* 1877 (February 2, 1927): 2–3.

Alexandrov, Vladimir E. *Andrei Bely: The Major Symbolist Fiction.* Cambridge: Harvard University Press, 1985.

———. "Nabokov's Metaphysics of Artifice: Uspenskij's 'Fourth Dimension' and Evreinov's 'Theatrarch.'" *Rossija/Russia* 6:1–2 (1988): 131–144.

———. *Nabokov's Otherworld.* Princeton: Princeton University Press, 1991.

———. "A Note on Nabokov's Anti-Darwinism, or Why Apes Feed on Butterflies in *The Gift.*" In G. S. Morson and E. C. Allen, eds., *Freedom and Responsibility in Russian Literature: Essays in Honor of Robert Louis Jackson,* 239–244. Evanston: Northwestern University Press, 1996.

———. "The Pleasures of Fate, or Why Free Will and Chance Are Incompatible with Nabokov's Artistic Form." In Michael S. Flier and Robert P. Hughes, eds., *For SK: In*

Celebration of the Life and Career of Simon Karlinsky, Berkeley: Berkeley Slavic Specialties, 1994. 41–50.

———. [Vladimir Aleksandrov]. "Spasenie ot èmigratsii u Nabokova." *Diapazon* 1 (1993): 24–29.

———, ed. *The Garland Companion to Vladimir Nabokov*. New York: Garland Publishing, 1995.

Andreev, Nikolai. "Sirin." *Nov'* (October 1930): 3.

———. "'Sovremennye zapiski' (Kniga 49, 1932 g.— Chast' literaturnaia)." *Volia Rossii* 4–6 (1932): 183–186.

Angell, Roger. *Nothing But You: Love Stories from the New Yorker*. New York: Random House, 1997.

Appel, Alfred, Jr. "Nabokov: A Portrait." In Rivers and Nicol, eds., *Nabokov's Fifth Arc*, 3–21.

Appel, Alfred Jr., and Charles Newman, eds. *Nabokov: Criticism, Reminiscences, Translations and Tributes*. Evanston: Northwestern University Press, 1970.

Apukhtin, A. N. *Polnoe sobranie stikhotvorenii*. Leningrad: Sovetskii pisatel', 1991.

Austin, J. L. *How to Do Things with Words*. New York: Oxford University Press, 1962.

Baboreko, A. I. A. Bunin. *Materialy dlia biografii (s 1870 po 1917)*. Moscow: Khudozhestvennaia literatura, 1967.

———. "Zlatoe drevo zhizni." In *Al'manakh bibliofila* 12:65–85. Moscow: Kniga, 1982.

Bahlow, Hans. *Deutsches Nameslexicon*. Hamburg: Gondrom Verlag, 1988.

Bakhrakh, Aleksandr. *Bunin v khalate (po pamiati, po zapisiam)*. Bayville, NJ: Tovarishchestvo zarubezhnykh pisatelei SShA, 1979.

———. *Po pamiati, po zapisiam. Literaturnye portrety*. Paris: La presse libre, 1980.

Bakhtin, M. M. *Literaturno-kriticheskie stat'i*. Moscow: Khudozhestvennaia literatura, 1986.

Barabtarlo, Gennady. *Aerial View: Essays on Nabokov's Art and Metaphysics*. New York: Peter Lang, 1993.

———. "English Short Stories." In Alexandrov, ed., *The Garland Companion to Vladimir Nabokov*, 101–117.

———. "A Skeleton in Nabokov's Closet: 'Mest'.'" Nicol and Barabtarlo, eds., *A Small Alpine Form*, 15–23.

———. "To Prince Kachurin—for Edmund Wilson." *The Nabokovian* 29 (Fall 1992): 30–34.

Barnstead, John A. "Nabokov, Kuzmin, Chekhov and Gogol': Systems of Reference in 'Lips to Lips.'" In Connolly and Ketchian, eds., *Studies in Honor of Vsevolod Setschkarëv*, 50–60.

Barthes, Roland. "The Death of the Author." In Roland Barthes, *Image, Music, Text*, ed. and tr. Stephen Heath, 142–148. New York: Hill and Wang, 1977.

Beaune, Danièle. "La publication de Nabokov: Un tournant dans l'orientation des *Annales Contemporaines*." *Cahiers de l'émigration russe* 2 [Special issue: *Vladimir Nabokov et l'émigration*] (1993): 57–65.

Beilage zur Franzenbader Kurliste für die Saison 1937. Franzenbad: n.p., 1937.

Beilage zur Marienbader Kurliste für die Saison 1937. Marienbad: Herausgegeben vom Stadtrat, 1937.

Belyi, Andrei. *Maski*. Moscow: GIKhL, 1932.

———. *Simvolizm kak miroponimanie*. Moscow: Respublika, 1994.

Bem, A[l']fred]. "O kritikakh i kritike (Stat'ia pervaia)." *Rul'* 20 (April 1931): 2–3.

Berberova, Nina. *Kursiv moi: Avtobiografiia*. 2nd ed. 2 vols. New York: Russica Publishers, 1983.

————. "Nabokov i ego 'Lolita.'" *Novyi zhurnal* 57 (1958): 92–115.

————. "Nabokov in the Thirties." In Appel and Newman, eds., *Nabokov*, 220–233.

————. Telephone interview. New Haven-Philadelphia, March 19, 1992.

Berdnikov, G. *Chekhov*. Moscow: Molodaia gvardiia, 1978.

Bethea, David M. "Bulgakov and Nabokov: Toward a Comparative Perspective." *Transactions/Zapiski of the Association of Russian-American Scholars in the U.S.A* 24 (1991): 187–209.

———— [Dèivid M. Betèia]. "Izgnanie kak ukhod v kokon: obraz babochki u Nabokova i Brodskogo." *Russkaia literatura* 3 (1991): 167–175.

————. *Joseph Brodsky and the Creation of Exile*. Princeton: Princeton University Press, 1994.

————. *Khodasevich: His Life and Art*. Princeton University Press, 1983.

————. "Nabokov and Blok." In Alexandrov, ed., *The Garland Companion to Vladimir Nabokov*, 374–382.

————. "1944–1953: Ivan Bunin and the Time of Troubles in Russian Emigré Literature." *Slavic Review* 43:1 (Spring 1984): 1–16.

Beyer, Thomas R., Gottfried Kratz, and Xenia Werner. *Russische Autoren und Verlage in Berlin nach dem Ersten Weltkrieg*. Berlin: Arno Spitz, 1987.

Bibliia: knigi sviashchennogo pisaniia vetkhogo i novogo zaveta. Moscow: Izdanie moskovskoi patriarkhii, 1992.

Bitsilli, P[ëtr]. "Neskol'ko zamechanii o sovremennoi zarubezhnoi literature." *Novyi grad* 11 (1936): 131–135.

————. *Tvorchestvo Chekhova: opyt stilisticheskogo analiza*. Sofia: Universitetska pechatnitsa, 1942.

————. "Vozrozhdenie allegorii." *Sovremennye zapiski* 61 (July 1936): 191–204.

Blake, William. *A Selection of Poems and Letters*. Ed. J. Bronowski. Harmondsworth: Pengiun Books, 1970.

Blok, Aleksandr. *Sobranie sochinenii*. Moscow/Leningrad: Gosudarstvennoe izdatel'stvo khudozhestvennoi literatury, 1960–1963.

————. *Zapisnye knizhki, 1901–1920*. Moscow: Khudozhestvennaia literatura, 1965.

Bloom, Harold. *The Anxiety of Influence: A Theory of Poetry*. London: Oxford University Press, 1973.

Bodenstein, Jürgen. *"The Excitement of Verbal Adventure": A Study of Vladimir Nabokov's English Prose*. Heidelberg: University of Heidelberg, 1977.

————. "Vladimir Nabokov, 'Spring in Fialta' (1947)." In *Die Amerikanische Short Story der Gegenwart: Interpretationen*, 90–100. Berlin: E. Schmidt, 1976.

Booth, Wayne C. *The Rhetoric of Fiction*. Chicago: University of Chicago Press, 1961.

Boyd, Brian. "Emigré Responses to Nabokov (I): 1921–1930." *The Nabokovian* 17 (1986): 21–41.

————. "Emigré Responses to Nabokov (II): 1931–1935." *The Nabokovian* 18 (1987): 34–53.

————. "Emigré Responses to Nabokov (III): 1936–1939." *The Nabokovian* 19 (1987): 23–38.

————. "Emigré Responses to Nabokov (IV): 1940–1984." *The Nabokovian* 20 (1988): 56–66.

————. *Nabokov's Ada: The Place of Consciousness*. Ann Arbor: Ardis, 1985.

————. "Nabokov's Philosophical World." *Southern Review* 14:3 (1981): 260–301.

————. *Vladimir Nabokov: The American Years*. Princeton: Princeton University Press, 1991.

————. *Vladimir Nabokov: The Russian Years*. Princeton: Princeton University Press, 1990.

Boym, Svetlana. *Death in Quotation Marks: Cultural Myths of the Modern Poet.* Cambridge: Harvard University Press, 1991.

Brodsky, Joseph. "Poetry in the Theater: An Interview with Joseph Brodsky." *Theater* 20:1 (Winter 1988): 51–54.

Bulgakov, Valentin. *Slovar' russkikh zarubezhnykh pisatelei.* Ed. Galina Veněčková. New York: Norman Ross Publishing, 1993.

Bunin, Ivan. *Bozh'e drevo.* Paris: Sovremennye zapiski, 1931.

———. *Chasha zhizni: rasskazy 1913–14 gg.* Paris: Franko-russkaia pechat', 1921.

———. "Genrikh." *Novyi zhurnal* 3 (1942): 5–19.

———. [Ivan Bounin]. "In the Forest." *Lovat Dickson's Magazine* 4:2 (February 1935): 221–234.

———. *Izbrannye stikhi.* Paris: Sovremennye zapiski, 1929.

———. *Lish' slovu zhizn' dana. . . .* Moscow: Sovetskaia Rossiia, 1990.

———. *Mitina liubov'.* Paris: N. P. Karbasnikov, 1925.

———. *Nachal'naia liubov'.* Prague: Slavianskoe izdatel'stvo, 1921.

———. *O Chekhove.* New York: Izdatel'stvo imeni Chekhova, 1955.

———. *Petlistye ushi i drugie rasskazy.* New York: Izdatel'stvo imeni Chekhova, 1954.

———. *Poslednee svidanie.* Paris: N. P. Karbasnikov, 1927.

———. *Roza Ierikhona.* Berlin: Slovo, 1924.

———. *Sny Changa.* Moscow-Leningrad: Gosudarstvennoe izdatel'stvo, 1927.

———. *Sobranie sochinenii I. A. Bunina.* 11 vols. Berlin: Petropolis, 1934–1936.

———. *Sobranie sochinenii v deviati tomakh.* Moscow: Khudozhestvennaia literatura, 1965–1967.

———. *Solnechnyi udar.* Paris: n.p., 1927.

———. *Tëmnye allei.* New York: Novaia zemlia, 1943.

———. *Tëmnye allei.* Paris: La presse française et étrangère, 1946.

———. *Ten' ptitsy.* Paris: Sovremennye zapiski, 1931.

———. *Vesnoi, v Iudee. Roza Ierikhona.* New York: Izdatel'stvo imeni Chekhova, 1953.

———. "Vne." *Zveno* (November 24, 1929): 2.

———. *Vospominaniia.* Paris: Knigoizdatel'stvo Vozrozhdenie, 1950.

———. *Zhizn' Arsen'eva. Istoki dnei.* Paris: Sovremennye zapiski, 1930.

Burns, Dan E. "*Bend Sinister* and 'Tyrants Destroyed': Short Story into Novel." *Modern Fiction Studies* 25:3 (Autumn 1979): 508–513.

Cave [?Leonid Kavetskii]. "Putevye zametki." *Zveno* (February 9, 1925): 4.

The Century Dictionary (New York: Century Co., 1911).

Chekhov, A. P. *Polnoe sobranie sochinenii i pisem v tridtsati tomakh.* Moscow: Nauka, 1974–1985.

Chekhoviana: Chekhov i Frantsiia. Moscow: Nauka, 1992.

Chernyshev, Andrei. "Ètomu cheloveky ia veriu bol'she vsekh na zemle." *Oktiabr'* 3 (1996): 115–156.

———. "'Kak redko teper' pishu po-russki . . .': Iz perepiski V. V. Nabokova i M. A. Aldanova." *Oktiabr'* 1 (1996): 121–146.

Chinnov, Igor'. Personal interview. Daytona Beach, Florida, March 15, 1994.

Chudakov, A. P. *Poètika Chekhova.* Moscow: Nauka, 1971.

Connolly, Julian W. "Bunin's 'Petlistye ushi': The Deformation of a Byronic Rebel." *Canadian-American Slavic Studies* 14:1 (Spring 1980): 52–61.

———. *Ivan Bunin.* Boston: Twayne Publishers, 1982.

———. "Nabokov and the Narrative Point of View: The Case of 'A Letter That Never Reached Russia.'" *Nabokov Studies* 1 (1994): 9–20.

———. *Nabokov's Early Fiction: Patterns of Self and Other.* Cambridge: Cambridge University Press, 1992.

———. "Nabokov's 'Terra Incognita' and 'Invitation to a Beheading': The Struggle for Imaginative Freedom." *Wiener Slawistischer Almanach* 12 (1983): 55–65.

———. "The Otherwordly in Nabokov's Poetry." *Russian Literature Triquarterly* 24 (1990): 329–339.

———. "The Play of Light and Shadow in 'The Fight.'" In Nicol and Barabtarlo, eds., *A Small Alpine Form,* 25–37.

Connolly, Julian W., and S. I. Ketchian, eds. *Studies in Honor of Vsevolod Setschkarëv.* Columbus, Ohio: Slavica, 1987.

Covell, Charles V., Jr. *A Field Guide to the Moths of Eastern North America.* Boston: Houghton Mifflin Company, 1984.

Croisé, Jacques [pseudonym of Zinaida Shakhovskaia]. "Le cas Nabokov ou la blessure de l'exil." *La revue des deux mondes* (August 15, 1959): 661–674.

Dal', V.I. *Tolkovyi slovar'.* 4 vols. Moscow: Gosudarstvennoe izdatel'stvo khudozhestvennoi literatury, 1935. (Rpt. of the 1882 Vol'f edition.)

Dante Alighieri. *The Divine Comedy of Dante Alighieri.* Tr. and comm. John Sinclair. New York: Oxford University Press, 1974.

Davidson, Hustav. *A Dictionary of Angels, including the Fallen Angels.* New York: Free Press, 1967.

Davydov, Sergej. *Teksty-Matrëški Vladimira Nabokova.* Munich: Otto Sagner, 1982.

———. [Sergei Davydov]. "Poseshchenie kladbishcha i muzeia." *Diapazon* 1 (1993): 36–39.

———. "Nabokov and Pushkin." In Alexandrov, ed., *The Garland Companion,* 482–496.

De Roeck, Galina L. "'The Visit to the Museum': A Tour of Hell." In Nicol and Barabtarlo, eds., *A Small Alpine Form,* 137–147.

Dolinin, Aleksandr. "Dve zametki o romane 'Dar.'" *Zvezda* 11 (1996): 168–180.

Dostoevskii, F. M. *Sobranie sochinenii.* Vol. 9. Moscow: Gosudarstvennoe izdatel'stvo khudozhestvennoi literatury, 1958.

Duperray, Max. "Au-dela du fantastique: La naissance douloureuse a l'écriture—'Cloud, Castle, Lake,' de Vladimir Nabokov." In Max Duperray, ed., *Du fantastique en littérature: Figures et figurations,* 161–165. Marseille: Publications de l'université de Provence aix Marseille I, 1990.

Eco, Umberto. *The Open Work.* Tr. Anna Cancogni. Cambridge: Harvard University Press, 1989.

Elms, Alan C. "Cloud, Castle, Claustrum: Nabokov as a Freudian in Spite of Himself." In Daniel Rancour-Laferriere, ed., *Russian Literature and Psychoanalysis,* 353–368. Amsterdam and Philadelphia: John Benjamin, 1989.

The Encyclopedia Britannica, 11th edition.

The Encyclopedia of the Jewish Religion. New York: Adama Books, 1986.

Engelking, Lescek. "Some Remarks on the Devil in Nabokov's 'The Visit to the Museum.'" *Canadian-American Slavic Studies* 19:3 (Fall 1965): 351–356.

Evans, Walter. "The Conjuror in 'The Potato Elf.'" In Rivers and Nicol, eds., *Nabokov's Fifth Arc,* 75–81.

Fasmer, Maks (Max Vasmer). *Ètimologicheskii slovar' russkogo iazyka.* Moscow: Progress, 1973.

Fet, Afanasii. *Polnoe sobranie stikhotvorenii.* Moscow: Sovetskii pisatel', 1959.

Field, Andrew. *Nabokov: His Life in Art*. Boston: Little, Brown and Company, 1967.

——. *Nabokov: His Life in Part*. Harmondsworth: Penguin, 1978.

——. *VN: The Life and Art of Vladimir Nabokov*. New York: Crown Publishers, 1986.

Foster, John Burt, Jr. "An Archeology of 'Mademoiselle O': Narrative between Art and Memory." In Nicol and Barabtarlo, eds., *A Small Alpine Form*, 111–135.

——. *Nabokov's Art of Memory and European Modernism*. Princeton: Princeton University Press, 1993.

Foster, Liudmila A. *Bibliografiia russkoi zarubezhnoi literatury 1918–1968*. 2 vols. Boston: G. K. Hall, 1970.

——. [Ludmila Foster]. "Nabokov in Russian Emigré Criticism." In Proffer, ed., *A Book of Things*, 42–53.

——. "O kompozitsii 'Tëmnykh allei' Bunina." *Russian literature* 9 (1978): 55–65.

——. "'Poseshchenie muzeia' Nabokova v svete traditsii modernizma." *Grani* 85 (1972): 176–187.

Foucault, Michel. "What Is an Author?" In Josué V. Harari, ed., *Textual Strategies*, 141–160. Ithaca: Cornell University Press, 1970.

Fowler, Douglas. *Reading Nabokov*. Ithaca: Cornell University Press, 1973.

Frank, Joseph. *The Idea of Spatial Form*. New Brunswick: Rutgers University Press, 1991.

Freedman, David Noel, ed. *The Anchor Bible Dictionary*. New York: Doubleday, 1992.

Frye, Northrop. *Anatomy of Criticism*. Princeton: Princeton University Press, 1957.

Garf, Andrei. "Literaturnye pelënki." *Novoe slovo* (March 20, 1938): 6–7.

Gay, Peter. *Weimar Culture: The Outsider as Insider*. New York: Harper and Row, 1968.

Geideko, Valerii. *A. Chekhov i Iv. Bunin*. Moscow: Sovetskii pisatel', 1976.

Genette, Gérard. *Palimpsestes: La littérature au second degré*. Paris: Seuil, 1982.

Gessen, I. V. *Gody izgnaniia: zhiznennyi otchët*. Paris: YMCA-Press, 1979.

Gibian, George, and Stephen Jan Parker, eds. *The Achievements of Vladimir Nabokov*. Ithaca: Center for International Studies, 1984.

Gilbert, Pamela. *A Compendium of the Biographical Literature on Deceased Enthomologists*. London: British Museum, 1977.

Gippius, Z. N. (see also "Krainii, Anton"). "Blagoukhanie sedin: o mnogikh." In *Zhivye litsa*, 117–170. Prague: Plamia, 1925.

Gippius, Z. N., and K. R. Kocharovskii. *Chto delat' russkoi èmigratsii?* Paris: Knizhnoe delo Rodnik, 1930.

Girard, René. "'Triangular' Desire." In *Deceit, Desire, and the Novel*, tr. Yvonne Freccero, 1–52. Baltimore: Johns Hopkins University Press, 1965.

Gitovich, N. I. *Letopis' tvorchestva A. P. Chekhova*. Moscow: Khudozhestvennaia literatura, 1955.

Gol'denberg, Mikhail. "Budem prezhde vsego sochiniteliami. . . ." *Vestnik* 7.2:16 (August 8, 1995): 44–48.

Grayson, Jane. "Double Bill: Nabokov and Olesha." In Arnold McMillin, ed., *From Pushkin to Palisandria: Essays on the Novel in Honor of Richard Freeborn*, 181–200. London: Macmillan/School of Slavonic and East European Studies, University of London, 1990.

——. *Nabokov Translated: A Comparison of Nabokov's Russian and English Prose*. Oxford: Oxford University Press, 1977.

Grebnev, G. *Propavsheee sokrovichshe. Mir inoi*. Moscow: Biblioteka prikliuchenii i fantastiki, 1961.

Grin, Militsa [Militsa E. Greene], ed. *Ustami Buninykh*. 3 vols. Munich: Posev, 1977–1982.

Gromov, Mikhail. *Chekhov*. Moscow: Molodaia gvardiia, 1993.

Grossmith, Robert. "A Future Perfect of the Minds: 'Time and Ebb' and 'A Guide to Berlin.'" In Nicol and Barabtarlo, eds., *A Small Alpine Form*, 149–153.

————. "Perfection." In Nicol and Barabtarlo, eds. *A Small Alpine Form*, 73–80.

————. "The Twin Abysses of 'Lik.'" *The Nabokovian* 19 (1987): 46–50.

Hagglund, Roger. "The Adamovič-Xodasevič Polemics." *The Slavic and East European Journal* 20:3 (1976): 239–252.

————. "The Russian Emigré Debate of 1928 on Criticism." *Slavic Review* 32:3 (September 1973): 515–526.

————. *A Vision of Unity: Adamovich in Exile*. Ann Arbor: Ardis, 1985.

Hanks, Patrick, and Flavia Hodges. *A Dictionary of Surnames*. Oxford: Oxford University Press, 1988.

Hansen, Ron, and Jim Shepard, eds. *You've Got to Read This: Contemporary American Writers Introduce Stories That Held Them in Awe*. New York: HarperPerennial, 1994.

Harvey, Sir Paul. *The Oxford Companion to Classical Literature*. Oxford: Oxford University Press, 1986.

Hastings, James, ed. *A Dictionary of the Bible*. New York: Charles Scribner's Sons, 1898.

————. *Encyclopedia of Religion and Ethics*. Edinburgh: T. and T. Clark, 1980.

The Herder Dictionary of Symbols. Wilmette, Ill.: Chiron Publications, 1994.

Hirsch, E. D., Jr. *Validity in Interpretation*. New Haven: Yale University Press, 1967.

Hüllen, Christopher. *Der Tod in Werk Vladimir Nabokovs Terra Incognita*. Munich: Otto Sagner, 1990.

Iablonskii, Sergei. Rev. of *Sogliadatai*, by Vladimir Sirin. *Rul'* 3050 (December 6, 1930): 2.

Ianovskii, V.S. *Polia eliseiskie. Kniga pamiati*. New York: Serebrianyi vek, 1983.

Il'in, I. A. "I. A. Bunin." In *O t'me i prosvetlenii. Kniga khudozhestvennoi kritiki. Bunin—Remizov—Shmelëv*, 29–77. Munich: n. p., 1959.

The Interpreters Dictionary of the Bible. New York/Nashville: Abigdon Press, 1962.

Iser, Wolfgang. *The Act of Reading: A Theory of Aesthetic Response*. Baltimore: Johns Hopkins University Press, 1978.

————. "Indeterminacy and the Reader's Response in Prose Fiction." In J. Hillis Miller, ed., *Aspects of Narrative. Selected Papers from the English Institute*, 1–45. New York: Columbia University Press, 1971.

————. "Interaction between Text and Reader." In S. Suleiman and I. Grossman, eds., *The Reader in the Text*, 106–119. Princeton: Princeton University Press, 1980.

Ivanov, Georgii. "Konets Adamovicha." *Vozrozhdenie* 11 (September–October 1959): 179–186.

————. *1943–1958. Stikhi*. New York: Novyi zhurnal, 1958.

————. Rev. of *Mashen'ka; Korol', dama, valet; Zashchita Luzhina; Vozvrashchenie Chorba*, by V. Sirin. *Chisla* 1 (1930): 233–236.

Ivask, Iurii. "V. V. Nabokov." *Novyi zhurnal* 128 (1977): 272–276.

————, ed. *Na Zapade. Antologiia russkoi zarubezhnoi poèzii*. New York: Izdatel'stvo imeni Chekhova, 1953.

Jackson, Robert Louis. "'The Betrothed': Chekhov's Last Testament." In Senderovich and Munich, eds., *Anton Chekhov Rediscovered*, 51–62.

————. "Chekhov i Prust: postanovka problemy." In *Chekhoviana: Chekhov i Frantsiia*, 129–140.

————. "'If I Forget Thee, O Jerusalem': An Essay on Chekhov's 'Rothschild's Fiddle.'" In Senderovich and Sendich, eds., *Anton Chekhov Rediscovered*, 35–49.

———. "Introduction." In Jackson, ed., *Reading Chekhov's Text,* 1–16.

———. *"The Seagull:* The Empty Well, the Dry Lake, and the Cold Cave." Robert Louis Jackson, ed., In *Chekhov: A Collection of Critical Essays,* 99–111. Englewood Cliffs, NJ: Prentice-Hall, 1967.

———, ed. *Reading Chekhov's Text.* Evanston: Northwestern University Press, 1993.

Jacobs, Louis. "The Hereafter." In *A Jewish Theology,* 301–322. New York: Behrman Publishing House, 1973.

Jakobson, Roman. "Shifters, Verbal Categories, and the Russian Verb." In *Selected Writings,* 2:130–147. The Hague/Paris: Mouton, 1971.

Janson, H. W. *History of Art.* 3rd ed. New York: Harry M. Abrams/Englewood Cliffs, NJ: Prentice Hall, 1986.

Johnson, D. Barton. "Belyj and Nabokov: A Comparative Overview." *Russian Literature* 9 (1981): 379–402.

———. "A Guide to Nabokov's 'A Guide to Berlin.'" *The Slavic and East European Journal* 23:3 (1979): 353–361.

———. "The Nabokov-Sartre Controversy." *Nabokov Studies* 1 (1994): 69–80.

———. "Preliminary Remarks on Nabokov's Russian Poetry: A Chronological and Thematic Sketch." *Russian Literature Triquarterly* 24 (1990): 307–327.

———. "Some Thoughts on Vladimir Nabokov's *A Russian Beauty and Other Stories.*" Rev. of *A Russian Beauty and Other Stories,* by Vladimir Nabokov. *Russian Literature Triquarterly* 10 (Fall 1974): 416–421.

———. "'Terror': Pre-Texts and Post-Texts." In Nicol and Barabtarlo, eds., *A Small Alpine Form,* 39–64.

———. "Vladimir Nabokov's *Solus Rex* and the 'Ultima Thule' Theme." *Slavic Review* 40:4 (1981): 544–556.

———. *Worlds in Regression: Some Novels of Vladimir Nabokov.* Ann Arbor: Ardis, 1985.

Johnston, Robert H. *New Mecca, New Babylon: Paris and the Russian Exiles, 1920–1940.* Kingston, Ont.: McGill–Queen's University Press, 1988.

Juliar, Michael. *Vladimir Nabokov: A Descriptive Bibliography.* New York: Garland Publishing Company, 1986.

Kaganskaia, M[aia]. "Otrechenie. Ot 'Mashen'ki' do 'Lolity.'" *Sintaksis* 1 (1978): 57–76.

Karlinsky, Simon. "Nabokov and Chekhov." In Alexandrov, ed., *The Garland Companion,* 389–398.

———. "Nabokov and Chekhov: The Lesser Tradition." In Appel and Newman, eds., *Nabokov,* 7–16.

———. "Russian Anti-Chekhovians." *Russian Literature* 15:2 (1984): 183–202.

———. "Theme and Structure in Vladimir Nabokov's 'Krug.'" In Kenneth N. Bronstrom, ed., *Russian Literature and American Critics,* 243–247. Ann Arbor: University of Michigan Papers in Slavic Philology, 1984.

Kashin, A. "O Nabokove." Rev. of *Vesna v Fial'te,* by Vladimir Nabokov. *Grani* 33 (1957): 223–224.

Kataev, V. B. "Frantsiia v sud'be Chekhova." In *Chekhoviana: Chekhov i Frantsiia,* 8–19.

Kauffman, Linda S. *Special Delivery: Epistolary Modes in Modern Fiction.* Chicago: University of Chicago Press, 1992.

Keats, John. *The Letters of John Keats.* Ed. Maurice Buxton Forman. 2nd ed. Oxford: Oxford University Press, 1935.

Kermode, Frank. *The Sense of an Ending: Studies in the Theory of Fiction.* New York: Oxford University Press, 1967.

Khodasevich, Vladislav. *Derzhavin.* Moscow: Kniga, 1988.

———. "Knigi i liudi: 'Russkie zapiski' kniga 2-aia." *Vozrozhdenie* 4107 (November 26, 1937): 9.

———. *Literaturnye stat'i i vospominaniia.* New York: Izdatel'stvo imeni Chekhova, 1954.

———. *Nekropol'.* Brussels: Les éditions Petropolis, 1939.

———. "O Sirine." *Vozrozhdenie* 4065 (February 13, 1937): 9.

———. *Sobranie stikhov.* Moscow: Tsenturion interpaks, 1992.

———. "'Sovremennye zapiski' kn. 61." *Vozrozhdenie* 4038 (August 8, 1936): 7.

———. "'Sovremennye zapiski' kniga 68-aia." *Vozrozhdenie* 4176 (March 24, 1939): 9.

K[hokhlov], G[erman]. Rev. of *Vozvrashchenie Chorba,* by V. Sirin. *Volia Rossii* 2 (1930): 190–191.

Kneeley, Richard J., and Edward Kasinec. "The Slovanská knihovna in Prague and Its RZIA Collection." *Slavic Review* 51:1 (Spring 1992): 122–130.

Kniazevskaia, Ta'iana. "Obraz Frantsii." In *Chekhoviana: Chekhov i Frantsiia,* 25–32.

Kostikov, Viacheslav. *Ne budem proklinat' izgnanie . . . Puti i sud'by russkoi èmigratsii.* Moscow: Mezhdunarodnye otnosheniia, 1990.

Krainii, Anton [pseudonym of Zinaida Gippius]. "Literaturnye razmyshleniia." *Chisla* 2–3 (1930): 148–154.

———. *Literaturnyi dnevnik (1899–1907).* St. Petersburg: Izdanie M. V. Pirozhkova, 1908. Rpt. Munich: Wilhelm Fink Verlag, 1970.

———. "Poèziia nashikh dnei." *Poslednie novosti* 1482 (February 22, 19252): 2–3.

Krasavchenko, T. N. "Zashchita Nabokova." *Russkoe literaturnoe zarubezh'e. Sbornik obzorov i materialov. Vypusk I.* Moscow: Institut nauchnoi informatsii po obshchestvennym naukam, 1991.

Kreps, Mikhail. "Èlementy modernizma v rasskazakh Bunina o liubvi." *Novyi zhurnal* 137 (1979): 54–67.

Kreyd, Vadim. "L'vova, Nadezhda Grigor'evna." In Marina Ledkovsky et al., eds., *Dictionary of Russian Women Writers,* 394–396. Westport, Conn.: Greenwood Press, 1994.

Kryzytski, Serge. *The Works of Ivan Bunin.* The Hague: Mouton, 1971.

Kuzmanovich, Zoran. "'A Christmas Story': A Polemic with Ghosts." In Nicol and Barabtarlo, eds., *A Small Alpine Form,* 81–97.

Kuznetsov, Pavel. "Utopiia odinochestva. Vladimir Nabokov i metafizika." *Novyi mir* 10 (1992): 243–250.

Kuznetsova, Galina. *Grasskii dnevnik.* Washington, D.C.: Viktor Kamkin, 1967.

Lee, L. L. "Duplexity in V. Nabokov's Short Stories." *Studies in Short Fiction* 2:4 (Summer 1965): 307–315.

Levin, Iurii I. "Bispatsial'nost' kak invariant poèticheskogo mira V. Nabokova." *Russian Literature* 28:1 (1990): 45–124.

Leyda, Jay. *Kino: A History of the Russian and Soviet Film.* Princeton: Princeton University Press, 1983.

"Literaturnaia anketa." *Chisla* 2–3 (1930): 318–322.

Literaturnoe nasledstvo. Ivan Bunin. Vol. 84, 2 parts. Moscow: Nauka, 1973.

"Literaturnyi vecher." *Rul'* 2818 (March 4, 1930): 6.

Liubimov, Lev. "Na chuzbine." *Novyi mir* 3 (1957): 135–205.

Lotman, Iuriii M. *Struktura khudozhestvennogo teksta*. Providence: Brown University Press, 1971.

Lucco, Mauro, and Carlo Volpe, eds. *L'opera completa di Sebastiano del Piombo*. Milan: Rizzoli, 1980.

Luther, Arthur. "Russische Emigrantendichtung." *Die Literatur* 36 (October 1933–September 1934): 146–150.

L'vov, Lollii. "Pil'gram V. Sirina." Rev. of "Pil'gram" by V. Sirin. *Rossiia i slavianstvo* 93 (September 6, 1930): 3–4.

Majhanovich, Ljubo Dragoljub. "The Early Prose of Vladimir Nabokov-Sirin: A Commentary on Themes, Style, and Structure." Ph.D. dissertation. University of Illinois at Urbana-Champaign, 1976.

Maliugin, L., and I. Gitovich. *Chekhov*. Moscow: Sovetskii pisatel', 1983.

Malmstad, John [Malmsted, Dzhon]. "Iz perepiski V. F. Khodasevicha (1925–1938)." *Minuvshee* 3 (1987): 262–291.

Malozemoff, Elizabeth. "Ivan Bunin, as a Writer of Prose." Ph. D. dissertation. University of California at Berkeley, 1938.

Mandel'shtam, O. E. *Sobranie sochinenii v chetyrëkh tomakh*. Vol. 1. Moscow: Terra, 1991.

Maria, mon[akhinia] [Mother Maria]. "Vstrechi s Blokom (k piatnadtsatiletiiu so dnia smerti)." *Sovremennye zapiski* 62 (October 1936): 211–228.

Marullo, Thomas Gaiton. "Crime without Punishment: Ivan Bunin's 'Loopy Ears.'" *Slavic Review* 40:4 (Winter 1981): 614–624.

Masanov, I. F. *Slovar' psevdonimov russkikh pisatelei, uchënykh i obshchestvennykh deiatelei.* 4 vols. Moscow: Izdatel'stvo vsesoiuznoi knizhnoi palaty, 1957.

Matterson, Stephen. "Sprung from the Music Box of Memory: 'Spring in Fialta.'" In Nicol and Barabtarlo, eds., *A Small Alpine Form*, 99–109.

Maxwell, William. *All the Days and Nights*. New York: Alfred A. Knopf, 1995.

May, Charles E., ed. *Short Story Theories*. Columbus: Ohio State University Press, 1976.

Meshcherskii, A. "Neizvestnye pis'ma I. Bunina." *Russkaia literatura* 4 (1961): 152–158.

Meyer, Priscilla. "The German Theme in Nabokov's Work of the 1920s." In Nicol and Barabtarlo, eds., *A Small Alpine Form*, 3–14.

Mihailovich, Alexandar. "Eschatology and Entombment in 'Ionych.'" In Jackson, ed., *Reading Chekhov's Text*, 103–114.

Monter, Barbara Heldt. "'Spring in Fialta': The Choice That Mimics Chance." In Appel and Newman, eds., *Nabokov*, 128–135.

Moser, Charles A., ed. *The Russian Short Story: A Critical History*. Boston: Twayne Publishers, 1986.

Mroz, Edith Maria Fay. "Vladimir Nabokov and Romantic Irony." Ph. D. dissertation. University of Delaware, 1988 (Ann Arbor: UMI, 1989, 8904598).

Mukařovský, Jan. *Aesthetic Function, Norm and Value as Social Facts*. Tr. and ed. Mark E. Suino. Ann Arbor: Department of Slavic Languages and Literatures, University of Michigan, 1970.

———. "Art as Semiotic Fact." In John Burbank and Peter Steiner, *Structure, Sign, and Function: Selected Essays*, 82–88. New Haven: Yale University Press, 1977.

Muliarchik, A. S. *Russkaia proza Vladimira Nabokova*. Moscow: Izdatel'stvo Moskovskogo universiteta, 1997.

Nabokov, Dmitrii. "Translating with Nabokov." In Gibian and Parker, eds., *The Achievements of Vladimir Nabokov*, 145–177.

Nabokov, Nicolas. *Bagázh: Memoirs of a Russian Cosmopolitan.* New York: Antheum, 1975.

Nabokova, Vera. "Predislovie." In Nabokov, *Stikhi,* 3–4.

Nal'ianch, S. Rev. of *Vozvrashchenie Chorba,* by V. Sirin. *Za svobodu* 209 (August 4, 1930): 3.

"Nashi pisateli o Chekhove: anketa 'Illiustrirovannoi zhizni.'" *Illiustrirovannaia zhizn'* 18 (July 12, 1934): 2–3.

Naumann, Marina Turkevich. *Blue Evenings in Berlin: Nabokov's Short Stories of the 1920s.* New York: New York University Press, 1978.

———. "Nabokov as Viewed by Fellow Emigrés." *Russian Language Journal* 28:99 (1974): 18–26.

Nazarov, Al. "V. V. Sirin—novaia zvezda v literature." *Novaia zaria* (August 11, 1934): 5.

Neider, Charles, ed. *Great Short Fiction from the Masters of World Literature.* New York: Carroll and Graf, 1995.

Newman, Charles. "Beyond Omniscience: Notes toward a Future for the Novel." *TriQuarterly* 10 (Fall 1967): 37–52.

Nicol, Charles. "Finding the 'Assistant Producer.'" In Nicol and Barabtarlo, eds., *A Small Alpine Form,* 155–165.

———. "'Ghastly Rich Glass': A Double Essay on 'Spring in Fialta.'" *Russian Literature Triquarterly* 24 (1991): 173–184.

———. "Nabokov and Science Fiction: 'Lance.'" *Science-Fiction Studies* 14:1 (1987): 9–20.

Nicol, Charles, and Gennady Barabtarlo. "Introduction." In Nicol and Barabtarlo, eds., *A Small Alpine Form: Studies in Nabokov's Short Fiction.* New York: Garland Publishing, 1993.

Nilsson, Nils Åke. "A Hall of Mirrors: Nabokov and Olesha." *Scando-Slavica* 15:5–12.

Noel, Lucie Léon. "Playback." In Appel and Newman, eds., *Nabokov,* 209–219.

Odoevtseva, Irina. *Na beregakh Seny.* Paris: La presse libre, 1983.

Opdycke, John B. *Harper's English Grammar.* New York: Warner Books, 1965.

Orlov, Vl. *Gamaiun. Zhizn' Aleksandra Bloka.* Leningrad: Sovetskii pisatel', 1980.

Osborne, Harold, ed. *The Oxford Companion to Art.* Oxford: Clarendon Press, 1970.

Osorgin, Mikhail. "'Sovremennye zapiski' (Knizhka 30-ia)." *Poslednie novosti* 2136 (January 27, 1927): 3.

———. "Sud'ba zarubezhnoi knigi." *Sovremennye zapiski* 54 (1934): 385–390.

O'Toole, L. Michael. *Structure, Style and Interpretation in the Russian Short Story.* New Haven: Yale University Press, 1982.

Ovid. *Metamorphoses.* Tr. Rolfe Humphries. Bloomington: Indiana University Press, 1983.

The Oxford English Dictionary. 2nd ed. Vols. 1–19. Oxford: Clarendon Press, 1989.

Paperno, Slava, and John V. Hagopian. "Official and Unofficial Responses to Nabokov in the Soviet Union." In Gibian and Parker, eds., *The Achievements of Vladimir Nabokov,* 99–117.

Parker, Stephen Jan. "Vladimir Nabokov and the Short Story." *Russian Literature Triquarterly* 24 (1991): 63–72.

Parry, Albert. "Belles Lettres among Russian Emigrés." *The American Mercury* 29 (July 1933): 316–319.

Pasternak, Boris. "Vstrechi s Maiakovskim." *Novaia gazeta* 5 (May 1, 1931): 12.

Petty, Chapel Louise. "A Comparison of Hawthorne's 'Wakefield' and Nabokov's 'The

Leonardo': Narrative Commentary and the Struggle of the Literary Artist." *Modern Fiction Studies* 25:3 (Autumn 79): 499–507.

Pifer, Ellen. "Shades of Love: Nabokov's Intimations of Immortality." *Kenyon Review* 11:2 (Spring 1989): 75–86.

Pil'skii, Pëtr. "Novaia kniga 'Sovremennykh zapisok.'" *Segodnia* 209 (August 1, 1930): 3.

———. "Novaia kniga 'Sovremennykh zapisok.'" *Segodnia* 309 (November 9, 1930): 3.

———. "V. Sirin. Novaia kniga V. Sirina 'Vozvrashchenie Chorba.'" Rev. of *Vozvrashchenie Chorba*, by V. Sirin. *Segodnia* 12 (January 12, 1930): 5.

Pimentel, Ken, and Kevin Teixeira. *Virtual Reality: Through a New Looking Glass.* 2nd ed. New York: Intel/McGraw-Hill, 1995.

Piotrovskii, Vl. (Vladimir Korvin-Piotrovskii). "Iz nochnykh progulok." *Rul'* 2458 (December 25, 1928): 2.

Poggioli, Renato. "The Art of Ivan Bunin." In *The Phoenix and the Spider*, 131–157. Cambridge: Harvard University Press, 1957.

"Polchasa s I. A. Buninym." *Illiustrirovannaia znizn'* 11 (May 24, 1934): 2.

Polnyi pravoslavnyi bogoslovskii èntsiklopedicheskii slovar'. Vol. 2. St. Petersburg: Izdatel'stvo P. P. Soikina, 1913. Rpt. by Variorum Reprints, 1971.

Polotskaia, È. A. "Chekhov v khudozhestvennom razvitii Bunina: 1890-e–1910-e gody." In *Literaturnoe nasledstvo. Ivan Bunin*, 2:66–89.

———. "Vzaimotnoshenie poèzii i prozy u rannego Bunina." *Izvestiia AN SSSR. Seriia literatury i iazyka* 29:5 (September–October 1970): 412–418.

Pol'skaia, Svetlana [Svetlana Polsky]. "Death and Immortality in Nabokov's 'A Busy Man.'" *Nabokov Studies* 2 (1995): 213–232.

———. "Kommentarii k rasskazu V. Nabokova 'Oblako, ozero, bashnia.'" *Scando-Slavica* 35 (1989): 111–123.

———. "Voskreshenie korolia Ofiokha: È. T. A. Gofman v rasskaze V. Nabokova 'Oblako, ozero, bashnia.'" *Scando-Slavica* 36 (1990): 100–113.

Poltoratskii N. P., ed. *Russkaia literatura v èmigratsii. Sbornik statei.* Pittsburgh: Department of Slavic Languages and Literatures, University of Pittsburgh, 1972.

Postnikov, S[ergei]. "O molodoi èmigrantskoi literature." *Volia Rossii* 5–6 (1927): 215–225.

———. "Russkaia zarubezhnaia literatura v 1925 godu (Pis'mo na rodinu)." *Volia Rossii* 2 (1926): 182–192.

Prince, Gerald. *Dictionary of Narratology.* Lincoln: University of Nebraska Press, 1987.

Proffer, Carl R., *Ada* as Wonderland: A Glossary to Allusions to Russian Literature." In Proffer, ed., *A Book of Things about Vladimir Nabokov*, 249–279.

———, ed. *A Book of Things about Vladimir Nabokov.* Ann Arbor: Ardis, 1974.

Proffer, Ellendea. "Nabokov's Russian Readers." In Appel and Newman, eds., *Nabokov*, 253–260.

———, ed. *Vladimir Nabokov: A Pictorial Biography.* Ann Arbor: Ardis, 1991.

Purdy, Strother B. "Solus Rex: Nabokov and the Chess Novel." *Modern Fiction Studies* 14:4 (Winter 1968–1969): 379–385.

Pushkin, A. S. *Stikhotvoreniia i poèmy.* Minsk: Mastatskaia literatura, 1978.

Rabaté, Laurent. "La poésie de la tradition: Etude du recueil *Stixi* de V. Nabokov." *Revue des études slaves* 56:3 (1985): 397–420.

Rabinowitch, Alexander. *The Bolsheviks Come to Power: The Revolution of 1917 in Petrograd.* New York: W. W. Norton and Co., 1976.

Raeff, Marc. *Russia Abroad: A Cultural History of the Russian Emigration, 1919–1939.* New York: Oxford University Press, 1990.

Raevskii, Nikolai. "Vospominaniia o Vladimire Nabokove." *Prostor* 2 (1989): 112–117.

Reaney, P. H. *A Dictionary of British Surnames.* London and Boston: Routledge and Kegan Paul, 1958.

Rennert, Hal H. "Literary Revenge: Nabokov's 'Mademoiselle O' and Kleist's 'Die Marquise von O.'" *Germano-Slavica* 4:6 (1984): 331–338.

The Revised English Bible with Apocrypha. Oxford/Cambridge: Oxford University Press/Cambridge University Press, 1989.

Rheingold, Howard. *Virtual Reality.* New York: Summit Books, 1991.

Richards, I. A. *Principles of Literary Criticism.* London: Routledge, 1989.

Rivers, J. E., and Charles Nicol, eds. *Nabokov's Fifth Arc: Nabokov and Others on His Life's Work.* Austin: University of Texas Press, 1982.

Rodnianskaia, Irina. *Literaturnoe semiletie.* Moscow: Knizhnyi sad, 1995.

Rodriguez, Johnette. "Iconoclastic Icons: Redefining Post-modern Fiction at Brown University." *The New Paper* (Providence, Rhode Island, April 13–20, 1988): 3–4, 6.

Rohrberger, Mary, and Dan E. Burns. "Short Story and the Numinous Realm: Another Attempt at Definition." *Modern Fiction Studies* 28:1 (Spring 1982): 5–12.

Ronen, Omry [Omri Ronen]. "Zaum' za predelami avangarda." *Literaturnoe obozrenie* 12 (1991): 40–43.

Rorty, Richard. Rev. of *Nabokov's Otherworld,* by Vladimir E. Alexandrov. *Common Knowledge* 1:2 (Fall 1922): 126.

Rubenstein, Joshua. *Tangled Loyalties: The Life and Times of Ilya Ehrenburg.* New York: Basic Books, 1996.

"Samoe luchshee proizvedenie russkoi literatury poslednego desiatiletiia (anketa)." *Novaia gazeta* 3 (April 1, 1931): 1–2.

Saputelli, Linda Nadine [Linda Saputelli Zimmermann]. "The Long-Drawn Sunset in Fialta." In Connolly and Ketchian, eds., *Studies in Honor of Vsevolod Setschkarëv,* 233–242.

Savel'ev, A. Rev. of *Vozvrashchenie Chorba,* by V. Sirin. *Rul'* 2765 (December 31, 1929): 2–3.

———. "'Sovremennye zapiski.' Kniga 43-ia." *Rul'* 2954 (August 15, 1930): 2–3.

———. "'Sovremennye zapiski'. Kniga sorok chetvërtaia." *Rul'* 3053 (December 10, 1930): 3.

Savel'ev, S. Rev. of *Sogliadatai,* by Vl. Sirin. *Russkie zapiski* 10 (1938): 195–197.

Schakhowskoij, Zinaïda. [Zinaida Shakhovskaia]. "Un maître de la jeune littérature russe Wladimir Nabokoff-Sirin." *La cité chrétienne* (July 20, 1937).

Scherr, Barry P. "Poetry." In Alexandrov, ed., *The Garland Companion,* 608–625.

Schroeter, J. "Detective Stories and Aesthetic Bliss in Nabokov." *Delta* [special Nabokov issue] 17 (October 1983): 23–32.

Senderovich, Savely. "Anton Chekhov and St. George the Dragonslayer (An Introduction to the Theme)." In Senderovich and Sendich, eds., *Anton Chekhov Rediscovered,* 167–187.

Senderovich, Savely, and Munir Sendich, eds. *Anton Chekhov Rediscovered: A Collection of New Studies with a Comprehensive Bibliography.* East Lansing: The Russian Language Journal, 1987.

Setschkareff, Vsevolod [Vsevolod Setschkarëv]. "Zur Thematik der Dichtung Vladimir Nabokovs (aus Anlass des Erscheinens seiner gesammelten Gedichte)." *Die Welt der Slaven* 25:1 (1980): 68–97.

Shakespeare. William. *The Complete Works of William Shakespeare.* London: Spring Books, 1972.

Shakhovskaia, Zinaida. *Otrazheniia.* Paris: YMCA-Press, 1975.

———. *Rasskazy. Stat'i. Stikhi.* Paris: Les éditeurs reunis. 1978.

———. *V poiskakh Nabokova.* Paris: La presse libre, 1979.

Sheldon, Richard, ed. and tr. Viktor Shklovsky. *Zoo or Letters Not about Love.* Ithaca: Cornell University Press, 1971.

———, ed. *Viktor Shklovsky: An International Bibliography of Works on and about Him.* Ann Arbor: Ardis, 1977.

Shepard, Jim. "'Spring in Fialta' by Vladimir Nabokov." In Hansen and Shepard, eds., *You've Got to Read This,* 401–404.

Shestov, Lev. "Tvorchestvo iz nichego." In *Nachala i kontsy: Sbornik statei,* 1–68. St. Petersburg: Tipografia M. M. Stasiulevicha, 1908.

Shklovskii, Viktor. *O teorii prozy.* Moscow: Sovetskii pisatel', 1983.

———. *Zoo or Letters Not about Love.* Ed. and trans. Richard Sheldon. Ithaca: Cornell University Press.

Shrayer, Maxim D. "'Cloud, Castle, Lake' and the Problem of Entering the Otherworld in Nabokov's Fiction." *Nabokov Studies* 1 (1994): 131–153.

———. "Conflation of Christmas and Paschal Motifs in Čechov's 'V roždestvenskuju noč'.'" *Russian Literature* 35:7 (February 15, 1994): 243–259.

———. "Decoding the Return of Chorb." *Russian Language Journal,* 51:168–170 (1997): 177–202.

———. "Ivan Bunin i Vladimir Nabokov: poètika sopernichestva." In *I. A. Bunin i russkaia literatura XX veka,* 41–65. Moscow: Nasledie, 1996.

———. "Mapping Narrative Space in Vladimir Nabokov's Short Fiction." *The Slavonic and East European Review,* 75:4 (October 1997): 624–641.

———. "Pilgrimage, Memory and Death in Vladimir Nabokov's Short Story 'The Aurelian.'" *The Slavic and East European Journal* 40:4 (Winter 1996): 78–104.

———. Rev. of *A Small Alpine Form,* by Charles Nicol and Gennady Barabtarlo. *Nabokov Studies* 1 (1994): 219–224.

———. "Two Poems on the Death of Akhmatova: Dialogues, Private Codes, and the Myth of Akhmatova's Orphans." *Canadian Slavonic Papers* 35:1–2 (March–June 1993): 45–68.

Sicker, Philip T. "Practicing Nostalgia: Time and Memory in Nabokov's Early Russian Fiction." *Studies in Twentieth Century Literature* 11:2 (Spring 1987): 253–270.

———. "Shadows of Exile in Nabokov's Berlin." *Thought* 62:246 (September 1987): 281–294.

Singer, Isaac Bashevis. *The Collected Stories of Isaac Bashevis Singer.* New York: Farrar, Straus and Giroux, 1982.

Sisson, Jonathan Borden. "Cosmic Synchronization and Other Worlds in the Work of Vladimir Nabokov." Ph.D. dissertation. University of Minnesota, 1979.

———. "Nabokov's Cosmic Synchronization and 'Something Else.'" *Nabokov Studies* 1 (1994): 155–177.

Slonim, M[ark]. "Literatura èmigratsii." *Volia Rossii* 2 (1925): 174–182.

———. "Literatura èmigratsii." *Volia Rossii* 3 (1926): 182–192.

———. "Molodye pisateli za rubezhom." *Volia Rossii* 10–11 (1929): 100–118.

Slovar' sovremennogo russkogo literaturnogo iazyka. Vols. 1–17. Moscow/Leningrad: Nauka, 1950–1967.

Smirnov, N. P., ed. "Pis'ma V. N. Buninoi N. P. Smirnovu." *Novyi mir* 3 (1969): 209–230.

Smirnova, L. A. *Ivan Alekseevich Bunin. Zhizn' i tvorchestvo.* Moscow: Prosveshchenie, 1991.

Smith, Barbara Herrnstein. *Poetic Closure: A Study of How Poems End.* Chicago: University of Chicago Press, 1968.

Smith, Gerald S. "Nabokov and Russian Verse Form." *Russian Literature Triquarterly* 24 (Spring 1990): 271–305.

Stepun, Fëdor. "Ivan Bunin." In *Vstrechi,* 86–122. Munich: Tovarishchestvo zarubezhnykh pisatelei, 1962.

Stevens, Wallace. *The Collected Poems.* New York: Vintage Books, 1954.

Stewart, Garrett. *Death Sentences: Styles of Dying in British Fiction.* Cambridge: Harvard University Press, 1984.

Struve, Gleb. "Current Russian Literature: II. Vladimir Sirin." *The Slavonic and East European Review* 12:35 (January 1934): 436–444.

———. "O V. Sirine." *Russkii v Anglii* 9 (May 15, 1936): 3.

———. "Russian Writers in Exile: Problems of an Emigré Literature." In Werner P. Friedrich, ed., *Proceedings of the Second Congress of the International Comparative Literature Association at the University of North Carolina, September 8–12, 1958,* 2:592–606. Chapel Hill: UNC Studies in Comparative Literature, 1959.

———. *Russkaia literatura v izgnanii.* 2nd ed. Paris: YMCA Press, 1984.

———. "Vladimir Nabokov po lichnym vospominaniiam, dokumentam i perepiske." Ed. Grigorii Poliak. *Novyi zhurnal* 186 (1992): 176–190.

———. "Vladimir Sirin-Nabokov (K ego vecheru v Londone 20-go fevralia)." *Russkii v Anglii* 3/27 (February 16, 1937): 3.

———. "Tvorchestvo Sirina." *Rossiia i slavianstvo* 77 (May 17, 1930): 3.

Struve, N[ikita]. "V. Khodasevich i V. Nabokov." *Vestnik R.Kh.D* 148:3 (1986): 123–128.

Sweeney, Susan Elisabeth. "The Small Furious Devil: Memory in 'Scenes from the Life of a Double Monster.'" In Nicol and Barabtarlo, eds., *A Small Alpine Form,* 193–216.

Tamanin, T. "Pravda Bunina." *Zveno* (March 30, 1925): 3.

Tammi, Pekka. "Chekhov's Shot Gun and Nabokov: A Note on Subtext, Motifs, and Meaning in the Novella 'Lik.'" *Notes on Contemporary Literature* 9:5 (November 1979): 2–5.

———. *Problems of Nabokov's Poetics: A Narratological Analysis.* Helsinki: Suomalainen Tiedeakatemia, 1985.

Tannakh: The Holy Scriptures. Philadelphia: Jewish Publication Society, 1988.

Terapiano, Iurii. *Literaturnaia zhizn' russkogo Parizha za polveka.* Paris/New York: Albatros-C.A.S.E./Third Wave Publishing House, 1986.

———. "O zarubezhnoi poèzii 1920–1960 godov." *Grani* 44 (October–December 1959): 3–12.

Terras, Victor. "Nabokov and Gogol: The Metaphysics of Nonbeing." In J. Douglas Clayton, ed., *Poetica Slavica: Studies in Honor of Zbignew Folejewski,* 191–196. Ottawa: University of Ottawa Press, 1981.

Tiutchev, Fëdor. *Stikhotvoreniia. Pis'ma. Vospominaniia sovremennikov.* Moscow: Pravda, 1988.

Todd, William Mills, III. *The Familiar Letter as a Literary Genre in the Age of Pushkin.* Princeton: Princeton University Press, 1976.

Toker, Leona. "Nabokov and Bergson." In Alexandrov, ed., *The Garland Companion,* 367–374.

———. "Self-Conscious Paralepsis in Vladimir Nabokov's *Pnin* and 'Recruiting.'" *Poetics Today* 7:3 (1986): 459–469.

———. "'Signs and Symbols' in and out of Contexts." In Nicol and Barabtarlo, eds., *A Small Alpine Form*, 167–179.

Tolstaia, Natal'ia I. "Sputnik iasnokrylyi." *Russkaia literatura* 1 (1992): 188–192.

———. "V. V. Nabokov Stages a Play: 'A Busy Man.'" In Nicol and Barabtarlo, eds., *A Small Alpine Form*, 65–72.

Tolstaia, Natal'ia I., and Mikhail Meilakh. "Russian Short Stories." In Alexandrov, ed., *The Garland Companion*, 644–661.

Tomashevskii, Boris. "Literatura i biografiia." *Kniga i revoliutsiia* 4 (1923): 6–9.

Tommaseo, Nicolò, ed. *Dizionario della lingua italiana.* Turin: Unione Tipografico-Editrice Torinese, 1915.

Tsetlin, Mikh[ail]. Rev. of *Vozvrashchenie Chorba*, by V. Sirin. *Sovremennye zapiski* 42 (1930): 530–531.

———. Rev. of *Korol', dama, valet*, by V. Sirin. *Sovremennye zapiski* 37 (December 1928): 536–538.

Tynianov, Iu. N. *Poètika. Istoriia literatury. Kino.* Moscow: Nauka, 1977.

Unbegaun, Boris. *Russian Versification.* Oxford: Oxford University Press, 1956.

Varshavskii, V. S. *Nezamechennoe pokolenie.* New York: Izdatel'stvo imeni Chekhova, 1956.

———. Rev. of *Podvig*, by V. Sirin. *Chisla* 7–8 (1933): 266–267.

Vasil'ev, G. K. "Stranitsa iz rasskaza Nabokova 'Vesna v Fial'te' (opyt lingvisticheskogo analiza)." *Filologicheskie nauki* 3 (1991): 33–40.

"Vecher v chest' Bunina v Berline." *Vozrozhdenie* (January 11, 1934): 4.

"Vecher V. V. Sirina." *Poslednie novosti* 4257 (November 17, 1932): 3.

Veidle, Vladimir. "Dvadtsat' let evropeiskoi literatury." *Poslednie novosti* 6528 (February 10, 1939): 3.

———. "Ischeznovenie Nabokova." *Novyi zhurnal* 129 (1977): 271–274.

———. "Na smert' Bunina." *Opyty* 3 (1954): 80–93.

——— [Vladimir Weidle]. "Russkaia literatura v èmigratsii. Novaia proza." *Vozrozhdenie* 1843 (June 19, 1930): 3–4.

———. "'Sovremennye zapiski' XLIII. Chast' literaturnaia." *Vozrozhdenie* 1878 (July 24, 1930): 3.

———. *Umiranie iskusstva.* Paris/Petseri: Izd. R.S.Kh. Dvizheniia v Èstii, 1937.

Verkheil, Keis. "Malyi korifei russkoi poèzii: zametki o russkikh stikhakh Nabokova." *Èkho* 4 (1980): 138–144.

Vishniak, M. N. *"Sovremennye zapiski." Vospominania redaktora.* Slavic and East European Series, vol. 7. Bloomington: Indiana University Publications, 1957.

Volkman, Hans-Erich. *Die Russische Emigrationen in Deutschland, 1919–1929.* Würzburg: Holzner-Verlag, 1966.

Vygotskii, L. S. *Psikhologiia iskusstva.* Moscow: Pedagogika, 1987.

Wehrle, Albert J. "Bunin's Story 'Petlistye ushi' ('Loopy Ears')." *Russian Literature Triquarterly* 11 (Winter 1975): 442–454.

Wellek, René, and Austin Warren. *Theory of Literature.* Harmondsworth: Penguin, 1993.

Wild, Henry D., et al., eds. *A Selection of Latin Verse with Notes.* New Haven: Yale University Press, 1914.

Williams, Carol T. "Nabokov's Dozen Short Stories: His World in Microcosm." *Studies in Short Fiction* 12:3 (Summer 1975): 213–222.

Williams, Robert C. *Culture in Exile: Russian Emigrés in Germany, 1881–1941.* Ithaca: Cornell University Press, 1972.

————. "Memory's Defence: The Real Life of Vladimir Nabokov's Berlin." *The Yale Review* 60:2 (December 1970): 241–250.

Wood, Michael. *The Magician's Doubts: Nabokov and the Risks of Fiction.* Princeton: Princeton University Press, 1995.

Yeats, W. B. "The Cold Heaven." In *The Collected Poems of W. B. Yeats,* ed. Richard J. Finneran, 125. 2nd ed. New York: Simon and Schuster, 1996.

Zaitsev, Boris. *Dalëkoe.* Washington, D.C.: Inter-Language Literary Associates, 1965.

————. *Moi sovremenniki.* London: Overseas Publications Interchange, 1988.

————. *Zolotoi uzor: roman, povesti.* Moscow: Interprint, 1992.

Zaitsev, K[irill]. "'Buninskii' mir i 'Sirinskii' mir." *Rossiia i slavianstvo* (November 9, 1929): 3.

————. *I. A. Bunin. Zhizn' i tvorchestvo.* Berlin: Parabola, n.d. [1934].

————. "'Sovremennye zapiski,' kn. 44." *Rossiia i slavianstvo* 103 (November 15, 1930): 4.

Zholkovskii, Alexandr [Alexander Zholkovsky]. "Philosophy of Composition (K nekotorym aspektam struktury odnogo literaturnogo teksta)." In Ronald Vroon and John E. Malmstad, eds., 390–399. *Readings in Russian Modernism: To Honor Vladimir Fedorovich Markov,* Moscow: Nauka/Oriental Literature Publishers, 1993.

Zholkovsky, Alekander. *Text Counter Text: Rereadings in Russian Literary History.* Stanford: Stanford University Press, 1994.

Zimmer, Dieter E. "L'Allemagne dans l'ouevre de Nabokov." *L'Arc* 99 (1985): 67–75.

Zimmermann, Linda Saputelli. "The Russian Short Stories of Vladimir Nabokov: A Thematical and Structural Analysis." Ph.D. dissertation. Harvard University, 1978.

Zlobin, V[ladimir]. "O nashem 'tolstom' zhurnale (Iz razgovora chitatelei)." *Mech* 8 (1934): 13–14.

Zorin, A. L. "Nachalo." In Khodasevich, *Derzhavin,* 5–36.

Zweers, A. F. [A. F. Zveers], ed., "Perepiska I. Bunina s M. Aldanovym." *Novyi zhurnal* 150 (1983): 159–191.

————. "Perepiska I. A. Bunina s M. A. Aldanovym." *Novyi zhurnal* 152 (1984): 153–191.

————. "Perepiska I. A. Bunina s M. A. Aldanovym." *Novyi zhurnal* 154 (1984): 97–108.

————. "Perepiska I. A. Bunina s M. A. Aldanovym." *Novyi zhurnal* 155 (1984): 131–146.

————. "Proustian Passages in Ivan Bunin's *The Life of Arsen'ev* in the Context of the Genre of Literary Memoirs." *Canadian Slavonic Papers* 30:1 (March 1988): 17–33.

Zverev, Aleksei. "Literary Return to Russia." In Alexandrov, ed., *The Garland Companion,* 291–305.

Index

Voloshin, Maksimilian, 334n.9
Voznesenskii, Andrei, 355n.36

Wilson, Edmund, 191, 239, 249–250

Yeats, W. B., 239, 359n.120; "The Cold Heaven," 239

Zabolotskii, Nikolai ("Circus" ["Tsirk"]), 232
Zaitsev, Boris, 242, 251, 271
Zaitsev, Kirill, 239–240, 352n.3; "'Bunin's' World and 'Sirin's' World" ("'Buninskii' mir i 'Sirinskii' mir"), 239–240

Zaitseva, Vera, 251–252, 271
Zak, Aleksandr, 104, 332n.11
Zamiatin, Evgenii, 86, 194
Zenzinov, Vladimir, 271
Zhirova, Ol'ga, 299
Zholkovsky, Alexander, 234, 352n.84
Zhukovskii, Vasilii, 101–102, 269, "Svet-lana," 101–102
Zimmermann, Linda Saputelli, 91, 254, 353n.14
Zlobin, Vladimir, 353n.12, 353n.13
Zorin, A. L., 171
Zurov, Leonid, 252
Zweers, A. F., 361n.150